Diversity in America

Diversity in America

Keeping Government at a Safe Distance

PETER H. SCHUCK

THE BELKNAP PRESS OF HARVARD UNIVERSITY PRESS

Cambridge, Massachusetts, and London, England | 2003

Library of Congress Cataloging-in-Publication Data

Schuck, Peter H.
  Diversity in America : keeping government at a safe distance / Peter H.
Schuck.
    p.   cm.
  Includes bibliographical references (p.) and index.
  ISBN 0-674-01053-1 (alk. paper)
    1. Pluralism (Social sciences)—United States. 2. Multiculturalism—United
States. 3. United States—Ethnic relations. 4. United States—Race relations.
5. United States—Religion. 6. Minorities—United States. 7. Immigrants—
United States. 8. Civil society—United States. I. Title.

E184.A1 S37 2003
305.8'00973—dc21   2002042684

CONTENTS

ACKNOWLEDGMENTS

Authors of serious books owe many debts. We may seem to entertain the conceit that we can repay these debts simply by acknowledging them, but we know better. In my case, I benefited enormously from the many individuals who generously commented on earlier drafts of parts of the manuscript. There are the readers, unknown to the author, whom publishers manage to dragoon into assessing the work. Then there are those whom the author recruits by ruthlessly exploiting friendships, playing the reciprocity card, staging academic workshops, and leaping on even the most casual or feigned expressions of interest. I plead guilty to all of these stratagems but am the richer for my shamelessness.

Among the individuals who read and commented on one or more chapters are Vicki Been, David Bernstein, Andy Beveridge, Derek Bok, Jon Butler, Jackson Carroll, Stephen Carter, David Del Tredici, Chris Eisgruber, Bob Ellickson, Nicole Stelle Garnett, Rick Garnett, Nathan Glazer, Kent Greenawalt, Philip Hamburger, Sam Issacharoff, John Jeffries, Rick Lempert, Jerrold Levy, Chip Lupu, Jerry Muller, John Noonan, Jr., Manuel Pastor, John Payne, Jonathan Rauch, W. Clark Roof, Jim Ryan, Mike Schill, Marcy Schuck, Steve Schuck, Dave Sheingold, Mark Silk, Peter Spiro, Stephen Sugarman, Harry Wellington, and Ari Zolberg. Special thanks go to Bruce Ackerman, who helped me think through this project when it was only a five-page outline; to John Skrentny, who commented on the entire manuscript; to my fine Yale Law School student research assistants Emil Kleinhaus, Jessica Sebeok, and Jacob Sullivan; to the participants in faculty workshops at Berkeley, Case Western Reserve, Columbia, Duke, Michigan, Notre Dame, NYU, Virginia, and Yale; and to the students in my Groups, Diversity, and Law seminar at Yale during the spring of 2002 who read a draft of most of these chapters. I was also privileged to present portions of the book as the Uri and Caroline Bauer Memorial Lecture at the Benjamin N. Cardozo Law School of Yeshiva University, the Alice Evangelides Lecture at Rutgers University, and the Harrington Lecture at Clark University. Earlier versions of Chapters 3, 5, and 6 were published in the *Cardozo Law Review*, the *Yale Law and Policy Review*, and the *Harvard Civil Rights–Civil Liberties Law Review*, respectively. I thank their staffs. I wrote much of Chapter 7 while doing hard labor as a resident of the Rockefeller Foundation's magnificent study center at Bellagio, Italy, in July 2001, made even more pleasant by the Bellagio staff, led by the redoubtable Gianna Celli. I am also grateful to Michael Aronson, my editor at the Harvard University Press, for sharing my own enthusiasm for this project and helping me bring it to fruition, and to Richard Audet, my eagle-eyed copyeditor. Tracy Thompson prepared the index.

I wish to express my boundless gratitude to the faculty, students, and staff of Yale Law School, my intellectual funhouse for almost twenty-five years, and especially to its dean Tony Kronman, who epitomizes its values of broad inquiry, high ideals, rich imagination, unflagging generosity, and the pleasures of the mind. I have also had the immense good fortune in recent years to be welcomed into the "penumbral family" of NYU Law School. This phrase coined by John Sexton, the school's visionary then-dean and now university president, aptly describes the network of personal affection and academic excellence that he, with his fine faculty and students, has fashioned there. I wrote much of this book in the library office that Dean Sexton kindly provided, and I drew upon the institutional resources he offered me. He and the school, which has become my intellectual second home, now led by the equally generous new dean, Ricky Revesz, have my heartfelt thanks.

I dedicate this book to my children, Chris and Julie, who are inheriting a far more diverse America than I did and will be the better for it, while enriching it further with their own love.

Diversity in America

I

THINKING ABOUT DIVERSITY

First Thoughts

America is probably the most diverse society on earth—certainly the most diverse industrial one. This is true regardless of how one thinks about or measures diversity or which kind of diversity is under discussion—issues I take up in the next section and in Chapter 2. Ask a random group of Americans or foreign visitors to name the most distinctive aspects of American society, and diversity will be high on everyone's list.[1]

This diversity is *itself* remarkably diverse—and dynamic. Like a blastula of cells undergoing mitosis, American society constantly proliferates new divisions and differentiations. Some of this merely reconfigures the familiar, reshuffling old decks, but much of it creates unprecedented forms of social life. Technological innovation both spurs some new differentiations and preserves some old ones.[2] Much differentiation reflects the greater confluence of peoples and cultures. Even here, technology plays its vital part by radically reducing communication and transportation costs, thereby facilitating encounters between previously separate people, activities, or information.[3]

Remarkably, this diversification is occurring amid social developments that commentators usually consider homogenizing. The national mass media, advertising, and popular culture penetrate every nook and cranny of our lives. Latinos, Asians, and other groups increasingly intermarry with whites and with each other. The federal government deploys much of its political, fiscal, and regulatory power in a quest for national uniformity. A steadily aging population buttresses familiar demographic patterns. Some pundits, eager to debunk Arthur Schlesinger's claim that diversity is unraveling the social fabric,[4] even assert that "[w]hile ideologically 'all are different,' Americans in fact are remarkably 'all the same.'"[5]

Yet diversity grows apace despite these homogenizing factors, and sometimes because of them. While the number of daily newspapers has declined, the number and variety of other mass media outlets—cable, radio, satellite, the Internet, films—have vastly increased. Advertising is more highly differentiated in order to reach diverse audiences, specialized interests, and niche

markets.[6] More diverse immigrants, religious sectarianism, linguistic enclaves, and ideological shifts make ethnic identity—a term hardly used before
the 1950s[7]—more salient. Women have entered and transformed previously
all-male occupations.[8] Congress has permitted states, localities, and private
actors to go their own separate ways in many policy domains. Economic and
medical advances for the elderly have multiplied their lifestyle choices. Fringe
groups, free to purify their political ideologies, can appeal to narrow, dis-
contented voter blocs. Suburbs, long derided by urban elites as the triumph
of bland uniformity over piquant diversity,[9] increasingly mimic the heterogeneous cities they surround.[10] Corporate culture, traditionally conformist,
now deploys the theory, practice, and rhetoric of diversity.[11] Popular culture
has become so transracial, according to one black commentator, that it spells
"the end of white America."[12]

   The growing social acceptance of diversity is nowhere more striking than
in the evolving views of openly gay relationships and lifestyles by a society
that harshly repressed them—and to an extent still does.[13] The number and
openness of gays have increased,[14] along with their status in popular and religious cultures,[15] social and governmental entities (including the military),[16]
and elite businesses.[17] A national outcry against the homophobia that inspired the brutal murder of Matthew Shepard led to passage of many hate-
crime laws[18] and the extension to gays of some civil rights protections.[19] Politicians of both parties avidly court gay voters.[20] Some national advertising of
major products celebrates gay life.[21] At least one gay commentator perceives a
pro-gay bias in the elite media,[22] and major TV networks air gay-friendly programming and are developing more.[23] Perhaps most remarkable, public and
religious support for normalizing same-sex unions is growing.[24] (Less encouraging, only 59% of Americans say they would vote for a gay presidential
candidate on their party's ticket, compared with 95% who would vote for a
black, 92% for a Jew, and 49% for an atheist.)[25]

   This flowering of diversity—particularly the diversities of ethnicity, race,
and religion with which this book is primarily concerned—does not mean
that it flourishes equally in all areas of American life. (The artificiality and per-
niciousness of the idea of race are important themes in Chapters 2 and 5. But
because race is the focus of most diversity talk, one simply cannot avoid using
it and I shall not try.)[26] The important exceptions to this flowering, however,
are few, narrowing, or debatable. Most Americans do live in demographically
similar neighborhoods, but social class explains more of this than ethno-racial
bias. (See Chapter 6; alas, the effects—racially identifiable neighborhoods
and schools—are often the same.) Social scientists vigorously dispute the
"bowling alone" claim that civic ties are fewer and less diverse, as to both the
character and direction of change.[27] Independent bookstores have declined,

but superstores and on-line booksellers provide greater choice and convenience to browsers and purchasers alike. When diversity is in jeopardy, it seems, we come to value it all the more deeply, debate its instances and status more seriously, and search for new ways to sustain it.

America does more than tolerate diversity.[28] Today, it also views diversity as constitutive of the national mythos and underwrites this by welcoming close to one million legal immigrants each year. (Canada, a vast, thinly settled land seeking more people, accepted 250,000 immigrants in 2001, constituting a much larger share of its much smaller population.) According to sociologist (and immigrant) Orlando Patterson, America's embrace of diversity "finds no parallel in any other society or culture in the world today."[29] We shall see that this is no exaggeration.

American society has always been diverse. Historian Jill Lepore reports that "the percentage of non-native English speakers in the United States was actually *greater* in 1790 than in 1990."[30] America, however, has not always celebrated this diversity. Slaveholders, eugenicists, racists, homophobes, xenophobes, church establishmentarians, monolingual diehards, and many others opposed it on principle. Many more feared the social instability it might cause. Shrewd nation-builders like George Washington and Benjamin Franklin were of two minds about diversity, sometimes praising it and at other times expressing skepticism or alarm. Their descendants harbor ambivalent feelings about diversity today, lauding it as a national tradition but complaining about its mundane forms and worrying lest it go too far.

Americans' hostility to diversity often took the form of opposition to immigrants, especially to those who seemed different from the dominant native stock. John Higham's chronicle of nativism in postbellum America[31] and Rogers M. Smith's magisterial survey of opposition to full citizenship for women and minorities[32] have turned bright spotlights on a dark, often neglected aspect of our social and political history. They and others have exhumed an ensemble of ways in which social and political elites, often joined tactically by working-class allies, managed to exclude, subordinate, and stigmatize racial and religious minorities, assertive women, gays, political dissidents, and others. Diversity's advances, Smith shows, were episodic, hard-fought, hard-won, and sometimes reversed by backlash movements advocating new forms of social hierarchy.[33] I discuss this history in Chapters 3 and 4.

The traditional resistance to diversity should not surprise us. As Chapter 3 recounts, few thinkers and fewer political or religious leaders in world history have considered diversity to be anything but a threat that should be suppressed or contained. Even today, most societies would view the claim that diversity is a social virtue as subversive, if not suicidal, nonsense. For them, toleration is but a survival tactic, a temporary expedient. Even in more liberal societies, toleration is a mild, though essential, sentiment. At best, E. M. Forster noted, it "is just a makeshift, suitable for an overcrowded and over-heated planet. It comes on when love gives out, and love generally gives out as soon as we move away from our home and our friends."[34] And *tolerating* diversity is not at all the same as *celebrating* and *promoting* it.

One can easily understand, then, why Crèvecoeur, Tocqueville, James Bryce, Dickens, and many other visitors to America have been perplexed as well as intrigued by our diversity. So far as one can tell from their writings, none of these close observers of American diversity ever endorsed it for their own societies. Even those who most admired it seriously doubted whether the United States could sustain a strong civil society and a democracy built with such disparate social materials. Tocqueville, who uncannily prophesied the long Russo-U.S. struggle, also predicted that America's diversity would culminate in a race war. The notion that American democracy and civil society could coexist with a far greater diversity than they or anyone else could then imagine would have struck them as lunacy.

Yet this is precisely what happened in the decades following Appomattox. Despite (or perhaps because of) a succession of crises—industrialization, mass immigration, the Great Depression, wars, the McCarthy era, the civil rights and antiwar movements, new waves of even more diverse immigration, and now a war on terrorism waged in regions from which many Americans and new immigrants come—the American polity's enduring stability and unity remain the envy of the world. At the dawn of the twenty-first century, every other polyglot nation—India, Indonesia, Russia, Nigeria, Turkey, South Africa, Sri Lanka, and even Canada—is at serious risk of fragmenting into ethnic shards.[35] (Australia and Switzerland stand, so far, as notable exceptions.) Indeed, even strong unitary states like the United Kingdom, Spain, France, and China, and religiously homogeneous states like Belgium, are being roiled by militant demands for devolution or even full independence.[36] In sharp contrast, the United States has maintained its social and political cohesion, even achieving a kind of cultural coherence (though this is more debatable). Moreover, it has done so without sacrificing its economic, social, and cultural dynamism.

How has this singular feat been accomplished? That question is among the most compelling and complex issues facing diverse societies like ours. This book analyzes an important part of the answer: the role of law. It examines the different ways and policy contexts in which we have used law to protect, import, define, certify, subsidize, mandate, exploit—in a word, *manage*—diversity. "Manage" is a serviceable term to characterize how government self-consciously approaches diversity—so long as one bears in mind that "manage" includes both decisions to make diversity a subject of active legal intervention and decisions to leave diversity to informal, unregulated choices. This spectrum of diversity management options is central to both my analysis and my policy prescriptions. Although I focus on how law manages diversity, my analysis necessarily considers how nongovernmental processes handle it. Indeed, a central theme of this book is that law's management of diversity takes different forms and is often perverse. For now four examples, which are more fully explained in Part II, will suffice to illustrate the point. Immigration law creates ethno-racial diversity by importing it, while bilingual education law often fails to integrate immigrants' limited-English children (Chapter 4). Ethno-racial preferences designed to increase one kind of diversity reduce other kinds of diversity and even tarnish the diversity ideal (Chapter 5). Fair housing law helps protect minorities from biased sellers, while courts that mandate housing those minorities in recalcitrant neighborhoods have aroused fierce opposition (Chapter 6). Some rules of general applicability unnecessarily burden religious minorities (Chapter 7).

This introductory chapter sets the stage for my analysis. First, I define what I mean by diversity, and then develop a distinction, which recurs throughout the book, between diversity *in fact* and *as ideal*. (For the most analytically minded readers, Chapter 2 develops many other diversity-clarifying distinctions.) Second, I discuss how Americans view the diversity ideal today. My claim here, particularized in Part II, is that diversity's rhetorical power and prestige are at their height, and that this exalted status is unique in history and in the world—a claim I support by comparing it to diversity's status in other liberal, democratic nations. A third point is that diversity talk in America today is superficial and largely tactical. To Jonathan Rauch's statement that "[w]e are becoming so diverse that we are no longer sure what we mean by diversity,"[37] I would add that Americans seldom even ask the question. We can no longer afford the luxury of intellectual laziness but must think more deeply and systematically about what diversity means, how it should be managed, and how law and other social processes can best contribute to that endeavor—thinking that this book is meant to provoke. The chapter concludes by sketching the book's structure.

THE CONCEPT OF DIVERSITY

It is time to say what diversity *is*. I define it as those differences in values, attributes, or activities among individuals or groups that a particular society deems salient to the social status or behavior of those individuals or groups. (Readers wanting a more extended discussion of diversity's conceptual taxonomies, sources, and abstract legal structures will find it in Chapter 2.)

Several features of this definition are noteworthy. It is empirical and social-psychological in character. That is, the definition refers to the actual facts of how a particular society perceives differences and which of them it considers salient to people's status, and the definition also refers to how people think about their relations to others, the boundaries between them, and the nature of their interactions. For example, people seek to maintain different levels and kinds of "social distance" from those whose status they think is lower,[38] and these distances affect how they think about diversity. People who interact frequently and intensively with others are generally less likely to think of them as different, but some interactions may convince people of the contrary—that the other group indeed follows different norms, and perhaps that the difference is not worth trying to bridge.[39]

The diversity definition is also contextual, instrumental, and tactical. Sometimes, for example, we praise or condemn diversity in order to express our values to others, perhaps signaling them about the kind of person we are—or want them to think we are.[40] Those who invoke the diversity ideal may hope to associate themselves with a political mood or constituency, to convey their adherence to the letter and spirit of pro-diversity laws, to avoid having to defend past conduct, to change the subject, and so forth. A university defending its affirmative action policy on diversity grounds may hope to avoid having to prove that it did not discriminate in the past or having to acknowledge that it did. Business leaders may laud diversity in order to appeal to consumers and forestall litigation or bad publicity.[41]

The definition is inevitably bounded. Any particular understanding of diversity will necessarily delimit its contours, focusing attention on certain attributes while minimizing or excluding others. Most laws that regulate biodiversity, for example, are concerned with the diversity of species, not habitat. As I discuss in Chapter 5, most affirmative action programs define diversity in terms of the "ethno-racial pentagon" (David Hollinger's phrase);[42] they treat religious, political, and other viewpoint differences as irrelevant. These definitional boundaries, moreover, are fluid and dynamic, not static. In the jargon of postmodernism (and traditional sociology), they are socially constructed and contingent.[43] Perceptions of difference can and often do change over time. Historians of ethnicity, for example, show that Jews, Italians, the Irish, and other immigrant groups were widely perceived as distinct (and inferior) races during their early migrations to the United States. (Indeed, Italians did not then think of themselves as Italians at all but as Sicilians, Calabrese, Abruzze, Romans, Venetians, and so forth; to some extent, they still do.) Over time, however, Americans came to view these groups as white, no longer differentiating their racial status from that of other whites.[44] Historians still disagree, however, about the meaning and significance of race, ethnicity, and the process of "whitening" during that period. One revisionist

claims that most pre–World War I immigration restrictionists targeted contract labor, not race, and indeed saw race not as immutable but rather as
characterological and thus transformable in the American setting.[45]

As this book reveals, diversity is itself a highly diverse phenomenon with
different meanings in different domains. For simplicity's sake, I shall usually
refer to diversity rather than diversit*ies* because my point will usually apply to
all kinds of diversity. In many instances the qualifiers "ethnic" or "ethno-racial" may serve my purposes reasonably well, and absent my use of another
qualifier, these will be my referents. Ethnicity, of course, is a notoriously elusive concept, at once ambiguous, capacious, shifting, and capable of political
mischief and abuse.[46] The authoritative *Harvard Encyclopedia of American
Ethnic Groups* describes ethnicity as "an immensely complex phenomenon,"
and goes on to list no fewer than fourteen indicia, some of them compound
ones.[47] After explaining many difficulties and indeterminacies of the concept,
the editors sensibly conclude that no single definition will do.[48] When I refer
to "ethnicity," I shall usually mean a group as to which there is both an internal (i.e., within the group) and an external (i.e., outside it) perception of
group distinctiveness based on some putative physical, ancestral, or cultural
feature common to the group. Greater refinement is unnecessary for my purposes here.

Some other preliminary clarifications are also in order. Diversity is a matter
of degree, not an absolute. Japan, for example, is far more diverse than ever
before in its long history as a nation-state but remains a singularly homogeneous society by American standards.[49] By the same token, the United States
is more ethnically diverse today than it was a mere generation ago, and will almost certainly be even more so a generation from now.[50] The amount and
kind of diversity in a community, of course, is to some extent a function of
the level of abstraction used by the analyst. Viewed from a high enough alti-
tude, even the most physically diverse communities look alike—absent special
equipment permitting detailed scrutiny of what is on the ground. Whether
one focuses on the 90% or more of DNA that is shared by all humans or instead on the small amount that differs determines whether one emphasizes
our genetic similarity or diversity.

A society that is highly diverse in some domains may be relatively homogeneous in others. A striking feature of American society is that it is diverse in
almost all of them. A possible exception is political ideology. America's two-
party system seems more homogeneous both on its face and in its centripetal
force than the systems in multiparty polities exhibiting and perhaps encouraging more ideological fragmentation. Although the party system in the
United States has been shaped in part by the first-past-the-post and winner-
take-all electoral rules, the reverse is also true. More to the point, those elec-

toral rules would probably not have survived so long absent a relatively centrist consensus in voters' underlying political beliefs. And America's remarkable demographic diversity surely helped to shape the conditions creating and sustaining those centrist dispositions. As Seymour Martin Lipset and Gary Marks put it in a recent book, "the American working class was exceptionally diverse ethnically, racially, and religiously even when compared to the working classes of other English-speaking settler societies. What was even more important, however, was that ethnic, religious, and racial cleavages were more powerful sources of political identity than was their commonality as workers."[51] For whatever reason, the United States does appear to be more ideologically homogeneous than most other societies, as evidenced by the failure of any enduring socialist or labor party to take root.[52]

The changing cultural meanings of diversity implicate a distinction that is central to Chapter 2 and helps structure the other chapters. "Diversity-in-fact" is diversity that people perceive as a reality worthy of notice, much as a demographer or anthropologist might perceive it. Diversity-in-fact may carry normative weight due to an observer's past experience or imagination of it, or it may be merely an observation *simpliciter,* as value-free as such a thing can be. While emphasizing diversity's perceptual, socially constructed character, I nonetheless use the term "in fact" in order to distinguish it from the ideal of diversity, to which I now turn.

People often entertain opinions and beliefs about diversity as an abstract principle. I call this generalizing concept "diversity-as-ideal." It is normative (we ascribe positive or negative values to it). It is also a second-order or instrumental value (our assessment depends on how we think it implicates more ultimate ends such as pleasure, beauty, interest, stability, competitiveness, productivity, and the like).[53] The distinction, then, is between perceiving meaningful differences (diversity-in-fact) and believing that diversity—in general or of a particular kind—is beneficial or not (diversity-as-ideal).[54] This distinction gains practical significance when we move from individuals' observations of and reactions to particular, actual instances of diversity, to public policy decisions based on how the society collectively values and wishes to influence the diversity ideal. Society's valuation will in turn depend on its political commitments—a dependency explored in Chapter 2's concluding section.

THE RHETORICAL POWER AND SOCIAL PRESTIGE OF DIVERSITY DISCOURSE

Americans tend to take diversity for granted. This is no more surprising than a fish's inattention to the water in which it swims. Diversity is so pervasive, so deeply embedded in everyday life, that we tend to ignore it until our attention is called to it, as when it was revealed that a large number of the victims of the World Trade Center attacks were not Americans. We overlook how diversity shapes our primary relationships, affecting the kinds of people with whom we work, converse, compete, do business, shop, attend school, reside, and worship. We also forget how recently we came to value it and how fragile our commitment to it might prove to be.

Our public square today teems with claims about the virtues of diversity—what I shall call diversity value. More specifically, diversity value is the sum of all of the social benefits associated with diversity.[55] My colleague Anthony Kronman goes so far (perhaps too far) as to say that

> in certain quarters, diversity is on its way to becoming not just a value but a supreme value, the yardstick by which all others are measured. From a commitment to the value of diversity there follows a certain conception of what political communities are for: they are for the cultivation of diversity, which some consider the highest and most valuable function that such communities perform. On this view, a state is not merely the guarantor of public order, protecting the rights of its citizens to live in private as they wish. It is also the guardian of an organized space for the display and celebration of diversity, whose aim is to promote the moral pleasure that citizens take in the diverse attitudes and achievements of others as well as in the pursuit of their own plans of life. This is the highest moral ambition of the state, and when that ambition is fulfilled, when the endlessly diverse human beings who are its citizens have been gathered into a community of mutual enjoyment and respect, the state reaches a goal that America's great prophet of diversity, Walt Whitman, describes as nearly divine.[56]

Diversity's prestige is evident in the continuing debate over affirmative action, detailed in Chapter 5. Proponents of preferences who are beleaguered by mounting judicial and political challenges now brandish the diversity justification much as medieval Christians thrust the cross before the Devil. Their opponents assail specific means of pursuing diversity but not the ideal itself. Diversity, according to law professor Sanford Levinson, "has joined 'family values' and 'good medical care' as something that everyone is for, as demonstrated by the fact that it is becoming ever more difficult to find anyone who is willing to say, in public, that institutional or social homogeneity is a positive good and diversity a substantive harm."[57] Advocates of diversity value play it as a political trump, a conversation-stopper, a desideratum so self-evidently compelling that only a churl or racist would question it. As we shall see in Chapters 4 and 5, leading politicians in both parties as well as educational, corporate, and minority elites have mastered diversity rhetoric; they know how to talk the talk and walk the walk. In the pantheon of unquestioned goods, diversity is right up there with progress, motherhood, and apple pie.

Do I exaggerate? Read President Clinton's celebration of diversity in his 2000 State of the Union Address[58] and the Republican Party's paean to it in the platform for the 2000 presidential election.[59] You will be hard-pressed to identify who authored which; the two statements are practically indistinguishable. And who wrote the following? "America has never been united by blood or birth or soil. We are bound by ideals that move us beyond our backgrounds. . . . Every citizen must uphold them. And every immigrant, by embracing these ideals, makes our country more, not less American." Not a left-wing, open-immigration universalist but George W. Bush, the leader of America's conservative and, for most of the past century, lily-white party, in his inaugural address.[60] Even more impressive under the circumstances was Bush's reaffirmation of the ideals of diversity, toleration, and inclusion in his address to the nation only two days after the catastrophic terrorist attacks.[61]

Encomia to diversity are exceedingly rare elsewhere in the world, even today. Indeed, they are hard to find outside of the United States and Canada.[62] Many regimes commit atrocities against their own minorities (sometimes, even against their majority), usually in the name of national unity, religious orthodoxy, historical destiny, or some other monistic ideal. Even a little diversity can elicit suppressive violence.[63] On the other hand, a cross-national study finds that civil violence is associated not with ethnic or religious heterogeneity but rather with political and economic factors favoring insurgency.[64] Nor are totalitarian or failed states the only ones to repress diversity. States seeking to liberalize and democratize unleash new competitive forces that often impel politically dominant groups to use their superior power to persecute politically weaker but more entrepreneurially successful groups.[65] Some states extend special rights to their unassimilated aboriginal peoples[66] but bar ethnically diverse immigrants.[67] Even states that tolerate diversity often do so for purely tactical, power-preserving, or security reasons. Most leaders reach some sort of modus vivendi with particular minorities in order to mute socially convulsive conflicts (e.g., Tito in the former Yugoslavia), but they know that the persistent allure of autonomy, independence, and irredentism to strongly identifying and well-armed minorities (e.g., the Tamils of Sri Lanka) makes such arrangements fragile, dangerous, and perhaps only temporary. In more liberal polities, toleration may be selective—extended perhaps to political, religious, and economic minorities but denied to ethnic minorities regarded as potentially destabilizing or untrustworthy.

Examples of selective toleration abound. Canada's province of Quebec, a liberal, immigrant-friendly, and cosmopolitan polity in many ways,[68] has harshly restricted the language rights of English-speakers in the face of high rates of francophone conversions to English.[69] Until very recently France ruthlessly suppressed linguistic minorities, viewing them as a threat to the nation's cultural unity and heritage, and the issue remains highly controversial.[70] Almost all Israeli Jews, even those friendly with Israeli Arabs, regard the prospect of an Arab majority with fear and loathing; they know that this would mean the end of a Jewish state that was prophesied in the Bible and served as a haven from the Holocaust and a homeland for the Jewish diaspora.[71] Turkey denies many basic cultural and political rights both to Kurds and to Islamic fundamentalists while according broad constitutional protection to almost all other minorities.[72] Even the most liberal European countries practice, or at least countenance, widespread discrimination against the Roma people.[73]

Most of the democracies that now tolerate ethnic diversity have done so only recently—and perhaps only temporarily. In Australia, which abandoned its white immigration policy only in the 1970s, the ruling conservative party has cut immigrant and refugee admissions, and nativist groups there fiercely oppose Asian migrants.[74] The German parties did not seriously consider allowing permanent ethnic diversity until the late 1990s when an immense cohort of long-resident but unassimilated Turks and Greeks, as well as newly arrived refugees from central and eastern Europe, made it impossible to temporize further on the issue. Even so, the long-dominant Christian Democrats there still oppose liberal naturalization rules while also seeking temporary skilled workers who are ethnically diverse and may want permanent residence. Every European state that imported temporary laborers has discovered, with Germany, that "we asked for workers but human beings came."[75]

Growing violence against recent migrants to countries unaccustomed to them suggests the possible limits of this tolerance. The hostility of many Germans, especially in the East, to migrants from the former Soviet bloc and elsewhere suggests that institutionalizing Germany's recent reforms will be difficult.[76] Austria, which prides itself on its "normalization" and liberal democracy that earned it membership in the European Union, turned to a governing coalition including an avowedly xenophobic party and leader, now out of the cabinet.[77] France, which like Germany recently liberalized its citizenship law and which proudly invokes its republican traditions and EU leadership, remains deeply divided over how to treat the large and growing number of Muslims and other minorities in its midst.[78] The same is true of Spain.[79] Denmark and the Netherlands, among the most liberal societies in the world, are reconsidering their relatively (for Europe) generous immigration and refugee policies because of the rapid rise of their foreign-born populations, mostly Muslim.[80] Switzerland, a linguistically diverse nation, allows its cantons to vote on the naturalization rights of individual long-term residents and to deny citizenship on ethnic grounds.[81] More than a third of Swiss voters supported a referendum in 2000 that would have capped the foreign-born population share.[82] Even Canada, arguably the most generous to immigrants of any major industrialized country, has tightened its borders.[83]

In truth, diversity has little support outside the United States and Canada; even inside them, the enthusiasm is quite recent. Outside North America, diversity's acceptance will require protracted political struggles whose outcomes are uncertain and may well turn out to be illiberal. India, the only other democratic mega-state with a highly diverse civil society and constitutional protection of it, is an ethnic and religious tinderbox in constant danger of violent conflagration. There, the state must stage-manage group relations with exquisite care in order to avoid communal warfare, an effort that often fails. This is also true of Indonesia, another large multiethnic state. The European states, confronted by rapidly growing illegal migration, have imposed ever-harsher restrictions on refugee and asylum claimants and on employers who hire undocumented workers.[84] These states are experiencing chronic labor shortages due to declining fertility and their citizens' unwillingness to take menial jobs, shortages that threaten the financial viability of their social insurance programs. Even so, they continue to resist establishing regular immigration programs other than for their co-ethnics,[85] those from former colonies, or temporary workers. A revealing exception is Germany's controversial decision in 2000 to offer 20,000 visas to high-tech foreign workers. Few of them have applied, however, in part because they anticipate that German society will not welcome even skilled non-Europeans.[86] Social homogeneity thus remains a compelling political imperative in Europe despite (actually, because of) the large migration to those countries in recent decades, most of it unauthorized. Some recent developments in Europe may augur greater openness to ethno-racial diversity in the future, but they remain embryonic and tentative.[87]

The belief in the diversity ideal, then, appears to be a distinctively, if not uniquely, American (or at least North American) theme. Even in the United States, as Chapter 3 shows, this ideal is a very recent invention; many Americans still oppose it, as many always have. Many others, moreover, support it only because they assume that it will be a merely temporary condition; newcomers, they suppose, will quickly assimilate to American mores, shedding their distinctive ones, and will soon speak English. Indeed, the question of diversity's duration is a focus of the fierce multiculturalism debate, discussed in Chapters 3 and 4. As noted earlier and discussed in Chapter 6, most of us, including many who profess a love of diversity, continue to live in racially isolated neighborhoods with racially isolated schools.

THE SUPERFICIALITY OF EXISTING DIVERSITY DISCOURSE

The diversity ideal is so new that Americans have had little occasion to think hard about it—about where it comes from, what it means, whether its meanings vary in different contexts, the values and disvalues it creates and the normative tensions it engenders, the conditions that influence these valuations and tensions, and the roles that law and government can and should play in managing it. Americans, in the clichéd depiction, are pragmatic rather than philosophical or reflective. On this account, our diversity talk is as superficial and casual as our talk about liberty, equality, fairness, and other values that pervade our public philosophy and policy debates. With an insouciance about diversity that perplexes other societies, we do not dwell much on its deeper social meanings.

A major exception is our strong tradition of First Amendment protection for diverse political speech. More than seven decades of often sophisticated public, judicial, and academic commentary have nourished this tradition.[88] Even so, efforts to stifle diverse speech persist—ironically, in the name of protecting ethno-racial, gender, or other diversities. Campus speech codes, restrictions on sexual speech in the workplace, laws against hate speech and hate crimes, and politically correct journalism in even the best papers are examples of this perverse trend.[89] Fortunately, staunch defenders of the free speech tradition, including many courts, have vigorously opposed these efforts and generated robust public debate on these political diversity issues, so I need not discuss them at any length here.

The free speech tradition aside, the diversity ideal is often trivialized even in academic precincts where deliberation, rationality, and a taste for complexity are dominant cultural norms and professional preoccupations. Here and elsewhere, diversity value may be treated as little more than a preference for a pleasant exoticism. This exoticism—call it diversity-as-taste—evokes the allure of new cuisines, pungent phrases, colorful costumes, unfamiliar music, unusual and euphonious names or phrases, vibrant neighborhoods, and attractive bargains. In this view, diversity is, well, diverting. It stimulates us. It possesses entertainment value. At least while the novelty lasts, it excites and unsettles the often bland, routinized, prosaic, monochromatic surfaces of modern life (as many see it). Like the orientalism and primitivism fads that swept the high cultures of eighteenth- and nineteenth-century Europe, and like the "ethnic chic" enthusiasms of recent years, diversity titillates the senses and provokes the imagination; it is another delectation to pursue, possess, consume, savor, and even flaunt.

Scholars, it is said, tend to be either lumpers or splitters. Lumpers emphasize the broad regularities of human institutions and behaviors, while splitters are more interested in the nature, causes, and consequences of particularity and variation. In this book, as in much of my other work, I try to do both. By definition, the subject of diversity demands the splitter's eye for arresting and important differences. But in order to say anything useful about how law does and should manage diversity, one needs the lumper's faculty for generalization. Readers will decide whether I have struck the right balance.

The book proceeds as follows. Like this chapter, the remainder of Part I is designed to clear the ground and build the necessary conceptual foundation for my analysis. This means distinguishing the relevant contexts, clarifying the necessary ideas, and identifying the sources and necessary preconditions for diversity value and disvalue. Chapter 2 discusses diversity's taxonomies, sources, and legal structures at levels of abstraction meant to provide some conceptual unity and clarity to the more policy-oriented, domain-specific chapters of Part II. Readers uninterested in these abstractions may want to proceed directly to Chapter 3.

Chapter 3 turns to the diversity ideal and the values that it implicates. Broadly surveying the historical evolution of views about the diversity ideal (at least the views that intellectual historians have managed to exhume), I show how the enemies and skeptics of this ideal, by far the dominant group in all times and places, have thought of it. This survey helps to explain an otherwise remarkable and puzzling fact that I mentioned earlier. Whereas other societies have almost always viewed diversity as a condition to be feared and eliminated or at least contained, government in the United States has come to see diversity as an ideal that public law should not only protect (a familiar role for liberal governments) but *promote* in a variety of new ways. I then identify the values and disvalues that diversity implicates by considering how liberals, communitarians, utilitarians, and functionalists tend to think about it. Again, readers eager to get to the case studies may want to skip this discussion and proceed to Chapter 4.

With these conceptual and normative foundations firmly in place, Part II presents my case studies, substantive analyses, and arguments. Each of the four case-study chapters in Part II—on immigration (Chapter 4), affirmative action (Chapter 5), residential integration (Chapter 6), and religion (Chapter 7)—deals with a policy domain where American society has made diversity a central goal and has deployed law as a major tool for managing it. Each chapter illustrates different legal-managerial approaches to diversity: importing and assimilating it (Chapter 4), defining and certifying it (Chapter 5), subsidizing and mandating it (Chapter 6), protecting and exploiting it (Chapter 7). Each chapter has a similar structure: it first describes the level of diversity-in-fact that exists in that policy domain, and then elaborates the diversity ideal or ideals that have taken hold there. Finally, each chapter focuses on specific diversity management issues or cases, and then assesses government's performance in terms of the goals that it set for itself.

Taken as a whole, Part II reveals diversity's different meanings, the values, disvalues, and interests that diversity implicates, and the challenges it poses for law. In each chapter I shall criticize certain legal and policy approaches that government has taken and propose superior alternatives. My principal aim, however, is less to defend these proposals (though defend them I will) than to reveal law's distinctive strengths and weaknesses as an instrument for managing diversity in particular ways and in various policy domains.

Chapter 4, on immigration, shows law trying to import and assimilate diversity. The 1965 immigration statute, whose basic structure remains in place today, was the key development. The chapter explores how admission and citizenship policies, interacting with other social changes, have precipitated a broad and often bitter contest over the competing values of diversity and assimilation—the "multiculturalism" controversy. After introducing this often abstract debate, I ground it in two specific multicultural policy issues: bilingual education and so-called diversity visas.

Chapter 5, on affirmative action, shows the law defining and certifying diversity. Here, I review the leading arguments for ethno-racial preferences, focusing on the diversity rationale at the center of today's constitutional and policy debates. After assessing the leading alternatives to existing preferences, I propose a novel reconciliation of the conflicting values.

Chapter 6, on residential communities, shows the courts using law to subsidize and mandate economic and ethno-racial diversity. Examining the epic *Mount Laurel, Gautreaux,* and *Yonkers* litigations, I conclude that the courts in *Mount Laurel* and *Yonkers* have tarnished the diversity ideal by using poorly conceived coercive remedies to implement it, while the *Gautreaux* court's approach, which relies on a voluntary, voucher-based, choice-enhancing mobility remedy for minorities and low-income families, is far more promising although still problematic.

Chapter 7, on religion, considers two issues: how law should reconcile diverse religious beliefs and practices with conflicting secular policies, and how law might affirmatively exploit existing religious diversity in order to improve social services delivery and education for the poor.

Chapter 8 gleans general lessons from my specific analyses of diversity.

Drawing on the case studies in Part II, I distill certain factual premises about the nature of diversity, the main principles that I believe should govern its management, more specific policy approaches for implementing those principles, and some private punctilios that I argue a diverse society should cultivate. Many of my conclusions—even the factual premises—are bound to be controversial. Given the complexity and delicacy of the subject, I offer them in a humble spirit and with the earnest hope that they will help stimulate much-needed and empirically based public and scholarly debates on government's role in managing American diversity.

CHAPTER 2

Taxonomies, Sources, and Legal Structures

In Chapter 1, I defined diversity and described the zeitgeist that impels this study and gives it contemporary significance. Some readers, however, will want further conceptual, causal, and structural clarification of our subject before I turn to the intellectual history and social valuations of the diversity ideal (Chapter 3) and then to law's efforts to manage diversity in particular policy domains (Part II). This chapter is for those readers. Others eager to get to the substantive analysis can safely skip this and proceed directly to Chapter 3.

I differentiate diversity along three dimensions. First, I explore its *taxonomies*—the various ways in which it can be defined, classified, and measured. I next discuss diversity's *sources*—its etiology, if you will. Finally, I abstract the *legal structures and techniques* used to manage it.

TAXONOMIES OF DIVERSITY

Diversity, like most other things, means different things to different people, so rendering the notion mutually intelligible is difficult. Much depends on the level of generality at which one discusses diversity and characterizes attributes and groups. But because diversity is context-sensitive, it can also mean different things even to the same person at a single point in time. Here I explore different ways of understanding diversity by introducing a number of analytical distinctions. Some of them relate to the idea of diversity itself; others relate to particular attributes (e.g., race, ethnicity) that a society may use to recognize, characterize, or measure it. Although these distinctions take the form here of fairly crude categories with simple labels, their more complex, particular applications are evident in the four case-study chapters constituting Part II.

Diversity-in-fact and diversity-as-ideal. This distinction, introduced in Chapter 1, affects the valence that diversity carries in public discourse. As noted there, the *fact* of diversity is ubiquitous, a function of socially conditioned perceptions. In contrast, as detailed in Chapter 3, the *ideal* of diversity is largely a post-1960s phenomenon in the United States and Canada, remaining alien to most other societies.

Normative and descriptive diversity. This dichotomy is closely related to the first. We often think about diversity normatively, assigning some personal or social value to it. Although we likely harbor ambivalent or conflicting feelings about diversity, we formulate a positive or negative "on balance" assessment (at least if we care to have a view, which we often do not). Officially at least, Americans, Canadians, and Indians apparently value diversity more highly than the Japanese and French do—even if the former are not very clear about what they mean by it.

We also sometimes think about diversity descriptively, simply observing differences among things or people without necessarily or consciously appraising those differences one way or the other. Although I say we observe differences "simply," our observations are anything but simple. As I note below, we do not yet clearly understand the cognitive processes through which we come to perceive things or people as being different (and hence remarkable), rather than as being the same (and thus unremarkable or even unnoticed). As a psychological, cultural, or aesthetic matter, moreover, we may be incapable of observing difference *simpliciter* without at the same time rendering some value judgment about it.

Indeed, at a deeper epistemological level, we may say that differences among people do not really exist independently of the social meanings that we impute to them. On this view, social cues, conventions, or understandings determine when we perceive that social phenomena (as distinct from simple objects) differ from one another. Many Asians, for example, are said to be able to detect subtle ethnic differences among individuals of different Asian nationalities who to the untutored European eye seem indistinguishable; perhaps all cultures have this ability. Skin color carries different significance in various cultures—consider Brazil and the United States, both of which are racially diverse and had long histories of race-based slavery.[1] Be that as it may, descriptive diversity is a useful analytical construct for certain purposes. At the very least, it helps us see that diversity possesses an empirical core that bears no normative weight unless and until we supply it.

Individual and group diversity. Individuals differ from one another in countless ways. They also constitute themselves, or are constituted by others, into groups that differ from one another; indeed, this differentiation is what defines them as groups in the first place. The number of such groups is vast, with the upper limit being the number of attributes individuals possess that they, or outsiders, consider salient to their group identities or memberships.[2]

When we speak of diversity, therefore, we must be clear whether we are speaking about diversity at the individual level or among groups.

This clarity, however, may elude even the most scrupulous analysis. Group definitions and boundaries are highly contested. Even if group boundaries were well defined, their memberships would overlap because individuals belong simultaneously to many different groups, including some that they may not even recognize as such or wish to join. Even within a particular, well-defined group, differences among its members may be greater than those between its members and outsiders. This fact may (or may not) call into doubt the utility of defining them as a group for certain purposes, or at all. In effect, then, some efforts to recognize or increase diversity among individuals may reduce group diversity, and vice versa—a point to which I shall return.

We, of course, do not view our own attributes or those we ascribe to others as an undifferentiated bundle. We imagine that some attributes are more central to our (and others') identities than other attributes are, that the former are more salient to how we think of ourselves (or others), and that without them we (or others) would be very different people. Or so we think. As Chapter 4 explains, the multiculturalism debate reveals much controversy over the empirical and normative issues surrounding individual and group identities both generally and in particular cases. Indeed, the debate's intensity reflects the widespread recognition that our views about identity affect, and are affected by, public policies concerning education, affirmative action, immigration, citizenship, and other multicultural issues.

Cultural identities—both individual and group—interact in complex and dynamic ways. In the United States, the nature and salience of group identities to putative group members ebb and flow over time and differ among its subgroups. Intermarriage, for example, is a major cause of mixed and diluted ethnic identities. The cultural norms and practices associated with a group evolve, as do the particular aspects of a group's culture with which individual members identify. This is especially evident among second- and third-generation immigrants.

These evolutions, however, are neither logical nor linear. K. Anthony Appiah suggests that the stridency of cultural identity claims may be *inversely* proportional to the robustness of their cultural content and their actual salience for the claimants; that this stridency is often greater for a group's rising and integrating middle-class members than for their poorer, more isolated co-ethnics; and that these assertions of cultural identity are sometimes nostalgic exercises concealing the erosion of the social infrastructure that supported and invigorated the culture in the past. "The new talk of 'identity,'" he says, "offers the promise of forms of recognition and of solidarity that could make up for the loss of the rich, old kitchen comforts of ethnicity." On this account, we must be careful to distinguish diversity of identity from diversity of culture. Noting the ethnic similarity of Tutsi and Hutu in Rwanda, Appiah shows that identity claims may misrepresent the cultures they invoke.[3]

Recognizing the complexity of identity (and hence of diversity), the economist Amartya Sen has made some conceptual distinctions that are useful in clarifying multiculturalism issues. He distinguishes three identity issues: how many groups can one identify with ("plural identity"); does one choose or discover identities ("identity choice"); and, among those people one does not identify with, do any have legitimate claims concerning one's behavior ("beyond identity"). Within the plural identity realm, Sen further distinguishes between "competing" and "noncompeting" identities, focusing our attention on how compatible they are. Concerning identity choice, he distinguishes between different levels of freedom and constraint in such a choice, between temporary and permanent identity choices, and between the different moral responsibilities entailed in defending chosen and discovered identities.

"Beyond identity" (or identity transcendence) has the greatest policy significance. Here Sen distinguishes between a moral or political concern for others and a concern based on a common identity, and relatedly, between epistemic and ethical uses of identity to determine moral or political obligations. "There is an inescapable crudity," he says, "in thinking that we cannot sympathize with the joys and the miseries, the predicaments and the achievements, of others without seeing them as some kind of an extension of ourselves."[4] Jim Sleeper, drawing on literary historian Daniel Aaron's analysis of how "hyphenated writers" evolve, makes a similar point: "There is the outsider who demands acceptance of his or her group; the more confident interpreter who builds bridges between that group and others, in an idiom all can share; and the seasoned writer who makes a fully American, if ethnically inflected, contribution to some vision of the whole."[5]

Demographic and substantive diversity. Most diversity discourse, especially that which is descriptive in the above sense, refers to demographic diversity. This is the distribution within a population of individuals who are grouped (by themselves or by others) according to a more or less objective and measurable attribute (e.g., age, gender, race, religion, nationality, language, income) that they seem to share with other members of the designated group. For example, one commonly describes an employer's workforce as diverse (or nondiverse) based on the extent to which members of various racial or gender groups (as demographers define them) are present in it. The law often relies on this demographic notion of diversity when it counts, classifies, and regulates, and this reliance produces, as we shall see in Chapter 5, a strong tendency to look to proportionality as the measure of the duties to diversify that the law may impose.[6]

Sometimes, however, the speaker is interested in what I shall call substantive, rather than demographic, diversity. One can use the idea of substantive diversity either descriptively or normatively. When used descriptively, it refers to the distribution of some attribute that is not demographic in the sense just discussed. Teachers who speak of diversity in the classroom, for example, might be referring not only (or not at all) to the distribution of such demographic characteristics among students but also (or instead) to the differences in the students' viewpoints, experiences, methodologies, or academic training. The fact that so much diversity discourse disregards this distinction is exceedingly important. Most proponents of diversity (and some opponents as well) seem to assume that demographic and substantive diversity are the same, or at least that the former is a proxy for the latter. This assumption is often based on ignorance, laziness, or (self-)deception. Occasionally, it is not an assumption at all but instead reflects a considered view that the proxy, while admittedly imperfect, is nonetheless good enough for the purpose at hand. An important, if controversial, example is the Supreme Court's ruling in *Hunt v. Cromartie* holding that state legislatures can consider race as a factor in districting where race "correlates closely with political behavior."[7] As Chapter 5 shows, however, the race proxy is extremely crude in many of its common uses; we pay a high price for pretending otherwise and an even higher price for embedding that pretense in law.

Official and unofficial diversity. Diversity, whether viewed normatively or descriptively, may be officially certified or approved as such by some authority. The demographic categories employed in the decennial census and in affirmative action programs are examples of official diversity. Throughout our history, the census has employed an ever-changing list of officially sanctioned categories for describing and enumerating the U.S. population.[8] In recent decades, this list has been caught up in partisan disputes, lawsuits, the administrative maw of the modern welfare state, and the shibboleths of identity politics.[9] Another example is the certification of Indian tribes by the federal government, which qualifies them for many economic and status benefits denied to other groups.[10] Indeed, the government goes so far as to delegate its race-certifying function to an undefined Indian "community" and to require, as a condition for Bureau of Indian Affairs hiring preferences, that the applicant produce a properly executed "Certificate of Indian Blood." As Peter Skerry points out, the officially designated tribes to whom the government has ceded this authenticating power thereby control access to federal funds and other economic spoils, including casino gambling.[11]

In contrast, the identities of groups that lack this authoritative status must find recognition, legitimacy, and sustenance in other ways. Even here, however, official categories often have a spillover effect in the private domain, where people may look to them for guidance or even adopt them outright. In this way, official group categories—for example, the "ethno-racial pentagon" used in affirmative action programs and discussed in Chapter 5—may serve as focal points that reduce uncertainty, coordinate behavior among competitors, and perhaps decrease regulatory compliance burdens. But as we shall see, official definitions and certifications of identities or diversities tend to impair their authenticity, legitimacy, and diversity value, to deform their meanings, and to skew peoples' incentives for self-identifying in particular ways.[12] Is it coincidental, for example, that the number of individuals who self-identified as Indians in the census more than tripled between 1960 and 1990, far greater than the population increase, or that the applicants to the University of California who declined to state their race more than doubled in 1998, the first year without affirmative action?[13]

Ascriptive and consensual diversity. Other people ascribe some attributes to us, officially or unofficially, without our consent or knowledge. Those who do the ascribing usually consider the attributes to be both objective and verifiable even when they are neither.

The commonplace category of race, for example, is in fact neither objective nor verifiable[14]—unless it is defined in an absurdly narrow and arbitrary way, as with the "one drop rule" that officials used to define Negroes in much of the United States both before and after the Civil War.[15] (Even there, of course, verification often required knowing the race of at least one of the individual's progenitors.) Indeed, the very concept of race has long been regarded by natural and social scientists as fictional and misleading, if not pernicious,[16] a conclusion fortified by recent DNA evidence.[17] Even if one accepts the concept of race—and American society manifestly does so today for (too) many purposes[18]—it becomes intelligible only in the context of culturally ascribed racial identities where the ascription accurately reflects the meaning the attribute carries in that culture. The category of race is socially and legally constructed,[19] not natural or scientific,[20] which is why, as noted earlier, skin color bears a different significance in Brazil than it does in the United States; Brazilians and Americans almost literally "see" skin color differently.

Unfortunately, however, the artificiality of race has little effect on public discourse, which usually treats it as if it were as objective and immutable as the skin pigmentation for which it often serves as a proxy.[21] In fact, as David Hollinger puts it, "Racism is real, but races are not."[22] Even more problematic than loose private talk about race, moreover, is the official administration of race in public programs. Christopher Ford, who has analyzed how this is actually done, reminds us of a far-reaching fact one is apt to forget when looking to law to administer race: legal classification requires an administrative *method,* and the available methods in the case of race are egregiously crude, are susceptible to strategic manipulation, and carry repellent historical associations.[23]

We believe, rightly or wrongly, that many other attributes are the product of individual choice. If we can acquire or shed such attributes more or less as the spirit moves us, then any social ascription is only provisional. Religion, at least in the United States, is an obvious example—though with a complication to be discussed momentarily. Historian Jon Butler notes, for example, that by the second generation in America, most French Huguenots had left their own Protestant congregations and joined other denominations.[24] A similar transformation occurs with ethnicity, at least once one has lived in a society long enough to lose one's distinctive ethnic language, accent, dress, and perhaps name,[25] and to assimilate into the dominant group's repertoire of sounds, appearances, and mores.

The distinction between ascribed and consensual attributes, although useful for certain purposes, is far from clear. Despite much evidence suggesting that individuals can and often do don and shed certain ethnicities as if they were garments (as in a sense they are),[26] many cultural theorists describe ethnic identity as if it were inscribed far too deeply to be effaced in this way. But the distinction's ambiguities go well beyond ideological confusions. In any given society, some people view their religion as primordial and divinely ascribed, while others consider it a matter of choice.[27] To take another example, the ascriptive category of race is consensual only for those who are in a position to "pass" (psychological coercion aside).[28] Gender and some other attributes once regarded as ascriptive are, through the wonders of modern surgery and biotechnology and the more glacial processes of social attitudinal change, becoming more consensual.[29] With genetic manipulation and cosmetic surgery becoming more refined and socially acceptable and affordable, even age (or at least some of its traditional indicia like wrinkles and farsightedness) is coming to be viewed as optional. Homosexuality, traditionally considered a matter of choice and harshly condemned in part for that reason, is now widely seen as a matter of genetic predisposition to some uncertain degree, but it is often stigmatized nonetheless. More generally, moral views about many behaviors (alcoholism is another example) often turn on whether or not we think they are consensual, yet scientists disagree on this issue and even on what consent means in these contexts.[30] Indeed, they increasingly view these behaviors as caused by a mix of genetics, environmental factors, and choice, with the proportions of each being difficult or perhaps impossible to ascertain.

Genuine and spurious diversity. Some attributes imputed to individuals by others or claimed by themselves seem (to an observer and perhaps also to the individuals) authentic and highly salient to their self-understandings, while others seem more attenuated or of marginal significance and thus not really a matter of identity at all. For want of better words, I shall call the former "genuine" and the latter "spurious." I recognize the conclusory, question-begging character of these terms but give them some content in Part II. Chapters 4 and 5, for example, show the spuriousness of the cultural diversity that the official ethno-racial pentagon claims to capture.

In a society that values individual autonomy, of course, this distinction and these labels will be problematic. After all, they suggest that an individual's self-understanding may in a sense be subordinated to an observer's judgment about who or what that individual "really" is and how the observer (perhaps an utter stranger) can know this. The possible injustice or intrusion is greatest when an official or other powerholder performs and authenticates the ascription and can use it to determine and justify how important social goods (and bads) are distributed in society. Illiberal polities often use such official ascriptions to define, manipulate, and conscript the social identities of individuals and groups. Indeed, totalitarian ones perfected these practices during the twentieth century, using them to inscribe much of that era's remarkably bloody record.

Judging the genuineness and salience of attributes claimed by others, however, is a universal human activity; it is not confined to officials. Even the earliest hunter-gatherer communities must have done so in order to distribute social status among their members. Such judgments abound in any civil society where people need to assess the influence, character, behavior, and reliability of others on the basis of imperfect information and ambiguous signals and clues—that is, in all societies.[31] Judgments about genuineness and salience are all the more inevitable in pluralistic societies where groups, often organized according to members' common demographic attributes, compete with other groups for influence and resources. This is true even where intragroup and intergroup diversities make such assessments problematic. Nor do the dangers of such judgments disappear simply because those who make them claim to be using them to promote socially valued diversity. Indeed, this ostensibly benign purpose may even magnify these risks by propelling, multiplying, legitimating, and ultimately politicizing those judgments.

In liberal societies, then, the genuineness and salience of the attributes deemed relevant to status and resource distributions are often at issue. The crucial questions are how such judgments are made, how authoritative and binding they are, and what social consequences turn on them. These questions are particularized in Part II, but some generalizations here can serve as useful first approximations. To begin with, an attribute is more likely to be viewed as genuine and salient when its possessor affirmatively and voluntarily embraces it. Religion is probably the clearest example. Yet even here, our judgments about genuineness and salience often turn not only on whether an individual has claimed the attribute but also on his motives for doing so and on how important we think it is to his identity. An example, briefly noted in Chapter 7, is the use of such criteria in assessing conscientious objectors' claims for military exemption.

Presuming to discern the motives underlying another person's self-identification and its salience to him is often intrusive and error-prone. If the costs of these intrusions and errors are high enough, they may be socially unacceptable. Accordingly, we may search for more objective criteria of genuineness and salience—for example, the personal costs and benefits the individual incurs in claiming the attribute, the duration and intensity of his putative identification, and so forth. Even these criteria may be unsatisfactory for a variety of administrative, moral, or other reasons, but the alternatives may be worse on balance. Economic need is a classic example of an attribute that is difficult to measure and verify for income transfer program purposes. Moreover, its genuineness—in the special sense that it is not due to one's lack of effort—is constantly in question where self-help is required by social morality or law.[32]

Protecting, promoting, exploiting, and empowering diversity. A society favorably disposed to diversity—and historically few have been—may approach it, generally speaking, in four different ways. First, society may use the law to *protect* existing diversities or those that might arise in the future. For example, the First Amendment permits diverse groups to express, organize, and conduct themselves largely as they wish, and it prevents the state or in some cases private entities from interfering with these beliefs and practices. Much of Chapter 7 deals with the law's protection of religious diversity. Civil rights laws use the nondiscrimination principle to protect certain minorities. These familiar legal instruments are essential features of a liberal democratic polity. In deploying them, the liberal state need not, indeed *should not,* advance any particular conception of how much and what kinds of diversity are socially optimal. Instead, informal social norms and market processes should determine which diversities, beyond the legally protected ones, people value. This precept is an important theme developed in Chapter 8.

In a second mode, the state may decide to affirmatively *promote* diversity rather than merely protect it. This term "promote" encompasses a number of different ways of using law to instantiate a particular conception or ideal of diversity. As illustrated in Part II, the government now seeks to promote diversity by importing it through immigration, perpetuating it through cultural maintenance programs, defining and certifying it through affirmative action, and subsidizing and mandating it through communities' land-use policies. In addition to these legal interventions, a promotion-minded government can use its "bully pulpit" to celebrate the diversities it favors and persuade the public of their value.[33]

Third, government may try to *exploit* the diversity that exists in order to advance its other programmatic purposes. In Chapter 7, for example, I consider how the federal government might draw on America's enormous religious diversity and its faith-based organizations in order to deliver publicly funded social services, including education, more effectively. As we shall see there, the purposeful exploitation of religious diversity to achieve secular public goals raises special—though not insuperable—constitutional and other difficulties.

Finally, government may *empower* diversity. In this mode, it helps people choose for themselves the kinds and levels of diversity that they prefer. It does so by distributing resources people can spend in ways that yield the diversity they desire—whether or not officials would have used those resources to pursue those particular diversities. In Part II, I propose a number of discrete policy changes whose common feature is that they would empower diversity in this sense. This too is a central theme that I generalize in Chapter 8.

The stakes in deciding whether government should protect, promote, exploit, or empower diversity could hardly be higher. This decision does not simply entail a choice among different conceptions or goals of diversity. It also entails a choice among different legal techniques that carry distinct normative connotations and empirical or even constitutional consequences that are quite independent of the diversity conceptions or goals themselves. I show in Chapter 5, for example, that the law protecting blacks and Hispanics from discrimination should not be used to prefer them over whites and Asians in the name of diversity goals.

Intergroup and intragroup diversity. Diversity today is usually discussed in group terms; a social unit is deemed more or less diverse depending on how many groups are represented in it. (This is not to say that diversity is solely a quantitative phenomenon—only that the number of groups or attributes is one measure of it, along with others.) Accordingly, the difference *between* groups is commonly taken as the most salient factor bearing on diversity. In an important sense, however, this way of thinking about diversity begs the more fundamental question of which attributes constitute a group in the first place. Indeed, the differences *within* conventionally defined groups are often at least as significant as those that mark the boundaries between them. This is especially true when a gross demographic category like "Hispanics"[34] or "blacks" is used as if it consisted of a discrete, homogeneous group when in fact it encompasses individuals whose commonalities are small compared to their differences. In fact, all of the conventionally defined demographic groups have become highly differentiated in almost every way. To cite just one of countless examples, Latino voters in the heavily Latino San Fernando Valley were sharply divided over a ballot proposal to secede from Los Angeles.[35] Indeed, as the case studies in Part II demonstrate, this fact of steadily increasing intragroup differentiation is perhaps the most important challenge to legal efforts to manage diversity by regulating, as the government typically does, on the basis of the conventional group categories.

Organized and unorganized diversity. Political struggle over the state's role in promoting diversity, of course, is intense and intricate. Individuals and groups that define diversity in certain ways and favor particular techniques for promoting or protecting it may organize politically to press those interests and approaches, or they may remain relatively inchoate or inactive. Political institutions and processes, moreover, may differ in how conducive they are to raising diversity issues, subjecting them to group competition, and resolving them. Both the former Soviet Union and Yugoslavia, for example, established political techniques to minimize overt ethnic competition within their polyglot states, whose collapse unleashed catastrophic ethnic strife.[36]

Enclave and larger-scale diversity. In discussing diversity, one should be clear about the unit of reference. Even if people were distributed randomly in geographical space (the very opposite is true), we would not expect a uniform level of ethnic or other kind of diversity throughout that space; demographic clustering occurs randomly, just as disease and coin-toss clusters do. Moreover, the attributes with which diversity discourse is concerned are not randomly distributed. Co-ethnics, for example, tend to cluster in the same urban neighborhoods, at least in the first and second generations before intermarriage and other forms of assimilation produce out-migration and diffusion into more ethnically differentiated communities. Ethnic cultures draw members of particular groups into certain occupations or neighborhoods and away from others, increasing the homogeneity of both.[37] As Chapter 6 notes, residential areas are highly stratified by income and by the many other demographic categories that correlate with income, such as education.

Since almost any kind of diversity will be greater in some geographic units than in others, the coherence of diversity discourse depends on the spatial and temporal[38] domains being discussed. This is most obviously true of descriptive statements ("The United States is more linguistically diverse than Sweden"), but it is also true of normative ones. To pick a more complex example, saying that Firm X's workforce should be more racially diverse makes little sense until one specifies the geographic area from which X can draw its workers and the racial composition of that area. In evaluating the moral implications of communities' actions toward would-be immigrants, Michael

Walzer has observed that achieving more diversity in the larger society may mean less diversity in particular neighborhoods within it because of people's wish to live with others like them.[39] Whether Walzer is right or wrong about this, the distinction between the diversity in a given society (or transnational or even global community) and that in some smaller area or enclave within it underscores the importance of spatial specifications in any discussion of diversity.

The size of the unit has another implication for diversity. Certain kinds of diversity cannot flourish or even exist unless the attribute is distributed on a sufficiently large scale. A language, for example, can only survive if enough people use it to communicate frequently and intensely enough to sustain it and transmit it to others. More generally, activities like computing and telephony whose value to people depends on the number of others engaging in them (thereby creating what economists call network externalities) require a certain scale to be sustainable. For this reason, enclave cultures may satisfy their members emotionally but nevertheless be too small to be economically viable.[40]

Hard choices between different sites of diversity are often inescapable. Under the Voting Rights Act, for example, legislatures and courts face the choice of increasing the racial diversity, demographically speaking, either of representatives in the legislature or of voters in many individual districts. If the former, concentrating voters of a given race into a relatively small number of districts may be necessary to assure legislative seats to representatives of that race (assuming racial bloc voting). If the latter, the preferred strategy will be to spread minority voters around in more districts, but this will reduce the probability of a racially diverse legislature. The necessity for such choices is not limited to voting rights. Another example is biodiversity policy, which may turn on judgments about the appropriate boundaries and scale of particular biological communities.

THE SOURCES OF DIVERSITY

If we wish to understand and manage diversity, we must consider its causes. Just as a physician must diagnose her patient's condition before treating it, and a track coach must learn about a runner's leg muscles before training her, a designer of diversity policy must know why some diversities exist and others do not.

We may define or understand diversity in the abstract, as the earlier discussion has done, but in reality diversity neither exists in the abstract nor comes preformed into our view. Things are diverse only if we perceive them as such. And perhaps paradoxically, we only perceive things as diverse (at least in the sense discussed in this book) if we think that they are sufficiently similar to something else to render them comparable—and thus possibly diverse within a category encompassing them both. When we behold or think about automobiles and fruits, we do not ordinarily consider them as a diverse unit because we normally place them in altogether different categories of things; they exhibit no shared properties that interest us. In contrast, we readily perceive Buicks and Saabs as diverse automobiles and perceive lemons and kumquats as diverse fruits. To be sure, if color or texture were the attribute of interest, we might well think of automobiles and fruits as being diverse within those particular categories. Indeed, such cross-category comparisons constitute much of what poets, entrepreneurs, advertising copywriters, psychiatrists, lawyers, and all other imaginative and conceptual thinkers do.

What, then, are the processes that cause us to perceive things as being comparable and thus possibly diverse in this sense? The answer is undoubtedly very elusive and complex; it is probably some uncertain combination of cultural, neurological, psychological, and other factors. I have already discussed how some disparate cultures experience skin color: they literally perceive it differently. Languages tend to generate vocabularies that reflect the more or less subtle differentiations that its speakers regard as salient to them.[41] Recent research by social psychologists and neuroscientists using brain-imaging techniques indicates that certain areas of the brain (particularly the amygdala) exhibit greatly heightened activity when individuals see people of a different race, regardless of their attitudes toward racial equality.[42] Evidently, our propensity to perceive differences among things or people is at least partly a function of some preexisting but poorly understood mental processes that organize experience for subsequent perception and thought. Appiah's observation, noted earlier, about the cultural similarity of Hutu and Tutsi suggests that we sometimes perceive differences for more mundane reasons such as confusion about cause and effect, or sheer ignorance.[43]

Let us put to one side the cognitive mysteries of how we come to perceive things as different and evaluate that difference. The next question is: what conditions account for the differences in things that we cognitively recognize as different? Much human diversity reflects, first, the almost infinite *genotypic variation* found in our species. Even with the recent coding of the human genome, scientists do not yet comprehend the full nature, extent, and behavioral significance of this variation. What is already known, however, indicates that genotypic variation accounts for a significant share of the interpersonal variations in intelligence, psychology, behavior, and a growing list of other variables; that the environment (usually defined to include whatever is not genetically determined) also accounts for a significant share; but that the relative proportions between genotypic and environmental causes—and more important, the nature of their interactions—remain very obscure and perhaps even unknowable.

But if *individual psychology* is perhaps the most fundamental source of diversity, *group psychology* is not far behind; indeed, the two cannot really be treated separately. Quite apart from the contribution of genotypic variation to individuals' emotional and psychological endowments, their experiences with and in groups help to shape how they perceive and evaluate themselves and others, and this in turn influences how they act in the world. Groups endeavor to forge particular collective identities among members and nonmembers as they compete with other groups for resources and programmatic agendas. This is clearest with religious organizations like the Catholic Church and ethnic advocacy groups like the NAACP that depend upon and encourage highly differentiated identities on the part of their members, but group identity formation and reinforcement are ubiquitous phenomena. We can see this in numerous autobiographical accounts of how individuals came to acquire their group consciousnesses and loyalties and how they struggled to achieve acceptance from the groups with which they identified, often through painful processes of separation and differentiation from their families and other primary groups.

Recent research by lawyer-economists like Richard McAdams, Eric Posner, and Cass Sunstein underscores the subtlety of the interactions between individuals' motivations and their behavior in group settings, stressing how individuals pursue social status, reputation, group consensus, and other goods. Some analysts explain these pursuits through game-theoretic and other rational-actor models of behavior,[44] while others emphasize the limits of economic analysis, instead using psychological and other theories to augment and in some cases refute rational-actor models.[45]

Geophysical factors—climate, topography, water and other natural resources, diet, urbanization, religious and ethnic mix, and many other conditions—also contribute to diversity. Indeed, an earlier tradition of social and political theory stretching back to Aristotle[46] viewed such factors as fundamental determinants of many or most of the important differences among people and among societies. Classic examples of this genre closer to our own time include Montesquieu's *The Spirit of the Laws,* Jefferson's *Notes on the State of Virginia,* the *annaliste* historians, and much environmental history.[47] The modern revolutions in telecommunications, transportation, agriculture, and other technologies, while reducing the significance of these differences, have by no means eliminated them.

In the American case, the vast landmass gives rise to more or less identifiable regions that differ from one another in geophysical terms. Together, these factors help to shape the distinctive economic, political, cultural, and even psychological characteristics of each regions's inhabitants and the social institutions that they create. Were no other diversifying influences operating, such geophysical factors alone would still differentiate Americans who live in one region from those who live in others, even in the same state. Many have remarked, for example, on the different attitudes, behaviors, and cultures between people in San Francisco and Los Angeles, in New York City and upstate, and in Pittsburgh and Philadelphia.[48]

Historical factors constitute an important part of this differentiation. Although a region's social profile partly reflects the kinds of geophysical factors just noted, other historical circumstances also play their part in shaping regional differences. American historians like Bernard Bailyn and David Hackett Fisher have traced these differences to the distinct migration streams that carried settlers from certain parts of the British Isles to particular parts of colonial America, settlers who brought with them cultural patterns that centuries later can still be observed in the areas where they originally settled.[49] Since colonial times, countless historical contingencies—westward expansion, the legacies of slavery and the Civil War, patterns of immigrant concentrations, the mechanization of agriculture, northward migration by southern blacks, the effect of air conditioning on the development of the Sunbelt, the interstate highway system, pension systems, religious sectarianism—have helped to propel the diversification of the American people.

The *market* is among the most powerful sources of American (and human) diversity, multiplying it rather than (as in planned economies) suppressing it. This is most obvious in consumer markets where the remorseless search for profits generates constant innovation, product and service differentiation, niche marketing, skills development, and cultivation of ever more exotic consumer preferences. In a consumer economy like that of the United States, these activities create both the illusion and the reality of variety on a bewildering scale.[50] Many critics maintain that powerful sellers and image-makers create artificial preferences, exploiting consumers' concerns about relative social status.[51] Even so, market diversity is largely epiphenomenal, reflecting preexisting diversities of the kinds discussed above, which in turn reflect the vast heterogeneity of consumer preferences that economists usually treat for methodological reasons as both given and exogenous.[52] As the saying goes, "there's no accounting for tastes."

The market is a source of diversity in two other senses. Benjamin Friedman shows that market-driven economic growth increases social and democratic morality, including a greater tolerance for minorities.[53] In addition, markets—more precisely, markets' limitations—create opportunities for an immense private nonprofit sector in the United States supplying a vast, stunningly diverse array of social services and other voluntary activities that also differ in important ways from the ostensibly similar services that public and private providers often supply.[54] Indeed, the Supreme Court has affirmed the enormous contribution of nonprofit groups to "the diversity of association, viewpoint, and enterprise essential to a vigorous pluralistic society."[55]

But diversity is *itself* a kind of good, and the economic laws of scarcity apply to it just as they apply to other goods. Each of us, moreover, values (or disvalues) diversity differently and each of us can produce (or reduce) it only by sacrificing other valued goods. And like many other goods (antiques, say), diversity's value depends on how we perceive its authenticity and provenance. This characteristic is highly relevant to government's efforts to use law to protect, promote, exploit, and empower diversity—as shown in Part II and emphasized in Chapter 8. As individuals and as a society, then, we must choose the kind and amount of diversity we are willing to pay for and the ways we want to encourage or discourage it. If we can clarify what diversity is, analyze its features and economy, and assess how well law manages it, these choices will be wiser—or at least better informed.

Diversity also emanates from the variety of people's *interests,* only some of which are manifested in market transactions. Again, these diverse interests are largely derivative of other diversities within society; they reflect our experiences, what we make of them, and the values they generate. These clashing interests, of course, account for most of the countless social conflicts that the law must help to resolve.

Constitutional structure is another powerful source of American diversity, although it is probably impossible to know precisely which way the causality runs. The remarkable diversities among states, regions, groups, and interests that antedated the framing of the Constitution[56] were well known, and the Framers' constitutional design sought not only to reflect those diversities but to protect and even perpetuate them.[57] The state constitutions were also written in light of the many intrastate conflicts between farming and mercantile interests, established and frontier communities, freemen and slaves, and so forth.

Several elements of the constitutional scheme encourage more diversity. The federal structure was established largely to inhibit the anticipated efforts by the national government to intrude on state and individual prerogatives. The separation of powers and checks and balances at the federal level (and similar, though not identical, conflicts encouraged by state constitutions), combined with different constituencies and terms for each of the political branches, enabled diverse groups to use multiple veto points to protect their interests. The Constitution also protected interstate diversity. Representation in the Senate, for example, was designed, among other things, to protect small states from domination by large ones. Provisions governing taxes, duties, and commercial arrangements sought to protect the economies of states located in the interior from exploitation by strategically located maritime states. Perhaps most important, the Bill of Rights—especially as later "incorporated" into the Fourteenth Amendment as a limitation on the states and not just the federal government—promotes diversity by protecting freedom of religion, thought, speech, privacy, and many other conditions that nourish a diversity of beliefs, ideas, associations, and practices among individuals.[58] At the same time, the incorporation doctrine also mandated interstate uniformity as to the practices that the doctrine either prohibited (e.g., restrictions on speech) or required (e.g., Miranda warnings by police).[59]

To cite these and other features of the constitutional structure that were designed to recognize, protect, and institutionalize diversity is by no means to suggest that the Framers were deeply committed to all kinds of diversity. Shrewdly assessing the competing claims of national uniformity and interstate diversity, they struck a delicate and pragmatic balance, one that has shifted considerably over time. The Supremacy Clause (to pick only the most obvious example) unequivocally ordains the primacy of federal power when Congress expresses a preference for uniform national policies. The same is true, broadly speaking, of the Commerce Clause. Recently, however, both clauses have been interpreted to permit somewhat greater scope for interstate differences.[60] Similarly, the Full Faith and Credit Clause, which requires states to effectuate other states' laws and decisions, strikes a flexible compromise, shifting over time, between uniformity and diversity.

Despite some pro-uniformity features of the constitutional order, the powerful dynamics favoring diversity often prevail. In this perennial struggle, diversity is encouraged not only by those structures but also by *subconstitutional structures and institutions*—many of which, of course, are shaped by the former. American political parties, for example, are largely organized on a state and local basis; even today, the national parties wield little power except during presidential election years.[61] Our legal system also supports diversity at subconstitutional levels. Law, to be sure, has strong generalizing and centralizing tendencies. After all, a rule's principal purpose is to secure uniformity and equal treatment by coordinating otherwise disparate behaviors. Nevertheless, important features of the American legal system strongly favor diverse values and outcomes. Most federal statutes, even those creating public entitlements, countenance considerable variation by giving the states important roles in financing, eligibility rules, benefit levels, administration, and enforcement. The precise mix between federal and state law, and between statutory and common law (especially at the state level), is always changing, but state and common law are still the defaults; federalization and statutes are usually seen as exceptions needing special justification. Even federal statutes and federal courts, despite promoting the value of national uniformity, draw many of their substantive rules from the state systems.[62] Both the federal and state judiciaries, which are highly decentralized and only weakly coordinated internally and with each other, produce much variation in legal rules, policies, and case outcomes even when uniformity is mandated in principle.

The particular forms of American law also facilitate diversity. Regulatory law will always proliferate detailed rules, but a strong reform trend has favored more flexibility with respect to what constitutes compliance, how it can be achieved, and whether exceptions are permissible.[63] Similarly, the common law's evolution from specific rules to broader standards such as "reasonableness" encourages diverse, context-sensitive outcomes at the expense of predictability, as does its case-by-case, fact-contingent, distinction-generating form of adjudication.[64] In this sense, then, the common law is fashioned bottom-up rather than top-down, and its pronounced contextuality assures that it will reflect the remarkable heterogeneity of American life in all of its manifestations.

Finally, the *ideology* of diversity, while celebrating that which already exists, also generates more of it. Through a combination of elite rhetoric, civic education, mass advertising, popular culture, and personal experience, Americans' taste for diversity now extends well beyond their private market role as producers and consumers to their public role as citizens. How we came to the novel view that the diversity ideal should be a compelling civic goal is the subject of Chapter 3.

THE LEGAL STRUCTURES OF DIVERSITY

Assuming that diversity—in any of the senses described here—is a value that society wishes to certify, preserve, promote, mandate, subsidize, or limit, society may choose to deploy the law toward that end. Through which techniques might the law do so?

Constitutional scholar Robert Post addresses this question in an essay mapping the contours of a democratic polity's capabilities in managing diversity.[65] Post's specific concern is with cultural diversity, but his discussion is schematic enough to apply to any of the diversities that law seeks to regulate. Setting to one side some techniques discussed in this book, such as the public subsidization of private choices in order to diversify communities (see Chapter 6), consider three other techniques that Post analyzes: individual rights, group rights, and devolution of sovereignty. Individual rights, of course, are the most familiar. They function by directly aligning individual behavior with cultural norms (e.g., reinforcing substantive values that society wishes to promote, as through contract and family law), or by sheltering individual decisions from state interference, preventing even the state from enforcing its cultural norms (e.g., creating a right to religious liberty). To Post's individual rights schema, I would add two other ways in which law often effectuates them—by *locating the rights enforcement power* (e.g., in the individual, a group, or the state), and by *specifying the remedies* for vindicating them (e.g., money damages and declaratory and injunctive orders).[66]

For our purposes, the most valuable part of Post's schema examines how the law can use group rights to influence diversity by recognizing interests that are meant to affect diversity, such as autonomy or religious liberty. He first clarifies the ambiguous distinction between individual and group rights, a distinction often invoked in debates over affirmative action and other diversity issues:

> Rights can be viewed as group rights because groups, as distinct from individuals, are the rights-holders. We can in this way distinguish rights held by churches, corporations, or tribes, from rights held by individual persons.
>
> But rights may also be considered group rights if they are designed to protect group interests, as distinct from individual interests. . . . We must . . . distinguish those interests that are understood to be shared, or potentially shared, by all persons within a political community, which I shall call "individual interests," from those interests that arise from membership in a group, which by definition is less than the whole community. . . . Group interests . . . are partial; they are not universally shared within the community.[67]

Post then combines these considerations into four possibilities: (1) individual rights-holders asserting individual interests; (2) individual rights-holders asserting group interests; (3) group rights-holders asserting individual interests; and (4) group rights-holders asserting group interests. He points out that (2), (3), and (4) represent three different kinds of what we loosely call "group rights."

Post explores these possibilities in nuanced ways, but for present purposes I shall confine myself to noting several of his points. First, the interests protected by (1) and (3)—Post's example is an interest in property—are the same, structurally speaking, whether they are asserted by an individual or by, say, a church. Second, the fact that a right in (3) is held by a group entails several structural consequences. It empowers the group that holds it. The group must organize or institutionalize itself in order to assert the right, which risks a split between the group's culture and its organizational agent. Disputes may arise over who properly represents the group, disputes that the state must resolve. This strategic position gives the state power to influence the group's identity and development, especially in (2) when the individual will be asserting the group's right and thus will both literally and figuratively "represent" the group.

In recognizing that the state gains the power to influence groups when it administers their rights, Post does not mention affirmative action, yet affirmative action—the subject of Chapter 5—exemplifies his point. Individual members of a protected group assert a claim to an affirmative action preference, which is in one sense (recognized in Supreme Court doctrine) their personal interest in vindicating their individual dignity and equality. In another sense, however, one can understand them to be asserting a group interest—namely, the group's interest in remedying discrimination based on the discriminator's invidious ascription to the individual of a group characteristic. But whether one views affirmative action as a group right or as an individual one, the claim cannot be resolved without some outsiders, ultimately state officials, having to define the group and characterize its interests because the group's contours and interests are socially contested.

This state power over group autonomy, moreover, is not peculiar to affirmative action claims; it also occurs when the state resolves a claimed right to nondiscrimination asserted by an individual member of a protected group —as in the *Dale* case when the Court upheld the Boy Scouts' right to exclude gays from its leadership positions.[68] The position advanced by the Scouts can also be understood as asserting a group interest—as a gay person's own claim can, albeit in the different sense just noted.[69] The fact that I view *Dale* as reaching the correct result even though I oppose the Scouts' policy[70] suggests the normative difficulties such cases present. But the key point here, which is also Post's point, is that a law allowing individuals to assert group-related rights inevitably insinuates the state into the group's identity, autonomy, values, and politics. This would be so *whatever* the decision in *Dale*.

Post says of state-created rights protecting group interests that they "intrinsically divide citizens into groups, and they divide groups from each other."[71] Equally true and perhaps even more troubling is that such rights may divide groups internally. Post also observes that the recognition of individually asserted group interests is most problematic "when the group interests protected by a right are those that go to the identity of persons."[72] But it is even more problematic, I would add, when the protected interests not only affect the right-holding individual's identity but also seem to deny the identity or interests of others. Unfortunately, this danger is increasingly common in a legal-political culture that manages diversity in ways that encourage people to define their identities and interests narrowly, exclusively, and militantly, and to defend them in the broad, uncompromising language of legal right. This is even true—perhaps especially so—when the interests in question are in a zero-sum conflict. In Chapter 8, I suggest some ways to minimize the problem.

The third legal technique for managing cultural diversity is the devolution of sovereignty, which I mentioned earlier in discussing federalism. This devolution, Post notes, can take different forms. It can allow groups to make law for group members, for all persons within a territory, or for group members within a territory; to make law but not to enforce it; to make law about some subjects but not others, and subject to constitutional or other side-constraints; and to interpret law more or less authoritatively. Only law (or war) can resolve these competing claims. How the legal system combines these and other variables, including the claims of "internal" minorities within a devolved group enclave, is historically and politically conditioned. The system's choices both reflect and in turn reshape the diversities at issue, determining the question of which forms of cultural diversity will receive legal protection.

This question is the focus of each of the chapters in Part II. They analyze how the law manages diversity with respect to immigration, citizenship, and multicultural issues; affirmative action; the integration of neighborhoods; and conflicts between religious and secular values.

CHAPTER 3

A New Ideal and Why It Matters

The dismal trail of hostility, fear, violence, and social upheaval aroused by ethnic, religious, racial, and other diversities is a very long one. The trail leads today from Sri Lanka, Rwanda, the Balkans, the Mideast, and many other dangerous neighborhoods[1] back to the earliest human communities. Countless blood-soaked battle monuments and endless graveyards mark the path. In this otherwise dark history, of course, one can also find many instances of what we now view as humane enlightenment. Moreover, because historians' attention, like ours, is drawn more to the drama of conflict than to the dullness of concord, such instances are probably more common than we can imagine, especially after having lived in the most murderous of all centuries.

Many peoples, cultures, and religious groups have dwelt peaceably near one another time out of mind, each absorbing and at the same time transforming aspects of the other's culture. Indeed, the most dynamic and durable civilizations in the modern world, including the United States, are mongrel cultures that borrow from, hybridize, and transform those of other societies. In most cases, this kind of successful cultural syncretism has followed in the wake of commercial relationships, which often flourish at the points where ethnic enclaves converge. In this sense, traders are the vanguard of a civilization. They penetrate the unknown culture, perform valuable reconnaissance there, excite curiosities and demands in both societies, and act as middlemen. In the short run, this engagement may engender intercultural conflict; in the long run, commerce tends to foster an appreciation of interdependence and a desire for material gain through exchange. These values encourage peaceful relations, a live-and-let-live tolerance, a longer-term perspective, and a respect for (the profitability of) differences.[2] Herodotus, historian of the Greek golden age, prefigured what we would now call a cultural marketplace where commerce mingles diverse ways of life—though he presumed that people, given a choice, would always prefer their own.[3]

Neither Herodotus nor subsequent historians, however, have identified societies valuing diversity as a positive ideal to be celebrated and actively and collectively pursued. Most often, diversity was seen as a potentially dangerous condition that threatened social turmoil and hence must be carefully controlled. Indeed, the principle that seems to have guided most societies in all other eras is that diversity means trouble and that, trading relations aside, diversity must be assiduously managed, often by seeking to repress or eliminate it. At best, societies practiced a grudging, highly selective toleration. To this nearly universal pattern, America in the twenty-first century is the great exception.

Until Charles Darwin's theories of biological speciation and competition and John Stuart Mill's broad vindication of religious and political liberty in the mid-nineteenth century, one finds little discussion of the diversity ideal. With a few visionary exceptions such as Ralph Waldo Emerson and Walt Whitman, it was not until the 1960s, and then largely in the United States and Canada, that ethnic, religious, cultural, and other politically controversial forms of diversity were widely hailed as goods in themselves that society should actively promote rather than curtail or eliminate.

The first section of this chapter offers a very schematic historical account of how the diversity ideal has evolved in America. I mean to show that this ideal, so familiar at the turn of the new millennium, has no real antecedent in American thought. (It is even more absent from the European intellectual tradition, as I show elsewhere.)[4] Hence public law's recent efforts to instantiate this ideal are truly unprecedented. The second section is normative. By analyzing how people who subscribe to a variety of social-political theories would evaluate diversity, I mean to identify the range of values and disvalues that might be ascribed to it—a normative audit of diversity, as it were. This will prove to be critical to understanding the policy conflicts detailed in Part II.

A BRIEF HISTORY OF THE DIVERSITY IDEAL IN AMERICA

America's diversity ideal, in its current policy-oriented robustness, is quite new. Until the 1960s, the history of race relations in the United States was stained by widespread hostility to blacks, browns, Native Americans, and those immigrants (including many who were then counted as Caucasians, albeit inferior types) who deviated from the dominant British-northern European archetype.[5] Racist currents ran deep in many northern communities as well as in the southern states, and the liberties of even free blacks were limited by law and persistent violence well into the middle of the twentieth century.

The persecution of religious minorities, like that of racial minorities, was also widespread from the earliest settlements in colonial America well into the middle of the twentieth century. This intolerance extended far beyond the harsh treatment of Jews and other non-Christians; targets also included Catholics and, to a much lesser extent, some evangelical Protestants. Indeed, before the Revolutionary War, almost every colony enacted anti-Catholic laws restricting certain religious practices, public and private activities, and some other rights of common citizenship. In the early Republic, most American states established tax-supported churches; only in the 1830s was the last of these disestablished.

Thomas Jefferson, influenced by the British theorist John Locke, favored a mild, tolerant, rationalistic kind of worship.[6] Unlike Locke, he opposed all doctrines at odds with his scientific convictions. He thus denied the authority of Scripture,[7] tolerated all religious dissenters including Catholics and atheists, and opposed any financial support for religion by the national government.[8] These views, however, in no way constituted an affirmative ideal of religious diversity. Jefferson disdained many Christian sects and doctrines and viewed Jewish theology as "degrading and injurious."[9] His famously inconsistent avowals concerning slavery could not conceal his deep fear of racial diversity.[10] Blacks, he insisted, were vastly inferior;[11] Indians, for whose culture he had more respect, would assimilate better with whites.[12] He would have regarded any claim that racial diversity was socially desirable as both absurd and vicious. This is even truer of Thomas Paine, the radical secular humanist.[13] James Madison, unlike his mentor Jefferson, was a devout Christian who deeply respected diverse religious convictions and practices and viewed religious conviction as a social and political virtue.[14] Like Jefferson, Madison believed strongly in protecting freedom of conscience and worship but was more consistently and publicly antislavery than Jefferson, although historians disagree about just how thoroughgoing his opposition was.[15] While evidencing no belief in the social value of racial diversity as such, Madison did analyze the role of diverse interests in political life. I discuss this below.

Throughout U.S. history, political minorities were vilified even more than racial and religious ones were.[16] Certain colonies, concerned about "fifth column" treason (a theme echoed in American anti-Catholicism and anti-Semitism), expelled some dissidents. The Alien and Sedition Acts of 1798, clearly unconstitutional by today's standards, sought to repress the emergent Jeffersonians. In the antebellum years, laws were targeted at various radical movements. After the Civil War, labor activists (many of them immigrants and thus easy targets) were violently attacked. Suspected radicals were prosecuted during and after both world wars.[17] Civil rights workers were targeted until the late 1960s. Only in 1964 did the federal government adopt strong legal remedies for unequal treatment of racial and religious minorities; only in 1991 did it ban discrimination against the disabled in federally funded programs.

Even today, relatively few jurisdictions have enacted laws protecting homo-sexuals against many forms of bias.[18]

The founding generation also understood the diversifying power of the market forces then emerging. Influenced both by the civic republican tradi-tion of James Harrington and by the Scottish Enlightenment, the founders crafted legal and political institutions to protect property and contract. Counting on a free, dynamic, and diverse civil society to limit the power of political and religious elites, they endorsed toleration to an extent remarkable for that time. (The Alien and Sedition Acts, notable exceptions, were soon repealed.) None of the founders, however, imagined that political and ethnic diversity was a good in itself. They supported the market not because it in-creased social diversity, but because it expressed individual liberty, created wealth, and fostered cooperation.

Foreign observers, not just native ones, had always remarked on America's diverse demography, and many went on to praise it in rhetoric, humor, story, song, and other cultural forms.[19] The late eighteenth-century Frenchman St. Jean de Crèvecoeur wrote admiringly of a newly amalgamated, vigorous race of Americans. Alexis de Tocqueville, writing in the 1830s during the Jackso-nian era, argued that political and class diversity helped to advance liberty and avert majority tyranny. He feared, however, that the American project of democratic self-government—and ultimately liberal freedom itself—would be undermined by the society's egalitarianism, mass opinion, legacy of slav-ery, and lack of an aristocratic class committed to distinct honor-driven val-ues. American diversity, then, was a mixed blessing.

A decade later, the American essayist Ralph Waldo Emerson, like de Crève-coeur earlier, praised the distinctive ethnic hybrid he saw emerging. Herman Melville, his contemporary, depicted the United States as a universal nation nearly 150 years before demographer Ben Wattenberg used the phrase as a book title.[20] Walt Whitman was perhaps the most ardent and lyrical of these celebrants of diversity. Influenced by Emerson and other transcendentalists who idealized nature's sublimity and man's authenticity and creativity, Whit-man's poetry depicted diversity, somewhat paradoxically, as a universal bond among people arising from an encounter between their irreducible unique-ness and differences, and their natural human sympathy based on a transcen-dent commonality.[21] Writing several decades later, cultural pluralists also ro-manticized American diversity, elevating it to the level of national myth and inspiring a generation of liberals who were searching for a new modernist, nonracist political identity.

These high priests of the diversity ideal, however, were decidedly the ex-ceptions, and their own enthusiasms were usually compromised by assumptions of racial superiority. From colonial times until the post–World War II era, non-Protestant, non-English-speaking immigrants, blacks, and Native Americans were treated with intolerance, violence, and demands for cultural extermination, isolation, or assimilation.[22] As Bonnie Honig shows, the iconic foreigner was a literary and ideological figure used both to affirm America's unique (and in Honig's view, often bogus) liberality and to exclude groups viewed as inferior.[23] Indeed, through almost all of this period, even white, Christian, English-speaking immigrants such as the Irish suffered pervasive discrimination of a kind almost unimaginable (and almost certainly illegal) today. Only with the huge influx of immigrants during the four decades between the 1880s and the 1920s, most of whom came from relatively poor areas of southern and eastern Europe, did ethnic diversity—as a socially desirable condition, not just as a demographic fact—become the subject of sustained debate among American public intellectuals.

More important for our purposes, even diversity's friends defined its scope and character differently than many of us do today. With Nathan Glazer, we can ask about Emerson the multiculturalist of 1845: Did he really mean it? Did he have any inkling of the disparate races and ethnicities that immigrants would bring here in the twentieth century and especially after 1965? And was his prefiguring metaphor for ethnic amalgamation, the "smelting pot," a celebration of diversity or its annihilation?[24] Whitman, for his part, evidently favored social diversity only by excluding nonwhites from its scope.[25] David Hollinger notes that some later cultural pluralists like Randolph Bourne and Horace Kallen "considered themselves radical for appreciating the cultural contributions of Jews, Irish Catholics, and various Slavic and Mediterranean peoples, yet were slow to conceive of the possibility that pluralism might provide legitimacy to peoples known today as African American, Asian American, indigenous, and Latino."[26] The diversity they valued extended beyond the white race, which, as we have seen, was then more narrowly defined than it is today, but it evidently did not include the black or Native American cultures, much less other non-European ones.[27]

Moreover, Kallen and Bourne conceived of this pluralism almost entirely as a matter of autonomous group activity undertaken in a private sphere. Insofar as group life was concerned, the laissez-faire state should be just that; it should not impinge on group autonomy. They wrote during and after World War I when governments, abetted by an often nativist, xenophobic, and reactionary public, frequently harassed, persecuted, and prosecuted groups they suspected of disloyalty, especially German immigrants like Kallen. Not surprisingly, the cultural pluralists regarded state intrusion into group life as a threat to diversity. The state's legitimate role, in their view, was to secure democratic citizens, not to influence group life. Not anticipating the creation of the New Deal administrative state a decade or more later, they never entertained the possibility that group diversity would become an affirmative government policy in which law would play regulatory, prescriptive, and promotional roles. Had they done so, they probably would have recoiled; recent history justified their fear that state intervention was a mortal threat to their project of preserving authentic group differences.

If the Whitmanesque idealization of diversity was monoracial and if the cultural pluralists feared any affirmative role for the state, the assimilationist vision sought to dissolve certain diversities altogether. Assimilationists, who have always dominated public attitudes toward newcomers to the United States, favor minimizing or eliminating many salient group differences in pursuit of a more or less homogenous national culture and political identity. Assimilationists disagree only about which methods should be employed and how long the molting of foreign customs should take. Some of the more extreme ones—Henry Ford was a notorious example—were avowedly racist, anti-Semitic, and nativist. Others, centered in the social work movement that marked the Progressive era, deeply sympathized with the immigrants and wanted them to prosper in America. Both of these extremes in the "Americanization" movement, and of course the many positions in between, expected immigrants to efface their provincial ethnic identities and submit to the dominant culture. Their goal was to produce the kind of "100% Americans" that Milton Gordon, a leading assimilation theorist, called "Anglo-conformity."[28] Until the "Americanization" movement turned reactionary in response to World War I and the Bolshevik Revolution, it did promote some genuinely useful integrative and educational innovations, especially English-language instruction.[29] Many of its true believers, however, were unabashedly intolerant and, by today's standards, offensively intrusive as they sought to eradicate the old cultures with swift and sometimes brutal efficiency.[30]

A much more tolerant form of assimilationism derived from what Gordon called the "melting pot" ideal. (This referred to Israel Zangwill's play of that name, which in turn recalled Emerson's metaphor. The play was staged at the height of the mass European migration.) Versions of Americanism like Zangwill's paid more respect to the diverse cultures that the new immigrants were bringing with them across the Atlantic. These assimilationists imagined that the unfamiliar ways of life would both transform and enrich the dominant one. This blend would constantly change as it absorbed and dissolved new groups over time—through civic education, social mobility, and even intermarriage—yielding a fresh and hopefully superior amalgam. The language and imagery of amalgamation, however, had an exclusionary implication; it was evidence that even the liberal assimilationist visionaries of the day like Frances Kellor, John Dewey, and Louis Brandeis did not really have blacks and other non-Europeans in mind.[31]

Lest we criticize the melting pot assimilationists too harshly in a spasm of "presentism," Michael Lind reminds us that "the then-new and progressive ideal of melting-pot nationalism . . . was centrist or liberal in a time when the right was still strongly racist and nativist." Most cultural pluralists, like most of today's multiculturalists, were attacking the melting pot from the left and emphasizing toleration, inclusiveness, and resistance to Anglo-conformity.[32] Hollinger notes some important differences within these reformist ranks. He shows, for example, that the more cosmopolitan Bourne feared that Kallen's pluralism might fall prey to its more ethnocentric tendencies and harden intergroup boundaries. John Dewey, Jane Addams, Louis Brandeis, Louis Adamic, and other liberals who shared Kallen's respect for diversity debated this issue as well.

With the imposition of the national origins immigration quotas in the 1920s, which favored pre-1890s American stock, and the virtual cessation of new immigration during the Depression (in some years, there was net outmigration), assimilation became less of an issue. And the antifascist propaganda of World War II, epitomized by the "foxhole" films featuring members of different ethnic groups sacrificing for the common good, seemed to assuage fears about the parochial, balkanizing possibilities of cultural pluralism.

These fears, however, were never fully dispelled, and they continued to haunt postwar liberalism. As Hollinger suggests, this is probably why a leading pluralist work of the 1950s, Will Herberg's *Protestant, Catholic, Jew,* confined its argument to the religious domain, avoiding the dangerous romanticism and cultural sectarianism of Kallen's approach. The same fears also help explain why the early civil rights movement emphasized black integration, the permeability of group cultural boundaries, and the galvanizing, encompassing unity of American ideals. Given the long exclusion of blacks from even most liberal versions of assimilationism, this was hardly a foregone conclusion.[33]

During the late 1960s and early 1970s, however, several developments clouded this optimistic, unifying vision and radicalized ethnic group politics. With the urban riots and the Nixon administration's accession to power, black separatism gained greater influence over the civil rights movement. The Vietnam War alienated many middle-class and elite Americans from a broad range of national institutions. Impatience with group inequalities grew even as those inequalities diminished. The Democratic Party changed its rules to increase the role of minority factions and women. The result was a dominant multiculturalist sensibility that left the old politically conservative, European-centered, patriotic cultural pluralism far behind. The differences between these positions obscured their commonalities. David Hollinger notes that

> [c]ultural pluralism had been a minor movement in the history of the American academic and literary intelligentsia. By contrast, multicultural-ism has proved to be a major preoccupation in American life as regis-tered in the deliberations of local school boards and in the professional journals of the humanities and social sciences.
>
> The triumph of basic multiculturalism has fostered a sensitivity to di-versity so acute that the deep differences between the various groups and subgroups are now being addressed with unprecedented ethnographic detail and theoretical sophistication. . . . The more these differences have come to be recognized, the more difficult it has become to convincingly represent American society in classically pluralist fashion as an expanse of internally homogeneous and analogically structured units, each autho-rized by an ancestral charter and each possessed of a singular mythology of diaspora.
>
> The heightened sensitivity to diversity fostered by multiculturalism has had the ironic result of diversifying diversity to the point that the ethno-racial pentagon can no longer contain it.[34]

These fears about the damage that a robust diversity might unleash on American society persist today.[35] Why, then, have so many Americans come to believe that diversity is a vital end in itself that public and private institutions should actively foster? What can explain the widespread currency of this un-precedented, even ahistorical, view? Why don't more Americans view diver-sity as a menace, as almost all other societies have always done and still do?

One possible answer is that many Americans *do* oppose diversity—that the 1965 reform of the immigration law did not mark the end of nativism, and the surge of newcomers since then has aroused latent fears about diversity. There is much truth to this answer. A recent study of nativism in the United States, France, and Germany finds that it survives in all of them, though it ebbs and flows.[36] It is also true that most Americans continue to favor lower levels of immigration.[37] Still, no one can doubt that the United States is far more receptive to diverse immigration than any other country, with the pos-sible exception of Canada. Nor is immigration the only domain of diversity in which American attitudes are distinctive. For example, American environ-mentalism differs from its foreign counterparts in a number of respects, in-cluding its emphasis on the use of law to protect species and habitat diversity, much as the American civil rights movement used it to promote racial diver-sity.[38] As we shall see in Chapter 7, Americans' religiosity is also exceptional among advanced industrial societies.

Another response to this question about American exceptionalism is to deny the premise that we know history's record of diversity-related violence. After all, we are often said to be an antihistorical people eager to efface our pasts, invent ourselves anew, and conquer the future. Perhaps we are a people so blessed that we can afford to disregard Santayana's oft-repeated dictum that "[t]hose who cannot remember the past are condemned to repeat it,"[39] ignoring many of the harsh lessons history has taught other peoples. Intoxicated by our sense of unique destiny, perhaps we assume that any such lessons simply do not apply to us.

Americans, however, are no more ignorant of the past than other people; indeed, the nation's ever-higher educational level suggests more exposure to these lessons, not less. Moreover, newspaper headlines and television reports about the use of American troops for international peacekeeping, humanitarian, military, and nation-building purposes have made us all too familiar with the risks of communal violence in societies that use force to extrude troublesome minorities from their midst. Americans today are more aware than ever before of our own grim history of discrimination.

The question thus remains: why have Americans come to believe that the communal violence associated with diversity throughout the world and throughout time will not happen here? We might begin with the human tendency to make a virtue of necessity—here, demographic necessity—to accept what cannot be changed and make the best of it. Ethnic and other diversities, greatly extended through the post-1965 migrations to the United States, are already so pervasive and entrenched today that the real question for pragmatic Americans is not whether they would have favored these diversities initially. It is how best to live with them now that they are in place and seem irreversible. This attitude helps explain public sentiments toward immigrants and immigration that might otherwise seem inconsistent. Most Americans tend to admire the immigrants they know and believe that immigration-related diversity has been good for the country, but they also wish there were less of it—and they have *always* felt this way. A leading student of public views on immigration puts it vividly: "We view immigrants with rose-colored glasses turned backwards."[40]

By itself, this explanation is unsatisfying. It begins with the post-1965 diversity regime when what needs explaining is why this regime has proved so durable and has become a policy platform for the promotion of further diversity. Much support for diversity is genuinely enthusiastic, more than a grudging surrender to demographic realities. There are other and better explanations for Americans' exceptional commitment to diversity. Indeed, there are too many of them, making it hard to be certain of their relative causal significance.

All polities, including our own, possess social resources for repressing and sublimating ugly and shameful memories. But a striking feature of modern life, especially after a growing understanding of the Holocaust spawned a truly international and militant human rights movement, is that such denials and concealments are now more difficult to maintain. Under these novel conditions, one should not underestimate the power of an aroused and mobilized public morality to shape a collective sense of guilt and injustice strong enough to influence national attitudes and policies. This reformist zeal has punctuated American politics from its colonial beginnings, especially during and after the recurrent periods of intense religious revivalism known as "great awakenings."[41]

Today, many Americans, largely but not exclusively on the political left, want to use immigration and other preferential policies as a way to acknowledge and rectify past wrongs perpetrated by the United States and its allies: the expropriation of Native Americans; the abominations of slavery and segregation; the internment of Americans of Japanese descent during World War II; the Vietnam War; support of tyrannical regimes in the Caribbean, Philippines, Central America, and elsewhere before and during the Cold War; historic discrimination against ethnic minorities and women; and newly disclosed atrocities during the Korean War. Animated by feelings of shame and a desire for reconciliation and reparation, the U.S. government has in all of these cases adopted remedial policies. Some of these policies—for example, affirmative action programs, civil rights laws, and immigration preferences for our Vietnam War allies, Amerasian children, and Cold War proxies in Central America—have predictably increased diversity.

Support for a diverse immigration policy, of course, is motivated by more than shame and guilt. Traditional interest-group politics explains much of it. Agricultural growers and many other businesses have long favored expanded immigration from countries that can supply needed workers.[42] Even some groups that traditionally opposed immigration now support it. Blacks, for example, are eager to cement political coalitions with Latino groups seeking more immigration from Central and South America.[43] Organized labor now views immigrants as potential members and even favors both a broad amnesty for many undocumented workers and the reform of the law imposing sanctions on those who employ them.[44] Much support, moreover, comes from relatively advantaged Americans who enjoy the economic and other benefits of immigration, including diversity values, without themselves having to compete with immigrants for housing, jobs, and schools.[45]

Celebration of diversity is closely related to the changing ideological status of the assimilationist ideal. A number of commentators like Peter Salins and John Miller claim that many Americans and newcomers alike have rejected that ideal, at least in its melting pot version.[46] It is difficult to parse this claim, which raises controversial, often unresolvable issues of fact, value, methodology, causality, and interpretation. At this point, my purpose is only to note some reasons why diversity has become a leading social goal, not to assess its complex relationship with assimilation. I have analyzed the latter question in some detail elsewhere,[47] and take it up again in Chapter 4, so I need only sketch the general contours of the debate here.

First, there are threshold definitional questions of what assimilation means and whether this meaning has changed since the proverbial good old days.[48] In fact, assimilation has always meant many different things, as my earlier discussion suggests. As a historical matter, Anglo-conformity, melting pot amalgamation, and cultural pluralism coexisted. They still do, although the mix varies. (Anglo-conformity, for example, is now out of vogue.)[49] Glazer notes that until the 1890s, Americans did not view assimilation as a problem because (quoting historian John Higham)

> [a]ssimilation was either taken for granted or viewed as inconceivable. . . . For European peoples it was thought to be the natural, almost inevitable, outcome of life in America. For other races assimilation was believed to be largely unattainable and therefore not a source of concern. Only at the end of the century did . . . large numbers of white Americans come to fear that assimilation was *not* occurring among major European groups and that it was going too far among other minorities, notably blacks, Orientals, and Jews.[50]

This earlier insouciance about assimilation now seems quaint but for altogether different and revealing reasons. Americans who want the newcomers to assimilate worry that multiculturalism is retarding assimilation, balkanizing American society, and weakening our civic culture. Many also fear that the children of immigrants are gravitating toward the deviant, dysfunctional enclaves of American culture, that they are assimilating all too well but to the wrong values, presaging their own downward mobility. Finally, many Americans who favor diversity oppose the tendency of ethnic political leaders to promote forms of separatism even though their rank-and-file desperately want to assimilate for economic and social reasons.[51] I return to these immigration-related issues in Chapter 4.

Another set of questions is empirical and methodological. How should we measure assimilation? Are immigrants in fact assimilating more slowly or differently than in the past? The standard criteria—intermarriage rates, English fluency, naturalization patterns, civic participation, moral values, noncriminal conduct, attenuation of ties to the country of origin—are not self-defining.[52] Moreover, the evidence on English acquisition is difficult to interpret. Some of it is self-reported, much turns on the age at arrival and length of time in the United States, and we know far less about English acquisition by pre-1960s waves of immigrants. With those qualifications, the first generation (the immigrants) seems as eager as ever to learn English, and the second generation (their U.S.-born children) are learning it quickly and prefer it to their parents' languages.[53] Finally, generalizations about assimilation rates can be misleading, as they vary considerably among different ethnic groups—another reflection of diversity's significance.[54]

However one plots the precise historical trajectory of the assimilationist ideal in its several forms, there is little doubt that the cultural pluralism version, with its enthusiastic affirmation of diversity values, enjoys far greater acceptance today than ever before. In large part, its current standing reflects the widespread belief among Americans that we can have it both ways, that the study, celebration, and maintenance of diverse traditions are compatible with assimilation to core American values. This belief has helped to legitimate what historian Thomas Archdeacon calls an "intermediate path" in which diverse groups affirm their distinctive cultural traditions while also integrating into the broader civic culture.[55] Advocates of this approach reject the traditional melting pot ideal in favor of other metaphorical visions: a mosaic composed of permanent, visible fragments, or a lumpy chef's salad containing diverse ingredients.

The central question is whether American society can successfully thread the needle socially and politically. Can it knit these disparate identities seamlessly and effectively enough to satisfy both the affective needs of parochial communities and the civic needs of the larger polities in which they are embedded? The analysis that can address this question turns primarily on the kinds of communal identities at stake, how robust the largely informal processes of political and social integration are, and which claims on present and possibly future members the polities need to make. In the chapters that follow, I answer the question with a qualified yes.

In explaining how diversity values came to be elevated in our public discourse, the civil rights movement in general and the evolution of black politics in particular are central. The story of the black struggle for equality has been told many times and never fails to inspire and instruct.[56] Black leaders, artists, and intellectuals of every kind have explored the complex feelings that blacks have always harbored toward an American society that for centuries enslaved, lynched, humiliated, reviled, and excluded them, and toward the alluring but distant prospect of ever becoming fully integrated members of it.[57] Given this long tradition of approach avoidance by black elites, it was natural for many black leaders to express frustration with the pace of integration, which relied largely on enforcement of a relatively passive nondiscrimination principle and had not seemed to work as well for blacks as for religious minorities and other ethnic groups. It was also natural for them to seek individual and group advancement instead through ostensibly more promising strategies. In this spirit, they sought to develop community cohesiveness by invoking racial pride and "black power," to foster self-help and racial identity by building exclusively black institutions, and to challenge the traditional accommodationist approaches of moderate black leaders.[58] They also adopted a more confrontational and ideological political style, along with a more radically redistributionist agenda including expansive welfare rights and affirmative action.

Although the black nationalist movement was always a minority fringe among blacks—a recent estimate places its adherents at no more than 50,000 people—its ideological influence was far greater, extending to other minorities and to whites seized by the fervor of ethnic identity-building.[59] This far-reaching idealization of diversity gathered steam in the late 1960s and early 1970s. It was generously supported—financially, ideologically, and rhetorically—by the Ford, Rockefeller, and other major foundations committed to fundamental social reforms. These powerful organizations promoted diversity as an integral element of a larger legal and political strategy. This strategy employed group mobilization, impact litigation, local control, and community action in an attempt to transform schools, voting, housing, and other social institutions of every kind. This approach soon spread to smaller foundations and university-based action projects as well.[60] It was also taken up by the public schools, which jettisoned a model of "intercultural education" that had been a product of the World War II struggle against fascism and was promoted largely by private elites, in favor of a more critical, state-driven "multicultural education" model. This avowedly pluralistic model advanced a pedagogical vision going well beyond the blander virtue of toleration to stress group recognition, respect, identity, and social mobility.[61]

All of this occurred at a time when blacks were making immense progress in political, economic, and social life.[62] One can view this conjunction of progress and ideological shift as a paradoxical fact. Alternatively, one can view it as an instance of rising but disappointed expectations fueled by a new kind of identity politics pursued by more confident, better-educated activists. I incline toward the latter view, in part because this same conjunction has been observed in the political movements of Mexican-Americans, Native Americans, gays and lesbians, the disabled, the elderly, and other groups.[63] Indeed, the black struggle for equality—its rhetoric of disadvantage and segregation, its assertion of group identity, its moral urgency, its legal strategy, and its programmatic direction—constitutes the template on which these other groups have tried to impress their own claims. Blacks' crusade to enforce America's ancient but still-unredeemed promises has become the model for other civil rights and human rights struggles not only in the United States but throughout the world.

Diversity values gained recognition in the U.S. Supreme Court in the 1970s. In *Lau v. Nichols,* a 1974 decision, the Court held that the civil rights laws required local public school districts to provide special programs to enable children with limited English proficiency to enjoy equal educational opportunity.[64] *Lau* drove a vast expansion of bilingual education programs in the public schools for the bewildering array of language groups that the post-1965 immigration brought to America. In the case of *Regents of California v. Bakke,* decided in 1978, the swing opinion of a sharply divided Supreme Court suggested that a public university's system of race-based admission preferences might be upheld against white applicants' claims of reverse discrimination if justified on the ground of student body "diversity."[65] *Lau* and *Bakke* are discussed in some detail in Chapters 4 and 5, respectively.

The new politics of black identity in the 1960s, as well as the adoption of affirmative action programs favoring nonwhite minorities, cast the pursuit of a diversity ideal in a more assertive, even belligerent light. This helped to energize in white ethnic groups their own identity politics, which celebrated their continuing "unmeltability," underwrote their opposition to affirmative action, and weaned many of them away from the Democratic Party.[66] Three decades later, the tremors from this political convulsion are still being felt—although, as sociologist Mary Waters has shown, there is reason to doubt the continuing robustness of some of these asserted ethnic identities.[67]

Several subsequent developments make the prospect of integrating diversity with a vibrant, cohesive civic culture seem less menacing and more feasible. The immense growth of the U.S. economy since the 1960s has softened the zero-sum competition for resources that pits ethnic groups against one another. Since 1970, the U.S. economy has absorbed more than 20 million new permanent immigrants, not to mention a vast increase in the number of women working outside the home. During this period, the economy generated about 55 million new jobs and expanded the GDP more than eightfold in current dollars, while maintaining unemployment at merely frictional levels and inflation generally at or below the level of productivity gains.[68] This stunning progress makes diversity seem perfectly compatible with, perhaps even a cause of, a steady rise in the standard of living of almost all Americans, including most of the poor.[69]

In addition, new technologies have familiarized more people than ever before with diversity in its most attractive forms, accustoming them to its importance in American life. With occasional (protested and publicly rebuked) exceptions, the mass media's depiction of ethnic, religious, and other diverse groups, if often stereotypical, tends generally to be positive or inoffensive. The not-so-subtle suggestion is that despite our superficial differences, we are all essentially alike beneath the skin, accent, or garb. In addition, the spatially diffuse nature of mass media means that they expose us to diverse peoples and cultures while keeping them at a safe distance. Viewing them in our dens or theaters, we can have diversity on the cheap and without risk. We can enjoy a kind of disembodied exoticism without actually having to live cheek by jowl with people whose different ways of believing and behaving make them distinctive and worth understanding but whose differences also create challenges for social integration, legal equality, and political unity.

In the nation's classrooms, as noted earlier, teachers in the 1960s and 1970s transformed their earlier commitment to "intercultural education" stressing toleration into "multicultural education" programs, including bilingual education, that went farther to celebrate, promote, and reinforce differences. More generally, larger cultural trends favoring an easygoing, libertarian, live-and-let-live stance toward diversity began to accelerate in the 1960s and have continued ever since.[70]

Corporate managers and their consultants, drawing on earlier organizational theories, have also developed a "diversity rhetoric" that views racial, ethnic, and many other diversities—including some that civil rights law does not protect—as a valuable business resource. This rhetoric holds that a diverse workforce facilitates the identification and solution of problems in all areas of the organization's activity, and also helps the organization to succeed in a "new economy" of globalization, intense competition, creativity, internal flexibility, and multicultural competence.[71] At a time when business enjoys immense social influence and rewards, corporate leaders' efforts to exalt and extend diversity's scope, meaning, and value and to exhort their employees to implement it is bound to affect how diversity is idealized. According to a recent study, "[d]iversity rhetoric replaced the legal vision of diversity . . . grounded in moral efforts to right historical wrongs, with a managerial vision of diversity . . . grounded in the notion that organizations must adapt to their environments in order to profit."[72]

For all these reasons, the abstract ideal of diversity, which was either opposed or peripheral in all cultures at all times, is now glorified in American ideals and practices. Where diversity was viewed at best as a necessary evil, it is now a goal of both private institutions and public policy. Consider the revealing mirror of everyday language. Diversity's antonym, uniformity, today tends to attract disparaging adjectives like "bland," "sterile," "boring," and "whitebread."[73] Another sign is the extent to which diversity-friendly public opinion, policy discourse, and technologies have discredited even established enclaves and dominant emblems of homogeneity in American life such as public school systems, heterosexuality, the English language, mainstream churches, network television, and even traditional family structures.

Nor is diversity merely a widespread ideal among social and educational elites. It is now an explicit political norm endorsed by both major parties and opposed by none (save Patrick Buchanan's wing of the Reform Party, which only 0.5% of the voters supported in the 2000 presidential election). Today, it is almost inconceivable that those who oppose more immigration, more integrated residential communities, or greater accommodation of religious practices or the disabled would express their opposition in terms of rejection of the diversity ideal as such. Elsewhere I have argued that in the late 1990s, the Republican Party at all levels of government turned decisively and permanently in a new direction that favors expansive, ethnically diverse immigration and greater solicitude for non-Cuban Latinos, Asians, blacks and other minorities, and women who have often voted against its candidates.[74] Economic historian Robert Fogel's assertion that "commitment to diversity is essential to any party that aspires to govern"[75] is confirmed by congressional Republicans' conspicuous failure in recent years to challenge affirmative action. This acquiescence, detailed in Chapter 5, reflects deep fears about the political consequences of being depicted as racist or antiminority.[76]

At the dawn of the twenty-first century, American politics has in effect installed a diversity ratchet. There is now no turning back.

DIVERSITY AS A CONTEMPORARY VALUE

We have seen that the ideal of diversity—diversity as an affirmative goal of civil society and of government—has gained broad acceptance in America only very recently and only after a very long struggle with the forces favoring ethnic and cultural homogeneity, forces that have almost always prevailed in virtually all other societies. The intriguing and compelling question remains—why?

I have already discussed some historical and sociopolitical causes: diversity's firm demographic grounding; the scruples prompted by national guilt; the nature of immigration politics; novel challenges to the assimilation ideal; the evolution of the civil rights movement; the success of other claimant groups in appropriating this movement's moral prestige and rhetoric; the softening of traditional resistance through corporate marketing, steady economic growth, and technological change. But we still cannot fully answer the "why" question until we understand the interests and values that Americans of varying ideological stripes think diversity serves and disserves. Even this, of course, cannot conclusively answer the "why" question; after all, Americans may misapprehend diversity's effects or may embrace it for other reasons.

Still, knowing the interests and values that diversity implicates will bring us as close as we can get to a sense of why we pursue it as avidly as we now do.

I am unaware of any systematic effort to analyze diversity in these terms.[77] Nevertheless, many of the positive values that diversity enthusiasts claim for it closely resemble, *mutatis mutandis,* certain values advanced by some familiar political and social theories. And although large gaps always exist between a society's avowed, abstract ideals and its actual behavior, we should still expect a strong correspondence between the values that we proclaim and the advantageous consequences that we *think* society would reap from their pursuit and realization.

Let us consider, then, how one would understand and assess diversity, both positively and negatively, under four different political-social theories: liberalism, communitarianism, utilitarianism, and what I shall call functionalism. I begin with two disclaimers. First, as will soon be apparent, I discuss each of these theories in a schematic and summary fashion, and I discuss each of them as if it were monolithic and canonical when in fact different theorists claiming to be liberals, communitarians, utilitarians, functionalists, or whatever advance different, often incompatible, versions of each. Such a simplifying treatment is justified, I think, by the very limited purpose for which I wish to use them—to reveal how thoughtful people holding different normative commitments might regard and evaluate diversity. For this purpose I need not explicate the theories systematically or at length but shall merely discuss them insofar as they bear on diversity values.

Second, I do not mean to suggest that most Americans actually think, much less theorize, in this way. Nor do I propose that these are the only theories that one might plausibly defend, or that they are internally coherent or empirically sound. Other ideological categories also speak to diversity issues, sometimes more directly than the theories I discuss. Instead, I simply assume that taken together the theories I discuss are likely to capture all of the diversity values, positive and negative, of which the vast majority of Americans are aware. For this reason, I discuss utilitarianism separately and very briefly, even though it is more a theory about how to define social welfare than a comprehensive social-political theory.

Liberalism

The relationship between liberalism and diversity is subtle and, as we shall see, multidimensional. Although many versions of liberal theory have been advanced, their common theme is the paramount value of individual freedom and autonomy. Competing versions of liberalism differ about the nature of individuals, the conditions conducive to this freedom, the nature, limits, and moral status of self-interest and other motivations,[78] the relationship between individual and group rights, government's role in defining and securing these rights, and many other ideas. They converge, however, on the centrality of individual flourishing, the free and independent wills of all persons, and their rights. In this sense, at least, libertarianism is simply a subset of liberalism; libertarians' approach to diversity does not differ significantly from that of more garden-variety liberals.

Most versions of liberalism do not really regard diversity as an independent or ultimate value. Rather, they view diversity as a possible, or even a probable, consequence of individuals' autonomous exercise of their wills and rights.[79] The reason is plain. As discussed in Chapter 2, all individuals possess a unique genotype, phenotype, and psychology. All are further influenced by different geophysical and historical forces and by social institutions and ideologies that lend structure to, and reciprocally affect, their particular interests. People who exercise their free wills in order to advance their perceived interests are bound to make diverse choices and commitments, pursuing their ends with more or less success.

These choices, according to liberal theory, constitute the authentic expressions of individuals' freedom and autonomy. To that extent, choices also constitute their social identities and their ways of life. Liberalism's respect for this freedom and autonomy implies a respect for this identity and the choices that constitute it. Liberal theorists disagree, of course, about the social, political, economic, and psychological conditions that must obtain before one can properly ascribe to individuals the genuine freedom of will that alone can legitimate their choices. They also disagree about the state's role in establishing, altering, and interfering with these conditions. But the diversity that flows from these exercises of individual freedom is presumptively valid, although the strength of the presumption and the circumstances under which it may be overridden depend on the particular liberal theory.

Liberalism, then, finds diversity not only congenial but also definitional or constitutive. For this reason, liberalism accords a special, even privileged role to markets. Markets, in this view, are highly responsive mechanisms for giving effect to individuals' diverse choices and assuring that buyers and sellers will only conclude transactions when both of them believe that they will advance their own interests by doing so. Because the diversity of individuals' interests and preferences is precisely what makes transactions possible and mutually advantageous, the more diversity there is, the more beneficial exchanges can occur.

Markets affect diversity in other complex and interesting ways—and vice versa. The existence and pursuit of comparative advantage and of scale economies among producers lead to specialization of functions, which in turn engenders the further diversification of skills, products, interests, and preferences. This specialization of functions, like the market itself, underscores the importance of the interdependencies among market participants, the self-interested value of cooperating with others, and the benefits of attending to their interests as well as one's own. In this often-ignored sense, the market is—as Adam Smith maintained—a civilizing, socializing, and pacifying process.[80] This is so even as it wreaks creative destruction (in Joseph Schumpeter's famous phrase) with remorseless efficiency.[81] In this important sense, the market makes the toleration of differences an economic virtue and not just a civic one, and it reserves its greatest rewards for those who are skillful at anticipating and promoting differences for which people are willing to pay.

Under certain conditions, however, diversity can impose significant costs and impair the market efficiency that liberalism prizes. Where interconnectivity and network externalities are significant (i.e., where an activity's value to individual participants increases geometrically as the number of participants increases, as with a telephone or computer network), market competition among different service or connectivity standards may be less efficient than having the state mandate uniform standards. Adverse selection in insurance is another diversity-related impediment to market efficiency. Where participants in an insurance pool are diverse in ways that pose significantly different risks of loss but their premiums are based on average risk rather than on their own risk, people who pose lower-than-average risks will want to avoid or abandon this pool in favor of insurance for which they can pay a premium reflecting their own, lower risk. This will leave only relatively high-risk people in the first insurance pool, unable to afford that high-cost coverage. Even liberal polities, which generally privilege market allocations over state-mandated equality, often find this outcome politically unacceptable and decide to subsidize coverage.

In the liberal conception, diversity is much more than just the result flowing from free individual choices in a market economy. Diversity also affects how individuals perceive the world, including what they assume is natural and what they think is possible. For this reason, diversity helps to shape our preferences as well as reflect them. People who have grown up in a homogeneous social, physical, or cultural environment form their assumptions about what is normal on the basis of their experience of sameness, which they take to be normal, even natural. Japanese people who have never seen Scandinavians are more likely to think of black as the natural hair color. Fundamentalist Muslims who have never seen women venture outside the home except in the company of a male family member are likely to think of females in the labor force not simply as irreligious but as unnatural. Those who have lived their lives in an isolated rural village are more likely to doubt the possibility of high-rise apartment living or air travel. The penetration of television into each of these settings has transformed these assumptions, of course, but that is precisely the point. Experiencing diversity causes us to think differently—and sometimes to desire different things.

In this sense, one may see diversity as a precondition for the genuine exercise of a fully informed, de-"naturalized" freedom that is liberalism's principal goal. Diversity's enlargement of freedom in this sense, however, will affect individuals in different ways. At one extreme, diversity can arouse awe and wonder about the sheer profusion, complexity, and ineffability of life that implicate spiritual values and engender the kind of world-love of which poets like Walt Whitman, who are particularly attuned to diversity, have sung. To observe people of different cultures, beliefs, and conditions going about the prosaic business of living is, I think, to gain greater respect for the resourcefulness, vitality, adaptability, resilience, humor, and courage of the species. A liberal society whose raison d'être is to enable individuals to pursue self-realization and material well-being has a special need to cultivate this kind of world-love and mutual respect. Diversity is among the most valuable resources for doing so.

But there is a much darker side to this diversity-inspired freedom, one that threatens the liberal project. The encounter with diversity is one of the most far-reaching elements of the larger process of modernization. In traditional, ethnically sequestered societies, as well as in traditional enclaves of already modernized ones, this encounter is jarring and disorienting. Instead of arousing solidaristic, humanitarian feelings, the experience may excite the very opposite—fear, repugnance, and intolerance—and impel a retreat to the comforts of familiarity, sameness, and a kind of primordial identification only with those whom one defines as one's own. At the extreme, this tribalism (as it is aptly called) cultivates a smouldering hatred of the other that, with little warning or pretext, can burst into a communal conflagration and even genocidal violence against newcomers, foreigners, or others deemed to be outside the tribe—even those who have been neighbors for centuries. The recent bloodlettings in Rwanda, Bosnia, Kosovo, Azerbaijan, Northern Ireland, India, Afghanistan, and other killing fields confirm these dread dangers.

Even in civil societies accustomed to and comfortable with it, however, diversity often sows conflict and discord that impose significant social costs and impede the attainment of individual goals that liberalism promotes. Within any particular group—whether public or private, profit or nonprofit—the existence of conflicting views and interests, mobilized by strategic behavior opportunities, magnifies the costs of internal governance, decisionmaking, and collective action. In the extreme, this can produce organizational paralysis or failure.[82] At a political or societal level, diverse interests typically organize into groups that seek to benefit themselves and their members by competing with others for resources, status, and various forms of power.[83] This competition benefits society in many important ways. For example, it can limit undue concentrations of political and economic power, increase accountability by elites, enhance the public's participation in decisions that affect them, encourage innovation, educate public officials about the consequences of their actions, and the like.[84]

But this same diversity-driven competition can also be socially damaging. The need for collective action to achieve social and individual goals is a perennial concern in a liberal society where free riding and other forms of opportunistic behavior by individuals and groups are endemic because of the limits on state power.[85] Sometimes only a sense of common purpose and commitment can overcome these obstacles and support the social undertakings and public goods essential to communal well-being. Recent social science has developed the notions of social and cultural capital, including trust, to describe the qualities of civic life that are required to forge and sustain these bonds.[86] Yet a diversity that is too widespread, too divisive, too inward-looking, and runs too deeply can narrow or dissolve these bonds—or even prevent them from forming in the first place. In an extreme form, we can see the high price that diversity exacts in Canada, Russia, Sri Lanka, Nigeria, Spain, and a host of other states vulnerable to secession movements. But this problem is also evident in much smaller social groups where diversity increases conflict levels and impairs group performance.[87]

Diversity also raises a host of practical and legal problems for societies committed to the liberal principle of equal treatment, dignity, and respect. In order to apply this fundamental principle, we must first decide which groups are similar enough that they must be treated the same, and which are sufficiently different that they fall into different categories justifying disparate treatment. Is a conscientious objector who is an atheist sufficiently similar to a member of a religious group like the Quakers that he, like them, should be draft-exempt, or does the nonreligious basis for his opposition to war make him more like individuals who have "merely" political objections to war?[88] Is the Boy Scouts sufficiently similar to the Rotary Club to be under the same duty to accept members it wishes to exclude (in this case, gays), or is the Scouts more like a religious group whose power to exclude is essential to its very meaning?[89]

Such questions arise constantly in a diverse, organizationally complex society like the United States, yet it is precisely this complexity that makes them so difficult to answer coherently. The more variables that are arguably relevant to the identity of an individual or group, the more indeterminate and controversial the judgment about how to classify and treat it will be. And the more indeterminate and controversial this judgment is, the more likely people are to view it as discriminatory and unfair. In a diverse, liberal society, this perception is particularly corrosive to faith in the rule of equality under law.

Consider the phenomenon of liberal citizenship in an era of massive migration by individuals from many different cultures.[90] On which grounds can a liberal state properly refuse to admit strangers? Is it ground enough that the state concludes through democratic processes that some groups are less likely than others to assimilate to the dominant culture? Once migrants are on the state's territory, can the state discriminate against them in its allocation of resources and status? Is it obliged to offer them full membership, and if so, what does full membership include? Which preconditions for citizenship can the state fairly require the migrant to meet? What level of cultural assimilation can it require and which are the appropriate indicia of this assimilation?

In a liberal polity, each of these issues (and a host of others) becomes more problematic because of three tenets of modern liberalism's "voluntarist conception of freedom" (in Michael Sandel's disapproving phrase).[91] First, state power to coerce individuals should be limited except when collective action to implement collective norms can be specially justified. Second, the scope of market and other consensual institutions should be correspondingly maximized. Third, the state should maintain a scrupulous neutrality as among different conceptions of the good out of respect for individuals' freedom and autonomy to choose their own ends. (As Chapter 7 shows, courts have interpreted this neutrality principle to support a variety of value-laden policy choices affecting religion.) When migrants are culturally and demographically diverse among themselves and are also differentiated from the native population in important respects, these difficulties are exacerbated by political ones. Natives more easily think of the newcomers (especially if they are undocumented)[92] not as members of the same community but as unassimilable, undeserving "others."[93]

In such societies, minority demands for special religious, linguistic, and other cultural rights, not to mention claims for political autonomy, inevitably arise. The law's management of multicultural and affirmative action claims in the United States is considered in Chapters 4 and 5. For present purposes, however, a threshold question is whether these are best understood as liberal claims on behalf of persons who seek to exercise their freedom as autonomous individuals, or instead as group claims that are not really intelligible on a liberal, individualistic account of value. I take the former, liberal view, at least insofar as a democratic society like the United States is concerned. In the most individualistic and market-friendly societies like the United States, people intensively crave—and must fashion for themselves—the affective and solidaristic ties to others that individualism inhibits and that people in more communitarian societies simply inherit and take for granted.

The fact that group life is important even in nonliberal societies does not mean that group interests cannot ultimately be reduced, as a normative matter, to the interests of individuals. It is true that individuals and their identities are constituted in large part by their group affiliations, and that a liberal legal system that protects individuals' freedom must enable them to associate with others to pursue commonly defined ends. It is also true that even a liberal system of law and politics must treat individuals as group members for certain purposes (e.g., barring discrimination on the basis of imputed group membership, or using groups as administrative categories). Such a system may confer certain rights on organizations such as limited liability, standing to represent members, perpetual existence, and even self-government. These group interests and rights, however, claim justification in terms of the interests and rights of their individual members.[94] Hierarchical organizations like the Catholic Church almost always have some norm (individual salvation through the Church) or mechanism (confession) that is meant to assure the group's fidelity to its members' interests, and vice versa. Even defenders of multicultural rights in modern democracies ultimately ground those rights in the welfare of individual group members, not of the groups themselves.[95] Will Kymlicka, for example, who insists that group rights are compatible with liberalism and may even be required by it, calls them "group-differentiated rights" and advocates them for certain "national minority" and immigrant groups. I discuss Kymlicka's theory in Chapter 4.

There may be a persuasive social theory that values groups *qua* groups quite apart from their value to individuals. Insofar as American society is concerned, however, I do not know what it would be.[96] Even pluralism, at least in its American form, values groups not for themselves but for how they affect individuals and the larger social system. My point is not that groups have no interest in diversity values. Indeed, their character, integrity, and perhaps even their survival vitally depend on how individuals and society think about diversity. The point, rather, is that diversity is ultimately valorized by individual or communal assessments.

To be sure, certain traditional societies do not conceive of individuals apart from the groups to which they belong, much less value their interests in opposition to those of the groups. New Zealand's Maoris are an example.[97] But such traditions have little to teach us about managing diversity in twenty-first-century America. Accordingly, we need not develop a separate group-

qua-group model to account for the diversity values that Americans find in the groups they inhabit or join. Liberalism adequately captures those values.

Communitarianism

Liberalism, of course, has spawned many critics. Liberalism's critics may differ over many things, but almost all of them—whether they call themselves civic republicans, cultural conservatives, fundamentalists, communitarians, socialists, communists, nationalists, fascists, monarchists, nativists, syndicalists, neo-Platonists, or something else—share at least two important things. First, they long for an integrative, soul-satisfying, character-cultivating community. Second, they agree that liberalism, with its emphasis on individuals' rights to pursue their own conceptions of the good without collective interference, is incapable of providing this community and may even destroy it. These critics, however, would (or at least should) concede that individual liberal citizens, in exercising their autonomous choices, may place a high value on communal encounters and solidarity. Such a valuation, although animated more by self-interest than by communitarian ideals, actually becomes more likely as a society becomes wealthier.[98]

Whereas liberalism is conducive and congenial to diversity, this communitarian vision (as I call it for want of a better label)[99] finds diversity problematic to its program of communal cohesion. This is so even when communitarians recognize, as many do, that diversity in today's America is a social fact and produces some of the benefits that liberals claim for it. At the heart of the communitarian vision, after all, are not individual purposes but common ones. In this view, these common ends are discovered, legitimated, and executed only through the active, shared participation of the polity's citizenry in collective life. Communitarians, especially the civic republican and statist varieties, ascribe to government a far-reaching responsibility to turn individuals into active citizens committed to deliberation and practical reason, to help form their character by cultivating civic virtues, and to forge communal identities throughout society.

Diversity does not necessarily prevent government from doing these things, but it does render each task more difficult to accomplish. Diversity tends to make the identification and pursuit of common goals elusive, if not illusory. This attenuation and fragmentation of common purpose, of course, is a matter of degree. Globalization has brought diversity to even the most communitarian societies; indeed, migration, telecommunications, and market culture are increasing diversity everywhere. For example, Japan, a notoriously extreme case of ethnic, cultural, and economic homogeneity, now includes a substantial and growing population of long-term foreign nationals (mostly Koreans) and guestworkers who are affecting the society in ways that many Japanese believe are insidious.[100]

A high level of diversity can undermine a communitarian ethos. Many Japanese fear that it is threatening theirs; others throughout the world blame globalization, especially global capitalism and labor migration, for the same reason.[101] The American Framers obsessed about the possibility that diversity would endanger their new regime. Assailed by internal and external sources of disorder and fragmentation, the young republic needed a strong civic integument to bind the national polity together. James Madison was perhaps the most astute in recognizing the threat that diversity posed to the fragile national unity and sound governance. In his Federalist No. 10, Madison famously analyzed the problem of economic and social diversity—its multiplication of narrow interests that might combine to subvert the broader public interest—and he devised a novel remedy.[102] By expanding the polity to include a broader range of interests, he wrote, a stable and monolithic majority could not as easily oppress the rights and interests of minorities that should be protected. Ironically and brilliantly, Madison's solution to the problem of social diversity was for the state to encompass more of it.[103]

Madison, however, was not a staunch communitarian. He endorsed communitarian values only in compromised, quasi-liberal form,[104] and feared that majoritarian or populist governments, no less than monarchical ones, might oppress important interests and liberties. Yet he saw the necessity for a vigorous central authority to discharge certain responsibilities. In order for more diversity to serve as the remedy for majoritarian dangers, Madison had to support a federal republic on a continental scale, one whose powers would largely concern national defense, foreign affairs, regulation of interstate commerce, and certain other areas in which federal authority and initiative were needed to blunt the parochial tendencies of individuals and states. Diversity was an attractive remedy to Madison, however, only insofar as its risks could be muted. He hoped that deliberative, civically engaged, virtuous, and patriotic elites at all levels—he regarded the state legislatures as special dangers—could achieve the requisite harmony, while the dispersal and limitation of governmental powers would tame their dangerous propensities.

Diversity poses other threats to the communitarian project. Vigorous public participation in civic affairs is the very essence of communitarian citizenship, yet diversity could discourage it. Citizens who do not share the common goals and values that the political community invokes to define itself are likely to feel estranged from it or oppressed by it. They may view politics as a futile, frustrating activity that compounds their marginality. Indeed, the more solidaristic the community, the more profound this alienation and oppression may be. Being (or being seen as) different creates psychological confusion within oneself and conflict with the larger group. This is the experience, for example, of many long-resident foreigners in Japan and even of Japanese nationals who, because of foreign parentage or otherwise, are viewed as different. They participate in civic life at low levels, mirroring their lack of social integration.[105] Closer to home, Indians in the United States who find tribal norms oppressive may have no choice but to leave the tribe.[106]

Reactions of this kind are common among newcomers to any social group who have not yet assimilated its norms, or who perhaps actively resist them. Often, they retreat from the dominant communities from which they are alienated into smaller normative enclaves where they can nourish their own values and live by their own rules.[107] This enclave strategy has been studied in many different kinds of social groups—for example, religious sects, spiritual cults, street gangs, immigrant neighborhoods, and the like. For all the affective and spiritual consolations of such a strategy, it may actually hinder the group's integration into the larger communal mainstream by accentuating and perhaps institutionalizing differences that might otherwise be transient or insignificant.

Certain radical forms of communitarianism, moreover, demand an ideological commitment to some monistic understanding of society, economy, polity, history, and in some cases God. In the United States, Old Order Amish and Orthodox Jewish communities have this character.[108] Classic Marxism envisioned a future in which social divisions, largely defined by economic classes and their distinctive interests and worldviews, would first sharpen and clash but, once the means of production were socially controlled, would give way to a harmonious unity of interests and worldviews. Many European socialist movements advanced similar, if less apocalyptic, visions. In general, communitarian utopianism has had little use for diversity except perhaps at the margins where it cannot threaten social harmony and collective authority. The teleology of these visions is almost always one of ever-increasing social harmony and unity.

Finally, this tension between communitarianism and diversity is even greater at the global level. The diversity of interests among, and not only within, states confounds their aspirations for a peaceful international community governed by international law. Indeed, even the growing integration of states into regional blocs that have achieved some degree of harmonization among themselves, as the European Union has, may exacerbate the bloc's conflicts and diversity of interests with its outside competitors—a dynamic illustrated, for example, by the European Union's growing tensions with the United States and even with potential members like Turkey and the

Czech Republic.[109] In this way, contriving regional uniformity may simply raise the struggle between community and diversity to a higher, supranational level.

Utilitarianism

In a utilitarian worldview, diversity is no different from anything else. Some people love it, some hate it, and most are somewhere in between. Some value diversity for its intrinsic merits and others only instrumentally because they hope to make a profit or otherwise gain from it. It confers some benefits and imposes some costs. The definition and incidence of these benefits and costs usually vary from person to person, from domain to domain, and from situation to situation. In this view, all of the possible effects of diversity that I have already discussed, as well as others still to be mentioned, are potentially relevant to the individual's or group's identification and calculation of benefits and costs.

I discuss utilitarianism separately in order to call attention to the interesting relationship that it bears to liberalism. Individual freedom, liberalism's ultimate ideal, is to the utilitarian merely an instrumental value. It facilitates the enlargement of one's utility but is not necessarily valuable in and of itself. Freedom, in the utilitarian view, is simply one of the innumerable human conditions to which people assign greater or lesser values, depending on their own preferences. Diversity is just another of those conditions. A utilitarian society would produce the amount of diversity (types, levels, and domains) that maximizes social welfare as expressed and measured through voting, market behavior, and other instruments of individual and collective choice.

It is hardly coincidental, of course, that this utilitarian conception of diversity closely resembles the economic notion of diversity, discussed earlier in connection with liberalism. Economic analysis begins (and ends, some would say) with a utilitarian methodology for measuring benefits, costs, and the efficiency of markets. The difference is that the utilitarian society must also devise some mechanism capable of aggregating these individual preferences into a political-policy decision. Neither markets nor simple majority rule can accomplish this.[110]

Utilitarianism, then, is agnostic about diversity. But the more diverse a utilitarian society is, the more difficult it will be for citizens to understand and identify with one another and thus to make collective decisions. In this sense, diversity poses much the same kind of political and decisionmaking problems for utilitarians that it poses for liberals and communitarians.

Functionalism

A functionalist theory posits that a society—usually viewed as an organic whole—orients its norms, practices, and institutions toward ensuring its survival and the successful attainment of its goals, whatever they may be. Every society, of course, is at least minimally functionalist in this sense. As many critics have noted, vulgar functionalism, like vulgar Darwinism, comes perilously close to tautology—and to a status-quo tautology at that. Whichever elements of a system exist for a long time are assumed to be functional, else neither they nor the system of which they are a part would have managed to survive.[111] On the other hand, diversity is not necessarily functional for a society; much depends on that society's particular values. As we have seen, certain kinds of diversity can, under some common social and political conditions, threaten the prosperity, harmony, governance, and even the survival of communities.

More sophisticated analysts of functionalism like Robert Merton have shown that all societies have dysfunctional aspects. If we focus on several features that any complex organism must possess in order to prosper, we can rescue a functional view of diversity from a tautological circle that obscures its distinctive social advantages, failures, and risks. Which are those features? The most important, I believe, is a society's capacity to learn and to adapt swiftly and creatively to changing conditions.[112] This learning capacity in turn depends on the society's ability to generate, aggregate, process, disseminate, deploy, and (as necessary) correct the information it needs in order to discover what its collective purposes are and might be, and then to pursue them effectively.

Social learning of this kind must be a central goal of every group, whether it be liberal, communitarian, utilitarian, or some other kind. Nevertheless, some groups are far better at it than others. I can best make this point by considering several domains in which diversity can facilitate this social learning process, even though it may at the same time create certain social problems. Diversity, for example, is important, even essential, to the strength and survivability of biological communities. We might usefully understand this as the functional equivalent of social learning in human communities, albeit in a form that processes and exploits new information through biological processes rather than through cognitive ones. Many people value the invigoration of the biota as an ultimate good, as something to be valued for itself. Some may conceive of this as part of a divine plan or manifestation. Others who are theologically agnostic or even atheistic may believe that humans owe a secular, moral duty of environmental stewardship to ourselves or to future generations. Still others may simply be awed by the sublime, ineffable beauty and power of the living world and feel obliged not to mar it.[113]

Diversity-driven strengthening of the biota can also be valued as an instrumental good, one that serves a variety of fundamental human needs: agricultural productivity, public health, medicinal innovation, natural resource management, and others. Until quite recently, for example, the level of biodiversity was widely thought to be relatively unimportant to the functioning of ecosystems. Darwin and other nineteenth-century scientists viewed the process of speciation as functional for subpopulations seeking a biological niche in which they could survive and reproduce in the face of scarce resources and other hostile environmental conditions. Seldom discussed was the notion that biodiversity not only benefits the species that occupy those niches, rendering the natural world more interesting, exotic, and beautiful for human observers, but also supports and promotes the health of the larger ecosystem.

Accumulating scientific evidence now strongly suggests that biodiversity contributes to the stability of larger ecosystems. In extreme cases, biodiversity may even prevent species extinction or accelerate the recovery from the biological effects of such extinctions. Like climate, soil type, moisture, fire, storm, and other such factors, species diversity seems to help cushion the damaging effects of environmental stresses, preventing the collapse or degradation of species into weakened states that are more vulnerable to temporary ecological disturbances.[114] Recent agricultural experiments, moreover, indicate that crop diversification can vastly increase disease resistance and yields, much more so than standard pesticide applications on monoculture crops.[115]

Diversity facilitates social learning in the economic domain as well as the biological. We have already seen how corporations have developed a managerial "diversity rhetoric" that affirms the problem-solving propensities of a diverse workforce and its conduciveness to the so-called new economy. But *homo economicus* finds other virtues in diversity. As individuals approach their decisions to invest, produce, and consume, they confront uncertainties that would be extremely costly, if not impossible, for them to resolve on their own. The price system in a competitive market, however, elicits, impounds, sifts, and transmits much of the information that they need in order to make these decisions, and it does so at a very low individual cost.

An interesting contemporary example of diversity's informational and learning value is Europe's experience with the euro, which it introduced in 1999, and specifically one of the structural reasons for its decline against other major currencies. Before 1999, Europe's currencies were diverse and uncoordinated, though of course influenced by one another. The market could evaluate each EU state's fiscal, trade, interest-rate, and other currency-related performance and respond accordingly by rewarding or punishing it. Although performance differences continue to exist, the states' adoption of a common currency means that the relationship of these differences to the euro market is more attenuated and opaque. Aggregating the states' performances reveals less discrete information than under the old system, making it harder for currency markets accurately to reward and punish the performance-relevant, state-specific economic policy decisions. This in turn reduces the markets' confidence in both the euro and in its underlying state-specific policy environments. By suppressing information about interstate diversity, the euro has dulled and confused the market signals that previously provided valuable learning and feedback mechanisms for individual states, signals that interstate diversity previously threw into sharper, clearer focus. This suppression of diversity also encourages states with weaker currencies to weaken them even more since their nationals receive the same valuation for a euro as do nationals of strong-currency states. Degrading market signals in these ways adds a cost to the euro, which in turn drives down its value against other currencies subject to more direct, transparent market disciplines. (Other factors, of course, may move the euro in the other direction.)

Other things being equal, the more numerous the market's participants and the more diverse their experiences, the better and more valuable economic information is likely to be. More participants bring to the market more diverse local knowledge and preferences that bear on economic decisions. The price system can quickly evaluate and aggregate this information, enabling participants to adjust their decisions swiftly. A competitive market also rewards success and punishes failure, as defined by participants; it encourages experimentation, enabling participants to refine their conduct and decisions in order to attract more resources. In contrast, a monolithic or thin market or one that is otherwise not workably competitive tends to weaken and distort these signals, inducing participants to learn the wrong lessons and make the wrong choices.

Religious diversity has also fostered social learning in numerous ways discussed in Chapter 7. These include the lessons the Framers took from the long history of religious wars in Europe and intolerance in early America, the role of religions in easing immigrant assimilation, the social reforms for which religious groups campaigned to great effect, and the work of faith-based organizations in providing public goods and social services that in most other advanced democracies are supplied directly or indirectly by governments. Without this extensive and growing network of privately provided public goods, America's tradition of limited government could not have been sustained into the twenty-first century, when the public demands more such goods.

Precisely because these religious groups address society's most fundamental needs, deal with its most intimate relationships, and effectuate its most important (largely noncommercial) transactions, they generate information that is of incalculable social value and cannot be obtained in any other way. In addition to their work on specific moral and policy issues, religious groups have often served society as a kind of canary in the mine, signaling hard-to-discern trouble ahead. Robert Fogel puts it this way:

> Evangelical congregations have been very effective instruments for detecting the negative effects of new technologies and changes in economic structure on the lives of their parishioners and for advancing programs of reform. These congregations might be called America's original focus groups. . . . Such interactions also made it possible for leaders to formulate programmatic demands and develop strategies that could mobilize home and far-flung congregations. It was this process of early program formulation and the preexisting network of organizations with passionate members and earnest leaders that made the evangelical churches the leading edge of populist reform movements.[116]

Social learning is also advanced by political diversity. The federal system, for example, both enables and encourages the states and other political subdivisions to experiment with their own programmatic approaches to a wide variety of public issues. Louis Brandeis's now-cliched view of the states as "little laboratories" of social learning is probably even truer now than it was in his day.[117] During the 1990s, social and political developments enhanced the states' policy autonomy and fiscal resources. At the same time, several new lines of Supreme Court decisions interpreting the Commerce Clause and the Eleventh Amendment to the U.S. Constitution began to constrain federal government authority over the states, an authority that had relentlessly expanded since the 1930s until it had come to seem virtually limitless. Concurrently, many states modernized their governance structures and processes in order to increase their effectiveness in policy initiation and implementation. These efforts have borne much fruit; state-level policy innovations now set the agenda for national debates in a host of policy areas. Some examples are term limits, health care regulation, voter registration rules, antismoking efforts, gun control, the death penalty, working conditions, environmental standards, tax law, consumer protection, campaign finance, special education, energy deregulation, conservation, and educational choice.

A particularly interesting and revealing instance is Congress's overhaul in 1996 of the welfare system. This was a far-reaching reform that followed—substantively as well as chronologically—several years in which different states experimented with a variety of approaches, sometimes under waivers granted by the Clinton administration to relieve those states of federal law requirements that all state programs conform to uniform national standards. In Wisconsin and some other states, these experiments showed promising results in moving welfare recipients into jobs and in reducing their dependency without generating the increased homelessness, child abuse and abandonment, and other indicia of immiseration that most commentators had predicted. Although powerful political pressures would probably have ensured a far-reaching welfare reform in any event, these experiments contributed greatly to the political viability and the specific programmatic content of the 1996 law.

The policy failures of states can be as influential in shaping national policy debates as their successes. During the 2000 election campaign, the Democrats were able to cite the inability of state programs to attract insurers into the market for prescription drug coverage for the elderly as evidence that could be used to discredit Republican proposals to extend that approach to the nation as a whole.[118] In the aftermath of the election itself, the failure of Florida's electoral machinery and the likelihood of similar failures in other states have spawned a political groundswell in support of national legislation to remedy the problem.[119]

For all of diversity's functional virtues in promoting social learning and adaptation, diversity can also be dysfunctional. Sanford Levinson points to many examples in the decision theory and organizational behavior literatures indicating that diversity can adversely affect group performance in a variety of contexts by interfering with the ability of people to communicate, define common goals, and pursue them effectively.[120] Indeed, the chaos of the Tower of Babel in Genesis made this now-obvious point long before social science confirmed it.

Finally, diversity may contribute to another, more ideological kind of chaos, which may be functional or dysfunctional depending on how the society values shocks and disruptions to its normative equilibria.[121] So-called "critical theory" seeks to create precisely this kind of disruption—one might call it the "shock of nonrecognition"—by insisting that diversity discourse, like other dominant discursive patterns, is a social construct that serves both to advance a particular political agenda or ideology and to disguise it. In the critical view, a discourse does this by normalizing and naturalizing itself, seeming to project a perspective on reality that is value-neutral, commonsensical, and unproblematic. Critical theory seeks to unmask this ruse so as to reveal what is "really" going on beneath the discursive surface. To be sure, the more candid of these theorists readily concede that they are, inescapably, as fully engaged in a power-seeking, ideological competition as those whom they criticize.[122]

To mention critical theory under the rubric of functionalism might seem very odd indeed. After all, opponents of critical theory often attack it for being cynical and nihilistic—a dog that has fun chasing its own tail when it is not busy denying its parents, eating its young, and covering its tracks. Yet a critical perspective on diversity remains functional. It tends to raise important questions about diversity discourse that a smugly integrationist society might otherwise miss or suppress.

The struggle to answer these questions can help to clarify diversity's various meanings—including some darker ones. One of my Yale colleagues, for example, has characterized diversity rhetoric as a misleading slogan that society's winners use to mollify its losers, tossing them some extra points for being different in some (irrelevant) way. Another critical take on diversity, akin to Robert Cover's warning that law wreaks violence on the distinctive ways of life *(nomei)* it regulates,[123] emphasizes what minorities lose when they assimilate and how and why they often resist doing so. Critical analysis, moreover, helps to expose the comforting but often unexamined assumptions that make different versions of assimilation and multiculturalism seem more natural, humane, and liberal than they truly are. The social functionality of such critical perspectives will become evident, I hope, in each of the chapters that follow.

II

MANAGING DIVERSITY

CHAPTER 4

Immigration: Importing and Assimilating Diversity

Of the many sources of America's rich demographic diversity, immigration is certainly the most fecund. The migrants who enter the United States, whether legally or surreptitiously, first create that diversity; they expand, refresh, and reform it when they help their kinsmen and countrymen enter. Once inside, immigrants fan out to countless communities where they live, worship, work, raise families, join civic groups, and reestablish links with their homelands. As we saw in the first two chapters, this demographic diversity was a striking feature of American life as early as the seventeenth century; linguistic diversity was even greater in 1790 than in 1990. Immigration in the nineteenth and twentieth centuries propelled ethno-racial diversity on a massive scale. The 2000 census enumerated 56 million foreign-born residents.[1] This total included at least 31 million long-term resident aliens, both legal and undocumented, and another million or so are added each year. These immigrants come from every country and culture on earth.

In this chapter I explore immigration diversity—as fact and as ideal—and then analyze some of the most important public policy issues raised by government's efforts to advance and achieve this ideal. The first section sketches the history of immigration to America. My brief *tour d'horizon* will limn several points developed more fully below. The long history of U.S. immigration and citizenship policies exhibits liberal, republican, and racist-patriarchal strands, with the emphasis on the latter until 1965. As Rogers Smith puts it, "for over 80% of U.S. history, American laws declared most people in the world legally ineligible to become full U.S. citizens solely because of their race, original nationality, or gender. For at least two-thirds of American history, the majority of the domestic adult population was also ineligible for full citizenship for the same reasons. Those racial, ethnic, and gender restrictions were blatant, not 'latent.'"[2]

The 1965 immigration law, the subject of the second section, broke decisively from this ascriptive tradition. The most powerful engine of ethno-racial diversification in the history of any nation, this law constitutes one of the great turning points of American history. Significantly, Congress has refused to repudiate it in the decades since enactment.

Even more interesting than the diversity spawned by the 1965 legislation is the diversity *ideal* it bespeaks. Unprecedented in America's (or any other society's) public philosophy, as Chapter 3 showed, the movements for civil rights and ethno-racial pride immediately embedded that ideal in public policy. I explore the meaning of this ideal in the third section of this chapter by analyzing how the ideal has evolved in three areas where the meaning of being an American is defined: immigrant admissions, citizenship policy, and the often bitter public debate over multiculturalism and political identity. In the fourth section, I show how government has tried to regulate and implement the diversity ideal in three other controversial domains: language policy, bilingual education, and "diversity visas" (a program that grants 55,000 permanent immigrant visas a year based solely on the applicants' diverse national origins). A concluding section summarizes my main findings and draws some general lessons about the ability of law, as a highly political technique of social control, to promote diversity in ways that advance our national purposes.

DIVERSITY-IN-FACT: A BRIEF HISTORY OF IMMIGRATION TO THE UNITED STATES

When the first Dutch and English settlers arrived in what is now America,[3] they found an indigenous population of some 500,000 natives divided into three decentralized cultural groups occupying the eastern seaboard: the Algonquians centered in New England but also including groups as far south as Virginia; the Iroquois nations in the Adirondack region of present-day New York State and running south; and the Muskogean group of tribes in the Southeast. Although the English preferred to purchase the natives' lands, they were also prepared to take the territory by force, and any violence by the natives, whom the English often likened to the Irish savages (as they viewed and treated them), brought awful retribution and sometimes extermination. The Dutch settlements, centered in New York, remained small and primarily sought to trade with the natives. The English and Dutch importation and trading of black slaves, mostly from West Africa, were greatest in the southern colonies and the Caribbean islands; but slavery also took root in the northern colonies. In an age when the Christian community frowned upon diversity, Africans were thrust entirely outside the bounds of approved religion.

Ethnic and religious diversity began early in the American colonies. By 1643, a Jesuit visitor to New Amsterdam remarked that eighteen languages were spoken on the streets. Jewish refugees from Brazil were also accepted there in the 1650s, as were Quakers, who had been persecuted in Puritan

Massachusetts. Some Swedes settled along the Delaware River in the 1630s. After the English took control of New Amsterdam in 1664, the colonies sought more English immigrants but depended increasingly on non-English sources, including German-speakers, French Huguenots (especially after Louis XIV revoked the Edict of Nantes in 1685), Scots (especially after their revolt was crushed in 1745), Scotch-Irish from Ulster (especially during the Irish famine of 1715–1720), and Welsh. These groups tended to migrate to the middle colonies rather than to New England, which was less tolerant and economically less promising. At one time or other, all of the colonies passed laws restricting Catholics' religious practices or political liberties, including Maryland, where Catholics were numerous.

Not until the eighteenth century, however, did the combination of immigration and increased religious toleration cause ethnic and religious diversity to really flourish. Indeed, by 1770 Britons composed only a third of all residents of the colonies; Germans were the largest other voluntary immigrant group and were viewed as being most different from the English, Scots, Irish, and other whites. "No other Old or New World society," Jon Butler observes, "knew such remarkable mixtures of peoples." Yet pre-Revolutionary ethnic relations were hardly harmonious, as Thomas Archdeacon notes:

> The servile condition in which many of the newcomers arrived, the proclivity of those who came independently to slip into the Back Country and to form isolated ethnic settlements, and the seemingly insatiable appetite of the New World for labor reduced the potential for conflict and eased the misgivings of the earlier arrivals. . . . But there were special areas of concern. The control of the black population always required attention. In addition, there was doubt about the suitability of some of the European servants who were imported. And, as tensions heightened between England and France, the Protestant provincials' terror of Roman Catholics flared. . . . The main objection that existed, however, was to the deportation of English convicts to the colonies [which] became common in the eighteenth century.[4]

All ethnic groups were divided on the issue of independence, but the Scots were notable for favoring the Crown. Many of the loyalists returned to England and many more fled to the Canadian territories, where they established a presence that would later attract some of the English migrants who might otherwise have gone to America. Although the first U.S. census in 1790, which counted almost four million inhabitants, distinguished only between whites, blacks, and black slaves (counted only as three-fifths of a white), scholars have used surnames to infer the nation's ethnic composition at that time. English-stock Americans accounted for only 49.2% of the total and

60.9% of the white total; the composition varied, of course, among the different states. Blacks constituted 19.3% of the total, and comprised over 40% in Virginia and South Carolina. The other major ethnic groups were Germans (7%), Scots (6.6%), Scotch-Irish (4.8%), Irish (3%), Dutch (2.6%), French (1.4%), and Swedes (0.5%).

Between 1790 and 1815, a combination of factors—the French Revolution and the ensuing Napoleonic Wars in Europe, emigration restrictions imposed by European states anxious to retain craftsmen and potential soldiers, refugee movements, the insurrection in what is now Haiti, repressions of Irish and Ulstermen, and the American War of 1812—made the migration flow modest in size and familiar in composition. After 1815 when peace was restored in Europe and the United States, migration increased briefly until the Panic of 1819 reduced the attractiveness of America. This situation continued until 1830, leading many Irish, Scots, and Welsh to go instead to England or Canada.

During the 1830s, especially before the Panic of 1837, four times as many immigrants came to the United States as in the 1820s. The number almost tripled again in the 1840s, especially in connection with the Irish potato famine, overpopulation and deteriorating economic conditions throughout Europe, and to a much smaller extent the 1848 revolution in Germany, with German-speakers constituting the first sizable influx of a non-British group since the colonial era. This large 1840s total doubled again in the 1850s, only to fall back in the 1860s due to the American Civil War. Two-thirds or more of the new arrivals landed in New York City, whereupon most of them migrated to other regions. In 1860, for example, New England, the middle Atlantic coast, and what is now the Midwest contained 81.1% of the foreign-born, compared to 63.5% of the native whites. Their regional distribution was highly ethnic-specific, a pattern that permanently affected ethnic concentrations in the country. The Irish and German immigrants dominated migration to the United States in the pre–Civil War years; by 1860 they constituted, respectively, 39% and 31% of the foreign-born population, distantly followed by those from England, Scotland, and Wales (14%), British Canada (6%), and France (2.5%). From the Civil War to the 1880s, the Irish and Germans continued to dominate the immigrant flow, followed by the English-Scots-Welsh group, Scandinavians, and both English- and French-speakers from Canada. By 1890, 32.7% of the almost 63 million residents (37.4% of the whites) were either immigrants or the children of at least one immigrant parent; for each ethnic group, moreover, immigrants exceeded the native-born by a considerable margin.

During the almost three centuries separating the earliest English settlements from 1890, the relations between natives and newcomers, as Archdeacon puts it, were a mixture of confrontation and accommodation. As the population stabilized ethnically before the new immigration of the 1830s, most white Americans, especially Protestants, became less tolerant of differences. Paradoxically, the position of blacks in American society reached new depths of isolation and vulnerability at the very time that slavery was coming under sustained attack. Contemporaneously, the new nation abandoned any thought of Indians' assimilation and accelerated their removal through wars and treaties, first to the west and then to reservations. Americans, convinced of the inferiority of the Spanish, Mexicans, and mestizo populations of Florida, Louisiana, and the Southwest and eager to control their territories, relegated these groups to the social and economic periphery.

Americans identified the European immigrants, especially Irish, French, and German Catholics, as the agents of crime, vice, disease, and disorder who flouted Protestant America's version of civic morality, resisted its ministrations, and opposed the use of public schools and other public institutions to propagate this morality. Catholics hardly seemed a threat to Protestant hegemony in 1790, when they constituted less than 1% of the population (the majority of those were in Maryland), and many Catholics in Protestant areas left the Church. By 1890, however, Catholicism was the largest Christian denomination in the United States.[5] Catholics were concentrated in the larger cities and were governed religiously by a national diocesan infrastructure. Protestants, who became increasingly evangelical during the early nineteenth century, reviled Catholics as not only theologically heterodox but disloyal, authoritarian, conspiratorial, morally depraved, and un-American. These conflicts, moreover, often pitted different immigrant groups against one another, occasioning violence and the burning and desecration of many Catholic churches. Bitter political struggles occurred over the Sabbatarian, temperance, and common school reform movements, as well as over the issues of naturalization reform and public funds for parochial schools.

An important battleground in the war against Catholics was slavery. Most immigrants, whether Catholic or not, opposed abolition for a number of reasons, including the fact that many abolitionists like Lyman Beecher and Arthur Tappan were ardent nativists, anti-Catholics, and Whigs. Indeed, the nativist American Republican Party's candidates, many of whom were abolitionists, won municipal elections in New York City and Philadelphia in 1844. The party—its adherents often called Know-Nothings because of their secret practices—won a large national following a decade later, sending seventy-five members to Congress, taking control of several state governments in the Northeast, and also doing well in other regions. The group failed, however, to enact its proposals, which politicians had promoted unsuccessfully since the 1830s, to impose twenty-one-year waiting periods for naturalization and to make aliens ineligible for political office. For a number of reasons, including the sharp decline in immigration after 1854 due to the end of the Irish famine and the Panic of 1857 in the United States, the party quickly faded.

Although immigrants were overrepresented in both the Union and Confederate armies, the Civil War was stridently opposed by many urban immigrants who rioted against conscription for a cause that was not theirs. Especially violent was New York's Draft Riot just after the Battle of Gettysburg in July 1863, which was led by Irish immigrants, claimed well over 100 lives, and gained infamy as the bloodiest episode in American urban history up to that time. After Appomattox, immigration resumed along now-familiar patterns, with somewhat larger infusions of Scandinavians along with Germans in the midwestern states and a large influx from Canada widely distributed among the states.

The 1870s and 1880s brought a number of important new developments. First, the groups that had naturalized in large numbers prior to the Civil War began to emerge as formidable voting blocs, with the Irish increasingly taking control in New York, Boston, and other cities where they were concentrated. By 1886, one-third of the police force of Chicago was foreign-born, largely Irish, and the remainder included many second-generation Americans. The Catholic Church, also Irish-led, achieved growing resources and influence, engendering internal conflicts over how much and on what terms to assimilate to American mores, to participate in the public schools and other Protestant-dominated institutions, and to relate to German Catholics and other ethnic coreligionists who viewed some of these questions differently. On a host of other issues, conflicts arose with non-Catholics fearful of the Church's rising power. German immigrants and second-generation voters became an important political factor in the Midwest, where they dominated the foreign-born in a number of cities and also, with their heavy employment in agriculture, in many rural areas.

A second development was Congress's enactment in 1875 of the first substantive federal limit on immigration. This law was expanded in 1882 and 1891 to bar criminals, prostitutes, idiots, lunatics, and persons suffering from loathsome or contagious diseases or those "likely to become a public charge." The law supplanted others that the states had imposed much earlier,[6] and although it only barred 1% of the immigrants who sought entry, it succeeded in establishing exclusive federal control over immigrant admissions, exclusion, and deportation. In 1903, the list of excludable aliens was again expanded to include epileptics, beggars, procurers, anarchists, and advocates of political violence.

Third, the first migration from an Asian country, China, began with the Gold Rush and grew to substantial numbers in the late 1860s. The Chinese were concentrated largely in California, and many were employed in mining and the construction of the transcontinental railroad, which was completed in 1869. The Panic of 1873, drought, and the depression of 1877 fostered extreme antialien fervor in the western states. Nativist and free labor groups demanded laws to expel the Chinese, who had been subject to often unconstitutional discriminatory legislation in California since the 1850s. By the mid-1870s, this anti-Chinese fervor began to affect the federal government, which had welcomed Chinese laborers to work on the railroad and for diplomatic reasons. In 1882, after the United States renegotiated an earlier treaty with China to allow limits on Chinese laborers, Congress enacted the Chinese Exclusion Act and then other laws that limited further migration and deprived those stranded in this country of the most basic elements of due process of law. The Supreme Court upheld these enactments, applying to them as well long-standing federal law that rendered the Chinese, along with other nonwhites, ineligible for naturalization. This disability remained in the law until 1943.

The immigration restriction movement during these years was by no means confined to California or the Chinese influx, nor was racism its only motive—or perhaps even its main one.[7] Businessmen, politicians, and others identified labor unrest, particularly in economic sectors manned mainly by foreign workers, with the radical ideologies of socialism, communism, syndicalism, and anarchism that they thought immigrants had brought with them. The perceived danger was not just reactionary Catholicism but also alien terrorism on the left and the threat to free labor posed by "white slaves." Many conservatives analogized the general railroad strike of 1877, which led to rioting in many cities, to the Paris Commune of 1871. Chicago's notorious Haymarket Riot in 1886, which killed seven policemen, was blamed on immigrant radicals. The American Protective Association (APA), organized in Iowa in 1887 to demonize Catholic immigrants, spread to other states, appealing to many earlier immigrant Protestant groups and reaching its zenith in the Panic of 1893 when it helped to secure victories for Republican candidates. When the APA passed from the scene, other nativist groups arose—for example, the Immigration Restriction League founded in 1894 by elite academics, blue bloods, and scientists propagating the new eugenics orthodoxy—that feared the demographic changes spawned by slavery, indentured servitude, imperial wars, and territorial expansion, as well as voluntary migration.[8] The assassination of President McKinley by an anarchist with a Balkan surname (in fact, he was a native-born U.S. citizen) prompted further exclusions on ideological grounds.[9]

Historians often view the decade of the 1890s, which perhaps not coincidentally also saw the closing of the American frontier, as a watershed separating the "old" immigration from the "new." More than 18.2 million new-comers entered the United States between 1890 and 1920, a total almost double that in the 1860–1890 period and quadruple that in the 1830–1860 period. This migration, which other receiving countries in the Americas, Australia, and New Zealand also experienced, was as striking for its ethno-racial and source-country diversity as for its size.[10] Most of these immigrants came from southern and eastern Europe, regions that previously had sent relatively few to the United States; some came from the Pacific and Caribbean islands conquered in the Spanish-American War. The old source countries, moreover, continued to send large numbers of migrants; indeed, after the Italians, "Hebrews," and Poles, the largest contingents came from Germany, Scandinavia, Britain, Ireland, and Canada. Farther down the list were the non-Polish Slavs, Mexicans (especially during and after World War I), Magyars, Greeks, and the Japanese, a group that arrived in significant numbers beginning in 1900. Most new immigrants were unskilled laborers, farm workers, or servants; Jews were a notable exception, as many were tailors, tradesmen, and merchants and very few were farm workers. Many of these groups, especially those from the Balkans, Rumania, Russia, Greece, Spain, Hungary, and Italy, returned home at very high rates.

Immigration fell sharply during World War I. As a result, the foreign-born population was still dominated by the "old" immigrants, especially German- and Irish-Americans. Archdeacon describes how the new immigrants had diversified America's demography by the eve of World War I:

A pair of relatively simple divisions had existed within the non-Indian population during the middle of the nineteenth century. In the North the native white stock faced newcomers from northern and western Europe, and in the South they held sway over several million Africans. But by the first year of the twentieth century, the non-Indian population was divided among the native stock, the descendants of the original old immigrants, latecomers from the old immigrant countries, Asians, Mexicans, blacks, and the new immigrants from central, eastern, and southern Europe.[11]

Deploring these changes, the proponents of immigrant restriction had already mobilized for political action. In 1907–1908, President Theodore Roosevelt responded to anti-Japanese pressure in California by negotiating a "Gentlemen's Agreement" that limited Japanese migration to the United States and its territories. In 1911, the Dillingham Commission, a statutorily created study group authorized in 1907 and appointed two years later, issued its recommendations along with forty-one volumes of monographs on specific subjects, including immigrants' criminogenicity, physical and intellectual inferiority relative to the native stock, and impacts on the economy. In addition, its findings that the new immigrants had high rates of illiteracy—from 25% to 50% for Italians, Jews, Poles, and Slovaks—fed the demand, advanced since the 1880s, for an English literacy requirement as a condition of immigrant admission, not just naturalization. This demand was strengthened by the fact that the foreign-born share of the total population had approached 15% before the war, and in 1916 over 2,200 Catholic churches were still worshiping in foreign languages. In this context the literacy requirement, which the Commission proposed but which for a quarter-century had been stymied by presidential vetoes, was finally enacted over President Wilson's veto in 1917—though it required only literacy in a language of the applicant's choice for those 16 or older. This law also banned immigration from the "Asia-Pacific triangle," a blatantly racist exclusion that would not be fully rectified until 1965.

Between the outbreak of World War I and America's entry in 1917, the bitter debate over foreign policy provided ammunition for those who questioned the loyalty of the old immigrant groups, particularly the Germans and the Irish, as well as of the new ones. Indeed, Roosevelt and Wilson condemned the immigrant groups' criticisms of America's pro-British tilt prior to joining the war as unpatriotic "hyphenism." Organizations like the American Protective League, which enjoyed semiofficial recognition from the government, engaged in a kind of vigilantism to ferret out alien subversives. Other civic and business organizations pressed "Americanization" agendas with more or less aggressiveness. With government encouragement, they provided English-language classes, citizenship training, and other forms of acculturation designed to efface ethnic identities.

Some states went farther by prohibiting instruction in German, bans that the Supreme Court struck down as unconstitutional. Occasional violence against German immigrants occurred, and lesser forms of discrimination were common. When the war ended, Archdeacon writes, "[t]he German-Americans . . . were finished as a culturally vital element in the United States. They could no longer pursue the illusion that success and acceptance in America did not demand complete Anglicization. After the war German-Americans did not dare to speak against the harsh terms imposed on the fatherland at the Versailles peace conference, and the disintegration of their separate identity . . . accelerated."[12]

Indeed, the postwar years were a period of growing assimilation by earlier immigrants, whose ranks were no longer being replenished. Nevertheless, a number of developments—labor strife, urban unrest, abhorrence at the Bolshevik Revolution in Russia, and a "Red Scare" campaign led by Attorney General A. Mitchell Palmer against suspected alien radicals—fed the popular opposition to immigration. The restrictionist cause was also aided by a resurgence of Protestant fundamentalism, the Ku Klux Klan, and support for prohibition, all of which were aimed in large part at the supposedly baleful influence on American values by immigrants, particularly urban Catholics and Jews.

In 1920, as the number of new immigrants rose despite the literacy test, the economy slumped, and organized labor pressed for suspension of all immigration, the politicians acted. Employing blatantly racist rhetoric, and over the veto of the lame-duck President Wilson, Congress enacted the Immigration Act of 1921, later extended for two more years, imposing an annual overall ceiling of 357,000 immigrants with additional per-country limits of 3% of the number of its foreign-born U.S. residents counted in the 1910 census. When restrictionists found that countries in northern and western Europe did not fill their quotas but those that sent the "new" immigrants did, they pressed for tighter limits. The result was the Johnson-Reed (or National Origins) Act of 1924, which passed by overwhelming margins. Significant opposition was confined to the Northeast, where so many of the "new" immigrants had settled. The new law set an annual limit of 150,000 Europeans, a complete prohibition on Japanese immigration, the issuance and counting of visas against quotas abroad rather than on arrival, and the development of quotas based on the contribution of each nationality to the overall U.S. population in 1890, thereby preserving the racial and ethnic status quo. A reluctant President Hoover put the new system into effect in 1929.

During the entire Depression-plagued decade of the 1930s, only 500,000 immigrants came to the United States, just over 10% of those who came in the 1920s, and many of these did not remain; in 1932 almost three times as many immigrants left the United States as entered it. Refugee issues came to the fore during this decade, and the U.S. response was decidedly ungenerous. Although some efforts were made to accommodate European Jews and other refugees—in 1940 the State Department permitted consuls outside Germany to issue visas to German refugees because the German quota sometimes remained unfilled—these measures were too little and too late. Indeed, recently published archival evidence suggests that expressions of racism and anti-Semitism had been common in internal government reports ever since World War I, when nativist xenophobia had led high army officers to consider Jews as a special national security problem.[13] In what may be the cruelest single action in American immigration history, Congress defeated a bill in 1939 to rescue 20,000 children from Nazi Germany despite American families' willingness to sponsor them—on the ground that the children would exceed the German quota! In addition, many refugees who might have been admitted under the quotas were excluded under the "public charge" provision.

The urgent political and economic needs generated by World War II affected immigration policy in several respects. The United States negotiated with Mexico a large-scale program for temporary farmworkers, known as *braceros,* in order to fill labor needs in the South and Southwest, a program that continued until 1964. In addition, the wartime alliance with the Chinese led Congress to repeal the legislation dating back to the 1880s that barred legal immigration from China. In the postwar years, the United States admitted hundreds of thousands of refugees under Cold War legislation aimed at Communist regimes, although the laws usually charged these admissions against the country of origin's quota as long as they did not exceed 50% of the quota for any one year. Another important contingent came from Puerto Rico, whose inhabitants had been statutory U.S. citizens since 1917 but whose migration to the New York City region, where most of them settled, was facilitated by declining airfares, the ease of returning to the island, and the much higher mainland standard of living.

The continuing support for the national origins quotas system was further demonstrated when Congress enacted the McCarran-Walter Act of 1952 preserving the system over President Truman's veto denouncing it. The new law adopted an annual ceiling of 150,000 immigrants from the Eastern Hemisphere, subject to a preference system emphasizing family ties and labor skills. Although most Western Hemisphere immigration remained unrestricted, a subquota was adopted for immigrants born in that hemisphere's colonies or dependencies. The 1952 law also repealed Japanese exclusion and established a small quota for the Asia-Pacific region. In 1953, a commission established by President Truman urged a complete overhaul of the immigration laws. Not until 1965 did this occur—and then only in the wake of the assassination of President Kennedy, who had advocated reform, the landslide victory of Lyndon Johnson in 1964, and the more enlightened attitudes toward minorities that led to passage of the Civil Rights Act of 1964.

The 1965 law abolished the national origins quotas, replacing it with a per-country limit of 20,000 on every country outside the Western Hemisphere, and an overall ceiling of 160,000 for those countries as well as a seven-category preference system based on family ties, labor skills, and Cold War refugee claims.[14] It established for the first time a ceiling of 120,000 on immigration from the Western Hemisphere, effective in 1968, but with no per-country limits. In 1976, the Western Hemisphere too was subjected to the 1965 law's per-country limits and preference system. In 1978, however, Congress replaced the hemispheric distinction with a single worldwide ceiling of 290,000, partly in order to facilitate the admission of Indo-Chinese refugees. And two years later Congress passed the Refugee Act of 1980, which expanded the definition of refugee beyond its Cold War limits, subjected refugee and asylum admissions to a more systematic process, and established a federal fiscal and administrative responsibility for the resettlement of refugees admitted under the Act.[15]

Since 1980, immigration legislation has been directed mostly at particular problems of administration and enforcement, especially with respect to undocumented and criminal aliens.[16] In 1986, Congress enacted the Immigration Reform and Control Act, which created a system of sanctions against employers who hire undocumented workers and against aliens who marry in order to obtain immigration benefits.[17] In the late 1980s and more systematically in 1996, Congress made it much easier to exclude and remove aliens who have committed crimes in the United States as well as asylum seekers with weak claims, and it mandated the detention of both groups pending their removal, perhaps indefinitely for those who cannot be repatriated. (Supreme Court decisions have eased some of these restrictions, and legislative proposals would ease others.)[18]

Major exceptions to this restrictive pattern include the Immigration Act of 1990,[19] which among other things substantially increased the number of immigrant visas to 675,000 plus refugees, asylees, and other ceiling-breaching categories, and a succession of legislated amnesties. The largest amnesty, enacted in 1986, eventually conferred legal status on over 2.7 million undocumented agricultural and other workers. Additional amnesties enacted in the late 1990s have provided millions of undocumented aliens from Nicaragua and other areas of Central America and the Caribbean with access to temporary, then permanent, legal status and eventually to American citizenship. Other forms of relief, including "temporary protected status," have provided at least short-term amnesty to many more.

These expansionist policies during the 1990s might suggest that the American public favors more immigration. This has never been the case, at least since polling on this question began. In fact, Americans' views on immigration closely track the overall U.S. unemployment rate.[20] Surveys consistently find that at least half (65% in 1993 and 1995) want to reduce the level of immigration and 10% or less want to increase it. A September 2000 Gallup poll shows 41% favoring the current level, only 13% wanting it increased, and 38% wanting it decreased. These were the most pro-immigration responses yet surveyed, presumably reflecting the very low unemployment rate at that time.[21] A recent survey of magazine covers depicting immigration since 1965 finds a recurrent use of alarmist imagery.[22]

In truth, the politics of immigration produces more expansionist policies than the general public supports. Groups with a special interest in immigration exercise great influence in the legislative process, just as counterparts do in other policy areas. In the case of immigration, these groups—agricultural growers and other employers, ethnic, religious, and human rights organizations, free market enthusiasts, and immigration lawyers—favor expansive policies; indeed, even organized labor, the main restrictionist lobby in the past, now supports new amnesties in the hope of gaining more members.[23] Almost everyone condemns illegal immigration, of course, but active opposition to legal immigration is now, even after September 11, 2001, confined largely to population control groups, some environmentalists, certain localities whose limited public services are under severe pressure, and nativists like Pat Buchanan.[24] Indeed, the reduction or elimination of welfare benefits for immigrants (and citizens) in 1996 weakened a popular argument against immigration.[25] A growing number of declining cities are actively seeking to attract more of it.[26]

THE CHANGES WROUGHT BY THE 1965 LAW

Few laws on any subject have had more profound consequences for American society than the 1965 immigration reform, which went into effect in July 1968. America's demographic diversity today is directly attributable to this legal change, yet its importance was not heralded at the time. A recent review of the statute's political history views it, in contrast with the civil rights law enacted just a year earlier, as "a low-profile negotiation driven by inside-the-beltway elites. It was covered only routinely by the press and was scarcely noticed in the television newscasts."[27]

Did the enacting Congress realize that the new law would effect this transformation, or is this one more instance of an even more notable law, the law of unanticipated consequences? Immigration scholars disagree on this fundamental question. Law professor Gabriel Chin describes the consensus view among the scholars this way:

> Although the 1965 Act is racially neutral on its face, a phalanx of scholars of otherwise diverse viewpoints agree with restrictionists that the Act was actually designed to increase the number of *white* southern and eastern European immigrants, not people from the third world. . . . David Reimers questions what "[Congress] would have done if this issue were clear in 1965," suggesting the possibility that the bill would not have passed, at least not without measures designed to minimize Asian and other non-white immigration. Roger Daniels has no doubts: "[H]ad the Congress fully understood [the 1965 Act's] consequences, it almost certainly would not have passed."[28]

Those who hold this view emphasize Attorney General Robert Kennedy's testimony to Congress predicting that "5000 [Asians] would come in the first year [under the new law], but we do not expect that there would be any great influx after that." In contrast, Chin's interviews with those who developed the 1965 law and his careful analysis of its legislative history demonstrate that Congress intended it as a genuine repudiation of the racist quota system and as an expression of America's global responsibilities and commitment to equal opportunity and fairness. Congress also recognized that the legislation would bring in substantially more Asians, although it probably did not anticipate that the number would be as large as it proved to be.[29] In the event, of course, the immigration flow from Asia was very heavy, not only in the family-based and skills-based categories but also in the refugee category with the admission of nearly one million people from Southeast Asia displaced by the Vietnam War and other conflicts. In addition, a significant group of Asians who were in illegal status in the 1980s received amnesty under the 1986 law.

Perhaps more unexpected by Congress in 1965 was the size and diversity of the impending migration from Latin America and the Caribbean region. Because the 1965 law imposed for the first time an overall numerical (though not a per country) limit on immigrants from the Western Hemisphere, Congress may have assumed that this stream would not grow. If so, it was very wrong, for several reasons. The 1965 law came only a year after Congress terminated the *bracero* program, which had regularized a large and patterned flow of Mexican workers to American farms, fields, and factories for more than two decades, and ending the program did not end the flow. Indeed, labor economists think the *bracero* program's demise may actually have increased the flow as many Mexicans, faced with the dire prospect of being cut off from desperately needed work in the United States, decided to enter or remain in the country both before and after the gate closed. As many migration specialists have shown, Mexicans and other nationalities have created strong and durable transborder networks of work, family, culture, and communication that are more or less impervious to the immigration law's prohibitions.[30] In addition, an explosive mixture of chronic political chaos, brutal guerrilla warfare, and worsening economic conditions generated a steady increase in migrants from Haiti, Cuba, El Salvador, Nicaragua, Guatemala, and other countries in the region that has continued for more than three decades.

The dramatic impact of these developments on America's demographic diversity can hardly be overstated. The 2000 census reported that more than 31 million foreign-born individuals lived in the United States. This number, which is 11.3 million more than in 1990, rises by more than a million each year. Immigrants' share of the total U.S. population was 11%, the largest since the 1930s, although still well below Canada's 17%. Immigrants' share exceeded 5% in twenty-seven of the states, up from fourteen states in 1980.[31]

The diversity of this influx can be seen through the standard demographic categories of flows and stock. In terms of flows: during the decade of the 1960s, one-third of the legal immigrants to the United States came from Europe, 40% came from Mexico, the Caribbean, and Central and South America, less than 12% from Asia, and almost all the rest from Canada. In a mere eight years between 1968 (the 1965 law's effective date) and 1976, the share of Europeans and Canadians fell by almost half, from 51.7% to 28.2%, while Asians' share rose *sixteenfold,* from 1.8% to 28.1%. By 2000, Europe's share of immigrants had fallen to about 16%, Latin America's had risen to 52%, Asia's had grown to 32%, and Canada's was negligible (0.2%).[32]

Even these numbers understate substantially the magnitude and regional diversity of the flow. First, they do not include the vast group of "nonimmigrants," more than 31.4 million in 1999, who enter the United States on temporary and restricted visas for a variety of business, diplomatic, and tourist purposes.[33] For our purposes, the most important nonimmigrant group is temporary workers, and specifically the contingent of technical workers, mostly Asians in the computer industry, who are admitted under the H-1B program. This program, which has been steadily expanded and liberalized until it is now essentially a prelude to long-term and often permanent legal residence, allows employers to import up to 200,000 skilled workers a year for up to six-year stays (which can be extended while their application for permanent residence is pending).[34] It also allows H-1Bs to change jobs in this country. About 163,000 H-1B visas were issued in 2001, and despite a "new economy"[35] slowdown that began in 2000, the demand for these workers continues in the United States and in other countries with which it competes for skilled labor.[36] Aided by their U.S. employers, many will become permanent residents despite the program's explicitly temporary character and without having to leave the country or even interrupt their employment.[37]

Second, almost a quarter of the foreign-born are undocumented aliens; each year, 200,000–300,000 of them settle more or less permanently in the United States. Estimates based on the 2000 census are that 8–9 million undocumented immigrants are living in the country, including 4.5–5 million Mexicans and the rest from Latin America, China, and all other parts of the world.[38] Hundreds of thousands of these migrants and their families will receive legal status under a series of amnesty laws enacted by Congress years ago—general amnesties in 1986 (whose coverage remains in dispute fifteen years later), and targeted amnesties for certain Central American groups in the late 1990s.[39] These amnesties will probably be extended to other groups, particularly the more than three million undocumented Mexicans whose legalization President Bush proposed before the World Trade Center disaster in September 2001 threw his plan off-course.[40] If recent immigration history is any guide, such an amnesty will spawn new illegal migration as amnesty-ineligible family members seek to join their eligible relatives.[41] Even with an enforcement budget that has been increasing more rapidly than almost any other in the federal government—and which President Bush proposes to increase to $5.3 billion in 2003—the Immigration and Naturalization Service cannot stem the illegal flow.

Indeed, a more robust political constituency favoring "regularization" (the now politically correct term) and other benefits for undocumented aliens living in the United States augurs well for their future status. Organized labor, traditionally the most powerful lobby for immigration restriction, now supports a broad amnesty for almost all illegal immigrants, to whom the unions look for new members.[42] In December 2000, Congress revived a lapsed provision (Section 245(i)) of the immigration statute to enable about 400,000 illegal aliens, who had been ruled ineligible for earlier amnesties going back to 1986, to obtain green cards nonetheless.[43] Then the new Bush administration twice mobilized Republicans in Congress to support extending the application deadline to April 2002; this rendered hundreds of thousands more eligible.[44] In March 2001, the Bush administration also gave temporary legal status to as many as 150,000 Salvadorans who were in the United States illegally.[45]

If the much-expanded temporary guestworker program proposed by Bush is enacted, it will not only benefit many Mexicans now in illegal status[46] but may be extended to other groups.[47] Past experience—especially the fact that even a much beefed-up INS with more than 34,000 employees manages to deport relatively few illegal aliens who make it past the border—indicates that a large number of those who are not legalized will remain permanently in the United States anyway.[48] Recognizing their permanence, a growing number of states are issuing driver's licenses to illegal aliens without Social Security numbers, which gives the aliens valuable documentation that they can use to engage with mainstream American society.[49] The Republican governor of New York, George Pataki, proposed using state funds to restore Medicaid assistance not just for legal immigrants whose benefits were repealed by states under the authority of the 1996 federal law but also for pregnant illegal aliens; other high-immigration states are likely to follow suit.[50] In 2002, California, New York, and some other states extended their much lower in-state tuition rates to illegal aliens who graduate from state high schools and apply for legal status.[51] The federal Victims Compensation Fund extended benefits for September 11 victims to illegal immigrants.[52] Measures like these evince a considerable sympathy for undocumented workers belying the common image of harsh legal sanctions.

Also contributing to the rising Asian, Latino, and Caribbean islander share of the U.S. population are their higher fertility rates, especially among the undocumented.[53] Although demographers expect these rates to decline with years spent in the United States, immigrant fertility will for some time remain well above American levels. Foreign-born residents constituted 43% of the New York City population in 2000, and another 9.2% were children of two foreign-born parents[54]—proportions exceeding those in 1910. The most rapidly expanding nationality groups in New York are those from the former Soviet Union, Mexicans, South Asians, and Dominicans.[55] As recently as 1990, Mexico did not even appear in the list of the first twenty sending countries to New York, yet by 1998 the number of Mexicans had grown to 200,000, constituting already the third largest group of foreign-born in the city (after Dominicans and those from the former Soviet Union).[56] In 1990, New Jersey, which was fourth among the states in the foreign-born share of its population, was first in source-country diversity *among* its foreign-born population.[57] These leading immigrant destinations, of course, are not demographically typical of the United States as a whole or even of other destination states like California and Texas, which are more heavily Mexican, or Florida, which attracts many Cubans and Haitians. Nevertheless, many other areas that until recently were racially rather homogeneous are also experiencing rapid diversification.[58]

A recent study comparing the recent immigration to New York City with that at the turn of the twentieth century demonstrates that the increased diversity goes well beyond countries of origin.[59] Two of the major groups in New York City today—blacks and Puerto Ricans—barely existed there a century ago, and the city now contains the largest urban concentration of Native Americans in the country.[60] Moreover, almost all of the immigrants in the city were then legal residents while many of today's immigrants are undocumented,[61] and the others occupy a bewildering variety of legal statuses.

In addition, the occupational and class characteristics of the new immigrants are much more diverse, ranging from illiterate peasants to physicians, computer engineers, and scientists in all fields. The 1990 census indicated that 43% of Mexicans in New York had less than a ninth-grade education and many other groups were not far behind. Most adult immigrants had a limited ability to speak, read, and write English. At the other end, almost 30% of the immigrants who entered in the early 1990s were professionals, executives, and managers. In 1990, 16% of the foreign-born, working-age people in New York were college graduates; more than a third of these had master's degrees. Nearly two-thirds of the post-1965 Filipino immigrants had college degrees. Indeed, many well-educated immigrants experience downward occupational mobility here.

The diversity *within* immigrating racial and national ethnic groups is also greater than ever. In the Asian grouping, the Indian subgroup more than doubled during the 1990s, bringing it close to the total for Filipinos (still the second largest subgroup, after the Chinese), while the Vietnamese increased 83%. Also growing rapidly was the "other Asian" subgroup, which includes Pakistanis, Cambodians, Malaysians, and others.[62] In New York City, urban anthropologist Nancy Foner notes, almost a third of the non-Hispanic blacks come from Jamaica, Haiti, Trinidad, Guyana, and other countries; a fifth of working-age, post-1965 immigrants from China had at least a college degree while one in four had less than a ninth-grade education; and "[b]efore 1975, Chinese restaurants in the United States were almost always Cantonese, but recent immigrants have brought myriad cuisines with them, including Szechuan, Hunan, Peking, and Shanghai."[63]

This geographic diversity of recent immigrants, moreover, extends to their destination cities in the United States. By 1998, the Washington, D.C., metropolitan area had become the fifth most common destination for immigrants (after the traditional enclaves of New York, Los Angeles, Chicago, and Miami), with the vast majority settling in the region's suburban communities. Nor is this influx concentrated among a few nationality groups; the immigrants come from 193 countries and territories, and the largest group, Salvadorans, comprise only 10.5% of the newcomers.[64]

The ethno-racial and national diversity that swiftly followed in the wake of the 1965 law has altered countless other aspects of American life. I mention but a few here. Most visible are the dramatic demographic consequences of the changes just discussed. As the 2000 census shows, Hispanics have already displaced blacks as the largest minority group in Florida and are about to do so in other states and in the nation as a whole.[65] Driving this development, of course, are the immigrants' relatively high fertility rates, noted earlier. In 2000, 16% of the nation's children were Hispanic, up from 9% in 1980.[66] By 2004, the two largest states, California and Texas, will have nonwhite majorities, and non-Hispanic whites are already a minority in California, New Mexico, Hawaii, and the District of Columbia.[67] This statistic, if taken to suggest the end of whites' demographic dominance, is quite misleading; as we shall see in Chapter 5, almost half of Hispanics and a growing number of Asian and other multiracial individuals consider themselves white as well, while most black multiracials consider themselves black.

Be that as it may, and despite racially inspired lamentations and urgent calls to action by some immigration restrictionists,[68] most Americans so far seem to be shrugging their shoulders at the prospect of these demographic changes. Indeed, it is noteworthy that the 1996 immigration reform law, which radically altered many aspects of U.S. immigration policy (especially enforcement against criminal aliens), did not tinker at all with the ethnic, racial, or national origins composition of the post-1965 immigration stream, which differs so remarkably from that of the general population. For many years now, the policy debate has instead focused on illegal migration, inter-governmental cost-sharing, criminal aliens, detention of asylum seekers, nonimmigrant employment visas, and other issues.[69]

Several other portentous immigration-related population changes are both increasing and integrating this demographic diversity. First, the religious affiliations of new Americans and recent immigrants are remarkably diverse.[70] The most dramatic example is the Muslim population, itself varied in numerous respects and geographically dispersed within the United States, which now amounts to about three million people, of whom immigrants constitute two-thirds to three-quarters.[71] As I will argue in Chapters 5 and 7, this religious heterogeneity is the greatest engine of the very kind of cultural and viewpoint diversity that maximizes diversity value for society. Second, the most reliable index of minority-group assimilation, intermarriage with whites, is very high and still rising for Asians, Hispanics, and Native Americans. More than in Asian families, the mestizo cultural norms of Latinos have long been open to intermarriage; today, two-thirds of intermarriages in California involve a Latino partner.[72] But intermarriage, far from reducing demographic diversity, projects diversity into society's most intimate and important enclaves (i.e., families) where it was previously absent, while increasing the number of individuals with multiple ethnicities and races. Indeed, it is estimated that by 2050 more than 40% of Hispanics in the United States will have multiracial ancestries.[73] Black-white intermarriage (especially between black women and white men) remains much less common but is also growing sharply.[74] And a July 2002 study indicates that Hispanics have already diffused residentially faster than any previous immigrant group—another sign of assimilation.[75]

The effect of these developments on the nature of American identity is immense and, as we have just seen, will accelerate in the future. As David Hollinger notes, it is not simply that there are so many descent communities or that people identify with more than one of them; it is also that the meanings of these communities change from generation to generation and that this fluidity of identities enables individuals, especially in the United States, to escape (if they wish) many of the limits imposed by imputed group membership.[76] The fact that this has occurred since 1965 for a large number of notably dark-skinned groups refutes "whiteness" theories contending that earlier European immigrant groups gained acceptance in America only by passing to a whiteness unavailable to those of other races. Sadly, it also underscores the relative isolation that persists for American blacks.[77]

In democratic politics, it has been said, demography is destiny. Immigration since 1965 has helped to fuel immense shifts of political power. At the national level, it has increased the congressional representation in many of the major receiving states, particularly in the Southwest and Florida, while slowing the decline of representation in New York, New Jersey, and other receiving states that have experienced diminishing native populations. The same is true, *mutatis mutandis,* at the state and local levels where changes in immigrant settlement patterns are altering not only districting patterns but also political styles, legislative coalitions, and issue agendas.[78] This demographic transformation is powering numerous policy debates in which the post-1965 diversity ideal is being defined. The rest of this chapter considers five of them—admissions; citizenship; political identity and multiculturalism; bilingualism; and diversity visas. Later chapters take up diversity-driven debates over affirmative action, neighborhood integration, and public law's treatment of religion.

DIVERSITY-AS-IDEAL

The provenance of diversity-as-ideal, Chapter 3 suggested, lies largely in the civil rights movement of the 1960s. We have just seen how notions of fairness, equal opportunity, and growing global responsibility manifested themselves in the legislative history and provisions of the 1965 immigration law, and how this law has driven America's demographic and political diversification-in-fact ever since. The 1965 law helps to fill in the substantive content of diversity-as-ideal by revealing what I take to be a rough approximation of the polity's actual preferences about immigration. These preferences include some level of illegal immigration, which many Americans treat as a kind of victimless crime.[79] But there are other immigration policy contexts relevant to the diversity ideal, and how the law manages them can give that ideal further content. This section discusses three of these contexts: who may come (admissions), who may naturalize (citizenship), and what American citizenship means in a multicultural society (political identity).

Admissions

Between 1975 when the first grounds for exclusion of immigrants under federal law were established, and 1990 when Congress eliminated some (but added others), immigration law saw a gradual but steady accretion of additional grounds for exclusion. Grounds for exclusion generally reflected the political obsessions and evolving social attitudes of particular eras. In 1990, for example, Congress eliminated homosexuality as a ground for exclusion and softened the grounds based on membership in subversive organizations, but strengthened provisions relating to terrorist activity, and in 1996, the year of welfare reform, Congress made it easier to exclude immigrants who might later need public assistance.

Beyond the grounds of inadmissibility, the law limits immigration to four main streams, which in 2001 totaled more than one million immigrants, with a huge backlog of almost 850,000 status adjustment applications still pending, virtually assuring that annual legal immigration levels will remain above one million for years to come.[80] Each stream receives a limited number of visas; would-be immigrants are further limited by the annual per-country ceilings of about 27,000. Each stream also has disparate impacts on different groups of would-be immigrants, but taken together they tend to assure considerable diversity of many kinds. First, employment-based visas (17% of the total) tend to favor those from more highly educated countries, although the most highly skilled from any country might qualify, and up to 10,000 visas are available to unskilled laborers. Second, family-sponsored visas (64% of the total) tend to favor those from countries that have previously sent the most immigrants, who can then petition for family members to join them. Third, humanitarian visas (10% of the total) are available to those who have fled persecution and who meet the additional criteria for refugee or asylee status. The overseas refugee program allocates refugee visas by region and sometimes by country, and the numerical ceilings are somewhat flexible. Tragically, people qualify from a very large number of countries, although certain source countries predominate. Some commentators have long criticized what they perceive as politically biased application of the refugee definition, especially in the asylum context, to serve the government's foreign policy interests. Finally, 50,000 diversity visas (5% of the total) are available to those who come from low-admission regions and countries. I analyze this diversity program later in the chapter.

In general, these visa programs favor certain types of individuals—those who are relatively well educated and highly skilled, have family members already in the United States, come from countries with well-established immigrant networks here, can afford to wait the often many years required for a visa to become available for nationals of their particular country, and have access to lawyers or agents who know how to work the intricate immigration system. This system also rewards those who can enter the United States on a tourist or other nonimmigrant visa and then, perhaps after a period of being out of status, find some way (e.g., marriage, employment, amnesty) to adjust their immigrant status to that of legal permanent resident. Indeed, 61% of the slightly more than one million immigrants who received green cards in 2001 were already in the United States, 215,000 of them illegally.[81] But beyond these hard-to-avoid biases, diversity (however defined) is on the whole well served by the immigration admissions system.

Citizenship

The admissions system is not simply a gateway to the United States; it is a pathway to becoming an American. Once immigrants enter as legal permanent residents, they will in due course and in all likelihood be eligible to naturalize. Their green card, then, is also their ticket to citizenship. In effect, the demographic diversity of the citizenry resembles that of the admitted immigrants, at least over time. This statement must be qualified in two respects. First, immigrant groups naturalize at different rates and after remaining in legal resident status for different time periods. Mexicans and Canadians, for example, are less likely to naturalize, and take longer to do so, than many Asian groups; this reflects, among other things, their greater geographic proximity and more enduring ties to their homelands.[82] Second, many of those who naturalize entered the United States without documents and subsequently gained legal status, and many others who entered on nonimmigrant visas but then violated visa conditions thereafter regained legal status.

Admission or legalization is not the only pathway to citizenship. Regardless of the parents' legal status, a child born on American soil becomes an American citizen at the moment of birth under the rule of *jus soli* (law of the soil), which dates back to sixteenth-century English common law. The American version of this rule is probably the world's most liberal. It is another route, albeit a relatively minor one, to the demographic diversification of the American polity—in this case *despite* our admission and enforcement policies, not because of them. At the margin, this version of the rule increases the incentives of undocumented aliens from the region to enter the United States.[83] (In addition to naturalization and birthright citizenship, one can become a U.S. citizen through a citizen parent under the rule of *jus sanguinis*, law of blood or descent.)[84]

Except for the provisions on immigrant admissions, the most significant law for infusing diversity into American political, cultural, and social life is the naturalization statute. It promotes diversity by providing eligibility requirements that are easy to satisfy relative to the naturalization statutes in Europe and Japan.[85] Although this has been true since 1790—at least for English-speakers who have not committed crimes—there have been some major and shameful exceptions to the naturalization law's openness to diversity:[86] a politically restrictive period between 1798 and 1802; exclusion of American blacks until 1870; exclusion of the Chinese and races indigenous to the Western Hemisphere until the 1940s; exclusion of all other nonwhites (other than those of African descent) until 1952; and provisions that automatically denationalized American women who married any alien (from 1907 to 1922) or an alien ineligible (usually for racial reasons) for naturalization (until 1931).[87]

Today, the English language and literacy tests are notoriously easy to pass —the naturalization statute mandates a "simple" literacy test and exempts many disabled individuals and older immigrants who are illiterate in English from having to take it[88]—and the American history and government test requires only rote responses. (Pending legislation would waive both tests for many more of the elderly.)[89] Indeed, a strong case can be made that making these requirements a bit more rigorous would actually strengthen the argument for more immigration, just as the 1996 welfare reform statute limiting immigrants' access to welfare benefits had the unanticipated effect of undermining a traditional argument for immigration restriction. In 2003, the INS will begin experimenting with a more rigorous naturalization examination.

The statute limits ideological diversity by disqualifying from naturalization those individuals and members of groups deemed subversive or "not attached to the principles of the Constitution." This bar, however, has been considerably narrowed by statute and judicial interpretation since the 1960s, and the possibility of denationalization due to the commission of "expatriating acts" has been practically eliminated. The "good moral character" required for naturalization is now interpreted quite generously with respect to noncriminals, although the statute flatly bars "aggravated felons," a category that Congress introduced into the law in the 1980s and then progressively broadened. Finally, the Supreme Court has interpreted the law to make it difficult to rescind citizenship, even of those who arguably procured their naturalization through fraud or misrepresentation.

The numerical results of this inclusive naturalization regime are impressive. Approximately 889,000 people naturalized in 2000, the last year for which data are available. (This total was exceeded only by the more than one million who naturalized in 1996.) In May 2002, more than 745,000 petitions were backlogged and awaiting decision.[90] The source-country diversity of those naturalizing is especially striking. In 2000 Mexicans accounted for about 21%, followed by those from Vietnam, China, the Philippines, India, the Dominican Republic, El Salvador, Jamaica, and Iran. All of Europe accounted for only 13.2% of the total.[91]

Another feature of naturalization law, dual citizenship, also helps to shape American diversity. Under a provision dating back to the first naturalization statute of 1790, all persons who take the oath of citizenship must "renounce and abjure absolutely and entirely all allegiance and fidelity to any foreign prince, potentate, state, or sovereignty of whom or which the applicant was before a subject or citizen."[92] Americans can acquire the nationality of two or more states in a number of ways—by birth in the United States to immigrant parents, by birth abroad to a U.S. citizen parent and a foreign parent both of whom can transmit their nationality to the child, by marriage to a foreigner who transmits his or her nationality to the spouse, and by naturalizing in another state after having acquired U.S. citizenship. In addition, the naturalizing citizen's renunciation oath in the United States may be legally ineffective in the state of origin; even if effective, the U.S. citizen may be able to reacquire nationality in that state. Because of international marriages, legal changes in other countries, and a softening of traditional opposition by the U.S. and other governments, a steadily growing number of Americans hold multiple citizenships. Indeed, nearly 90% of legal immigrants to the United States today come from states that allow dual citizenship; under a recent legal change, Mexico even promotes it for the U.S.-born children of its nationals.[93] Such laws are increasing naturalization in the United States by Latin American immigrants.[94] As more U.S.-resident children with multiple citizenship are exposed to their parents' countries, languages, and traditions, America's cultural diversity may broaden even more.[95]

We have seen that immigration and citizenship policies combine with illegal migration to produce high levels of demographic diversity. By itself, this diversity-in-fact is merely that, a fact; it is simply a matter (as Jim Chen puts it) of counting and classifying.[96] But it is a fact whose greatest significance is normative, not empirical. What matters most are the social values diversity serves, not the bare facts denoted by ethnic statistics. We want to know how diversity does and should affect how Americans think of themselves as a political community, the political values they share, the rights they demand and the duties they accept, what they expect of new members, and how they design their institutions, including law, to serve those expectations. We want to know, in short, our collective answer to the vital question Crèvecoeur asked in 1781, "What, then, is the American, this new man?"[97]

In the next section I explain why our vastly more diverse society must seek new answers. In developing my own, I argue that the law should, insofar as possible, leave minority cultures to their own devices, consistent with the overriding need to maintain public order and uphold constitutional values. This position means, among other things, that government should not promote or even preserve cultural diversity beyond what is necessary to vindicate individuals' constitutionally guaranteed autonomy, freedom of speech, and equal protection of the laws. It should limit itself to dismantling public policies that inhibit individuals' ability to define and act upon their own cultural commitments. In later sections I apply this approach to two specific diversity policy issues, bilingual education and diversity visas. Chapters 5 through 7 take up similar issues in the contexts of affirmative action, residential integration, and religious practices.

Multiculturalism and Political Identity

Every modern state obsesses about its own political identity and destiny in its own way. Still, among the relatively few whose national unity is secure, America's preoccupation is perhaps the most insistent. A frequent explanation for this is that other states' unity is based on sturdy, indeed primordial, commonalities like language, religion, and ethnicity, while America's is based on a more fragile foundation: a common commitment to a set of civic ideals that speak in universal terms and are accessible to all of humanity.[98] To many theorists of American exceptionalism, these ideals constitute a civic nationalism or ideology suitable to what Ben Wattenberg calls "the first universal nation."[99]

Concern is often expressed about the continuing capacity of these civic ideals to define, fuse, and inspire a polity as liberal, decentralized, and aggressively diverse as ours.[100] To begin with, these ideals—democracy, the rule of law, pragmatism, the spirit of compromise, respect for differences, equality of opportunity, freedom—are rather abstract. Such values can mean different things to different people; indeed, the openness of these values to interpretation is surely part of their enduring strength, allowing them to evolve over time to accommodate emerging social needs. But this also means that these values can be rhetorically hijacked and politically compromised more easily, leaving their defenders without a fixed, authoritative standard to which they can appeal.

Second, these ideals are no longer unique to America. Some other states now pursue these same values, albeit through different institutions and political cultures. Some of these other states are more egalitarian than the United States,[101] and claim to embody democratic values as much as or more than the United States does. Such claims, which depend on debatable definitions, cannot easily be refuted.

Third, the challenges to national unity are probably greater than at any time since the Civil War and these challenges are in their own ways unprecedented.[102] Many enclaves in which immigrants now live are large and self-sustaining enough to attenuate, at least in the short run, their economic, linguistic, and cultural integration with the larger, more assimilated community. Many immigrants and their children maintain transnational ties that are stronger and easier to sustain than ever before. As the United States and sending countries accept multiple citizenship more, naturalized immigrants can retain (or regain) their old nationalities. Immigrants without traditions of democracy in their home countries—Haiti and Pakistan, for example—may find America's political values harder to comprehend and practice.

Other changes may also make American political identity less robust. In the absence of war, a military draft, external threats, a strong communitarian ethos, robust public rituals, or other communal experiences to galvanize a unified political identity, being American may seem less central to citizens' self-definition today than in the past—though the war against terrorism may heighten that solidarity. Because citizenship law itself is so undemanding and illegal immigrants can secure citizenship for their children even more easily simply by giving birth to them here, that law contributes little to shaping this identity.[103]

Finally, globalization is exerting new pressures on national values, institutions, and practices, pressures that are difficult for any individual nation-state, even the United States, to control. The world economy is increasingly integrated. International trade accounts for a growing share of the economy, now over 20% of GDP (though still much lower than other first-world economies). Immigrants in the United States send more than $13 billion a year home, dwarfing U.S. foreign aid to those countries.[104] Environmental pollution, migration, organized crime, weapons proliferation, public health, and many other problems transcend national and even regional boundaries. Supranational institutions, some exercising coercive legal and political authority of great consequence, now regulate in a host of policy domains that were traditionally governed almost exclusively by domestic politics.[105] To some observers, these developments prefigure an inevitable shrinking of national sovereignty and loss of cultural distinctiveness. Even those who believe that the globalization phenomenon is exaggerated, however, acknowledge that both the autonomy of national ideals and the freedom of action to pursue them are under pressure, even for the sole remaining superpower.[106]

The contemporary debate over what American political identity now means, what it should mean, and how that meaning can be attained (or preserved) is conducted daily in homes, workplaces, college campuses, mass media, politics, private associations, places of worship, and every other corner of American life. Its special urgency reflects the diversity that recent immigration has wrought.[107] What frames this debate is the overarching, multidimensional question of American citizenship. Earlier, I discussed how citizenship is acquired, drawing certain inferences from how its availability has evolved, and I noted that immigrant groups differ as to naturalization rates and other socio-political behaviors.

Certainly the most far-reaching dimension of citizenship, however, concerns assimilation to American culture. This subject raises many difficult questions. They begin with the word "assimilation," which, like "Americanization," carries some unpleasant historical associations. It often evokes the memory of coerced adherence to some dominant but dubious ideal (Anglo-conformity) through pressures on newcomers to shed their ethnic identities, sometimes incurring deep emotional, cultural, and psychological losses in the process.[108] (Using a less loaded term like "integration" might elide these associations, but such euphemisms cannot help resolve the genuinely knotty issues lurking beneath any such term.) Sociologist Alan Wolfe notes that assimilation "is a form of symbolic violence. Like the actual violence of war, assimilation is disruptive and heartless, the stuff of tragedy."[109] Much imaginative literature on immigration plays on this theme.[110] One is not surprised, then, to find Nathan Glazer reporting that a large majority of his Harvard students (an elite group, to be sure) react negatively to the term, that "[n]either liberals nor neoliberals, conservatives nor neoconservatives, have much good to say about assimilation, and only a branch of paleoconservatism can now be mustered in its defense."[111]

Conceptually, then, what does assimilation mean? Normatively, what are its purposes? Emotionally, why should we care about it? Morally, how can we demand it? Practically, how can we assure it? Empirically, what kind and how much of it is occurring? The answers to these questions matter enormously not only to the immigrants who enter the culture from abroad but also to Americans who live and raise their children in it. If we could authoritatively answer them, we would conjure not only the nature of our political identity but also the future of diversity-as-ideal. We could foretell whether this ideal will retain its recently acquired social legitimacy and inspirational power or will instead return to the disrepute in which the world has held the ideal time out of mind.

Alas, no agreed-upon answers to these questions exist—although certain things are fairly clear. By almost any definition, assimilation of immigrants to American life is proceeding rapidly, fueled by market incentives, the need and desire to learn English, the allure of sports, and a powerful, mass-media-shaped national culture. As noted earlier, the rates of intermarriage among different ethnic groups and with whites are both high and increasing, especially for Asians and Hispanics, as is the rate of residential diffusion and integration by these recent immigrant groups. As sociologist Stanley Lieberson shows, immigrant families soon choose their children's names from the general inventory rather than using ethnically distinctive ones.[112] Also facilitating immigrants' assimilation, perhaps, is the fact that two-thirds of the foreign-born population self-identified as white in the 2000 census, compared with only half ten years earlier.

But as always, the pace of assimilation is faster for some than for others, with low-skill and Mexican groups tending to remain more isolated. Although this swift pace is generally desirable, it becomes problematic when very young immigrants and the young children of immigrants (the "one-and-a-half" and second generations) adopt norms and conduct, all too common and dysfunctional in the United States, that may bar their future mobility and integration—what immigration sociologists call "downward" or "segmented" assimilation.[113] Here, immigrants who want to facilitate healthy assimilation by their children must try to use the cultures of origin to inoculate them against these dangerous aspects of American life, providing a cultural shelter and breathing space in which their youngsters can flourish. Indeed, research indicates that immigrant achievers tend to be the ones who assimilate more slowly to American culture, while delinquents tend to abandon their ethnic heritage more quickly.[114] The central questions about assimilation, then, are not just how quickly it will occur but, perhaps more important, which aspects of American culture—the more wholesome, or the more deplorable—immigrants will embrace.

If this were the whole story, multiculturalism, with its celebration of diverse ways of life, would not be the *casus belli* in the culture wars it has become. But certain forms of multiculturalism can also impede assimilation and even discredit it as a social goal. Even more confusing, multiculturalism can both promote and impede assimilation at the same time. We must explore multiculturalism more deeply, then, as a particular way to understand, express, and institutionalize identity in an ethnically diverse society.

Multiculturalism, in one form or another, boasts an ancient pedigree. From the first European settlements in America, managing conflicts among different cultures has been a vital social and political project. Its salience has increased as immigrants' transplanted cultures have grown more diverse and as group demands for recognition and protection have become legally and politically more strident and found greater social and political acceptance. But if multiculturalism is an old problem, its contemporary status is quite new. Like the cognate diversity-as-ideal that animates it, multiculturalism has only recently become a freestanding public policy goal. And like the diversity ideal, its meaning is contested even in specific contexts like education. K. Anthony Appiah explains why:

> [Multiculturalism] is now used . . . to cover an extraordinary range of educational practices from the anodyne insistence that American students should be taught something of the history of all the world's continents to the kooky suggestion that they should learn that the Africans who built the pyramids did so by telekinesis. But because the word has become a term of ritual abuse for some conservatives and a banner

for many on the left, there is not much hope of agreement on its core meaning.[115]

Today, multiculturalism is perhaps best understood as a set of ideas whose common theme is respect and toleration for cultural differences—globally,[116] nationally,[117] locally,[118] or individually.[119] Its common claim is that a nation should accommodate (to some extent) most (if not all) of the distinctive values and practices of culturally diverse groups in its midst. As these qualifications suggest, multiculturalism is a matter of degree. Multicultural policies are of many kinds; they may be designed to facilitate the integration of group members into the national culture, recognize their cultural identity as a vital end in itself, or even help groups wall off their cultures from the mainstream. Moreover, such policies can promote a wide range of values—liberal, communitarian, or even conservative—depending on how they are defined and justified.[120]

Multicultural policies may be pursued in common or in separate institutions, and they can accommodate more or less diversity.[121] Canada is officially, indeed constitutionally, committed to multiculturalism, and other states like Australia affirm it at a subconstitutional level.[122] Although the United States has no explicit constitutional provision of this kind, the Supreme Court broadly interprets constitutional and subconstitutional principles to protect cultural diversity in religion, dress, language, and other areas; in addition, federal and state laws have established (and sometimes disestablished) specific multicultural policies like bilingual education. Indeed, so widespread are these policies in the United States that Nathan Glazer, an early skeptic concerning many of them, was able to write a book entitled *We Are All Multiculturalists Now*[123]—though Glazer recognizes that this thin consensus ends as soon as discussion of specific policies begins.

The seminal analysis of contemporary multiculturalism in the United States is historian David Hollinger's *Postethnic America*, an avowedly "Americocentric" essay on cultural diversity.[124] A pastiche of intellectual history and group sociology, Hollinger develops five major themes that comprise a "postethnic" or "cosmopolitan liberal" vision of multiculturalism. One theme is the centrality of individual choice in determining our ethnic affiliations and identities. With the major exception of blacks, whose ethnicity is inescapable to the extent that it is racially defined by hostile others, Americans have over time been able to choose and shape the ethnic affiliations that they most valued while discarding others. Normatively, Hollinger claims, this is how identities ought to be constituted; they should be more fluid, consensual, revocable, and multiple than more rigidly "pluralistic" models allow.

A second theme is that the ethno-racial pentagon, originally adopted in a spirit of "enlightened antiracism," soon ceased being a merely technocratic device for integrating certain minorities more completely into American society, and took on a life of its own as a kind of embedded end in itself. Among the pentagon's most pernicious consequences is the promotion of the false idea that a race is equivalent to a culture. This notion ascribes a spurious solidarity to each of the pentagon's blocs, denying the fluidity of affiliations that facilitates individual fulfillment.

A third theme is that the postmodernist emphasis on the historicity and situatedness of all truth-claims has been taken so far as to discredit the notion of universal truths or values on which any genuine equality among individuals and groups depends. Hollinger puts the point this way:

> The less one's raw humanity is said to count for anything, the more important one's affiliations become. The more epistemic and moral authority is ascribed to historically particular communities, the more it does matter just who is and is not one of "us." The more detached truth and goodness become from the testimony and tastes of any population outside our own tribe or club, the more is at stake when that tribe or club defines itself in relation to other human beings. How wide the circle of the "we"? This may be *the* great question in an age of ethnos-centered discourse.[125]

A fourth theme is that immigrant-driven multiplication of diversity has fostered notions of multiculturalism and cosmopolitanism that harden the boundaries between the pentagon's blocs while at the same time rendering those blocs more incoherent. This hardening is particularly perverse, Hollinger emphasizes, because demographic changes are blurring these boundaries and the growing number of multiethnics are rejecting them altogether. He buttresses this concern about group boundaries in responding to Will Kymlicka, a Canadian philosopher who argues that even a liberal state must guarantee certain rights to immigrants and to national minorities (defined as groups that functioned as complete societies in a historic homeland before being incorporated into a larger state, usually involuntarily).[126] Hollinger notes that those of greatest concern, blacks and Hispanics, fall into neither category and also are too heterogeneous to easily justify group (or group-differentiated) rights.[127]

Hollinger's final theme is to insist that the United States is a civic nation, not an ethnic one (a distinction that Kymlicka rejects),[128] and that contrary to many multiculturalists' claims, the United States exhibits a distinctive national culture. This culture, Hollinger says, is located between ethnic particularity ("the ethnos") and universality ("the species") and can creatively mediate between them. Endorsing philosopher Michael Walzer's view that

American solidarity is "profoundly nonprimordial" and individualistic in character, Hollinger concludes that this nonethnic nationality reflects many ethnic histories but offers a "postethnic opportunity"—a unity "tight enough to mobilize action on common challenges and loose enough to militate against a replay of the chauvinisms of the past."[129]

Hollinger's vision of American cultural identity resembles in important ways the more robust and programmatic "new nationalism" advanced in Michael Lind's impressive 1995 book, *The New American Nation*.[130] Both reject a fixed, state-regulated, state-fostered structure of ethno-racial identity in favor of a more fluid, individualistic, voluntary, and privatistic set of affiliations. I ardently share their common commitment to this version of what Alan Wolfe describes as a "soft multi-culturalism [that] is the friend of civic nationalism, not its enemy."[131]

Indeed, as I discuss below, I take this position farther (though they might well agree) by rejecting the view, held by many multiculturalists, ethnic chauvinists, and educators, that government has a legitimate role in helping immigrants retain their cultures of origin. Immigrants' desires to maintain those cultures are perfectly natural, socially desirable, and may be fully compatible with the level of assimilation that Americans have a right to expect and that benefits both citizens and immigrants. This cultural maintenance, however, is not an appropriate public goal; it should be entirely a private matter for the immigrant family to pursue (if it wishes) at home or in its ethnic community, not in the public schools.

The normative privatism of cultural maintenance reflects a number of considerations. Immigrant cultures, indeed *any* cultures, are very difficult for outsiders to comprehend.[132] As I contend in Chapter 8, we cherish cultures insofar as they are authentic and spontaneous, two values that public law cannot readily promote. The problem is not so much that the state must be rigorously neutral in matters of culture. In reality, strict neutrality is neither possible nor desirable. The state is necessarily in the business of maintaining the dominant English-speaking culture, and it properly insists that newcomers wishing to become citizens must demonstrate some English-language ability, a basic knowledge of American political institutions, and a commitment to certain civic principles. These tools are necessary, though not sufficient, for successful assimilation—a fact that today's immigrants, eager to learn English, seem to understand no less than their admired predecessors did—and government has a vital interest, often neglected in practice, in helping them do so.[133]

If past is prologue, immigrants will shed some aspects of their ethnic identities as they live here; this molting process will be particularly rapid in the second and certainly the third generation. The melting pot metaphor, then, is not altogether inapt even today when many immigration advocates and scholars deride it. The swift, complete, and identity-stifling assimilation demanded by some in the first Americanization movement was sometimes bigoted and often oppressive.[134] Still, it was quite effective at a time when the stakes in rapid assimilation were very high. As the late Barbara Jordan urged on behalf of the U.S. Commission on Immigration Reform, more nuanced, well-designed, and diversity-friendly versions of Americanization would be welcome today.[135]

Hollinger's essay, while justly celebrated, disappoints on a few counts.[136] Concerned primarily with multiculturalism's ideological origins and internal coherence, he remains well above the messy realms of policy formulation or implementation where empirical evidence and institutional practice matter and where values must be defined and their conflicts resolved through hard choices. His ideas about cultural diversity would be more readily tested if grounded and elaborated in some specific issue context. Indeed, affirmative action is the only specific multicultural issue he discusses (and then only in his "postscript"). Supporting it without any analysis or even definition, he does not consider—to pick one example—the irony, absurdity, and incoherence of a policy that accords to almost three-quarters of post-1965 *immigrants* (26 million strong) valuable, zero-sum ethno-racial preferences in jobs hiring and promotion, government contracts and loans, and higher education admissions—even though, by definition, they have not experienced the historic discrimination that gives those preferences whatever moral legitimacy they have.[137] I examine affirmative action at length in Chapter 5, where I reject Hollinger's casually offered conclusion.

IMPLEMENTING THE DIVERSITY IDEAL

Today's unprecedented levels of immigration and immigrant diversity pose immense challenges to American society as it seeks to integrate the newcomers into a civic culture that is dynamic, competitive, and highly individualistic. These challenges are manifest in many different areas of public and private life. In this section, I consider two domains—language policy and bilingual education—where the diversity ideal continues to be fiercely contested, and a third, diversity visas, where the ideal has become surprisingly uncontroversial even while being implemented in a foolish way.

Language Policy

Language policy can serve as perhaps the leading paradigm of America's approach to the management of diversity. The reasons are plain. In a polity that prides itself on a civic conception of citizenship in which any individuals who subscribe to the principles of American constitutional democracy can be full members regardless of their group identities, a working knowledge of the English language is the essential glue that binds diverse citizens into a political community where they can communicate with one another about matters of common interest. Legal and practical considerations also underscore the centrality of English. The language test constitutes the main legal barrier to naturalization for many immigrants. Even more important, English is indispensable to immigrants' full integration into American society. They may be able to survive and even prosper in immigrant enclaves without speaking English, but their inability to venture outside those enclaves must severely limit their life chances and civic contributions.[138] Accordingly, the teaching of English in the public schools that most immigrant children attend is the key to their integration—and often that of their non-English-speaking family members as well. (Europeans evidently find the need for English fluency essential to *their* integration into the global economy.)[139]

Language policy imposes a different constraint on the state than other policies.[140] A state can adopt more or less neutral stances with regard to diverse religions, races, and other attributes in society, but it must prefer one or more languages. (India's constitution lists sixteen official languages.) The costs of accommodating a multiplicity of languages are significant, and the state, as Aristide Zolberg puts it, "cannot choose to become mute or deaf."[141] A people's language, moreover, has extremely powerful symbolic, instrumental, ethnic, and political associations and effects. Indeed, throughout history language has *constituted* peoplehood and ethnicity more than any other attribute, including religion or state jurisdiction. For this reason, state builders have always had to develop language policies to define the desired relationship between the center and the periphery, create a national identity, reduce political fragmentation, conduct revenue, military, and other governmental activities, and make necessary concessions to subnational groups.

The goal of modernization, however, increased states' determination to achieve linguistic unification, which they equated with it. States have pursued these two goals through administrative technique, educational policy, and repression. With an estimated 6,700 languages in the world but only 225 nation-states, linguistic conflict is inevitable.[142] Linguistic unity has become even more urgent as these states seek to mobilize their people in support of more ambitious programmatic and nation-building agendas, and as globalism enhances the economic value of linguistic skills, especially English fluency. Today, Zolberg points out, over three-fourths of the world's countries are officially or effectively unilingual; half of these contain linguistic minorities of 10% or more; in about one-third of unilingual countries, most inhabitants do not use the official language in their everyday speech; and even the languages recognized by officially multilingual states rarely encompass the full range of the population's everyday speech.

Until recently, language policy in the United States was episodic and for the most part low-key. After all, 87% of its residents now speak English as their first language, English is by far the dominant language used on the Internet,[143] and half the planet is expected to be somewhat proficient in English by midcentury, compared to roughly 12% now.[144] Even at the founding when only 40% of the people living within America's boundaries spoke English, the Constitution's framers thought it unnecessary to designate English as the official language.[145] At all times, many of those who opposed immigration or particular immigrant groups cited the divisiveness and cultural inferiority of non-English-speakers as reasons for excluding or restricting them; American anti-imperialists also made such arguments in opposing the acquisition of Spanish-speaking territories during the nineteenth century. Despite (or because of) these concerns, English was imposed as a matter of course on non-English-speaking dependencies such as Indian reservations, Hawaii, and Puerto Rico. Especially during World War I, some states enacted laws restricting the teaching of any language but English in public and private schools, but the Supreme Court invalidated them in 1923 as an infringement on parents' privacy.[146] Zolberg describes some state and local deviations from the English-only norm:

> Spanish was recognized in New Mexico's constitution; numerous school boards provided a modicum of bilingual public education to their immigrant communities; the use of foreign languages in the press and private education was unquestioned; language requirements for naturalization were minimal, if they existed at all; and foreign language ballots occasionally appeared as well. German was particularly widespread among public institutions throughout the Midwest. . . . Nevertheless, . . . the educational community overwhelmingly supported unilingualism on pedagogic grounds. Notwithstanding acceptance of cultural pluralism in other spheres, an English-only regime prevailed throughout the country [until the 1960s] except for the recognition of Spanish as the language of Puerto Rico in the New Deal era.[147]

This linguistic history of the United States has produced an intriguing paradox. The world's most diverse industrialized country, which attracts immigrants speaking as many as 329 languages,[148] is almost entirely monolingual in all of its governmental and major social institutions. This linguistic homogeneity at the institutional level is almost unique among large, populous, and ethno-culturally diverse polities. (This last qualification excludes China and

Japan; France's case is discussed below.) Compare, for example, monolingual America to bilingual Canada and multilingual India, Indonesia, Russia, and the European Union. It is in this linguistically homogeneous context that the demands for public recognition of the Spanish language arise—and arouse resistance.

Like so much else in American life, this monolingual tradition was called into question in the 1960s. A larger, more diverse immigration stream, coupled with a growing social acceptance of civil rights and egalitarian ideals, inspired new calls for the recognition of minority language rights. This led to the enactment of two important federal laws: the Bilingual Education Act of 1968,[149] which provided funds for programs designed to meet the special educational needs of children of "limited English-speaking ability," and the 1975 amendments to the 1965 Voting Rights Act,[150] which provided for bilingual ballots for four "linguistically disadvantaged" groups (including Asians and people "of Spanish heritage") in certain districts and authorized Justice Department intervention to protect those linguistic minorities from voting rights violations.[151] Although almost 300 counties and municipalities in thirty states used multilingual ballots for the November 2002 elections—Los Angeles County issued them in seven languages (English, Spanish, Tagalog, Vietnamese, Chinese, Japanese, and Korean)—such ballots have aroused relatively little debate in recent years.[152]

Bilingual Education

The same cannot be said of bilingual education. Indeed, it has become one of the most divisive issues in American politics, particularly at the state level. Sociologist John Skrentny observes that bilingual education "has been at the center of a storm over what it means to be an American, over assimilation, the 'melting pot' and the nature of American culture, over the proper duties of citizens and immigrants, over the legitimate uses of taxpayer dollars, and over the efficacy of 'liberal' pedagogy."[153]

Ostensibly, the issues are technical and pedagogical. First, there is the choice between teaching English through "immersion" with instruction entirely in English, or instead through English as a Second Language (ESL) with some instruction in a student's native tongue. Second, there is the choice between continuing native language instruction throughout a student's schooling ("maintenance") or instead only until the student masters English ("transitional").

In fact, the real choices are not this stark; hybrid forms of instruction are common. For example, "sheltered" immersion usually involves a period of time, often a year, of concentrated training in English with some use of the native language, at the end of which students enter mainstream classes. Because native language instruction is typically used to teach about the student's native culture, this form is sometimes called bilingual-bicultural education. Inevitably, as Nathan Glazer shows, "the reality of bilingual teaching . . . had substantial consequences for *what* was taught. Bilingual instruction for students speaking Spanish also meant to some degree instruction in Puerto Rican or Mexican culture and history."[154]

With the expansion of immigrant communities and their growing political, economic, and cultural influence, the question of how well and how quickly bilingual education programs teach English literacy and fluency has become much more salient. (The challenge is even greater, of course, for those who are illiterate in their native language.)[155] Concern focuses mostly on Spanish-speakers who are far more numerous than other language groups and whose continuing ties to their cultures of origin are strengthened by geographic proximity, much Spanish-language mass media, and transnational communities based on family and trade relationships. In fact, there is no convincing evidence that the continued primacy of English in the United States is endangered by this growing linguistic diversity. Almost all studies of English proficiency among legal immigrants indicate that the first generation acquires fluency at roughly the same rate as earlier waves did, that the "one-and-a-half" (people brought to the United States as young children) and second generations learn it at school and strongly prefer it to their parents' native language, that 98% of the second generation speak it proficiently by the end of high school, and that the third generation is largely monolingual in English and likes it that way.[156] (Alarmingly, however, 10% of students with limited English proficiency—LEP—are third generation.)[157]

Immigrants, however, are not the only targets of concern. An estimated three million or more LEP students are native-born U.S. citizens who entered public school at an age when children can learn English easily, even if their parents cannot.[158] Moreover, the 1990 census found that almost eight million households, 8.3% of the U.S. total, were "linguistically isolated," meaning that no person 14 or older spoke English well.[159] Given this linguistic dysfunction, it is small comfort that the rest of the world is busily learning English.[160]

As with affirmative action and some other diversity policies, the federal commitment to bilingual education began in the 1960s, and at a modest level.[161] A few cities had taught immigrant children in German in the nineteenth century but these were local efforts.[162] Although German-speakers were a much larger share of the population than Spanish-speakers are today, constituting more than 35% in some states, and although they used their often considerable political influence to demand bilingual education in the public schools, their proposals were rejected at the federal and state levels.[163]

In the early 1960s, a bilingual education program in Dade County, Florida seemed to enjoy some success with Cuban students whose parents—who presumably expected a swift return to Cuba once Castro fell—wanted them to retain their Spanish fluency. Drawing on this success, national program advocates persuaded Senator Ralph Yarborough of Texas to champion their cause.[164] When Congress passed the Bilingual Education Act of 1968 (BEA), there was no direct precedent for federal support of bilingual education, and it provided a modest $7.5 million for demonstration projects in 1969, the first year. Ten years earlier, the National Defense Education Act (NDEA),[165] enacted in response to Sputnik and national security concerns, had provided funds for foreign language development and also presaged greater federal involvement in the quality of education. In the Elementary and Secondary Education Act of 1965,[166] Congress not only plunged further into the field of foreign language development but also institutionalized categorical programs targeted at disadvantaged children.

John Skrentny shows that the BEA, which generated little opposition at the time, was produced by a number of converging developments: a United Nations–centered network of international bilingual education professionals, programs for Cuban refugee children in Florida, growing support by teachers' unions, Yarborough's tireless advocacy, foreign policy symbolism, a linkage to the ethno-racial justice and recognition ideals associated with the black civil rights movement, and political appeals to Latinos. The new Nixon administration also saw political opportunity and supported a small increase in funds for BEA implementation.

Hispanic advocacy groups, however, soon made bilingual education a focus and symbol of ethnic solidarity. They were remarkably effective, helping to mutate a limited educational benefit for a relatively small number of children provided voluntarily by some local school districts into a civil right to federal support for one's native language. The key step came in 1970. The federal Office of Civil Rights (OCR) issued "guidelines" informing federally funded school districts with more than 5% national origin-minority group children that it now considered the failure to act affirmatively to accommodate LEP children to constitute a violation of Title VI of the Civil Rights Act of 1964, which barred discrimination on the basis of national origin.[167] Lower federal judges drew on civil rights principles established earlier by black litigants in interpreting the 1970 guidelines to mandate Latino cultural maintenance and promotion, not just effective English instruction.[168]

The Supreme Court upheld the guidelines in its 1974 decision in *Lau v. Nichols,* which involved Chinese students.[169] Henceforth, language discrimination would constitute national origin discrimination. (Interestingly in light of his later pronouncements, then-Solicitor General Robert Bork urged the Court to adopt this position as a matter of *constitutional* law, not just statutory interpretation.) Later that year, Congress broadened the BEA to include nonpoor children and a right to be taught about the culture of origin. It also enacted the Equal Educational Opportunity Act, which applied the new right to all public schools.[170]

In 1975, the government issued new guidelines designed to help school districts implement the *Lau* decision. These "*Lau* remedies" were remarkably expansive, intrusive, and prescriptive. Going well beyond *Lau* itself, they covered *all* schoolchildren in homes where English was not the primary language, not just LEP students. They required the schools (among other things) to "determine the language most often spoken in the student's home, regardless of the language spoken by the student, the language spoken by the student in the home and the language spoken by the student in the social setting (by observation)," and the particular "cognitive learning style" and "incentive motivational styles" to which each student best responded. And they directed the schools to end ESL for grade-school students, supplement ESL for high school students, maintain each student's language and culture while English was being taught, and eliminate transitional programs absent a special showing. Finally, they endorsed the illiberal principle that only co-ethnics could truly understand the Latino language and culture, and created strong incentives to hire only Latinos as teachers. Skrentny summarizes the remarkable history leading up to the *Lau* remedies:

> [L]anguage accommodation became a right without public debate and public involvement. OCR issued an order, and the courts affirmed it. At this stage, and in the origins of the [BEA], resistance was almost nonexistent. . . . The [BEA] became law about a year after anyone in Congress had even heard of bilingual education. The OCR issued its memorandum declaring a right to language accommodation only a few months after Latino advocates first spoke to OCR officials. While it took longer to gain implementation, there was no organized resistance to these moves at the federal level. Nothing came this easy for black Americans.[171]

OCR proceeded to negotiate hundreds of plans with local school districts. The plans prescribed, among other things, how the schools must implement the *Lau* remedies. In effect, OCR created a virtual monopoly for bilingual education by designating it as the clearly preferred method. Districts could substitute other approaches only by making a special showing, a burden few districts would undertake. In the *Aspira* case,[172] brought by the Puerto Rican Legal Defense and Education Fund against the New York City Board of Education, the parties agreed to a consent decree in 1974 requiring the Board to provide an effective program for teaching all Spanish-speaking and Spanish-surnamed LEP students, then about 150,000 in number, to speak, understand, read, and write English. This decree, combined with program funding patterns, gave the city powerful fiscal incentives to maximize the number of students in bilingual education and to keep them there for many years. The decree also shifted key policymaking and implementation responsibilities from professional educators to the court. Almost thirty years later, the decree remains in effect, entrenching some of the most dubious pedagogical choices made by New York's judges and city officials, most notably the mandate to enroll LEP students in bilingual education classes taught almost exclusively in Spanish and to emphasize cultural maintenance.[173]

Other court decisions throughout the country accepted the advocates' claim that bilingual, and especially bicultural, education was good for Hispanic children regardless of how well they could speak English, a claim that Congress seemed to accept. The new orthodoxy, according to educational historian Diane Ravitch, operated on four assumptions:

> first, that Hispanic children did poorly in school because they had a "damaged self-concept"; second, that the negative self-appraisal occurred because the child's native tongue was not the language of instruction; third, that the appropriate remedy for this problem was bilingual instruction; and fourth, that children who were taught their native language (or their *parents'* native language) and their cultural heritage would acquire a positive self-concept, high self-esteem, better attitudes toward school, increased motivation, and improved educational achievement.[174]

Within a few years of the *Aspira* decree, this approach had come under fire from many education specialists, politicians, and parents. At one level, the debate concerned the appropriate balance between two goals: rapid transition to English-speaking and cultural maintenance. The combatants disagreed about the relationship between these goals—proponents of bilingual education viewed the two goals as entirely consistent—and about which classroom methods were most effective in achieving them. Bilingual education enthusiasts argued that children cannot learn a second language until they have mastered the first, and that special English instruction should continue for six or seven years. Their opponents, citing among other things the experience of earlier generations of immigrants, favored a more rapid transition to English.

In 1977, the critics of the bilingual programs mandated by the *Aspira* decree were buoyed by a long-awaited, federally funded report by the American Institute for Research (AIR) based on a large-scale study of programs that had been in operation since at least 1971. AIR found that the programs keeping LEP students in regular classes were more effective in teaching English than were the bilingual education programs, and that the bilingual programs were more effective in teaching them to read in Spanish (as well as learn mathematics). The study also found that two-thirds of Hispanic children in bilingual education classes were *already* proficient in English, and that 86% of the programs kept children in bilingual classrooms even *after* they had achieved English proficiency. The orthodoxy Ravitch described seemed to rest on a foundation of sand. According to one commentator, "[e]xperts interpreted these findings to mean that bilingual education had an overall segregative, rather than inclusive, effect on the classroom . . . [and] the AIR evaluation destroyed whatever consensus there had been regarding the educational benefits of bicultural-bilingual education."[175]

Some supporters of bilingual education programs, thrown on the defensive by the AIR report, criticized its methodology. Others, however, made a more radical critique, arguing that numbers had no place in the debate because bilingual education was a civil and cultural right of Spanish-speakers. The growing dominance of this latter view in the pro-bilingual education camp transformed the public debate. What had begun as an ostensibly professional-pedagogical dispute over how best to help children transition quickly to the agreed-upon goal of English proficiency now became a struggle over the value-laden and ideologically divisive issues of multiculturalism, the nature and pace of assimilation, and even the character and future of American citizenship. The cultural maintenance argument for bilingual education most unsettled those (like me) who favored a vision of multiculturalism that respects and tolerates the cultures of origin as much as liberal principles permit but that leaves the task of defining and transmitting those cultures to families and private institutions, not to government—a vision to which American public policy has adhered, with few exceptions.[176] Nonetheless, Congress in 1978 extended the program pretty much as the advocates wanted, even expanding its coverage to include students who spoke English so long as their reading and writing in English remained inadequate.

In the debate over bilingual education, the argument that earlier generations of immigrant schoolchildren had learned English through immersion was more than a pedagogical claim. It also caused some to question whether the newcomers were less committed to joining American society than their predecessors (many of whom, of course, were among the debaters) had been. The doubters also suspected that the newcomers were being misled and disabled by some of their own advocates, whom they accused of sometimes being more interested in preserving jobs for bilingual teachers and scoring ideological points than in promoting their co-ethnics' assimilation.

The debate heated up even more during the Reagan years. In 1981, a comprehensive Department of Education review of the published studies on bilingual education cast serious doubt on its effectiveness. In April 1982, Education Secretary T. H. Bell instructed OCR to renegotiate the *Lau* remedies with local school districts, allowing them to use ESL programs to satisfy their bilingual education mandates. Congress was disturbed by the Department's findings on bilingual education's ineffectiveness and took due note of President Reagan's strong opposition to the program. Marching under the banner of the "new federalism," Congress passed the Bilingual Education Improvement Act of 1984, which gave state and local agencies more discretion in shaping education for LEP students.[177] Although these agencies could not discriminate against such students, they could decide for themselves how to serve them. In 1988, Congress sought to move the political struggles over bilingual education to the state and local levels by allowing substantial BEA funds to be spent instead on English immersion and other programs not relying on native language instruction. Despite this new option, however, many state and local agencies, notably in Los Angeles and New York City, took the opposite tack; they reinforced and expanded their commitments to the bilingual education and cultural maintenance approaches.

Several developments during the 1980s indicated a hardening of attitudes in other domains of language policy. First, many employers promulgated some version of an "English only" rule for their workplaces, a practice whose legality under the civil rights laws has divided the courts.[178] Second, many states enacted "official English" laws that affirm the primacy of English as the language of the state. Most of these laws are largely symbolic gestures but some of them go farther, requiring government business and public education to be conducted in English. The constitutionality of these laws remains an open question,[179] and their wisdom, at least as presently written, seems doubtful. Surely many situations arise in which a government agency's refusal to communicate with members of the public in a language other than English is counterproductive, if not alienating or demeaning. The popularity of such laws, however, is broad-based; in 2002, Iowa became the twenty-seventh state to declare English its official language, the tenth state to do so since 1995.[180] Conservatives favor these laws much more than liberals do, but they draw support from across the political spectrum. Thus 29% of "strong liberals" and 39% of Hispanic voters favored California's measure in 1986.[181]

During the 1990s, the bilingual education controversy boiled over in some states, fueled by the unprecedented levels of legal and illegal migrants, mostly from Latin America, and by the ineffectiveness of existing programs. The number of non-English-speakers in American homes and schools increased sharply. According to the 2000 census, 18% of the population (40% in California) do not speak English at home; 43% of these say they do not speak English "very well."[182] Today, more than 20% of schoolchildren are children of immigrants, compared with 6% in 1970 and 14% in 1990.[183] Three-fourths of all children in foreign-language-speaking homes—an estimated 5.6 million—lived in Spanish-speaking ones, an increase of 64% since 1980.[184] In 1997, an estimated 40% of foreign-born students—3.5 million, or about 5% of all students—were LEP, 57% more than in 1990. The total enrollment of LEP students in the United States, by one estimate, more than doubled during the decade of the 1990s, reaching a total of 4.1 million in 1999–2000.[185] (On the brighter side, the foreign-born share of the Hispanic population evidently peaked in the 1990s and is now declining, so that a rising proportion will be second- and third-generation English-speakers.)[186]

The prospects for LEP students are dismal. They are left back and drop out of school four times more frequently than their English-proficient peers, and many of those who remain attend linguistically segregated schools; almost half of LEP students attend schools where at least 30% of the students are LEP. Within their schools, they are segregated from English-proficient students.[187] Most shocking, as noted earlier, 10% of LEP children, disproportionately of Hispanic descent, appear to be the third generation in America (i.e., native-born children of native-born parents).[188]

The public investment in bilingual education has grown rapidly—even as its failures have become more evident. Federal spending under the BEA, which declined briefly in the mid-1990s when Republicans gained control of the House, has nevertheless grown 50% since 1994 (in nominal dollars), reaching $296 million in fiscal year 2001—making a total of $4.5 billion since 1969.[189] Other federal programs, such as refugee assistance and the Immigrant Education program, provide additional funds. Spending on Immigrant Education tripled between 1996 and 1998 when it reached a total of $150 million; the number of eligible students grew by more than 11% between 2000 and 2001.

This increased federal spending on bilingual education, however, must be kept in perspective. First, state and local spending on bilingual education is at least three times the amount of federal spending.[190] A 1993 survey found that about half the states required their schools to provide special services to LEP students, and most other states encouraged or promoted such services.[191] California alone spends about $50 million a year on this.[192] Second, the services funded by the federal government probably reach at most 25% of the 4.1 million LEP students, and the amount spent per LEP student is very low. The median extra outlay per LEP student by state and local programs in the early 1990s was only $373.[193] Third, federal BEA spending per LEP student, which as just noted is a small part of the total funding, has not kept pace with the increased number of eligible students; it is now only 70% of the 1991 per-student figure.[194] Finally, the federal government has no reliable data on how much it spends on bilingual education—the vast majority of federal funds spent on LEP students comes through Title I (assistance to schools with low-income students) rather than through the much smaller BEA—nor does it know the extent to which its BEA, Immigrant Education, and Title I funds are spent on native-language, English-only, or other methods of instruction.[195] Urban Institute researchers estimate that in 1993–1994, 29% of LEP students were in ESL-only classes, 10% were in bilingual-only classes, 25% were in both, and 36% were in either regular or English-immersion classes.[196]

It is instructive to compare France's approach to linguistic diversity. Aristide Zolberg has noted that although the share of foreign-born residents in the United States and France are similar, France takes a far more monolingual stance in part because most of its immigrants come from the Maghreb, where French is usually both the language of instruction and the lingua franca. It does not provide for public services in other languages, except for criminal defendants: "Bilingual education, even of a transitional sort, does not exist; the only concession made to immigrant communities at the elementary level is to allow the teaching of 'languages and cultures of origin' as an elective subject outside of regular school hours."[197]

A galvanizing, convulsive political response to bilingual education programs' rapid growth occurred in 1998 when California's Proposition 227 was approved by 61% of its voters over the strong opposition of both gubernatorial candidates and President Clinton. This measure, which the courts upheld,[198] amended state law to require that public schools teach a single year of intensive English to LEP students and then place them in English-speaking classrooms. Parents of children in these sheltered immersion programs can seek waivers or extensions from the school district if they can demonstrate special emotional, psychological, or educational needs dictating a different kind of program for their children. Two years later, Arizona voted by a wider margin for Proposition 203, which resembles California's measure but provides fewer waiver opportunities and mandates that ESL teachers teach in English in all academic subjects. English-immersion measures were on the November 2002 ballot in Colorado and Massachusetts.[199]

English-immersion advocates will surely point to early results from California, where LEP students in districts that most fully implemented Proposition 227 seem to be raising their standardized test scores more than the others are.[200] Some researchers also conclude that the kind of sheltered English-immersion programs that the law mandated are more effective than traditional bilingual education,[201] a position strongly argued by political opponents of bilingual education.[202] On the other side are academics who hold that the relative merits of sheltered English immersion are exaggerated, as well as others who view cultural maintenance as a vital public educational goal.[203]

Because the arguments over bilingual education's effectiveness are an amalgam of social science claims, ethnic politics, educational theory, nostalgic immigration history, and sheer ideology—and also because effectiveness depends so much on the quality of specific teachers and local programs—they may never be resolved.[204] For what it is worth (and I think it is worth a great deal), the public, including Latino parents who have the greatest stake in effective programs, seems to have made up its mind. Public opposition to bilingual education has been both persistent and widespread.[205] In 1980, Gallup reported that 82% of the respondents favored requiring children who cannot speak English to "learn English in special classes before they are enrolled in public schools." In 1988, only 42% favored "providing instruction in a student's native language, whatever it is, in order to help him or her become a more successful learner." A 1993 poll found that 27% favored bilingual education (described as teaching students in their native language with a gradual transition to English), 46% favored English immersion (defined as teaching students in English while providing intensive training in how to read and speak English), and 25% favored requiring students to learn English before enrolling in public schools. In 1998, 75% of foreign-born parents (66% of Hispanics) favored teaching children "English as quickly as possible, even if this means they fall behind in other subjects." Only 21% favored teaching them "other subjects in their native language even if this means it takes them longer to learn English." In another poll, English immersion was favored by 63% of respondents and opposed by 33%, closely mirroring the ballot results in California's Proposition 227, where the split was 61%–39%. Whites and nonwhites differ little on bilingual education but age groups do differ, with the 18–29 group significantly more favorable to it.

Most Latinos evidently oppose bilingual education. Polls indicate that 84% of them supported Proposition 227 in 1997, 60% opposed it in the actual vote a year later, and more than 60% of them approved once it was implemented.[206] A survey of Latino attitudes published in 2000, while not asking specifically about bilingual education, found that nearly 90% of recently arrived Latinos "believe it is important to change so they can fit into the larger society."[207] Other polls indicate that Latinos overwhelmingly reject programs that emphasize cultural maintenance.[208] All the more astounding, then, that California Governor Gray Davis would seek in effect to nullify Proposition 227 by having his State Board of Education appointees vote in February 2002 to allow bilingual education teachers rather than parents to exercise the right to apply for waivers placing children in such programs, and also to rescind the rule that LEP children under the age of 10 be taught English for at least the first month of every school year—this at a time when the changes effected by 227 were raising Latino student performance substantially.[209] When it comes to educating California's LEP students, Davis seems to think, nothing succeeds like failure—and vice versa.

Bilingual education has become especially polarized in New York City,[210] where public school students, either immigrants or the children of immigrants, speak more than 140 different tongues.[211] Today, almost 160,000 of them, 15% of the city's school population, are considered LEP and are enrolled in programs offered in a dozen different languages, or in ESL classes. About 65% are Spanish-speaking.[212] Many have mild or moderate disabilities. The school system places many in the programs arbitrarily, without the parents' consent or even over their vehement objections. The schools find it easier to teach LEP students in language-segregated classes, of course, but there is also a fiscal incentive: the schools receive additional funding for each LEP student they enroll in bilingual classes. In 2000, the cost of bilingual and ESL programs was $45.6 million and $123.3 million, respectively, largely to pay the 6,000 teachers, of whom 4,700 are certified to teach bilingual or ESL classes. According to the city, "no significant state funding for such programs has been forthcoming" despite the state's oft-stated concerns about the LEP problem.[213] The shortage of qualified bilingual and ESL teachers in the system is both chronic and growing. Moreover, the changing composition of the large Hispanic community in New York, now dominated by Dominicans with many Mexicans and South Americans, has led to bitter local disputes challenging the *Aspira*-centered approach of the Puerto Ricans who dominated Hispanic life when they secured the consent decree in that case almost thirty years ago.[214]

Although New York's current programs are billed as transitional, about half of the students in bilingual and ESL programs are still there after three years. (In a classic glass half-empty or half-full exercise, the Chancellor of the system noted that 50% exit the programs within three years, calling this evidence of "substantial effectiveness.")[215] Indeed, about 10% of the students, disproportionately Spanish-speakers, remain in the programs after seven years or more! The one-in-eight LEP students who are "inconsistently served," moving between bilingual and ESL classes, have especially low exit rates. These problems are particularly acute for immigrants who enter the city schools at grade six or above; only 45% of LEP children who enter in middle school and 15% who enter in high school exit the programs at all. For linguistic and other reasons, they drop out of school at alarmingly high rates with predictably crippling effects on their life chances. Indeed, many enter these programs more proficient in English than in their parents' tongue and proceed to *lose* their English proficiency after years of supposedly transitional classes.[216]

Not surprisingly, support for bilingual education in the New York City system, which was always lukewarm, is cooling further, especially among better-educated Hispanics. English immersion is strongly favored by many parents, especially Russians and others who are less eager to retain their ties to the mother country. The published studies on the comparative effectiveness of different teaching methods is not very helpful, much less dispositive. "Much of the research," according to a recent Chancellor's Report, "can be characterized as 'advocacy research,' lacking in scientific rigor. Methodological weaknesses in the research include lack of conceptual clarity, failure to control for important interactive factors such as students' socioeconomic status, inconsistency of programmatic approach and quality, and small sample sizes."[217]

New York's mayor, education establishment, and even some former bilingual education advocates have proposed far-reaching reforms in the city's programs. These include providing parents with more choices among programs, placing strict limits on the number of years students may remain in them, raising the amount of instruction time using English, and replacing bilingual classes with sheltered but virtually total English immersion, as California and Arizona have done. Early in 2001, the Board of Education adopted a policy requiring students in bilingual programs to remain there for no longer than three years under normal circumstances. But this "new" policy, as bilingual education opponent Ron Unz has noted, was already dictated by state law (although local school districts often waived it) and does nothing to change the twenty-seven-year-old *Aspira* decree, which leaves many LEP students to languish in bilingual programs indefinitely unless and until their parents manage to get them out.

While bilingual education is under vigorous attack and additional states are considering "official English" laws, the federal government would greatly expand its use of other languages in order to accommodate the linguistic needs of limited-English speakers. In August 2000, President Clinton issued Executive Order 13166 requiring every federal agency, as part of its civil rights compliance obligation, to examine the services it provides and to develop and implement systems enabling LEP individuals, adults as well as children, to gain meaningful access to those services, perhaps by using English *less*. This order, which also applies to the vast number of state and local agencies and private entities that receive federal funds, could become a critical element of U.S. language policy. President Bush, who is attempting to woo Hispanic voters,[218] is assessing its implementation.[219]

The executive order, coupled with Bush's highly symbolic decision in 2001 to deliver his weekly radio address in Spanish on the Mexican national holiday of Cinco de Mayo (with the Democrats replying in kind) and thereafter to give his speech in both languages each week, marks an important inflection point for language policy.[220] The same is true of the decision by both gubernatorial candidates in the Texas Democratic primary to debate in Spanish as well as in English—including an ensuing tiff over whose Spanish was better and more authentic.[221] The fact that these actions were taken by the leaders of both major parties, notoriously cautious politicians who continually monitor and court public opinion, demonstrates two important points. First, this affirmative multilingualism is a new public value embraced by the educational and political establishments, not just by Hispanics.[222] Only a generation ago, these same elites forbade many schoolchildren to speak Spanish, as did many immigrant parents.[223] Second, even after thirty-five years of high Hispanic immigration, the public's strong opposition to bilingual education apparently reflects not xenophobia but a negative appraisal both of its pedagogical merits and of its use as an instrument of government-promoted cultural maintenance—an appraisal plainly shared by Hispanic voters and parents, who are the central parties in interest. Similarly, as noted earlier, the support for official-English measures cuts across all partisan and ideological lines.[224]

If the federal government has a special role to play in spurring linguistic assimilation, that role is not to place its heavy thumb on the pedagogical scales at the local level. Washington should leave school districts and individual schools free to experiment with different methods of teaching English to immigrant children. As we saw earlier, the policy evaluation research is by no means unanimous on this subject, and few if any of the studies are sufficiently well designed to support a categorical choice of pedagogic method. Indeed, the clearest findings are that excellent teaching can make most methods effective and that hybrid approaches often work well.

Educators attempting to manage diversity in their local schools, then, should neither be bound nor fiscally motivated by some transient orthodoxy devised elsewhere. Instead, the federal government should continue to sponsor research on and evaluation of "best methods," and disseminate the results widely. Even more important, it should expand its fiscal support for local programs that, regardless of methodology, seem effective in teaching English to adult immigrants. Improving adults' English fluency would also make the task of teaching English and other subjects to their children that much easier. Many locally funded adult education programs already exist, of course, and most immigrants learn English on their own. Still, the nation has a strong independent interest in promoting immigrants' English fluency. Yet despite these high stakes in expanding such programs, long and growing waiting lists exist in many communities.[225] Few policy anomalies are more striking than insisting on the hegemonic status of English while also limiting access to programs that would help to assure it.

The most important step in reforming bilingual education, in my view, would be to furnish parents of LEP children with vouchers, equal in value to the special per-pupil cost of instructing LEP students in that system. The parents could then use the voucher to purchase any accredited English-language instruction, public or private, that they prefer to the public school's bilingual or ESL offering. Parents who select total English immersion for their child in mainstream public school classes could use the voucher instead to purchase accredited supplementary ESL, tutoring, or other educational services. In addition to prescribing the amount and parameters of the LEP voucher, governmental responsibility would focus on basic and applied research about the effectiveness of different approaches and providers, on disseminating the results to parents and providers, and on policing fraudulent providers. Indeed, the $75 million bilingual education reform approved by the New York City Board of Education in February 2001 includes an ambitious "informed consent" component, which would hold school districts accountable for providing clear, detailed information on all available program options, including extensive data on exit rates and other indicia of programs' effectiveness.[226]

The advantages of LEP vouchers, like those of school vouchers more generally,[227] will depend crucially on the details of the program's design, but they are likely to include broader parental information and choice, services tailored more closely to individual need, greater accountability by providers, lower-cost and less politicized services, and salutary competitive pressure on the public schools. These advantages, moreover, in no way depend on the existence of the kind of broader school choice programs, discussed in Chapter 7, that some communities have already established. In any event, an LEP program should arouse fewer objections than these broader plans generally do. Almost by definition, LEP vouchers would target the neediest children, those most at risk of dropping out and of related problems, without spreading limited funds over the great majority of non-LEP children whose families already have more and better choices (a feature that plagues many broader voucher proposals). LEP vouchers, moreover, would be less vulnerable to challenge on various constitutional grounds,[228] and since they would be of lower value and apply only to a single service (English instruction) rather than to the entire curriculum, they would be less likely than broader voucher programs to move children to a religious or other private school.

Finally, and for our purposes most relevant, such vouchers would foster genuine diversity in several senses. They would allow different families to pursue different avenues to English-language competence according to their distinctive needs and values as *they* define them; leave to parents the choice of precisely how much and what kind of cultural maintenance their children should have; invite competition among many potential service providers with respect to quality, cost, convenience, and other aspects of language instruction; and encourage experimentation and research on more effective instructional methods. This last is particularly valuable in a pedagogical area in which the only expert consensus seems to be that no consensus yet exists.

Diversity Visas

Until the 1965 immigration reform law, diversity—however one might choose to define it—was not an immigration policy goal. Quite the contrary. The diversity that flourished before the United States imposed general immigration restrictions was simply a consequence of policies designed to attract immigrants who would settle and cultivate a vast continent and man the factories and construction gangs of a rapidly expanding, industrializing economy. And the express purpose of the quota system that Congress maintained between the early 1920s and 1965 was to reverse the profusion of ethnic and national origins diversity by returning to the relative demographic homogeneity of an earlier day. Indeed, even the Congress that enacted the 1965 law foresaw neither the number of Asians who would come nor the great surge of immigrants from Latin America and the Caribbean. Congress intended to repudiate the racist quotas and affirm a new nondiscrimination principle as applied to national origins, not to promote diversity as an independent policy goal. It extended this nondiscrimination principle in 1976 when it ended the Western Hemisphere's exemption from the limits that applied elsewhere, and in the Refugee Act of 1980, which sought to equalize the treatment of refugees throughout the world.

An augury of a more affirmatively pro-diversity approach first appeared in the 1981 report of the Select Commission on Immigration and Refugee Policy, which Congress had established three years earlier. The Commission's report enunciated three immigration policy goals, one of which was cultural diversity consistent with national unity. Although the report failed to define or elaborate on this,[229] its rationale was probably to augment the existing system of employment- and family-based admissions with some visas for "new seed" immigrants, and also to redress what many perceived as a bias against European ethnic groups caused by the large flows from Asia and Latin America resulting from the 1965 law.

These "new seed" and "discrimination against European immigrants" arguments had been invoked back in the late 1960s and early 1970s by several members of Congress who represented Irish and Italian constituencies, but the legislation they introduced went nowhere.[230] By the mid-1980s, however, the number of Irish immigrants in illegal status had grown quite large and the amnesty provisions of the pending Immigration Reform and Control

Act of 1986 (IRCA) provided this group's advocates, who wielded the new rhetoric of diversity as well as the old themes of new seeds and discrimination, with a political opening.

Their efforts culminated in Section 314 of the IRCA, which proponents and opponents alike saw as a kind of special amnesty for the Irish.[231] This provision, which was added at the last minute and had not been considered by any committee in either house during the six years of debate over the IRCA, authorized a program providing for 10,000 visas over a two-year period above the existing worldwide ceiling to go to natives of countries "adversely affected" by the 1965 law; those within that category would be selected by lottery.[232] The IRCA conference report defined the intended countries as those "which enjoyed favorable quotas and/or whose nationals received significant numbers of visas prior to the 1965 amendments." The State Department, which would administer this "NP-5" program, then defined "adversely affected" to mean a country whose average annual rate of immigration from 1966 to 1985 was less than its average annual rate from 1953 to 1965. This standard excluded most Central and South American countries and all Asian countries except Japan. The three largest recipient countries of NP-5 visas were Canada, Ireland, and the United Kingdom. Although the IRCA did not provide for an annual upper limit on the number of visas that an individual nation could receive, the State Department set one based on the amount by which its average rate had declined in the later period. In terms of these limits, sixteen out of the top seventeen nations were European. Demand for the NP-5 visas was immense. Due to security concerns at U.S. embassies, mail applications were required, and more than 1.3 million people applied for the 10,000 visas during a two-week period.

In 1988, Congress extended the NP-5 program for two more years and expanded it to 30,000 visas. Congressman Brian Donnelly of Massachusetts, who had been mainly responsible for inserting Section 314 into the IRCA, offered three arguments for extending the program, none of which had anything to do with diversity. The goal of legalizing out-of-state aliens was meant to benefit illegal Irish immigrants in New York, Boston, and other cities; the goal of fair competition for visas was refuted by the program's clear Eurocentric bias; and the goal of reintroducing the old stock into the new immigration stream was hardly diversity-enhancing, as the old stock was by definition already disproportionately represented in the population. Indeed, advocates of the old stock sometimes invoked the rhetoric of affirmative action opponents, claiming that the 1965 law had caused "reverse discrimination" against their groups.[233]

Concerns about this Eurocentric bias in NP-5 visas led Congress to create in the 1988 law another program, also ostensibly aimed at diversity. Known as OP-1, it authorized 20,000 visas over a two-year period, to be distributed by lottery, for natives of "underrepresented countries," defined as countries that in 1988 used less than 25% of the maximum number of visas available to them. By 1990, when both programs expired, four countries accounted for over 75% of the NP-5 visas: Ireland (40.8%), Canada (17.6%), Great Britain and Northern Ireland (9%), and Poland (8.5%). The twenty-seven European nations took up 68% of them. Indonesia, the only non-European winner, took 8.4%. The OP-1 program, in contrast, did benefit non-European nations, led by Bangladesh, Pakistan, Egypt, Peru, and Trinidad and Tobago; a European state, Poland, followed close behind.

In the Immigration Act of 1990, Congress again expanded and extended the NP-5 lottery for "adversely affected" countries by providing 40,000 diversity visas each year for three years as a transition to a permanent program.[234] Congress made Canadians ineligible for these "AA-1" visas in order to support another change, which starkly reveals that the program was driven by ethnic group politics—and *white* ethnic groups at that. With strong political ties to Irish groups and key positions as chairs of the immigration subcommittees, Senator Edward Kennedy and Congressman Bruce Morrison of Connecticut, along with Congressman Donnelly, included a provision guaranteeing that at least 40% of the visas, which came to be known as "Donnelly visas," went to natives of Ireland—without actually naming the country![235] Because the law did not limit the number of visa applications an alien could submit, some 19 million AA-1 applications were filed during the program's first year. In 1991, Congress tried to stem this tide by eliminating multiple applications and making other technical changes to the lottery.

In addition, the 1990 Act provided for a permanent "diversity visas" program beginning in 1994 and modeled on the OP-1 program. Each year, 55,000 diversity visas (50,000 since 1999) are available to natives of low-admission states in low-admission regions (not counting diversity visas); determinations are based on a very complex formula. In another special-interest provision, the statute treats Northern Ireland as a separate state from Great Britain, thus making it eligible for these visas for which it would be ineligible if considered part of Great Britain. The program divides the diversity visas among six geographic regions, setting upper limits on each region, awarding the visas on a first-come, first-served basis up to the region's ceiling, and excluding potential immigrants from certain countries that fill their yearly quota of family- and employment-based visas. No single country may receive more than 7% of the total visas (now 50,000) in any one year, but certain countries do tend to dominate the visa lottery.[236]

The individual eligibility criteria are remarkably undiscriminating. Applicants need no more than a high school education equivalent or two recent years of work experience at a skilled job; even these minimal requirements were imposed only at the conference committee stage. More than 13 million foreigners applied for the lottery for the 50,000 diversity visas for 2002, and 3 million of these were disqualified for failing to follow directions, which may be an index of how complex the lottery application process is. For some reason, the number applying for the 2003 lottery was "only" 8.7 million. Family members can join the winners but they count against the visa ceiling.

For the past decade, the diversity lottery has remained beneath the congressional radar. Neither the House nor the Senate has exhibited any real desire to alter the program's scope or shape.[237] In 1994, the Jordan Commission opted not to propose any significant amendment to the diversity lottery, choosing instead to focus on the problem of illegal immigration.[238] Despite the apparent lack of congressional interest in the program, the State Department believes that the lottery, which it administers, creates poor public relations by offering admission to the United States based on a game of chance.[239] Immigration experts and legislative aides, however, think the program will retain its current form until Senator Kennedy, an architect of the lottery system, leaves office.[240] Even then, inertia may defeat reform; there is simply no evidence that any senator or representative wishes to push for large-scale changes.[241] Unless and until Congress decides to undertake a full-scale overhaul of the immigration system, the diversity lottery is probably here to stay. Its persistence is due not to strong affirmative support but rather to a lack of any impetus for reform.

The diversity visas program was never about diversity, especially at its inception when the program was the ethnic equivalent of pork-barrel politics. Like traditional rivers and harbors construction projects that use lofty national defense or environmental rhetoric to disguise their nakedly political motivations, the program sought legitimacy by wrapping itself in the growing social prestige of the diversity ideal in hopes of concealing its more mundane political origins. (Some have suggested more pernicious motives, including racism.) Supposedly, the diversity visas program served to redress what its supporters claimed was an unfair imbalance between high-admission and low-admission regions and states. The claim was that this imbalance (if that is what it was) reflected unfair advantages that post-1965 immigrants enjoyed in petitioning to bring their family members here compared with pre-1965 immigrants who were less likely to still have immediate family in their countries of origin.

This view, however, ignored several crucial facts. First, the national origins quotas that prevailed prior to 1965 conferred an unfair advantage on most of the low-admission states that the diversity visas program originally favored. They had become low-admission states precisely because they were high-admission states under the same, discredited pre-1965 system that enabled their immigrants to be admitted and then bring in their family members. Second, the program's favoritism toward the Irish, many of whom were and are illegally in the United States, is entirely inconsistent with this justification. In reality, immigration policy experts say, the program was designed to create a new white, European, English-speaking, largely Irish immigration stream to balance, albeit in only a limited way, the unexpectedly large nonwhite Asian and Latino migrations in the 1970s and 1980s.[242] Calculations at the time by then-Congressman Charles Schumer of New York predicted the ensuing Eurocentric regional allocations.[243]

Indeed, the remedial, antidiscrimination rationale for the diversity program never made much sense. After all, the major goal of the admission system created by the 1965 law was nondiscrimination among countries of origin, and in this it has succeeded admirably. Although the system, like any complex practice, affects different states differently, the important point is that its disparate impacts result not from invidious discrimination but from the differential effects of the per-country ceilings, the timing of earlier migrations, their demographic mix, and other such factors. If anything, the diversity program created a new and genuinely perverse form of discrimination, as immigration law expert Stephen Legomsky noted:

> But even if the kind of "diversity" that the 1990 Act seeks to attain is accepted as a valid goal, the [program's] machinery . . . is difficult to fathom. The Irish citizen who has been waiting for several years to join her permanent resident alien husband in the United States might be forgiven for wondering why another Irish citizen, without any specific equities, will be able to skip ahead of her and immigrate immediately on the basis of a lottery. The explanation that "we want an ethnically diverse immigration stream" will not dispel her confusion. . . . Since many more Americans already trace their ancestry to Europe than to Asia or Latin America, the statutory "diversity" program is in truth an *"anti-diversity"* program; it causes the resulting population mix to be *less* diverse than it would otherwise be.[244]

During the late 1990s, the diversity program shed its unjustified Eurocentrism in general, and its bias in favor of Ireland in particular. The lottery now excludes any country whose nationals have used almost all of the visas allotted to it during the preceding five years; in 2002, this excluded Canada, China (except Hong Kong), Colombia, the Dominican Republic, El Salvador, Haiti, India, Jamaica, Mexico, Pakistan, the Philippines, South Korea, the United Kingdom (except Northern Ireland), and Vietnam. The leading sending countries under the program in 2002 were Ghana, Nigeria, Sierra

Leone, Ukraine, Bangladesh, Ethiopia, Poland, Russia, Bulgaria, Kenya, Albania, Iran, and Peru, in that order; Ireland (which has not used up its allotted visas in recent years, presumably because of its prosperity and easy access to other EU countries) is far down the list. The regional caps, which are based on the number of eligible applicants, are now 19,930 for Africa and 10,520 for Asia (India and China are excluded), compared with 20,000 for Europe (almost all in eastern Europe), 845 for Oceania, 15 for North America (i.e., the Bahamas), and 1,600 for South and Central America and the Caribbean. Even without the diversity visas, the percentage of visas accounted for by a few top sending countries declined after 1965—a small number of sending countries had been the norm throughout U.S. immigration history—but the diversity visas have helped reduce the concentration even further.

Even before this change, of course, both American society and the current immigration stream were already about as diverse, ethnically speaking, as anyone committed to genuine diversity might wish—a fact so obvious that the program saw fit to soft-pedal its diversity rationale in favor of a new goal of admitting "new seed" immigrants, those who have no other means to obtain a permanent visa to the United States because they lack any family or employment connection here. Although many genuinely support this new-seed justification for the program, it is only slightly more defensible than the pretextual diversity rationale. It appeals to a nostalgic romanticism among many Americans who recall that their ancestors came to the United States without visas, much less prearranged jobs. (Indeed, an 1885 statute barred immigrants who had contracted for jobs in advance.)[245] The vast majority of immigrants who came before 1952, when a system of family- and employment-based visas was established, came to join family members already in America and thus were not "new seed" in that sense.

More to the point, the immigration context has radically changed in the half-century since then. Today, a visa to the United States is the most valuable resource that mobile foreigners can ever hope to obtain—the right to permanent residence, citizenship, and further family migration here. No convincing conception of justice demands (nor was any seriously offered by the program's proponents) that this precious asset should simply be given away at random and without reference to any benefits for American society. Indeed, this farce became tragedy in July 2002 when an Egyptian gunman, who had avoided deportation when his wife won a visa in the diversity lottery and was a member of an Egyptian terrorist group, killed two people at the Los Angeles International Airport.

No other country allocates its valuable visas by lottery. Moreover, no studies support the notion that new seeds will germinate and flourish in the

United States as well as other immigrants do;[246] reasons to doubt this include the minimal education, job skills, English fluency, and work experience requirements, and the fact that family and job supports in the United States make immigrants' prospects of success more likely. In addition, the injustice noted earlier by Legomsky applies to lottery-based visas, whether new seed or diversity. A program that favors lottery winners over individuals who have patiently waited in line for family- and employment-based visas, often for many years, can hardly be called fair. If anything, it magnifies their existing temptation to jump the queue and take their chances as undocumented migrants, a calculation that accounts for much of our existing illegal immigration population.

Despite the program's recent makeover, it continues to suffer from fraud and procedural maladministration.[247] In the lottery's early years, the government failed to set a limit on the number of applications that a given individual could submit. Immigration lawyers found out the location of the post office receiving applications and delivered carloads of them there, while individual applicants carried shopping bags filled with them. After two years under this notorious free-for-all system, the State Department imposed a "one-per-customer" limit on visa applications, but fraud has persisted. Many immigration lawyers counsel clients to submit a number of applications under slightly different variations of their name (e.g., John Smith, John W. Smith, J. W. Smith, J. Smith) because the computer will reject only identical names. In response to these stratagems, the State Department now requires a photograph with each application, but African and Asian applicants still find ways around the system by submitting slightly different ones, while certain countries such as Bangladesh, a perennial winner in the diversity lottery, use their well-developed false document industries to fake the job or education histories. Multiple applications remain a problem; the only way to catch somebody is if the government happens to accept two or more of their applications. Document substitution, in which diversity visa recipients agree to sell their successful applications to home-country firms that then resell them, is a growing practice. Corrupt governments sometimes intercept incoming mail containing winning visa notices and then redistribute them. In countries like Sierra Leone, outgoing mail with visa applications is sometimes destroyed.

The single most important determinant of how many people from a given country apply for the lottery is the level of involvement of that country's immigrant community in the United States; the Polish and Bangladeshi groups are particularly active in counseling their compatriots about how to use the program. Because the application process can now be completed on the Internet, many immigration lawyers in the United States have stopped handling diversity applications except as a lure for clients who need other legal advice. Many of those who received diversity visas were already in the United States, most of them out-of-status. As we have seen, this is a feature of other permanent visa programs as well.

The diversity visas lottery program should be jettisoned and its 50,000 visas allocated according to some more plausible conception of the public interest. A number of reformers have proposed a kind of point system used in Canada and Australia but never adopted here that ranks potential immigrants according to age, family ties, residential destination, English fluency, and other policy-oriented criteria. (Notably, Canada stiffened its point system in 2002.)[248]

The simplest, most incremental reform option would be to distribute these visas among the existing family- and employment-based categories. (I assume here that the admission of refugees, asylees, and others on humanitarian grounds, which operates differently and less predictably than family- and employment-based admissions, would continue to be handled through quite distinct decisionmaking processes.) A more radical alternative would use the diversity visas, or some portion of them, to experiment with an auction-based system that, if effective, might supplant or augment the existing labor certification process. Organized labor and other interests have rendered labor certification notoriously bureaucratic, inefficient, costly, and slow in order to obstruct the hiring of foreign workers. This process, which forces time-sensitive employers to try to circumvent the system, now burdens both immigrant and American workers, consumers, and the economy.[249]

In one possible auction, the government would specify the criteria that bidders (i.e., would-be immigrants or their employers) must satisfy in terms of job skills, language competency, years spent on a visa waiting list, or other desiderata, and then allow all eligibles to bid for the available visas—subject, of course, to the usual grounds of excludability applicable to all intending immigrants.[250] In an auction, the enormous surplus value of a visa—its value in excess of the immigrant's opportunity cost—would be captured not by the immigrant but by the United States, which could then use the surplus to upgrade American workers' job skills or for other social purposes.[251] It seems likely that these employment-based visas would be won by the most productive workers whose labor most helps the U.S. economy, as they would find it easiest to finance their bids.

To address fairness concerns, the government might subsidize the bids of productive workers who for good reasons cannot fully finance their own.[252] Any perceived unfairness of this scheme, moreover, must be compared with the existing system, which favors workers who are in the United States already (often illegally) and can get employer sponsors and lawyers to navigate the immigration and labor bureaucracies. If the auctioned visas were added to the existing ones, no one would be worse off and those who have been waiting for visas might be better off.[253] Successful bidders, whether employer-sponsored or not, would likely have greater skills and perhaps even family ties than holders of diversity visas, who often possess only minimal skills, need not have any prior ties to American society, and create only a spurious diversity ("anti-diversity," in Legomsky's phrase).

Any auction proposal will face strong political and ideological objections. Opponents can easily disparage it as allowing people to buy their way into the United States, which is anathema to our traditions, and to do so at a time when close family members of legal immigrants must wait for years to rejoin them here. Proponents would try to meet these objections by using the auction to replace only the existing diversity visas, allowing government to subsidize certain categories of bidders, pointing to the investor visa program which already allows people to obtain visas by agreeing to create new jobs in the United States, and explaining how the existing system operates much more unfairly in reality than appears on paper. These defenses of an auction, however, are unlikely to assuage public misgivings—and perhaps they shouldn't. Miss Liberty holding aloft an auctioneer's gavel rather than a torch of liberty would be a less inspiring icon.

CONCLUSION

Almost four centuries of immigration to America have produced an array of ethno-racial and other diversities whose richness probably has no equal in world history. To twenty-first-century Americans, this diversity is a priceless legacy akin to our fertile soils, powerful rivers, and abundant minerals. Its social value, moreover, exceeds the value of all the individuals who have comprised it. Even recognizing the bitter intergroup conflicts that immigration occasioned in the past, America's heterogeneity has over time nourished a high degree of social tolerance for and among ethnic and religious minorities. In this sense, immigration diversity has contributed not only incalculable human capital to the United States but also social capital, the reservoir of civic trust and interactivity that supports political stability and a rich civil society.

It would be odd to call this diversity "natural." After all, immigration policy reflects political, legal, economic, ideological, and other forces. The 1965 immigration law, however, did succeed in largely removing the government from its traditional business of engineering the ethnic composition of the nation according to some vision of a past golden age when the American stock was superior. In this important respect, America's current demography is more "naturally" diverse than it has been in almost a century. Relatively permissive and inclusive citizenship policies assure that this diversity will be fully reflected in the America of the future.

Language policy, however, is another story altogether. Far from retiring from the field of ethnic engineering, government at all levels has actively entered the fray wielding blunt instruments—"official English" and bilingual education policies—in ham-handed fashion. Official English, while doubtful on a number of grounds, is innocuous compared to bilingual education, which is far more perverse. In New York City, where any delay in learning English can only have dire consequences both for the large new cohorts of immigrants and for the society that they and their children are joining, longstanding language policy failures are only now being addressed. New York's response, moreover, is tentative, partial, and seemingly oblivious to the fact that other states, no less concerned about immigrant assimilation, are eliminating bilingual education altogether in favor of more or less complete English immersion.

This chapter provides a number of lessons about law's capacity to promote diversity. First, law is a technique of social control that radically simplifies complex realities by adopting formal definitions, regulatory classifications, and rules. Even where the rules are intricate, as with the formula for allocating diversity visas among countries, law's animating conceptions tend to be reductionist and its implementing categories rudimentary, usually binary (e.g., high- and low-admission countries). Lawmakers know that the world of immigration is more complicated, but the law can only regulate through broad categories—at wholesale, as it were—if it is to make itself intelligible to ordinary people and easy for ordinary officials to administer. Through these characteristic modalities, then, law suppresses diversity in the name of advancing it.[254]

Second, a law that seeks to promote diversity, like law generally, is unavoidably political. To begin with, law must make normative choices, if not explicitly then implicitly. The law could not do otherwise given the diversity of the world it regulates. Thus all rules, including those designed to be neutral, will affect different people and interests differently. Whether the rules anticipate these differences or overlook them, the inevitable consequence is to favor some values and interests over others. Sometimes this favoritism is explicit or ludicrously obvious despite its disguise, as with the special treatment of the Irish in the diversity visas program. At other times, the bias may be unexpected, surprising even the lawmakers—for example, the large increase in Hispanic immigration resulting from the 1965 law. In either case, such favoritism engenders political conflict and feeds public cynicism.

Law is also political in a second sense: it invites symbolic or rhetorical manipulation by groups seeking competitive advantage. The diversity ideal especially lends itself to such manipulation. Because it is so new as a public value, its social meanings and consequences are more opaque than with ideals such as equality and due process that society has debated and applied longer and more carefully, albeit still inconclusively. Examples include the ability of the diversity visas program to hijack the diversity ideal, and the initial success of Hispanics in using diversity rhetoric to sell bilingual education and cultural maintenance to willing legislators and courts.

Finally, the law is political in that it not only reflects competing interests but also vests and entrenches them, providing them with the inertial advantages and other tools to resist further change. Bilingual education's long career in the face of persistent failure would have been impossible had the law not provided its advocates with the funds, authority, jobs, patronage, pedagogical status, and public legitimacy that they could use to leverage their programs into a dominant, if not monopoly, position and discredit alternative approaches. The diversity visa program has similarly perpetuated itself. These themes are further developed in Chapter 8.

CHAPTER 5

Affirmative Action: Defining and Certifying Diversity

Affirmative action policy is even more divisive and unsettled today than at its inception forty years ago. This is a remarkable sociopolitical fact. I know of no other public policy since the rise of the administrative state during the New Deal that has remained so intensely unpopular both among whites and among many minority individuals, yet has survived so long.[1] Equally remarkable, its current unpopularity coincides with strong support for ethnic diversity in all areas of public and private life and with unprecedented social progress by blacks[2] and other minorities.[3] This chapter analyzes the true nature of this conflict, how it arose, why it endures, and the role that law has played in fomenting and perpetuating it—often and increasingly in the name of diversity.

I set the stage by defining affirmative action, distinguishing it from nondiscrimination, and identifying the most important forms and policy domains where it appears. I then discuss the importance of context to a normative assessment of affirmative action and emphasize several developments that create a new setting: immigration and intermarriage patterns, more fluid notions of identity, greater socioeconomic convergence of protected minorities with whites, and recent studies revealing the actual magnitude of college and professional school admission preferences. In this new context, I argue, the ethno-racial categories on which affirmative action relies are losing whatever coherence and normative appeal they may once have had.

Next, I develop the principal rationales and normative justifications offered by affirmative action's advocates, as well as the counterarguments. I focus here on the diversity rationale, particularly in the domain of higher education, where it now assumes the central justificatory role. In an effort to understand how so unpopular a policy could have survived for so long, I describe the policy's political and regulatory past and how the public views it today. After reviewing what is known about the actual consequences of affirmative action, I consider two vital issues—what an America without it would look like, and whether attractive alternatives exist—and then propose my own approach, which I summarize in the next few paragraphs and defend at greater length in a later section of this chapter.

I conclude the analysis by explaining why race is a singularly and increasingly problematic principle of distributive justice in America. My own view, as will emerge, is that affirmative action, although well intended, is hard to square with liberal ideals in general and the diversity ideal (properly understood) in particular. The social benefits are too small, too arbitrarily and narrowly targeted, and too widely resented to justify the costs that it imposes—its unfairness to other individuals, its propensity to corrupt and debase public discourse, its incoherent programmatic categories, and its reinforcement of the pernicious and increasingly meaningless use of race as a central principle of distributive justice rather than the other distributive principles, particularly merit, with which most Americans, whites and minorities alike, strongly identify. (I analyze the highly contested ideal of merit below.)[4]

My chief concern here is not with the constitutionality of ethno-racial affirmative action, but with its wisdom as public policy. In my view—much too briefly stated—the Constitution should be interpreted to permit Congress to adopt a law preferring blacks so long as it does not violate the heightened constitutional protection that other racial minorities enjoy. At the time of the Fourteenth Amendment, after all, Congress enacted laws to protect and benefit the newly freed blacks.[5] Congress enacts laws every day that favor one group over another, laws that if rational are constitutional. That being so, Congress has the power to favor blacks at the expense of the white majority if it believes that this would be sound policy and if this would meet the other constitutional tests applicable to racial classifications. Whether Congress can favor blacks over other disadvantaged ethno-racial minorities, as affirmative action sometimes does, is less clear, as is the states' power to do so.

Be that as it may, the question I ask here is whether, assuming mandatory preferences would be constitutional, Congress (or a state) *should* enact them. In explaining why my answer to this question is no, I focus on the diversity rationale for affirmative action both because of my larger interest in how law manages diversity, and because diversity is the only broad rationale that the Supreme Court has not yet rejected. This rationale, I find, is too flimsy and poorly tailored to the relevant social facts to satisfy the current constitutional standard for affirmative action. But even if an ethno-racial preference were constitutional, it should not be adopted. Furthermore, most proposals for reform would be impractical, ineffective, or make matters even worse.

For sound *policy* reasons, then, I would bar government from sponsoring affirmative action, as distinguished from nondiscrimination, a crucial distinction discussed in the next section. A possible exception[6] to this bar is a carefully tailored, time-limited remedy for the continuing effects of past bias in the kinds of situations where the Supreme Court has long permitted it.[7]

In contrast, the law should allow private institutions that are associational in nature—organized primarily for purposes of fellowship or the expression or promotion of group values rather than profit—to use affirmative action for diversity, exclusivity, or other associational purposes so long as the association meets the larger community's most fundamental normative commitments, including nondiscrimination against racial minorities. Specifically, the law should permit private affirmative action by associational groups if they publicly disclose the nature and magnitude of their preferences and do not discriminate against minorities entitled to the highest level of protection under the equal protection principle. The category of private associational groups permitted to engage in this limited form of discrimination (for that is what it is) would include religious organizations, universities, clubs, and a melange of nonprofit entities, but would not include commercial employers.

No sensible person who carefully considers the evidence and arguments I marshal here can be wholly satisfied with either the status quo or the position I espouse. The cruel legacy of 250 years of slavery in America has proved more stubborn than even Frederick Douglass, a former slave and consummate realist, imagined. Affirmative action, for all its problems, promises to do something to repair this incalculable damage. This explains why thoughtful individuals like Orlando Patterson, Sanford Levinson, David Hollinger, Nathan Glazer, Derek Bok, and many others continue to support it even though, as I shall show, the empirical and normative premises of their own arguments have become harder and harder to sustain. Reasonable people can and obviously do differ about these premises and about the trade-offs that any new policy would entail. My ambitions here are to dispel some of the misunderstandings that plague the debate, to clarify what is actually at stake, and to propose a better reconciliation of the conflicting social values.

DEFINITIONS, DESIGNS, AND DOMAINS

Definitions

By affirmative action, I mean a program in which people who control access to important social resources offer preferential access to those resources for particular groups that they think deserve special treatment.[8] In this context, then, I use the terms "affirmative action" and "preferences" interchangeably.[9] By affirmative action, I also refer to its typical programmatic forms—

more or less systematic, continuous, bureaucratized, rule- or routine-governed, and often outcome-determinative.[10]

I also focus on ethno-racial preferences, particularly on programs favoring blacks, rather than those that target income, age, gender, or disability. There are several reasons for my focus on blacks. First, as discussed below, blacks present the strongest case for preferences. If the case for preferring them is weak, as I maintain, then the case for other groups is even weaker. Second, although some of my analysis also applies to attributes other than race, some of it does not—or at least it involves different considerations that I cannot take up here.[11] Unless the context indicates otherwise, I use race to include blacks and the other groups ordinarily favored by affirmative action.

As the adjective "affirmative" suggests, I mean to distinguish affirmative action from a more passive practice, nondiscrimination, in which the normative principle is simply to refrain from treating people differently on the basis of their race or other protected characteristics.[12] The distinction between affirmative action and nondiscrimination is clear and important both in politics and in principle, though not always in practice.[13] In sharp contrast to affirmative action, nondiscrimination is no longer a controversial norm in American society except among bigots and some extreme libertarians.[14] The punctilio of public discourse severely condemns any hint of antiblack or antiminority attitudes. As Alan Wolfe observes, "No credible public figure— literally none—seeks to bind white Americans closer together by means of rhetoric that sets them against blacks."[15] The public associates nondiscrimination with the universally praised norm of equal opportunity, while it generally disparages preferences as a demand for equal outcomes or special treatment. Some strong egalitarians favor affirmative action precisely because they think that it will equalize results, but most affirmative action proponents make a more limited argument—that it is essential to achieve genuine equal opportunity.

Both proponents and opponents of affirmative action define nondiscrimination in ways they hope will exploit its greater legitimacy.[16] Proponents claim that affirmative action, by leveling the playing field, is simply another form of nondiscrimination. Opponents define nondiscrimination to include greater outreach to minority communities in hopes of going beyond "old boy" networks and enlarging the pool of minority applicants who will then have an equal opportunity to compete for the prize on the basis of merit. Outreach, in this view, includes more minorities, vindicates the nondiscrimination, equal opportunity, and merit principles, and leaves no one with a legitimate claim to the prize worse off—whereas preferences, quotas, and goals subject to sanctions violate all of these principles. This makes it easy, then, for affirmative action critics to support outreach.[17]

Not so fast. In fact, greater outreach is neither cost-free nor neutral. In order to reach out, one must expend additional resources, targeting them on some groups and not on others and, as with affirmative action, increasing the probability that members of the target group will win the prize. If we dismiss this problem as de minimis because only limited resources are involved, we should nonetheless recognize that we are now on a slippery slope that could move us toward preferences of a more robust sort.[18]

Evidentiary problems can also propel us from nondiscrimination toward preferences, especially when proof of intentional bias is required. Antidiscrimination enforcers need baselines or other indicia of bias to help them gauge its extent, the need for remedial measures, and the measures' effects. They naturally prefer numerical benchmarks—in employment, for example, a group's share of the working-age population in the relevant labor pool—as a basis for inferring whether the employer discriminated against the group. In antidiscrimination programs, and also in voluntary affirmative action programs, these benchmarks may take the form and rhetoric of mere "goals" toward which firms should strive but which do not necessarily trigger sanctions if they are not met. The "not necessarily" is the qualifier that can push the antidiscrimination program toward preferences. For legal and psychological reasons, soft, tentative goals tend to become harder, more rigid standards that raise a presumption of bias if not reached. The strength of the presumption, the kind of evidence that can rebut it, the effect of rebuttal on the burden of proof, and other technical issues are the province of an increasingly arcane antidiscrimination law. Goals that at their inception were merely aspirational become more binding and consequential. These goals may mark "safe harbors" where firms meeting them can expect protection. Or the goals may condemn firms that do not meet them, or at least shift the burden of proof to such firms.[19]

Although the government does not impose specific goals on private universities but exhorts them to set their own, admissions officers nonetheless feel external pressure and internal compunction to use preferences to meet the goals they set.[20] Under these various pressures, three related distinctions—between nondiscrimination and affirmative action, equality of opportunity and equality of result, and goals and preferences—blur at the edges. Some affirmative action advocates use this blurring to deny that the distinctions exist; others recognize the distinctions but define nondiscrimination, equal opportunity, and goals in ways that imply greater normative and programmatic scope for affirmative action.[21] In contrast, I view these distinctions as foundational (though again, blurry at the borders) and believe that the values they represent condemn affirmative action. Americans overwhelmingly agree, and they have organized a philosophy around these three distinctions.[22] Public convictions, of course, may still be false; our history is replete with collective delusions—norms favoring racism and subordination of women, for example. All I claim here is that these distinctions matter a great deal to almost all of us.

Another principle, merit, is central to the foundational character of these distinctions.[23] Although I discuss the merit principle at length below, I do not provide a categorical definition of it for one simple reason: decisionmakers who allocate a job, admission slot, or any other scarce resource on the basis of merit define it in their own ways. Merit's content is wholly and properly contextual; it derives meaning only from one's particular conditions and purposes.[24] We may criticize particular conceptions of merit in context; these critiques sometimes persuade the decisionmaker to change its conception, which is why some colleges decided to recruit women and why others are abandoning standardized tests.[25] Rather than dispute the prevailing definition of merit in a specific context, we may instead argue that a particular applicant satisfies it. To assess affirmative action, then, we must begin with the definition of merit on which it implicitly rests and proceed to analyze how well this definition serves the policy's purported rationales. This will be my approach.

Designs

Affirmative action programs are structured differently, depending on how they combine a number of distinct features. I note five of them here.

Favored groups. The usual favored groups, which David Hollinger calls the "ethno-racial pentagon,"[26] track the major census categories: blacks, Hispanics (although the census requires them to pick a race as well), Native Americans, Asian and Pacific Islanders, and women. Other groups (e.g., Arabs and others of Middle Eastern descent) have demanded inclusion,[27] and particular programs may include fewer or more groups. Some preferences cover the disabled and the economically disadvantaged; homosexuals, however, are seldom if ever covered even when nondiscrimination laws protect them.[28] Which groups should be covered and how they should be defined are highly controversial issues. Blacks and perhaps to a lesser extent Native Americans are always covered but consensus ends there. Immigrants are included, although even some proponents of preferences doubt that they should be, for reasons discussed below.

Kind of actions. The program may direct or permit decisionmakers to report data on the composition of their populations; engage in outreach and dissemination of information to the general public and members of the favored groups in particular; set goals and timetables; impose numerical quotas—or other things in between.

Mandatory, voluntary, or prohibited. Compliance with affirmative action may be voluntary, legally mandated, or legally prohibited. I use the term "voluntary" loosely here to mean an absence of legal sanctions for noncompliance, such as ineligibility for participation in public programs or subsidies. Programs mandated by legislation or regulation raise the most difficult legal and policy issues, of course,[29] but voluntary programs like those in private higher education raise some as well.

Kind and weight of preference. Preferences may affect individuals' eligibility for employment or housing, bids for contracts, college admission, or many other public and private advantages. Preferences may add weight to any beneficiary's claim or may instead function only as a tie-breaker when competing claimants are otherwise equally qualified.

Methodology, exemptions, and duration. Programs differ in how they measure membership in favored groups, rank claimants according to various eligibility or performance criteria, and so forth. Programs may exempt small businesses, permit religious institutions to employ only coreligionists, or include other special provisions. Most are open-ended, but some can be time-limited, becoming inapplicable once certain conditions are met (e.g., when a firm's minority employees reach a level equal to their share of the relevant population).

Domains

Federally mandated affirmative action was first established in the employment area, and the scope of affirmative action in both public and private employment vastly expanded thereafter, as detailed below. It now covers much of the nation's workforce in both public and private employment, protects not only the ethno-racial pentagon but religious and national origin affiliations and the disabled as well. It extends beyond recruitment and hiring decisions to include promotions, terminations, in-service training, and other workplace practices. The U.S. military establishment is the work setting where affirmative action has been particularly pervasive and arguably most successful.[30] In public and private contracting, federal, state, and local laws often impose set-asides, quotas, and other preferences for minority contractors and subcontractors.[31]

Affirmative action operates in all parts of the educational system; no other domain practices and supports it so enthusiastically.[32] Public education systems often mandate it to assign pupils to different schools and school districts and to structure their programs in order to achieve and then maintain some ideal of racial or ethnic balance in the face of enrollment changes that might "tip" this carefully engineered balance and precipitate white flight. These assignment policies have generated bitter political and legal conflicts in Boston, San Francisco, and many other cities.[33] Colleges and universities with selective admissions criteria—a minority of institutions, but exercising disproportionate social influence—use affirmative action to select students, balance residential units, award financial aid, employ administrators, recruit and promote faculty, run athletic programs, staff student organizations, award contracts, and conduct other aspects of their institutional lives. A few states bar affirmative action in college admissions, as we shall see, and others mandate it only for public institutions. Nevertheless, selective private institutions, including their alumni, are among its most committed advocates. Affirmative action even extends to shaping how university scientists conduct their research; a 1993 law requires the National Institutes of Health to ensure that women and minorities are involved in clinical studies as researchers and as subjects of research.[34]

Banks and other lenders are required to use affirmative action in their programs, including mortgages, construction and auto loans, and the like. Under the Community Reinvestment Act, financial institutions must, on pain of losing their public charters, assure that their facilities and investments are located in minority and low-income communities.[35] Public housing projects are subject to affirmative action requirements, and private developers receiving public credit, funds, or other public assistance must assure that members of favored groups enjoy equal access to their projects, sometimes including set-asides and quotas.[36] The law's effort to diversify housing racially and economically is the subject of Chapter 6.

Electoral districting is another affirmative action venue.[37] Federal courts have interpreted the Voting Rights Act of 1965 and its 1982 amendments to require the states to draw electoral lines for legislative districts and other decisionmaking bodies so as to maximize the number of "majority-minority" districts, those with a sufficient concentration of the favored minority group that one of its members is very likely to win.[38] Since 1993, however, Supreme Court decisions have cast doubt on the extent to which districting may take race into account.[39] The situation is complicated by the fact that the Court allows the line-drawers to use partisanship, which for blacks, who overwhelmingly vote Democratic, has been easy to predict. Growing evidence, however, suggests that at least 20% of whites vote for black candidates even in some Deep South states (which weakens any justification for packing so many blacks into majority-minority districts) and that packing them in this way has undercut blacks' interests.[40] In the redistricting cycle that began in 2001, the Court's mixed signals have sowed enormous uncertainty and confusion.[41]

The Federal Communications Commission (FCC) administers affirmative action programs governing the agency's award of television and radio broadcasting licenses. The agency extends its diversity requirements to programming content, the employment and investment practices of potential and existing licensees, and the financing of auction bids by potential licensees. Although the federal courts have sometimes invalidated FCC programs not authorized by Congress,[42] the agency, citing the need for more diversity in broadcasting, has pressed ahead with them anyway—with little success.[43] Indeed, on the very day that the FCC suffered a major defeat in court,[44] the U.S. Department of Commerce reported that the number of television stations owned by minorities had dipped to the lowest level in more than a decade, while minority ownership of radio stations had risen marginally in the preceding two years, with industry consolidation and deregulation making further minority ownership gains more difficult.[45] The FCC's programs, moreover, face rough sledding under the new agency leadership installed by President Bush.[46]

The magnitude of FCC preferences is huge. By awarding licenses for the spectrum it controls, it confers enormously valuable economic rights on a very small number of individuals and firms. In recent years, it has awarded much of the spectrum by auctioning off licenses to the highest qualified bidder, and it has created programs to subsidize minority groups so that they can compete in the auctions as "designated bidders." This status gives them bidding credits such that they need pay the government only a fraction of the winning bid and can pay in installments over a long period at favorable interest rates. Combining both of these advantages enables the designated bidder to pay the government only 50% of its winning bid. Given the economic value of the licenses, these advantages are worth scores of millions of dollars to those who can use them.[47]

Because the programming diversity rationale for preferences is so poorly supported by the evidence,[48] even some who defend affirmative action in general have excoriated the FCC's preferences in particular. For example, Michael Kinsley, editor of *Slate* magazine, an avowed liberal, and supporter of some affirmative action programs, views the FCC's as

> especially farcical. Members of favored groups who get valuable licenses, for nothing or at a discount, are more or less free to resell them, at market rates, to white males or anyone else. The policy amounts to the simple anointment of black millionaires. And, because black-millionaire businessmen are such an obvious exception to the generalization that "black equals disadvantaged," these policies help to discredit affirmative action even in situations where the generalization makes more sense.[49]

These abuses, moreover, extend beyond race-based affirmative action to FCC programs that give extremely valuable preferences to small minority-owned firms. Many large companies have helped to organize small companies with token minority leadership to front for them in bidding at auctions of wireless frequencies for which the large companies are legally disadvantaged or ineligible.[50]

Finally, the law requires many private groups that receive government grants or contracts to engage in affirmative action. Much litigation has challenged the implementation of these programs. Courts, for example, have ordered labor unions to undertake affirmative action, sometimes even appointing special masters to supervise compliance.[51] Private groups often press for affirmative action even when the law does not require it. The American Bar Association, for example, seeks to increase the minority representation among judicial law clerks, who are surely among the most privileged young people in America.[52]

THE IMPORTANCE OF CONTEXT

Should all of these domains (and others not mentioned here) be governed by the same principles, or should those principles instead differ depending on the particular domain at issue? This "metaquestion" relates closely to the question of merit, which I discuss below. In his well-known book *Spheres of Justice,* philosopher Michael Walzer persuasively argues that a liberal society should aspire to a "complex equality" in which different domains ("spheres" in his parlance) are governed by different principles of justice depending on the social meanings and competing values implicated in each domain and the different balances that may be struck among those values.[53] Few advocates, for example, would suggest that morality requires us to practice affirmative action in our own families, homes, or friendships. Parents looking for baby-sitters or people seeking professional services are seldom equal opportunity employers. On the other side, few opponents of affirmative action object on moral grounds to the traditional practice of ethnic ticket-balancing by political parties or to special efforts by urban police departments to recruit minority and female officers. People who take these views are not necessarily moral hypocrites or even logically inconsistent. They recognize that different principles are appropriate in different public and private domains by virtue of the distinct values that are morally relevant there.[54]

Certain preferences engender little public controversy—although some of them *should*. Veterans' preferences for civil service jobs, for example, have been in place for many decades and remain politically and legally secure despite the fact that they greatly disadvantage women who could not serve in the armed forces in significant numbers until very recently, but who wish to compete for those jobs.[55] Many colleges and universities give admission preferences to athletes, alumni children, and those from remote areas.[56] However one views the merits of these preferential practices (I am quite dubious about the first two), each is rationalized on the basis of particular contextual facts— veterans' sacrifices and interrupted careers, the capacity of college athletics and kinship to cement alumni loyalty,[57] and the supposed value of geographic diversity—that have some normative weight relevant to one's overall evaluation of the practices.

In assessing (and reassessing) affirmative action, then, context matters. In reality, its policy context is being transformed in ways that greatly weaken its empirical, conceptual, and normative underpinnings. First, new patterns of immigration, intermarriage, and identity are completing the process that science long ago began—rendering affirmative action's ethno-racial categories ever more incoherent. Second, recent studies show that the size of the preferences, at least in higher education admissions, are now very large. Third, only a tenuous connection exists between being in a favored category and being socially disadvantaged enough to need preferential treatment at the expense of others with their own justice-based claims. Fourth, mounting evidence suggests that many of the policy's supposed benefits are exaggerated, imaginary, or even socially harmful, while its social costs are substantial. This section discusses the first of these changes; I consider the others below.

Scientists have long discredited the notion of race that underlies affirmative action policy, and the latest DNA research provides further evidence, were any needed, of its artificiality and incoherence. Science aside, centuries of immigration and miscegenation, and the recent rise in intermarriage rates by all groups, render the conventional racial categories increasingly arbitrary today as bases for social policy.[58] Indeed, so many Americans now consider themselves multiracial and wish to be identified as such (if they must be racially identified at all)—seven million in the 2000 census, including nearly two million blacks (5% of the black population) and 37% of all Native Americans[59]— that advocacy groups desperate to retain the demographic status quo mounted a fierce political campaign to preempt a multiracial census category.[60]

Although these monoracial groups did not decisively win that battle—the census allowed people to indicate more than one race but did not include a "multiracial" category[61]—they seem to be winning the war. In a grimly ironic aspect of the new demographic dispensation, the government adopted something like the one-drop rule that helped enslave so many mulattos and self-identifying whites before Emancipation. (As Malcolm X quipped, "That must be mighty powerful blood.")[62] In March 2000, the Office of Management and Budget (OMB) issued rules providing that for civil rights enforcement purposes,[63] any response combining one minority race and the white race must be allocated to the minority race.[64] This, despite evidence that 25%

of those in the United States who describe themselves as both black and white consider themselves white. And minorities other than blacks are even more likely to be multiracial. Indeed, 48% of Hispanic respondents to the census self-identified as white; another 42% said "some other race." In a survey by highly trained census enumerators of Hispanic households that had failed to respond to the mail questionnaire, 63% considered themselves white and 29% said "some other race."[65] Almost half of Asian-white people and more than 80% of Indian-white people self-identified as white.[66] This is the racial equivalent of an enduring sociological reality: almost 95% of Americans, including many who are poor by standard "objective" measures, consider themselves solidly working- or middle-class.[67] Just as class warriors prefer to brush by this fact, administrators of affirmative action programs, who desperately need to race- and ethnic-code in order to meet their targets or quotas, choose to ignore the "whitening" and "multiracializing" of many of those whom we insist on treating as minorities.[68]

No allocation rule can be neutral, of course; OMB's rule effectively maximizes the size of minority groups and minimizes that of the white group. But where multiracial individuals chose their own racial identities, the government's allocation rules now decide this matter for them in order to preserve racial preferences. The new rules introduce other changes that will further complicate future race-coding by the government and hence by the many others who rely on these racial data for affirmative action and other purposes. By recognizing no fewer than 126 group combinations under the Census 2000 system, these rules encourage many other eager groups (Arab-Americans, for example) to demand their own specific listing in the census form. The government will now find it harder to resist these demands than when the ethno-racial pentagon was its exclusive taxonomy. The new system, then, is inherently unstable.[69]

The number of actual and self-designating multiracial individuals will surely grow rapidly in the future due both to intermarriage and to younger respondents' greater propensity to intermarry and to self-identify as multiracial. Sociologist Amitai Etzioni predicts that even if current trends do not accelerate, 14% of the population will identify as multiracial by 2050.[70] Forcing them into the increasingly arbitrary categories to which traditional racial classifiers tenaciously cling will spur them to seek even more fundamental changes in the ethno-racial pentagon, including a separate multiracial category or perhaps even eliminating racial categories altogether, as a proposed initiative in California hopes to do. The government's insistent pigeonholing, which clashes with the robust and, for Americans, compelling rhetoric and ideology of freedom of choice, will further erode the already weak public support for preferences.

Some analysts wishfully think that the multiracial phenomenon does not threaten the viability of the traditional civil rights programs that rely on racial data, both because the cohort of self-reporting multiracials is relatively small and because OMB's allocation rules further reduce their numerical significance.[71] Although this may well be true for the immediate future, advocates of the ethno-racial pentagon have only a temporary reprieve. New demographics and identities mean that as time goes on, the government's use of the standard racial categories as a pivot of social policy will become ever harder to justify logically and sustain politically.

The effort to control racial profiling by the police through the gathering of race-coded identity information, while aimed at discrimination and not affirmative action, reveals an important irony about the latter as well.[72] Just when the accuracy, coherence, and social value of racial information are rapidly declining, even as to blacks, but especially for other groups, the law is demanding more of it and using it more intrusively. State and city police departments must now collect data on the race, ethnicity, or national origin of all drivers or other individuals whom they stop. In order to do so, the officer must decide what the motorists' race, ethnicity, or national origin is and then record the data for the profiling monitor—without asking them, much less allowing them, to self-identify. To a lament by the president of the Los Angeles Board of Police Commissioners (himself multiracial) that "[w]ith all the racially mixed people in L.A., and Latinos coming in all shades, the data will be garbage in, garbage out," a Harvard law professor responds that "[w]e're not trying to get at truth, we're trying to get at bias."[73] But the legitimacy of the search for bias has everything to do with the kind of information that the naturally confused police will record and how accurate it is. Of the other techniques that may be used to obtain racial data, the *least* chilling is already in place: New Jersey taxpayers paid for all 2,700 state troopers to receive mandatory "instruction on how to classify a motorist's race by judging 'skin color' and 'facial characteristics.'"[74] In the name of racial justice, one supposes, every bad idea must be taken seriously and even subsidized, at least until the inevitable political backlash against this new policy erupts—perhaps in the form of a voter referendum that will ratchet up the political rhetoric, racial bitterness, and group alienation. In this way, we are told, America will somehow "get beyond racism"[75] and enhance racial equality.

THE SIZE OF AFFIRMATIVE ACTION PREFERENCES

When competing claims for scarce resources—jobs, admission to higher education, financial aid, public and private contracts, broadcast or other spectrum licenses, credit, housing, and the like—are weighed, how heavy a thumb does affirmative action actually place on the scales? This question is important for at least two reasons. First, the larger the preference, the greater is its tension with the merit principle—and this is so however one conceives of merit. Indeed, a preference may be large enough to flatly contradict certain conceptions of merit, in which case preference advocates must invoke other rationales such as diversity that either reject or redefine those conceptions. It is one thing to use a preference merely as a tie-breaker between two equally qualified candidates, another to use it to enable a relatively unqualified one to win. (The tie-breaking case is very rare, as candid advocates of preferences will concede.)[76] Some might oppose the preference in both of these situations, of course, but most will view the tie-breaker case more favorably just as most will support greater outreach and candidate pool-enlarging efforts more than they favor preferences.[77]

A second reason why the size of a preference matters is that the larger it is, the more obvious the competing interests and values that are being sacrificed. This can be a decisive factor in the highly politicized environment of affirmative action debates.[78] In fact, as we shall see, the preferences received by minority applicants in higher education are so large that their defenders have reached and passed a rhetorical tipping point. Rather than deny the preferences' size, they use this fact to argue that eliminating the preferences would resegregate the institutions.[79] I closely examine this important argument for preferences later in this chapter.[80]

Measuring the size of a preference is more difficult in some domains than in others. I have already discussed the quantification of minority bidders' discounts in some FCC spectrum auctions, and I shall later discuss the efforts to determine what efficiency losses, if any, affirmative action imposes in particular work settings. The most extensive studies, however, have focused on higher education admissions where schools have traditionally used standardized tests to measure students' aptitude, preparation, and achievement. In 1998, William Bowen and Derek Bok, the former presidents of Princeton and Harvard, published a book-length study based on the academic records of more than 80,000 students who entered twenty-eight highly selective institutions (large public universities, private universities, co-ed liberal arts colleges, and women's colleges) in 1951, 1976, and 1989, augmented by some other data.[81] Affirmative action, Bowen and Bok say, has little or no relevance outside of such institutions because the vast majority of undergraduate institutions accept all qualified candidates and thus have no need to prefer any group of applicants.[82] On the other hand, a recent study suggests that the practice may be much more widespread, including some second- and third-tier schools.[83]

A large literature reviewing the Bowen-Bok analysis now exists. There is little disagreement about the actual magnitude of the preferences enjoyed by black applicants (the authors did not break out other minorities): by any objective standard, the preference is very large—one might say *immense*—although its precise magnitude probably cannot be determined.[84] Bowen and Bok, who strongly support affirmative action, find a difference of almost 200 points in the average SAT total test scores of the black and white applicant groups in these schools. But the difference between the two applicant groups is even starker. First, the deficit for black applicants with respect to high school grade-point average (GPA), the other major admission criterion, is even larger than for SAT scores. Thomas Kane, a researcher in this field, finds that black applicants to selective schools "enjoy an advantage equivalent to an increase of two-thirds of a point in [GPA]—on a four-point scale—or [the equivalent of] 400 points on the SAT."[85] Second, at every SAT score level, the test, which has long been criticized as being culturally biased against blacks, in fact *over*-predicts their actual academic performance in college. The same is true of GPA scores.[86]

Another way to characterize the difference between the two groups is to compare their prospects for admission to the schools in the Bowen-Bok sample. Terrance Sandalow, a professor and former dean at the University of Michigan Law School, summarizes the Bowen-Bok data this way:

> Thus, a black applicant with a score between 1400 and 1449 had nearly a 75% chance of admission, while a white with a comparable score had approximately a 40% chance. In the 1250–1299 range, the odds that a black applicant would be admitted remained at the 75% level, while the odds for white applicants dropped below 25%. The comparable percentages for applicants with scores between 1100 and 1149 were approximately 15% for whites and just under 50% for blacks. Viewing the same data from a slightly different perspective, the odds were approximately even that black applicants with scores between 1100 and 1199 would be admitted. The odds for whites did not reach that level until they had scores in the 1450–1499 range.[87]

Sandalow does not mention a further finding—that with a score of 1500 or above, more than a third of whites were rejected while every single black gained admission.[88] The University of Michigan, whose affirmative action program is detailed in a pending lawsuit,[89] weighs race even more heavily than the average school in the Bowen-Bok sample. At Michigan, the admissions advantage of being black, Hispanic, or Native American is even larger than Kane's estimate; these applicants receive the equivalent of a full point of GPA, and the school permits minority status to override any SAT score deficit.[90] A recent study of forty-seven public institutions, moreover, found that the odds of a black student being admitted compared to a white student with the same SAT and GPA were 173 to 1 at Michigan, and 177 to 1 at North Carolina State.[91]

These preferences continue, broadly speaking, at the graduate and professional school levels. Bowen and Bok document the encouraging fact that an identical percentage (56%) of black and white graduates of the institutions in their sample earned graduate degrees, and the percentage of blacks earning professional or doctoral degrees was actually slightly higher than for whites (40% versus 37%). But because the black students' college grades and graduate- and professional-level admissions test scores are usually much lower, preferences strongly affect their admission to programs, especially at top-tier institutions. Because of financial aid and other factors that affect applications and admissions, we cannot know the exact size of their preferences at this level with certainty, but it is surely very large.[92]

The leading study of law school admissions in the early 1990s found that only a few dozen of the 420 blacks admitted to the eighteen most selective law schools would have been admitted to those schools absent affirmative action.[93] And although a high percentage of blacks who graduate from these law schools eventually pass the bar examination, only 61% of black law graduates pass it the first time (compared to 92% of whites) and 78% pass it on the second or subsequent attempt (compared to 97% for whites). In short, over 20% of the blacks who take it never pass, almost seven times higher than the never-pass rate for whites.[94]

It is true, of course, that institutions, especially selective ones, take other factors into account besides race, that some whites who are admitted have academic credentials that are no better or even worse than the blacks admitted under preferences,[95] and that if one compared the credentials of the blacks who were just barely admitted with those of the whites who were next in line for those slots, the credentials gap, while still significant, would be much smaller.[96] It is also true that minority graduates of the selective institutions whose alumni have been studied, like the University of Michigan Law School, achieve high professional status, income, civic participation and leadership, and career satisfaction.[97]

These studies, however, do not examine how these schools' preferences affect the institutions and students that are lower down the academic food chain. The less selective institutions must admit many minorities who will have academic difficulty, are likely to fail the bar examination (some of them repeatedly), and may be marginal professionally. Because there simply are not enough academically qualified minorities to go around, Richard Sander notes, "the success of affirmative action at Michigan comes at the cost of making integrated education more problematic at weaker law schools."[98] This also means that any school that opts out of the preferences competition—for any reason—ends up with few or no black students, which of course just reduces racial diversity at those schools.

These large disparities in high school and college academic records and professional entry rates are profoundly disturbing and tragic measures of the persisting social disadvantages of blacks in American society. They reveal the inferiority of their earlier schooling, their desperate need to be better matched with or better prepared for the academic programs in which they enroll, and the deceptiveness of preferences' ostensible inclusiveness. To many affirmative action supporters, these disparities, far from weakening the case for preferences, constitute the strongest argument in their *favor* by indicating how lily-white and Asian the student bodies at elite campuses would be without preferences.[99] This "resegregation" argument is certainly troubling—indeed, there is no wholly satisfying rebuttal to it—and, as noted earlier, I discuss it in a later section.

My purpose at this point is not to make an overall assessment of affirmative action, but only to establish that the preferences it confers tend to be very large and thus are extremely valuable to the recipients and disadvantageous to their competitors. I discuss the magnitude of this disadvantage below when I consider how preferences affect those who do not receive them.[100] To say, as Stanley Fish does, that a preference simply allows a decisionmaker to "take minority status into consideration" within a pool of "qualified applicants"[101] is to beg the key question: how far can one stretch the meaning of "qualified" and "consideration" before they lose their notional integrity?

RATIONALES AND COUNTERRATIONALES

Affirmative action's supporters have advanced many different rationales for preference programs in light of a changing mix of ideological, tactical, moral, political, and legal considerations over the course of more than three decades of public debate. Perhaps the most candid, powerful, and comprehensive defense of affirmative action is that by sociologist Orlando Patterson, who advances almost all of the rationales in one form or another.[102] These rationales overlap to some extent, and any given advocate is likely to invoke more than one of them. Still, it is useful to distinguish among them according to their different claims. Because their opponents often counter these claims, I can consider both sets of arguments together. Some of the arguments against affirmative action, however, do not line up quite so neatly; they are more usefully discussed below in my analysis of its consequences. Because the case for affirmative action is strongest for blacks,[103] though by no means limited to them, I shall discuss the rationales for race-based programs, unless otherwise indicated.

Restitution

Affirmative action is often justified as a means of compensating groups that have been victimized in the past by persecution and discrimination inflicted by the dominant majority. This rationale looks *backward* and is an argument for reparations. It is to be distinguished from another rationale, which I call "anticaste" and discuss below, that emphasizes the consequences *today and in the future* of past injustices. In this view, what connects past, present, and future is the bitter irony, if not arrant hypocrisy, of ruling out the use of race now when it is used to rectify egregious wrongs that were perpetrated in the past on that very basis. It is easy to understand why affirmative action advocates see opposition to this use of race as the cruelest kind of catch-22. Their morally grounded skepticism deserves a serious answer, but it cannot be a simple one. It will take me the rest of this chapter to provide it.

The restitution rationale applies with special force, of course, to blacks whose ancestors were brought to the United States in chains and suffered unspeakable degradation over many generations, including the era of Jim Crow that ended as recently as the 1950s and 1960s.[104] Although these monstrous wrongs can never be truly or precisely rectified, the argument runs, the simple but compelling imperative of compensatory or corrective justice requires society to do what it can to restore the victims' descendants to the positions they would have occupied had the wrongs not been committed. Although this remedy is not feasible as a practical matter, a program of affirmative action is. Distributive justice considerations, moreover, also justify such a restitution-oriented program both because blacks as a group are especially needy[105] and because government has often been an active agent or a passive participant in their subordination.[106]

Opponents of the restitution rationale counter with several arguments. First, the history of human communities is replete with great wrongs. Were we to take the project of restitution seriously, we could not stop with slavery but must also rectify the violence and destruction inflicted on Native Americans, their lands, and their cultures; the harsh subordination of the Chinese, Japanese, Irish, Jews, and many other immigrant groups; and the discrimination against women that severely limited their opportunities outside the home and their freedom within it.

Second, affirmative action programs cannot rectify past wrongs because their beneficiaries are not the victims in any straightforward sense; indeed, preferences can only commit new wrongs because the cost-bearers are innocent. Some program advocates insist that the notion of "innocent victim" that underlies such concerns is itself problematic and that today's whites are the unwitting, continuing beneficiaries of the crimes committed by white slaveholders and their segregationist successors.[107] Opponents respond that it would be impossible to conduct the kind of complex causal analysis necessary to support any fair calculation of historical advantages and disadvantages,[108] that attributing them to broad racial groups would be egregiously crude, and that so gross an assessment could not satisfy even the most minimal demands of a very rough justice.

Third, even if these objections could somehow be met, some opponents say, the restitution rationale could at most justify affirmative action for the descendants of American slaves and perhaps Native Americans. It could never justify extending protection to immigrants, linguistic minorities like Hispanics, or geographic origin groups like Asians and Pacific Islanders. Yet tens of millions of immigrants become automatically eligible for preferences the moment they set foot in the United States, competing for preferences with blacks whose families have been in America since antebellum times. For example, a University of Michigan faculty study found that almost 20% of black faculty and more than half of Asian-Pacific Islander faculty were immigrants.[109]

The U.S. Supreme Court has accepted a limited version of the restitution rationale, permitting or mandating affirmative action as a constitutional matter where it is shown that the actor has specifically engaged in identifiable past discrimination against a favored group, this discrimination continues to affect individual victims, and the preference is carefully tailored to remedy this particular wrong.[110] In the context of elite professional schools that draw from a national, indeed international, pool of candidates, the required nexus between discrimination and preference can become quite attenuated and farfetched.[111]

Merit

Most affirmative action advocates challenge the fundamental assumption of its opponents that merit selection—as conventionally understood and as implemented—is a valid and compelling principle of distributive justice with respect to certain kinds of social goods. This challenge takes at least three forms; some advocates use all of them.[112] First, they contend that accepted understandings of merit are arbitrary, unduly narrow, and unjustly disadvantage minorities. "Merit," Nicholas Lemann writes, "is various, not undimensional. Intelligence tests, and also education itself, can't be counted on to find every form of merit. They don't find wisdom, or originality, or humor, or toughness, or empathy, or common sense, or independence, or determination—let alone moral worth."[113] Stanley Fish adds that when disputes arise over merit, "the dispute is between different versions of merit and not between merit and something base and indefensible."[114]

Like Lemann and Fish, defenders of preferences particularly object to notions of merit that rely heavily or exclusively on certain kinds of mental and physical tests or that demand certain academic, experiential, and other traditional credentials. This argument for redefining merit may invoke efficiency as well as fairness values. The claim is that those who administer conventional merit standards ignore or reject many individuals who, were merit properly defined, would be found to possess it and thus would perform the task perfectly well.[115] By excluding them, more radical advocates say, the supposedly race-neutral merit standard in fact operates as a "white-people's affirmative action" program.[116]

Second, some argue that what we conventionally think of as merit is actually a composite of different ingredients, some of which have little or nothing to do with the kinds of virtues that society should reward with material or status advantage. Ronald Dworkin, for example, condemns the notion that what he calls "wealth-talents" (which would include scholastic aptitude or achievement) should be rewarded because they are praiseworthy attributes. "What counts as a wealth-talent," Dworkin writes, "is contingent in a hundred dimensions. . . . Luck is, anyway, by far the most important wealth-talent in this catalogue—being in the right place is often more important than being anything else at all."[117] Even apart from luck, he argues, it is hard to justify conferring such social advantages on those whom such contingencies happen to favor. In short, merit is not an appropriate principle of distributive justice for the social rewards that wealth-talent receives.

Third, advocates of racial preferences maintain that conventional merit standards are routinely violated by other preference practices that bear little or no relation to any defensible conception of merit and that exhibit few if any of affirmative action's virtues. I have already noted some examples in higher education—lower admissions standards for athletes, legacies, and geographic diversity—but exceptions to the merit principle also abound in other areas like employment, where governments and private firms often recruit, hire, and promote through veterans' preferences, old boy networks, nepotism, and favoritism.[118] And as journalist Michael Kinsley has noted (with barely disguised glee), the Republicans endorse even race-based affirmative action when it suits their purposes.[119]

Some defenders of preferences do not so much challenge traditional notions of merit as they argue pragmatically that the likely alternatives to preferences would be even worse. In Jeffrey Rosen's view, for example, state universities' programmatic responses to the ending of preferences coupled with continuing political pressures to keep minorities on flagship campuses threatens to "turn the leading state universities into remedial academies. . . . [A]ffirmative action represents a lesser compromise of meritocratic standards than the alternatives that are almost certain to follow its elimination."[120] I discuss alternatives in a later section.

A willingness to disregard or redefine the merit principle, then, knows no ideological and partisan boundaries. Does this bespeak a context-sensitive flexibility in the notion of merit, as Fish maintains, or is it just hypocrisy? The answer is—it depends. Universities, employers, and other decisionmakers are in the best position to define and measure merit in whatever terms they deem most relevant to their own institutions because they must bear most if not all of any efficiency losses and other costs arising from any errors in definition or measurement. Thus what outsiders may view as arbitrary and hypocritical exceptions to the merit principle presumably advance the institutions' broader interests. In this sense, these "exceptions" can be seen as part of a defensible, institution-specific conception of merit. A preference for legacies and athletes, for example, may maximize the alumni contributions and loyalty that in turn support the institution's academic mission. By the same token, a preference for racial minorities may reflect the institution's belief that their presence will somehow enrich campus life. If so, the merit principle remains inviolate, although its precise definition depends on the particular social context in which it is invoked and the mix of values that the institution seeks to promote.

This contextualized conception of merit is more than just window-dressing. A university president may well believe that admitting athletes, legacies, and minorities who do not meet the school's highest academic standards would nonetheless advance its overriding academic and social missions. Indeed, many university presidents do take this view. For myself, I could not reach this conclusion without strong evidence that admitting them was both necessary and sufficient to advance those missions without eroding those standards. My sense—based partly on the academic and fiscal success of elite schools that abandoned single-sex admissions over initial alumni opposition, and partly on the scandalously low academic standards for athletes on many campuses[121]—is that such evidence does not exist and that most of the special treatment for athletes and legacies bears no relation to a defensible conception of merit. Evidence of the contribution of minorities to campus life does exist, however, and I discuss it below.

In defining the academic mission, I personally place a very, very high weight on intellectual achievement. I say "very, very high," not exclusive; I might also give points to applicants who play in the school orchestra, come from rural backgrounds or foreign countries, or exhibit unusual leadership abilities. Doubtless others, mindful of their own institutions' distinctive goals and traditions, would strike these balances somewhat differently, and variations of this kind are to be encouraged. An institution's choice should only be considered hypocritical (as opposed to arguably misguided) when it violates the institution's proclaimed values or when the institution does not demand hard evidence to justify departures from those values, as may well be the case with some universities' athletic programs. The important point is not merely that, as Lemann and Fish rightly argue, different institutions (and the people within them) can plausibly define merit in different ways, but also that the integrity of those definitions depends partly on the underlying facts. In a later section of this chapter, I combine this point and my defense of diverse institutional identities to justify allowing private entities, but not public ones, to adopt ethno-racial preferences under certain defined conditions and in certain contexts.

Defenders of traditional merit make several dignity-based and consequentialist arguments against preferences. One of them counters Dworkin's contingency argument, contending that it assigns insufficient importance to the role that individual efforts play in academic and other success. Such efforts should be rewarded both on efficiency and fairness grounds; those rewards send socially desirable signals to others in the community. If society deems the rewards excessive, it can best reduce them by taxing the excess, not by disparaging a principle that helps motivate socially valuable activity. Once this merit principle is abandoned or discredited, it cannot readily be restored or replaced. No alternative principle, in this view, is as socially functional or morally attractive as merit.

Another argument against preferences holds that departures from traditional merit tend to demean and stigmatize the program's beneficiaries—including those who would have qualified under the traditional merit standard.[122] Since preferences' categorical nature prevents others from telling which members of the favored group were hired or admitted on the basis of merit and which on the basis of the preference, observers assume the worst. (This assumption, of course, might itself be considered discriminatory but it may instead reflect a nondiscriminatory aversion to risk.) In a reverse twist on the economic theory explaining why "lemons" are hard to detect in the market,[123] a preference tends to reduce the returns to true merit. A similar argument of this kind notes that many who take advantage of preferences will perform poorly or fail, further stigmatizing the group and demoralizing the individuals.[124] Stanley Fish's riposte to the stigma argument is worth quoting:

> Some beneficiaries of affirmative action will question their achievements; others will be quite secure in them; and many more will manage to have low self-esteem no matter what their history. Affirmative action is a weak predictor of low self-esteem, and even if there were a strong correlation,

you might prefer the low self-esteem that comes along with wondering if your success is really earned to the low self-esteem that comes from never having been in a position to succeed in the first place. At any rate, low self-esteem is at least in part the product of speculation about it.[125]

I consider these and some other consequentialist arguments in more detail below.

Anticaste

Most advocates of affirmative action seek to justify it as a powerful tool for dismantling what they view as a racial caste system in which blacks continue to be subordinated not just by individual racist attitudes, but also and more importantly by intractable hierarchical and institutional structures that a more passive, slow-moving nondiscrimination principle cannot effectively dislodge.[126] In contrast to the backward-looking restitution rationale, the emphasis on eliminating tenacious caste structures is more forward-looking and remedial. However labeled, this rationale aims at promoting integration with the goal of genuine democratic participation on the basis of equality.[127]

Indeed, even today when defenders of affirmative action use diversity rhetoric in part to avoid legal pitfalls, the heart of the case for affirmative action is unquestionably its capacity to remedy the current effects of past discrimination. One advocate, the former chancellor of the University of California at Berkeley, likens a university without affirmative action to a form of educational apartheid "almost as pervasive and insidious as the strictest segregation in South Africa."[128] Others, less hyperbolic, believe that affirmative action on campus "may well be . . . the best long-term remedy for the private beliefs and behavior that perpetuate the effects of racial caste."[129]

Somewhat subtler is Orlando Patterson's argument for affirmative action, based on the small number of blacks in the workplace relative to whites. Since there are on average more than six white employees for every black one, Patterson contends, even nonracist employers will likely promote whites more often than blacks, especially if they think that whites will "fit in" better with a predominantly white workforce. When one adds to this "the fact that Euro-American workers have a hard time taking orders from Afro-American supervisors," affirmative action is the only way to break the statistically driven and sometimes vicious circle.[130]

Advocates who rely on the anticaste rationale contend that the intractability of these social structures—what Martin Duberman calls racism's "terrifying agility"[131]—demands special and energetic interventions to dismantle them. Perhaps conceding that affirmative action is problematic in certain respects, they nonetheless insist—in the spirit of Justice Harry Blackmun's claim that "[i]n order to get beyond racism, we must first take account of race"[132]—that the imperative of true integration and the prospect of genuine equality are overriding ends and that affirmative action is the only practical way to achieve them. For constitutional support, they point to Reconstruction-era legislation, contemporaneous with the Fourteenth Amendment's adoption, that seemed to establish racial preferences for the freedmen.[133]

The political leaders of minority groups have clearly viewed affirmative action as a rallying point, a basis for group solidarity, that can galvanize the ethnically defined organization of minorities into an effective political force.[134] This tactic succeeded in extending the scope of affirmative action from public sector to private sector, from hiring to promotion, from college admissions to graduate and professional school admissions, and in other dimensions,[135] while institutionalizing it more firmly than its supporters could possibly have predicted at its inauspicious inception.[136] Indeed, some use these anticaste arguments to justify giving preferences even to middle-class blacks.[137]

Opponents counter with several arguments. None of these counterarguments denies America's dark history of racial caste. All of them, however, emphasize changes that cast doubt on the merits of affirmative action today. Some, for example, point to the stunning political, economic, and social advances by blacks both individually and as a group, concluding that special preferences are no longer warranted (if they ever were), especially in light of their social costs.[138] Some cite the historical experience of immigrant groups that also suffered harsh racial and other discrimination but still managed to advance without the benefit of these kinds of affirmative action programs.[139] Others argue that any caste effects today are based more on class or cultural practices than on race,[140] or more on spiritual than economic deprivation.[141] Still others, like Cass Sunstein, who strongly supports the struggle against caste, concede that racial preferences often fail and prefer "race-neutral alternatives."[142]

Affirmative action advocates do not concede these points. They note, correctly, that many substantive inequalities remain[143] and contend that affirmative action's social costs are minimal. Immigrants, they say, came to America voluntarily and optimistically, not in chains and in trauma, and they insist that slavery's acids continue to corrode the foundations of the black family and of black culture even six or seven generations after Emancipation.[144]

Leadership Cadre

A variant of the anticaste rationale is the claim that affirmative action is effective in producing a cadre of black professionals who can form a nucleus of group leaders and serve as role models for other members of the group, especially the young who need to have high aspirations and confidence that others have succeeded despite their common legacy of group disadvantage. This rationale, which has its skeptics,[145] applies most strongly to the domain of higher education, which of course is an important training ground for leaders. Studies on how well such programs perform this function have been chewed over by proponents and opponents of affirmative action alike.

There is something to the role-model argument. Group members who have succeeded are surely a source of encouragement to young people thinking about their futures. If this is true, however, it is true not just for the groups preferred by affirmative action but for all low-status groups. This argument, moreover, cannot be separated from questions about the other social signals youngsters receive from role-modeling. A role model might signal: "If you study and work hard and keep your nose clean as I did, you too can succeed." But in a society where preferences are both pervasive and normative, another signal might be: "You get points for having a certain skin color or surname, so you should emphasize that identity and learn to play the ethno-racial card." How do youngsters in such a society in fact read role-model signals and how do they integrate conflicting ones? These are important questions to which we do not know, and have not really sought, the answers.

Role-modeling aside, affirmative action proponents point to the Bowen-Bok data on the career achievements of blacks admitted to the selective schools in their sample during the affirmative action era, graduates whom Bowen and Bok characterize as "the backbone of the emergent black . . . middle class."[146] Their data clearly establish that the vast majority of the individuals who graduate from baccalaureate and postbaccalaureate programs to which they were admitted through affirmative action do enter the middle class, participate in community life, and presumably function as role models for young blacks.[147] A further argument in this vein is that the presence of minority group members in visible roles of leadership and influence is conducive, if not essential, to the legitimacy of America's social and political institutions. For minorities to accept their outcomes as minimally just or at least acceptable, they must view these institutions as inclusive and procedurally fair. Being governed by minority legislators, taught by minority teachers, and tried by minority judges, for example, may advance that goal. Minorities must perceive that they are not merely invisible servants of the regime but are, along with their fellow citizens, its masters as well. A related, though slightly different, argument, which is particularly applicable to affirmative action in public universities and other public programs, is that minorities pay taxes for these mobility-enhancing public services, entitling them to fair representation in those programs.[148]

This, then, is the core of the leadership cadre rationale for affirmative action. There are at least three reasons, however, to doubt how much of this mobility and participation is due to affirmative action. First, the propensity to participate and lead in the civic sphere reflects factors that are usually evident in high school and that therefore presumably increase the chances that individuals will be admitted to the selective institutions in the first place, with or without the boost of affirmative action—although without it, many fewer would be admitted.[149] Second, the vast majority of the black students admitted to these institutions (86%) are *already* from middle- and upper-class families (although they are still poorer and more needful of financial aid than their white peers),[150] a background that correlates with both participation and leadership. Third, absent affirmative action, these students would presumably have attended other institutions that graduate many more blacks than the ones in the Bowen-Bok sample do, blacks who succeed both professionally and civically.[151] Indeed, a striking fact is that historically black colleges, which account for only a sixth of total black college enrollment, produced 43% of the 1995 Congressional Black Caucus, 39% of black officers in the U.S. Army, and a quarter of black MacArthur "genius" grantees in the last two decades.[152] Although these successful graduates were educated some time ago, their alma maters are now more intensively recruiting and often enrolling the most outstanding black students, many of whom could gain admission to predominantly white institutions through affirmative action programs —or, in some cases, without them.[153] The nonflagship campuses of public university systems, where most of the direct affirmative action beneficiaries would end up absent affirmative action, also produce successful graduates.[154] In short, the vast majority of those admitted to select institutions may well have succeeded, participated, and been leaders *anyway* even without the preferences. Still, there is no denying that some of them, perhaps because of reduced financial aid opportunities at less select institutions, would have succeeded less.

Market Failure

Some analysts of an economistic bent emphasize that affirmative action can be justified as a response to a defect in the markets for labor, college admissions, credit, and other goods. Their argument is that a decisionmaker who rationally relies on group stereotypes—because the savings in search and other information costs in doing so exceed the costs of missing some qualified members of the stereotyped group (false negatives, as it were)—is not internalizing the full social costs of her discrimination. Those costs include the demoralization of excluded, but qualified, group members, underinvestment by stereotyped group members in education and other qualifications that would disproportionately benefit them and society, and so forth. Affirmative action, in this view, is a way of obliging decisionmakers to bear the full costs of these externalities and thus to make economically efficient choices.[155] But even if some externality adjustment were desirable, the one effected by affirmative action is, as we shall see, far too crude, costly, and inefficient in its own right to rectify the problem.

Institutional Pragmatism

Some have defended affirmative action as a necessary, prudent resolution of the competing values to which certain institutions are committed. Focusing on elite universities, for example, law professor Samuel Issacharoff, echoing Nathan Glazer, argues that

> affirmative action represents a point of compromise in the contradictory missions of the elite universities. They serve as both the guardians of a meritocratic vision of achievement and as the guarantors of opportunity so that the elites of the society may be replenished from the diverse groups that have built this country. Affirmative action grows out of the frustration with the apparent intractability of this country's inability to achieve these twin objectives with regard to black Americans. It is a pragmatic and oftentimes messy accommodation of two of the central values of higher education.[156]

Issacharoff's plea for granting institutions some discretion in deciding how to balance competing considerations that are peculiar to them is convincing, and I endorse this approach below for private institutions.[157] And his description of the moral and political impulses motivating many proponents of affirmative action is surely correct. But as we shall see, most Americans and even most racial minorities oppose affirmative action as a matter of principle. Moreover, Issacharoff's pragmatic judgment rests on certain premises: that affirmative action is necessary to create black mobility, that the preferences are "modest," that they only "operate on the margin of established selection criteria," that they have "an end-point that will prevent affirmative action programs from becoming institutionalized as a racial spoils system," and that they do not have other negative consequences that might affect the prudential balance.[158] My analysis casts serious doubt on all of these premises.

The Diversity Rationale

The institutional pragmatist will often seize on diversity as a more satisfying, more substantive rationale for affirmative action. Its appeal is readily apparent. Even more obvious, however, are its flaws—so obvious, in fact, that many of affirmative action's more forthright defenders readily concede that diversity is merely the current rationale of convenience for a policy that they prefer to justify on other grounds.[159]

Until the late 1990s, when federal courts began striking down affirmative action programs in public institutions of higher education as unconstitutional reverse discrimination, advocates had focused their arguments more on the restitution, anticaste, merit, leadership cadre, market failure, and institutional pragmatism rationales for such programs than on diversity. These other rationales were more attractive to the advocates because they seemed morally compelling, remedial, and based on the demands of justice. Diversity, in contrast, was essentially a functional rationale whose force depended on a number of plausible but controvertible empirical propositions. Equally problematic, this functional account of diversity was geared less to how affirmative action benefited the victims of past discrimination than to how it benefited other institutions or people (e.g., students and faculty), including many who may have either participated in that discrimination or been advantaged by it.[160] Functional arguments for diversity suffer not only from this distasteful aspect, but also from the distinct possibility, which I develop below, that these arguments fail according to their own functional criteria. Arguments supporting preferences because of diversity's supposed effects may turn out to discredit them if and when those effects do not materialize.[161]

In fact, the diversity rationale is being used as a rhetorical Hail Mary pass, an argument made in desperation now that all other arguments for preferences have failed. Although this rationale had been advanced earlier, proponents turned to it in earnest beginning in 1989 when a series of adverse court rulings cast serious constitutional doubt on other legal arguments for preferences. By 1998, voters in California and Washington State had adopted laws barring affirmative action in state programs.[162] Casting about for a safe harbor, defenders of preferences seized upon the diversity justification offered by Justice Powell in 1978 in his plurality opinion for the Supreme Court in the *Bakke* case.[163] There he stated that "a diverse student body . . . clearly is a constitutionally permissible goal for an institution of higher education" and observed that "[t]he atmosphere of 'speculation, experiment and creation'— so essential to the quality of higher education—is widely believed to be promoted by a diverse student body."[164]

Today, Michael Selmi explains, "diversity has quite clearly become the most heralded of all justifications for affirmative action."[165] In large part, this is because

> relying on diversity rather than discrimination places affirmative action programs on more solid legal and perhaps political grounds. It is the rare case in which a university will have engaged in systematic discrimination

against a particular group recently enough and in other particulars that a court may accept as sufficient to justify a race-conscious measure. It is rarer still that a university defending a plan will be willing to assert its own past discrimination as justification for affirmative measures.[166]

The diversity rationale, in contrast, entails a fresher, more "future-oriented vision."[167] As law professor Eugene Volokh says, "it ascribes no guilt, calls for no arguments about compensation. It seems to ask simply for rational, unbigoted judgment."[168] Judge Alex Kozinski adds that "everyone likes diversity, so long as it falls within a fairly narrow ideological range."[169] And depending on how diversity is defined, preferences for middle-class minorities might fall within the rationale, possibly facilitating public acceptance of the policy.[170]

The diversity rationale attracts supporters, especially in higher education, for another reason. Whether or not professors agree with Kenneth Karst that the conventional affirmative action categories are good proxies for the kinds of diversity that enrich teaching, learning, and social interactions in and outside the classroom,[171] and whether or not they are persuaded by the non-diversity arguments for affirmative action, most of them are profoundly uncomfortable at the thought of teaching a class or being on a faculty containing only whites and Asians. (Whether this also troubled professors in the days before preferences helped put racial minorities in their classrooms is less clear.) As we shall see below, resegregation of the more elite private and public institutions, absent preferences or other policies, is a genuine concern.[172] I am a teacher at such an institution and experience the same anticipatory discomfort.

What is the source of this discomfort? Here, I enter the realm of speculation (or more precisely, introspection), although survey evidence does shed some light. College and university professors tend to be ideologically and politically far more liberal, Democratic, statist, and secular than other Americans, and this bias is even more pronounced at the more elite institutions. For example, in a recent study of party registrations, only 3% of faculty registrations at Cornell (my alma mater) were as Republicans or Libertarians; at the University of California at Santa Barbara, the figure was only 1%. Professors tend to be knowledgeable about and sensitive to the historical injustices inflicted on blacks by slavery, Jim Crow, and the legacy of racism in America, and to support affirmative action and other remedial and egalitarian policies. Many of us came of age in the 1960s and believe profoundly in integration and civil rights.[173]

It is not cynical, I think, to add that tenured professors have little or nothing to fear personally from affirmative action for students or faculty. Indeed, it benefits them by eliminating the discomfort they would feel in classes and faculty meetings without non-Asian minorities, and they bear few of the program's costs.[174] Many genuinely believe that the benefits of ethno-racial diversity justify preferential admissions. Their reactions are perfectly predictable and understandable, and I share some of them.

What independent weight should these professorial feelings carry in the affirmative action debate? Not much, in my view. For the diversity rationale to justify affirmative action in higher education, it must do so because of the genuine *diversity* benefits that flow to students and faculty, especially those in the favored groups. The diversity rationale means that the benefits relevant to a diversity assessment must be the educational and social advantages that interactions among diverse students and faculty supposedly produce. The benefits from allaying the anxieties of white faculty members who are already highly privileged in so many respects should not count heavily (or perhaps at all) because such benefits bear only the most tenuous relation to the values that underlie the diversity rationale, properly understood.

What, then, are the benefits—from a diversity perspective—that *should* count in favor of preferences in higher education admissions? To answer this question, we must first address three other closely related ones. What does diversity mean in this context? What is it about a group that accounts for its diversity value?[175] (Groups, after all, are what diversity-based affirmative action programs are all about.) And what diversity value do the groups favored by affirmative action actually create?

Diversity's meaning. Diversity, like equality, is an idea that is at once complex and empty until it is given descriptive and normative content and context.[176] Unfortunately, most discussions of diversity and the diversity rationale for affirmative action do not explain what diversity actually means, much less which groups with what kinds of attributes create diversity value.[177] Nevertheless, the ways that affirmative action programs are designed and defended leave little doubt that program advocates almost always mean *ethno-racial* diversity, with little regard to the many anomalies, evasions, and confusions that attend most ethno-racial discourse in America.[178]

This preoccupation with race by proponents of the diversity rationale is also anomalous because other attributes are also predictive of one's experiences, outlooks, and ideas. According to an unpublished study by lawyer-sociologist James Lindgren of the demographic correlates of viewpoint differences, political affiliation accounts for the largest cleavages, with religion and race producing cleavages of similar magnitude.[179] The failure of diversity-based affirmative action programs to base preferences on religion is among the most revealing facts about them.[180] (Alas, this immense failing extends as well to most of the other debates over multiculturalism.)[181] The programs' lack of interest in our rapidly growing religious diversity[182] casts some doubt on the bona fides, or at least the coherence, of the diversity rationale as now implemented,[183] and may reflect the unusual religious composition of university faculties.[184] A priori (which is how programs select the groups to be preferred), doesn't the perspective of a Muslim or fundamentalist Christian applicant have at least as much diversity value as that of a middle-class black or Hispanic?[185]

Sanford Levinson, an affirmative action supporter, puts this point another way: "One sometimes gets the feeling that ostensible defenders of 'diversity' and 'multiculturalism' have no real idea of how truly diverse and multicultural the United States has become, fixated as they are on the 'traditional' racial and ethnic cleavages within this country." Levinson's use of scare quotes around "traditional" reminds us how much more complex and numerous America's social cleavages are than those presupposed by diversity-based affirmative action programs.[186] This complexity also underlies David Hollinger's critique of the official ethno-racial pentagon.[187] And if we want to stick with simple but perspective-relevant cleavages, why not diversify the student body through preferences according to political party affiliation?

Diversity value in general. Just how many blacks or members of other favored groups must be present in order to establish the requisite diversity? Because the value of diversity surely depends on various factors, any sensible answer must be context-specific.[188] Unfortunately, law and practice offer a wholly reductionist answer to the question. They simply count the number of group members in the relevant community (or their percentage of the community total) and demand proportional representation, at least as a default but often, in effect, as the final answer.[189] Defining the relevant community— that which will be used in making the proportionality assessment on which the legal obligation will directly turn—almost always entails highly controversial judgments, if not arbitrary empirical and normative ones. The relevant baseline for judging proportionality, for example, can only be defined in terms of a number of elusive, hard-to-measure, and internally competing parameters, including group definition, geography, qualifications, attitudes, applicant pool, and others. Rhetoric aside, the task of actually administering affirmative action requires, ironically, that a program first combine many complex determinations that as a practical matter it can only make through almost comically arbitrary judgments,[190] and then come up with a bottom-line number that is certain to be breathtaking in its simplicity and abstraction from context.

This, emphatically, is *not* what Justice Powell had in mind in his *Bakke* opinion, although in other respects it is not altogether clear what he *did* have in mind[191] or how binding his opinion is as precedent.[192] In *Bakke,* he insisted that simple numerical quotas could not be used to achieve diversity; institutions must instead look at the individual as a whole and her potential to contribute effectively to educational diversity.[193] Institutions that invoke diversity, Powell added, must also pursue nonracial diversity.[194] Both factors led him to condemn the University of California at Davis system that precluded whites from competing for the set-aside slots and to praise Harvard's system because there race was only a tie-breaking factor.[195] More recently, the Supreme Court held, as Powell had argued in *Bakke*,[196] that all race-based preferences are subject to strict scrutiny, the most demanding constitutional test.[197]

The diversity that Powell seemed to have in mind was not the pure ethnoracial diversity that affirmative action programs now prize.[198] The fact that affirmative action programs have bureaucratized diversity does not mean that it is a hollow ideal unworthy of society's aspiration. It does mean, however, that these programs may in fact be pursuing a spurious or formalistic kind of diversity. Indeed, for institutions that must process thousands of applications for relatively few slots in a very limited period of time, it could hardly be otherwise.[199] As a practical matter, then, diversity admissions may mean color-coding and color-counting in service of a predetermined color-targeting.[200]

How, then, does a favored group in fact confer diversity value on a community? A group can only create diversity value if it possesses certain desired qualities *qua* group. It seems to follow that a group can only do this if those qualities inhere in all members of the group (else the group should be redefined to exclude those who lack them).[201] To affirm that a quality inheres in a racial group, however, is to "essentialize" race in a way that utterly contradicts liberal, egalitarian, legal, scientific, and religious values (at least in the "Abrahamic"—i.e., Jewish, Christian, and Muslim—traditions). Together, these values hold that all individuals are unique and formally equal regardless of genetic heritage, and that their race causally determines little or nothing about their character, intelligence, experience, or anything else that is relevant to their diversity value. Indeed, for employers to use racial stereotypes in this way would be flatly illegal—even if the assumptions underlying the stereotypes were true. (As Eugene Volokh says, "It's hard enough to persuade people to give up their irrational prejudices; it's harder still to persuade them to give up their rational ones.")[202] The best that can be said of advocates' using diversity in this way is that they have "reproduced the most gross and invidious of popular images of what makes human beings different from one another" for a putatively benign purpose.[203] They are propagating a socially inflammatory stereotype that, even when fairly accurate, invites decision-makers to violate people's claims to be judged as individuals, not as members of ascribed groups. On a parity of reasoning, legitimating the use of this proxy might equally justify racial profiling by police if it were intended to fight crime and were sufficiently accurate.[204]

Diversity value in particular. This, then, brings us to the third of the questions I posed at the outset of this discussion: what diversity value does a favored group actually confer? Affirmative action programs attempt to finesse the essentialism difficulty by assuming certain facts that might make the use of race as a proxy more defensible. They assume, first, that black students bring to campus histories and viewpoints that are unique to and nearly universal among black students, even though those histories and viewpoints are not racially or genetically hardwired into them. They then assume that all of these students have the common experience of growing up black in America and the special perspectives that go with that experience—what Yale Law School dean Anthony Kronman calls value diversity.[205] Educational institutions and their black members, they further assume, should help nonblacks to comprehend this experience, and campus diversity can strengthen the foundations of good citizenship in a pluralist democracy.[206] Finally, they assume that race can serve under these circumstances as a rough but serviceable proxy for both diversity value and value diversity. Although Sanford Levinson doubts that anyone "is so stupid as to believe that all (or even most) members of any given group necessarily have similar opinions on a variety of important issues,"[207] most defenses of preferences based on viewpoint diversity seem to reflect precisely this belief. Levinson makes a more limited claim—that the presence of blacks and other groups on campus fosters some educational values in certain contexts while having less effect in others.[208]

The Bowen-Bok study strongly defends these assumptions. Using broad-question surveys conducted in 1995–1997, it asked three age cohorts of former students how they assessed their experiences on racially diverse campuses. Large majorities—especially among blacks and in the more recent cohorts—thought that it was important or very important in life "to work effectively and get along well with people from different races and cultures," and that their college educations helped to cultivate this ability to a significant degree. Bowen and Bok also find that the more blacks in an entering class, the more likely that white students in that class would know two or more blacks well; that 56% of all the white students responded that they knew two or more blacks well; and that the percentage who did so increased with the school's selectivity. These interactions occurred, moreover, even though black students represented fewer than 10% of the students in the schools studied.[209] Relying on a "contact theory" holding that increased contact among racial groups should decrease prejudice, a theory with uncertain empirical support,[210] Bowen and Bok develop a model to predict how the amount of contact would change if admissions were instead race-neutral. Finding that the 56% figure would fall by several percentage points, they conclude that "the drop in interactions would certainly be substantial."[211] These findings support the notion that affirmative action cultivates interracial socialization skills that both white and black students value and that they enhance by attending racially diverse institutions.[212]

This conclusion, which is also supported by a study done to bolster the University of Michigan's defense in the courts of its preferential admissions systems,[213] has been challenged from at least six directions. The first is empirical; a recent review of existing survey data shows that most students and faculty place little weight on ethnic diversity as a cause of positive educational outcomes, and its regression analysis of peer-group racial composition effects finds no positive effect on any of the eighty-two outcome variables used by the American Council on Education.[214]

The second challenge is comparative. Stephan and Abigail Thernstrom, prominent critics of the Bowen-Bok study and authors of an earlier analysis of American race relations that strongly opposed affirmative action,[215] point to a 1997 national survey in which 86% of white adults reported having black friends, and to a 1994 survey in which 73% said they had "good friends" who were black.[216] To the Thernstroms, the Bowen-Bok findings justify a different inference: "By these standards, the elite schools are hardly in the proud vanguard of progress. To the contrary, they are lagging woefully behind."[217] Interestingly, the Bowen-Bok and Thernstrom data on college-age and adult friendships both overlook the increasing interracial friendships among youngsters even *before* they reach college,[218] which would suggest that the college experience may be less central to such friendships than *either* camp supposes.

A third challenge examines how the education process actually works on campuses. Terrance Sandalow maintains that any experiential differences between white and black students "are simply irrelevant to most of what students study in the course of their undergraduate careers. The irrelevance of those differences is perhaps most obvious in the study of mathematics and the natural sciences, but it is no less true of most of the humanities and the social sciences."[219] Sandalow goes on to consider the argument, crucial to the diversity rationale, that blacks are likely to advance different ideas unfamiliar to whites. His reply accords precisely with my own experience:

> [E]ven though the subjects I teach deal extensively with racial issues, I cannot recall an instance in which, for example, ideas were expressed by a black student that have not also been expressed by white students. Black students do, at times, call attention to the racial implications of issues that are not facially concerned with race, but white and Asian-American students are in my experience no less likely to do so.[220]

To some scholars, however, Sandalow's empirical observation is beside the point because only racial preferences can secure minority students their "free exercise of race."[221] Mary Anne Case, invoking an analogy to religious freedom, even suggests that barring racial preferences "may work a denial of equal protection to some [students] for whom race is a particularly salient characteristic."[222] But although race is surely quite salient for some students, the admissions office almost never asks about their ideas or points of view, much less how salient race is to them, so this rationale seems even weaker.[223] Outside the classroom, of course, race-based experiential differences might encourage empathy and openness to diversity of all kinds.[224] On the other hand, those differences might promote greater conflict.[225]

The diversity rationale, as deployed by some of its advocates, masks a deeper confusion about the diversity value arising out of social interactions. In this view, which Justice Stevens has avowed, diversity demonstrates to people that despite our superficial differences, we are really all alike under the skin.[226] This proposition is clearly true in many respects—recall, for example, the DNA evidence on the similarity of our genetic endowments—but the diversity value that the diversity rationale invokes is supposed to grow out of decidedly different viewpoints that diverse people are said to bring to these interactions. If we take the rationale seriously, then similarity under the skin may confer negative, not positive, diversity value. The very logic of this rationale dictates that we should seek *differences* under the skin, since those differences constitute the payoff to diversity. At the very least, those who espouse pieties like that of Justice Stevens should be clearer about what they mean.

Two other challenges contend that the schools with diverse student bodies are not fully realizing the pedagogical possibilities this diversity creates,[227] and that students admitted on diversity grounds may suffer special burdens from having to serve in a "representative" capacity[228]—although Bowen and Bok find that low-scoring students admitted to elite schools later express great satisfaction with their college experiences.[229] Finally, the dismaying evidence of persistent racial self-isolation on campuses, including those with affirmative action, also raises questions about the interracial socialization thesis. Orlando Patterson, who supports affirmative action, ruefully concedes that "no group of people now seems more committed to segregation than Afro-American students and young professionals."[230] Jack Citrin, an opponent, believes that the 250-point gap in SAT scores created "a caste system" at Berkeley:

> Intellectual Balkanization with large ethnic differences in majors and grades was the outcome of Berkeley's version of affirmative action. Underrepresented minorities did not often major in subjects such as philosophy, mathematics and chemistry, while they were heavily clustered in such areas as sociology and ethnic studies.
>
> Of the Berkeley freshmen admitted in fall 2000 [without affirmative

action], by contrast, 14.9 percent were members of underrepresented minority groups, but the ethnic gap in test scores was slashed by more than one-third. The smaller number of minority students admitted are more competitive with their peers than previously, a necessary start to ending the academic caste system.[231]

After carefully interrogating the diversity rationale for racial preferences, then, one is left with serious doubts about its coherence and persuasiveness. There is something to it, surely, but not much. Recognizing this problem, some advocates seek to reconceptualize diversity as something else. In philosopher Elizabeth Anderson's view, for example, diversity is really "another way of talking about integration," a way that can link diversity to the advocates' "core social justice and democratic concerns."[232] In the same spirit, Robert Post sees diversity as the seedbed of "a democratic public culture."[233] But this discursive move is really an effort to change the subject; it defends racial preferences not as a way to enrich the experiences of students and teachers but as a remedy for social inequalities and generalized discrimination. That the Supreme Court has expressly and repeatedly prohibited this general remedial justification, of course, is not a conclusive argument against it; the Court, after all, is notoriously fallible.[234] My point, rather, is that the diversity rationale is weak even in its own terms.

THE POLITICS OF AFFIRMATIVE ACTION

The political dynamics of affirmative action policy have been much studied in recent years,[235] and I have reviewed these studies in detail elsewhere.[236] My analysis here consists of three parts: the political, bureaucratic, and legal history of affirmative action; public attitudes; and the reasons for affirmative action's political survival in the face of widespread public opposition. I summarize that analysis very briefly here, and urge interested readers to consult the full version.

Affirmative action was initiated as a voluntary program in 1961, giving no hint of the expansions in coverage, preferences, and legal controls that were to follow. Later, the Johnson administration created a bureaucratic apparatus in the Department of Labor to administer affirmative action requirements being imposed on federal contractors. The program began to assume its current form in the Nixon administration, which mandated preferences with several political objectives in mind. It hoped to avoid urban unrest and, by not including white ethnics and religious minorities, to drive a wedge between white and black Democratic voters. Congressional expansion of Equal Employment Opportunity Commission (EEOC) powers, and the ensuing enforcement, led to litigation during the late 1960s and 1970s challenging the constitutionality of affirmative action in a variety of employment settings.

A series of Supreme Court rulings left its legal status murky, and the Reagan administration attacked affirmative action on a number of fronts but did not succeed in derailing it. Similarly, the first President Bush opposed affirmative action preferences but felt compelled to sign the Civil Rights Act of 1991 even though he feared that it would encourage quotas.[237] In 1989, the Supreme Court dealt affirmative action a severe setback in the *City of Richmond v. J. A. Croson Co.* decision.[238] In 1995, the Court inflicted another wound in its *Adarand Constructors v. Pena* ruling, where it imposed a high standard of justification even on programs established by Congress.[239] Seeking to retain preferences in the face of these decisions, President Clinton ordered restrictions on numerical quotas while supporting enforcement based on specific findings of discrimination in particular industries. Beginning in the mid-1990s, a combination of hostile lower court decisions, ballot initiatives, and legislative actions in California and other states put the legal and political future of affirmative action in great doubt. The second President Bush entered office after a campaign in which he strongly opposed preferences. As this book went to press, the constitutional issue was pending before the Supreme Court.

Affirmative action has never had much public support,[240] "with little evidence of change over time."[241] The vast majority of Americans, including more than a third of blacks and more than 70% of Hispanics, oppose racial preferences in hiring and promotion, with the level of this opposition rising somewhat over time.[242] A leading study of public attitudes toward affirmative action finds, consistent with other studies, that "the most fundamental factor behind opposition to affirmative action is one of principle."[243] That is, the opponents view preferences, rightly or wrongly, as inconsistent with the ideals of equal opportunity and merit that almost all strongly endorse.[244] Indeed, even affirmative action supporters feel obliged to honor, affirm, and somehow reconcile these principles with their program—usually by suggesting that, because of racism, the merit and equality of opportunity values can only be achieved through preferences. Researchers on public attitudes toward affirmative action understand that the phraseology of the question asked, as well as other contextual factors, can affect survey results and that multiple interpretations of the data are possible.[245] For this reason, it is hard to know the precise division of opinion. No researcher in this field doubts, however, that the public's opinion remains decidedly and intensely negative,[246] pretty much regardless of how the questions are formulated, the state of the economy, or personal financial conditions.[247] Indeed, researchers find that "opposition to, and anger over, affirmative action is pervasive among the white public and is just as strong among whites on the political left as among those on the political right"—the former being the ones that have the most positive views of blacks and the firmest commitment to racial equality.[248] Here are the conclusions of a recent study by political scientists Paul Sniderman and Edward Carmines, who employ a variety of survey-based experiments in order to tease out public attitudes in a more nuanced way:

> (1) The role of racial prejudice in promoting opposition to affirmative action is minor. (2) Rather than opposition to affirmative action signaling a refusal to acknowledge the discrimination and exploitation that black Americans have suffered, a substantial majority of white Americans believe that an extra effort should be made to see that blacks are treated fairly. (3) Opposition to affirmative action is not peculiar to Americans. (4) Opposition to affirmative action does not hinge on the race of the group who benefits but rather on whether the procedures involved are judged to be fair. (5) In addition to dislike of blacks leading to dislike of affirmative action, dislike of affirmative action fosters dislike of blacks. (6) Opposition to and resentment over affirmative action has burst conventional political channels—it is now as prevalent on the left, among liberals and Democrats, as on the right, among conservatives and Republicans.[249]

The large size of racial preferences in certain domains, coupled with their clear offense to principles in which the public fervently believes, means that Americans in varying degrees—blacks and whites, liberals and conservatives, men and women, rich and poor—regard affirmative action's methods to be not merely misguided but morally wrong. Indeed, if the public knew how large affirmative action preferences in selective college admissions and some other areas actually are, opposition would probably be even more intense than it is. This is bound to taint the diversity, real and spurious, that preferences produce and to discredit the larger liberal project.[250] The value that Americans ascribe to diversity surely depends, among other things, on how they evaluate the process and criteria that produced it.

If public attitudes dictated policy outcomes in some straightforward fashion, race-based preferences would not have been adopted initially, much less survived for four decades. How, then, can we account for their survival and even, in many communities, their expansion?[251] More than twenty-five years after Nathan Glazer first posed this question,[252] there still is no simple answer.

Accounts of affirmative action's survival based on its initial lack of transparency and its largely incremental and bureaucratic growth are certainly plausible, but they can take us only so far. At some point, particularly after the 1978 *Bakke* decision, the earlier veil lifted. This alerted the public to how the policy had evolved and expanded, and informed politicians of voters' opposition to it. Why did the politicians not turn decisively against affirmative action at that point? More explanation is needed. Interest-group politics, analyzed in the light of public choice theory, provides additional insights. Affirmative action may be a classic case of what James Q. Wilson called clientist politics, in which a policy's benefits are concentrated on a relatively small but intense group while its costs are spread among a much larger but more diffuse, hard-to-organize group for which the issue is less salient.[253] We saw that the number of white workers, college applicants, and others potentially disadvantaged by affirmative action is large, but that relatively few report actual disadvantage, perhaps because the statistical probability of such disadvantage *to an individual white* is quite small. (As we shall also see, this statistical result is less true of Asians, which may make them a more potent source of future opposition.)[254]

Powerful political interests have indeed supported affirmative action. According to Lemann, "[t]he new meritocratic elite didn't resist affirmative action at all—in fact it voluntarily established affirmative action in every institution under its control."[255] In time, liberal advocates for minority groups placed it high on their policy agendas. As Orlando Patterson explains, black perceptions of white racism are probably heightened (and distorted) by the proportion of the two groups in the population, which increases the policy's salience to blacks. The status quo has been sustained by strong support by ethnic organizations, national media, leading educational institutions, large corporations, government bureaucracies,[256] mainstream foundations,[257] and other opinion leaders. It has been further fortified by the growing acquiescence (and in the districting area, connivance)[258] of national Republican politicians and the inertial advantages of any long-established policy.[259]

Large corporations' strong support for affirmative action might seem counterintuitive. After all, employers must bear most of the direct compliance costs, and affirmative action often places them between contending employees in an awkward damned-if-you-do, damned-if-you-don't position. Nevertheless, some large companies support affirmative action even in non-business settings.[260] Their leaders emphasize the benefits of ethno-racial diversity in a global market,[261] and the programs are promoted by powerful internal and external constituencies, including some customers.[262] The programs also tend to advantage large companies by imposing onerous reporting, staffing, and other compliance costs on smaller competitors who cannot bear them as easily.[263] Firms also see affirmative action as a safe harbor sheltering them from Title VII claims, helping them to "keep the peace" and avoid adverse publicity. Absent allowable preferences, these claims would come not only from black workers but also from the vastly larger number of white workers who might allege reverse discrimination.[264] In a notoriously uncertain system, firms favor almost anything, even regulations, that can clarify their legal duties.[265]

All of these corporate interests, taken together, surely help to explain the failure of President Reagan and both Presidents Bush to move vigorously against affirmative action—except through judicial appointments—despite numerous opportunities to do so.[266] (Presidents Johnson, Nixon, Carter, and Clinton supported it in varying degrees.) Today, most politicians, with their eyes on Hispanic and Asian voters (and money), are unwilling to rock the affirmative action boat and risk being pilloried by ethnic group advocates as racist or insensitive to minority interests on an issue that is highly salient to the advocates but not to most minority voters.[267] This helps to explain why the battles against affirmative action (and bilingual education) in California and elsewhere have been spearheaded primarily by private political entrepreneurs in ballot referenda, not by elected politicians.

A final explanation of affirmative action's political survival transcends the interests of particular groups and politicians and is undoubtedly important. Many who might otherwise oppose preferences simply do not see any viable alternative, and others see them as "easier than the slow acculturation that would naturally prepare blacks to compete at school and on the job."[268] Advocates of preferences have skillfully exploited a deep reservoir of elite guilt about past discrimination. Charles Fried notes this dilemma: "[w]ithout preferences, the elite institutions of this country might rapidly be stripped of much of their African-American presence . . . [and] a society that is segmented by race, with all the best jobs, places, honors, and titles going to whites (and Asian Americans) is simply not an integrated society, whatever the reason for the segregation. It is two societies, separated by race."[269] As we saw, this concern is especially acute at the elite schools where the credentials gap makes the resegregation scenario seem quite plausible.[270] This issue is discussed further below.

THE CONSEQUENCES OF AFFIRMATIVE ACTION

I have considered some of affirmative action's consequences, such as the increase in black representation at selective undergraduate, graduate, and professional institutions; the entry of their graduates into the black middle class; and the public's views on race issues. But these hardly exhaust the consequences; three others remain to be discussed: the rate of black progress, the distribution of affirmative action's benefits, and the incidence and distribution of its costs.

Rate of Black Progress

The improvement in American blacks' social and economic conditions has been, in Orlando Patterson's words, "nothing short of astonishing" in almost every respect.[271] The relevant question for present purposes is: how much of this progress is due to affirmative action? Since affirmative action in some domains has been in place as a national policy for more than three decades, this is a difficult question to answer. Two ways to approach it is to compare the trajectory of black progress before and after the policy was established, and to analyze the backgrounds of those who benefited from it in order to draw inferences about whether and to what extent they would have improved their positions without preferences. Both methods produce interesting but uncertain results.

Affirmative action preferences, we saw, have unquestionably had a large effect on the number of blacks admitted to selective institutions. The evidence is murkier in the employment area. Economists John Donohue and James Heckman sought to discover how much of blacks' economic gains since 1940 were due to federal civil rights policy and enforcement under the Civil Rights Act of 1964, particularly Title VII barring employment discrimination. They concluded that this federal activity was "the major contributor to the sustained improvement in black economic status that began in 1965," while noting the difficulty of controlling for important contemporaneous developments such as black migration to the North, selective attrition of older, less skilled blacks from the workforce, improvements in black education, the rise in wages resulting from Vietnam War–related shortages, and underlying attitudinal changes among whites.[272] A recent study, using outcome variation among states passing antidiscrimination laws instead of the time series methodology employed by Donohue and Heckman, finds smaller positive effects on blacks than they did; moreover, almost all of the gain was by black females.[273] Some studies, comparing outcomes before and after Title VII, have found negative effects on blacks.[274]

An even greater challenge is to distinguish between gains attributable merely to nondiscrimination and those attributable instead to affirmative action preferences.[275] In the South, where Donohue and Heckman found the major gains, nondiscrimination presumably was the major enforcement thrust; remedies taking the form of numerical preferences were often upheld, but only to rectify specific instances of past discrimination.[276] Another economic analyst finds that affirmative action has not improved the employment prospects for the most disadvantaged blacks but has instead redistributed black workers from small and medium-sized firms to large employers and federal contractors most aware of legal requirements, without increasing black employment rates overall.[277] The econometric studies of affirmative action find modest gains for favored groups in employment, government contracting, education, and entrepreneurship, with inconclusive evidence on efficiency effects.[278] Again, however, it may be impossible to disentangle the effects of nondiscrimination and affirmative action policies.

Distribution of Benefits in and outside the Favored Group

If we wish to know whom preferences directly benefit, we must first disaggregate the broad favored group (e.g., blacks, Hispanics) in order to determine which of its members are helped by the program. Disaggregation is especially necessary with respect to affirmative action. First, even its proponents concede that only a very small fraction of the group can hope to take advantage of it. This is most obvious with selective college admissions and FCC broadcast licenses, discussed immediately below, but it is bound to be true as well for employment that requires special job skills or a certain level of education. Second, preferences effect a redistribution of opportunity and status *within* the favored group; as discussed below, the program's mere existence makes some members worse off—particularly those who, rightly or wrongly, are stigmatized as needing special help when in fact they do not need it and can qualify under conventional race-neutral standards. Again, the Bowen-Bok study shows that affirmative action in admission to selective colleges and universities largely benefits students from middle- and upper-class families.[279] This is hardly surprising, as these students are best equipped to apply to such competitive and costly schools. This pre-college advantage is then multiplied when these students, now graduates of the selective schools, go on to apply to selective professional and graduate programs and then proceed with their careers. As we saw, most of them graduate from these programs and do well, but a disproportionate number (at least in law) do not gain entry to the profession.[280]

The skewed distribution of benefits from FCC licensing is even more dramatic, as they are enjoyed by a handful of black entrepreneurs who are already sufficiently successful to be able to meet the complex bidding and licensing standards. Indeed, the black bidders or licensees are sometimes little more than fronts for white business interests seeking to exploit the economic value of preferences.[281] Similar abuses have been documented in preferences applying to tens of billions of dollars in federal, state, and local government contracts,[282] and to additional billions intended for minority-owned small businesses under the scandal-ridden Section 8(a) and other set-aside pro-grams.[283] Such programs are designed to help a relatively small number of people who can only take advantage of them if they are already fairly sophisti-cated and well connected.[284]

A preference program, moreover, is a zero-sum game in two senses. It not only pits favored groups against nonfavored groups as they compete for a fixed set of resources or advantages—a competition that foments complaints of reverse discrimination—but it also pits each favored group against the other favored groups. Blacks' success in gaining a preference is at the ex-pense, not only of whites, but also of Hispanics, Asians, and other preference-eligible groups—and vice versa. This intergroup competition is most notori-ous in higher education and contract preference programs.[285] Such rivalries exacerbate the already tense conflict over politically distributed, racially de-fined spoils.[286]

Racial preferences' skewed benefits can also be seen in officially sanctioned or officially required racial gerrymandering of legislative districts that seeks to benefit blacks. As noted earlier, analysts disagree over whether this form of affirmative action helps black voters by packing them into a small number of majority-minority districts where they can easily elect black representatives, or whether their interests would be better served as a substantive matter by line-drawing that leaves them as a significant minority in a larger number of white-majority districts. Those who favor this latter approach find grow-ing empirical support in studies showing that the majority-minority districts benefit the few black politicians who occupy or aspire to the safe seats they yield, but not their black constituents who would be better represented sub-stantively by representatives, white or black, in districts where black voters constitute a significant minority.[287] Indeed, many analysts hold the majority-minority strategy partly responsible for the unseating of a large number of liberal Democratic members of the House by conservative Republicans in 1994.[288] Another example of the conflict of interest for the few black politi-cians (and others) who benefit from policies concentrating blacks geographi-cally occurs in affirmative action remedies that have the effect of keeping blacks in their isolated neighborhoods rather than moving them to better, hopefully more integrated ones.[289]

This problem—the small numbers and relative affluence of those within the broader preferred group who actually benefit from the preferences—is probably endemic to all such programs rather than being confined to Ameri-can ones. Will Kymlicka, a Canadian proponent of preferences there (and in the United States), reports that the same is true of Canada's programs.[290] Studies of preferences in other countries, including less developed ones like

India, find much the same thing.[291] Again, this is predictable; the supply of preference slots and the qualities needed to gain access to and use them are in very limited supply relative to demand.

The Incidence and Distribution of Costs

I have been discussing affirmative action's beneficiaries. I now ask what are its costs, and who bears them? This is a much more difficult question to answer than on the benefits side. There is, first, a conceptual and normative difficulty. Consider those applicants—the "losers"—who would have been hired or admitted on the merits (however defined), but who are not hired or admitted because of preferences given to others. Should (and do) the losers think of themselves as members of a demographic group and assess their loss in terms of that group's changed probability of admission, or should (and do) they view themselves as individuals and assess their loss accordingly?

In thinking about these questions, two empirical factors might seem to support the argument for preferences. First, only 7% of whites surveyed in 1990 claimed to have experienced any form of reverse discrimination themselves, 16% knew of someone close who had, and fewer than 25% said it was something they had witnessed or heard about in their workplaces.[292] Some analysts, however, attribute the low complaint rate of whites to the policy's informality, their reluctance (common to other discrimination victims)[293] to get embroiled with the law, and a dose of "you can't fight City Hall" fatalism.[294]

Second, preferences only slightly reduce the ex ante statistical group probability of elite school admission of whites: eliminating preferences would increase whites' probability of admission only from 25% to 26.5%.[295] This increase is so small, of course, because the white applicants and admittees vastly outnumber the black ones. Affirmative action advocates correctly argue that when the program is viewed in this ex ante, probabilistic, group-centered way, whites suffer a trivial reduction in their chance of admission in order that blacks can more than triple both their ex ante group chance of admission and their representation on campus.[296] Whites might still argue, of course, that this reduction is unfair to them because at the margin and thus for some, it means the difference between admission and rejection. But from the ex ante group perspective, no white can properly claim an individual expectation of admission, much less a right to it, since the individuals who lose slots as a result of the preferences will never know whether they would otherwise have been admitted. Given the losers' anonymity, the most that any one of them can claim is that absent affirmative action, more whites would have been admitted and he might (or might not) have been one of them, depending on how his application compared to those of other disappointed white applicants.[297]

We must complicate this picture of group consciousness and competition in several respects. First, the 1.5% decline in probability of admission seems trivial, but when applied to the entire group of white applicants it means that a significant number of people are affected[298]—and many more will *think* they were affected (the flip side of the "anonymous loser" factor). Second, substituting Asians for whites makes the picture look very different and more troubling. Indeed, relatively high-achieving Asians are probably the group most unfairly treated by preferences for blacks. During most of the nineteenth century, many Asian laborers endured a kind of servitude and subordination that was only a cut above slavery.[299] The *Chinese Exclusion Case*, sometimes called the Dred Scott decision for Asians, rivals the Japanese internment cases for harshness and injustice.[300] Until 1952 (for the Chinese, 1943), Asians could not naturalize as American citizens. Increasingly, affirmative action in effect punishes the stunning academic and economic achievements of many Asians by excluding them from eligibility for preferences. Because the number of Asian applicants is so much smaller, preferences for blacks reduce the ex ante admission probability of Asians as a group and as individuals as much or more than they do for individual whites.

A third and related complication arises from the growing possibility that, contrary to my assumption in this scenario, the whites disadvantaged by preferences may in fact think of themselves not as whites but as members of some other group—say, New York City public school students, Muslims, whites with SAT scores of X, outwardly gay women, or any group that they believe is salient to their applicant-identity. Because these nonpreference groups are so much smaller than the white group, the preference for blacks may create a much greater disadvantage for them than the 1.5% for whites.

Now suppose that we instead imagine that the white losers think of themselves as individual applicants, not as members of the demographic group "whites." I would expect them to feel a more profound sense of unfairness and personal loss, if not bitterness.[301] Regardless of how large or small their racial group disadvantage was, they will think that it may account for their rejection, depriving them of admission on what most will regard as a nonmeritorious, hence illegitimate, basis. In psychological reality, and not just by hypothesis, they will not have thought of themselves as "whites" in this connection, at least until they realize that affirmative action disadvantages whites as a group. Perceiving their group membership as a reason, if not *the* reason, for their rejection is bound to demoralize and anger them in a way that would not occur to those who conceive of themselves not as unique individuals, but rather as members of a specific demographic group that has a statistical chance of admission.[302]

In a culture that ardently affirms the principles of individual freedom, merit, and equality of opportunity, this demoralization and anger must be counted as a very large social cost. It is no less a cost because it is borne by whites, and often less privileged whites at that. If these principles make it unfair to impose this cost, the fact that the unfairness is spread across a large group of people may not make it any more palatable. In fact, diffusing the unfairness in this way simply increases the number of people who feel themselves aggrieved. The most powerful groups among them may seek protection by seeking new preferences for themselves. These incentives do not fully explain the politics of affirmative action, but they surely are part of the story.

Other costs of affirmative action are also diffuse, invisible, hard to measure, or ineffable. Here as elsewhere, we do well to remember the laws of unintended consequences, of inertia, of program politicization, and of reinforcement of existing advantage—laws that are as implacable and distort affirmative action as much as other well-intended policies.[303] Black students' much higher drop-out rates from the selective schools represent a large financial and psychological cost to the students and to the schools.[304] Shelby Steele, who firmly opposes affirmative action, sees it as an "iconographic" policy aimed at enhancing whites' virtuous self-image and blacks' sense of power—"the precise qualities that America's long history of racism had denied to each side."[305] The fact that affirmative action is a feel-good policy for white elites, of course, tells us nothing about whether or not it is moral, rational, or effective. Many socially desirable behaviors are actuated by guilt or by the desire to be esteemed by others and by oneself as righteous and generous. Indeed, no community can flourish without such motivations.

Some of affirmative action's iconographic elements, however, are less uplifting. What signals does society send when it exempts one from the normal rules of the game, treats one as a kind of ward of the state or of some other institution, presumes that one needs special help because one cannot make it on one's own, subjects one to others' lowered expectations for oneself, and segregates one—paradoxically, in the service of the integration ideal?[306] No one really knows how program beneficiaries decode the subtle semiotics of preferences; they surely read them in many different ways. Indeed, because these signals are multiple, intricate, and perhaps internally contradictory, the beneficiaries may be as confused as the rest of us about what preferences actually connote.

In any event, one must wonder about the iconographic authenticity of a policy in which most of the feel-good benefits go to those who bear few if any of its costs. Most of affirmative action's costs are borne by young people struggling to reach the first rungs of the long ladder to success, while many of its most influential supporters are relatively privileged whites, elite universities,[307] and large corporations.[308] In these institutions, domestic tranquility, good governmental relations, and a public image of rectitude are paramount considerations. The best-off members of these institutions, moreover, are the ones least likely to be displaced by the policy. Again, this fact does not mean that they are wrong to defend affirmative action; it only means that they free-ride on it.

Another subtle aspect of affirmative action is how it reshapes the ways in which merit is defined, measured, and discussed. An example is the trend for select institutions of higher education to move away from national testing toward a consideration of "the whole person,"[309] something that elite institutions, of course, always sought and can best afford to do. Which criteria of merit will take the place of testing, however, remains conspicuously unexplained. This question is especially important for large institutions. The University of California cannot realistically consider 68,000 applicants for about 28,000 freshman places[310] on any meaningful "whole person" basis. Alternative criteria like personal interviews, recommendation letters, high school rank, and extracurricular activities are likely to have other, perhaps greater, disadvantages for applicant pools drawn from very diverse, hard-to-compare high schools.[311] These questions, of course, intersect with the robust, politically salient national debate over educational standards and testing, which became a centerpiece of the 2000 presidential election. In less rarefied contexts like police departments, the practice of racial or gender norming of qualifications is now common and breeds cynicism, resentment, and uncertain effects on the quality of public services.[312]

Yet another hard-to-measure effect of affirmative action, especially at select institutions of higher education, is the pervasive dissimulation and deformation of thought on all sides due to the felt need to deny or ignore the fact that racial preferences play a large, often decisive role in many admissions decisions.[313] Even more pernicious—and tragic for the individuals involved—is the denial that the preferentially admitted students, as we have seen, tend to have much lower academic performances and higher drop-out rates. These evasions in turn create a perverse rhetorical incentive that encourages double-talk. Below, I discuss a current example of this—California's constant revision of its admissions criteria in order to get the "right" ethno-racial mix.[314]

A cost of preferences that is impossible to measure is the insidious innuendo about the deserts of almost all but the most unquestionably superior performers in the preferred group—and perhaps even of them.[315] Ironically, this innuendo tends to perpetuate the very stereotypes that affirmative action was supposed to dispel. That these costs are often invisible and unacknowledged does not make them any less real and cruel—or hypocritical, given athletic and other types of preference with even less justification.[316] Stanley Fish dismisses this stigma by saying that a particular beneficiary may prefer to bear that cost in order to gain the preference, and that it would not exist if people just stopped thinking that way.[317] The problem, however, is that even unbigoted people *do* think that way—they still believe in merit despite efforts to discredit the ideal, and they are right to think that preferences often violate it. Moreover, the stigma attaches to *every* member of the preferred group whether she is willing to accept this bargain or not.

More generally, affirmative action has contributed to the relentless racialization of discourse on a vast range of public and private subjects, some of which actually have little or nothing to do with race. The felt need to defend affirmative action against strong public opposition has encouraged many advocates to play the race card at every turn and with a desperation that grows with the effectiveness of the critique. When opportunities are made to depend on officially sanctioned categories of race or ethnicity, one is more likely to emphasize one's racial identity rather than the many other identities that one naturally acquires in a society as fluid, complex, and individualistic as ours. Orlando Patterson, a proponent of temporary affirmative action, captures this discursive tic so astutely and succinctly that I can do no better than to quote him at length:

> Any reference to Afro-Americans by Euro-Americans that does not acknowledge the totality of racism or flatter all things Afro-American risks sneers of contempt or the charge of racism. Any but the most professionally qualified expression of sympathy is likely to be dismissed as liberal patronage. Any suggestion that an Afro-American person might be responsible, even in some minor way, for his or her condition invites the knee-jerk response that one is blaming the victim. The result is that no Euro-American person, except one insensitive to the charge of racism, dares say what he or she really means. . . . So much "race" speech has become ritualized and rhetorical. . . . The overwrought nature of ethno-"racial" talk results in curious forms of self-censorship and privileged speech among ethnic groups in their interactions with each other. . . . [A]n Afro-American person is privileged to say, "I love my blackness," or "I take pride in the great cultural achievements of my race," or any such chauvinistic clap-trap. No Euro-American person dares say the very same thing, not if she cares about her reputation, even though it is true that nearly all Euro-Americans cherish their appearance and cultural heritage. . . . Every Afro-American is presumed to be an expert on all aspects of the subject of "race." . . . When they are not proving that "race"

as a concept has no scientific meaning, most social scientists and even medical researchers are busily controlling away all other variables in a relentless effort to prove that one, and only one, variable explains the condition of Afro-Americans: "race." Having abolished the ontological basis of "race" in biology, American social scientists vie with each other to reestablish its ontological essence as a social fact. . . . American social science is either uninterested in, or befuddled by, the fact that the vast majority of Afro-Americans, including the majority of those born and brought up poor, overcome their circumstances and lead healthy, happy, productive lives.[318]

Patterson's insistence on the reality of black progress brings us to what may be the most important question of all about affirmative action: What would happen if it were eliminated? What would workplaces, high schools, legislatures, college campuses, and other purlieus of American life look like without affirmative action—or at least without the kinds of preferences that are now in place?

THE RESEGREGATION NIGHTMARE

The prospect of all-white (and Asian) institutions is deeply repellent to everyone I know. Most Americans who oppose affirmative action in principle, the evidence suggests, are likewise appalled at the thought of returning to a world in which whites seldom interact with minorities, and almost never as social equals. As we have seen, this nightmarish prospect accounts for much of the support for affirmative action. Do we actually face that prospect?

Knowing precisely what America would look like without government-mandated ethno-racial affirmative action is impossible. The difficulty is increased by the rhetorical strategy of preference defenders like the University of Michigan, who shift uneasily between arguing that (1) preferences confer only a marginal advantage on minority applicants, and (2) resegregation would occur absent those preferences. In making predictions, however, we must not lose sight of how much American institutions have changed since the 1950s and how strong the nonlegal incentives for maintaining and increasing diversity are today. If diversity depended on racial preferences as much as some advocates imply, even the levels of diversity that now prevail in colleges, workplaces, politics, and communities would simply be inexplicable. A key question is how the more selective institutions would react to a ban on ethno-racial preferences. Since private institutions often engage in affirmative action now when they are under no legal mandate to do so, it is safe to predict that they would continue the practice, and perhaps even increase it if public institutions could no longer do so. Many private institutions evidently find the organizational, political, and moral considerations compelling, and there is no reason to believe that their reasoning would change.

An across-the-board ban on ethno-racial preferences by public institutions would reduce the now-preferred minorities on flagship campuses, though it is impossible to know how much. A study of the effect of *Bakke* found that the decision changed little about minority admissions; the best predictor of an institution's post-*Bakke* pattern was its pre-*Bakke* pattern.[319] The same is true today. Public universities, most notably in California and Texas, have already demonstrated their determination to maintain their black and Hispanic enrollments even in the face of legal prohibitions against preferences. They have substituted other criteria that are not explicitly ethno-racial but effectively maintain or raise the previous levels of minority admissions. Texas changed its system to admit the top 10% of graduating high school seniors to the public campus of the students' choice. A recent study of admission data through 1999 finds that the program has had "mixed results" at the flagship campuses there and has helped Asians as much or more than blacks and Hispanics.[320]

California's approach was more restrictive; it was limited to the top 4%, excluded students who had not taken certain preparatory courses, and did not guarantee enrollment at the campus of the students' choice.[321] Even so, using greater outreach, more individualized review, and "holistic" criteria, the share (18.6%) of "underrepresented minorities" admitted to the California system in 2001 was essentially the same as the 18.8% in the last year of affirmative action (1997), although their distribution among the various campuses in the system was different.[322] In 2002, their share rose above the 1997 level, to 19.1%.[323] Under less political and legal pressure to abandon preferences, Florida adopted a plan that admits the top 20% from each high school to the state system, yielding more than 40% minority incoming students and raising black enrollment at its flagship campuses.[324]

But even if the new "percent plans" (as they are called) succeed in maintaining or increasing black and Hispanic enrollments, they will not necessarily be a cause for unequivocal rejoicing. First, they may simply preserve the same objectionable use of ethno-racial preferences by disguising them and effectuating them indirectly. In addition, these programs enable many students who graduate from uncompetitive high schools to gain admission to institutions for which they are ostensibly unqualified, with all the difficulties this entails for them and the institutions. Those admitted under the programs, moreover, will still constitute but a very small fraction of their groups' cohorts. After all, only 6% and 7% of black and Hispanic students, respectively, who graduated from high school in 1998 scored at least 900 (out of a possible score of 1600) on the SAT and ranked in the top 20% of their classes.[325]

Another dismaying and perverse feature of these plans is that their ability to raise non-Asian minority enrollments depends on the existence of segregated neighborhoods and high schools, and also on school districting practices that officials can manipulate to qualify students under the plans.[326] Furthermore, these plans disadvantage minority students (especially those attending good integrated high schools) who fall just below the new cutoff but could succeed academically at the more selective schools. Also disadvantaged are those white students who are more qualified than the whites who, because of their higher class ranking at inferior schools, will be admitted in their place. Indeed, one can predict that the state university systems, under great pressure from minority caucuses in the legislature, will lower academic standards further by raising the percentages specified in the plans and by again reducing the percentage of students who must be admitted on the basis of academic criteria. For all these reasons, the new rules seem likely to lower the credentials of whites as well as minorities in the state system.[327]

Manipulation of the new emphasis on class rank and holism rather than higher standards is already evident,[328] and the California system has countenanced if not conspired with these stratagems even when they violate the principle of equal opportunity.[329] Consider, for example, one ruse that benefits Hispanic applicants to the disadvantage of blacks and most whites.[330] High school students who speak Spanish at home are now encouraged to take Spanish as one of their three SAT II tests, which are designed to measure achievement in a specific subject matter area. Not surprisingly, they score very well on the Spanish SAT II as well as on the Spanish advanced placement test (which also strengthens their applications) without ever having taken a course in the subject! Students in one low-performing Los Angeles school who took the Spanish SAT II averaged 715 out of a possible score of 800 compared to an average of 396 on the SAT, far below the national norm. Since the California system now weighs the SAT II scores more heavily than the SAT scores, many Hispanic students win a guaranteed slot in the system despite extremely low SAT scores. Other language-minority students, such as Chinese, Koreans, and Japanese, are doing the same thing where the SAT II offers a test in their language, sometimes after heavy ethnic group lobbying and subsidization of test development.

In California, the end of legally mandated ethno-racial preferences did not significantly reduce minority admission to the public university system overall. This outcome, however, rests on two conditions. First, minority students' distribution among the system's campuses changed. At Berkeley, for example, the demise of preferences substantially reduced black enrollment there, especially at its law school,[331] but most of the students who no longer could get into Berkeley attended other schools in the system instead.[332]

One would expect this to happen, and it is not necessarily regrettable. Dropping down a rung on the academic ladder in the public systems does not necessarily damage a student's educational and life opportunities. The data presented earlier on academic performance, drop-out and bar passage rates, and the educational and career paths of black leaders, suggest that the opposite may be true, at least for those who would have done poorly at the flagship campuses. Homogeneity in academic ability among students in the same program is pedagogically desirable, less qualified students are more likely to succeed or excel academically at less demanding schools, and failing at a more prestigious school is probably worse than succeeding at a lesser one.[333] In the year before preferences ended at the University of California, only one black freshman at the San Diego campus had a GPA of 3.5 or better, as compared with 20% of whites. In 1999, after Proposition 209, 20% of black freshmen at San Diego had GPAs of 3.5 or better, and an internal administration study found no substantial GPA differences based on race or ethnicity.[334]

This outcome, I contend, benefits the minority and white students and the larger society. Even so, of course, this will no more assuage such students' disappointment in not being admitted to their first-choice school than white students will be mollified by being told that affirmative action reduces their ex ante chances by only 1.5%. At the lowest rungs of the ladder, to be sure, the most marginal minority students, like their white counterparts, may not gain admission to *any* of the system's campuses, and some of them may be unable to afford the tuition at any of the vast number of nonselective private colleges that admit all applicants. We do not know how many are in this predicament and what they will do about it.

The second reason why California has been able to maintain overall minority enrollments in its public system without formal preferences is that it has kept jiggering its admissions criteria in a determined search for a formula that will produce the numbers it wants.[335] I have already explained why I think this well-intentioned tactic will lower academic standards, disserve and stigmatize those minority students who are unprepared for the schools they attend, engender deep resentment on all sides, encourage subterfuge and dissimulation, have perverse effects at the high school level, and eventually bring a once-great university system into disrepute. My belief that this game is not worth the candle is fortified by the system's ability to maintain or even expand minority enrollments by appropriately redistributing them among its different campuses while also trying to improve their pre-college preparation (discussed below). Obviously, many others disagree.

If past is prologue, the remarkable and hard-won achievements of minorities should lead in the future to greater diversity in higher education, workplaces, and other social institutions—with or without racial preferences. This diversity will occur with or without new antidiscrimination remedies.[336] Existing remedies should be strengthened wherever possible. In addition to the usual law enforcement strategies, for example, the government could deploy many more trained testers disguised as job applicants, homebuyers, borrowers, and so forth to gauge discrimination in various markets, while increasing the penalties for violations.[337] Violators could be required to publicize their violations to suppliers, customers, and communities. Other remedial reform proposals have been advanced and should be seriously considered.[338]

ALTERNATIVES

The real choice for America, then, is not between the status quo and a return to the 1950s—or even the 1980s. The powerful processes of immigration and social change, augmented by more vigorous enforcement of the antidiscrimination laws and voluntary private affirmative action, promise to expand diversity in higher education and other areas of American life. By the same token, we need not choose between existing forms of affirmative action and none at all. Indeed, many proposals to reform affirmative action have been offered by its defenders and critics alike. I discuss these proposals under six broad rubrics: (1) better targeting within currently favored groups; (2) disadvantage-based preferences; (3) lotteries; (4) addressing root causes; (5) time-limited programs; and (6) voluntary programs.

Better Targeting within Favored Groups

Many of the proposals take cognizance of the overbreadth of the coverage and definition of favored groups—for example, as noted earlier, more than 75% of the post-1965 immigrants to the United States qualified for preferences as soon as they arrived—and seek to focus more narrowly on particularly compelling claims for preference. The most important of these proposals would limit the preferences to blacks (and, for obvious historical reasons, to Native Americans) by virtue of the disadvantages they have suffered from the legacy of black enslavement and pervasive race discrimination.[339] On this reasoning, one might further limit preferences to nonimmigrant blacks (i.e., those descended from Afro-American slaves), but programs seldom if ever make this distinction.[340] Any who oppose affirmative action in principle but who also recognize blacks' special moral and historical claims might well support this approach as a better compromise. But the growing political influence of Hispanics, whose leaders often couch the group's claims for preference in similar terms,[341] makes such a change less likely. Distinguishing among blacks in this way might also be administratively unworkable.

Other proposals illustrate just how fine-grained and also how crude these targeting efforts might need to be. Orlando Patterson, for example, would exclude "first-generation persons of African ancestry from Africa, the Caribbean and elsewhere . . . [but] [l]ike Mexican-Americans, their children and later generations should be eligible in light of the persistence of racist discrimination in America." He would also exclude from preference all Hispanics except for Puerto Ricans of any generation, Mexican-Americans of second or later generations, and "all Asians except Chinese-Americans descended from pre-1923 immigrants."[342] With due respect for Patterson's pathbreaking work on race, his specification more resembles a tax code provision governing depreciation expenses than a coherent, workable formula for promoting social justice.

Another recent proposal for an alternative form of affirmative action in legal education would grant admissions preferences on the basis of three criteria: whether the applicant has experienced the effects of racial discrimination; is likely to contribute a perspective or viewpoint on racial justice that is currently not well represented in the classroom; and is likely to provide legally underserved communities with services and resources.[343] The advantage of these criteria, according to the proposal, is that they target qualities for which law schools have traditionally used race as a proxy, without themselves being racial classifications and thus constitutionally suspect. This scheme might indeed pass constitutional muster, although this would depend on how it was administered and whether it can be shown to be anything more than a transparent disguise for the kinds of racial preferences that courts have rejected. One wonders, however, how schools—as a practical matter and without relying on impermissible racial stereotypes—would determine the answers to the three questions. The proposal, one suspects, would simply invite institutions, parents, and students to dissemble, with a resulting increase in demoralization of the participants and system.

Rather than amending the categories of favored groups, some targeting proposals would demand more rigorous proof of actual discrimination-based disadvantage before affirmative action could be upheld,[344] a requirement that the Supreme Court has imposed in any event, especially with regard to race-based preferences.[345] President Clinton's proposal to "mend, not end" affirmative action took this approach.[346]

Disadvantage-Based Preferences

Perhaps the most alluring proposal for targeting would shift the focus from preferences based on race or ethnicity to race-neutral preferences based on economic or other disadvantages (e.g., disability).[347] Not only would this limit preferences to those in the currently favored groups who most need help; it would also extend them to low-income whites, the disabled, and oth-

ers who are not now favored by affirmative action. Because blacks are disproportionately poor, the thinking goes, they would disproportionately benefit
without incurring the hostility that attaches to race preferences. Most Americans, after all, are morally more inclined to assist people on the basis of their
economic need than on the basis of their skin color, language, region of origin, or gender.[348]

Despite these supposed advantages of class-based preferences, however,
they would be neither administrable nor advantageous to many blacks. First,
as others have noted, most poor people are white, not black, so a class-based
program would disproportionately favor whites. In response to this problem,
some supporters emphasize that poor blacks, unlike poor whites, are separately disadvantaged by race and by class, so their predicament should be assessed on a different scale.[349] In itself, of course, this aspect of class-based
programs is not a good argument against them—poor people are poor whatever their color—but it does reduce the enthusiasm for such programs on the
part of many affirmative action proponents who primarily want to benefit
blacks.[350] For example, Berkeley's law school, Boalt Hall, like the rest of the
California university system,[351] experimented with a socioeconomic disadvantage criterion (among others) instead of race, but abandoned it after one year
when it produced no additional black admissions—thereby signaling both
the inefficacy of this particular targeting strategy and the institution's determination to find some way to get the numbers that it wanted. A somewhat
different, possibly more promising approach, initiated by the University of
Vermont and a few other institutions, is to form a partnership with particular
high schools in low-income areas that can feed economically disadvantaged
minority and white students to the university.[352]

Second, determining economic need would be a very tricky business, as it
has proved to be in the administration of need-based social welfare programs
more generally.[353] For all the arbitrariness and overbreadth of existing affirmative action categories, they are far more objective and administrable
than a need-based program would be. After all, it is much easier and less contestable for a bureaucrat accurately to detect one's skin color, language, ethnicity, and gender than to make the kinds of empirical and normative judgments necessary to determine the extent and, even more controversially, the
causes of one's economic need.[354] Morally, it matters to most people whether
another's poverty is due, for example, to discrimination or to drug abuse.
Journalist Michael Kinsley, who favors some forms of affirmative action,
imagines what would happen:

> Is it worse to be a cleaning lady's son or a coal miner's daughter? Two
> points if your father didn't go to college, minus one if he finished high
> school, plus three if you have no father? (Or will that reward illegitimacy,

which we're all trying hard these days not to do?) Communist societies tried this kind of institutionalized reverse discrimination—penalizing children of the middle class—without any enviable success. Officially sanctioned affirmative action by "disadvantage" would turn today's festival of competitive victimization into an orgy.[355]

Some targeting proposals would focus on "place, not race," allocating government contracts to companies located in economically distressed areas rather than according to their owners' race.[356] Some propose distinguishing between jobs that merely require an employee to be competent, for which preferences could be used, and those for which a high level of performance is necessary and merit is an overriding value. The locational proposal, however, seems suspiciously similar to an economic development program for distressed areas, which has little or nothing to do with the rationales for affirmative action; moreover, such programs have often been shown to be problematic in their own right. The competence-achievement job distinction, like the class-based program, would be very difficult to administer. It would also place even more of affirmative action's burdens on low-income workers who happen to be white while leaving well-off workers unaffected, an outcome that seems distributionally perverse.

Lottery

Lani Guinier, noting that affirmative action is a winner-take-all, us-against-them system, has proposed substituting a lottery to allocate slots in desirable schools. The school would allow all students scoring above the minimum total that now secures admission to compete by random selection, with the school allocating additional lottery tickets to students it thinks possess special talents. Under this system, Guinier says,

> no one would feel "entitled" to admission; nor would anyone feel unjustly excluded. Such an approach recognizes that claims of "merit" and "diversity" are equally legitimate. It does not set "us" against "them." It does not assume that only one group wins. It avoids a zero-sum solution in favor of a positive-sum solution that more broadly accommodates the goals of diversity and genuine merit.[357]

Although Guinier's proposal does possess the virtue, lacking in some reform proposals, of assuring that all admittees would possess at least a minimal level of merit (as defined by the school), it is objectionable on both practical and principled grounds. By flooding the applicant pool with whites who are only minimally qualified and who would not otherwise have applied, it would reduce the overall quality of admitted students without necessarily increasing black admissions at all—and perhaps decreasing them. Americans, moreover, emphatically do *not* believe that the claims of merit and demographic diversity are equally legitimate; they value diversity only when it is achieved in ways that are consistent with deeply held moral values like merit (however defined). Guinier offers no moral justification for denying people who excel by dint of hard work and sacrifice the fruits of their efforts, nor does she consider that her plan sends the wrong messages and creates the wrong incentives for people to strive for excellence, not just minimally satisfactory performance.

Root Causes

Other alternatives to affirmative action are more attractive on their merits and may be more politically feasible. One might be called a "root cause" strategy; it begins from the premise that the main reason why affirmative action seems necessary is the inadequacy of the education and training received by youngsters in the favored groups, which renders them unable to compete on equal terms with their counterparts. In this view, affirmative action is simply a poultice that not only fails to treat the underlying wound but also conceals its true dimensions. A root cause strategy would emphasize the desperate need to improve the schools that low-income children attend, provide remedial assistance to those who cannot progress without it, expand job training for low-skill workers who cannot otherwise compete in the labor market, and help minority entrepreneurs build stable, competitive businesses.[358]

No one really doubts that these are essential elements of any effective solution to the inequality problem that affirmative action seeks to remedy, or that the root causes of this inequality begin to operate very early in a child's life. Adopting this cause approach to reforming affirmative action, however, yields the same difficulties that this approach faces in other social policy areas. Root causes usually remain root causes for one of three reasons: we do not know how to eliminate them, or we (think we) know how but consider it too costly to do so in terms of resources or competing values, or we believe it worth doing but simply cannot muster the necessary political will. When these impediments to attacking root causes exist—with violent crime, for example[359]—our best course may be to focus on managing symptoms until we can figure out how to remove the more fundamental causes. In such cases, insisting on a root cause strategy may in effect be a prescription for inaction, futility, rhetorical excess, and (because root causes are hard to understand) sloppy analysis.

To the extent that the academic performance of low-income children can be improved by remediation and educational reform, this is clearly the road that we should travel—and hopefully *are* traveling[360]—even as we search for other ways to improve their life prospects. But to the extent that we do not understand the causes of their inferior performance, or those causes seem to lie in the more recalcitrant social structures of low-income neighborhoods, or the politics of educational and social reform impede desired solutions, such measures may be ineffective—or worse.

Time Limits

Another alternative approach to affirmative action is to concede its offense to liberal values but insist that it is desirable if it is temporary. This, of course, is hardly a novel proposal. I know of no proponent of affirmative action who does not endorse this objective; the program is always defended as a short-term remedy, as a temporary expedient to be continued only until the favored groups can achieve . . . what? Very few proponents have specified, even in principle, which conditions would trigger its termination. They seem disinclined to speculate, perhaps because they believe that existing inequalities are so large and intractable that they will not be erased in the foreseeable future. Indeed, Justice Thurgood Marshall spoke in this spirit when he remarked that eradicating them would take at least 100 years.[361]

Still, many Americans worry about the indefinite continuation of a policy that raises the most difficult moral and political questions and that has always been rationalized as a temporary remedy. They have good reason to ask, and are entitled to know: what measure of equality would be enough to end affirmative action? My point is not that this question is unanswerable—indeed, one can easily imagine any number of plausible answers—but that almost no proponent of preferences seriously addresses it.[362]

I say "almost" because at least one individual, Orlando Patterson, has done so—although his fifteen-year termination date is actually a conversion date on which race-based affirmative action would become a wholly class-based program that would continue indefinitely. In light of his conviction that affirmative action "is a major factor in the rise of the Afro-American middle class, the single greatest success story of the past forty years," and that its benefits "far outweigh its costs," one is struck by Patterson's failure to explain why he would phase it out at all, much less in fifteen years.[363] Is the desired equality now in view? Or is it simply that he and affirmative action's other defenders can no longer hold off the incessant attacks by its misguided and gullible assailants? In short, is his phaseout a principled proposal consistent with his praise of the policy, or is it instead merely a pragmatic concession to political reality? One cannot tell.

Whatever the content of Patterson's proposal, the political reality is that once affirmative action preferences are established, they are almost impossible to dismantle. So far as one can tell, this has been the universal experience of the other countries that have established them.[364] The United States is no different. As we saw earlier, when conservative Republican presidents and congresses have been in power, they have not seriously challenged existing preferences despite their avowed opposition to them. The logic of coalition-building among groups and don't-rock-the-boat politics dictates that these preferences will remain with us for the foreseeable future.

Voluntary Programs

Voluntary affirmative action is a final example of another approach that might meet or minimize some of the objections to current programs, particularly the criticisms that they are coercive, legalistic, inflexible, and insufficiently sensitive to specific contexts. Strong reasons exist to believe that many, though certainly not all,[365] educational institutions and businesses that now practice mandatory affirmative action would continue to do so without legal compulsion if the law permitted it.[366]

The fact that much affirmative action would exist without legal compulsion, of course, is not a conclusive argument against mandating it. For one thing, a program might be quite different depending on whether it is voluntary or mandatory. For another, as I have been at pains to show, even voluntary preferences are problematic, especially when they are used as the basis for allocating valuable social resources whose principle of distributive justice is and should be merit, properly defined. In addition, mandating preferences would address the market failure argument discussed earlier.

Be that as it may, entities often have their own political, ideological, and self-interested reasons, quite apart from legal considerations, for seeking to diversify (as they define the term) their student bodies, faculties, workforces, and markets.[367] Corporate leaders, for example, have been expanding their management desiderata to include diversity of thought, lifestyle, culture, dress, and other attributes not covered by affirmative action law even as they explicitly disassociate themselves from affirmative action mandates.[368] Indeed, employer-sponsored "diversity training," which was hardly known until the late 1980s, has quickly become a sizable industry. A 1995 survey of the largest corporations indicated that 70% had already initiated formal diversity management programs and another 16% were planning to do so—at costs sometimes amounting to $500,000 a year.[369]

More generally, elite institutions, as we have seen, are among the most influential groups that favor affirmative action, along with the Democratic Party even (or especially) in its Clintonian, "New Democrat" makeover.[370] Sociologist Alan Wolfe, who calls this voluntary approach "prudential affirmative action," notes that it has the additional advantage of not requiring American society to take a clear-cut principled position on a policy for which in truth no favorable political consensus exists or is ever likely to form.[371]

Certain arguments for making affirmative action voluntary are a bit too facile. I believe that private entities (e.g., Stanford University, the Boy Scouts, or the Catholic Church) should be able, as a legal and a policy matter, to make many choices that the government may not properly make. Nevertheless, this cannot explain why *as a matter of principle* private decisions to allocate resources and opportunities on the basis of skin color are any less objectionable than governmental ones. After all, a large body of public law, now more than three decades old, prohibits not only governmental discrimination but also much private, voluntary discrimination in areas like employment, public accommodations, some contracting, and government-assisted activities covered by the Civil Rights Act of 1964. The coverage of state antidiscrimination laws is sometimes even greater. Even if we put the law to one side, why are preferences that are arbitrary and morally wrong when government employs them not at least prima facie arbitrary and morally wrong when private entities do so? To many people, private voluntary affirmative action is no less problematic than a governmental mandate, and there is no satisfying normative basis for distinguishing between them.[372]

I disagree. A racial preference mandated by public law is much more objectionable than one that a private entity decides to establish to reflect its own values and for its own purposes. Let me be clear about why this is so. Governmental preferences are more objectionable, in my view, not because they deploy public funding or authority while private entities do not, and not because public institutions are invariably more powerful than private ones. In fact, public law pervasively shapes private entities, and private influence in society may match or exceed that of government agencies. Critics often use these facts to discredit both the public-private distinction and its constitutional analogue, the "state action" doctrine, under which the Constitution's due process and equal protection guarantees do not limit private conduct.[373] Although the state action doctrine has a dubious constitutional pedigree, the Court has reaffirmed it so often and recently that its continuing authority cannot really be doubted.[374]

But even if no state action doctrine existed, a liberal polity with a genuine commitment to diversity would have to invent something very much like it to permit private associational choices to exclude members of groups not entitled to heightened constitutional protection. Such permission safeguards the autonomy and freedom that are diversity's lifeblood. Mandatory racial preferences threaten these values more than otherwise similar private ones do. In part this difference reflects the nature of all legal regulation. Mandates are more coercive than voluntary actions not only by definition but as a quantitative matter; they regulate more people and more activity than voluntary options that govern only those who elect them and apply only to activities they choose. Prima facie, they offend liberal values more.

Other differences are qualitative. For reasons I have explained elsewhere,[375] legal rules issued from the center tend to be more simplistic, slower to develop and to correct, and less contextualized than voluntary practices that can be tailored to specific needs and situations. A legal rule reflects interest-group politics or the vagaries of judicial decision, whereas a voluntary practice is the product of the chooser's own (albeit socially conditioned and economically constrained) assessment of benefits and costs. One who opposes a voluntary practice can avoid its burdens more easily than one who opposes a mandatory rule.[376] Voluntary practices can assume more diverse forms than mandated ones; this facilitates social learning and problem-solving.[377] When change is desirable, a voluntary practice is easier to reform or abandon than a legal rule. For example, Hispanics now find that rules and formulas designed to benefit them as a minority disadvantage them in communities where they are now a majority and are thus losing the preferred access to magnet schools and other programs guaranteed them under the old rules.[378]

Most important, public law speaks authoritatively for the entire society, binding all who are subject to it. Indeed, many legal theorists maintain that law's expressive and symbolic functions, by signaling community values and commitments, shape social behavior. It does so quite apart from—and perhaps even more powerfully than—the sanctions it may impose.[379] While a public law preference does express a certain kind of compassion for and commitment to the preferred groups, other signals dominate its message— among them, that American society thinks it just to group people by race and ethnicity, to treat those groups monolithically, and to allocate precious resources and opportunities accordingly; that it holds equal treatment and individual merit as secondary, dispensable ideals; that the preferred groups cannot succeed without special public favors; that such favors do not stigmatize them in the minds of fair-minded others; that those who oppose preferences thereby oppose the aspirations of the preferred groups; and that society can assuage old injustices by creating new ones. When public law says such things, it speaks falsely, holds out vain promises, and brings itself into disrepute.

A private, voluntary preference is very different. Rather than sending a strong, authoritative signal about what society does and does not value and how social goals should be pursued, it expresses only the values of those who choose to engage in it. Because most of my substantive objections to public preferences apply to private ones as well, I would probably not choose them for my own academic institution. But many others who also cherish the non-discrimination and merit principles and who conscientiously weigh the competing values reach different conclusions.

One who affirms, as I do, the broad freedom of an individual, group, or entity to choose how to order its own affairs cannot simply dismiss such conclusions out of hand. Suppose that a private university chooses to sacrifice some level of academic performance in order to gain greater racial diversity and whatever educational or other values it thinks this diversity will bring.[380] (If the university perceives no sacrifice, then it follows that there is no problem and no need for a preference, except perhaps in the rare case of a tie-breaker.) I may view its choice as profoundly misguided and think it will disserve many of those it prefers because of their skin color, unjustly harm those rejected for that reason, diminish its own institutional values, and erode over-riding social commitments. But I cannot say categorically that its choice is morally indefensible. More to the point, the law should not categorically say this either.

This distinction between public and private morality, between the values law should mandate and those it should leave to the disparate choices of a diverse civil society, lies at the core of a liberal society. Tamar Jacoby, who studied affirmative action and race relations in three cities, put it well:

> No one who understands what makes America great can quarrel with ethnic pride. At home, on the weekend, in the family and the neighborhood, Jews will be Jews, Italians Italian—and there is no reason blacks should be any different. Religion and ethnicity are essential parts of our lives, and government should not curtail how we express them in the private sphere. But when it comes to public life, even the benevolent color coding of recent decades has proved a recipe for alienation and resentment. . . . Society need not be color-blind or color-less, but the law cannot work unless it is color-neutral, and the government should not be in the business of abetting or paying for the cultivation of group identity.[381]

Americans, Jacoby suggests, must each find their own ways to reconcile their ethnicity and their common citizenship. Preferences, many believe, promise to accelerate this process, but in fact there are no shortcuts.[382]

A post-affirmative action law, I believe, should harmonize the nondiscrimination principle with the important liberal principle of private ordering (or autonomy) by preserving a limited space for private, voluntary preferences that meet minimal conditions of norm compliance and public accountability. The private ordering principle holds that society must respect a private entity's decision about how to conduct its own affairs, absent some overriding public justification for regulating that decision (laws barring racial discrimination, for example, or First Amendment neutrality requirements in intra-church property disputes).[383]

How much private ordering through preferences can the nondiscrimination principle accommodate? So far, federal law has said "very little," allowing a private entity to use preferences only if it does not receive federal funds or is remedying its own past discrimination. Private ethno-racial preferences have largely escaped judicial scrutiny, but it is only a matter of time before they too are challenged in the courts. Such preferences may be upheld on the basis of the kind of "expressive association" defense that the Supreme Court recently extended in *Boy Scouts of America v. Dale*,[384] but the availability of that defense to large private universities and other diverse organizations is by no means clear.[385] For example—and perhaps ironically—the diversity of a large private institution might militate against recognizing an expressive association defense for a preference rationalized on diversity grounds; the argument would be that the institution's very diversity precludes the kind of coherent, self-defining point of view that the expressive association defense is meant to protect.

I want to suggest another exception to the nondiscrimination principle for private preferences, one that depends on their *transparency*. Private entities that now use preferences seldom admit this fact to the public, preferring obfuscation and outright deception to candor. One may argue that silence is golden here, that opacity about racial preferences minimizes social disputes over abstract, irreconcilable principles and sustains desirable social myths.[386] Although this argument for opacity has force in some contexts, it is notably weak as applied to affirmative action. There, divisions and suspicions already abound and dissimulation serves only to magnify and multiply them, as people who assume that preferences are even more widespread than they actually are stigmatize even those who did not receive them. Concealment of the truth about preferences inflames these social conflicts and injustices.

The relative benignity of private voluntary preferences justifies allowing them as an exception to the nondiscrimination principle, but only on two conditions. First, the entity must publicly disclose the preference in advance; it must describe its criteria and weighting system and state why it thinks the preference serves its goals. Second, the preference must not disadvantage a group that enjoys the highest level of constitutional protection against discrimination.

The first condition, transparency, is designed to discipline the granting of preferences by forcing institutions to be more candid about their value choices and by triggering reputational, market, and other informal mechanisms that make the entity bear more of the costs of adopting preferences instead of shifting them to innocent third parties. Customers, students, alumni, investors, journalists, and other interests to which the entity must be attentive can then hold it accountable, rewarding, punishing, or ignoring the preferences, as they see fit. I can only agree with my colleague Jed Rubenfeld, a grudging advocate of preferences, when he writes that "[i]nstitutions with affirmative action plans should be open about them or scrap them."[387] The same is true, I believe, of legacies and other kinds of nonracial preferences, though it is doubtful that federal law can or should compel disclosure in those situations.

Disclosure, of course, is no panacea for the moral and other problems that preferences create, and it would entail some problems of its own. Institutions presumably dissemble for reasons they think are important, perhaps even humane. Harvard, for example, believes that it would be poor educational policy to reveal to the public high school students from Boston and Cambridge to whom it gives admission preferences that they are less academically qualified than others.[388] And someone—a legislature, agency, court, or contracting parties—will have to decide what full and accurate disclosure means. Even so, challenges would go to the nature of the preference and whether it was fully disclosed, issues that are simpler and less costly to resolve than the legality issues under the current affirmative action regime. The law might promote transparency in other, possibly less intrusive and litigious ways. Adequate disclosure, for example, might be a defense in a subsequent civil rights challenge or at least limit damages, much as some retraction statutes do in libel cases.

The second condition, nondiscrimination against groups entitled the highest level of constitutional protection, underscores the important distinction between nondiscrimination and affirmative action preferences discussed early in this chapter.[389] This will not persuade those who deny this difference and believe that preferences are as normatively compelling as nondiscrimination. But others like me who view the distinction as fundamental (while conceding that it can blur at the edges) should favor a strong presumption that the value of nondiscrimination against groups that society believes need special constitutional protection must trump the value of private ordering. With this constraint satisfied, the law should accommodate fully disclosed voluntary affirmative action preferences that do not discriminate against those groups for whom the Constitution demands the highest solicitude.

Whether voluntary affirmative action can survive under these conditions is an empirical question. Under this regime, a private educational institution wishing to prefer ethno-racial minority students or those suffering from disabilities for diversity, anticaste, or other reasons could presumably satisfy both conditions, as could a private employer wishing to favor such minorities or the disabled. But an institution or employer that wanted to favor whites would violate the second condition. Although whites are protected by the same nondiscrimination principle that protects everyone else, they do not enjoy the highest level of protection that the Constitution owes ethno-racial minorities and thus could not qualify for an exception to the presumptive ban on even private preferences.

I have explained why preferences by public entities differ normatively and empirically from preferences adopted by private ones, and why the law should treat them differently. This means barring government-sponsored preferences except in the relatively narrow remedial situations that the courts now permit, while permitting private ones that can satisfy the two conditions just discussed. This distinction places great weight on the "state action" line, and some will say that the weight is more than it can bear. Nevertheless, the liberal goal of individual autonomy demands that it be drawn, and the courts long ago grew accustomed to doing so. The line can be blurry when, as with subsidies, the public and private spheres converge. One can certainly argue that courts have drawn it poorly in particular cases. That, however, is a different question than whether the line should be drawn at all. I hope I have convinced the reader that it should.

CONCLUSION

It would be comforting if the arguments about preferences on one side or the other were compelling and conclusive, but in truth they are not. Most advocates of affirmative action, one suspects, feel some discomfort at the tension (if not contradiction) that the policy creates with the values of individualism and merit that command such powerful, almost universal allegiance in American culture. We can see this in much of the dissimulation about affirmative action[390] and in the support by many advocates for a more targeted and temporary policy.

On the other side, even the vast majority of Americans who oppose affirmative action in principle also exhibit some ambivalence about it, seeking to hedge their bets against the dread possibility that social institutions without affirmative action would be almost lily-white or would further inflame the sense of injustice that many blacks already feel and that most whites acknowledge. In their more candid moments, the opponents may concede that merit is to some degree in the eye of the beholder and that American society has sometimes compromised the merit principle when it kept a group down or gave a group some political advantage. Opponents may also acknowledge that the alternative to existing affirmative action programs, at least in higher education, may be something worse because of institutions' determination to reshuffle the deck or dissemble until they get the demographic representation they want. Finally, opponents may recognize that our system of pluralist, interest-group politics is just that, a politics of *groups*—one in which individuals seek politically allocated benefits by aligning themselves with others who they think are similar in relevant respects.

But to say that the arguments over affirmative action are more evenly balanced than most disputants will admit is not to say that these arguments are equally persuasive. The debate over affirmative action is not simply about how the law should allocate scarce resources and opportunities, important as that allocation decision obviously is. An even greater stake, important in voluntary programs as well, is how society should encourage us to think of ourselves, organize ourselves, and present ourselves to others. Viewed this way, the issue is whether, for example, society should promote policies and norms that encourage individuals and groups to compete with one another in comparative victimization, with all of the demoralization, distortion, and dependency that this kind of competition tends to foster. Shaping and communicating these self-understandings, incentives, and interactions are among the most vital functions both of law[391] and of the informal social norms with which law interacts.[392]

Race is perhaps the worst imaginable category around which to organize group competition and social relations more generally. At the risk of belaboring the obvious, racial categories in law have played an utterly pernicious and destructive role throughout human history. This incontrovertible fact should arouse wonder at the logic of those who view racial preferences as no more troubling than athletic scholarships,[393] and at the hubris of those who imagine that we can distinguish clearly enough between invidious and benign race discrimination to engrave this distinction into our constitutional order.[394] Vast human experience mocks this comforting illusion, as does the fact that most Americans, including many minorities, think racial preferences are invidious, not benign. Whether benignly intended or not, using the category of race—which many affirmative action proponents depict both as socially constructed and as primordial and immutable—to distribute advantage and disadvantage tends to ossify the fluid, forward-looking political identities that a robust democratic spirit inspires and requires. Justice Blackmun's earnest hope that we could get beyond race by emphasizing it[395] has not been borne out.

Quite the contrary. Today, ironically, the proponents of affirmative action have the greatest stake in infusing our private and public discourse with a relentlessly racialist rhetoric and sensibility that, in my view, deform the debate and impede further progress. This vested interest in racialism often deploys the diversity ideal in a dubious way. Christopher Lasch observed that "'[d]iversity'—a slogan that looks attractive on the face of it—has come to mean the opposite of what it appears to mean. In practice, diversity turns out to legitimate a new dogmatism, in which rival minorities take shelter behind a set of beliefs impervious to rational discussion."[396]

Let us come at the problem of racial preferences in another way. Suppose that we stood behind John Rawls's famous veil of ignorance in order to frame rules of justice for our society.[397] Suppose further that we knew only three things about the society: that legally countenanced race consciousness had caused incalculable suffering and injustice in the past; that the society still contained many inequalities, some (but not all) of them caused by racism; and that it was seeking to redress these inequalities through various individual and collective actions. Finally, suppose (as the veil image and logic invite us to do) that we were ignorant of our own demographic traits and thus could not frame the rules opportunistically. Under these conditions,[398] how likely is it that we would adopt a rule permitting the government to use race as the basis for allocating scarce resources and opportunities? I think that we would view such a rule as terribly misguided,[399] and that almost any other plausibly fair distribution rule would strike us as both wiser and more just.

Even as traditionally defined, race's correlation with social disadvantage is weaker than it once was, and there is every sign that it will weaken further in the future.[400] By almost any measure, and despite frequent denials of this fact, racism in the United States has declined dramatically in recent decades.[401] Those accused (however unfairly) of racism and racial insensitivity must propitiate public opinion through public rituals of apology and self-abasement—like the earnest District of Columbia official who felt obliged to resign after a barrage of criticism for having used the word "niggardly" in a correct manner.[402] Data from the 2000 census will likely confirm that this decline in racism, which has been occurring since at least World War II, is accelerating. The effects of this decline are apparent everywhere. The income of young, intact black families already approaches the income of demographically similar white families. On almost every other social indicator, the black-white gap has narrowed significantly.[403] For young black women, the gaps have largely disappeared.[404]

Even these comparisons understate the prospects for closing the black-white gaps in the future, for several reasons. First, much of racism's cruel legacy is permanently impounded in the low education and income levels of retirement-age blacks who grew up under Jim Crow and who, economically speaking, bear little resemblance to their better-educated children and grandchildren. Second, blacks are considerably younger than whites on average and thus are less likely to have reached their peak earning years. Even in residential housing where black isolation has remained stubbornly high, the long decline in residential segregation nationally seems to have continued in the 1990s, particularly in the fastest-growing population areas.[405]

My point, emphatically, is not to deny that appalling inequalities of opportunity persist;[406] no informed person could possibly do so with a straight face. Rather, it is to insist that race today is a poor proxy for the conditions affirmative action is supposed to remedy and that it is steadily becoming an ever cruder and more misleading proxy as the number of multiracial Americans increases and as intragroup differentiations proliferate. At some point, the arbitrariness of the traditional race-as-proxy-for-egregious-disadvantage becomes so unmistakable and insupportable that it must fail legally, politically, and morally.

Each of the race-related changes I have just discussed adds to the already heavy burden of showing that preferences are also "narrowly tailored"—even assuming, contrary to the earlier analysis, that they can be shown to implement a compelling governmental interest in diversity.[407] The Supreme Court has cast serious doubt on whether race preferences can still meet this demanding constitutional test. As I have tried to show, this doubt is well justified.

On a strictly consequentialist view of affirmative action, reasonable people will surely assess its costs and benefits differently. These differences will reflect not only people's diverse values but also their empirical uncertainty on at least two important points: first, how much of blacks' progress is due to affirmative action, as distinct from migration to better jobs in the North, improved education, reduced discrimination, and other factors; and second, how segregated American society would be if mandatory affirmative action were now eliminated. In some cases, the consequentialist verdict seems quite clear—and clearly negative. For example, affirmative action's benefits in the spectrum licensing and minority business set-aside programs discussed earlier seem so marginal if not irrelevant to any defensible conception of social justice that they are almost certainly outweighed by the cynicism and abuse (and possible inefficiency) that have widely discredited such programs. Most racial gerrymandering practices under the Voting Rights Act also fail a consequentialist test, not just a constitutional one, albeit for quite different reasons.[408] As we shall see in the next chapter, class-based and race-based preferences designed to integrate housing also seem to have had disappointing, not to say corrupting, effects.[409] One could cite many other examples along the same lines.[410]

Affirmative action in initial[411] hiring and college admissions presents much closer cases, for it is in these areas that the evidence best supports the view that blacks as a group gain more from preferences than whites as a group lose. As we saw, these are precisely the areas in which considerable internal pressure, self-interested as well as ideological, would remain to maintain or increase existing levels of diversity, at least if voluntary affirmative action were constitutionally permissible.[412] Proponents of affirmative action hope, in Hollinger's words, that we can avoid "mistaking a tactic for a truth."[413] But after four decades of affirmative action, this understandable hope remains a vain one. The diversity rationale has transformed a temporary, limited tactic into an almost theological orthodoxy that skin color per se confers diversity value, an orthodoxy affirmed by many elites who should, and do, know better. This is not the first time that hard cases and wishful thinking made bad law and policy.

I have explained why this comparison of group gains and losses from affirmative action, while significant as far as it goes, is both misleading and even irrelevant when we consider how most Americans (black and white) conceive of themselves and compete with each other, how the ethnic composition of the United States is changing so much faster than the law, and how short-term group benefits can turn out to be long-term group costs. For better *and* for worse, and recognizing the complications and ambiguities, American culture remains highly individualistic and liberal in its values and premises, even at some sacrifice (where compromise is necessary) to its goal of substantive equality.[414] One need not ignore the illiberal strands in our tangled history, which enslaved, excluded, and subordinated members of despised groups[415] in order to conclude that racial preferences increasingly compromise our deeply engrained but incompletely realized commitment to legal-formal equality. The progress of this principle has advanced only through long and heroic struggle. It has served Americans well—even though, tragically, it has not yet served all of us equally well.

CHAPTER 6

Residential Neighborhoods: Subsidizing and Mandating Diversity

Using the law to promote diversity in residential communities is probably more difficult than promoting it in any other public policy domain. Many reasons for this difficulty arise from the distinctive nature of housing markets, which in turn reflects the unique ethos that surrounds housing in American culture. Other problems are endemic to public law generally. In this chapter I discuss how the law has defined and handled the goal of residential diversity, a project in which the courts have taken a remarkable degree of policy initiative rather than simply reacting to or implementing the policies of politicians and bureaucrats.

This chapter is divided into five sections. In order to frame the discussion that follows, the first section sketches the nature of housing markets and the regulatory context that shapes and constrains residential diversity policies. The second examines the actual extent of America's residential diversity, finding much racial and social class diversity *across* residential communities but far less diversity *within* them. Here we see how Americans, as individuals and as communities, actually define the residential diversity they seek in the market. The third section discusses how various theorists have formulated an ideal of residential diversity.

The fourth section, the heart of this chapter, is historical-empirical. I use three protracted litigations to show how governmental entities deploy law to pursue and instantiate the diversity ideal—almost always as a way to remedy past and continuing discrimination. The first, *Mount Laurel*,[1] began as a state court challenge to income-based discrimination in suburban housing under New Jersey law, but morphed into a permanent regulatory program to promote affordable housing in all developing towns. The other two litigations, *Gautreaux*[2] and *Yonkers*,[3] were federal court challenges to the placement of public housing in areas where racial minorities were already concentrated. Because these cases took quite different remedial paths, they invite comparison.

The concluding section distills from these case studies several lessons for efforts to increase residential diversity. Litigation against recalcitrant communities is a crude, costly, often counterproductive tool for diversifying them. Resistance to diversity is greatest when communities think that the government is forcing on them members of a social class who cannot afford the neighborhood housing. The government can minimize this resistance by providing new entrants with rent-equivalents that they can use, with the aid of mobility professionals, to negotiate quietly with landlords on a unit-by-unit basis.

NATURE AND REGULATION OF HOUSING MARKETS

This section provides a schematic account of the highly complex, diversified, fragmented, and intensely competitive residential housing market.[4] In 1999, there were 119 million units in the nation's housing stock. Of these, about 12% were vacant, 59% were owner-occupied, and 29% were rentals. That year, construction began of more than 1.6 million privately owned housing units (three-quarters of them single-family houses); moreover, 5.1 million existing one-family houses were sold and 225,000 apartments were completed and rented. In 2000, home ownership reached 67.5%, with 69.8 million homeowners.[5]

The residential housing industry, broadly defined, consists of literally millions of firms, most of them small and specialized. Home assemblers include homebuilders, contractors, home manufacturers and their dealers, and mobile home producers. These assemblers procure their materials from a network of specialized wholesalers and retailers that distribute the materials of a huge number of manufacturers and processors. Land acquisition, preparation, and construction involve real estate developers, brokers, advertisers and marketers, lawyers, title insurance companies, zoning officials and experts, surveyors, designers, civil engineers, and possibly land planners and landscape architects. Much on-site construction work is performed by specialty subcontractors. Financing needed by builders, land wholesalers, developers, and buyers of completed sites and units is available through an array of lending institutions. Operation of apartments may involve superintendents, management firms, and maintenance workers.

The supply side of the market is risky, and profits are commensurate with this risk. Construction schedules depend on weather, deliveries, bureaucratic delays, and unions. Builders often work with thin capitalization, much of which comes from large financial institutions with great leverage over them. The industry's financing and costs, like consumer demand, are sensitive to the business cycle in general and to interest rates in particular. An immense stock of existing housing looms over and competes with the market for new units. Builders, developers, and contractors are in effect tied to specific land parcels and regulated by local building codes and zoning rules that are highly discretionary and whose administration depends on local knowledge and influence.[6] Although builders and developers have some exit power, their businesses tend to be territorially fixed and captive to local conditions.[7]

The distinctive character of housing and the regulatory environment that constrains it make the demand side of the market well informed, competitive, and deliberate. The typical homeowner is very undiversified in an economic sense. Housing represents the single most costly item that most consumers will ever purchase (or rent) and becomes by far their greatest asset. Homeowners or buyers usually expect to remain in a unit for a long time (even though Americans move every six years on average).[8] Housing is among Americans' most important sources of enjoyment, security, and emotional well-being. Not surprisingly, then, Americans tend to shop for housing conservatively and carefully. We search out alternatives and compete against others for the most desirable units. Perhaps more so than for any other economic decision, consumers usually obtain considerable market information before making their decisions. The Internet is steadily reducing consumers' search costs while improving their ability to make informed decisions. Once a home is acquired, real or perceived threats to its value can create genuine financial and psychological risks to the family that owns it.

If homeowners are financially undiversified, their housing choices in the market are just the opposite. Housing demand is so individualized that the industry must offer an exceptionally wide range of units in terms of price, size, quality, amenities, and type. Mass-produced standardized units are often difficult to market because of the variations in consumer demands. Housing units increasingly are single-family homes, and more of these are custom-tailored to the desires of their first occupants. The era of Levittown-type cookie-cutter homes is over; today, even builders of tract homes usually offer potential buyers a range of different models and options from which to choose.

Residential housing is probably regulated more heavily than any comparably diverse, fragmented, and competitive market. Although much of this regulation—especially zoning, building codes, development standards, tax programs, and other exactions and fees that shift infrastructure costs to developers—is local, all levels of government intervene in this market. They do so in many ways and with different policy goals, so it is not surprising that their interventions often have conflicting purposes. Some regulations are designed to reduce housing costs (e.g., financing disclosure requirements), some are designed to increase costs (e.g., the Davis-Bacon Act,[9] which stifles wage competition). Some subsidize relatively well-off homeowners (e.g., the Federal Housing Administration mortgage interest deduction), others subsidize groups thought to have special housing needs or claims to assistance (e.g., veterans, the elderly, the poor, and the disabled). Some hope to revitalize declining urban neighborhoods (e.g., subsidies to inner-city housing), others promote suburbanization (e.g., the Fair Housing Act of 1968).[10] Some are intended to reduce sprawl (e.g., growth controls), others encourage it (e.g., large-lot zoning and duty-to-serve-all-comers rules). Some look to reduce negative externalities like pollution and noise (e.g., environmental and nuisance laws), others encourage them (e.g., development subsidies). Some seek to reduce health risks (e.g., building codes), others increase such risks (e.g., industrial development bonds). Some would entrench existing residential patterns (e.g., rent control), others facilitate mobility (e.g., tax rollovers of gains on sales of homes). Some defer to the desire to exclude poor people (e.g., large-lot zoning), others constrain those desires (e.g., inclusionary zoning).

The conflicting *purposes* of these policies say nothing about their conflicting *effects*. This distinction is important because housing policies, mediated as they are by robust market forces and powerful political constituencies, often have unanticipated effects that deviate sharply from their animating purposes. New York City rent regulation is a particularly notorious and well-documented example. This scheme subsidizes more than one million units. Many of them are occupied by middle-class families fortunate or wily enough to have rent-controlled or rent-stabilized units at the expense of others, including low-income families whose access to affordable units is reduced because of the scheme's development disincentives.[11] The *Mount Laurel* case study provides a second example of unanticipated effects: the conflict between exclusionary zoning and other laws often justified by environmental and aesthetic considerations, and the goal of improving access for low-income people to the suburbs by reducing their housing costs.[12] A third example, striking because of its magnitude, is the policy of subsidizing home ownership but not tenancy, which probably exacerbates the racial segregation that civil rights programs seek to combat.[13] The Office of Management and Budget estimated that the mortgage interest deduction alone cost $67.5 billion a year by 2000,[14] with the tax benefits concentrated among high-income owners in a few large metropolitan areas.[15]

For present purposes, my interest is in the particular regulatory policies that are driven by an affirmative commitment to one or another diversity ideal. These policies are few and far between because the ideal of residential diversity, which I elaborate below, is weak compared to two other, less integrative norms: the nondiscrimination principle and what I call classism.

These two norms require explication. Both federal and local legislation seek to implement a policy against housing discrimination. The Fair Housing Act of 1968 ("FHA"), also known as Title VIII, prohibits discrimination in housing on the basis of race, color, religion, sex, family status, age, national origin, or handicap.[16] Some state and local fair housing laws extend protection to other characteristics, like sexual orientation.[17] Such laws assume that one should make one's housing choices in markets unimpeded by the bias of others. From this nondiscrimination perspective, whatever diversity is produced by independent market choices is optimal.

In contrast, classism countenances discrimination on the basis of wealth, income, social class, or perceived ability to pay.[18] Classism is not only descriptive but normative as well; in a capitalist society it seems like the natural order of things.[19] A classist believes that one improves one's housing by ascending a ladder, reaching higher rungs only when one's ability to pay rises. Government, in this view, has no business inserting people who have not climbed the ladder in the customary way into a neighborhood they cannot afford among people who can afford it through their own (or family) efforts.[20] Such government action, Nathan Glazer writes, is "opposed by the strongest motives that move men and women, their concern for family, children, [and] property."[21] These motives animate virtually all Americans regardless of race or ethnicity.

The case studies detailed in this chapter demonstrate the truth of Glazer's assertion. They illustrate the immense difficulties that arise when courts translate the nondiscrimination principle into an affirmative mandate to reconstruct residential neighborhoods that, like almost all neighborhoods in America, are deeply committed to classism. The nondiscrimination principle, which is also very widely held, does not translate well into an affirmative judicial mandate to reconstruct residential neighborhoods on more diverse lines. The judicial tools for undertaking this reconstruction are clumsy at best, and often perverse; they can even delegitimate judicial authority and the diversity ideal it invokes. In *Mount Laurel*, the New Jersey Supreme Court invoked a principle that it created out of whole cloth and that enjoys little political or moral support in an individualistic, market-oriented society—equal access to suburban communities regardless of ability to pay. In *Yonkers*, a defiant community and a strong-willed judge transmogrified the shining ideal of diversity as a remedy for past wrongs into a costly, protracted struggle over which of them would control the community's future, with the market serving as a silent, disciplining referee. The verdict in *Yonkers* seems clear: everyone lost. Even the rule of law emerged in a weakened state. In *Gautreaux*, a similar debilitating struggle eventually produced a more hopeful solution, one that seeks to promote diversity by using the law to work imaginatively with the market, not, as in *Yonkers*, against it.

RESIDENTIAL DIVERSITY TODAY

This section describes the extent of racial segregation and isolation in neighborhoods today. It then considers this phenomenon in light of four likely contributing causes: racial prejudice, traditional residential clustering, the complex dynamics of white flight, and classism.

In 1993, sociologists Douglas Massey and Nancy Denton published an important book about racial segregation in residential communities entitled, provocatively, *American Apartheid*.[22] To anyone who values community diversity, their findings were alarming. Relying mostly on 1980 census data and employing a variety of segregation measures, they found that "a substantial and marked decline in black segregation" occurred in certain smaller metropolitan areas between 1970 and 1980 but that segregation "continue[d] unabated" in the largest ones.[23] Based on their limited analysis of 1990 census data, they found that segregation dissipated very slowly in northern cities during the 1980s and that "modest but significant declines" had occurred in six of twelve southern cities.[24]

Not included in Massey and Denton's study are preliminary data from the 2000 census that show some reduction in minority segregation, particularly in high-growth areas. The data also suggest that the suburbs of major metropolitan areas are becoming much more racially and ethnically diverse. Minorities now constitute 27% of their population, up from 19% in 1990, with the greatest increase occurring, again, in high-growth areas.[25] Over half of Asians, almost half of Hispanics, and 39% of blacks in these metropolitan areas live in the suburbs, with Hispanics showing the greatest increases.[26] Nevertheless, blacks' residential isolation (one measure of segregation) is greater than that of other minority groups, and has declined more slowly than for any other minority group, including nonblack immigrants.[27] The racial isolation that the preliminary 2000 census data suggest clearly has a number of causes, but there is little consensus on their relative significance.

American Apartheid has been widely praised and much cited.[28] Nonetheless, even some of the authors' admirers have challenged their methodology, interpretations, and prescriptions, as well as the book's claim that racial prejudice is the overwhelming cause of residential segregation.[29]

Racial Prejudice

The history of racial prejudice, enforced by both public policy and the practices of private developers, brokers, and housing consumers, surely explains much of today's segregation.[30] Although racism's extent and intensity have declined markedly in recent decades, the residential patterns it produced have great staying power. Because people make large investments in their housing and plan to occupy it for many years, the effects of individual, group, and neighborhood choices may persist much longer than the racial attitudes that originally influenced them. Neighborhood demographics constantly change, of course, but the process is usually quite gradual.

Clustering

Much of the observed racial isolation might be caused by other, less invidious factors and even benign ones. Family composition, income, property and income tax rates, access to jobs and transit, and other seemingly neutral market factors powerfully affect housing choices. Ethnic groups in the United States have always clustered together in enclaves until they felt comfortable in the dominant culture—but they have also clustered afterward to some extent. For straightforward economic and social reasons, as well as for more elusive psychological ones, much of this clustering would occur even in the absence of discrimination, as the clustering of even higher-income Latinos and Asians today suggests.[31] For small entrepreneurs trying to gain a market foothold, ethnic affinities can create a natural customer base. This is especially true for those who provide food, clothing, housing, and personal services for which knowledge of the ethnic group's distinctive preferences, speech patterns, and customs is highly valued. Ethnic networks in the community constitute efficient sources of information about religious, social, and economic opportunities. For many products and services, ethnic enclaves also generate scale economies such as personal and business reputation, whose reliability and value depend in large part on the number of people who know the individual or firm from repeated, face-to-face contacts, family ties, and back-fence gossip.

Perhaps ironically, America's ethnic diversity contributes to this clustering. Pietro Nivola contends that the flow of immigrants to American cities helps to explain the greater urban sprawl compared with European cities, and that this sprawl facilitates clustering even as it reduces population density.[32] People from very diverse backgrounds, Nivola says, want to live near those with whom they have ethnic ties and choose to spread out rather than live close to those who are different. "Plainly stated, a good deal of sprawl in this country may be a necessary complement to its extreme multiculturalism."[33] But the racial and ethnic clustering in neighborhoods is more complex even than this; for example, economic segregation is growing *within* racial groups.[34]

The Dynamics of White Flight

More than three decades ago, economist Thomas Schelling analyzed a social process that leads ineluctably to more racial segregation than people actually want.[35] Individual choices in the housing market, Schelling demonstrated, can transform small differences in groups' attitudes about neighborhood diversity into relatively high levels of segregation. Under such conditions, according to Schelling's analysis, almost all configurations will be unstable and vulnerable to rapid change: "A moderate urge to avoid small-minority status may cause a nearly integrated pattern to unravel and highly segregated neighborhoods to form."[36] Unless blacks and whites do not have any preferences about neighborhood composition or their preferences happen to converge on the identical integration level, the unraveling process—also called "tipping"[37]—will ensue and segregated housing patterns will persist or even grow. In fact, however, the groups' preferences differ significantly. Nathan Glazer has noted, "the neighborhood that blacks would like, 50 percent black, is one that most whites would move away from, making it close to 100 percent black."[38]

Efforts to arrest this seemingly inexorable process almost always fail. As Schelling emphasized, the dynamics of flight in such communities reflect what game theorists call a collective action problem that rationality deepens rather than solves. Each family, prompted by self-interest, will act in ways that leave it worse off (fleeing) than the family would have been had it agreed with its neighbors to do what would make them all better off (remain). The problem arises because such an agreement is hard to enforce. Each family has an incentive to defect from the agreement unless it knows that all families will comply, yet all the other families have the same incentive to defect. Thus a white family may be perfectly happy to remain in a town into which black families are moving. But if it thinks that (1) other white families are ready to flee, (2) it has no way to prevent them from doing so, and (3) it will be worse off if they do flee, then the white family will want to flee first, and no agreement by others to remain will dissuade the family from doing so.

Can the law solve this problem by enforcing an agreement to maintain racial balance? Probably not, *Starrett City*[39] suggests. Starrett City, a very large development in New York, aimed at a middle-class market and was heavily subsidized by the state and federal governments. It maintained a "managed waiting list" for admissions designed to ensure that 70% of its occupants were white. Using separate waiting lists for whites and blacks, Starrett City let apartments sit empty and kept prospective black tenants waiting until it could find white families to fill the quota. Supported by some strong advocates of housing integration, Starrett City claimed that its system, which community leaders had demanded as the price of overcoming their opposition to the project, was essential to forestall white flight and maintain integration. Indeed, the state housing agency had subsidized the vacancies resulting from this system to help Starrett City attract and retain middle-income (mostly white) tenants who would only move to the project if they were assured that it would not "tip" racially, causing other whites to flee. In 1988, the United States Supreme Court let stand a Second Circuit decision invalidating the quota system under the Fair Housing Act even though the system's purpose was to prevent white flight and promote racial integration.[40]

The metaphors of white flight and unraveling, however, are a bit misleading, or at least are incomplete insofar as the actual dynamics of racial segregation in housing are concerned. Ingrid Gould Ellen, an analyst of neighborhood transitions, has shown that racial composition affects entry decisions more than exit decisions: "white avoidance"—the decisions of whites living in all-white neighborhoods *not to move into* integrated neighborhoods—contributes more to the racial composition of those neighborhoods than white flight. She has found that this is also true, albeit to a much smaller extent, of black avoidance of all-white neighborhoods.[41]

The analyses of Schelling and Ellen raise an extremely important question going to the very essence of racism: is the fact that one has a preference about the optimal level of racial or ethnic integration in one's community proof of racism or ethnic bias? To put the question more provocatively: would even white persons who want to live in a neighborhood that is 90% black, or black persons who want their neighborhood to be 90% white, be guilty of racism simply because they are not indifferent to the racial composition of the neighborhood or because they prefer a mix that differs from the demographic distribution of society as a whole?

There is no agreed-upon answer to this question but some answers are more convincing than others. In thinking about this question, we must be mindful of Schelling's ultimate irony: one who wants to live in an integrated neighborhood, or (to avoid a circular definition) a neighborhood in which no resident has any preference concerning its racial composition, cannot be indifferent to the race of her neighbors lest she end up with more segregation than she (and perhaps they) wants. For so long as the neighbors have preferences about this, their preferences (if different from hers) can trigger a process that will remorselessly generate less integration than she (and perhaps they) would like. If merely having a preference for some degree of racial diversity indicts one as a racist, then most blacks, and not just whites, are guilty—including those who desire a high level of integration.[42]

The point of Schelling's analysis, and my use of it, is *not* to deny the existence of racism in housing decisions but rather to suggest how misleading it would be to infer racism simply from one's choice of neighborhood. In fact, the problem is even more complex. To see why, we need look no farther than Jonathan Rieder's fine ethnography of Canarsie, a working-class Brooklyn neighborhood into which blacks were beginning to move when he studied it in the early 1980s.[43] Canarsie's resistance in the face of what it saw as convulsive change is a finely etched and dismaying portrait of racism—a racism so explicit in the residents' words that one need not infer it from their conduct. Rieder also shows, however, that even in Canarsie, some motives had less to do with racial hostility per se than with anxieties familiar to all Americans, black or white, that arise out of their predictions about how the independent choices of their existing neighbors will affect them, their children, their neighborhood, their vulnerability to crime, and their property values. Nor are such predictions limited to whites. One would expect middle-class blacks, no less than whites, to resist the building of nearby housing projects or the in-migration of poor people, and for the same reasons.[44] The fact that these predictions become self-fulfilling prophecies, or might have proved wrong had not so many made and acted on them, is tragic but in Schelling's sense, irrelevant. The people doing the predicting are not social scientists, and the accuracy of their predictions depends on the choices of others who are keenly aware of white flight and unwilling to behave heroically in the face of risk.

The notion that race per se plays only a secondary role in causing racial and economic change in urban neighborhoods is a central finding of a study published in 1984 by Richard Taub and associates. The Taub study used statistical techniques and cross-community analyses to compare eight neighborhoods in Chicago that varied in crime rates, racial stability, and housing market trends,[45] and it sought to disentangle the complex factors that cause neighborhoods to tip. It found that individual residents make the decisions contributing to neighborhood change largely on the basis of their perceptions of the risk of crime and deterioration; that both blacks and whites know that these problems tend to be more severe in minority-concentrated neighborhoods; that racial stereotypes, while operative, influence these decisions less than the realities of crime and deterioration; and that "once forces are set in motion for the withdrawal of white residents, there is little individuals acting alone can do to reverse the pattern, nor are there likely to be many who would be willing to try."[46] The Taub study concluded that "[e]ven with higher levels of tolerance and a substantial black middle class, some sort of firm undergirding is necessary to allow citizens to take hold."[47]

Ingrid Gould Ellen's research confirms a similar race-based neighborhood stereotyping model. According to this model, blacks and whites alike associate predominantly black neighborhoods with high crime, poor schools, and declining property values, and on this basis they decline (if they have a choice) to move there.[48] Sound policymaking requires a distinction between aversion to black neighborhoods and aversion to blacks as individuals, but doing so, as Ellen emphasizes, is both morally and empirically complex.

Indeed, integrating residential neighborhoods is even more difficult. The

Taub study found that corporations, universities, and other institutions with major fixed assets and stakes in neighborhoods can provide the necessary signals to trigger a virtuous cycle that sometimes enables even neighborhoods with large low-income populations to remain racially integrated.[49] On the other hand, Celebration, a planned community in Florida that went to extraordinary lengths to foster racial diversity, abjectly failed to achieve it. Celebration's experience suggests that even strong institutional commitment is often insufficient to overcome the forces impelling suburban segregation. Despite pro-integration advertising, an integrated sales force, inclusion of affordable units near more expensive homes, and even a buyers' lottery to prevent racial discrimination, only 1% of Celebration residents are black and 7% are Hispanic in a county that is 6% black and 29% Hispanic.[50]

Classism

Classism explains much residential segregation. Indeed, the distinction between racism and classism is pivotal. American popular culture, morality, and law treat them very differently, particularly as concerns residential choices. Although racism is categorically illegal in all but the most private contexts, the law bars classism only when it works to deny voting rights, access to the courts, legal counsel in serious criminal cases, and a few other basic incidents of common citizenship.[51] In all other respects, the law protects, or even promotes, classism.[52] Housing is no exception. Residential isolation by class is the norm, especially at the building or block level, and even advocates of class integration of communities seek to do so only at the level of the neighborhood or larger community.[53] Whereas many minorities live in predominantly white neighborhoods, unsubsidized lower-income people cannot afford to live in more affluent areas. Moreover, the federal government strongly reinforces this class stratification, "spending" more than twice as much on the mortgage interest deduction than on all housing programs for the poor, such as Section 8 rental vouchers and public housing, discussed below.[54]

Distinguishing racism from classism is no easy matter. Racial isolation in neighborhoods is overdetermined. With race and income highly correlated,[55] minorities and the poor are often the same people and thus the targets of both racism and classism. Racism and classism, moreover, may prompt identical behavior. A decision that disadvantages a racial minority may have been motivated by classism rather than racism.[56] Still, classism cannot fully explain blacks' residential isolation; some analysts think it only explains a small part.[57] Solving this causal puzzle requires, at a minimum, a much clearer definition of classism and its normatively proper limits than we now possess. Another complication is that racists can try to escape the moral censure (and sometimes illegality) that racism now arouses by couching their words in more acceptable classist terms. Finally, there is a problem of asymmetric information between whites who already live in a community and blacks seeking to enter it. Well-publicized government efforts to increase residential diversity by building affordable housing projects may lead some whites to assume that all blacks moving into their community are government-subsidized and of a lower social class, especially when the blacks cannot readily signal the contrary and the whites cannot easily ascertain the truth of the matter.[58] For this reason, subsidizing through vouchers, discussed below, may be preferable. After all, vouchers make it hard for anyone other than a landlord to identify who is being subsidized.

Whatever the precise mix of causes for racial isolation, it constitutes one of America's most serious social problems. Racial isolation practically ensures the continuation of inequalities in education, employment, culture, personal networks, freedom from crime, and the many other opportunities, amenities, and freedoms that are related to location. The interaction of classism and racism makes racial isolation in neighborhoods and attendant social inequalities both socially destructive and difficult to remedy. As the case studies will reveal, however, some solutions are more promising than others.

IDEALS OF RESIDENTIAL DIVERSITY

This section explores different visions of why communities do and *should* seek visual, functional, demographic, and other kinds of diversity. I discuss the visions advanced by four leading theorists of residential community that have influenced judges, politicians, interest groups, commentators, and the public. Along with the norms of nondiscrimination and classism, these ideals—localism (Charles Tiebout), demographic and activity diversity (Jane Jacobs), neighborhood connectivity (Andres Duany, Elizabeth Plater-Zyberk, and Jeff Speck—collectively representing the New Urbanism movement), and dispersal of low-income and minority communities to the suburbs (Anthony Downs)—help to shape the competing conceptions of neighborhood diversity that collided in *Mount Laurel, Gautreaux,* and *Yonkers.*

Charles Tiebout

In a famous 1956 article, economist Charles Tiebout proposed a model to account both for how individuals decide among the variety of communities in which they might choose to live, and for how different communities decide, through their local governments, which public goods and services to provide to their residents.[59] He addressed the free-rider problem that afflicts "public goods": everyone shares an incentive not to pay for goods such as clean air or police protection, if they can enjoy them without paying their costs. Because the market will not provide such goods, and government will be unable, for the same reason, to convince voter-taxpayers to pay for them, they will either be underprovided (relative to people's preferences) or not provided at all.[60]

Tiebout's innovation was to suggest that local governments might not be subject to the free-rider problem for a large class of public goods. Each community offers residents a distinctive package combining different types and levels of public goods and taxes, and potential residents "vote with their feet" for whichever package they prefer. This behavior, Tiebout argued, enables residents with similar taxing and spending preferences to group themselves in communities that satisfy them.[61] Subsequent research by others showed that intermunicipal differences in local taxes and spending are capitalized in housing prices, that zoning restrictions help to stabilize these arrangements and keep the poor from upsetting a community's equilibrium too much, and that the model must include political factors affecting a community's ability to make collective decisions of this kind.[62] For our purposes, Tiebout's model has an important, empirically demonstrable implication: in a society like the United States, which localizes taxing and spending decisions, people use their housing market choices to express their preferences for different kinds of communities.

Tiebout's choice model helps to explain why different communities permit diverse patterns of property use. In almost all communities, some combination of private developer, neighborhood group, and public zoning board decisions restricts numerous aspects of property use and activity, such as aesthetics, animal ownership, signage, subdivision, lot size, building materials, setbacks, commercial activity, household composition, and environmental controls. Courts, moreover, may augment these restrictions through nuisance law. Although the power of communities to impose such restrictions is limited by various constitutional, statutory, and other common law principles, they still enjoy broad discretion.[63] Property-use decisions, like decisions concerning taxes, spending, and public goods, are mostly left to individual communities. By allowing each community to reduce its *internal* diversity in property use and activity, the system enlarges the diversity *among* communities. Again, some trade-off between these diversity goals is inescapable.

Tiebout's choice model contrasts starkly with what Robert Ellickson and Vicki Been call a "Waring Blender model." In this model, each neighborhood would have all types of land uses and all types of households in proportion to its representation in the entire metropolitan area. Unlike Tiebout's model, the "Waring Blender model produces great diversity *within* neighborhoods, but no diversity *between* them, and thus may limit the variety of residential choices available to households."[64] In the case studies that follow, I explore this crucial distinction and the trade-offs that it entails.

Jane Jacobs

Jacobs is the most influential analyst of neighborhoods. Her 1961 book, *The Death and Life of Great American Cities*,[65] quickly achieved the status of a classic. A paean to diversity within and among urban neighborhoods, this book analyzed the conditions that generate and sustain diversity and rendered a withering indictment of the top-down, monochromatic (as Jacobs saw it) visions of urban planners. Jacobs's ideal of diversity revolved around the communities that she believed arise naturally and spontaneously in urban neighborhoods when they are left free to meet felt human needs defined by ordinary people from the bottom up. These needs include the desire for frequent and casual interactions, unexpected encounters, heterogeneous vistas, a jumble of mixed land uses, uncoordinated sidewalk activity, reduced auto traffic, a profusion of small neighborhood meeting places and institutions, buildings of varying age and composition, short blocks and frequent turnings, irregular lots, "eyes on the street" to look after children and assure safety, and density of population and activities.[66] Jacobs excoriated the urban renewal and massive highway construction projects that were substituting artificial, sterile, homogeneous, oversized, and predictable districts for these more natural conditions.[67]

In light of the analysis in the remainder of this chapter, it is significant that the diversities Jacobs extolled in her ideal neighborhoods had everything to do with the diversity of land uses, visual factors, and intensive human interactions, and little to do with the racial and class attributes of the denizens per se. This is not because Jacobs was indifferent to race and class integration; she clearly placed a very high value on it. But she thought that such integration results from the presence of *other* diversities. Absent those diversities, segregation will continue. If they can be encouraged, however, "no . . . slum need be perpetual."[68]

James Scott's critique of "high modernism" in city planning finds additional virtues in Jacobs's ideal of neighborhood diversity:

> While Jacobs makes a convincing case for mixed use and complexity by examining the micro-origins of public safety, civic trust, visual interest, and convenience, there is a larger argument to be made for cross-use and diversity. Like the diverse old-growth forest, a richly differentiated neighborhood . . . is, virtually by definition, a more resilient and durable

neighborhood. Economically, the diversity of its commercial assets . . . makes it less vulnerable to economic downturns. At the same time its diversity provides many opportunities for economic growth in upturns. Like monocropped forests, single-purpose districts, although they may initially catch a boom, are especially susceptible to stress. The diverse neighborhood is more sustainable.[69]

Economic stability, then, may be another benefit of Jacobs's vision of diverse land uses and organic neighborhood development.

New Urbanists

The architects, city planners, and other urbanologists who constitute the New Urbanism movement endorse some of Jacobs's diversity values but diverge from her in important respects—in part because of their preoccupation with suburban rather than city neighborhoods. The movement's leading exponents, Andres Duany, Elizabeth Plater-Zyberk, and Jeff Speck, identify the great vice as suburban sprawl that is caused by federal policy, local zoning laws, and the demands of the automobile. In its stead, they propose six fundamental rules for suburbs in their 2000 book, *Suburban Nation:* (1) a clear neighborhood center or focus; (2) pedestrian-friendly policies that place life's daily needs within walking distance; (3) a street network, preferably a grid, with relatively small blocks, straight streets, and connectivity of all compatible land uses; (4) narrow, versatile streets with trees; (5) mixed-use zoning that clusters buildings of similar size and ordinarily brings them close to the sidewalks; and (6) special siting for civic buildings, which represent the collective identity and aspirations of the community.[70]

Unlike Tiebout and Jacobs, New Urbanists explicitly denounce the income segregation of communities and of neighborhoods within communities. They advocate several measures designed to integrate affordable units into relatively wealthy blocks and neighborhoods. For example, they propose to scatter affordable units among market-rate units in a 1:10 ratio, and to eliminate restrictions on outbuildings and on apartments that are above or below stores.[71]

Anthony Downs

Anthony Downs, an innovative economist and real estate industry expert, has focused more than Jacobs and the New Urbanists on the social and economic evils of segregating communities by income and race. In a 1973 book entitled *Opening Up the Suburbs,* Downs detailed what has come to be known as the "geography of opportunity."[72] Facilitating the ability of low- and moderate-income people to move to more prosperous, largely white suburbs, he claimed, would increase their social and economic mobility and opportunities. In turn, this suburban diversity would ameliorate other conditions associated with recalcitrant inner-city poverty and eventually produce racial integration. More recently, analysts such as William Julius Wilson, Gerald Frug, Michael Schill, and Richard Thompson Ford have reached similar conclusions, though by somewhat different analytical paths.[73]

A broad consensus has long existed that greater residential mobility and access to suburban jobs for low-income families and racial minorities, especially blacks, is essential not only for them but also for American society as a whole. In this sense, residential diversity is a leading policy goal. What remains to be considered is what role law can and should play in pursuing it.

Of all the diversity ideals being actively debated in the area of housing policy, the most controversial and difficult are those relating to class and race and the relationship between them. A community's diversity ideals regarding the design, size, and cost of homes, the mix of publicly provided goods, services, and amenities, and the patterns of property use and activity are largely defined by people's individual choices in the housing market. These choices instantiate a kind of metadiversity ideal. Residential diversity should be a function of personal predilection, which no independent, communal ideal of diversity can override. Although ideals such as nondiscrimination against protected minorities, nuisance law, and environmental safety can trump individual choices and affect residential diversity, these ideals promote values other than diversity. Nondiscrimination, for example, may have the effect of increasing diversity but this is not its central justification.

Much the same is true of choices about the ethnic, racial, or class characteristics of one's neighbors. In selecting neighborhoods, individuals consider the kinds of people with whom they want to interact, taking into account whatever personal factors they deem relevant. With limited exceptions, the law enforces such choices. But it has sometimes formulated different diversity ideals regarding race or class, and then ordered communities to implement them. The following case studies provide examples.

THE LAW AND RESIDENTIAL DIVERSITY:
THREE CASE STUDIES

In the first section of this chapter I noted that the nondiscrimination principle embodied in fair housing laws is a constraint on all housing markets. The law, however, has sometimes gone beyond the nondiscrimination principle to impose an affirmative obligation on government to increase diversity in ways that judges, not markets, define and implement. The tasks of defining and implementing diversity, however, have proved far more difficult than the courts imagined. Their Herculean efforts have borne little fruit. Indeed, Promethean might be a more apt adjective, as their efforts have entailed compulsive persistence, mythic hubris, and tragic failure.

I illustrate these points by examining three examples of judicial policy-making aimed at increasing demographic diversity in housing. I begin with the epic *Mount Laurel* litigation,[74] which involved a state law remedy—first judicial, now administrative—for what the court viewed as class discrimination against low- and moderate-income families in suburban housing in New Jersey. By way of comparison, I discuss *Gautreaux*,[75] which challenged racial bias in Chicago's public housing projects and fashioned a different, more effective remedy aimed at both racial and class barriers to the migration of black families to Chicago's suburbs. The *Gautreaux* strategy devised a more successful, though not unproblematic, path largely through a remedy that relied more on market mechanisms and less on legal compulsion. Finally, drawing on my own fieldwork, I turn to the torturous *Yonkers* litigation, which I describe in much greater detail. Like *Gautreaux*, the *Yonkers* court found racism in the placement of public housing developments. Yet the *Yonkers* court failed to learn *Gautreaux*'s lesson, and decreed a remedy similar to one that the *Gautreaux* court originally ordered but ultimately found unavailing.

Mount Laurel

In the quarter-century since the initial decision, *Mount Laurel* has become the icon of legal, and especially judicial, approaches to the economic integration of communities in the face of classist practices.[76] In 1971, a group of low- and moderate-income families sued Mount Laurel, a sprawling, developing suburban township in New Jersey, claiming that its zoning practices excluded them from the community in violation of the state constitution. Exclusionary zoning practices take a variety of specific forms, including limitations on nonresidential uses or housing types, requirements for maximum building or occupant densities, and requirements for minimum lot sizes, building setbacks, or floor areas. Each type of exclusionary zoning has the effect, and often the purpose, of increasing housing costs, which inevitably reduce the number of affordable units for low-income persons.

The cost-increasing effect of exclusionary zoning creates a formidable obstacle to any legal challenge to such practices. First, as noted earlier, most Americans do not regard classist exclusions, as distinguished from racist ones, as a social problem.[77] They do not think it unjust if people live only in communities that they can afford.[78] Second, the law permits communities to pursue a variety of legitimate purposes (e.g., limiting pollution or congestion) through zoning techniques that sometimes have intended or unintended exclusionary effects. This means that even in a community that bars zoning for classist purposes, an effective legal challenge must show that the community's facially neutral, ostensibly legitimate purposes are in fact pretexts for a classist one.

Nevertheless, the trial court upheld the plaintiffs' claim in 1972, and three years later the New Jersey Supreme Court affirmed in what is called *Mount Laurel I*.[79] The court assumed that Mount Laurel's zoning was designed not to exclude the poor or minorities but to minimize the tax burdens occasioned by the additional public services that a more populous and congested community would require.[80] The court held that Mount Laurel had violated a state constitutional provision that required all police powers, including zoning, to promote the general welfare. Significantly, the court based its decision entirely on exclusionary zoning's adverse effects on general welfare, not on its racially discriminatory effects.[81]

> As a developing municipality, Mount Laurel must, by its land use regulations, make realistically possible the opportunity for an appropriate variety and choice of housing for all categories of people who may desire to live there, of course including those of low and moderate income. It must permit multi-family housing, without bedroom or similar restrictions, as well as small dwellings on very small lots, low cost housing of other types and, in general, high density zoning, without artificial and unjustifiable minimum requirements as to lot size, building size and the like, to meet the full panoply of these needs.[82]

The court went on to impose an affirmative duty on every developing municipality to bear its "fair share" of the regional burden, without defining this critical concept. It allowed Mount Laurel ninety days to amend its zoning system to correct the constitutional deficiencies. The court held that in the future a municipality would have the heavy burden of justifying its system once a plaintiff demonstrated that the system prevented the creation of affordable housing for low- and moderate-income families.[83]

The many procedural, substantive, and remedial uncertainties that *Mount Laurel I* failed to resolve unleashed a flood of litigation by would-be homeowners and builders seeking to invalidate municipal zoning restrictions. In 1981, the New Jersey Supreme Court consolidated six of these, ordering the litigants to participate in a highly unusual three-day legislative-type hearing and to answer twenty-four questions put to them in advance.

Two years later, the court issued its decision in *Mount Laurel II*.[84] This ruling surely is one of the most extraordinary judicial opinions ever written. In scathing terms, the court denounced the state's developing municipalities for their blatantly exclusionary zoning laws and their determination to exclude the poor.[85] The court chastised the state legislature for failing to protect the constitutional rights of poor people.[86] Additionally, the court criticized the lower courts for having allowed the municipalities to delay and defeat the plaintiffs' *Mount Laurel I* claims through endless and costly litigation.[87] More than ten years after the trial court's order in *Mount Laurel I,* the New Jersey Supreme Court's ruling had not been implemented.[88]

In order to cut through this morass, the court performed what Rutgers Law School professor John Payne calls a "gut rehab" of *Mount Laurel I.*[89] Abandoning most of the decision, it prescribed a remarkably detailed set of rules that municipalities and the lower courts must follow in implementing its order. The court divided New Jersey into three areas, assigned a trial judge to each, and ordered that any future *Mount Laurel* litigation was to be assigned to the judge according to the area in which the case arose. The judge, assisted by special masters, was to determine the numerical fair shares of affordable housing for each municipality located in a growth area (no longer just developing municipalities) in each housing region. The court left key regulatory definitions to future elaboration based on the State Development Guide Plan (SDGP), a regional planning document that a state agency had drawn up several years earlier for more limited purposes.

For municipalities to meet their fair-share obligations, the court noted, they might have to do more than eliminate excessive zoning, subdivision restrictions, and exactions that impeded the construction of affordable housing:

> Affirmative governmental devices should be used . . . including lower-income density bonuses and mandatory set-asides. Furthermore the municipality should cooperate with the developer's attempts to obtain federal subsidies. For instance, where federal subsidies depend on the municipality providing certain municipal tax treatment allowed by state statutes for lower-income housing, the municipality should make a good faith effort to provide it.[90]

Municipalities had to offer "affirmative inducements to make the opportunity real," including subsidies.[91] It would no longer suffice for a municipality to rezone land to permit low-income housing as well as other, more profitable and more expensive housing.[92]

Most important, the court evidenced a firm resolve to use the profit motive to power the reform process. Lower courts, it held, must allow a direct remedy to builders who propose projects that include a "substantial amount of low-income housing"[93] consistent with "sound zoning and planning concepts, including its environmental impact."[94] Such builders could legally challenge the validity of municipal laws and conduct. If they prevailed, they could proceed with their projects, which usually included "inclusionary zoning" provisions requiring that at least 20% of the units be affordable to lower-income families.

While warning the lower courts to prevent abuses of this "builder's remedy," the New Jersey Supreme Court surely anticipated that this would prove to be the most powerful lever for change under *Mount Laurel*. The court's predictions proved accurate—developers rather than poor people or nonprofit groups have filed nearly all of the subsequent lawsuits.[95] In effect, the court empowered the lower courts to rewrite municipal zoning ordinances within ninety days when necessary to produce the required low-income housing.[96]

Mount Laurel II was a breathtaking assertion of judicial power, policy-making initiative, and remedial innovation. Even Charles Haar, a Harvard Law School professor and admirer of the decision, concedes that the court was so determined to put "steel into its Mount Laurel Doctrine" that it invited the legislature to undertake the task, while warning that the constitutional duty must not be compromised by conventional remedial limitations.[97] Eager builders, taking the court at its word, filed about 140 lawsuits by June 1985.[98]

Application of the *Mount Laurel II* formulas to particular municipalities, laws, and proposals generated a new round of conflicts. Two book-length studies of this period emphasize the unprecedented demands that these tasks placed on the three judges and their special masters.[99] They had to set fair-share numbers for each town, assess the adequacy of existing zoning ordinances and proposed revisions to them, and supervise their implementation. To do this, they transformed the courts into something like three streamlined regional administrative agencies. Each performed economic projections, estimated job availability, assessed housing needs, prepared environmental impact statements, used planning criteria for suitable sites including judgments about soils and infrastructure, analyzed whether the incentives offered by municipalities to prospective developers were sufficient, and addressed countless other issues. As a result, *Mount Laurel II* severely strained the traditional conception of judicial competence. The ruling encouraged judges to assume a heroic, often imaginative, and only occasionally successful role in increasing the supply of affordable housing for the poor.[100]

New Jersey politicians, like many other observers, found the judges' improvisations problematic.[101] Indeed, *Mount Laurel II* and its early implementation by the courts ignited a political conflagration.[102] With suburban communities lobbying furiously for legislation that would get the judges off their backs, and citing the court's invitation in *Mount Laurel II* to come up with a better solution, the New Jersey legislature enacted its own Fair Housing Act.[103] The Act was the product of a grudging, grueling political compromise between resolute *Mount Laurel* opponents in the suburbs and a coalition of pro-development, realtor, and civil rights groups brandishing the *Mount Laurel* decisions as their weapon.

The Act created a new agency, the Council on Affordable Housing (COAH), and granted it the responsibility to assign, calculate, adjust, certify, and decertify the municipalities' fair shares.[104] Although COAH was given few remedial powers, the Act created incentives for municipalities to comply voluntarily. These included the prospect of immunity from further *Mount Laurel* litigation for six years, a strong presumption of validity for COAH-certified fair-share plans, a temporary cap on the number of affordable units required, and financial subsidies.[105]

In addition, the Act placed a temporary moratorium on the builder's remedy. This had the effect of postponing the program until after the real estate boom of the mid-1980s had passed. The Act also gave communities a number of ways to reduce or eliminate their fair-share obligations. For example, they could get credit for protecting historic sites, environmentally sensitive sites, established development patterns, farmland, and open spaces. They could show that they lacked vacant and developable sites. They could enter into "regional contribution agreements" (RCAs) under which they paid another community (typically a poor, minority, largely urban locality like Trenton) to discharge up to half of their fair-share obligation.[106] Because of these reduction mechanisms for established communities, the fair-share quota primarily affected newly developing suburbs.[107]

A year later, the New Jersey Supreme Court upheld the Act in *Mount Laurel III*.[108] Repeating the mantra that a legislative solution would be better than a judicial one, the court signaled its intention to retreat from the field and to cede responsibility to the cautious politicians. According to John Payne, a long-time advocate of low-income housing, a participant in the litigation since 1983, and a sympathetic critic of the *Mount Laurel* approach, "COAH was set up to dissipate constitutional pressure, not to further expand constitutional confrontation by pursuing aggressive new policies."[109] Almost twenty years after *Mount Laurel II*, few analysts of the affordable housing problem find much to show for all the time and trouble.[110]

The first special judge to decide a case after *Mount Laurel II* developed a "consensus methodology" for determining affordable housing need; it was based on the number of low-income households spending more than 30% of their income on housing.[111] This produced a ten-year, statewide need estimate of 243,736 units, not counting the homeless.[112] The state has not come close to meeting the targets. In July 2001, fifteen years after COAH began, 28,392 units (accessory apartments, group homes, mixed-income development units, municipal- and nonprofit-sponsored units, and buy-down units) had been built or were under construction to satisfy the mandates of challenges brought before COAH or the courts. Another 13,056 units had been zoned for or approved but not yet built, 11,245 had been created through rehabilitation, and 7,396 had been transferred under RCAs from suburbs to Trenton, New Brunswick, Jersey City, and some smaller communities.

Compared to the estimated need for affordable housing in New Jersey, these figures suggest that *Mount Laurel* and COAH have not made much of a dent. Beyond this, however, appraising the program's success or failure depends, among other things, on one's view of how the program's costs affect building activity, how many units would have been built without the program, and how many of its beneficiaries would have obtained affordable units through the filtering process triggered when new market-rate units were built. The realities of the New Jersey housing market suggest that few of the roughly 1,890 units of low-income housing built annually during the fifteen-year period would have materialized without the COAH incentives. In comparison, very few publicly funded units were built in this period and 25,000–30,000 privately owned units *not* under COAH were begun each year during the late 1990s.

What are the demographics of the people who occupy the *Mount Laurel* housing? Commentators and COAH (in its pleas to suburban municipalities) characterize the beneficiary households as being of relatively high socioeconomic status but at a low point in their lifetime earning potential. They are people whom Charles Haar described as "junior yuppies, the recently divorced, graduate students, [and] the retired."[113] The most recent study of the situation, published in 1997 by Naomi Bailin Wish and Stephen Eisdorfer,[114] confirmed this characterization using data from a state agency, the Affordable Housing Management Service (AHMS), that qualifies and places applicants for low-income housing. Specifically, the Wish-Eisdorfer study found that although households headed by persons aged 62 or over constitute only 17% of the applicant pool, they occupy 27% of all AHMS-administered units and 39% of the suburban ones. Elderly white females living alone account for only 4% of the pool but occupy 10% of the units and 15% of the suburban ones. Another group that seems to have benefited are local middle-class people who could not otherwise afford to live in the towns where they worked.[115]

Mount Laurel and COAH have moved few poor people from cities to suburbs. For those households for which Wish and Eisdorfer could determine both current and previous residence as well as race and ethnicity, 47% previously lived in urban areas but only 15% of these (7% of the total) moved to units in the suburbs. Two-thirds of those who did move to suburbia were white, 23% were black, 2% were Latino, and 9% were classified as "other."

Notably, almost as many black households decided to move in the *other direction,* from suburbs to cities. Of all those households that did move from suburbs to cities, 90% were black and none was white.[116] Thus *Mount Laurel* enabled some low-income suburbanites to remain in suburbia and a handful of city-dwellers to move to it. Indeed, by helping low-income people, mainly whites, move from the cities to the suburbs, *Mount Laurel* may even have exacerbated residential segregation by race—though this segregative effect would be small, given the low migration totals.[117]

John Payne, reflecting on an academic symposium that reviewed the Wish-Eisdorfer study, notes the limitations of the AHMS definitions and data (particularly their skewing toward those living in urban projects). As to *Mount Laurel's* demographic effects, he reports that "the general feeling among the commentators is that the results of the study, troubling as they are, probably overstate *Mount Laurel's* accomplishments, rather than the reverse."[118] For example, Payne challenges the view of Haar and other analysts who praise the builder's remedy for its boldness in using builders' profit motives to propel law reform far beyond where public interest lawyers could have taken it.[119] In Payne's view, the builder's remedy is "potentially a Faustian bargain with the developers."[120] It has excluded organizations and lawyers representing racial minorities, renters, and poor people in *Mount Laurel* litigation by making cases more costly to bring and harder to settle. Payne argues that, contrary to what the court had intended, the builder's remedy provides a decisive advantage to developers, as opposed to the supposed beneficiary groups, by allowing them to supply large tracts of land for new inclusionary zoning projects and by excluding most older, built-up parts of the state. The remedy is also land-intensive, requiring four market-rate units to assure one *Mount Laurel* unit. For this reason, inclusionary zoning projects arouse fierce opposition by environmental and antigrowth groups and supply a useful pretext to those with other exclusionary motives. Finally, Payne contends that the builder's remedy "drove out all strategies other than inclusionary zoning."[121] This, despite the fact that, as we shall see, better strategies do exist.

The court in *Mount Laurel* did not just select the wrong tool for reforming affordable housing markets generally. It also chose the wrong target and offered the wrong justification for what it was doing. As noted earlier, the court decided for tactical and doctrinal reasons to attack exclusionary zoning's classism, not its racism, and framed both the indictment and the remedy accordingly. As Payne notes, this was a fateful choice.

> Simply put, there are so many more poor White families than there are poor minority ones that, absent a massive infusion of resources into producing affordable housing that has not happened and realistically could not have happened, it was foreseeable that the lion's share of the hous-

ing that could be produced would go first, whenever possible, to White households, which, if suspect because of their poverty, were nonetheless not so frightening to many middle-class suburbanites as poor Black families.[122]

Payne is correct as a matter of fact, but he fails to explain why, as a matter of substantive policy and justice, New Jersey housing law should have less solicitude for poorly housed whites than for poorly housed blacks. He contends that the court should have repaired a structural defect in the representation of low-income people: the state's "failure to provide them with a political forum in which they can fairly compete with other interest groups for their 'fair share' of society's beneficence."[123] It should have done so, Payne argues, by invalidating the delegation to municipalities of the power to adopt exclusionary zoning policies.[124] Yet it strains credulity to imagine that such a radical decree, in the face of overwhelming public support for local, class-sensitive zoning power, would have aroused less opposition than did *Mount Laurel* itself.

Of greater interest is Payne's claim that the court, by relying on the "general welfare" clause of the state constitution to fight class discrimination in housing, earned less public legitimacy than it might have earned through a frontal challenge to racial discrimination. Payne asserts that this doctrinal bastardy of *Mount Laurel* weakened its moral force and effective implementation—and by extension, that of COAH. Lacking this legitimacy, he says, *Mount Laurel* was "a public relations disaster."[125] *Mount Laurel* would have succeeded in integrating the suburbs, Payne suggests, had the court only justified it on the basis of racial equity, which carries a deeper moral resonance among Americans than class integration does.[126]

There are several reasons to doubt Payne's assertions. First are the many problems with the builder's remedy that Payne himself points out. Absent this remedy, the drive for housing integration beyond what nondiscrimination produces would have to be fueled by government litigation or public interest groups. Yet such litigation might have been even less effective than the builders' cases, given the limited resources available to such groups and the municipalities' strong resistance. Another reason to doubt the efficacy of a race-based strategy is the immigration-driven demographic change that has been transforming New Jersey even more than most other high-immigration states.[127] As the 2000 census shows, blacks are no longer the only large minority group able to assert race-based claims to special benefits like inclusionary zoning, nor are the traditional racial categories as administratively useful or morally compelling as they once were.[128]

A third cause for doubt is legal. The Equal Protection Clause severely limits government's power to distribute special benefits to groups on the basis of race. As a constitutional matter, government may do so only as part of a care-fully designed, victim-tailored remedy for intentional, purposive, racial dis-crimination in housing.[129] As a statutory matter, proof of discriminatory im-pact without discriminatory intent may suffice to establish a violation of the federal Fair Housing Act of 1968 and perhaps justify a race-based remedy.[130] It will be the rare case, however, especially under exclusionary zoning laws, when plaintiffs can prove discriminatory intent and when defendant munici-palities cannot justify those laws on legitimate, nondiscriminatory grounds. This fact best explains the decision by the *Mount Laurel* plaintiffs and the New Jersey Supreme Court to focus on income-based rather than race-based discrimination,[131] although, as Anthony Downs and others have contended, there are also strong policy grounds for this decision.[132]

Mount Laurel's minimal effect on the production of affordable housing in New Jersey is not surprising. Other states have attacked exclusionary zoning in a variety of other ways, yet they too have had little effect.[133] Indeed, inclusionary zoning laws are likely to harm those members of the eligible in-come class, the vast majority of whom do not receive subsidized units.[134] Be-cause high land and construction costs and other factors besides exclusionary zoning are also responsible for the affordable housing deficit in the more prosperous suburbs, we should not expect that reducing exclusionary zoning will solve the problem.[135] This presumably is why Anthony Downs devotes little attention to courts and zoning changes in his comprehensive analysis of the policies needed to truly open up the suburbs.[136] Nonetheless, Payne and other housing advocates who prosecuted the *Mount Laurel* litigation have not given up on either the courts or zoning reform. Insisting that "*Mount Laurel* never really reached our clients at all," the developers and their allies in the affordable housing movement won another round in August 2002 when the New Jersey Supreme Court, in the first significant *Mount Laurel* dispute to reach that court since 1985, allowed them to override environ-mental and zoning restrictions on multifamily housing in the suburb of West Windsor.[137]

Gautreaux

Of our three case studies, the only one that seems to have succeeded in moving a significant number of blacks to previously white suburbs is *Gau-treaux*.[138] The court there granted a race-based remedy only after proof that a government agency had intentionally isolated low-income blacks in black neighborhoods. *Gautreaux* employed a very different approach to integrat-ing minorities into white suburbs than did *Mount Laurel* or *Yonkers*. In doing so, it seems to have succeeded where the others failed.[139]

In 1966, black residents of public housing in Chicago brought a class action suit against the Chicago Housing Authority (CHA) and the United States Department of Housing and Urban Development (HUD) alleging a conspiracy to locate public housing and assign tenants to projects on a racially segregated basis.[140] Three years later, a federal trial judge dismissed HUD but agreed with the plaintiffs and ordered the CHA to build and buy low-rise, small buildings on sites that were far more "scattered" than in previous programs. In addition, because half of the units in any CHA scattered-site development were reserved for low-income families (presumably whites) who were already living in the new neighborhoods, the court ordered CHA to assign occupants on a desegregated basis so that black families could move into predominantly white neighborhoods in Chicago rather than remain concentrated in a few black neighborhoods. These provisions were designed to foster peaceful, stable integration, minimize white "fight and flight," reduce public housing's stigma, and reassure the community about the neighborhoods' futures.[141] Even so, much political resistance impeded the program's implementation, and in 1987 the judge appointed a receiver to administer it.[142] Opposition continued, however, not only in white neighborhoods but also in Latino and black ones.

The case against HUD moved on a separate track. In 1971, the court of appeals ruled that HUD should not have been dismissed and was indeed liable.[143] It ordered the agency to establish and fund a program enabling low-income black families to relocate beyond the city limits and throughout the Chicago metropolitan area, largely into rental housing.[144] In 1976, the United States Supreme Court upheld this remedy,[145] the first time it had ever authorized a school or housing desegregation plan to extend beyond the community where the legal violation took place. A consent decree was entered in 1981, and this metropolitan-wide remedy, which soon eclipsed the troubled CHA scattered-site program, became known as the Gautreaux Assisted-Housing Program (GAHP).

Although the GAHP continued the scattered-site approach that emphasized existing housing and gave receiving suburbs little reason to fear additional migration by non-*Gautreaux* blacks, it used a new funding and delivery mechanism known as Section 8, which Congress created in 1974.[146] Under Section 8, the public housing authority (here, CHA) provides vouchers to income-eligible families. Generally, the vouchers' value equals the difference between 30% of family income and an agency-prescribed payment standard defined as some percentage of the "fair market rent" figure determined by the agency. Armed with vouchers and assisted by a nonprofit fair housing agency, families in the GAHP would enter the market and negotiate five-year renewable leases with landlords for housing units they wanted and could afford. Because the GAHP lacked *Mount Laurel*'s power to invalidate exclusionary zoning practices, the voucher and traditional fair housing laws were the families' only ticket for entry to the white suburbs.

In the fall of 1998, when HUD's obligation to fund the GAHP ended and the last relocation was completed, the program had moved 7,100 low-income black families out of inner-city neighborhoods (over 90% black). Most participants moved to more than 100 suburban communities (96% white on average), and the rest (a comparison group) moved to other neighborhoods within Chicago (99% black on average) that were demographically similar to the neighborhoods they had left. In contrast, most families who left CHA housing with Section 8 vouchers but did not participate in the GAHP and therefore did not receive mobility counseling, ended up moving to other black, high-poverty neighborhoods.[147]

Long-term research on the GAHP has documented many of the effects on both the suburban movers and the city movers.[148] The results are more encouraging than those in *Mount Laurel* and compare especially well to the public housing status quo, which is more expensive and less socially integrative. First, in exchange for a much-reduced risk of the crime, violence, and gunfire that pervaded daily life in their original communities, the suburban movers experienced a higher risk of racist encounters. These encounters, however, while upsetting, were infrequent and nonviolent. Second, suburban movers initially experienced more harassment than city movers, but after the first year the two groups experienced similar levels. Third, both groups experienced similar levels of social integration in terms of number of friends made, levels of interaction with neighbors, and feelings of acceptance. Suburban movers tended to have more white friends than city movers, but some of the suburban movers had more black than white friends.

Fourth, the suburbs offered safer schools, smaller class sizes, and higher educational standards, but the movers found this a mixed blessing. Although these benefits helped children achieve far beyond what the city schools even aspired to attain, many quickly realized that their performance was substantially below the new schools' expectations, and they doubted their capacity to meet them. The children of suburban movers were more likely than their city counterparts to be in high school, on a college track, in a four-year college, in a job, and in a job with benefits. Nonetheless, they had very similar rates of behavior problems, similar grades, and similar class ranks. Given the much higher standards the suburban movers faced, however, this ostensible equivalence probably reflects a higher level of performance.[149]

Galvanized by the promise of the GAHP approach, some courts, HUD, and other public and private agencies throughout the country are seeking to create similar "mobility-based housing" programs. Their approach is to use direct tenant subsidies to help low-income black families move to predominantly white, middle-class, suburban communities. Federal policy has moved strongly in this direction, marshaling Section 8 as the programmatic vehicle for almost all new assistance since the mid-1980s. According to a General Accounting Office study, 1.4 million low-income households were using housing vouchers in 2000, down from 1.7 million in the early 1990s, but still surpassing the number living in public housing.[150] The study also found that the total per-unit costs for housing voucher programs are from 32% to 59% lower than the unit costs for bricks-and-mortar production programs in the first year and from 12% to 27% lower over thirty years.[151] Voucher-based mobility programs, coupled with new funds for counseling and housing search assistance, become even more important as the units available to low-income renters dwindle. These units are becoming scarcer because public housing projects are slated for demolition or revitalization with fewer units, troubled subsidized private buildings are being closed, and viable ones are being converted by their owners to market-rate status.[152]

Initially, reformers' enthusiasm about the GAHP approach was somewhat muted by fears that its success might have been due in part to self-selection into the program by more highly motivated, easily integrated black families. In order to find out, Congress enacted the "Moving to Opportunity" program (MTO) in 1992, establishing a controlled experiment to help low-income families living in concentrations of poverty move to areas of lower poverty.[153] Under the experiment, three distinct groups of low-income families in five different cities were randomly chosen, with one group moving to designated areas, a second group moving any place they chose, and a control group not moving at all. The MTO programs differ from the GAHP in that they are not instituted through a court decree, they are smaller (approximately 5,000 families), they seek to remedy proven racial discrimination, and they are not limited to racial minorities. The results of MTO programs have been mixed. The programs have encountered even more of the obstacles that faced *Gautreaux,* including limited Section 8 funds, landlord resistance to Section 8 tenants, a declining stock of affordable units, and concentration of even Section 8 recipients in racially and income-segregated neighborhoods. In 2000, voucher-holders' success in finding leaseable, program-eligible units ranged from 37% in some locales to 100% in others; the success rate has been declining, largely due to tight rental markets.[154] Nevertheless, and despite fierce opposition to the MTO in the Baltimore research site, the early results are encouraging.[155]

More generally, conventional Section 8 programs have succeeded in improving housing quality and affordability for low-income minorities, the elderly, families with children, and the disabled. Section 8 tenants are far less concentrated in high-poverty neighborhoods than are public housing and unassisted tenants, and the relative invisibility of vouchers diffuses opposition by making it harder for neighbors to detect whether newcomers are subsidized. Despite this success, the programs' growing emphasis on dispersing assisted tenants into higher-income communities has increased their clustering there, which engenders some opposition. At the same time, recipients of Section 8 vouchers have increasingly used their vouchers in low-income areas, resulting in clustering in high-poverty neighborhoods. Both kinds of clustering reflect various factors that policymakers are beginning to address such as high rents in more desirable areas, recipients' wishes to retain family and social networks, discrimination based on race, class, and Section 8 status, community opposition, ignorance about housing options, high search costs, and poor program administration.[156] The *Yonkers* case, discussed immediately below, illustrates some of these challenges to Section 8's effectiveness—particularly community opposition and administrative challenges—but more fundamentally demonstrates the dearth of better alternatives.[157]

Yonkers

As noted earlier, housing patterns are intricate mosaics in which the pieces are shaped and fitted together by many private choices of individual consumers, commercial and industrial firms, property owners, developers, insurers, lenders, the construction industry, utilities, and other institutions. These private choices are in turn influenced by public policies directed not only, or even primarily, at housing, but also at economic development, transportation, infrastructure, energy, recreation, environment, schools, hospitals, and other public services. And although a city's residential patterns change over time, those changes tend to occur almost imperceptibly. The private and public choices of long ago create a path of dependency that blunts the effectiveness of more recent ones.

As a practical matter, and perhaps as a matter of professional training as well, lawyers and judges generally can only focus on a few of the mosaic's more visible shards. The rest remain unexamined and their complex linkages go unexplored. In *Yonkers*, the lawyers focused almost exclusively on one set of choices—the forty-year sequence of municipal decisions about whether and where to build subsidized (i.e., public and assisted) housing. The evidence about those choices clearly established many "who did what to whom, when, and why" kinds of facts. As to this, the factual record was immense; the judge, Leonard B. Sand, later required more than 250 pages of double-columned, small-type, printed opinion simply to describe and evaluate it.[158]

My necessarily schematic review, then, is like a topographical map that must suppress many arresting details in order to render the main contours intelligible and useful.

The *Yonkers* story confirms the adage that geography is destiny. The city's political, social, and ethnic divisions reflect its physical features and topographical contours to a remarkable extent. It is ribbed by a series of natural barriers, almost all of which run from north to south. Relatively prosperous blacks clustered in the Runyon Heights area of east Yonkers between the Nepperhan River and the railroad line. This enclave, which flourished most in the period from 1910 to 1925, boasted some lawyers, doctors, and numerous Pullman porters and remains prosperous today. The vast majority of blacks and Hispanics have long been concentrated in west Yonkers, an area near the dilapidated remains of the old commercial and industrial core where the city built the public housing projects from the 1950s to the 1970s that became the focus of the *Yonkers* litigation.

In the southeast, Lincoln Park became a white middle-class neighborhood populated mainly by people from New York City who moved to Yonkers to avoid the increasing number of public housing projects for low-income families that were being built in their old neighborhoods. These new residents became some of the most vocal opponents of the Lincoln Park public housing sites proposed during the *Yonkers* litigation.

The northeast sector developed into the more exclusive white neighborhoods. These include Lawrence Park, which is next to Bronxville, where Sarah Lawrence College is situated, and Crestwood, which abuts Eastchester in the north. The residents of these more affluent neighborhoods opposed public housing in their areas, though less militantly than the residents of Lincoln Park.

These physical, economic, social, and ethnic divisions generated a remarkable amount of civic organization and activity in Yonkers in response to the litigation. Writing in August 1988 at the height of the controversy, a *New York Times* reporter found no fewer than fifty civic groups operating in the city, four or five times the number that had been active prior to the litigation.[159] Eight of these groups joined to form Citizens and Neighbors Organized to Protect Yonkers (CANOPY), an organization opposed to public housing in members' neighborhoods but committed to improving the city's image by supporting the court's orders. Most of CANOPY's members were professionals who lived in the affluent neighborhoods in the north and far south of the city. The remaining forty-plus groups formed the Save Yonkers Federation (SYF), which strongly opposed the court. SYF had a diverse membership: many were teachers, police officers, electricians, secretaries, and owners of small businesses, and many owned modest, well-kept homes. SYF drew its greatest support from southeast Yonkers neighborhoods where some of the proposed sites were to be located—a fact many SYF members saw as hardly coincidental.

Planning the litigation. Lawyers in the United States Department of Justice (DOJ) under President Jimmy Carter knew nothing about these divisions when they conceived the *Yonkers* case in 1980. They and some old-line civil rights organizations had become frustrated by the limited capacity of school desegregation cases and fair housing cases to improve the actual conditions of racial minorities. For more than twenty-five years, they had brought and won school desegregation cases, but racial isolation in urban school systems remained endemic. Several related obstacles hobbled DOJ's efforts. Segregated school systems almost always reflected segregated residential patterns, so little could be gained by dismantling the former without altering the latter. Yet even successful Title VIII cases did not have much impact on the racial composition of communities. Intentional discrimination, usually required in order to establish a constitutional violation,[160] was also important, if not always strictly necessary, to support a Title VIII claim, yet it was ordinarily very difficult to prove. In addition, the wrongdoers subject to court decrees often were not the ones primarily responsible for, or able to rectify, the condition, while the responsible ones—often politicians—were not always haled into court as defendants.

The DOJ staff recommended a suit against Yonkers to Drew Days III, the assistant attorney general for civil rights and a former NAACP Legal Defense and Education Fund litigator. Days, who did not have to obtain the attorney general's approval, accepted it. He thought the case against Yonkers was "a strong one as northern cases go," but he anticipated problems in proving discriminatory intent.[161] "There are usually more footprints than there were in Yonkers," he later recalled, "and there was no history of de jure discrimination and no smoking guns."[162] In their memo to Days supporting their recommendation, moreover, the staff lawyers had been quite vague about the housing remedy that DOJ should seek from the court. They were no clearer in the documents they filed with the court during the next several years. The lawyers foresaw a long, difficult journey before they could hope to reach the remedial stage. They could worry about an appropriate remedy, they reasoned, if and when they proved liability.

Still, it is striking—especially in light of the legal novelty of their housing claims and the ferocious struggle that ensued—that the lawyers finessed the remedial issue when the government planned and then prosecuted the case. They did not officially consult with HUD, nor did they seek advice from a housing consultant about the nature of housing markets. The lawyers relied for their information largely on public documents, newspaper articles, community leaders, state and local civil rights agencies, and the local chapter of the NAACP.

Low-income housing in Yonkers. Yonkers has a long history of public housing and urban development. At first, the city sought public housing largely as an adjunct to its program of slum clearance and redevelopment in southwest Yonkers. The projects would help relocate those displaced when their homes were razed. Whenever the city government or the (at least formally) independent Yonkers Municipal Housing Authority (MHA) proposed a site for a new project outside of southwest Yonkers, opposition by residents and community groups in the targeted area quickly arose. The city council was almost always sympathetic and responsive to this opposition and indeed sometimes instigated it. Opponents feared that building public housing in their neighborhoods would adversely affect the resale and loan value of their homes by bringing into their areas a different "class of people."[163] They also feared increased crowding in their local public schools, hospitals, streets, and other public services. Moreover, they believed the sites would be more valuable if used for tax revenue-generating activity instead of for housing that must be subsidized through tax abatements.[164]

Resentment also simmered, and occasionally flared, out of a widespread belief that other, more prosperous communities near Yonkers, especially White Plains, were using their federal urban renewal funds to push welfare families out of those communities and into Yonkers.[165] Most alarming to many Yonkers residents was the prospect that more public housing would lead to a rapid, irreversible "Bronxification" of the city, attracting (at the taxpayers' expense) the same criminal, drug-dependent, and rootless people from whom many Yonkers residents had only recently, and with extraordinary effort and sacrifice, managed to escape.[166]

Yonkers residents of all income levels and all races shared these sentiments to some degree, but the ardor with which they felt and expressed them varied. Groups representing blacks were in a particularly delicate position. They wanted to expand housing opportunities for low-income people, many of whom were black, but the politics of doing so created genuine dilemmas. At first blush, it seemed fair and sensible to disperse public housing into east Yonkers, where the superior schools, safer streets, and more desirable neighborhoods were located, rather than to build more public housing in southwest Yonkers, which might well accelerate racial tipping by causing the remaining whites there to leave.

But there were also strong countervailing considerations. Dispersal would dilute black voting power in the southwest sector and drain support away from businesses and churches there. More money for public housing could mean less money for assisted housing for working- and middle-class blacks.

Many blacks in the east who had managed to distance themselves from the culture of poverty feared that public housing, by concentrating and perhaps perpetuating that culture, might threaten their own hard-won gains. Indeed, the black community in Runyon Heights, which had to absorb a large public housing project in the 1960s, advanced many of the same arguments used by the SYF.[167] The leading black civil rights groups opposed to the sites in the southwest also advanced these arguments. But blacks faced a more poignant dilemma. Those who saw the need for more public housing and wanted it sited in east Yonkers had to accept an increasingly obvious political reality: unless it were built in southwest Yonkers, it probably would not be built at all.[168]

For the city, the lure of federal and state funds was irresistible. Although almost all vocal groups in Yonkers opposed new public and assisted housing, certain locations and target populations proved to be politically acceptable. These included state-subsidized (Mitchell-Lama) projects for middle-income residents in southwest Yonkers, and public housing for senior citizens rather than families—although even some seniors' projects were defeated out of fear that they might eventually be occupied by poor families. Most striking—and most significant to U.S. District Judge Sand, who presided over the entire litigation—was the location in the black middle-class neighborhood of Runyon Heights of the only public housing project built in east Yonkers.[169]

The legislative and bureaucratic politics of these siting controversies also followed a fairly consistent script, which the lead plaintiff's lawyer later called "the dance."[170] As the concentration of sites in the southwest sector became too obvious for even HUD to ignore, it rejected the only proposals that the city council was prepared to approve. In a political climate that would later shape Judge Sand's legal decision and to an extent his remedial strategy, community opponents always mobilized to defeat any siting ideas floated at the staff level by lobbying the planning board and the MHA, which were both wholly or largely mayor-appointed. Especially in a weak-mayor government, such as the Yonkers system during most of the period in question, professional siting criteria were simply no match for aroused, politicized community indignation.

When Congress enacted the Housing and Community Development Act of 1974,[171] however, it adopted a fundamentally different approach to federal housing assistance and priorities. Instead of promoting construction of public housing and directly subsidizing builders, the new statute directed HUD to place its primary emphasis on two new programs: Community Development Block Grants (CDBG) and Section 8 rent subsidies and vouchers (described earlier in connection with the *Gautreaux* remedy). The CDBG program supplanted a large number of urban renewal–related categorical programs with a single grant that localities could use in a more flexible, discretionary manner for nonhousing community development programs. To receive a CDBG, a locality had to submit to HUD an annual Housing Assistance Plan (HAP). The HAP identified the community's low-income housing needs, indicated where the HUD-assisted housing would be located, and helped HUD to decide whether to make or renew a grant.[172]

These new programs transformed the regulatory environment for low-income housing, but Yonkers officials responded to the new programs as if little had changed. Yonkers housing officials filed HAPs that emphasized the need for new housing in east Yonkers, outside the southwest sector, and city planners proposed sites that would meet those specifications. The city council, however, rejected the proposals. HUD acquiesced; it funded projects that the council supported in the southwest sector and did not fund the others. In 1979, the council approved a public housing project sited in east Yonkers over strong community opposition. But this decision was consistent with the traditional pattern—the housing was for senior citizens rather than for families. The pattern was evident in Yonkers' response not only to the new supply-side CDBG program but even more so in its response to the highly flexible demand-side Section 8 program. As Judge Sand would later point out:

> [T]he certificates . . . imposed no financial burden on the City. No tax abatement was required, as in the case of most subsidized housing projects, and included with the grant of the certificates were funds payable to the City for the cost of administering the program. . . . Section 8 Existing Certificates offered a way to disperse low income housing without adding to the density of a neighborhood (as a subsidized housing project might) and without raising any other real or imagined physical planning problems.[173]

On the other hand, if the city council wished to keep poor or minority people from residing in certain areas, it would regard Section 8's purchasing power and locational flexibility as a threat rather than an opportunity. In fact, this was precisely how the council seems to have viewed the program. Again, Judge Sand's opinion makes the point:

> [F]or three years, the City refused entirely to apply for Section 8 Existing Certificates for families; failed to use many of the certificates eventually applied for; failed to make any significant efforts to promote their use outside Southwest Yonkers; sought to conceal from HUD the extremely limited geographic scope of its outreach efforts; resisted efforts by HUD to transfer the program to an agency perceived by the City to

be less "responsive to elected City officials" and opposed the efforts of that agency to obtain certificates on its own.[174]

By mid-1980, when DOJ decided to investigate Yonkers, the city's approach was transparent. DOJ's interest in the Yonkers housing patterns was beginning to embarrass HUD, which saw that the federal government would challenge as racist a housing policy that HUD had richly subsidized for decades. For political and perhaps constitutional reasons, DOJ did not sue HUD, although it recognized that it must implicate HUD in order to defeat Yonkers.[175] In response to this pressure, HUD insisted in June 1980 that it would not grant Yonkers its next round of CDBG funds unless the city agreed to do what it had already promised in its HAP: "take all actions within its control" to build 100 units of subsidized housing for low-income families "located outside of areas of minority concentration."[176] It was never clear whether this HAP statement constituted an enforceable commitment by Yonkers to build the housing, and if it was enforceable, whether the city could have pointed to the ferocious political opposition to east Yonkers siting as a legitimate reason for noncompliance.[177] What is certain is that, as Judge Sand later put it, "[i]n the two years following the imposition of the 1980 contract conditions, the City Council failed to support a single site for subsidized housing for families,"[178] again reflecting the now familiar patterns of bowing to constituent pressures and ward courtesy.

The Yonkers litigation. As the Carter administration wound down following Ronald Reagan's victory in the 1980 presidential election, the DOJ filed a school and housing desegregation suit against Yonkers on December 1, 1980, in the U.S. District Court for the Southern District of New York in Manhattan.[179] Judge Sand was assigned to both parts of the case and a legal marathon was off and running. (Although the housing and school cases were very much linked in the minds of DOJ lawyers, this chapter deals only with the housing side of the case.)[180]

The first year was dominated by the city's unsuccessful efforts to have the case dismissed, along with the normal run of procedural gambits, tactical maneuvers, and initial discovery. Two important developments occurred during that year. First, the NAACP, aware that the Reagan administration might drop the case, intervened as a plaintiff. This addition of a well-respected civil rights group, along with a very talented and zealous young lawyer from Yonkers, Michael Sussman, greatly enhanced the plaintiffs' resources, effectiveness, and public legitimacy.[181] Sussman was to become the dominant force in the legal assault on Yonkers.

Second, Yonkers brought HUD into the case as a codefendant. Pointing to the numerous HUD approvals of its public and subsidized housing projects over the years, Yonkers argued that HUD's policies, by emphasizing the need to locate those projects in areas with relatively low land-acquisition costs, had actually *encouraged* the city to concentrate the projects in minority areas. If Yonkers were found liable to the plaintiffs, the city argued, HUD should also be liable as the truly responsible party.

Sussman knew that Yonkers would try to deflect blame by showing that it had simply complied with HUD's directives. If the court accepted this argument, the plaintiffs would lose the case because they had to prove the city's racial animus, not just its passive acquiescence and complaisance. To surmount this obstacle, Sussman had to show that HUD was *independently* liable, whether or not the city was also liable.

In Sussman's view, the decisive development in the entire case occurred in December 1982 when the city tried to sell the Public School 4 (P.S. 4) site.[182] More than two years earlier, just before the suit was filed, the city had responded to HUD's request for an inventory of sites available for public and assisted housing. Of the fourteen locations listed by the city, HUD had found only two to be acceptable—a McLean Avenue property and the vacant P.S. 4 site. When the city permitted the McLean Avenue site to be developed as a shopping center, P.S. 4 remained as the only HUD-approved location for low-income housing. Then, when the city moved to sell it to a developer for condominiums, HUD did not object. Sussman, however, did. He swiftly moved to enjoin the sale, insisting that the city had a responsibility to preserve what might be the only site with which it could meet its 1980 commitment to HUD. In discovery, several members of the committee that the city council had appointed to screen potential developers of the site admitted to Sussman that the committee's real purpose was to bypass the normal processes and get the property into private hands where it could not be used for public or assisted housing. Confronted with this evidence, the city's lawyer attempted to persuade the city council to consent to the preliminary injunction. When the council refused to drop its plan to sell, the lawyer quit. This episode, Sussman says, "vividly illustrated everything we were trying to tell the court about why the city was liable and why HUD, which did not even object, was also liable. And it happened right before the judge's eyes, two years after the case started."[183]

The trial began in August 1983 after the judge's strenuous efforts to promote a negotiated settlement failed. Positions had hardened. Yonkers pointed the finger at HUD, which had approved all of the sites. HUD insisted that it had no way of knowing that the city's site selections were a pretext for discrimination. Sussman contended that the city and HUD were equally to blame. He opposed settlement on principle and felt that the Yonkers community would never accept liability and a far-reaching remedy unless the whole story could be laid out at a trial and confirmed in the court's opinion.

The HUD consent decree. There was another defendant in the case, however, and as settlement pressures mounted, HUD's role in the litigation took center stage. As discussed above, the city had maintained that the concentration of housing in minority areas was a condition for which HUD was ultimately responsible. As the city's litigation prospects grew ever bleaker, its hope of exculpating itself by inculpating HUD became even more fervent.

Little evidence supported the strongest version of Yonkers' claim—that HUD had directed it to site public housing in or near urban renewal areas. Rather, HUD in more recent years had actually asked Yonkers to avoid concentrating minorities. But even Judge Sand found some validity in a weaker form of the city's claim. It was "reasonable to assume," he later wrote, "that HUD may have encouraged the City to put some of its relocation housing near the major urban renewal areas."[184] In rejecting Yonkers' argument, however, Judge Sand emphasized that HUD's policy did not *require* the city to build in any particular area and that the city had actually considered siting some projects in nonrenewal areas.[185] None of this necessarily relieved HUD of a shared responsibility—perhaps legal but certainly moral—for the housing patterns it had financed and approved, so Yonkers wanted to keep HUD in the case as a codefendant.

Once Sussman put his case against HUD into evidence, however, he had compelling reasons to settle with the agency. In the final analysis, only HUD had the funds to provide the particular relief—more housing for low-income and minority families in scattered sites—that the NAACP had entered the lawsuit to obtain. As the price for allowing HUD to exit, Sussman hoped to extract from it much of these housing funds. Indeed, settling with HUD might actually produce more low-income housing than would a successful trial. After all, even if Judge Sand ruled for the plaintiffs on the liability issues, it by no means followed that he would issue a remedial order going as far as HUD might be willing to go in a settlement.[186]

Sussman plunged into intensive negotiations with HUD, and early in 1984 they reached an agreement and submitted it to Judge Sand for the requisite court approval and entry of a consent decree. At its core, the agreement provided that within forty-five days, HUD would "make available solely" to Yonkers, and would invite the city to apply for, funds for 200 units of two-bedroom and larger family public housing, which might or might not require new construction, "to be located east of the Saw Mill River Parkway within the City of Yonkers."[187] HUD also agreed to work with the city to bring any unsatisfactory proposals up to HUD standards; encourage the city to use its CDBG funds to develop this housing; refrain from seeking to recapture any unused funds for these units unless it concluded (after giving the NAACP an opportunity to object) that there were "no developable sites" in east Yonkers; invite the city to apply for 175 Section 8 certificates for families and to limit their use during the first 120 days to units located in east Yonkers; allow exceptions to the certificates' maximum gross rent limitations; require the city to affirmatively assist certified families to find units in east Yonkers; and report on how those certificates were being used.[188] Although the agreement did not specify that the new units be occupied by racial minorities, those on the waiting list for public housing would have priority, and they were mainly blacks and Hispanics.

The consent agreement represented a great victory for the NAACP. It not only committed HUD to fund additional public housing and rent supplements for east Yonkers, it also protected the plaintiffs from rising housing costs by defining HUD's obligation in terms of a specific number of units rather than a specific level of funding. In addition, it envisioned that the funds would flow quickly, on a preferential basis, and at a time when new federal housing assistance throughout the nation was being curtailed. But there was a hitch. HUD would not have to act on most of these commitments unless Yonkers took the initiative to apply for funding and meet the requisite timetables and regulatory standards. In short, HUD's promises would be meaningless unless the city government took HUD up on them, which it was not inclined to do. In light of subsequent events, however, the consent decree's importance can scarcely be exaggerated. It legitimated giving the plaintiffs more relief than the law might have allowed the judge to order on his own. It also moved Judge Sand down a remedial road that at the time appeared better marked, straighter, and shorter than it turned out to be. And it kept him there long after its destination ceased being a worthwhile goal. The court would learn a painful lesson: it was far easier to influence the lawyers and the other professionals in the case than to motivate the politicians in Yonkers to comply.

Although HUD was now out of the case (at least as far as the NAACP's claims were concerned), it was not yet in the clear. Dismissing HUD, Judge Sand took pains to emphasize that if its future participation in the litigation became necessary, the court "would not be without means to obtain" it.[189] The ink was hardly dry on these words when the NAACP took the judge up on them. HUD responded to the decree by inviting Yonkers to apply for Section 8 certificates, but when the city applied, HUD did not issue them. Insisting that HUD had "subverted" the decree, the NAACP asked the court to compel HUD's compliance. In court, HUD contended that the law did not authorize it to approve and issue certificates in excess of those called for in a city's HAP. Yonkers' failure to amend its HAP goals to include the new certificates, HUD said, prevented their issuance.

Judge Sand would have none of this. Castigating HUD for its position, he found that the decree had envisioned the Section 8 certificates "as relief that could be provided expeditiously, and without the need for any action on the part of the City."[190] HUD, Judge Sand ruled, must take certain specified steps to persuade Yonkers to amend its HAP. If the city did not respond, HUD must threaten to disapprove any HAP that did not provide for the Section 8 certificates available to the city under the decree.[191]

This contretemps, and others still to come, signaled the nature of the game that the defendants were playing in 1985—and continued to play for many years after. The MHA, the city's housing agency, was prepared to build public housing wherever the politicians would allow the agency to build, provided HUD came up with the necessary funding. The MHA was ready to receive and distribute the 175 certificates provided under the decree, although it warned that east Yonkers landlords might not accept them.[192] Most members of the city council, including Mayor Angelo Martinelli, did not want to build public housing *anywhere*, even in southwest Yonkers. Like many Americans, they viewed public housing projects as a breeding ground for crime, drug use, and dependency. They also believed that the city already had too much public housing, draining its limited resources.[193] Concurrently, HUD entered the second term of a Reagan administration that had built only 5,000 units of public housing, almost all on Indian reservations. HUD had no interest in building more, preferring to use Section 8 certificates.[194] It had no wish to penalize Yonkers for following its lead and was especially reluctant to impose sanctions against cities at a time when it was already reducing funding for other construction programs in which cities like Yonkers had far more interest.[195] HUD saw Yonkers as a normal grantee to be dealt with under normal rules and arrangements. But Judge Sand clearly regarded Yonkers as a special case demanding unique treatment and placed HUD under a court order that the agency feared to defy.[196]

The decision imposing liability on the city. On November 20, 1985, fourteen months after the trial ended but only two weeks after the municipal elections, Judge Sand issued his decision. Given the testimony by Mayor Martinelli and other top officials conceding that racial factors influenced the city council's siting decisions, only the ostriches and the incurably optimistic in city hall could have been surprised at the final peroration of the housing portion of Judge Sand's gargantuan opinion:

In sum, the record clearly demonstrates that race has had a chronic and pervasive influence on decisions relating to the location of subsidized housing in Yonkers. While the precise configuration of subsidized housing which would have arisen in the absence of that influence necessarily remains a matter of speculation, it is clear that "but for" that influence, a significantly different result would have obtained.[197]

The influence of race on housing decisions, Judge Sand emphasized, was intentionally discriminatory, not merely incidental or adventitious; the pattern of segregative intent was so clear that his judgment condemning the city was "a relatively easy one."[198] Considering that Judge Sand's judgment would later be affirmed by both the court of appeals[199] and the United States Supreme Court,[200] his confidence in his judgment seems justified. The evidence indeed supported his findings about "who did what to whom and when" and that race was a motivating factor in the city's placement decisions.

More doubtful was Judge Sand's belief that residential neighborhood segregation in Yonkers would not have occurred in the absence of the city's racism—or, to put it another way, that racism was the necessary and sufficient precondition for this segregation. Although the legal validity of his ruling depended on such a finding, Judge Sand did not spell out this belief, much less defend it. Nor is it likely that he could have done so persuasively. As we saw earlier, residential segregation can be caused by a number of factors other than racism: private preferences for ethnic homogeneity, income-based differentiation of neighborhoods, land-use decisions driven by tax and other economic factors, and a widely shared classist value system with respect to housing that claims to legitimate existing housing patterns.

Judge Sand's ruling illustrates an unfortunate social and legal compulsion to use simple dualistic categories to explain complex phenomena. Here, characterizing the city's conduct as racist (and hence legally culpable) became essential to the case, even though that conduct almost certainly reflected some mixture of racism and classism.[201] Legal remedies premised on such simplifications are poorly tailored to the realities they seek to regulate and transform. I have explained this problem elsewhere:

> Ordinarily we assess people and things according to the numerous dimensions along which they vary, for example, size, strength, beauty, speed, intelligence, morality, humor, culpability, and value. In contrast, law—especially regulatory law—usually attempts to govern complex reality through simple binary, yes-or-no categories; it seldom uses the kinds of continuous categories of more-or-less that refine our perceptions and discourse and render everyday life intelligible and nuanced. The citizen beholding law's artificial, reductionist classifications often

protests in the name of common sense: "The real world isn't black and white; it is all a matter of degree." Law knows this, of course, but it pretends otherwise. There are plausible arguments for using simplistic classifications, and they have usually carried the day.[202]

This analysis, if correct, may shed light on the remarkable fact, detailed below, that even after fifteen more years of litigation and political turmoil over implementing the court's decision, low-income blacks have little more access to housing in Yonkers' white neighborhoods today than they did before the litigation.

To the question of why the law has yielded so little, the short answer is that the city militantly and recklessly defied it. But this answer only pushes the "why" question back a step—for as Jonathan Rieder notes, the "rising up of a placid community, the breaking of lawful and routine patterns of making wishes known, is an event of remarkable singularity that demands explanation."[203]

One could tell many explanatory stories. The most straightforward is that the citizen resisters in Yonkers were simply recalcitrant racists. But although Yonkers (and especially SFY) certainly had its racists, the city was neither a moral backwater nor a lawless, hate-filled enclave. Before the housing crisis erupted, its public and private life seemed indistinguishable from that of other American communities where racism has declined dramatically. A second story emphasizes the intolerance and lawlessness of the city's elected officials. Yonkers voters, however, ratified the politicians' open defiance, even though they knew how costly this defiance would be to them and their city. For all that appears, the city council voted for what most of its constituents seemed to want.

I wish to propose a third story in response to Rieder's demand for explanation—one that I cannot prove but that is nonetheless consistent with my fieldwork in Yonkers. Let us suppose that most people in Yonkers genuinely believed (1) that the city's residential patterns resulted mainly from conventional private and public choices based on economic and classist, "not-in-my-back-yard" (NIMBY) values, with racism only a marginal factor—or put another way, that those conventional reasons were a necessary and sufficient cause of the residential patterns; (2) that Judge Sand was wrong, demeaning, and morally obtuse to insist that these choices and values were racist; and (3) that his remedy was ill-founded, unfair, and jeopardized their hard-earned property and sense of well-being. My hypothesis is that citizens who believed these things might also have believed that if Judge Sand's law violated the norms of their community about how neighborhoods should form and develop, how diverse they should be, and how diversity must come about in order to be valued, then so much the worse for his law and so much stronger the reasons for resisting it.

I do not know whether the people of Yonkers actually believed these propositions nor do I know whether the propositions were in fact true. Judge Sand made a strong finding of fact that intentional racial discrimination played a role in Yonkers housing patterns. This finding seems clearly correct, and the appeals court fully affirmed it. But what is also arguable, and what is probably impossible to prove, is that conventional market dynamics would have caused these patterns *anyway,* with or without such discrimination. If this was so—or even if reasonable people thought it was so—then this might well explain why so many people in Yonkers defied the law in ways that, in Jonathan Rieder's sense, are otherwise inexplicable.

The decision on remedy. Judge Sand ordered the parties to convene on December 18, 1985, to discuss how to proceed with the remedial phase of the case. His remedial powers, everyone knew, were awesomely broad. Indeed, in certain respects they were far broader than those of city officials, including the city council. In principle, at least, he could exercise them unilaterally; legislative, administrative, and judicial authority were fused in him. He did not have to fashion a legislative majority, nor would he face reprisals at the polls. Perhaps most important, he alone defined the limits of his own authority, subject only to reversal by the appeals court.

The prospect of appellate review, however, did not pose much of a threat. The city's appeal on liability could not be filed until Judge Sand issued his remedial order, and two more years would elapse before the appeals court finally ruled. A district court has very broad discretion to decide precisely which policy instruments and implementation processes are necessary and appropriate to remedy intentional racial discrimination. In *Gautreaux,* for example, the U.S. Supreme Court allowed the trial judge to extend his already broad remedy beyond the boundaries of Chicago to include the entire metropolitan housing market.[204]

Even so, the politics and mechanics of implementing whatever housing remedy the court eventually adopted would be complicated and protracted. At a minimum, it would be necessary to agree upon a plan, negotiate with HUD for funding, select and acquire sites, solicit bids from contractors, obtain building permits and zoning approvals, and clear other administrative hurdles in order to reach even the construction stage. No city had ever done this before under the compulsion of a court order. The court's mandate might speed things up, or it might slow them down. Nobody really knew.

Disputes began to surface even before the parties could submit housing plans or discuss settlement. A spirit of compromise, which Mayor Martinelli and others had discerned shortly after the liability ruling, vanished as quickly as it had appeared. The most important conflict was fiscal, all the more so because there was a serious question about whether HUD would defray all of the housing costs to be mandated. Moreover, because the city council must approve the financing of any housing remedy, electoral politics would surely pervade any remedial plan.

On May 28, 1986, after a six-day remedial trial, Judge Sand issued his housing order.[205] He began by finding that the city's violations of minority rights had continued beyond 1980, when the suit was filed, up to the present. In support of this finding, he noted that the city had failed to designate two acceptable public housing sites in east Yonkers, an action that it had agreed to take in 1980 to receive CDBG funds from HUD. He found, in addition, that Yonkers had failed to submit its HAP to HUD and had also failed to procure the Section 8 certificates for use in east Yonkers. Observing that "political paralysis" had "stalemated" the city's decision process, and citing Yonkers' housing needs and financial straits, Judge Sand found it "unthinkable" that the city, by its inaction in selecting sites or filing required documentation, would forgo "scarce federal funds that would be of significant assistance" in providing the additional housing required by his order.[206]

Building on these findings, Judge Sand enjoined the city from confining public or subsidized housing to southwest Yonkers for racial reasons and from otherwise promoting residential segregation. He ordered Yonkers to create an ambitious fair housing program with educational, informational, marketing, and complaint-generating components to be administered by a Fair Housing Office (FHO) committed to nondiscrimination. The FHO's director and program would be selected under court supervision (the judge even exempted the FHO from civil service restrictions). The FHO would work with Yonkers' MHA, to which Sand ordered the city's Section 8 program transferred. Together, the agencies would work to aid families who wished to use Section 8 certificates for units located in east Yonkers.[207]

Most of Judge Sand's order, however, involved a *class* integration remedy that emphasized bricks-and-mortar construction of public housing in east Yonkers and not the dispersal of low-income families into existing private units through the use of Section 8 certificates. The city, Judge Sand decreed, must build 200 public housing units east of the Saw Mill River Parkway. This was the number to which the city had earlier agreed in order to obtain HUD funding and to which HUD had agreed in its consent decree with the NAACP.[208]

Remarkably, Judge Sand also authorized the plaintiffs to prepare the necessary proposals and documents for the implementation of these decrees and announced that if he approved of these proposals and documents, he would order the actions directly into effect through the fictive device of "deeming" the city and HUD into compliance. Judge Sand also used this device to "deem" the city to have taken certain actions—the submission to HUD of certain funding applications and other documents, the designation of at least two sites for 140 family units for preapproval by HUD, and the submission (through MHA) of site development proposals—in the face of the city's failure to take them. He also "deemed" those actions to be in compliance with HUD's legal requirements. Judge Sand ordered that if the city failed to designate approved sites promptly, the court would "deem" the city to have designated a combination of P.S. 4 and two other school sites, and any other available sites recommended by the plaintiffs and approved by the court.[209]

This approach was highly controversial, if not unprecedented. The traditional remedy for a defendant's obduracy or inaction was to hold it in contempt and then enforce that contempt by imposing fines, imprisonment, or both. But Judge Sand anticipated, correctly, a guerrilla strategy of contemptuous behavior on the city's part. He was unwilling to tolerate the protracted, debilitating struggle that a sequential, incremental use of the contempt sanction would almost certainly entail. In addition to the use of the "deeming" device, Judge Sand warned that if the city did not comply, "the Court may appoint a person expert in such matters to assist the Court and the parties in the preparation of the materials required pursuant to this Order, whose reasonable compensation shall be paid by Yonkers."[210]

Judge Sand also encouraged the city to provide most of the public housing units through an inclusionary zoning approach. The designated sites could contain market-rate units as well as assisted ones so long as at least 140 of the 200-unit total were assisted units. He hoped that integrating public housing with private housing would reduce the former's stigma in the public mind and thus ease political opposition. He also hoped that this would encourage the city, in accordance with the prevailing city-planning wisdom, to scatter the units among a number of sites rather than building one obtrusive highrise. Finally, he hoped that this approach would enhance the social and economic integration of low-income tenants into the surrounding community. As for the remaining sixty units, Judge Sand ordered the city to submit proposed sites from a list of six available privately owned sites that the city's planning director had indicated were suitable for development of public housing.

In addition to mandating public housing, Judge Sand required the city, not HUD, to subsidize "affordable" housing for low- and moderate-income people by creating an affordable housing trust fund, to be run by the FHO in cooperation with HUD and the MHA. The trust fund would initially consist of at least 25% of Yonkers CDBG moneys for a three-year period.[211] Through this trust fund, Judge Sand sought to encourage private development of affordable housing and to advance racial and economic integration. Therefore, he required the city to use the trust fund to induce developers to designate at least 20% of their units as affordable units by giving them certain concessions.[212] Moreover, Judge Sand required the city to quickly develop a detailed plan for creating subsidized family housing units beyond the 200 units of public housing already mandated. He insisted that these units be located "in existing residential areas in east or northwest Yonkers" and allowed them to be financed out of the trust fund or out of other public or private resources.[213] For example, they could be included in developments containing market-rate units, and the city could use inclusionary zoning arrangements to provide these units. As with the new public housing, Judge Sand mandated occupancy priorities for the new units in order to use his housing remedy to help integrate the public schools.

This was a stunningly broad order, perhaps the most sweeping ever entered by a federal court.[214] For our purposes, what is most striking about Judge Sand's housing remedy, other than the "deeming" technique mentioned earlier, was his decision to broaden the focus of the case and the ambit of his power in three ways. First, he extended the remedy well beyond public housing, which had been the cynosure of the legal claims and the factual evidence, to also include subsidized private housing. This extension would benefit a larger group of people, including some who were neither poor nor black. Second, he expanded the targets of his remedy far beyond the now-familiar city council and Yonkers housing bureaucrats, who could be subjected to court orders. His decree encompassed the private housing market, an amorphous set of actors who operated according to very different incentives and whom he could not place under his direct control. This would have enormous ramifications.

Even more importantly, Judge Sand reached far beyond the goal that had justified his imposition of liability. He transmuted the lawsuit's goal of ending housing discrimination against poor blacks into a far more ambitious commitment to integrate lower-class blacks and whites into middle- and upper-class neighborhoods by locating new housing for them there. This goal, which was similar to the class-based integrations sought in *Mount Laurel* but employed an altogether different means, was far more difficult to achieve and required much more complex governmental interventions into neighborhoods and housing markets. The particular form of intervention that Judge Sand chose was a structural injunction mandating specific numbers, types, configurations, and income compositions of housing units, and even controlled all private development in the city that might be conscripted into advancing his remedy.

In moving beyond nondiscrimination to class integration, Judge Sand must have known that he was taking on a daunting task—though just how daunting he could never have predicted. Surely he knew that almost twenty years after the original remedial order in *Gautreaux,* virtually none of the mandated public housing had been built despite prodigious efforts by the judges in the case. At the very least, the *Gautreaux* problems would reach his attention a year later when the new judge in that case took the highly unusual step of putting the Chicago Housing Authority into receivership in an effort to gain compliance.[215]

Implementing the housing remedy. By September 1986, the city's requests for a stay of Judge Sand's orders pending appeal had been denied, [216] but the city failed to file the site designations or to do the rezoning required of it by the remedial order. Sussman prepared to return to court. In December 1986, several weeks after the city missed the deadline for filing a subsidized housing plan, the DOJ asked Judge Sand to hold Yonkers in contempt and to appoint a "housing master" as a court expert to develop the required inventory of available sites at the city's expense.[217]

The NAACP supported the request for a housing master, but it did not seek a contempt citation. This decision prefigured a major tactical dispute with DOJ, one that would recur throughout the long remedial phase. Sussman felt that litigating contempt would be a political and legal sideshow. In his view, it would only delay implementation and ensure the reelection of lawless city councillors by making martyrs of them. The parties and the court knew what needed to be done, he argued, and Judge Sand should do it directly through his own appointee rather than give the city more opportunities to temporize. Judge Sand, while noting that contempt always remained a possibility, agreed with Sussman. He named Oscar Newman, the author of several books on city planning and an expert witness in *Starrett City* and other housing integration cases, as his housing master. He directed Newman to submit a ranked list of potential sites within ninety days. Newman envisioned two- or three-story semidetached or townhouse configurations to be occupied mostly by one-parent households with children. The units would be built on eight scattered sites, where they would be integrated into middle-income developments targeted at families earning $25,000–35,000 a year and would be subsidized through the city's use of its CDBG funds and inclusionary zoning deals with builders.

HUD, which would have to fund Newman's plan, had little enthusiasm for it. HUD's strict federal guidelines had been developed with more traditional, higher-density projects in mind. The agency doubted that the higher land and development costs of low-density units, especially in Yonkers' inflated housing market, could meet these restrictions.

Newman anticipated HUD's reaction, but Sussman's criticism of the planner's approach came as something of a shock. Sussman thought Newman's preoccupation with low density was "foolish."[218] The important goal, the lawyer said, was to maximize the number of units built with the limited funds available; "feasibility," not "the ideology of housing forms," should drive the court's decision.[219] This conflict between Newman and Sussman was as much political as it was legal or technocratic. Although east Yonkers residents would find low-density developments far more acceptable than high-rises, the former would inevitably increase the number of sites and thus the number of neighborhoods affected, with predictable opposition. For Sussman, aesthetics and planning principles had to take a backseat to a more mundane imperative: maximizing the number of his clients who would get housing units.

But as "final" deadlines came and went without the city either acquiring potential sites or adopting the necessary zoning changes, Judge Sand's patience wore thin. On July 1, 1987, he threw down the gauntlet: the city's choice, he said, was "compliance or receivership."[220] The city, hoping to avoid public criticism for targeting particular neighborhoods for the housing, urged Judge Sand to impose his own housing plan but he refused to take the bait. The city must designate the sites, rezone for denser public housing, and take the political heat. And if the city failed to submit its long-overdue affordable housing plan by mid-July, he would hold it in contempt and impose a fine of $100 per day that would double each day thereafter. These fines would exhaust the city's entire $306 million budget by the twenty-second day. Tightening the screws even further, Judge Sand ruled that the city could not issue any more building permits with respect to any city-owned or city-controlled property, nor could it sell, transfer, or encumber (e.g., mortgage) such property without his prior approval. Finally, he instructed Newman to submit his final site proposals for the 200 units and to identify surplus county-owned land in Yonkers that the city might use for the additional affordable units that his remedy required.

With this order, the city once again tottered on the rim of fiscal disaster. Sensing that Judge Sand would not hesitate to push it over the brink, the city council pulled back. It approved, and Judge Sand accepted, a plan to build semidetached duplexes or townhouses on eight sites.[221] In a community seemingly addicted to reenacting the "Perils of Pauline," disaster had been averted. Within a week, however, the agreement had begun to unravel as political, legal, and jurisdictional problems arose around each of the eight sites. Sensing trouble ahead, Judge Sand began to retreat from the city's alternate plan. Saying the plan might be revised, he solicited public comments on it.

When the November elections placed more defiant politicians on the city council and replaced the relatively conciliatory mayor with Nicholas Wasicsko, a 28-year-old councillor who had gained election by cultivating a less compliant image, Judge Sand concluded that Yonkers would respond only to persistent pressure. In order to force Yonkers to the point where it might think more clearly about its future, he barred the city from using zoning changes, variances, tax abatements, industrial bonds, or other incentives to assist four pending private developments or any other projects. This moratorium was categorical, with an exception only if a particular project site was unsuitable for public housing. And he was prepared to go even further. If the city remained defiant, he might extend the freeze to "any and all action with respect to any real estate in Yonkers."[222] Judge Sand knew that his step would probably bring major development in Yonkers to a grinding halt at a time when its economy was starting to boom and its budget was running a $20 million surplus. He had raised the stakes once again, threatening to punish the city not by regulating its housing decisions but by strangling its economic development in nonhousing areas.

Although *New York Times* editorials praised Judge Sand's moratorium as a creative answer to Yonkers' defiance,[223] this tactic raised very serious questions of law, policy, and morality. Was his remedial authority broad enough to allow Judge Sand to control *everything* the city did, including mass transit, health care, and sanitation? Were there no narrower remedies that would achieve the desired result? Who would suffer most from the moratorium— city officials, private developers, or poor people living in southwest Yonkers where one of the frozen developments was to be located? And was it just or sensible to impose the burden of public and affordable housing on Yonkers while its far wealthier suburban neighbors sat back and did nothing?

Shortly after Christmas, the Second Circuit gave Judge Sand a much-wanted gift: it unanimously affirmed his liability and remedy decisions in all respects, calling them "exhaustive and well documented."[224] This approval strengthened Judge Sand's hand, making it easier to deal effectively with the more recalcitrant city council that would assume office on New Year's Day. The Second Circuit could hardly have been more deferential to Judge Sand's rulings on law, on facts, on liability, and most remarkably, on remedy. The appellate court had given Judge Sand the whip insofar as remedy was concerned, and he lost no time in cracking it.

The Yonkers consent decree. The Second Circuit's ruling, coupled with Judge Sand's increasing pressure on the Yonkers economy and the city council, had an immediate, unmistakable effect. To the new mayor, Nicholas Wasicsko, it "changed the landscape."[225] The city's litigation strategy, which had produced nothing but $15 million of lawyers' bills, had essentially come to an end. Idled developers and community groups that favored compliance swung into action. The CANOPY group, for example, distributed 60,000 fliers, one to almost every family in the city, urging immediate compliance and a scattered-site solution.

On January 20, 1988, the city council threw in the towel—or so it seemed. Amid a clamorous chamber filled with citizens opposed to the measure, and citing the threat of large fines, the council voted 5–1, with Councillor and Vice Mayor Henry Spallone opposed, to approve the HAP that Judge Sand had mandated years earlier. Five days later, after around-the-clock negotiating sessions and only one hour before the court's deadline, the council agreed to seven specific sites for townhouse-style public housing. The seven sites, each with an agreed-upon number of units, included P.S. 4 and two other public school sites and four privately owned properties. In addition, the city council agreed to adopt an ordinance requiring that all multifamily developments designate at least 20% of the units as affordable units until a total of 800 such units was achieved within four years. In addition, the council agreed not to seek Supreme Court review of Judge Sand's decisions.[226]

Announcing the settlement in open court, a lawyer for Yonkers reported that several pro-compliance council members had received threatening phone calls and envelopes containing bullets.[227] Expressing concern about this intimidation, Judge Sand announced that he would end his freeze on private development, although not the freeze on transfers of city-owned property. As recriminations and accusations between old political allies intensified, the city council fractured along new fault lines.

After a long, raucous January 28 meeting held amid bitter taunts and shouts of "Resign! Resign!" by 800 enraged spectators under the watchful eyes of police officers, the council voted to formally accept the negotiated agreement.[228] When the meeting ended at almost 1:30 A.M., only Spallone, who was loudly cheered, and another councillor who switched his vote at the last moment, Edward Fagan, opposed the resolution. All but one of the councillors who supported the resolution had campaigned against it less than three months earlier, and the sobriquets "wimp" and "liar" were constantly hurled at them. With this vote, the city could sign the consent decree.

Within two months, however, several developments brought the city back to court. With the deadline for appealing to the Supreme Court rapidly approaching, the city now sought to renege on its commitment to forgo that appeal, a commitment that had infuriated many in Yonkers who bitterly resented Judge Sand's orders. The mounting opposition to the consent decree, it argued, was causing "near chaos for the Council in its attempts to govern the city."[229] Few expected the city to win an appeal, but it would be politically popular and might delay the inevitable. To add to the crisis, HUD now refused to provide funds beyond those necessary to build three-story walkups.

New rounds of siting and funding proposals, and counterproposals, culminated in a dramatic motion by the city to vacate the recent consent decree and to return the $30 million HUD grant it had won for the housing.

Judge Sand declined to alter the consent decree. Instead, he entered an order requiring the city council to enact into law a housing plan that he had drafted in consultation with the parties. The council refused to do so and proposed that the court should order the necessary legislation into effect. On July 26, 1988, Judge Sand issued an order giving the council until August 1 to enact the legislation, known as the Affordable Housing Ordinance. If it failed to do so, the city and each councillor failing to vote for it would be punished with contempt citations and heavy fines. On August 1, the council voted 4–3 not to comply, and Judge Sand held the city and four councillors in contempt and imposed the fines. The Second Circuit upheld Judge Sand's sanctions in virtually all respects.[230] The city and councillors appealed to the Supreme Court.

With the city's appeal pending, the fines rapidly growing (those imposed on the councillors were stayed pending appeal), and drastic cuts in core city services looming, the city council purged itself of contempt by enacting the Ordinance. Councillors Spallone and Fagan voted no, remaining in contempt. Spallone's obstinacy was rewarded politically in November 1989 when he ousted the pro-compliance incumbent mayor, Nicholas Wasicsko.[231]

Mayor Spallone and the city continued to defy the court. Judge Sand responded by in effect stepping into the council's shoes. He directly ordered the city housing agencies to implement his instructions on requesting bids for site development, choosing among the bids, transferring the building site titles to developers, issuing building permits, and a host of other matters. HUD, which would have to fund the housing, opposed many of Oscar Newman's design and development plans on bureaucratic, procedural, and cost grounds. It second-guessed him even on matters of detail, such as the quality of fencing around the yards. When construction began on the first site in April 1991, weekly protest marches and more threats of violence followed, but to no avail. In November, Spallone was defeated for reelection.

The 200 units of scattered-site public housing that the court had mandated back in 1985 were built on seven sites that contained fourteen to forty-eight units each and were not fully occupied until the mid-1990s. Sited in overwhelmingly white, middle-income neighborhoods in east Yonkers, they were two- and three-bedroom, factory-built brick townhouses featuring small private backyards and other features designed to make them look like single-family homes and blend into the neighborhood. The tenants were low-income black and Hispanic families whom the MHA chose by lottery, half from existing public housing tenants and half from the waiting list.

Yonkers in the 1990s—developments and reflections. In any moral accounting of the city government's behavior, it has long been bankrupt. Its defiance flagrantly violated the constitutional rights of its minority residents, demonstrated contempt for the rule of law, and nearly destroyed the community, leaving wounds that may never heal. That said (and it can hardly be said enough), any inquest on the law's effectiveness in promoting diversity must ask some other questions. What has Judge Sand's public housing remedy actually wrought? Was it worth the price that the entire Yonkers community— rich and poor, minority and white, racist and integrationist—has paid? Were there other ways through which the court could have better vindicated the law's promises?

The first two questions have an empirical core that social science can help reveal. A study of how the public housing was affecting the surrounding neighborhoods in 1994–1995, shortly after the last mandated tenants moved in, concluded that the housing "has not wreaked havoc in any of the ways that opponents of the court order claimed it would. Most importantly, there are no signs of neighborhood tipping or significant white flight. . . . [A]ny negative price effects not apparent in our statistical models should be short term."[232] Other analysts, however, have examined the data on property value effects and concluded that such declines did occur, especially around the public housing sites in the less prestigious neighborhoods.[233]

Be that as it may, Xavier de Souza Briggs reported in 1997 on how the social integration of these neighborhoods had progressed several years after the moves:

> [F]ew of the movers interact with whites in the new neighborhoods beyond their public housing complex, and few report having white friends or acquaintances in any domain (neighborhood, school, etc.). . . . Also, the movers do not attend neighborhood churches, which help neighbors get acquainted in many American communities. Rather, they go back to their old churches across town. . . . But partly because of their ethnic isolation, one-half of the mover youth (and an equal proportion of stayers) cannot think of a single adult they could count on to provide helpful advice about a school program or getting a job.[234]

Lisa Belkin, *New York Times* journalist and author of a book on Yonkers, conducted extensive before-and-after interviews with the tenants and their opponents and described the situation in 1998:

> In short, the tenants in the townhouses live in a bubble within a bubble. They are still visitors in their new neighborhoods, and they have almost

no interaction with the white homeowners whose world they were sent east to change. Was this what Judge Sand envisioned when he wrote his 657-page opinion? Was it worth ten years and $260 million so that two hundred families could live in nicer homes and be ignored by their neighbors?

I asked Sand a version of this question . . . and it was the only moment during hours of conversation, that made his tone go sharp. The number of townhouses—two hundred in a city of nearly 200,000 people—was chosen by the NAACP and the Justice Department, he said. He accepted their number, but he did not choose it, and he would not comment on whether it was sufficient to remedy the perceived wrong. What he did say was that the point of all this was never *integration*. It was *desegregation*, and the differences are not merely semantic. Yonkers is, technically, desegregated. A group of people, a category if you will, is now allowed in where before it was deliberately kept out. But Yonkers is *not* integrated. Black and white are not woven into the same fabric, the same community. Time might accomplish that. A judge cannot.[235]

The third question, in the inquiry about the law's effectiveness, concerns the availability of more effective remedies and is more easily and categorically answered. Better alternatives existed. The *Gautreaux* plaintiffs, minority and low-income families who were no more welcome in white, middle-class neighborhoods than were their counterparts in Yonkers, used Section 8 vouchers and mobility counseling to rent private units located twenty to thirty miles from their previous central-city neighborhoods in suburbs with a higher quality of life for them and their children. Earlier, we saw that a Section 8 approach has its own serious problems. The families need help finding new housing, getting it inspected, negotiating with landlords, defraying moving expenses, and settling into an alien environment. Often, the vouchers' value is too low to pay market rents and overcome landlords' suspicions about subsidized tenants and the program's administration. That said, the results are still encouraging.

Judge Sand did not have to look to Chicago for proof of this proposition. From the mid-1990s on, the proof was right there in Yonkers—literally under his nose—in the form of the Enhanced Section 8 Outreach Program (ESOP). ESOP was created in 1993 in the wake of a suit against HUD and state, county, and Yonkers Section 8 agencies. The suit claimed that the entities were preventing families from using their Section 8 benefits to move into racially and economically mixed neighborhoods.[236] The suit charged that these agencies refused to approve rent exceptions that could raise the vouchers' value so that tenants could rent in such neighborhoods, steered tenants to southwest Yonkers neighborhoods, did not do the HUD-mandated out-reach to landlords in other areas, and discouraged landlords from accepting vouchers. Under the consent decree in that case, ESOP would do what the city had failed to do—try to help Section 8 tenants move out of southwest Yonkers by seeking higher voucher values, recruiting and negotiating with landlords on behalf of Section 8 tenants, advising, screening, and prioritizing the tenants for reliability, not concentrating too many of them in a single building or neighborhood, and helping them gain access to other benefit programs that might make them more attractive to landlords.

After eight years and operating with only three people on a $236,000 annual budget, ESOP has replicated *Gautreaux*'s relatively successful mobility program. It has moved approximately 250 families to housing outside south-west Yonkers, including many into other racially and economically mixed Westchester County communities. Utilizing a higher payment standard approved by HUD in April 2002, it is now placing 65 families a year in such communities.[237] In stark contrast, the city's own non–Section 8 rental assis-tance program had moved only 22 families out of southwest Yonkers by Oc-tober 2002, fifteen months after the city grudgingly established the pro-gram.[238] This paltry outcome is hardly surprising given the agency's political incentives to keep them in their ghetto.

The city's dismal performance extended as well to the separate affordable housing part of the remedy. In 1997, a new mayor, John Spencer, took office. Spencer convinced Judge Sand to allow the city to fulfill its obligation largely through its own agencies and by using existing units in order to minimize the delay and political turmoil involved in acquiring sites and building new units. Under a new plan, New York State, which Judge Sand had previously found to be partly responsible for Yonkers' housing segregation, would designate 740 affordable units (some existing and some new, at the city's discretion) and would pay half of their $32 million cost. Simultaneously, other sources of potential funding arose: Sussman brought the Urban Development Corpora-tion, a potentially substantial source of new funds, into the case. Additionally, the Emergency Financial Control Board, which under state law had super-vised Yonkers' finances since 1975, decided to restore fiscal control to the city. With these developments producing some tendrils of optimism, even Judge Sand now foresaw an end to the saga.[239]

Judge Sand should have known better. Disputes with the city continued. The Fair Housing Implementation Office (FHIO), which Judge Sand estab-lished in the late 1980s to secure the mandated affordable housing through some combination of public subsidies and private developers, was utterly in-effective. It generated almost no affordable housing units outside southwest Yonkers. Judge Sand seemed surprised at FHIO's failure. But his surprise itself is surprising: many experts had predicted its failure because it took a financial approach that made little sense even to fair housing advocates and because of the perceived incompetence of Karen Hill, the FHIO director. Hill wanted families to *own* the affordable units. Yet FHIO's eligibility criteria gave priority to public housing families with no ownership experience, in whom potential developers, co-op converters, and lenders had little interest. Many of the families, moreover, were understandably skeptical about a program that saddled them with mortgage payments and limited their ability to accumulate equity and sell at a profit. To them, FHIO's program seemed to be mostly a downside risk.

With Judge Sand's approval, Spencer fired Hill and assigned FHIO's duties to a city housing agency.[240] The city agency, however, did only a little better than FHIO. Beginning in 1998, it offered ownership of existing affordable units to 175 families. Few observers were surprised by the program's slow pace given its continued stress on ownership and a widespread belief that the city wanted it to fail. In December 1999, an increasingly frustrated Judge Sand issued his third supplemental affordable housing order. The order imposed a new, racially defined system of priorities and city compliance bonuses. Both the city and the NAACP appealed. The city argued that the order violated the 1988 consent decree and unconstitutionally used racial criteria; Sussman attacked the order as too lenient. The Second Circuit upheld the order early in 2001.[241] The race-conscious remedy was proper, the court held, because of the city's repeated defiance of Judge Sand's earlier orders, the resegregative effects of its placements, and the fact that Yonkers public housing was still substantially segregated.[242] When the Supreme Court declined to hear either side's appeal in December 2001, this decision became final.[243]

Meanwhile, the ostensible point of all this legal wrangling—more affordable housing in east Yonkers—was as far from fulfillment as ever. Efforts during the late 1990s by the DOJ to get HUD to issue special Section 8 vouchers to implement the Yonkers housing decree failed when HUD insisted that it lacked the authority to issue them for this purpose. DOJ lawyers then met with ESOP to explore the possibility of having the city hire ESOP to move Section 8–eligible families into better neighborhoods. Given ESOP's track record, the DOJ's aim to place twenty-five to thirty families a year in this fashion seemed eminently feasible. The city, however, flatly refused either to hire ESOP or to use Section 8 vouchers. Instead, it hired a private nonprofit organization, the Housing Action Council, to run a new city-regulated, city-funded rent assistance program that drew families from the court-mandated priority list. Sussman acquiesced in this and the DOJ did not object.

The city had also managed to whittle the consent decree's original target of

800 affordable units down to 600 existing units—100 units per year for six years beginning in 1997. As of August 2002, the final year of this remedial schedule, the city had provided only 233 of the promised 600 units. As noted earlier, its alternative to Section 8 had managed to move only twenty-two families into rentals in desegregated neighborhoods as of October 2002.[244] After a generation of litigation and fifteen years of resolute supervision by a resourceful judge whose far-reaching remedies were affirmed by the nation's highest court, the remedies remain mostly empty words, the DOJ remains frustrated, and the minorities in Yonkers remain where they were when the litigation began, perhaps even more so because of the departure of so many whites from the city.

CONCLUSION

In a review of the *Yonkers* case written in 2001, two political scientists provide a sweeping and pessimistic appraisal:

> To the degree that any locality can stand in for the whole, Yonkers is a microcosm of the United States on [the desegregation] issue. Its history demonstrates that, even with the best intentions and a lot of power, over the long term political actors cannot or will not extensively desegregate public schools and public housing. If Americans are serious about implementing the principles of equal opportunity and racial integration, they must find other means than the forms of desegregation with which our nation has been preoccupied since the 1960s. Mandatory school desegregation and quasi-mandatory public housing desegregation are dinosaurs appreciated by many, laughed at by some, but doomed in any case to extinction.[245]

This is a harsh verdict but astute advice to anyone who would look to the courts to promote racial and class diversity and social integration in residential communities. Yonkers is indeed a microcosm of America, but fortunately its officials' open, protracted, and contemptuous defiance of the law is probably unique since the end of massive resistance to the civil rights laws of the 1960s.

This chapter has discussed three prolonged, high-visibility legal conflicts involving roughly similar social, economic, and political constraints on courts' ability to protect and implement the legal rights that the judges defined, substantively or remedially, in residential diversity terms. In *Mount Laurel*, the New Jersey courts tried to enforce a substantive right of low- and moderate-income families to live in residential communities that they could not afford without public subsidies. In *Gautreaux* and *Yonkers*, the courts tried to enforce a substantive right to equal treatment through remedies that measured families' equal protection rights and community integration levels by racial- and income-diversity indices. *Gautreaux* has improved housing options for thousands of low-income minority families who now enjoy some of the hoped-for social, economic, and educational benefits of integration. In contrast, endless litigation in *Mount Laurel* and *Yonkers* has yielded little housing improvement and even less genuine integration. What accounts for the different outcomes?

In each case, of course, one can point to contextual differences that complicate efforts to compare and generalize, such as idiosyncratic judges, distinctive communities, and unique political and economic conditions. Four commonalities are striking nonetheless. First, the market's pervasive influence over housing choices powerfully constrains, and often distorts, efforts by government generally and courts in particular to shape those choices. Second, a ubiquitous classism rejects the idea that people should have a right to live in a neighborhood they cannot afford. Third, politically mobilized communities strongly oppose the kinds of diversity the courts have mandated. Fourth, courts possess only the crudest, most limited tools for constructing a new vision of diversity amid these obstacles. In effect, they are trying to erect a large tent with one hand in the middle of a hurricane.[246]

In *Mount Laurel*, the legislature sized up these four conditions and promptly supplanted the courts with an administrative agency, albeit one still unable to grapple effectively with the housing market's remorseless logic. In *Yonkers*, a determined judge promoted his remedy with every weapon in his arsenal (plus some that arguably were not), yet they proved abjectly inadequate for the task. Like Canute facing the turbulent sea, like a general without an army, Judge Sand could not master the forces on which his plan's success depended. He had to contend with the powerful self-interest of thousands of ordinary people fearing inner-city contagion, people whose locational choices were constrained only by their income and willingness to move. He was also opposed by the city politicians who reflected and fed those anxieties, by the developers who saw little profit in low- and middle-income housing, by the neighboring, resource-rich communities to which his writ did not run, and by the city bureaucracies with incentives to delay and subvert but not to comply. His main vision, scattered-site housing for minorities and the poor, did little more than expand subsidized housing into older, blue-collar neighborhoods near the inner city while leaving more affluent areas almost as economically and racially homogeneous as before.[247]

Indeed, Judge Sand's efforts probably made matters much worse. This criticism seems amply warranted when we consider the opportunity costs of his remedial decisions—particularly the better, more integrated housing that a mobility remedy would have provided to minority and other low-income families; the scarce resources squandered by the interminable legal proceedings, most of which were paid by the city's working-class taxpayers; the political scars left by the conflict; and the further segregation of a city that was 79% white in 1980 but only 50% white in 2000.[248] Additionally, over two decades of litigation of both school and housing issues have left the public schools even more segregated than the city generally. In 2002, when the school side of the case was finally settled (largely for cash)—and after city and state desegregation expenditures estimated at $500 million—white students comprised only 25% of the school population, down from 65% in 1980 when the case was filed.[249]

Seldom, if ever, has so much judicial power been exerted for so long against so many officials and produced so little progress as in *Yonkers*.[250] The culprit, of course, has always been the city government itself, not the judge who sought tirelessly, if often fecklessly, to uphold the law. This cannot be emphasized enough. But neither this fact nor the fact that *Yonkers* is an unusually pathological case should blind us to the deeper, more structural problems that arise when the law defines, promotes, and mandates diversity in certain ways. We must go on to ask whether, taking the city's flagrant defiance as a given, Judge Sand could have fashioned a more promising remedy.

Gautreaux suggests an affirmative answer. The court there faced similar resistance and seemingly endless temporizing by Chicago politicians and public housing bureaucrats. Yet, after some false starts, the court managed to regroup and refashion its remedial approach by establishing an outreach-focused mobility program based on Section 8. This program, despite its problems, became a national model for diversity programs (like ESOP in Yonkers) that arm families with vouchers and support services, and accompany them into the market where they can rent housing from those landlords who can be induced to accept them. Section 8 vouchers still encounter resistance from some landlords even though the program has been changed to make it more market-friendly—for example, by letting landlords use their own leases with Section 8 tenants and not requiring renewal at the tenant's option.[251] But landlord resistance tends to be isolated, of low visibility, and sometimes tractable to negotiation by groups like ESOP on behalf of voucher-holders.

As discussed above, Judge Sand's approach was very different. His was a bricks-and-mortar, fixed-site, take-it-or-leave-it, top-down, court-designed, court-managed remedy for public housing. He did not empower the low-income families to carry money-equivalents into the market and to negotiate with landlords with the sustained assistance of highly motivated outreach and mobility specialists. Rather, he empowered the very same officials who created the problem in the first place, who had repeatedly defied the law and the court, and who had neither political nor market incentives to promote the families' interests. In addition, although Judge Sand did initially look to Section 8 as part of his affordable housing remedy, he surrendered to Yonkers' resistance to using vouchers, and then allowed the city to substitute a limited, demonstrably failed rental assistance program of its own and to continue to violate its own promises and timetables.

Indeed, Judge Sand's tenacious effort to manage Yonkers housing markets from his courtroom was even less auspicious than the command-and-control regulation that has performed so poorly in so many different policy domains.[252] By forcing families into public housing clusters, he created a highly visible target that the community could easily stigmatize and mobilize against, a target with few defenders besides the court. Had Judge Sand deployed his legal authority on behalf of a well-designed, well-supported Section 8 remedy as forcefully as he deployed it in pursuit of his bricks-and-mortar approach, the result would almost certainly have been better for low-income and minority residents of Yonkers.

Diversity policymakers can draw at least one clear lesson from my three case studies of residential integration. Neighborhoods are complex, fragile, organic societies whose dynamics outsiders cannot readily understand, much less control. A court demanding the implementation of a diversity ideal that a neighborhood's residents do not share, and will strenuously resist, cannot conscript the housing market to do its bidding as it might be able to do with a public bureaucracy (though problematically, and in Yonkers' case, perversely). A court that mandates this diversity over such resistance is bound to impair its legitimacy and effectiveness. Recalcitrant neighborhoods are more likely to allow for diversity when it comes with money or other things of value, although even this may not assuage residents' fears.[253] Government-sponsored dispersal and integration of poor and minority families into resistant white, middle-class neighborhoods can succeed, if at all, only when done in a small, carefully orchestrated, and low-visibility way. Voucher-type mobility remedies are *necessary* for this even if they are not always *sufficient*. The alternative, alas, is probably some version of the ongoing Yonkers imbroglio.

CHAPTER 7

Religion: Protecting and Exploiting Diversity

America is an anomaly among modern postindustrial societies, in at least three respects. It is more religious,[1] its religiosity is more diverse,[2] and its separation of state from religion is more rigorous and complete.[3] This religiosity, diversity, and separation—which contrast sharply with the European experience—did not come immediately or naturally. The zealous Puritans who founded American society were soon reduced to a minority even in the Plymouth Colony, and their descendants conducted a constant and for the most part unsuccessful struggle with secularism, indifference, and declining church attendance.[4] The only doctrine they valued was their own—or as the nineteenth-century minister Henry Ward Beecher put it, "Orthodoxy is *my* doxy and heterodoxy is *your* doxy, if *your* doxy is not like *my* doxy."[5] Themselves antiestablishment dissenters, many colonists nonetheless did not shrink from persecuting, expelling, and even killing those whose worship differed from theirs[6]—an intolerance widely practiced, *mutatis mutandis,* in Massachusetts, Maryland, Virginia, New Amsterdam, and other colonies.[7]

What brought religious diversity to America was not so much toleration as immigration, which the colonies desired primarily for its economic value to thinly settled frontier communities and their entrepreneurial merchants and real estate speculators. As we saw in Chapter 3, toleration for the unusual beliefs and practices of other Christians, not to speak of non-Christians and nonbelievers, came only slowly and, even then, incompletely.[8] Americans, literally repelled by the religious wars that had butchered and benighted so many of their ancestors in Europe, gradually found their way to the live-and-let-live acceptance of heterodox beliefs and disparate practices that marks our constitutional tradition—and, today, our dominant social ethos.[9] The dramatic declines in anti-Catholicism and anti-Semitism during the last half of the twentieth century were important signs of this attitudinal change. If any more proof of the new ethos were needed, recall President Bush's speech to the nation only two days after the September 11 terrorist attacks, praising Arab-Americans and Islam while declaring war on their violent coreligionists.

Traditionally, most religious believers have wanted others to embrace their faith. They viewed religious diversity as a troublesome social reality to be hemmed in and if necessary suppressed (as in the case of Mormon polygamy and the church itself).[10] What is decidedly untraditional is to regard religious diversity as an affirmative social good. Indeed, until quite recently, only a relative handful of visionaries held this view, and some of them were not themselves religious people. Rather, their perspective on religious diversity proceeded mainly from practical concerns. They hoped that civil society, by harboring many contending beliefs, would neutralize and domesticate their dangerous propensities. Peacekeeping motives for protecting religious diversity have long existed—although it is worth recalling that the Supreme Court did not protect a minority religion under the Free Exercise Clause until the 1940s.[11] In contrast to grudging or necessitous toleration, the embrace of religious diversity as an affirmative social ideal is a very recent concept dating back only to 1965. In that year, Congress abolished the national origins immigration quotas (see Chapter 4), and Vatican II issued *Dignitatis Humanae Personae,* urging religious freedom for all individuals.[12]

Today government proposes to do something even more novel than preserving, protecting, and accommodating religion. It seeks to exploit our religious diversity in order to advance certain secular policy goals. This creates problems for the public management of diversity that are different from those encountered in the earlier chapters. For example, officials who make immigration, citizenship, and language policy must decide which kinds of diversity will promote our cultural and demographic goals and which of them threaten national identity, solidarity, and other overriding imperatives. Affirmative action policy must decide which groups will be preferred in the face of sharp zero-sum conflicts and constitutional constraints. Officials who would integrate residential communities in order to rectify past discrimination are stymied by people who can flee when faced with unwanted kinds of diversity.

Compared with these challenges, the task of protecting religious diversity has been a simpler (though not simple) matter. Historically, Steven Smith notes, "the ferment that caused religious diversity to flourish–and that is largely responsible for the condition of religious freedom we enjoy today–was a product of pluralism; it owed little or nothing to judicial review, or to the legal elaboration and enforcement of any constitutional 'principle of religious freedom.'"[13] Religious minorities now have vast breathing space where they can cultivate their distinctive beliefs and practices. No one group exercises hegemony. The First Amendment protects dissenters, and strong social norms favor religious autonomy and pluralism. As we shall see, politicians often respond favorably to even small religious groups. I do not mean that it is easy to define the shifting, porous boundary between public purposes and religious liberty and then defend it with workable rules of accommodation. Hard cases do arise and the stakes for people of deep faith are very high. Nevertheless, accommodation is a familiar task for courts engaged in routine case-by-case adjudication. Far more daunting are legislative efforts to mobilize diverse religious groups as affirmative instruments of secular policy. Such efforts are highly controversial even when the policy goal is widely accepted—for example, public support of social services.

In order to contextualize these accommodation and mobilization strategies, I first develop the facts about religious diversity—the multiplicity of faiths and their fragmentation into numerous smaller units (alongside the rise of mega-churches); the social forces driving this fragmentation; and the nature of American religiosity. Second, I discuss the ideal of religious diversity, developing the general concepts and principles that together define it. As the courts implement this ideal under the aegis of the religion clauses,[14] they must referee a robust, incessant competition for public allegiance between civic and religious values. In this competition, I maintain, judges' regulatory lodestars must be two kinds of neutrality—among religions, and between the religious values of a pious people and the secular values of a liberal civic culture.

As an ideological matter, the value of neutrality is not terribly controversial in a liberal society like ours. But defining neutrality in a way that decides hard cases without appealing to some non-neutral value is more than difficult. To Stanley Fish, it is "mission impossible" because *all* values are non-neutral—despite the best efforts of their proponents to depict them as universal.[15] When I speak of neutrality, then, I do not mean to deny Fish's incontrovertible point. Indeed, Fish acknowledges that some understandings of neutrality are more plausible and persuasive than others; he simply refuses to claim for them a transcendence they do not possess. Nor do I mean to deny a cognitive point about neutrality—that its meaning depends on how one frames the particular comparisons in the neutrality analysis.[16] This is simply an instance of a more general difficulty encountered when we reason by analogy: judgment, not logic, determines which features of the arguably analogous cases should be regarded as salient to the comparison.

Neutrality, then, is a norm whose content and application are often highly contestable. This is almost always true where disputes over government regulation affecting religion are concerned. In this context, I define neutrality to mean a requirement that the law accommodate any religious practice or claim that does not threaten compelling governmental interests. This standard did not seem neutral enough to the Supreme Court in its 1990 ruling, *Employment Division, Department of Human Resources of Oregon v. Smith*, which rejected it.[17] The pre-*Smith* Court had used this "compelling interest" standard but had generally applied it to reject the religious claim and uphold the government's refusal to accommodate.[18]

Notwithstanding the possible deference to governmental interests in the application of this standard, its formulation did—and still does—underscore the public value of preserving a broad private sphere of religious autonomy where the law tolerates some deviant practices that offend our general policies and civic sensibilities. In this view of neutrality, government must not coerce a religious practice, of course, but neither should it sponsor or endorse it, favor one religion over another, or favor religion over nonreligion or the reverse. (As use of the "In God We Trust" motto on U.S. currency suggests, exceptions to the neutrality norm exist, usually rationalized on grounds of the Framers' usage, hoary tradition, or *de minimis* offense.)[19] A neutral law would leave individuals, families, and communities to work out their own solutions to disputes over student-led prayers, moments of silence, and other such practices[20]—even though believers sometimes discomfit, isolate, or stigmatize religious or atheistic minorities.[21] The law's province should not extend to regulating informal sanctions of this sort, however deplorable.

Finally, I examine two proposals that would go beyond merely protecting religious diversity; they would also use it affirmatively to achieve certain secular policy ends. "Charitable choice" seeks to recruit faith-based organizations (FBOs) to deliver publicly funded social services to individuals and families. It would try to exploit FBOs' experience in providing direct, person-to-person interventions designed to improve clients' behaviors by altering their moral and spiritual beliefs. "School choice," particularly in the form of tuition vouchers, would give families alternatives to their local public schools, such as private religious schools. As with charitable choice, voucher advocates hope to use religious (and secular) diversity, which proliferates different educational approaches, to advance the secular policy goal of improving the educational experiences of children in all schools.

RELIGIOUS DIVERSITY-IN-FACT

To understand the still-evolving ideal of religious diversity in America, one must first consider the social facts that surround it. As already noted, these facts largely reflect historical patterns of immigration. Native Americans' religious diversity was vast before the Europeans arrived and remains so today.[22] European settlers brought with them quite disparate cultural, linguistic, and confessional traditions, and the churches they established in America were ethnically parochial in these senses. For example, Catholic immigrants from France, Italy, Bavaria, Puerto Rico, and South America naturally preferred to worship with coreligionists from the old country—although they used the

Latin liturgy until after Vatican II. These imported religious traditions have achieved a critical mass in the United States that is now more easily sustainable than ever before—although the assimilation process may in time efface some of their ethnic distinctiveness. Globalization, Diana Eck notes, "enables an immigrant from India to read the *Times of India* every morning on the Internet, to subscribe to Indian cable news on the satellite dish, to bring artisans from rural India to work on Hindu temples in suburban America, and to return home for a family wedding."[23]

America's religious diversity also reflects the fierce, fractious ethos of its Protestantism, an ethos refined through almost four centuries of sectarian struggle as well as by American society's distinctive racial, class, ethnic, and regional cleavages.[24] This history precipitated a vast number of sects and denominations (a term I use loosely here to mean large confessionally related groups). This heterodox pattern was apparent as early as the seventeenth century with the migration of Huguenots, Quakers, Mennonites, and other dissenting groups to the American colonies.[25] Nor is this fragmentation diminishing today. During the twentieth century, the Pentecostal movement produced more than 300 distinct denominations,[26] and a significant dissident faction has recently arisen within the Southern Baptist Convention, by far the largest Protestant group.[27]

Indeed, further fragmentation seems likely as the forces of secularism, pluralism, and bureaucratization transform the nature, function, and relationships of religious groups. Thirty-five years ago, Peter Berger described them as "marketing agencies" working in a "system of free competition very similar to that of *laissez-faire* capitalism," one in which "[r]eligious contents become subjects of 'fashion.'"[28] On the supply side, denominations seek more distinctive niches or "brand identities" with which to hold and attract members. On the demand side, individuals in what Wade Clark Roof calls the "questing culture" pursue a bewildering variety of customized mixes of meditation, therapy, counseling, self-help, behavior modification, fellowship, and a search for "spirituality without religion."[29] The power of this competitive, individuating impulse helps to explain why so little has come of formal ecumenical efforts among American churches, most of which have involved restoring relations broken by the Civil War.[30]

These centrifugal forces extend far beyond Protestantism. American Judaism, for example, long ago split into four major streams—and a fifth, "humanistic Judaism," is now seeking recognition.[31] Some of these, like Reconstructionism, have no real counterparts in other countries, while others, such as Orthodoxy, are divided into so-called "black hat," Lubavitcher, modern, and many other sects led by particular rabbis, with the greatest growth occurring in the more conservative sects. As this example suggests, the fragmentation is by no means confined to liberal, congregational-oriented, and decentralized groups; it also extends to the more hierarchical Catholic and Orthodox Christian churches and especially to the evangelical and Pentecostal sects, which are the fastest growing of all in the United States and are rapidly expanding overseas.[32] Indeed, the largest gains in the evangelical sector have occurred in nondenominational groups, which have tripled as a percentage of the total since 1965.[33] The degree of fragmentation is further underscored by the fact that once we set aside a few large denominations—Catholics (22%), Baptists (18%), and Methodists (9%)—no single religious group exceeds 5% of the population.[34]

Even within the most hierarchical of American religions, diverse views abound. Today's Catholic Church has been described, perhaps hyperbolically, as "a federation of internally divided quasi denominations. . . . [P]eople who identify as Catholic are more liberal on sexual morals than Protestants as a whole. Birth rates and opinions on abortions are virtually the same. Like Protestantism, the American Catholic Church today seems to be many denominations, loosely united."[35] A 1996 survey finds an almost even split between "traditional" and "progressive" Catholics on basic issues of faith, and much the same is true among other putatively conservative groups:

> For example . . . one-third of committed evangelicals and 41% of committed Catholics believe that legal abortions should be available to women in at least some circumstances other than rape, incest, or to save the life of the mother, and well over half of the members of these two groups support the distribution of birth control information in public schools. Thirty-three percent of committed evangelicals—and nearly as high a percentage of Mormons—believe that government regulation is necessary for the public good, and 28 percent of both groups think that the federal government does a better job than it is often given credit for. Similarly, about one-fourth of committed black Protestants believe that the government cannot afford to do more for the needy, and almost one-third feel that African Americans are largely responsible for their own economic circumstances.[36]

Truly, American Protestantism's intradenominational differences are greater than their interdenominational ones.[37]

In addition, the religious practices and views within most religious groups in America are far more heterogeneous liturgically, doctrinally, organizationally, demographically, and in their geographic distributions than the same groups are elsewhere in the world—and this diversification is accelerating. For each church that amalgamates with others today, many more are born afresh or separate from their parent congregations. An estimated 1,600 religions and denominations exist in the United States, a far cry from the "three-religion country" proclaimed by Will Herberg in the 1950s. About half of them were founded after 1965.[38] Indeed, as Richard Ostling points out, each of two dozen denominations has as many local congregations today as made up the whole of American religion in 1776.[39] Here, as elsewhere in American life, technological and market forces have played their part in spawning diverse forms of worship—tele-churches, mega-churches, and pastoral teachings on the Internet.

Reflecting international trends,[40] the mainline Protestant denominations—predominantly white, relatively affluent, ecumenical, affiliated with the National Council of Churches, and leaders in college and seminary education—have experienced markedly declining population since the 1960s. (Most of them, however, grew during the 1990s, even in percentage terms.)[41] The American Episcopal Church, for example, has lost 23% of its members in the last thirty years; just during the 1990s, the Presbyterian Church USA declined by 11.6% and the United Church of Christ declined by 14.8%.[42] Catholicism, with more than 62 million adherents and new concentrations in the South and Southwest, is holding its own demographically with the help of immigration; about 3% of its seminarians are Vietnamese.[43] The share of Baptists and Methodists did not change during the 1990s.[44]

At the same time, the shares of fundamentalist, evangelical, pentecostal, and charismatic sects have grown dramatically; the Mormons' share has doubled, the Assemblies of God's has more than tripled, and the Church of God in Christ's has risen almost ninefold.[45] Ecstatic Christianity is resurgent. These dramatic demographic and ideological shifts within Protestantism, as we shall see, are having far-reaching effects on the balance between secular and religious values in contemporary American politics.

Christianity still utterly dominates religious affiliation throughout America. In 2001, 82% of those polled described themselves as Christians; this share, although down from 89% in 1947, represents 100 million more adherents.[46] Indeed, more Christians live in the United States than in any other country in the world,[47] and virtually every U.S. county is predominantly Christian.[48] Even so, non-Christian, non-Jewish religions have grown rapidly here. Almost one million Hindus live in the United States today compared with only 70,000 in 1977; most of the world's diverse Hindu traditions are practiced here, as are the Sikh, Jain, and other offshoots of Hinduism. The Muslim population is now roughly two to three million.[49] Like Protestants, they are divided by ethnicity, race, and language; one-third are from South and East Asia, 30% are African-American, and 25% are Arabs. Significant tensions, moreover, exist within and among these groups.[50] There soon will be more Muslims in the United States than in the small Arab countries.[51] As with Hinduism, all branches of Islamic worship can be found here. An estimated four million practicing Buddhists live in the United States, representing the whole range of Asian Buddhist traditions, along with many indigenous American ones.[52] Only twenty-one Buddhist study centers existed in the United States from 1900 to 1964, but more than 1,000 exist today; American-born Buddhists recently consecrated an immense stupa in a Rocky Mountain valley.[53] The Federation of Zoroastrians in North America has established many Zoroastrian temples here,[54] and more Baha'i live in the United States than in Iran.[55] Even pagan religions seem to be flourishing in the United States; the Pagan Educational Network estimates 600,000 practitioners here.[56]

But even this denominational variation understates the amount of religious diversity in America. Worshipful energy, liturgical innovation, and even governing authority have gravitated steadily from the national organizations to their regional and local units[57]—a devolution that religious organizations in America share with secular ones.[58] Even the Jesuits, the most disciplined, hierarchical, and orthodox of Catholic groups, have come under the spell of these fragmenting, individualizing conditions of modern American religious life.[59]

To an extent, the devolution of even highly centralized religious authority rests on practical, structural, and ideological considerations. The Episcopal Diocese of New York, for example, conducts its Sunday worship in fourteen languages, and U.S. Catholics, who are increasingly Spanish- and Asian-language speakers, come from twenty-three different countries of origin.[60] Another powerful diversifying force is Americans' traditional personalization of their religious practices, whether as members of organized denominations or not—a remarkable phenomenon famously analyzed by philosopher William James a century ago in *The Varieties of Religious Experience*.[61] No other society on earth has experienced this vast proliferation of sects, which usually break away from more mainstream denominations, and "new religions" or cults, usually centered around charismatic leaders.[62] In Alan Wolfe's study of middle-class suburbanites, he found that "this strong strain of individualism . . . helps explain why, as religious as Americans are, they also distrust organized religion: in 1990, as few as 23 percent of the American population expressed a great deal of confidence in religious institutions. . . . Americans would be more comfortable living next to blacks than to religious sectarians."[63] Even traditional sectarianism cannot wholly satisfy this radical religious individualism, which Wolfe finds to be distinctively privatistic, voluntaristic, nondogmatic, and separate from organized religion.

Indeed, sociologists have argued that all religions in America, including

those with strong hierarchical organizations, become de facto congregation-
alist in form and practice.[64] Even the Catholic Church in the United States,
which for centuries has successfully resisted devolving power over diocesan
decisions, may have to cede more authority to parish and lay groups in the
wake of the pedophilia scandals roiling it.[65] In Protestant congregations, a
liberal-conservative divide commonly forms, and "special purpose groups,"
which reflect members' diverse interests but also create more divisions,
abound.[66] Still further along in the process of congregational fragmentation
is the apparently growing number of "home churches" where a single family,
sometimes joined by a few others, constitutes its own unique congregation
and liturgy.[67] The ultimate destinations of this implacable individualism, it
appears, are the narcissistic, spiritual wanderings of the individuals and families who populate the growing questing culture discussed earlier.

This chronic dissatisfaction with religious institutions bears a striking resemblance to the populist, antihierarchical, maverick, and competitive impulses that Americans exhibit in other spheres. Their mistrust of mainline religions probably springs from many of the same social, psychological, and
ideological sources as their suspicion of large corporations, political parties,
professional expertise, and government. This may help to explain a striking
fact: Americans profess strong religious convictions but appear to know little
about basic religious ideas and facts. Fully 96% of them say that they believe
in God—about the same as fifty years ago—with 90% believing in heaven,
65% in the Devil, and 75% in angels that affect human affairs. In 1996, religion accounted for 16% of all television programming in the United States
and such programming appeared on 257 stations, up from 1% and nine stations in 1974. Sales of "Christ-honoring products" had quadrupled to $4
billion since 1980.[68] In 2001, 25% of adult Internet users, about 28 million
people, had gone online to find religious and spiritual material—more than
the number who had visited gambling sites, participated in online auctions,
or traded stocks online, and a sharp increase from the number in 2000.[69]

More than 40% of Americans have been telling pollsters for six decades that
they attend religious services each week. Although the accuracy of this figure
has been doubted, its consistency over time is striking. In any event, church
attendance is higher, often much higher, than in any other industrialized
country other than Ireland and Poland,[70] as are other indicia of religiosity.[71]
The United States is the only advanced Western industrial society with an important fundamentalist movement.[72] Thus Americans' theological ignorance
is all the more remarkable. Although 93% of their homes contain at least one
Bible and a third claim to read it at least once a week, 54% cannot name the
authors of the Gospels, 63% do not know what a Gospel is, 58% cannot name

five of the Ten Commandments, and 10% think Joan of Arc was Noah's wife! Indeed, a recent survey found an astonishing number of born-again Christians whose views seem to flatly contradict the Bible.[73]

Although some regard this religiosity, especially the growth in evangelical membership, as proof of another "great awakening,"[74] the data suggest otherwise. Mainline denominations, now quite liberal theologically, are losing members to indifference or to more conservative breakaway groups. Secularism continues to rise, most notably among influential university and media elites.[75] The share of those self-describing as atheists, agnostics, and "no preference" has almost doubled since 1965, and a large and growing minority of younger Americans consider themselves "spiritual" rather than religious.[76] Even among the religious, a significant decline in traditional religious beliefs, practices, and commitment has occurred during this period. For example, Gallup polls indicate that in 1993 only 46% of Catholics in the United States said they regularly attended Mass, down from 74% in 1958.[77] At the same time, however, many religious beliefs seem to have intensified.[78] Today, some social analysts think, America's great cultural divide is not among different religions but between believers and nonbelievers.[79]

Whether all of this amounts to paradox, a deeper consistency, inartful survey techniques, or arrant hypocrisy is uncertain. What is clear is that Americans profess respect for the religious diversity around them.[80] Wolfe describes it this way:

> When we consider how many people have died in the name of religion over the years, the acceptance of so many different kinds of belief in America is remarkable. One is tempted to call it real diversity, not because the idea of diversity is inappropriate to race, gender, or sexual orientation, but because religion claims to speak to what really and truly matters in life. I confess that at some level I did not fully understand the non-judgmentalism of middle-class Americans . . . [but] what comes along with it [is] a strong commitment to the principle that a wide variety of religious views ought to be allowed to flourish.[81]

Indeed, recent research suggests that this diversity actually promotes church attendance and religious commitment.[82] Perhaps religious pluralism sends a social signal that a robust norm of belief exists, one that confers status regardless of what the beliefs are. Alternatively, this diversity may trigger a more straightforward economic dynamic in which churches and sects compete for parishioners by emphasizing their differences—their unique "brand identities"—in contrast to the similarities that ecumenical movements emphasize. Some, for example, have launched costly identity-building campaigns—casting off bland, generic texts and hymns in favor of more sect-specific ones, and requiring sect-specific courses for adults and children.[83]

Scientific, technological, and material progress since the nineteenth century has affected the nature of American religious belief and practice in many ways. But what is most striking, particularly when compared with other developed societies, is the persistence of Americans' fervent, quirky, diversified quest for spirituality and transcendence in the face of this progress. There is little sign that this quest is abating.[84]

RELIGIOUS DIVERSITY-AS-IDEAL

A remarkable degree of religious diversity, then, is a continuing, distinctive fact of American life. I now take up religious diversity as an affirmative ideal, which as I noted earlier emerged in a strong form only as recently as 1965. I ask what it is about this diversity that Americans want to actively protect and promote.

Diana Eck, a professor of religion at Harvard, offers one answer to this question. As director of the Pluralism Project, a long-term research effort supported by mainstream liberal foundations since 1991, Eck's studies of changes in American religious life have led her to a vision of its future course. The ideal, she says, is not diversity, mere tolerance, or relativism, but "internal pluralism," which to her means transcending religious differences "to create a society in which we actually know one another. . . . Being a Christian pluralist means daring to encounter people of very different faith traditions and defining my faith not by its borders, but by its roots." This in turn means protecting religious freedom, improving our provincial understandings of other faiths, and actively engaging all religions in the common work of civil society.[85]

One can hardly disagree with the notion of diversity-as-ideal at this level of generality. As a matter of ethical exhortation, moreover, it seems fully compatible with the liberal, communitarian, functional, utilitarian, and even libertarian social understandings discussed in Chapter 3. Eck's vision, however, says less about why we should affirmatively value religious diversity than about how we should deal with it now that it exists. Many familiar encomia to religion—that it propounds fundamental truths, creates essential meaning, prescribes moral conduct, strengthens family and communal feelings and institutions, encourages personal humility and respect for divine law and legitimate authority, inculcates awe and reverence for life, creates sublime beauty, and many others—explain why *religion* is valued, even by many atheists. The question here is why we value religious *diversity*.

The question is pertinent because diversity might threaten some of these religious values, as different traditions affirm different truths and morality, create competing institutions, and so forth. After all, war, violence, repression, and political turmoil in almost all societies throughout history—including the United States, albeit to a far lesser degree—have occurred under religious auspices. (The issue of causality, of course, is more complex.) Setting communal conflict to one side, religious differences might facilitate logrolling tactics among religious groups—what Kenneth Karst calls a "religious spoils system"[86]—that could expand their political influence to levels that even those favoring a robust role for religion in public life may find troubling.

Another problem is that group autonomy, self-government, and other conditions needed to protect and promote religious diversity sometimes conflict with the principles of nondiscrimination, nonviolence, openness to conflicting views of the good, protection of children, and other liberal norms. Almost all religions, including mainstream ones, are deeply illiberal in certain respects. We accept this only because we think membership, at least for adults, is voluntary, and perhaps because we think that religious values demand some exemption from secular precepts.

Given such difficulties, why might we nevertheless want government to protect religious *diversity*? To reply that the Constitution demands this protection, of course, simply pushes the question of justification back a step: why is protection of religious diversity a constitutional value? We might value diversity as an independent social ideal for several reasons. Liberal groups like Unitarians and Reform Jews hold that diversity, even of religious beliefs, manifests the fecundity of the divine spirit[87] and thus confirms and extends their own religious beliefs. Then there is the "different strokes for different folks" factor: people respond spiritually to certain religious stimuli but not to others, so diverse religious communities increase the number who will find one that is congenial. Human nature, James Madison observed, entails "[a] zeal for different opinions concerning religion."[88] Indeed, this zeal for diversity in spiritual matters is one reason why ecumenical movements usually fail. (Another is the organizational competition mentioned earlier.)

Among the many signs of the persistent demand for religious diversity, and of diversity's propensity to maximize "religious capital," are Pope John Paul II's failed efforts to draw more Eastern Rite churches back into the fold; the furor created by the Vatican's recent indictment of relativistic toleration; the dismay of even liberal theologians and ecumenists over a "lightweight pluralism" that downplays sectarian differences; and non-Christians' growing impatience with traditional deference to Christian holidays and other majoritarian prerogatives.[89] Even the Catholic Church has embraced some diversities, as a Notre Dame professor explains: "The Church does not simply tolerate diversity as a way to aid conversions (like using 'saints' to replace ancestor worship) and prevent schisms (by sanctioning non-Latin rites), but cultural differences should now be incorporated into worship because different cultures have developed different practices that please God by their uniqueness."[90]

James Madison advanced what is perhaps the most powerful defense of the religious diversity ideal. His defense is notable not just because of his prominence in the framing of the Constitution but also because of his instrumental view of religious diversity. Madison likened religious diversity to the diversity of social interests more generally, which he thought would best secure liberty and justice in both government and civil society: "In a free government, the security for civil rights must be the same as for religious rights. It consists in the one case in the multiplicity of interests, and in the other, in the multiplicity of sects. The degree of security in both cases will depend on the number of interests and sects."[91] Just as a plethora of competing parties and secular interests would forestall majoritarian tyranny by placing them at cross-purposes, so a "variety of sects dispersed over the entire face of [the country], must secure the national Councils against any danger from that source."[92] Significantly, however, Madison valued religious diversity as a barrier to government overreaching, not as an independent good. Historian Gordon Wood doubtless exaggerates in writing that "[Madison and other] secular reformers and deists yearned for a homogeneous society, as Jefferson did, in which all Americans might become Unitarians,"[93] but the instrumental justification for religious diversity surely predominated.

Another support for the religious diversity ideal is its link to immigrant assimilation, a related ideal discussed in Chapter 4. Historically, the religious identities nourished by the churches, synagogues, mosques, and other communities of worship that immigrants join upon their arrival have played important, often decisive roles in orienting them to American civil society, effecting their integration into it, and eventually incorporating them into the polity. Religious groups provide emotional and spiritual resources that newcomers desperately need in order to endure the wrenching experience of casting off the familiar. As in the nineteenth and twentieth centuries, the groups also constitute communal enclaves that can provide immigrants the essential breathing room and mundane integrative resources they need in order to learn English, access social services, gain job, social, and networking skills, consolidate their families in America, and adapt their distinctive liturgical, linguistic, and ethnic traditions to the mores of their new society.[94]

This process of change, moreover, is a two-way street. Even as American religion alters the immigrants, the immigrants alter their religions, both in the United States and abroad. American social and ideological conditions helped liberalize the Catholic Church, itself an event of world historical significance.[95] Similarly, Judaism was "Americanized" during the twentieth century, and much the same is occurring today with Islam, Hinduism, Buddhism, and other world religions. Their diasporas in America are not only transforming their religions here but are also catalyzing religious changes in their civilizational homes.[96] Countless local, ethnically defined churches founded by immigrants during the pre–World War I period of high immigration helped to smooth the always rough path of assimilation. Although most of these religiously conditioned group adaptations succeeded, many failed (at least in secular terms), particularly among the more millenarian and socialistic sects.[97]

But the encounter between diverse religions and American culture is not always mutually enriching nor does it always promote the diversity ideal. One might argue that America absorbs all religions by assimilating them to a democratic culture that demands fealty to individualism, formal equality, common morality, and other liberal orthodoxies. Respect for religious diversity, in this view, embraces only practices and beliefs that are broadly consistent with these orthodoxies but does not extend to exotic ones like polygamy, the sacramental use of peyote, and withholding of medical care from children. It is in this sense a domesticated, denatured diversity, confined to respect for what does not threaten. More generally, the law compromises the diversity ideal whenever it mediates among religions and between religious and secular values. We can only understand these compromises if we first analyze the general concepts and norms that give them meaning: definition of religion, separation, accommodation, neutrality, judicial review, choice, and establishment by exception.

Definition of Religion

Defining religion ordinarily presents no special difficulties. (Regulating it with the requisite degree of neutrality, however, is another story.) In common parlance, a religion is a set of beliefs organized around the existence of God, a Supreme Being, or some other notion of deity. Typically, religions have institutional or physical forms—organizations, edifices, sacred texts, liturgies, holy days, spiritual leaders—that make them easily recognizable as such and qualify them for full constitutional protection. The hardest cases usually involve individuals who do not express their beliefs and practices in such forms or may even worship alone, yet even here the law has tended to interpret "religion" inclusively.

Perhaps the most revealing disputes of this kind concern the interpretation of the federal statute defining individuals' eligibility for exemption from military service as conscientious objectors.[98] These cases, after all, pit the government's undeniably compelling need to defend itself and to distribute the risks of violent injury and death from war equally among its citizens, against the individual's equally compelling conscientious refusal to inflict violence. The 1917 conscription statute, which had exempted only members of "any well-recognized religious sect . . . whose creed or principles forbid its members to participate in war in any form," was broadened in 1940, 1948, and 1967 to reflect intervening judicial glosses on the law. These amendments exempted those "who, by reason of religious training and belief" conscientiously oppose participation. Religion, under the law, entails "belief in a relation to a Supreme Being involving duties superior to those arising from any human relation, but do not include essentially political, sociological, or philosophical views or a merely personal moral code." Cases mostly involved questions about the content and authenticity of particular beliefs held by undeniably religious people, not about whether arguably nonreligious individuals' conscientious beliefs nevertheless had the requisite relation to religion to qualify for an exemption.

The U.S. Supreme Court faced this more difficult issue in *United States v. Seeger*,[99] a 1965 decision where the applicant said that his creed was purely ethical and philosophical "without belief in God except in the remotest sense." In awarding the exemption from service in Vietnam, the Court defined the test: "A sincere and meaningful belief which occupies in the life of its possessor a place parallel to that filled by the God of those admittedly qualifying for the exemption." In 1970, the Court granted relief to one who said his objection was "nonreligious," based on his reading of history and sociology.[100] In a nondraft context, even the nontheistic practices of Scientology, transcendental meditation, and the Unification Church have been deemed religious; communism and other totalizing, secular worldviews have not.[101] The law, then, holds that a religion provides a more or less comprehensive account of how humans should relate either to a deity or to its ethical equivalent—prescriptions that occupy a central position in their lives.

No such consensus exists, however, on the proper relationship between religious beliefs and values, on the one hand, and our political, collective life, on the other—or in our terms, on the significance that American society should accord to religious diversity when that diversity impinges on its secular interests. Indeed, the vigorous debates over this issue during the last two decades have served only to underscore the chasm separating the disputants. As Alan Wolfe puts it, "[t]wo hundred years after the brilliant writings of

James Madison and Thomas Jefferson on the topic, Americans cannot make up their minds whether religion is primarily private, public, or some uneasy combination of the two."[102]

Separation and Accommodation

We can best map this chasm by exploring what it is that seems to divide the disputants. The polar positions are "separation" and "accommodation," but people's positions ultimately depend on how they define and apply the neutrality principle (discussed below) that the courts require government to observe, and in which contexts.[103] For example, Justices William Brennan and Thurgood Marshall were strong separationists in Establishment Clause cases but vigorously favored accommodation in Free Exercise Clause cases.[104]

Separationists tend to think that religion is a potentially divisive force when brought into public life; they wish to consign it to the private realm where, like other forms of expression and activity, law would protect it on the same neutral terms that liberalism applies to other views. Invoking Jefferson's famous metaphor, separationists believe that both religion and politics gain when the law erects between them "a wall . . . which must be kept high and impregnable." They also draw on Jefferson's equally famous distinction between belief, which the government cannot regulate, and conduct, which in this view it can regulate. In 1990, the Court affirmed this distinction in _Smith_[105] after having criticized it in the _Yoder_ and _Sherbert_ cases noted below.

Accommodationists claim that Jefferson's wall metaphor, which he used in a letter to the Danbury Baptists in 1802, is both ahistorical and misleading. Legal historian Philip Hamburger, in a new study of the church-state relationship, shows that neither the Framers nor subsequent constitutional understanding favored such a wall. Jefferson was not a member of the Constitutional Convention or the Congress that adopted the First Amendment, and the Danbury Baptists rejected Jefferson's strict separation ideal and did not disseminate his letter. Indeed, Hamburger shows that this ideal was first advanced by anti-Catholic nativists and the Ku Klux Klan in the nineteenth century.[106]

Accommodationists also believe that religion generates enormous public and private benefits (a claim many separationists concede—up to a point). Accommodationists insist, however, that religion can only retain its meaning-creating, value-conferring force and integrity if it enjoys considerable breathing space in which to pursue distinctive beliefs and practices. The law, accommodationists say, should create a strong presumption favoring even those practices that seem illiberal or in some cases are illegal—although just how strong it should be is a question that divides Congress and, as we shall see in the next section, has recently set it against the Court.[107]

Separationists reply that such accommodation is not neutral as between religion and nonreligion or perhaps even as among religions; far from merely tolerating religion, they say, accommodation may unconstitutionally "establish" it. The most notorious example of this position is probably the June 2002 federal appeals court decision in *Newdow v. U.S. Congress*, striking down the teacher-led Pledge of Allegiance in public schools as an unconstitutional establishment of religion because the phrase "under God" endorses monotheism.[108]

Neutrality

Beneath these antipodal positions lie deeper conceptual, empirical, normative, and political cleavages. As an initial matter, separationists and accommodationists differ over three things: what neutrality means, whether it is really possible in religiously diverse America today, and if so whether it is a defensible public value or legal standard where religion is concerned. Because these three issues are not always distinguished, separationists like Stephen Macedo, a liberal defender of civic values against the inroads of religion, and accommodationists like Stephen Carter, a religious conservative who wants to broaden religion's role in public life, can end up agreeing on a number of points even as they present their positions as strongly antagonistic.[109] I shall use recent work by Carter and Macedo to focus the debate.[110]

The first commonality is that, as Carter approvingly puts it, "religion has no sphere. It possesses no natural bounds. It is not amenable to being pent up. It sneaks through cracks, creeps through half-open doors . . . and it flows over walls. . . . Rushing past boundaries is what religion does."[111] Macedo acknowledges this leakage but decries it, warning that it poses a mortal danger to the ideal of civic liberalism.[112] They also agree that strict state neutrality—basing government policy solely on secular ideas and disregarding its effects on religion—is in an important sense illusory. Religion is inevitably political in that it helps shape our public and private values.[113] To Carter, "[n]eutrality is a theory about freedom of religion in a world that does not and cannot actually exist" because the state cannot act without taking account of religion. A pretense of neutrality, Carter argues, is used to override deep convictions for little governmental gain, as when the Supreme Court invoked neutrality to uphold military discipline against an Orthodox Jew for wearing a yarmulke while in uniform.[114] Macedo also doubts the possibility of strict neutrality but wants to contain this leakage lest it contaminate both sides, especially the liberal polity, which needs inoculation against certain sect values. The state, he argues, must promote civic virtues, not comprehensive ideals of the good life, but even this civic promotion affects religious beliefs and practices non-neutrally.[115]

Carter also claims that the neutrality norm favors big, influential religions over small, defenseless ones. (Interestingly, separationists say the same about accommodations of religion,[116] although this theory has trouble explaining *Yoder*'s accommodation of the Old Order Amish—hardly a political powerhouse, even in Pennsylvania—and their practice of leaving school after eighth grade.) Historically, prohibition laws did allow mainstream believers to drink sacramental wine, and *Smith* did refuse to extend unemployment benefits to drug counselors for a minor, peyote-eating Native American sect.[117]

Carter's larger hostility claim, however, is weak.[118] Long before *Smith*, many federal and state laws gave religions in general and small sects in particular special consideration.[119] The Religious Freedom Restoration Act (RFRA) was enacted to overrule *Smith* and to protect (among others) the same obscure Native American sect, as both Congress and some states had already done.[120] Courts, to be sure, tend to be less accommodating than legislatures; even under the pre-*Smith* compelling interest test, courts almost always upheld the government.[121] But this may be changing. In 1993, the Supreme Court upheld a small sect's ritual practice against a local ban.[122] Four years later, in the important case of *City of Boerne v. Flores*, the Court rejected a claim by the powerful Catholic Church, America's largest denomination. Indeed, the claim it rejected was based on the RFRA, precisely the kind of religion-friendly law that Congress was emphatically trying to protect and that the Court then struck down for exceeding congressional power.[123]

Separationists like Macedo also agree with accommodationists like Carter on religion's manifold virtues. Indeed, Macedo maintains that the separatist project "depends upon the support of religious reasons and religious communities—a support that can be encouraged by a liberal public philosophy but not altogether justified by it."[124] Liberalism, he says, depends on the reasons, norms, and moral convictions generated by religious communities, and also on the political and moral education that such communities provide. Macedo holds that even Catholicism, whose earlier illiberalism he strongly condemns, has strengthened the American polity. Its natural law doctrine checks the moral excesses of democratic majoritarianism, its "subsidiarity" principle supports devolution of power, and it rightly insists that human values transcend the political, justifying why one should not invest politics with all of one's moral energies.[125]

Beyond these convergences, however, separationists and accommodationists disagree sharply.[126] To someone like Carter, the state that Macedo wants to protect poses a far greater threat to religion than religion does to the state, and the state's putatively civic projects, which Macedo wants to promote, are in fact pervaded by assumptions of value and fact that are hostile to religion. To Carter, these assumptions cohere to constitute a comprehensive, secular worldview that not only competes with religion in defining the meaning of life but remorselessly deploys secularism's monopoly of coercive power, together with a conviction of the state's superior rectitude, to establish and maintain its dominance.[127] To Macedo, in contrast, this competition is disciplined by the ground rules of separation, and the hegemony of an activist state is required to sustain his vision of "liberalism with spine," which goes beyond promoting tolerance, freedom, order, and prosperity. It must also secure "the preconditions of active citizenship," including the state's "educative" interests in citizens' character, in order to pursue society's collective ends. Some religions, notably fundamentalist groups that insist on subordinating the state's educational and moral authority to that of the group and family, are anathema to this vision and must be overridden in the name of civic liberalism.[128] Which values civic liberalism includes, of course, is itself a hotly disputed issue.[129]

I am tempted to suggest that despite these sharp rhetorical conflicts, and except at the extremes, most separationists and accommodationists differ only in degree. Militants of both stripes doubtless will reject this pacific suggestion. Unlike Macedo, for example, many separationists categorically oppose the use of government-funded vouchers in religious schools, and unlike Carter many accommodationists demand school prayer. Nor do I mean to deny that such differences can produce quite disparate views about particular cases or policy disputes, as with the charitable and school choice proposals discussed in a later section of this chapter. My suggestion, rather, is that the precise location of the lines that the law must draw depends in the end on principles that come down to matters of degree, of more or less.

Carter, for example, concedes that there are limits "beyond which no claim of religious freedom will be recognized," citing the case of religiously mandated murder. One could cite more difficult cases like church-sanctioned child and spousal abuse, racial segregation, and female genital mutilation, but the point would be the same: lines must be drawn and someone with temporal authority must draw them. But having acknowledged this, Carter then complains that it is the courts that eventually will do the line-drawing and that they inevitably "center their concern on the needs of the state, not the needs of the religionist."[130] But Congress and the states, as we have seen, often do precisely the opposite. Courts, moreover, must review these legislative choices. The real issue for the courts, then, is the legal standard for reviewing them.

Judicial Review

Here is where we can see the *casus belli* dissolving into a difference of degree, albeit a consequential one. Stephen Carter seems to favor the "compelling governmental interest" standard that the Supreme Court applied until its controversial 1990 *Smith* ruling,[131] a standard he says most accommodationists endorse. According to this standard (also called the *Sherbert-Yoder* test, after earlier decisions that elaborated it),[132] a law may substantially burden the exercise of religion only if that burden furthers a compelling governmental interest and is the least restrictive means of doing so. Stephen Macedo argues that this test is too demanding of the state and too accommodating of religious practices that run afoul of secular law. This ignores the fact, emphasized by the Court first in *Smith* and later in *City of Boerne,* that governments almost always prevailed under the compelling interest standard, unless the restriction implicated some other constitutional right—and *no* federal statute has failed to satisfy it.[133] Macedo proposes instead an "intermediate standard" now used to assess discrimination claims asserted by some nonracial minorities; it would ask "whether the law being challenged advances important governmental objectives in a reasonable manner."[134] Both Macedo and Carter, then, support tests under which courts draw lines by identifying, weighing, and balancing competing interests much as legislatures do. They differ only over whether the state's interest must be "compelling" or merely "important" and whether the burden must be "the least restrictive means" or merely "reasonable."

Let me be clear. In calling attention to the small differences between the two standards' operative phrases and to the even smaller differences between how judges might actually apply them after identifying, weighing, and balancing interests, I am not denying that outcomes in particular cases may turn on these differences. The *Mozert* case, a much-discussed 1987 appeals court ruling,[135] is a telling example. *Mozert* involved the claims of fundamentalist Christian parents who wanted to opt out of a mandated public school reading program designed to teach tolerance of diverse views. They insisted that the readings contradicted their understanding of God's word, which denied the truth of other views. The required readings, they argued, would lead the children astray. As an alternative, the parents proposed that their children use other state-approved texts, cover any missed work at home, and take the same reading tests as other students. Although the court applied the accommodating compelling interest standard, it rejected their claim because the texts taught only tolerance and did not assert the truth or falsity of any particular view. Merely exposing children to diverse views, the court felt, could not be constitutionally objectionable.

Macedo and Carter, our proxy separatist and accommodationist, take opposing views on *Mozert*. Macedo notes that the parents' proposed accommodation "did not seek to impose their ideas on anyone else through the public school curriculum and did not (apparently) challenge the general legitimacy of secular public schooling. They wanted only to opt out of a particular program while remaining in public schools—how much harm could there be in that?" Macedo quickly answers his own question: "And yet, the *Mozert* objections went to the heart of civic education in a liberal polity: how can tolerance be taught, how can children from different religious and cultural backgrounds come to understand each other and recognize their shared civic identity, without exposing them to the religious diversity that constitutes the nation's history?"[136] In a liberal polity, he argues, fundamentalist parents have "[no] right to shield their children from the fact of reasonable pluralism. . . . We are dealing with children who are not mere extensions of their parents. The parents' religious liberty does not extend with full force to their children."[137]

Carter, however, will have none of this. Rejecting the *Mozert* court's view that teaching tolerance could not be objectionable, he asserts the primacy of the parents' claims: "We flout the ideal of genuine diversity when we strip mothers and fathers of their freedom to limit the exposure of their children to what is not, according to the judgment of the parents, true and noble and right. . . . [T]he religious should unite behind a very strong norm elevating parental interests above the interests of the state (except in extreme cases, such as physical abuse), so that dissenting religious communities have the chance to survive and thrive rather than drowning in the cultural sea that, if left unchecked, will eventually overwhelm them all."[138]

Note that although Macedo and Carter would have decided *Mozert* differently, this difference seems quite unrelated to any distinction between the "compelling governmental interest" and intermediate scrutiny legal standards. It is not the legal standards that do the analytical work for them but their deeply held moral convictions about the competing claims of family, state, and community. Note also that both would countenance exceptions: Macedo would justify some accommodation of the parents' claims on prudential grounds, while Carter would override parental sovereignty in "extreme cases, such as physical abuse." But these concessions raise further questions. To Macedo: Why is the reasonableness of a proposed accommodation a merely prudential consideration? Why is it not also relevant to defining the parent's constitutional right under the intermediate scrutiny balancing test that he supports? To Carter: Why is state intervention justified for conduct that the state considers physical abuse but that the parents consider divinely ordained discipline? Would he also justify state intervention to prevent what it considers psychological abuse or unusually harsh but presumably loving rigor? Carter might reply that we have laws, reflecting a moral consensus, against physical abuse but not against the others, but this response, of course, simply begs the same question that he purports to be answering: what is the legitimate scope of the state's power to regulate religiously motivated diversity?

Both Macedo and Carter might concede that their grandly opposed separatist and accommodationist principles ultimately come down to largely subjective judgments about relatively small differences of degree. This, I believe, is true—and also is cause for optimism. Like Carter, I think that accommodation was warranted in *Mozert*. The notion that all diverse ideas about truth, morality, and authority should be treated with equal respect and given equal time is itself a distinctive and dubious ideal, one that even the most flexible accommodationists—or at least anyone who has been responsible for designing a school curriculum for students who have only limited classroom time—cannot persuasively defend. In the real world, we must choose among competing versions of truth, and neither flat-earthism nor cannibalism (to pick extreme examples) should be taught in a public school—*at least until the state gives parents who favor those subjects a genuine choice, through tax dollars, to send their children elsewhere.* The state can and should provide this choice, as I maintain later in this chapter. But until it does, the public schools have a special obligation to accommodate parents in cases like *Mozert*.

It is true that diverse religious beliefs "are as infinite as the imagination,"[139] and that the genie of opt-outs and exceptions to general rules (or standard curricula) cannot easily be confined once it is out of the bottle.[140] Indeed, this was one of the strongest arguments against the RFRA, where Congress sought to resurrect the more accommodating "compelling interest" standard that *Smith* had jettisoned. (After the Court in *City of Boerne* invalidated the RFRA, Congress enacted a much narrower version, the Religious Land Use and Institutionalized Persons Act of 2000, which rests on a different source of legislative power.)[141] The Court's concern about the RFRA reflects a legitimate anxiety about line-drawing in an area fraught with constitutional constraints, but this concern is best addressed not by in effect barring accommodationist exceptions, as *Smith* seemed to do, but by requiring those who seek them to present strong supporting evidence of religious need.[142] More secular objections to RFRA—that its accommodationist protection of religious autonomy would weaken antidiscrimination safeguards for minorities—are considered in the section on charitable and school choice.

Choice

A society that truly values diversity, and whose Constitution is expressly committed to religious freedom, must do all it reasonably can to accommodate deeply held but deviant worldviews—including secular ones as well as, say, the Old Order Amish.[143] This is best accomplished through techniques that respect and expand the diversity of individual and family choices in settings that otherwise tend toward monolithic, hegemonic solutions. Choice, of course, is always a matter of degree and constraint. The Mozerts, for example, could always move to another community with a different reading program that they preferred. The constitutional issue is how much the government may or must burden a private choice that bears on fundamental interests like religious freedom.

Choice has enormous normative power in American life—so much so that it has become something of a fetish or shibboleth. It is deployed constantly and to great effect in public debates ranging from abortion to zoning; its flexibility and social prestige can often defuse otherwise knotty social conflicts (though notably not in the case of abortion). Unsurprisingly, advocates of public funding for FBOs and vouchers label their proposals as "charitable choice" and "school choice."

Choice, then, can be highly relevant to legal and policy disputes concerning religion. Consider the Supreme Court's decision in *Goldman v. Weinberger,* which rejected an Orthodox Jew's challenge to an Air Force rule prohibiting religious head-covering for uniformed soldiers.[144] One can criticize this decision from an accommodationist perspective; after all, the practice was central to the soldier's faith while the military could make an exception without endangering security.[145] But the fact that Congress had substituted a voluntary military for the draft may help to explain the Court's ruling. The soldier's choice to serve in the military when he knew the prohibition was in effect should, other things being equal, weaken his claim for accommodation. Were he a conscript, the case might be different.

By facilitating choice by individuals among the normatively diverse systems in which they (or their children) may conduct important parts of their lives, society can reduce, though not wholly eliminate, demands for exceptions to generally applicable laws. The more job choices a religious minority has, the weaker its claim for special treatment in the workplace. Where employers compete for workers in part through their policies on work dress, for example, a worker who demands the right to wear a head scarf along with her uniform may have to accept a position away from customers or look elsewhere for work.[146]

This choice-facilitating approach to the accommodation issue is not, I hasten to add, a perfect solution that resolves all disputes. One difficulty is the need to make the kinds of balancing judgments required by even (or especially) an exception-friendly "compelling state interest" test.[147] Courts can reduce this problem somewhat by deferring more than the Court did in *City of Boerne* to laws that provide useful guidance about how society wishes to strike those balances. Legislation is not the full measure of constitutional meaning, of course, but the fact that it is enacted in conditions of profuse religious and secular diversity provides strong security against discriminatory or preferential laws—indeed, far more security than Madison, mindful of other structural checks,[148] thought sufficient in his far less diverse society. Today's diversity is not a perfect safeguard but it greatly limits possible legislative abuses.

Establishment by Exception

There is also the constitutional issue of when government violates the Establishment Clause by exempting a religious practice—door-to-door proselytizing and Sabbath observance, for example—from legal sanctions or other disadvantage in order to avoid Free Exercise Clause problems. Legal scholars are notoriously divided on the Framers' original understanding of establishment,[149] but many would surely agree with John Jeffries and James Ryan that the modern Establishment Clause jurisprudence of thoroughgoing, not to say radical, separationism dates only from the 1940s and bears little relation to the Framers' original intent.[150] In any event, a growing consensus holds that the long-dominant *Lemon v. Kurtzman*[151] test—especially the parts that ask whether the law's primary effect advances or inhibits religion and whether it fosters excessive government entanglement—defines establishment too broadly, arbitrarily, and unpredictably.[152] Most of the Justices now proceed cautiously in a fact-sensitive, domain-specific manner as they search for a different approach for deciding Establishment Clause cases. (In later sections I consider two such domains: social services and education.)

The courts, I maintain, should not use the Establishment Clause to reject accommodations that respond to genuine free exercise concerns, modify legally imposed impediments, and implement nondiscrimination principles fairly, evenhandedly, and under demanding evidentiary standards.[153] In this spirit, Congress in the 1964 Civil Rights Act required employers to reasonably accommodate their employees' religious practices and beliefs,[154] and the courts have held that the Free Exercise Clause not only permits some accommodation but may require it.[155] In addition, the Supreme Court's recent *Good News Club, Rosenberger,* and *Lamb's Chapel* decisions held (correctly, in my view) that public officials allowing private groups to use public school or public university premises to air their views must not treat groups that express religiously informed views on religious or secular subjects any differently than they treat purely secular groups.[156] These decisions, which rely more on free speech and equal protection principles than on religious accommodationism, tend to be as fact-specific as the nonreligion cases they resemble.

I would contrast these decisions with the *Kiryas Joel* case,[157] involving a more difficult conflict between the Establishment and Free Exercise Clauses. There, the Court rejected a special school district created by New York at the behest of a community of Satmar Hasidim to enable them to provide special education to their disabled children in public schools that would consist almost entirely of Satmar children. The Court's decision, however, was complicated by an earlier ruling *(Aguilar)* that had condemned the kind of accommodation at issue in *Kiryas Joel* but that a majority of Justices clearly wanted to abandon (and would do so three years later in *Agostini*).[158] It also seemed clear that in gerrymandering a district to include only the politically active Satmar community, the legislature gave that group a dispensation it would not have given less influential sects.[159]

An approach that would make the availability of choice a weightier factor in the analysis of accommodation claims must of course determine when one has enough choice to warrant denying the accommodation, as the Court did in *Goldman v. Weinberger,* involving the Jewish soldier's head covering. On the choice issue, as on some issues in Establishment Clause cases, judges who tend to have the last word sometimes misapprehend the stakes and thus the relevance of choice. In two recent Supreme Court decisions—*Lee v. Weisman,*[160] which barred a school-sponsored clerical prayer at a high school graduation ceremony, and *Santa Fe Independent School District v. Doe,*[161] which barred a student-delivered prayer over the school's public address system before school football games—the Court found that students who are free to remain seated or silent if they do not wish to participate are nonetheless psychologically coerced—deprived of choice—in a constitutionally decisive sense.

Reasonable people can differ about whether the state's role was sufficiently neutral on the specific facts of these cases, but the Court's approach to the choice issue is more troubling. It trivializes the ideas of coercion and harm, presumes that young adults are more fragile than the vast majority are, and seeks to protect them from having the courage of their convictions even to the minimal extent of possibly courting some unpopularity by maintaining those convictions. If the state neither sponsors nor sanctions particular views but simply allows their expression on a sufficiently neutral basis, the law should not elevate even the desire to avoid predictable feelings of discomfort into constitutional rights. Such rights will not reduce these feelings but will likely multiply them and make them even more unappeasable, while limiting the prerogatives of others who do not share them. The law does better, as the *Lee* dissenters urged, to limit the idea of coercion to a threat of official sanctions, not expand it to include a contest among competing, informal norms.[162]

Religious practices that might threaten the lives or well-being of small children whose choices are largely controlled by their parents raise some of the most difficult questions for a choice approach.[163] The real issue is whether the law should recognize parental prerogatives to choose what they believe is in the best interests, both spiritual and temporal, of their child without state interference or second-guessing. Although there are no simple or categorical answers, the easier cases (for me) are those like *Mozert* in which the parents' choice only minimally impairs, and might even serve, the state's interest, properly conceived. Much harder are those involving parental choices that arguably threaten a child's life or safety; here the courts usually uphold state intervention.[164] This interventionism, which is often premised on Jefferson's distinction between protected beliefs and unprotected conduct, is a slippery slope. A paternalistic state is often tempted to substitute its majoritarian view of the child's interests for that of majority-deviant parents. Parents, however, have a more sustained moral, physical, and financial commitment to their children, and their judgments deserve deference except in clear cases of abuse or neglect.[165] (An even more vital parental prerogative, the choice of schooling, is discussed in a later section.) Disagreement with some of their choices is a price society pays for respecting family autonomy that serves the best interests of children in the vast majority of cases. Law should preserve this general principle while targeting and regulating the narrow exceptions.

In sum, the demands that religious diversity and the state place on one another in our constitutional regime can be made more manageable by providing or facilitating greater choice to those who feel constrained to pursue religious as well as secular values and who integrate those values in different ways. Although the law, as we saw, sometimes favors religion even after *Smith* and *City of Boerne,* society's secular goals are also advanced when government affords greater expression to diverse values of all kinds. I now consider how this can best be accomplished.

MOBILIZING RELIGIOUS DIVERSITY TO ADVANCE SECULAR POLICY GOALS

The 1980s and 1990s were decades of unprecedented innovation in the ongoing project of American politics to define the appropriate public role of religion in the expansive domain of today's administrative state. A period of great doubt and discontent about the moral direction of society on the part of religious and nonreligious Americans alike, the dominant moral concerns of those decades spurred a growing militancy on the part of religious groups in politics, as they linked what they decried as the remorseless secularization of American life to the weakening of families, the coarsening of behavior, the decline of traditional values, and the erosion of authority.[166]

National politicians both fed and responded to these anxieties. In order to signal that they shared such concerns, they deployed religious rhetoric and symbolism and initiated concrete actions designed to promote religious freedom and values. They brought religion into the public square in new ways. Consider the succession of pro-religion statutes passed during this period. The RFRA was surely the most far-reaching federal statutory protection of religious freedom law in the nation's history until the Supreme Court invalidated it in 1997, whereupon Congress enacted the Religious Land Use and Institutionalized Persons Act of 2000 in an effort to restore the RFRA's accommodationist stance in certain narrower contexts. In 1998, Congress unanimously passed the International Religious Freedom Act requiring the State Department to monitor and oppose religious persecution abroad and to promote religious freedom.[167] The American Indian Religious Freedom Act of 1994, seeking to overrule *Smith* on its specific facts, authorized tribes to use peyote sacramentally.[168] The Church Arson Prevention Act of 1996 increased federal penalties for such attacks.[169] The "charitable choice" provisions of the 1996 welfare reform required federal agencies to give religious groups equal access to contracts funding work-related programs.

These religion-friendly federal statutes, augmented by many state laws enacted during this period,[170] are just the tip of the iceberg. Congress passed many others, and presidents (especially Clinton) took many formal and informal actions in the name of protecting or promoting religion.[171] George W. Bush's administration, which sees conservative Christian churches as a core political constituency, is at least as ardent. Early in 2001, President Bush proposed to extend "charitable choice" to many more federally funded social services, and to give tuition support to parents with children in religious schools. I discuss these proposals below.

This cascade of federal, state, and local governmental measures to protect and promote religion just within the last decade makes it hard to credit the complaints by many religious conservatives that government systematically discriminates against religion, or Stephen Carter's worry that "religious expressions in our public debates [will] be greeted not merely with derision but with hostility."[172] If anything, the opposite is true. To be sure, no one with eyes to see and ears to hear could possibly deny that rap music, films, television, mass entertainment, and other effusions of popular culture often deride and debase traditional religious values, or that many influential journalistic and intellectual elites are aggressively secular, regarding religion, as Carter put it, as a kind of quaint hobby in which some (other) people take an interest. It is also true that the courts have rendered some decisions like *Mozert*, denying some religious groups exemption from laws that fall especially hard on them.[173]

But these examples are far from telling the whole story, or even the greatest part of it; they must be balanced against numerous religion-promoting examples. In addition to the vast amount of contemporary religious activity noted in the first section of this chapter, and the burst of pro-religion legislation just discussed, religious programs abound on network and cable television and radio,[174] and numerous Internet sites are religious in content. Religious books and other publications sell briskly, and religious colleges are thriving.[175] Religion courses offered by secular institutions have rising enrollments.[176] And with the important exception of the *Smith* decision—to which Congress, the president, and the states responded promptly and forcefully, albeit with limited effect—the Supreme Court's protection of even exotic religions against discriminatory laws has not noticeably flagged, as exemplified by the Hialeah animal sacrifice case.[177] (*City of Boerne* is not to the contrary; it rested on the RFRA's unconstitutionality, and did not decide either the accommodation claim or the validity of state-level RFRAs.) Finally, and most strikingly, government wealth transfers to religion are multifarious, enormous, and increasing.[178] Michael Kinsley's rejoinder to Carter's complaint is perfect: "Does anybody really think it is harder to stand up in public . . . and say, 'I believe in God,' than it is to stand up and say, 'I don't'?"[179]

In this religion-friendly social and political environment, the issue of the limits of the religious diversity ideal has been brought into sharper focus by two current policy proposals—charitable choice and school choice—that would bring the state, religious groups, and secular elements of civil society into ostensibly new relationships. I say "ostensibly new" because, as we shall see, both proposals arise in a historical context rich in precedents, familiar practices, long-standing relationships, age-old hopes, and persistent anxieties. Exploring the merits of these proposals provides an excellent way to better understand not only the contemporary promises and perils of religious diversity in America but also the role of law in realizing the one and controlling the other.

What, then, are these promises and perils? Even before turning to the specifics of the charitable and school choice proposals, we can identify some of the important, recurring themes in these debates. First, the promises. Many Americans believe that FBOs can do a better job of educating their children and serving the needy in their communities than secular organizations can, and they want their tax dollars used to make this happen. As we shall see, some evidence supports this view, at least with respect to schooling. Even more Americans, both religious and secular, see much in contemporary life to worry about, regret, and even loathe. The litany of social ills—crime, substance abuse, in-family violence, neglect and abandonment, sexual promiscuity and provocation, teen pregnancy, out-of-wedlock births, single-parent families, easy divorce, betrayals of public and private trust, grotesque materialism, a coarse and profane popular culture and mass media, a public square not fit for children, to name a few—is all too familiar and I shall not either belabor it or analyze its accuracy, causes, and possibly cures.[180] For my purposes, it is enough that most Americans ardently want something done about it.

Social scientists may offer secular explanations for this pathology, but many Americans think that much of it is fundamentally moral in nature and can only be cured through moral regeneration (reinforced in some cases by legal sanctions).[181] Religion, they think, may not be the only way to cultivate this morality but it is the oldest, most tried and true way. Or rather *ways*. No less than Americans generally, religious people are divided over how moral regeneration is best achieved, and the division usually proceeds along familiar liberal-conservative fault lines. Liberals tend to favor the "Social Gospel" approach, which looks to more egalitarian social structures to produce more moral individuals, whereas conservatives emphasize the need for individual spiritual conversions and commitments, one heart and soul at a time.[182]

The reasons for looking to religion to do some of society's regenerative work are as ancient and as numerous as the reasons why all successful societies value religion, reasons discussed earlier. The most straightforward, surely, is that religiously inspired moralism and political action have played a leading role in most of America's most idealistic public causes and reforms, and this remains true today. The burst of evangelical energy known as the Second Great Awakening,[183] beginning in the early 1800s and continuing through most of that century, sought to educate the public on a massive scale about the need for moral uplift, religious enthusiasm, and building social institutions. Their many causes included abolition of slavery, Bible literacy, temperance and prohibition, child labor, control of prostitution and other forms of vice and crime, urban political reform, public health, universal public education, female suffrage, financial support and moral tutelage of the indigent and wayward, missionary work here and abroad, and many others. More recently, religious enthusiasms have propelled the antiwar, antiabortion, and civil rights movements, as well as campaigns for arms control, international human rights, and elimination of the death penalty.

One characteristic virtue of religion deserves special attention in this connection, as it is particularly relevant to the case for charitable and school choice. Religions are by nature *communal*. Any religion is a set of beliefs and practices that, perhaps by definition, are shared by and constitutive of a faith community that elaborates institutions designed to perpetuate that community's highly particularistic ways of life, death, memory, learning, interpretation, childrearing, family relations, worship, and so forth. Religious communities place distinctive demands on their members and promise them soul-satisfying rewards and consolations. They provide the discipline and structure of relationships, expectations, routines, reciprocities, and moral codes.

Religions in the United States tend to be highly inclusive in their recruitment of new members, imposing few if any of the kinds of ascriptive barriers that might exclude or alienate their recruits in other societies or settings. Instead, these religions usually offer acceptance and at least a notional love to anyone who is prepared to subscribe to their tenets. For individuals whose poverty, isolation, crime, or other antisocial conduct has cut them off from any spiritual life and community of meaning, a religious connection may offer emotional, psychological, spiritual, and social succor and survival, literally a godsend. Even more striking, members can hope to find this fellowship regardless (within very broad limits) of the specific content of a religion's beliefs and practices. Small wonder, then, that religious ministries have been established, with varying success, in prisons, hospitals, skid rows, addiction treatment centers, and other venues in which outcasts congregate. The distinctive promise of religious organizations is especially apparent in their school systems, among their most important communal supports. I discuss this in more detail below in connection with school choice proposals, but at this introductory stage the important point is this: the success that religious schools have enjoyed in educating students who would probably fail in the secular ones they would otherwise attend seems to reflect many of the same factors I have just discussed—particularly, discipline, structure, clear expectations, and a pervasive sense of community, shared values, moral and pedagogical seriousness, and mission.

What, then, of the perils? Can it be a bad thing to invite FBOs into areas of what modern welfare state liberals think of as secular values and state responsibility? The many affirmative answers tend to fall into two categories to which the religion clauses of the Constitution are attentive: dangers to the state and civil society, and dangers to religion. These two dangers are related, and separationists usually stress both. For purposes of discussion, however, it is useful to treat them as analytically distinct.

The Framers were of course exquisitely conscious of the bloody history of religious strife in Europe and even in colonial America, a history in which dominant religions, having accumulated great wealth and social influence, used their resources to bend the state to their special interests, which often included persecuting dissenters, controlling education and property, dispensing patronage, fomenting war, and securing a share of state revenue. Leonard Levy, Marci Hamilton, Kenneth Karst, and other separatist scholars frequently point to the writings of James Madison, who warned against pressures on government by powerful religions, which were then established in many states. (The last disestablishment did not occur until the 1830s.)[184] Stephen Macedo describes the nineteenth-century struggles among the Protestant elite, a reactionary Catholic hierarchy, and secular civic liberals in American cities over the proper conception of the common school and over specific issues of funding, curriculum, prayer and Bible reading, teaching methods, and the Blaine Amendment, which would have barred the use of public funds to support sectarian schools. The civic, nonsectarian ideal so essential to a liberal polity, he argues, only narrowly survived these "school wars," and was challenged throughout the twentieth century by religious fundamentalists demanding school prayers, the teaching of creationism,[185] special political favors (as in *Kiryas Joel*), and other concessions.[186] Many who oppose expanded funding of FBOs for education and other social services fear that competition among religious groups for dollars, congregants, and souls will compromise certain civic values of the liberal state: equal access, noncoercion, and neutrality. Many also resent seeing their tax dollars go to support groups (as one skeptic put it) "who think I am owned by the devil because I am, dare I say it, a secular humanist"—although such complaints do not prevent many other things that government does, such as fight wars or run programs, to which some taxpayers object.

But state support of FBOs also poses some dangers to religion, as many accommodationists as well as separationists maintain. One of these dangers, according to Stephen Carter, is the seduction of political power leading to an exhaustion of religious commitment:

A religion that becomes too settled in the secular political sphere, happily amassing influence and using it, is likely to lose its best and most spiritual self, as has happened to established churches all over Europe, which nowadays find themselves virtually without a voice—small wonder, as they have relied on man rather than God for their sustenance. In consequence, they have redefined their role, trying to please humans instead of pleasing God. . . . [T]he same has happened to so many of today's organizations of conservative Christianity, so delighted with their political prominence that they have decided to try to keep it, resulting in a predictable softening of the hard, clear, Bible-based message that led to their prominence in the first place. . . . Secular politics is a very dangerous place for institutions concerned with spiritual matters that transcend ordinary human striving.[187]

A related danger, often mentioned (as we shall see) in the debate over charitable choice, is that religious groups overeager to obtain public dollars will submit to state-imposed conditions designed to protect secular values. These conditions may divert them from their distinctive religious approaches to the social problems that the state wishes to solve. This diversion deprives the groups of their authenticity and society of effective religious solutions. State support may also inhibit religious groups from vigorously protesting public policies that harm their interests or those of the larger society. Religious groups in politics may not only lose their souls, purity, and programmatic punch but may also invite persecution, retribution, or investigation by the state when they cross politicians, are on the losing side of political struggles, take politically incorrect positions, engage in taxable activities, or run afoul of other secular regulations. Recent examples include the Clinton administration's effort to use the campaign finance laws to bar the Christian Coalition's voter education pamphlets, and the Internal Revenue Service's continuing pursuit of the Church of Scientology.

With these promises and perils of religion in politics in mind, I turn to the debates over how religious groups can contribute to the delivery of education and other vital public endeavors. Two recent proposals—charitable choice and school choice—are particularly notable because they seek to exploit religious diversity to accomplish secular public purposes. (In sharp contrast, this same religious diversity dooms certain other proposals, such as allowing school-sponsored vocal prayer.)

Charitable Choice

FBOs have provided an array of social services for as long as religious communities have existed in America. Today, the volume and variety of these services are astonishing. A recent study sampling the country's approximately 300,000 congregations found that 91% offered some sort of social service and that most offered five or more. Each congregation donated an average of 148 work-hour equivalents per month, the work equivalent of $140,000 a year.[188] Another study, however, found that fewer than 10% of these programs, concentrated in the larger churches, took on persistent problems of poverty like drug abuse, health care, domestic violence, and lack of job skills, while the smaller ones emphasized soup kitchens and other short-term emergency programs.[189] "The hard social work can be done only by big congregations," according to one commentator on these findings, "and they are already doing a lot."[190] FBOs also vary enormously in how intensely their faiths are infused into their social services.[191]

Governments have been supporting FBOs' communal efforts since America's earliest days. For example, the Massachusetts colony appropriated funds for Harvard College, then a college primarily for training ministers,[192] Congress sent Congregational ministers to proselytize the Cherokees,[193] and state and local governments supported religious schools through most of the nineteenth century, stopping only when immigrant Catholic schools demanded their fair share of any such funds for their own sectarian teachings.[194] Governments funded private religious agencies for a broad range of child welfare services, care of the sick and destitute, education and training of Native Americans and low-skill workers, relief of war refugees, and community-based programs for the mentally and physically disabled, elderly, homeless, and hungry, and other needy populations.

A leading student of the FBO-government relationship, Stephen Monsma, estimates that in 1993 two-thirds of all voluntary, charitable giving went to nonprofit entities with a religious base; a third of all child-care providers were church organizations; the New York Roman Catholic archdiocese obtained 75% of its $1.75 billion budget from government (most of it from federal Medicare and Medicaid payments to Catholic health-care agencies); and Jewish organizations received roughly the same share of their budgets from government sources.[195] Some 63% of wholly religious child welfare agencies receive at least 20% of their budgets from public funds.[196]

During the 1980s and 1990s, political pressures to increase federal government funding of FBO social service programs grew. This pressure came not only from church groups that hoped to use the new resources to expand their programs but also from politicians seeking to identify themselves with religious values, the vibrant, expanding evangelical movement, and the many religious swing voters who had supported both Jimmy Carter and Ronald Reagan. In the Senate, this initiative brought together people of different political stripes like Republican Dan Coats of Indiana and Democrat Joseph Lieberman of Connecticut; similar coalitions formed in the House. President Clinton won the 1992 election with the support of many former Reagan voters in the evangelical movement and joined forces with, indeed mobilized, religious conservatives on many domestic and international free exercise issues.[197] In 1996, Clinton signed into law provisions that encouraged states to use FBOs in moving the needy "from welfare to work" under federally funded antipoverty and social welfare programs. The new law made FBOs eligible to receive various forms of government funding on an equal basis with other private providers, and protected "the religious integrity and character" of FBOs providing these services while barring FBOs from religious teaching, proselytizing, or coercing clients into participating in religious practices.

The push for a broader "charitable choice" law was a largely conservative initiative in Congress, and most liberals opposed or ignored it. Its political appeal became so obvious, however, that Al Gore endorsed the idea, though not all the details, of George W. Bush's proposal in the 2000 presidential campaign. This support from the left may not be so surprising. A year earlier, sociologist Mark Chaves had predicted that politically conservative congregations were much less likely to apply for these funds than middle-of-the-road or liberal congregations, especially predominantly black ones with strong traditions of social services to the poor and support for government spending.[198] This prediction seems to have been borne out.[199]

Shortly after President Bush's inauguration in January 2001, he established a White House Office of Faith-Based and Community Initiatives directed by John DiIulio, Jr., and proposed legislation to expand the 1996 provisions to all federal programs and to increase tax incentives for charitable donations to FBOs. Bush's FBO program encountered strong opposition in the public and in Congress. On July 19, a bill passed the House by a vote of 233–198 but only after the administration was forced to accept many compromises in the House. In August, the White House issued a report finding that the 1996 law had failed to dismantle the widespread barriers to FBOs' participation in federal programs,[200] but the September 11 terrorist attacks derailed this debate, delaying Senate consideration until 2002.[201] The House bill granted up to $13 billion in tax relief aimed at increasing charitable donations; a pending Senate bill, sponsored by Senators Lieberman and Rick Santorum of Pennsylvania, would raise this to $50 billion.

Political problems dogged the administration's original proposal. Members of both parties worried about its constitutionality, questioned its exemption of churches from employment discrimination laws (even though such an exemption had been in the law since 1964 and was upheld by the Supreme Court in 1987),[202] and complained that reduced program funding due to the administration's recently passed tax cut raised more acute questions about allocation of the remaining funds. The White House was widely criticized for appearing to favor a Salvation Army request to be allowed to exclude gays and lesbians from its federally funded programs, overriding local nondiscrimination laws. Conservative evangelical churches feared that the government would monitor how they pursued their religious missions and might fund programs run by Muslims, eastern religions, the Church of Scientology, and the Unification Church.[203] They were further shocked when DiIulio announced that FBOs emphasizing religious conversion of clients would be ineligible for direct grants under the program and must compete for clients' vouchers. Media reports of abuse in some FBO youth programs, notably in Texas where private accreditation had replaced public licensing of such programs, also threw the administration on the defensive.

The Bush proposal was also criticized by certain liberal and moderate Baptist leaders, some other mainstream Protestant groups, the Catholic Charities USA, liberal Jewish groups, the American Civil Liberties Union, the NAACP, and even a coalition of Wiccans and pagans.[204] Many feared that conservative causes would receive a new source of funding and at their expense, or harbored a class-based animus against the kinds of programs and schools that evangelical groups catering to low-income people might establish. Democrats also charged that it had become a partisan measure designed to woo black, traditionally Democratic voters in inner-city churches. Amid persistent reports of presidential concern about the program's progress, DiIulio resigned in August 2001; a successor was not named until February 2002.[205] Ambivalence about the Bush proposal was evident even among those who favored the basic approach.[206]

In addition to political obstacles, the merits of the measure are controverted.[207] Social scientists who study existing FBO programs, including DiIulio himself, agree that there is little or no reliable research establishing their effectiveness; until recently, few funds were devoted to studying FBOs. Researchers have not systematically compared the performance of these programs with the performance of secular programs treating the same populations. Such comparison may be impossible if, as some claim, FBOs limit their clientele more than secular programs do. Even the much-praised Teen Challenge, a substance-abuse program that is a model for what the initiative hopes to support and is one of the few FBO programs to open itself to researchers, has not been studied in this way. Although most social programs, not just FBOs, lack reliable effectiveness data, the lack of data is especially problematic here where a government agency that chose grantees based on theology, secularism, favoritism, or familiarity rather than effectiveness would risk a constitutional violation.[208] And the rich diversity of religious groups and approaches, which Bush has touted as an opportunity to discover which social programs work best, turns out to be something of a liability, or at least a point of vulnerability; this diversity facilitates challenges to broad generalizations about the success of FBO programs that lack strong empirical support.

No one can seriously doubt that FBOs should receive public funds to do the public's secular work. The United States wisely took this road a long time ago; indeed, as time goes on, FBO services become more and more indispensable to our social well-being. The real questions are about the terms on which they should receive government support, whether the law can specify and enforce those conditions effectively, and whether, in light of such conditions, FBOs will be prepared to participate.

Several of these conditions seem clear enough, although interpretation and implementation problems are inevitable.[209] First, the service must be secular in the sense of having a predominantly nonreligious purpose (serving the disadvantaged). Very often, however, this secular purpose coincides with a religious one (doing God's work on earth), a fact that should not, without more, disqualify the FBO. Second, client participation must be voluntary, informed, and uncoerced. This means, for adult clients, that an FBO must clearly disclose its religious orientation before rendering the service. The government must give clients secular alternatives wherever possible; if none is available, the government must devise other ways to assure voluntariness. Children served by FBOs must look to parental choice to protect their autonomy interests. If no competent parent exists, a legal guardian must fill the gap. Protecting children against FBO overreaching, abuse, or neglect is a daunting challenge; indeed, even legal fiduciaries for children sometimes abuse their trust.[210] The relevant comparison, however, is to public agencies and other secular alternatives whose performance in this respect may be no better, and possibly worse.[211]

Third, FBOs must have equal opportunity to compete for social service funds under established, objective criteria that neither favor nor disfavor religion. To make this competition most meaningful and responsive to clients' interests, government should give those funds in the first instance not to the service providers but to the eligible clients to spend on the program-qualified providers and services they prefer; information about the various providers should also be made available. Where a client's mental condition impairs exercising this kind of autonomy, a legal guardian or protective agency must decide on the client's behalf.

Fourth, if these limits are observed, the law should not bar FBO services that mention God, display sacred symbols (e.g., a cross, crescent, or cassock), or include other religious elements. Both common sense and anecdotal evidence suggest that religious appeals sometimes increase the effectiveness of prison ministries, youth workers, and other programs. Flat bans are hard to enforce. They require factual distinctions that government is ill-equipped to make and that entangle it with religion in undesirable, perhaps even unconstitutional, ways. By the same token, and consistent with the Civil Rights Act exemption permitting religious institutions to discriminate in favor of coreligionists when hiring, an FBO should be able to prefer coreligionist employees where this affinity promotes its mission,[212] but should have to disclose this policy. Unfortunately, political opposition persuaded the Bush administration to yield on this point.[213]

A harder question concerns proselytizing. As a legal matter, no government funds should be used to support FBO efforts to recruit new members. The difficulty is that using religious appeals in an effort to induce moral conduct can be tantamount to recruitment. A law allowing an FBO to exhort clients to abandon child abuse or some other depravity only if it calls the behavior "antisocial" rather than "sinful" or "against God's will" would be foolish. And since applying such a test would turn on the speaker's precise wording and intent, it would be even harder to enforce and more entangling even than a ban on displaying religious symbols. Indeed, it is not clear that the Constitution would permit government to distribute public funds on the basis of neutral secular criteria but then to proscribe spending those funds on a service provider that spoke approvingly of God's will.

Perhaps the best the law can do in this situation is to (1) bar the use of federal funds to proselytize, defined as recruitment activity exceeding what is necessary to provide the secular service effectively; (2) monitor FBO compliance, perhaps through unidentified market testers; and (3) focus enforcement on FBO overreaching rather than challenging, say, a caseworker's invitation to clients to attend a meeting held in a church basement or her mention of God's blessings. This solution, to be sure, is neither neat nor altogether satisfactory. Rule (1) is somewhat ambiguous (how much praise of God is "necessary" for effectiveness and when does it constitute "recruitment"?), which will make rules (2) and (3) indeterminate. Moreover, the constitutional constraints on the use of government funds under such conditions are not entirely clear. Nevertheless, this approach strikes a prudent balance between two compelling but competing goals: exploiting the immense social value of FBO-provided services in a spiritually inclined, religiously diverse society where the sacred and secular often converge, and keeping religion and government in their appropriate spheres.

School Choice

No one can doubt that the key to America's future is quality education for all young people. Education is our cultural transmission belt—perpetuating the best of our inherited ideas, values, artistic expressions, and traditions, fueling our imagination, creativity, and enjoyment, and generating human capital, which economists estimate accounts for two-thirds of the U.S. gross national product. Precisely because education is the major form of nonfamily socialization, it is not just a matter for professional judgment but is at the center of a struggle over the propagation of diverse and often inconsistent worldviews.[214] Given the immense stakes, it is hardly surprising that defining, measuring, and producing quality education is one of the most hotly debated of all policy issues.

Efforts to improve access to high-quality schooling are no less controversial. No one doubts that access to a fine education for all who want to pursue it is a compelling social ideal. Nor has our commitment to this ideal been merely rhetorical. Governments at all levels have spent trillions of dollars under Title I of the Elementary and Secondary Education Act of 1965 (ESEA)[215] and other programs aimed at closing the vast educational achievement gap between low-income children and their more fortunate peers. But more than thirty-five years later and after countless policy studies and programmatic reforms aimed at equalizing pre-college educational opportunity,[216] the chasm between the quality of inner-city public schools and their suburban counterparts remains almost as large as before—this despite inner-city per-pupil expenditures (PPEs) that sometimes equal or exceed those in the suburbs. After all of these efforts, Harvard educational psychologist Howard Gardner can still say, "Tell me the ZIP code of a child and I will predict her chances of college completion and probably income."[217]

What has all this to do with law and religious diversity? A great deal, as it turns out. I contend that we cannot hope to improve the quality of schooling for educationally disadvantaged children unless and until we give their parents the power, not just the right, to send them to schools other than the ones to which their local school boards now consign them. If parents had this choice and the wherewithal to exercise it, many, perhaps most of them, doubtless would continue to send their children to the assigned public school, others would opt for alternate public schools such as magnets or operationally independent "charter" schools, and still others would choose private schools, secular or religious.

Many private schools—and most relevantly those with tuition low enough to be affordable by low-income families—are religious in educational mission, institutional sponsorship, or both. Therein lies both the opportunity and the problem. The opportunity arises because some religious schools, particularly Catholic parochial ones, have demonstrated comparative success in educating the same kinds of low-income children whom public schools have manifestly failed to reach—whether the students are Catholic or non-Catholic, minority or white, immigrant or American, urban or suburban. The sociologist James Coleman and his colleagues documented the Catholic schools' remarkable record in educating socially and educationally disadvantaged children in his classic 1982 study drawing on data from 893 public schools, 84 Catholic schools, and 27 other private ones, covering almost 60,000 high school students.[218]

For our purposes, the most important findings of Coleman et al. were as follows. Black, Hispanic, and other minorities accounted for approximately 15% of students in Catholic schools, 24% in public schools, and 11% in other private schools. The median family income of Catholic school students was somewhat higher than for public school students ($22,700 compared with $18,700), but over 38% of the former had median family incomes below $20,000. Catholic schools had slightly higher teacher-student ratios than public schools and offered more mathematics and far more advanced language courses. Catholic school students reported much more school discipline and effective enforcement than public school students did, and both administrators and students at public schools reported much more absenteeism, verbal abuse of teachers, fighting and disobedience, drug and alcohol use, and vandalism of school property than their Catholic school counterparts. Almost twice as many Catholic school students reported doing five hours of homework per week than did public school students; the two groups watched a similar amount of TV. Educational outcomes, measured by standardized tests and future educational attainment, were better in Catholic schools, even controlling for a range of family factors and minimizing the possibility of selection bias.[219] In later analyses, Coleman argued that parochial schools were relatively effective because they served as "functional communities," creating social capital—relationships generating obligations, trust, and norms that an individual can draw on when needed—which complemented what students' families provided and enabled even children from dysfunctional families to perform well.[220] Researchers have long speculated that this "Catholic school effect" could be biased by the kinds of youngsters who attend the schools, but efforts to account for this possible selection bias have not yet fully accounted for the effect.[221]

The problem arises because only government can create the conditions under which educationally disadvantaged children have genuine opportunities to attend better schools, including religious ones. Even the most generous private philanthropy for this purpose—and there is much of it, now supporting about 60,000 low-income students throughout the United States—can reach only a tiny fraction of these children. In reality, their parents cannot exercise genuine choice unless government provides it in one form or another. Yet each of the four main kinds of government-supported choice plans—intradistrict choice, interdistrict choice, charter schools, and private school tuition support—is hobbled by legal, political, and practical obstacles that seriously reduce their availability and potential effectiveness.[222] (Home schooling, a growing choice, is generally not publicly supported.)

Although all four of these school choice mechanisms are important, the discussion here will focus on tuition support through vouchers, though it can also take the form of tax credits. The idea of vouchers is an old one[223] that has new salience in an era with widespread libertarian, egalitarian, antibureaucratic, religious revivalist, parental authority, and family choice ideals. The vast majority of students with vouchers use them in religious schools.[224]

(Maine and Vermont, however, bar their high school students from so using them.) Catholic schools' share of private school enrollments has declined since the 1960s, but they still account for almost half the total while other religious schools account for another 35%; nonreligious schools account for only about 16% of the enrollments.[225] This is why vouchers, unlike other choice forms, remained under a federal constitutional cloud until June 2002 when the Supreme Court upheld a Cleveland program that gives vouchers to parents who can use them in schools of their choice;[226] their possible invalidity under some state constitutions may also help explain why more states have not adopted voucher programs.[227]

This stigma is rich in irony. First, public support for Catholic and other religious schools was a common practice historically, ending only in the mid-nineteenth century due, among other things, to a virulent nativist, anti-Catholic politics conducted in the name of liberal theology and values.[228] As one historian of the period puts it, "the disinheritance of the church-related schools, a doctrine born of bigotry at the state level, was transmuted by the U.S. Supreme Court into high constitutional principle."[229] A related irony is political. Religiously conservative Protestants who once fiercely opposed public aid to religious schools (because those schools were Catholic) now support it (because they fear Catholicism less and have established their own academies since the 1960s, originally to avoid integration and busing).[230] John Jeffries and James Ryan note the political transformation on this issue, as revealed in positions on the RFRA:

> In an earlier time, the Republican Party, backed by Protestants of all stripes, supported the Blaine Amendment, which would have explicitly prohibited any and all forms of financial assistance to religious schools. A century later, a different Republican Party again sought to amend the Constitution, only this time to provide that religious institutions be entitled to [government aid to their schools].[231]

A third irony is economic. By the time vouchers' political viability is accepted, there may be few inner-city parochial schools around to accept them. Because these schools are under great financial pressure,[232] Andrew Greeley's prediction a decade ago that "the first voucher will arrive on the day that the last Catholic school closes"[233] must be taken seriously. A final irony is comparative. Many other liberal democracies, including those where religious divisions were historically deeper than in the United States, have long funded private school tuition for numerous students.[234]

The political success of voucher opponents to date has limited the amount of empirical evidence on vouchers' effectiveness.[235] Still, new studies are appearing, and vouchers show much promise.[236] Researchers assessing the publicly funded programs in Milwaukee, Cleveland, and Florida that extend to religious schools, and the privately funded ones in Washington, D.C., Charlotte, Dayton, New York City, and San Antonio, have reached what one education policy scholar calls a consensus about their positive effects on pupils, parents, and public schools,[237] although some more recent studies find inconclusive effects on academic achievement.[238] Since voucher applicants are typically selected by lottery, random-assignment studies, unique in educational policy research, have been possible. These studies "unambiguously and overwhelmingly" find improvements in both parental satisfaction and standardized test scores. This surely is why almost half of blacks support vouchers (48% generally, with higher support among young adults).[239] Cleveland's experience is typical: nearly 50% of the parents of the 4,000 participating students reported being very satisfied with the academic program, safety, discipline, and teaching of moral values in their private school, compared to 30% of those in the public schools. As to test scores:

> There have been seven random-assignment and three nonrandom-assignment studies of school choice programs in the last few years. The authors of all ten studies find at least some benefits from the programs and recommend their continuation, if not expansion. No study finds a significant harm to student achievement from the school choice programs. The probability that ten studies would find benefits and no significant harms if there were no benefit from school choice is astronomically low. Furthermore, the [participating] private schools tend to have [PPEs] that are nearly half the [PPE] in the public schools. Even if no significant academic benefit came from school choice, the policy would find support because parents like it and it costs half as much money to produce the same level of academic achievement.[240]

In fact, the cost is often less than half; for example, Cleveland's vouchers are worth only $2,250 a year, or 25% of the PPE in the public schools there. The amounts in Florida ($4,000) and in Milwaukee ($5,300) are also low relative to the public school PPEs.

In the discussion that follows, which largely concerns the secular advantages of vouchers and other school choice proposals, one must remember that although diversity in general and religious diversity in particular often go unmentioned in the public debate over vouchers, these diversities are in fact central to the debate. First, most families receiving vouchers will use them in relatively low-cost private religious schools; in Cleveland, the figure is 96%—although including in the denominator students who enroll in public community and magnet schools and voucher-funded tutorial programs in public schools reduces the percentage who chose religious schools to under 20%.[241]

This is largely because the few public programs that now exist allow vouchers to be used only within the student's district, and their monetary values are well below both the tuition most secular private schools charge and public schools' PPE. Second, religious schools' distinctive communal commitments, pedagogical missions, authority, teaching methods, and discipline seem integral to their comparative success in educating low-income children. If so, the diverse educational approaches needed to reach such children, which public school monopolies discourage, may depend on diverse religious and other normative communities with different pedagogical theories. Third, diverse religious communities are central players in the political coalition favoring vouchers.

As a policy matter, the case for funding further experiments with vouchers is compelling. Both the Bush administration, which proposed vouchers but did not fight very hard for them, and the Democrats, who with a few exceptions opposed even small experiments with vouchers, should be strongly condemned for failing to authorize them in the education legislation enacted in December 2001.[242] No one has explained why the government should prevent low-income parents from gaining access to better educational alternatives for their children just as more affluent families who send theirs to good suburban and private schools can—especially if this access, as in existing programs, does not necessitate higher public outlays and may actually cost less. Although voucher opponents advance a number of policy and political arguments against them, none is at all convincing. We have seen that low-income parents think that vouchers improve their children's educational experience —although the data on academic performance are not yet conclusive. Nevertheless, opponents say, vouchers will destroy the public schools by "creaming" off the best students and moving them into private schools, thus concentrating the neediest ones in the public systems and abandoning the civic ideal according to which youngsters in common schools learn secular values, a trans-ethnic, trans-class citizenship, and a familiarity with different cultural traditions.

The research on voucher programs refutes this argument in all of its particulars. It is rather late in the day to lament creaming. After all, higher-achieving students from better-off families have long chosen public or private alternatives; almost 60% of all students now attend "chosen" schools, including at least 25% of public school students.[243] In any event, voucher users are decidedly disadvantaged in terms of family income (averaging $10,860 in the Milwaukee program and even less in New York), family composition (about 75% are single, female-headed households), and test scores (students generally were in the bottom third academically). It is true that many low-income parents whose children would be eligible do not even bother to sign up for the lottery for vouchers, but those who do sign up (both winners and losers) are unquestionably poor.[244] "The most damaging thing one could say . . . with respect to 'creaming,'" education researcher Jay Greene writes, "is that [voucher programs] probably attract the more capable of the disadvantaged poor. But if this is 'creaming,' then [virtually all] anti-poverty programs engage in creaming."[245]

How does the *prospect* of vouchers affect the public schools and the children who remain in them? This issue is difficult to study, so researchers either examine programs that make vouchers available only after a public school fails a series of state tests, or they compare public school performance in areas with more public and private school choices with their performance in areas with fewer choices. The leading researcher on this issue, Harvard economist Caroline Hoxby, has found that "[i]f private schools in any area receive sufficient resources to subsidize each student by $1,000, the achievement of *public* school students rises."[246] When public providers must compete for scarce dollars with private ones, performance tends to improve. This is one reason why public colleges are now good and cheap enough to attract 80% of U.S. college students. Still, competitive effects have been, and are likely to remain, small until the amount of choice—and thus the threat it poses—increases.[247]

For people who enjoy choice to argue that low-income children must be denied choice and locked into the public schools in order to save those schools is not simply wrong as an empirical matter (as we have just seen, choice can improve those schools) and as a historical matter (choice was common until the mid-nineteenth century).[248] It is also morally perverse, at least in the context of a public entitlement like education. Those taking this position seem to prefer the welfare of an institution (the school system) to that of the children it is meant to serve. They would allow parents with choice to impose the burdens of nonchoice on the families who can least bear them, and would violate the basic moral premise of most social programs, which opposes wealth-based barriers to essential public services. For example, most Medicaid recipients go to private health-care providers, and many low-income families use housing vouchers to rent private units.[249]

Most Americans think of public schools as sites where young people of different social and ethno-racial backgrounds can come together to learn a common liberal citizenship.[250] Stephen Macedo, whose religious separatist views I discussed above, ardently advances this vision, which entails a "hidden curriculum" of "mutual understanding, respect, and cooperation among reasonable fellow citizens who may disagree about their ultimate religious and philosophical commitments."[251] Common schools, he insists, must teach tolerance, pluralism, inclusiveness, social mixing, and critical thinking. This in turn requires that children be detached, while in school, from the beliefs of their parents and the particular normative communities with which their families identify. Children, Macedo emphasizes, "are not just family members pursuing common family goals: they are independent individuals with their own lives to lead, and they are future citizens." This creates an overriding social interest in their civic education to which parental prerogatives, like those of the Mozerts, must yield.[252]

Unlike many who invoke this ideal, Macedo recognizes that in reality today's public schools, at least in low-income urban areas, fall far short of it—though he is less than candid about just how vast the shortfall actually is and how urgent is the need for a remedy. While rightly worrying that high school has become a diffuse, liberal "shopping mall" where mindless, undiscriminating toleration flattens and bleaches the moral and intellectual landscape, he barely mentions the illiteracy, innumeracy, indiscipline, violence, and astronomic drop-out rates in these schools. These conditions explain why a steadily rising share of black children (now about 10%) attend private schools,[253] why 52% of public school parents, and 67% of inner-city ones, would choose a private school if they could afford it, why 77% of the latter, especially black parents, favor the voucher approach when it is explained to them, and why young black adults are even more pro-voucher than older ones.[254]

Macedo is spooked at the thought of a choice-oriented system "guided by the peculiarities of a small number of people [like the Mozerts] whose needs for psychological closure place them in opposition to liberal democratic civic practice and virtues, including mutual respect amidst diversity and cooperation across group lines"[255]—as if this were the most serious risk facing American education rather than being a remote, peripheral risk involving only a relative handful of families. (Even the Mozerts sought to keep their children in the public school rather than isolating them.) Indeed, by enabling families like the Mozerts to "exit" to a religious school rather than exercising "voice" in the public one, vouchers help the public school to maintain its civic and secular emphases.[256] In turn, this specialization of functions among schools may better reconcile the conflicting goals of different families and of society.

As it happens, the research on vouchers indicates that the risk to civic ideals that so preoccupies Macedo is not at all a problem. The claim that a public school monopoly is necessary to promote these ideals has no empirical support and is refuted by the experience of other democracies where governments pay private school tuition for large numbers of students—76% in the Netherlands, 58% in Belgium, 30% in the United Kingdom, 25% in Australia, and so on.[257] As Macedo reluctantly concedes (in an endnote),[258] the available evidence in the United States indicates that private schools and religious schools are *more* successful than public schools at teaching civic virtues, community service, tolerance—and even feminism!—and that these teachings seem to persist into students' adult years.[259] Even more striking, and perfectly predictable, is the fact that private schools in communities with choice are more integrated both racially and by income than the public schools there.[260] After all, public school enrollments both reflect and reinforce the racial isolation of neighborhoods. Choice systems, in contrast, aim to decouple good schooling from residence.[261]

By detaching schooling from housing, school choice makes it easier for wealthier families to stay in economically mixed neighborhoods. And by reducing the financial premium placed on housing in areas with good schools, vouchers make it easier for poorer families to move into those areas. No wonder that vouchers are most strongly supported by poor inner-city residents and most vigorously opposed by well-to-do suburbanites. Ohio, for example, invited suburban public schools to accept Cleveland's voucher students but none agreed to do so.[262]

Suburbanites' resistance to paying more taxes to support private school tuition for other people's children, their reluctance to encourage low-income urban children to join theirs in suburban public and private (including religious) schools, and the job-anxiety opposition of the teachers' unions are already crippling nascent voucher programs. This is simply the latest chapter in an old political story; suburban interests derailed earlier efforts to improve urban schools through cross-district busing and school finance reforms.[263] Indeed, these same interests are also limiting the scope of *public school* choice programs—even in states strongly committed to school integration.[264] Joined by teachers and traditional civil rights groups, suburban forces marginalize vouchers or, more often, defeat them altogether[265]—even though they would never send their own children to the failing public schools to which low-income urban children are now condemned.[266] They refuse to allow those children the same choice of secular and religious education that they enjoy—even when they will not foot the bill. As a result, fewer than 15,000 students, or less than 0.1% of students nationwide, receive vouchers in the three publicly funded programs (private philanthropists fund four times as many vouchers!), and of these, relatively few can be used outside the students' local districts, much less in the suburbs.

This opposing coalition of suburbanites, teachers, and civil rights groups has defeated (at this writing) every single proposal for large-scale voucher programs by wide margins in legislatures or ballot initiatives. It has prevailed even when voucher proponents outspent it and even when Republican governors not beholden to these interests seemed open to vouchers.[267] The power of this coalition was most evident in 2001 when, with bipartisan support, it quickly and easily sank President Bush's high-profile proposal to fund vouchers of up to $1,500 per year for low-income children in persistently low-performing schools; indeed, it defeated even a very limited pilot program.[268]

Poor plan design has added to vouchers' political vulnerability. The problem is not so much that the voucher values are too low. Although existing vouchers do not cover the tuition at Andover or elite New York City academies, they suffice to cover full tuition in the vast majority of private schools in America. Voucher amounts, moreover, could be raised significantly without even approaching the PPE in most urban and suburban public schools. Any remaining gap (whose precise size depends on how the public system's fixed costs are allocated) would still leave the public schools with more money to spend per pupil than before—another reason, if one is needed, why vouchers should help them, not destroy them. A greater problem is that the most prominent voucher proposals, like the ones rejected in Michigan and California, were universal rather than being targeted, as they should be, at the most needy children in the worst-performing public schools. Universality greatly magnifies a plan's cost, diffuses its rationale, and weakens its likely impact. For the foreseeable future, at least, vouchers should be means- or school-tested. They should also be only one part of a much wider choice program that includes public schools through out-of-district options and charter schools, as well as efforts (vain so far in Cleveland's program) to secure suburban communities' participation.

Finally, the private schools where publicly funded vouchers are used must of course be accountable to public standards of fiscal responsibility, transparency, due process, and the like. (Public schools, for their part, are hardly accountable to those who cannot afford to exit from them.) There are many different ways to combine public and private standards, resources, and energies.[269] In general, government should not demand too much control and standardization of education in exchange for its funds. Perhaps the most alluring promise of voucher programs is their capacity to draw on private schools' diverse missions, values, curricula, and educational techniques, yet exploiting this diversity requires that they be free to disregard certain orthodoxies of public institutions. Just as the government has a right and a duty to enforce public standards of legality and safety, it can properly insist that the schools it supports meet minimum levels of curricular coverage (including civics instruction) and educational effectiveness. Regulation should focus on disclosure of information about schools and on educational outcomes like student achievement, not on input or process measures like teacher certification that often bear little or no relation to those outcomes.

A school probably cannot be effective, however, unless it or its sponsor is free to define its mission and propagate its values, including some that the majority may deplore. For example, a Catholic school's performance may depend on its power to send clear moral signals condemning premarital sex, divorce, homosexuality, and other conduct that most non-Catholics (and some Catholics) accept. But a genuine respect for diverse moral visions and educational ideals would allow public funds to be used in a school promoting core Catholic beliefs to the children of informed, consenting parents if it meets secular educational standards and neither endangers third parties nor violates norms to which our Constitution is unequivocally committed such as racial equality. But beyond this, a voucher law should be substantively agnostic, allowing the use of religiously driven admissions or hiring criteria if a school can show that the criteria genuinely advance a genuine, legitimate educational mission. It is hard to see how an all-white school could qualify under this standard but a single-sex or all-black program or one that will not hire unwed mothers to teach might qualify, depending on the strength of its rationale.[270]

School vouchers are certainly no panacea for the failure of inner-city public schools,[271] any more than charter or magnet schools are.[272] Diversity is not the same as excellence. Many religious schools where parents will use vouchers, like the secular schools they reject, will be mediocre or worse, and some of them will propound values that many in the community may find repellent. Some schools will engage in fraud or fail financially. Not all parents will make wise educational choices, nor will vouchers free their families from crime, substandard housing, and limited economic opportunities in declining neighborhoods. In addition, many religious schools may decline to participate for fear that government funding will subject them to controls and monitoring that they deem inimical to their autonomy. In short, the design of specific voucher programs and of their regulatory safeguards is crucial to their success. The same is true, of course, for public school programs.[273]

What vouchers can do is to enlarge the sadly limited options of low-income families, enabling them to seek schooling that may redeem their children's lives—choices that other Americans routinely make for their own children. Vouchers are by no means the only way to provide such choices. Indeed, as I noted earlier, a healthy respect for diversity values means that the state should support, under appropriate regulation, a variety of other approaches to school choice including charter and magnet schools, choice among public schools, home schooling, and other forms of subsidized access to private schools.[274] Accomplishing this would be no small thing, and we cannot afford to foreclose it by demanding an educational orthodoxy that defies our normative diversity and that so far has failed its own minimal civics test.

CONCLUSION

The combination of proliferating religious diversity and expansive government regulation multiplies the occasions for conflict between secular rules of general application and deviant religious practices—and hence for the regulation of that diversity. Legislatures and courts, I have argued, should endeavor to accommodate deviant religious practices and claims like those in *Mozert* and *Smith* unless they genuinely threaten compelling state interests (which in my judgment was not so in those cases). Congress and state legislatures, aroused by *Smith*'s abject deference to the asserted governmental interests in uniformity, perceived a fact that courts sometimes overlook. In a vast, diverse society like ours, the nonendangering practices and claims of (usually small) religious groups seldom threaten overriding secular values—and when they do, adequate legal and political remedies exist. Indeed, absent such a threat, a state should be seen as having an *independent* governmental interest in *making* such accommodations, insofar as they facilitate religious commitments that tend to benefit secular society in many important ways.

Finally, I maintain that although constitutional or political reasons may demand a strict neutrality, government can draw upon the diversity of religious groups in order to advance certain vital but elusive public purposes. Under contracts drafted to vindicate public values, qualified religious organizations can use public funds to provide social services that promise succor, fellowship, and meaning to those who seek them, and perhaps a kind of spiritual identity that most secular groups eschew. Many religious organizations project their distinctive beliefs and practices into their social service programs, increasing the chance that people in need will find one that "works" for them. They may also succeed in teaching many children whom the public schools have not reached or whose parents want, but cannot otherwise afford, civically adequate but faith-based education for their children. The risk of coercion can be avoided by assuring full disclosure and genuine choice with secular alternatives to adult clients and parents or guardians of students. Religious providers' autonomy and integrity can be protected if the government's rules are clear enough that a group can decide for itself whether participation will promote its distinctive values or compromise them.

These hopes are not Panglossian. Failures and frauds there certainly will be—just as there are in the existing public system despite formal accountability systems. The appropriate standard for assessing the more diverse, choice-oriented system I propose is not Plato's academy in Athens but the status quo in twenty-first-century America—a status quo that is demonstrably failing our children.

CHAPTER 8

Concluding Thoughts: Premises, Principles, Policies, and Punctilios

Diversity, we have seen, is not one thing but many things. It is also not what it used to be. Changes in American life have transformed diversity's social meanings since the 1960s—and especially during the last decade. The chief causes are clear enough: massive immigration, growth of the administrative state, the rise of identity politics, a new "great awakening" in matters spiritual, the differentiation and expansion of consumer markets, the emergence of choice as a dominant public value, greater toleration of minorities, and the celebration of diversity as an iconic, constitutive American ideal. Far less clear is what we are, literally, to make of this diversity. How should we understand and manage it through law and other social processes?

In Part II, I sought answers to these questions in specific areas where government has attempted to deal with what it views as serious threats to the diversity ideal, as it has defined that ideal. These threats include the linguistic deficits of immigrants, especially immigrant children, and the competition for visas among national origin groups (Chapter 4); the effects of past and present discrimination against ethno-racial minorities and their representation in social institutions (Chapter 5); the exclusion of minorities and low-income people from suburban communities (Chapter 6); and the blurring of church-state boundaries (Chapter 7). In these cases and in many others, public officials have used law to import, assimilate, define, certify, subsidize, mandate, protect, and exploit diversity. Each chapter reviewed these diversity-regulating efforts in great detail and assessed their effectiveness in achieving the government's diversity goals.

This final chapter draws on these particular assessments in order to distill the general lessons that I believe they hold for diversity management—recalling my point in Chapter 1 that this concept includes not only government actions to protect, promote, or regulate diversity but also government's willingness to stay its hand and defer to private, informal interactions among different individuals and groups. I present these lessons in three forms: (1) factual *premises* on which our management of diversity should be based; (2)

normative *principles* that should shape our diversity ideals and prescriptive *policies* that should guide our diversity management; and (3) private *punctilios* that we should observe as we interact in an increasingly diverse civil and political society. These lessons are tendentious, of course, as lessons usually are. The reader must decide whether my evidence and analysis adequately support them.

PREMISES

Diversity in America Is Immense and Increasing

I began this book by asserting that "America is probably the most diverse society on earth—certainly the most diverse industrial one." Chapter 1 presented evidence to justify both this claim and the related claim that American diversity, which we saw was remarkable even in early colonial days, is growing in almost every domain and despite some socially homogenizing tendencies. Our astonishing ethno-racial-linguistic diversity, Chapter 4 showed, is a direct result—some would say, an explicit goal—of admissions, citizenship, and language policies adopted since 1965, policies strongly influenced by egalitarian civil rights ideals. Turning to affirmative action in Chapter 5, we saw that what began as an equal opportunity remedy for the descendants of black slaves excluded from the full bounty of American life has evolved into an instrument—ethno-racial preferences—for infusing social institutions with broader demographic diversity. The 2000 census data on multiracialism revealed the paradoxical fact that this demographic heterogeneity, among other factors, now confounds the ability of these preferences to implement a constitutional and coherent diversity goal. Chapter 6 revealed that the ethno-racial diversity of residential neighborhoods is growing steadily, though more slowly for blacks than for other groups, and that much black isolation reflects a classism shared by almost all Americans, regardless of race, as well as race-specific differences in defining the optimal level of residential integration. And in Chapter 7, we saw that the dynamism of religious heterogeneity, which may be the most remarkable American diversity of all, presents valuable opportunities for social policy.

The Affirmative Ideal of Diversity Is New

Chapter 1 introduced an important distinction between the fact and the ideal of diversity. In explaining the diversity ideal, I further distinguished between tolerating differences, which is common in most liberal democracies, and viewing diversity as an end in itself with independent social value. This latter diversity ideal, Chapter 3 shows, is a very recent cultural innovation confined largely to North America.

Its novelty helps to explain why Americans have paid so little attention to the issue of diversity management. Because neither the United States nor any other polity even attempted to promote diversity until a few decades ago,[1] it should not surprise us that Americans do not agree about what diversity means or how the law should approach it. As we gain more experience, our views about diversity and its proper management will surely change.

The Social Value of Diversity Depends on the Dominant Political Theory

As Chapter 3 showed, diversity is neither good nor bad in itself. Its value (or disvalue) depends entirely on the appraiser's understandings of and beliefs about the competing ideals and complex notions that are the preoccupations of political theory. These ideals and notions include liberty and obligation; nature and convention; individual and group; polity and society; citizen and alien; and law, market, and culture. We saw that liberals, utilitarians, communitarians, and functionalists tend to disagree strongly about what diversity means, which values it promotes and in what amounts, what the empirical relationships among those values are, and how society should resolve the resulting conflicts.

The law systematically favors homogeneity over diversity. First, regulatory law tends to use uniform rules, which are easier to administer than rules that differentiate according to regulated entities' disparate circumstances. Second, the supreme liberal value, individual freedom, is often exercised in ways that subordinate diversity and even equal protection values. There is a world of difference, morally and legally speaking, between being subjected to an imposed homogeneity and freely choosing it for oneself, between mandated segregation and self-segregation. The historical shame of Jim Crow may affect whether we think today's choices are free enough to be given legal effect, but it does not negate the fundamental value of choice. This is why the law still allows people to choose same-sex schools, predominantly black colleges, religiously defined programs, and heterosexual-only groups. Third, the law often limits diversity in order to promote other public ends. Election laws seriously disadvantage third parties.[2] Labor law makes the choice of a majority of workers the exclusive bargaining representative for the entire unit.[3] In the interests of national uniformity, federal law frequently preempts states from adopting their own solutions to policy problems.[4]

Finally, the law must often protect homogeneity in one realm in order to promote diversity in another—a phenomenon noted in Chapter 2 and exemplified throughout Part II. Homogeneity in some enclaves, we learn, is essential to diversity in society as a whole. Protecting people's right to associate with those sharing a salient (to them) trait by forming groups that exclude those who the members think do not share it actually engenders society-wide diversity. This is so for at least two reasons: the community constituted by such homogeneous groups is itself diverse, and such groups afford people a normative and psychological breathing space that helps them become more tolerant, diversity-friendly citizens in the larger society. Indeed, protecting homogeneous groups against the universalizing demands of antidiscrimination law may sometimes even be constitutionally required. Religions define themselves by excluding nonbelievers, of course, but some secular groups also possess this right, according to the Supreme Court's recent decision in *Boy Scouts of America v. Dale,* briefly discussed in Chapter 5. This tension between the right of association and the right to be free of discriminatory treatment renders the task of managing diversity even more complex and challenging.

Diversity Is Often a Zero-Sum Game

This last example reveals a simple but pivotal fact about diversity, one that seriously constrains law's ability to promote it affirmatively or sometimes even to protect existing diversity. When law increases diversity of one kind or at one level, it often reduces diversity of another kind or at another level. This constraint occurs because of the nature of the diversities, the empirical relationships between them, or the multiple levels of government with different goals (a form of political diversity). Seldom can we reconcile conflicts between competing diversities without limiting at least one of them. This clash of diversities may be "zero-sum"; the gains of one kind or level of diversity may entail and equal the losses of the others. (I say "may" to recognize several possibilities: the diversity gains and losses—or both—may not materialize; if they do materialize, they may be unequal; or more than two kinds of diversities may be in conflict.)

Unfortunately, zero-sum and negative-sum conflicts (i.e., those in which the losses exceed the gains) between diversities are quite common. First, consider conflicts between different kinds or conceptions of diversity. In what William Galston calls the "paradox of diversity," a law that favors one diversity inevitably sacrifices all other diversities that are either normatively or empirically inconsistent with it.[5] The First Amendment protects political viewpoint diversity, but should it protect viewpoints like Leninism that advocate the elimination of diversity? If so, and if those viewpoints triumph, they may then suppress diversity. If they do not triumph or do not suppress opposing views, then protecting them will increase viewpoint diversity without any off-setting loss. Another example of such conflict occurs in antidiscrimination law, which seeks to enhance minorities' employment opportunities and create a more ethnically diverse workplace. It does so, however, by preventing minority (or other) entrepreneurs from using ethnically defined, often exclusionary, recruitment techniques or performance criteria.

Now, consider the controversy over same-sex public education. Many advocates justify it on the basis of diversity values. Different students, they believe, need different kinds of academic settings in order to flourish socially and develop their full educational potential. But opponents of same-sex schools invoke diversity values with equal fervor; they believe that gender-segregated environments adversely affect schoolchildren.[6] Indeed, as this example suggests, a particular policy issue may implicate more than two conflicting diversity ideals. Thus in the name of diversity, same-sex schooling advocates may also want government to fund parents directly so that they can choose among many different schooling options for their children—public or private, integrated or same-sex, and so forth. In contrast, other advocates may insist that facilitating parental choice does not significantly advance, or may even retard, the diversity ideal.

These conflicts can also arise within a single kind of diversity. As we saw in Chapter 6, housing developers desiring a racially diverse tenant mix in their buildings sometimes seek to control the racial composition of their tenants by rejecting members of certain races (usually blacks) in hopes of maintaining what the developers (or the law) deem an appropriate racial "balance."[7] Public school systems sometimes establish similar programs—again, in diversity's name.[8] As we also saw in Chapter 6, such racial sorting reflects a fear, well-founded both in theory and social experience, that such controls are necessary to prevent the interacting, cascading decisions of individuals that produce "tipping" where most whites move out of a neighborhood, leaving an equilibrium of racial "imbalance." This may even occur among homeowners who prefer more integration, so long as different groups prefer different levels of integration, perhaps for nonracist reasons.

Sometimes the law reduces diversity in one area on the supposition that this will increase it in others. We saw in Chapter 5, for example, that courts sometimes require an election *district* to be drawn so as to "pack" racially similar people together in order to diversify the racial composition of the *legislature* by assuring that such districts will elect minority representatives. Federalism may produce conflicts over even a single kind or locus of diversity. A national civil rights law promoting workplace diversity, for example, bars states and localities from addressing workplace diversity in other ways. In this structural sense, national uniformity and local option are locked in a zero-sum conflict over diversity even if governments at all levels value it.

In other situations, the conflict between or among different diversities arises not because of any normative or structural tension between them but because of the way they happen to interact in the real world. James Lindgren, for example, shows that among faculty at the top 100 law schools in the mid-1990s, 80% of law professors identified themselves as Democratic or leaning Democratic and 13% identified as Republican or leaning Republican. Republican women and Republican minorities were particularly underrepresented compared to both the general public and the full-time workforce.[9] A school's effort to diversify its faculty in terms of race or gender, then, will almost inevitably reduce political diversity—at least until the views of the preferred groups become more internally heterogeneous. As an empirical matter, a school valuing these different diversities must decide how to trade them off against one another; it cannot maximize them all.

The fact that pursuing diversity is often a zero-sum game, however, does not mean that all laws that promote one conception of diversity undermine competing conceptions equally. Laws can strike different balances between uniformity and diversity values. For example, one law might adopt a default rule and permit people to contract around it. Another might authorize or invite exceptions, or might allow alternative solutions to the problem at issue. How much a law treats diversity, then, will depend on precisely how it is framed and applied, the realm in which it operates, and the institutional apparatus. Any restriction on individual choice, however, means a potential loss of diversity.

A variant of this trade-off occurs when a law seeks to promote equality by requiring people to act or be treated the same even though they see themselves (or others see them) as different. This is not very troubling in the relatively easy case of a civil rights law barring racial discrimination. Denying bigots the right to practice racial exclusion, after all, will not strike most of us as causing a significant social loss; racial nondiscrimination is a principle that enjoys nearly universal allegiance, one that the law, correctly, seldom compromises.

A harder case arises when individuals want to do something that is more widely valued but that the majority nevertheless restricts. Such conflicts are common at the permeable border between religious practices and state-enforced secular values, as Chapter 7 revealed. Because deviant traditions often flourish in relative isolation from more cosmopolitan cultures, a society wishing to cultivate a truly robust and genuine diversity may need to protect these self-isolating traditions as much as possible from the intrusion of more universalistic norms.[10] Law can confer this protection.

Existing Diversity Management Is Eclectic

Another factual premise emerges from Part II: current diversity management efforts are not ideologically pure, analytically crisp, and internally coherent. Instead, they are decidedly messy and dissonant. This should not surprise us given the varied contexts in which diversity values affect policy, and given Americans' pragmatic, compromising approach to most public issues.

Ideological eclecticism about diversity is historically rooted. As Chapter 3 showed, American society has always mixed liberal inclusionary and exclusionary elements in its views of and policies toward ethnically, religiously, and otherwise diverse groups. Political leaders combine these elements differently and opportunistically in order to promote "people-building." At every turn, Rogers Smith reminds us, advocates of racial and religious hierarchy have challenged liberal immigration and religious toleration, and their challenges have often succeeded.[11] For much of American history, chattel slavery, race-based immigration and naturalization restrictions, ineligibility of women and the foreign-born for the highest political offices, segregation, and many other forms of civic subordination persisted:

> [W]hen restrictions on voting rights, naturalization, and immigration are taken into account, it turns out that for over 80 percent of U.S. history, American laws declared most people in the world legally ineligible to become full U.S. citizens solely because of their race, original nationality, or gender. For at least two-thirds of American history, the majority of the domestic adult population was also ineligible for full citizenship for the same reasons. Those racial, ethnic, and gender restrictions were blatant, not "latent." For these people, citizenship rules gave no weight to how liberal, republican, or faithful to other American values their political beliefs might be.[12]

Even today, when Americans have largely put behind us the most violent and intolerant reactions to diversity, the mixture of our attitudes toward it is bewildering. For example, we welcome (or at least tolerate) different ways of speaking, dressing, eating, praying, working, and living, which seems to evince a remarkably easygoing, shoulder-shrugging attitude toward cultural differences that many first-time visitors find striking. At the same time, however, we increasingly hive ourselves off into gated residential communities and other enclaves where uniformities of economic class and lifestyle mute, conceal, and even banish these differences. It is as if we like the *idea* of diversity more the less we have to *live* with it.

Other ostensibly paradoxical stances toward diversity abound. Consumers who support the world's richest smorgasbord of goods, services, and communications channels nevertheless patronize vendors that separate them into highly segmented "niche" product and media markets, which in turn construct them and their interests as narrowly and exclusively as possible. The best-educated, most secure, and most cosmopolitan generations in American history seek or cling to the most parochial, self-isolating identities, and seem determined to project such identities onto others. We honor the universal human rights that our Constitution and laws proclaim, yet we resist those rights when we think that extending them to others might detract, however slightly, from our national sovereignty.[13] We laud the diversity created by small, entrepreneurial enterprises as we countenance consolidation and concentration in vital economic sectors. Our public and private institutions adopt preferences for certain forms of diversity (e.g., skin color, surname, and athleticism) while ignoring or even discouraging other diversities that are— or in my view ought to be—more closely linked to these institutions' goals. Faculties that should thrive on viewpoint diversity seem to have little taste for it or even for closer diversity proxies like religious affiliation—or indeed for religiosity itself![14]

The convergence of these different attitudes and behaviors about diversity does not necessarily imply that Americans are irrational, hypocritical, or self-contradictory—though we may be. Some of these patterns are consistent with more general principles, as when we prefer one market to be concentrated in order to create scale economies (e.g., missile production) while favoring more fragmentation and competition in another market (e.g., movie theaters). But other positions are in strong tension—for example, human rights and national sovereignty claims. Still others are flatly inconsistent, as when affirmative action justified on diversity grounds ignores diversity's most valuable aspects. And some patterns, like the tendency of faculties to declare the virtues of diversity while strongly preferring politically like-minded colleagues, seem downright hypocritical.

Technology's effects on diversity are notoriously hard to predict. Consider the Internet, for example. On the bright side, certain ways of organizing the Internet's architecture promise to diversify content for consumers.[15] Advances in software now facilitate methods of automated loan underwriting that prevent lenders from observing applicants or their ethno-racial attributes and discriminating against them.[16] On the other hand, some observers think the Internet is diversity-unfriendly. In 2000, legal scholar Cass Sunstein lamented that computer filtering programs are enabling Americans to personalize incoming news and other information flows in ways that threaten democracy by screening out diverse viewpoints and the experiences of fellow citizens. People, he wrote, will in effect limit their information source to a solipsistic publication he mockingly called "The Daily Me." Sunstein's prediction was based on a very limited view of human ingenuity, imagination, and curiosity, and he soon recanted it. The Internet, he now concedes, "is allowing millions of people to expand their horizons and to encounter new worlds of topics and ideas."[17]

Many commentators worry that advances in genetic engineering, including cloning technologies, will have the pernicious effects that Sunstein originally predicted for the Internet. These changes, they fear, will replicate the safe and familiar, eliminate the unexpected, homogenize human physiology and experience, and even program the destiny of species, including our own. At this point, the only certainty is that these technologies, like the Internet and most earlier technologies from the wheel to digital electronics, will augment our choices. But how we shall use these new choices—whether for or against diversity, or indeed in ways that redefine its meaning—remains anyone's guess.

Existing Diversity Management Is Largely a Civil Society Function

The eclecticism of diversity management has forced government to develop a repertoire of legal and policy techniques that it hopes will bear some coherent relationship to one another. Part II discussed many examples: the First Amendment, immigration quotas, antidiscrimination laws, affirmative action and bilingual education programs, naturalization policies, inclusionary zoning laws, housing vouchers, court-ordered desegregation, and many others. But focusing on public law measures of this kind can give a seriously misleading picture of how Americans actually go about managing diversity.

Compared to other nations, the United States looks more to the fragmented, integrative processes of civil society than to programmatic initiatives launched from the center, but these low-level, informal processes are easy to miss unless one carefully looks for them (as sociologists do). Consider some ubiquitous examples of these processes. Members of different ethno-racial groups intermarry, blending their traditions. Immigrants learn English, and their children do so rapidly—especially if the schools do not mire them in native language ghettos. Daily interactions in schools, workplaces, churches, and other cultural entrepôts mute ethnic differences. Religious communities energetically recruit new members to share their beliefs and practices. Mass media and commercial advertising disseminate a steady stream of common cultural symbols. Popular sports and music become foci for allegiances and interests that transcend group boundaries. Private institutions, serviced by a growing army of "diversity consultants,"[18] engage in self-conscious efforts to understand and mediate cultural conflicts. Neighbors trade experiences and interpretations of events. People form nonprofit organizations to pursue a breathtaking variety of communal goals.

America's largely hands-off approach to managing diversity is consistent with its laissez-faire orientation toward numerous other arenas of social conflict, arenas that in other societies elicit active governmental intervention. Whereas the state of Israel manages almost every aspect of immigrants' integration (language, housing, job training and placement, income support, social clubs, religious affiliation, and much more),[19] nonrefugee immigrants to the United States are largely on their own except for public schooling.[20] Much the same is true, *mutatis mutandis,* of religious institutions, political parties, mass media, the working poor, the elderly, health care, education, and most other markets for services that are publicly provided or highly regulated elsewhere. In this respect, diversity management, like so much else, is part of an American public philosophy that emphasizes disparate values and private responsibilities.

Diversity's Value Depends on Its Provenance

If diversity were simply an instrumental value, we would be relatively indifferent to its origins. Our interest would only be in how effectively it produces the ultimate end for which we deploy it. But while diversity is instrumental to other ends, it also possesses a normative and expressive character that cannot be reduced to its instrumental value. This helps explain why a well-meaning judge who contrives ethno-racial diversity by manipulating jury selection violates the Constitution,[21] and why a housing complex's putatively diversity-friendly effort to avoid racial tipping by limiting the number of black tenants suffers the same fate.[22] In short, diversity's value to people depends on its perceived genuineness and lack of legal contrivance. This in turn depends on where it came from, how it came about, and the process that produced it. I refer to this as diversity's *provenance.*

Americans evidently care a great deal about the provenance of their most identity-salient diversities: race, ethnicity, religion, viewpoint, language, and politics. In Chapter 2, I distinguished between genuine and spurious diversity while noting some of the difficult conceptual, political, and social questions that the distinction raises and offering some preliminary answers to those questions. With the benefit of the studies in Part II, I can now refine those answers.

The three case studies of neighborhood integration reviewed in Chapter 6 demonstrate that people perceive, value, and react differently to a legally imposed diversity (say, race or income level) than to an otherwise similar but freely chosen diversity. Although few Americans endorse racism, almost all of us endorse classism—the notion that one may properly choose to live with others of one's wealth or income level but has no moral claim to live in a community one cannot afford. Recall that the court in *Mount Laurel* mandated inclusion of those who *by definition* could not afford the housing in question, and the plaintiffs in *Yonkers* and *Gautreaux* could not afford it *in fact*. The most plausible account of the disputes that arose in these communities, then, is that the mandated diversities seemed inauthentic precisely because they *were* mandated and lacked the only provenance, ability to pay, that Americans value as a legitimate eligibility criterion for residential communities.

The same analysis applies to ethno-racial preferences in higher education, although the form of legitimation there is less clear-cut. Academic achievement or promise (however measured) is the credential that most strongly legitimates admission, but it is not the only one. As we saw in Chapter 5, many academics, administrators, and members of the public view race, ethnicity, athletics, parentage, and some other nonacademic factors as morally relevant to admission. Many others in the academic community, however, stigmatize members of preferred groups who do not earn admission through academic achievement or promise. Even some beneficiaries of ethno-racial preferences endorse this perspective. Again, diversity is not self-authenticating. Its value ultimately depends on its provenance.

The analysis of immigration-related diversity in Chapter 4, however, suggests a further refinement in how we understand the significance of diversity's provenance. Provenance is less important where no other baseline norms of legitimacy exist. A nation that admits only a limited number of immigrants must decide which groups to select and which to exclude. The United States uses nationality, family relationships, skills, humanitarian need, priority of application, and other such criteria, while some other countries screen for ethnicity and language. The point is that all use certain selection criteria and that the ensuing diversity is simply a product of these political choices. Absent a strong competing norm, then, diversity's provenance is not an issue in immigration policy. If the selection criteria are legitimate, it follows that the diversity these criteria produce is also legitimate. Americans primarily debate how many visas we should assign to each admission category, not the validity of the categories themselves. This contrasts sharply with housing markets and universities where widely shared norms of classism and merit, respectively, undermine law's legitimacy when it substitutes other, more controversial distributive criteria.

PRINCIPLES AND POLICIES

I now turn from description to prescription—from a relatively objective account of how diversity is actually manifested and organized in American society, to some general principles and then to more specific policies that I believe should guide our management of diversity.

Government Should Not Try to Create, Certify, or Cultivate Specific Diversities

As we saw in Chapter 3, diversity generates many social values and disvalues, depending on the political and social norms people embrace. An economist would say that diversity is a collective or public good in the technical sense that many of its benefits and costs are externalized to the society as a whole. It follows from this, the economist holds, that voluntary actions alone cannot produce the "right" amount or kind of diversity; only government can do so by promoting good diversity and limiting bad diversity.

But this is what philosophers call a category mistake. Unlike other public goods whose value does not depend on who produces it or where it comes from, diversity's value depends on its provenance. Genuine diversity (hence diversity value) is a far more fragile thing than lawmakers often seem to suppose; the crude regulatory resources and techniques at law's disposal are more likely to asphyxiate it than to invigorate it. For this reason, precisely how government conceives of and implements diversity management matters a great deal. Some efforts meant to increase diversity value may indeed do so but others may debase or destroy it. The fact that diversity is a public good, then, does not imply that government should manage it. It is always an open question whether a particular form of public law increases or reduces diversity value.

Let us distinguish among different ways in which government can and does approach diversity. We saw in Chapter 4 how the immigration laws literally *import* diversities that persist even as the process of assimilation transforms those diversities in complex ways. Our immigration stream is now so diverse in terms of ethnicity, language, race, religion, and national origin that efforts to diversify it further cannot yield much additional diversity value. In Chapter 7 we also saw that the religion clauses of the First Amendment, taken together, *protect* an extraordinarily diverse mélange of religious groups, beliefs, and practices—even though, as I argued there, the U.S. Supreme Court could and should protect even more religious diversity than it does now. By barring discrimination against minorities, the law also protects diversity. Political diversity, which is largely outside the scope of this book, receives strong legal protection from American law. Indeed, the Court's fidelity to the protection of flag burning, hate speech, and other political deviance is praise-worthy.[23] It is also remarkable, given the statist values of most of the current Justices.[24]

Sometimes, however, government seeks not simply to protect an existing diversity but to create or promote a new one. These two enterprises are very different. In order to promote a particular diversity, government must *define, measure,* and *certify* it as one deserving special legal recognition and support. This requires it, in turn, to make determinations about provenance and authenticity that it is singularly ill-equipped to make. The Bureau of Indian Affairs, for example, decides which groups it will recognize as tribes for purposes of various federal benefits, with the most valuable benefit today being tribal eligibility to establish potentially lucrative gambling casinos. These incentives have embroiled the Bureau, tribes, and individuals in high-stakes disputes over who is and is not an Indian and which groups of Indians constitute tribes, disputes sometimes resolved in highly politicized, even corrupt ways.[25]

Perverse certification is also exemplified by the recent decennial census, discussed in Chapters 2 and 5. This reveals how official definitions, measurements, and certifications of ethno-racial groups can reify and (at least for a time) ossify anachronistic categories, distort behavioral incentives, and politicize identities that, I have argued, should be matters of private, unsubsidized choice. The census's handling of the Indian, black, and Hispanic groupings is particularly problematic.[26] (The fact that the census was conducted with great professionalism only confirms that these distortions are systemic, not incompetent.) An equally troubling, if no less well-meaning, instance of official certification of diversity, also noted in Chapter 5, is New Jersey's new policy of training state troopers to determine and then code each driver's race for purposes of antiprofiling statistics.

Having certified a certain kind of diversity for promotion, government will then either *subsidize* or *mandate* it—particularly if it is a kind that the relevant community is inclined to resist. The detailed analyses of mandatory ethno-racial preferences (Chapter 5), court-ordered integration of residential neighborhoods across class lines (Chapter 6), and required bilingual education for cultural maintenance (Chapter 4) reveal the disappointing outcomes of these efforts. That the government had plausible reasons and better remedial alternatives makes these outcomes all the sadder.

Why is it so much harder for government to promote new diversities than to protect old ones? I have already discussed one largely structural reason: the tight link between diversity's value and its provenance. We value diversity only if and to the extent that we think it arises from a legitimate source and perceive it as authentic, natural, and uncontrived. We care about where the diversity comes from and whether the process that produced it comports with deeply held norms about moral desert and instrumental appropriateness. We value diversity that seems to reflect human spontaneity, personality, and achievement (e.g., performance-based selection of students and workers, or cultural maintenance managed by immigrant families) more highly than diversity that government designs, manufactures, certifies, and mandates (e.g., choosing students by skin color, or using public schools to maintain immigrant children's Spanish when their parents want them to learn English quickly).

Although law has many strengths, the ability to create the values and experiences we associate with genuine diversity is not one of them. To contemporary Americans, law is not a mystical emanation from a majestic sovereign. Instead, we regard it as a technocratic, artifactual tool of social control to be assessed according to the more mundane criteria of consent, efficiency, fairness, and effectiveness. Democratically legitimated law carries moral force, to be sure, but law's ubiquity and instrumentalism have disenchanted and demystified it. We no longer stand in awe of law; we are disenthralled.[27]

Law cannot easily extract diversity value from processes that make the resulting diversity seem artificial to people who believe in academic or occupational merit, class-based neighborhoods, immigrant assimilation and economic mobility, and other values. Coercive law has failed (though certainly not for want of trying) to legitimate ethno-racial preferences, integrate east Yonkers or New Jersey suburbs, and educate LEP children—even when wrapping itself in the mantle of constitutional principle. This inability to create diversity value, as distinguished from protecting it from suppression, may be part of a larger limitation endemic to law. Robert Fogel suggests that while the law successfully redistributed material gains in the past, it has less purchase on the spiritual values that contemporary Americans increasingly seek.[28] Fogel's insight, I maintain, also applies to diversity value.

These findings bespeak a paradox about diversity and law. The harder the law tries to create or promote diversity, the more law magnifies and highlights its own weaknesses, and the more law reveals as inauthentic, illegitimate, and disvalued the diversity that it fashions. When Judge Sand increased the legal pressure on Yonkers, he succeeded only in ratcheting up the city's defiance. Like a man caught in quicksand, his remedial flailing simply worsened his predicament. The more he brandished the law to quell the city's defiance, the more he risked discrediting both the law and the diversity it demanded. Resisters in Yonkers sought to personify the law and hence demystify it by depicting Sand's court orders as *his* law imposing *his* diversity. Sand, for his part, naturally saw the mandated diversity as nothing more than the law's just remedy for past wrongdoing. His claim of authority was perfectly correct as a legal matter, and as a legal matter the city eventually had to capitulate. As a practical matter, however, the city's compliance was—and remains—as slow, grudging, and incomplete as it could manage. The city simply moved the venue of resistance, with Sand's acquiescence, from his court to the city bureaucracy. Far from vindicating either law or diversity in Yonkers, public esteem for both has probably declined.

This paradox about diversity and law is also evident, albeit far less dramatically, in the other diversity-mandating efforts we reviewed. In hopes of rescuing affirmative action from the grim reality of sharp differentials in group academic performance, the University of California has repeatedly resorted to new manipulations and dissimulations that must sow cynicism about both law and the diversity ideal. The same is true, *mutatis mutandis,* when government sacrifices immigrants' assimilation and education in order to maintain an important culture whose authenticity and hence value derive from a provenance of unregulated, unmediated efforts by motivated families and communities, not from government mandates.

Indeed, the paradox of an earnest government defeating its own best efforts is even crueler than this. In truth, government and law are natural enemies of diversity, especially when they are most eager to create it. This has nothing to do with motives or incentives and has everything to do with the nature of law, government, and diversity. Consider, for example, the categories that law uses to structure legal discourse, doctrine, and responsibility.[29] These legal categories, of course, perform many valuable functions. They allow us to make, apply, and comprehend law more cheaply and more predictably than if the rule traced the bewildering variety and semiotic complexity of social life. Public law's hope is to use simplistic categories to facilitate legislators' control of regulators and regulators' control of the rest of us. Certain legal techniques, of course, can temper the reductionism of rules. Lawmakers, for example, can include more categories, replace bright-line tests with more flexible, contextual standards, and permit exceptions to be made. These techniques, however, have their own drawbacks. A nuanced law is more complex and costly to understand and apply. Moving from clear rules to vague standards delegates discretion to those who apply and enforce them, such as citizens, juries, or bureaucrats, thus reducing accountability and inviting arbitrariness and unpredictability. Exceptions may swallow, weaken, or delegitimate the rules to which they apply.

Even at the most formal level, then, it is more problematic for public law to define, certify, and promote diversity than it is to protect (and, in some cases, exploit) a diversity that has already been defined, authenticated, and valorized by civil society. Genuine diversity value is a product of an opaque, complex, dynamic, mysterious realm of human meaning and identity that we call culture. Where the goal of generating diversity value is concerned, law is seriously disabled. This disability, moreover, cannot be overcome or accommodated. We can only hope to understand its sources and minimize its worst effects.

Government Has an Essential Role in Protecting Diversity from Discrimination and Monopoly

Government, I have argued, should use its bully pulpit to praise diversity in general and even particular diversities, as President Bush did shortly after September 11 when he exhorted Americans to treat Muslims with respect. But it should not try to create or promote any *particular* kind of diversity. I have explained why this is not a proper public function in a society committed to liberal and democratic values and why, in any event, law is a singularly poor instrument for performing that function.

This does not mean, however, that government has no role to play in protecting diversity or indeed in promoting it as a worthy social ideal. Far from it. Government is indispensable to protecting existing and emerging diversities from suppression, and it can open the channels through which new diversities may be born.[30] Indeed, *only* government can protect groups whose beliefs and practices differ from those of a dominant group that wants to use the law to impose its own.[31] I do not mean, of course, that all majority impositions are impermissible; almost all of them are perfectly appropriate in a democracy. Rather, I simply want to underscore the conventional constitutional rule that such impositions must meet a higher-than-usual standard of justification where they are regulating ethno-racial, religious, political, or associational diversities.

Government's management of diversity, then, should take two general forms. First, it should protect existing diversities against invidious discrimination. Second, it should clear a path for the emergence of other, privately generated diversities (most of which it will be unable to predict) by challenging various forms of monopoly power. I shall discuss each of these in turn, highlighting the role of enhanced choice.

Antidiscrimination. I emphasized in Chapter 5 the fundamental, normatively compelling distinction between nondiscrimination and affirmative action, even as I noted how the two are often conflated for evidentiary and other reasons. In a society strongly dedicated to genuine equal opportunity, the law must assure individuals that they will not be denied it on the basis of attributes used historically to stigmatize, subordinate, or otherwise disadvantage the group. This means creating a system of antidiscrimination remedies like the Civil Rights Act of 1964 and the Americans with Disabilities Act of

1990 and ensuring their effective enforcement.[32] The goal of antidiscrimination law is justice conceived of as equal opportunity for individuals, not diversity. Although employers and others who comply with antidiscrimination law may well end up with more demographic diversity than otherwise, this is beside the central point, which is justice. (By definition, as we saw earlier, the law often *reduces* diversity in another sense, as when it prevents employers or others from using certain screening criteria—a reduction that is sometimes necessary to prevent discrimination on the basis of group characteristics.)

In contrast, affirmative action—at least in its more robust, preferential forms—promotes many new injustices in the name of remedying an old one. It does so by favoring one ethno-racial group over others either for historical reasons that are incoherent as applied to most of the beneficiaries, or for diversity reasons that government, as I explained above, can neither effectively nor legitimately mandate. And it does so at a time when rapid demographic changes in American society make the system of preferences increasingly difficult to administer justly or even rationally.

The *Yonkers* and *Gautreaux* litigations are cases of court-mandated affirmative action. The Supreme Court permits this use of affirmative action when the trial court can narrowly tailor it to remedy specific acts of past discrimination, but bars its use as a remedy for past societal discrimination of a more diffuse sort. This distinction is justified in principle, in my view, although like many sound rules it is hard to apply in particular cases. I criticized the *Yonkers* court not because it used affirmative action to remedy the city's past discrimination against minorities, which under the circumstances was wholly justified. My criticism, rather, was that the court chose a particular remedial form—which I described as "a bricks-and-mortar, fixed-site, take-it-or-leave-it, top-down, court-designed, court-managed" remedy—that predictably would exacerbate the minorities' plight and increase the impediments to meaningful residential diversity. The New Jersey court's mandate of affirmative action in *Mount Laurel* was, if anything, even less justified and more fruitless than Judge Sand's regime in Yonkers because the New Jersey court demanded a kind of diversity remedy—forced integration of upper-income communities by lower-class families—that violated a norm of class-based residential patterns reflecting a conception of fairness endorsed by almost all Americans.

If we truly value diversity, however, we must impose certain limits on the scope of the nondiscrimination norm. Antidiscrimination law was originally intended to protect blacks and other minorities who are most vulnerable to majority oppression, and whom the Equal Protection Clause of the Fourteenth Amendment was meant to protect against exclusion and subordination on the basis of group membership. More recently, antidiscrimination remedies have been extended to many groups, such as parents, that do not and should not receive the same level of constitutional protection.[33] This may be because the group (e.g., parents or women) can more adequately protect itself in the political process and in the market, or it may be because forcing others to transact with the group (e.g., homosexuals, families with small children, Medicaid recipients, the obese, members of motorcycle gangs) would violate their principles, identities, or interests in freely choosing their own associations. The nondiscrimination norm, as I argued in Chapter 5, is very powerful and widely embraced in American society, as it certainly should be. But so is the norm favoring group autonomy in the enjoyment and promotion of common values, as is implied by the religious exemption and other statutory limitations on the scope of antidiscrimination laws.[34] This norm is also explicit in recent Supreme Court decisions recognizing individual and group rights of "expressive association."[35] These rights should be extended, for example, to allow experimentation with single-sex schools, which reflect a plausible educational theory designed to address an urgent social problem and advance equal opportunity.[36] The government's role, however, is not to promote such schools but only to eliminate discriminatory rules that unfairly inhibit them.

The Supreme Court has only begun to flesh out the nature and scope of the expressive association right as it probes the constitutional boundaries between a group's power to define and express its members' values through association of like-minded people who therefore exclude others, and an excluded individual's claim under antidiscrimination law to equal treatment. This task presents a difficult judicial challenge. The contours of a group's expressive association right will likely depend on factors such as the characteristic on which the exclusion is based, the effect of that characteristic on the group's values, coherence, and identity, the clarity and consistency of the group's identity, and the kind of evidence required to establish these facts. Developing distinctive identities in association with others will often demand the exclusion of individuals who the group believes, rightly or wrongly, possess different traits, viewpoints, or interests. These exclusions may cause pain to some of the excluded and may also offend many in the general public, as the Boy Scouts' exclusion of avowed homosexuals evidently does.[37] But if valuing diversity in a liberal society means anything, it means assuring people's freedom to form exclusive groups that embrace unpopular beliefs and to act on those beliefs in ways permitted by the Constitution and without undue interference by the law. Within those very broad limits, a diversity-friendly law must protect not only those values that the majority favors, but also those that it abhors.

The law should define rights of expressive association broadly enough to give individuals the breathing space they need to join with others in private groups that they think can affirm and sustain their values, meanings, and solidarities. In a liberal society, these norms will often be different from (though not necessarily inconsistent with) those enforced or proposed by the state, and a liberal law must protect people's right to maintain these differences between their own norms and those demanded by the state. Helping them preserve these normative differences is one way for the law to counter the state's tendency to try to monopolize norms in an increasingly diverse America. I now turn to other ways.

Antimonopoly. The principle that the law should prevent public and private entities from exercising monopoly power over others is not really debatable—although precisely how this should be done certainly is. In the economic domain, this principle motivates antitrust law, which is a charter for economic diversity (or at least for efficient levels of it) in the interest of consumers. The government, of course, is an important enforcer of antitrust law. In the political domain, a similar principle animates the Free Speech Clause of the First Amendment, which bars the state from using public power to impose its views on the citizenry, prefer some groups over others, or stifle speech and viewpoint diversity.

Indeed, a robust First Amendment is the most powerful legal instrument for protecting many other kinds of diversity. The government, usually a defendant in First Amendment cases, should do much more than refrain from violating the Amendment. It should also act affirmatively to vindicate the Amendment's antimonopoly principle. For example, government could diversify campaign finance by giving citizens more control over the allocation of campaign dollars.[38] It could ensure that when it speaks,[39] it speaks in diversity-friendly ways—even when the Constitution does not require it to do so, as when it sponsors public art or funds legal services.[40] It could begin planning a phase-out—or at least an appropriate disclaimer—of ethno-racial statistics and categories whose growing artificiality, crudeness, inaccuracy, and capacity to mislead are already distorting public policy discourse.[41] Government can also nourish institutions and practices in which diverse visions of the good can meet, compete, and interact—sometimes in the "public square," sometimes in private ones—at a subconstitutional level and in ways that the First Amendment permits but does not necessarily require. Perhaps most important, it should indulge a strong though rebuttable presumption favoring decentralized decisionmaking in both the polity and the market, and it should support educational systems that prepare young people for the different ways in which they can comprehend and live in a world far more diverse and dynamic than that inhabited by their parents.

This book has been concerned less with economic and political diversities than with the diversities of race, ethnicity, language, religion, and class. Here too, government can use the law to challenge monopoly power—especially its own. It can empower diversity by enhancing *choice*.

Choice. The attentive reader has surely noticed that this theme of using choice to empower diversity, along with enhancing enforcement of the non-discrimination principle, links many of my otherwise disparate policy propos-als for improving diversity management. Individuals should be allowed to self-identify as they wish rather than having government impute to them ra-cial or other identifiers that they may reject. Parents should have more say about the linguistic education of their LEP children. So-called diversity visas should be auctioned to qualifying worker-bidders. Private expressive associa-tions that seek to restrict their staff or membership in order to strengthen their common identity should be allowed, as religious groups are, to do so without violating antidiscrimination law. Housing integration should be pro-moted by giving discrimination victims and other target groups vouchers for rent, search, and other mobility services. Religious practices that do not vio-late a compelling public interest should be accommodated. People who re-ceive social service subsidies should have equal access to FBO providers. Par-ents of children in failing public schools should receive tuition vouchers that can help them to choose better schools. All of these proposals have a com-mon feature and goal—to increase the meaningful, autonomous choice of people who now enjoy little choice because the government preempts or mo-nopolizes it.

Americans, more than perhaps any other society, recognize that absent market failure or other overriding reasons for government choice, social wel-fare is maximized by having resource allocation decisions made by the af-fected individuals and firms, not by government. In the liberal tradition, moreover, the normative value of choice transcends economic efficiency. As Chapter 3 explained, choice is the means to liberalism's ultimate end, auton-omous freedom, whose exercise almost inevitably generates diversity.

The fact that Americans venerate individual choice is evident in numerous public debates—over abortion, smoking, gun control, and school vouchers, for example—where competing interests jockey for the political advantage of justifying their causes in choice rhetoric. But an equally important and less obvious point is that a society that relies on decentralized choice gains an in-calculable value—political conflict reduction—that goes well beyond the ef-ficiency and autonomy values enjoyed by those who exercise it. This muting of political conflict is essential to the survival of a polity as diverse and com-petitive as twenty-first-century America.[42]

In the United States, many institutional arrangements are designed for this purpose.[43] Federalism and a decentralized party system manage much political conflict by channeling it to the states and localities rather than elevating it to the federal level where it would be magnified by the higher stakes in a single national solution. Judiciaries at all levels resolve litigation, much of it political in nature, in a fragmented, low-visibility fashion. Juries, used far more widely in the United States than anywhere else, diffuse (and conceal) responsibility for what are often political decisions through their local and independent character, notably ad hoc form, Delphic opacity, and the subjective nature of many legal rules that they apply.[44] The separation of powers also distributes responsibility for political decisions, though it does encourage interbranch conflicts. Many activities that in other countries are matters for political decision are privatized in the United States; they are governed more by contract law and markets than by public law and politics. The private sector itself is also relatively decentralized; small firms account for most economic activity, nonprofit groups proliferate, religions are organizationally and often liturgically decentralized, and laws mandating information disclosure help to facilitate and educate private choice.

The decentralization of choice to private individuals and groups and to lower-level governments, then, is a vital element of America's approach to conflict reduction. When politicians cannot agree on a uniform decision rule to resolve a controversial issue, they often leave it to be decided by the concerned individuals or groups, using phrases like "freedom of choice" and "local option" to describe and dignify their deference. The growing diversity, complexity, and competitiveness of American society make it more urgent to extend this conflict-reducing technique (as well as to find others).

For this reason, I have proposed in Part II a number of programmatic devices designed to move the *loci* of choice from politicians, bureaucrats, and judges to individuals and private groups, thereby reducing political conflict and empowering diversity. These include full First Amendment protection for private expressive groups with exclusionary membership policies; promotion of cultural maintenance by families, not government; means-tested vouchers for housing, schools, bilingual education, and other publicly funded benefits; broader accommodation of deviant religious practices; greater use of the voluntary choice factor in analyzing church-state disputes; and elimination of mandatory affirmative action (except in the narrow remedial usage now authorized by the courts).

Expanded choice can also be used to diffuse other kinds of disputes. Consider the bitter conflicts that rage in numerous communities over school curricula, particularly over whether to teach Darwinism, creationism, "intelligent design," or some other (pseudo)scientific creed.[45] Like most educational policy issues, this one is resolved by local school boards, which obviates the need for a national consensus but of course engenders a large number of local conflicts producing some dubious decisions. The ferocity of these conflicts, however, is largely due to the monopolistic nature of the existing public school system in these communities. This monopoly raises the stakes by mandating a single, one-size-fits-all curriculum.

In principle, a public school system does not require this monistic solution. It could allow different schools in the system to teach different versions of science; charter schools sometimes enjoy this freedom. In practice, however, political and bureaucratic factors almost always dictate a uniform system-wide curriculum. By relaxing its monopoly over the curriculum and giving low-income families financially viable choices among schools offering different curricula and other controversial features, government could defuse many such conflicts, including that presented in the *Mozert* case discussed in Chapter 7. Subsidized choice could have much the same effect on conflicts over public housing, public transportation, and many other public services that government now provides in relatively monolithic form on a take-it-or-leave-it basis to those whose poverty limits them to the public system.

I am not suggesting that enhanced choice is equally compelling in these different policy domains. Officials must always weigh the value of a national, uniform, or mandatory rule against the value of a decentralized, variable, or permissive rule—or of no rule at all, leaving the matter entirely to individual choice. The advantages of diversifying school curricula, for example, must be balanced against the desire to equip all students for a common democratic American citizenship—although the data reviewed in Chapter 7 suggest that this particular conflict is more apparent than real. Spillover effects are common in complex, interdependent societies and often can be effectively regulated only through a mandatory rule preempting local or individual choices.

In contrast, there is little or no social value in uniformity of some public goods and services; indeed, diverse responses to the different needs and desires of different individuals and groups are very desirable. Even when government decides to regulate private conduct through a mandatory rule, as it often does, it should authorize exceptions to the rule where such exceptions will not defeat the rule's underlying policy.[46] More generally, government should not demand uniformity and limit choice beyond what a suitably refined, targeted policy requires. This principle is neither anodyne nor tautological. Taken seriously, it would condemn or alter an immense body of public law.[47]

In urging government to facilitate diversity by deferring more to private (and lower-level governmental) choice, I do not mean to fetishize either diversity or choice. Diversity is not always an unalloyed virtue; it also imposes costs that may be severe, as I explained in Part I. Choice, for its part, only merits its elevated normative status in the liberal tradition when it is sufficiently voluntary and informed to vindicate individual dignity and autonomy. (I say "sufficiently" because choices are almost always constrained and based on imperfect knowledge, so voluntariness and information are inevitably matters of degree.) And although more choice is generally desirable, there can be too much of a good thing. (Mae West famously retorted that "too much of a good thing is wonderful.") Too many choices, empirical evidence suggests, may increase anxiety, not just decision costs.[48] Moreover, certain of the choices opened up by new technologies may create grave moral and political dilemmas, as the debates over cloning, late-term abortion, surrogate motherhood, and many other issues suggest. But while we should always bear in mind these "dark sides" of more choice, they have little or no relevance to the kinds of enhanced choice that I have proposed here.

PUNCTILIOS

Much of the work of diversity management must be done not by government but by *us*. Most conflicts that diversity engenders occur as almost 300 million Americans and more than 30 million aliens interact with one another in countless workaday, informal ways as they proceed with the ordinary business of life. Relatively few of these interactions, one assumes, are problematic for society. Fewer still are suitable for legal intervention. Indeed, this book strongly suggests that further intrusion by the law into these low-level interactions would in most cases make the formidable challenge of managing diversity more difficult to meet. The vast range of such interactions is much too complex, opaque, unpredictable, and resistant to formal sanctions to be well regulated by legal rules. Even if that were not so, the Constitution and practical politics severely constrain such intrusions into private conduct and relationships.

Inevitably, then, these interactions will be governed less by legal rules than by the intricate, often ineffable punctilios of everyday life—what Alan Wolfe calls "morality writ small."[49] If law cannot much affect these punctilios, what can? Novelists, social scientists, humanists, pundits, experts on etiquette, and politicians make their living by seeking answers to this question, of course, yet the reasons why people think, feel, and behave as they do remain remarkably obscure. If it is rigorous explanation and prediction that we want, we are likely to be disappointed. But if what we want are normative prescriptions about how people in a diverse America should treat one another, we shall find an overwhelming social consensus on some basic precepts.

These precepts are perfectly serviceable for practical purposes even though —perhaps *because*—they leave some important terms undefined. Here are some of the most important. All people, regardless of race, religion, ethnicity, or other particularity, are entitled to respect, dignity, fair treatment, and the benefit of the doubt unless and until they show by their conduct that they do not deserve these things. Diverse cultural practices and beliefs should be permitted so long as they neither violate the law nor moral decency as defined by an increasingly latitudinarian American society. The law and those in authority should not play favorites. People should feel free to identify with racial, religious, ethnic, and other limited groups so long as this does not prevent them from also identifying with the larger American community. People's private feelings and thoughts are their own business, not the government's, but behavior that adversely affects others may be subject to censure or sanction. Religion—almost any religion—is good for society, as are hard work and strong families. People are responsible for their behaviors and destinies— or at least we should treat them as if they were. Government should not interfere with people's freedom except in unusual situations. People should not look to the government to do for them what they can do for themselves. People should cultivate an interest in and sympathy for those who are different, trying by an act of moral imagination to put themselves in the shoes of strangers before judging them. Private and public charity to the poor is desirable if it does not undermine their dignity, self-reliance, work incentives, and moral responsibility.

These punctilios are hardly exhaustive. Nor are they unique to today's diverse America. Indeed, most of them would likely have been endorsed even by a generation of Founders who owned slaves, denied women full citizenship, barred nonwhites from naturalizing, established state churches, viewed Englishmen as a superior breed, and thought it obvious that their own language revealed a special genius for liberty and self-government. But if most of the precepts I listed have a long pedigree in America, the same cannot be said of either the fact or the ideal of American diversity today. As we saw, they are largely post-1965 phenomena.

Their new prominence necessitates, in my view, at least two new precepts: more candor in debating how to manage diversity, and thicker skins as we conduct this debate. Both of these changes are essential; indeed, more candor will increase our need for thicker skins.

Candor

Candor is the easier to justify, as it seems like an unquestioned virtue. It certainly should be, yet as we have seen, there is remarkably little of it. In order to manage diversity intelligently, citizens and officials must identify and confront squarely the inescapable value conflicts, empirical trade-offs, and confounding ironies generated when diversity policies are implemented. For example, ethno-racial profiling is morally justified in certain situations, and our leaders do the public no service in pretending otherwise.[50] Laws that respect family and group diversity by protecting their autonomy also enable private powerholders to behave illiberally toward those subject to their authority in these domains. More generally, acute, endemic, and largely unacknowledged conflicts exist between diversity and equality values.[51] The crucial question of precisely how to compromise these competing values needs careful normative and empirical exploration, and then frank appraisal. This requires that we tease out the relevant interests, comprehend the precise nature and extent of the conflicts, and consider alternative ways to strike acceptable compromises. This in turn demands honesty and rigor, not evasion and superficiality. Hopefully, this book will move the public debate in that direction.

Thicker Skins

The need for thicker skins is more complicated and controversial than the need for more candor, and it is also harder to achieve. As we interact in an increasingly diverse world, we should strive to cultivate in individuals a capacity for greater resilience, not greater delicacy. Unfortunately, as one commentator puts it, the United States has become "a world of endless slights."[52] Of the myriad examples of this, I shall mention just a few that have come to my attention recently even without my searching for them:

- A group of Holocaust survivors expresses horror and indignation about an exhibition of artistic uses of Nazi imagery mounted by the Jewish Museum in New York City.[53]
- A Korean-American student at Yale takes such offense at a college dining hall worker's joking proposal to add "dogs and kimchi" to the menu that he protests to the worker's superior. Although the worker apologizes as soon as he learns that offense has been taken, the student still files a report that will go on the worker's record.[54]
- A group, "9/11 People Against Racism," posts a large sign near a New York State thruway exit ramp in New Paltz proclaiming "This community does not tolerate racism against Muslims, Arabs and people of color," only to elicit protests by Jews, gays, and lesbians complaining that they also face discrimination and should not be left out if others are being named. The *New York Times* reporter who interviews community residents finds that "many residents read the sign to mean that it was O.K. to discriminate against everyone else—so long as they were not Arabs or

Muslims or people of color. Others took it as a reprimand and bristled that it was done in such a public way, as if accusing the good people of New Paltz of being bigots in need of character education."[55]

- A Chinese-American complains that the term "Chinese wall," used in its ordinary colloquial sense in a lawyers' magazine, is a "euphemism for exclusion" and is "insensitive, outdated, and outright offensive."[56]
- An earnest District of Columbia official feels obliged to resign after a barrage of public criticism for having used the word "niggardly" correctly.[57]
- A large school district adopts an "antiharassment" policy barring any verbal or physical conduct that creates an intimidating or hostile environment, including jokes, name-calling, graffiti, and innuendo, as well as making fun of a student's clothing, social skills, or surname, with punishments ranging up to suspension, expulsion, or firing.[58]
- A regular *Yale Daily News* columnist who is a woman of color recounts how she reacted when four white boys in a car turning into a parking lot waited and whistled while a group of white girls on the sidewalk ahead of her walked past the lot entrance, but said "No, no, no. We go first" when she tried to do the same. Saying nothing more about the boys' behavior than this, she describes the deep emotional crisis (weeping, hatred, physical collapse, intense bitterness, and inconsolable sadness) into which this incident propelled her.[59]
- A law professor taps a female student on the shoulder in class to illustrate the principle that even an innocent touching, if unconsented and unprivileged, constitutes a tort, and she sues him for assault and battery, seeking compensatory and punitive damages because, according to her lawyer, the touching "exacerbate[s] and bring[s] to the surface once again her vulnerability to men with authority and power."[60]
- Under "sensitivity guidelines" issued by New York's education agency, the Regents examination for English must delete from an Isaac Bashevis Singer excerpt all references to Jewishness and Polish nationality, and make similar excisions or substitutions ("heck" for "hell" in a Frank Conroy quotation, for example) in the work of numerous other famous authors.[61]

I shall not attempt to persuade the reader that these examples describe egregiously intolerant, uncharitable, self-absorbed, self-indulgent, silly, and irrational (not to say humorless) conduct on the part of the complainants, and unconstitutional overreaching in the case of the school district. Nor shall I try to prove that such examples abound in American life today. The reader who denies these two propositions need not read any farther, for I shall proceed as if they were true. The reactions I describe—and much conduct that is less extreme—are corrosive in a society as diverse, interactive, plainspoken, casual, and freewheeling as ours. When used to justify political, legal, or even heavy social sanctions against the putative offenders, such behavior is not only perverse but dangerous. It chills personal interactions by denying them the lubricating pleasures of spontaneity and humor. It discourages candid discussion or artistic expression on vital public issues. It enlists formal and informal sanctions in order to reduce what should be robust give-and-take. It invites us to open our wounds, magnify our fears, and parade our sensitivities, to imagine injuries and motivations that do not exist and to view others, without basis, as enemies. It rewards cant, hyperbole, and reductionist rhetoric while penalizing moderation and reason. It denies others the slack that it allows oneself. It encourages us to seek security in groups of people who look, think, or worship like us rather than to venture out into the more diverse public square where our common citizenship is forged. It makes a mockery of the law when the law is brandished to penalize what often is only just ignorance, boorishness, interpretive confusion, ill-considered speech, clumsy provocation, misjudgment, rough or poor humor, and other unfortunate infelicities.

As individuals in a turbulent, vibrant, feisty, competitive, jostling society of diverse strangers, we do better to respond to such conduct with constructive engagement, forceful rebuke, pointed rebuttal, and internal shrugging of shoulders and biting of tongues. Even when the offender intends to humiliate or dehumanize, the schoolyard adage "sticks and stones can break my bones but names will never hurt me" is a much sounder foundation for coexistence in such a society than the swift turn to law and other strong reprisal that marks so many interactions today. This means developing thicker skins and deeper tolerance, reserving the law and other heavy artillery for dealing with incitements to violence, traditional defamations, and other extreme cases.[62]

It is unfair that the people who need the thickest skins and the most self-restraint are often those who already feel under siege. To them, more self-restraint will seem like an added burden and an unjust imposition on their all-too-vulnerable status. Why, they may ask, should they have to forbear it rather than those who offend them?

Four considerations, however, can help palliate this unfairness, if not assuage the hurt and indignation. The first concerns the value of speech. Those who practice incivility are morally obligated not to offend others without justification, and under certain conditions this may even amount to a legal duty.[63] But the arguments for and against tolerating such incivilities are not equal; they generally favor the speech (if not the speaker). There is a compelling social interest in people feeling free to express themselves without undue external or internal censorship. This interest in spontaneous expression is compelling not only because of the truth-value the speech may contain (even very offensive speech may contain some), but also for other reasons. The offense may provoke socially useful speech in response. (Self-)censorship risks inhibiting more than what is false or offensive. The social interest in spontaneity is shared *ex ante* by *all* members of society, including those who *ex post* will be offended by particular incivilities that result. This interest, moreover, extends beyond constitutionally protected speech to include inhibitions of expression caused by informal norms and practices. Sometimes other values such as privacy and modesty override the interest in spontaneous speech, but this interest remains one with which we must always reckon.

A second consideration reducing any unfairness from the thicker skin punctilio is that incivility today transcends class, status, and ethno-racial grouping. Indeed, this transcendent rudeness has always marked American popular culture to some degree. Exalted social status has never protected a group from crude and hurtful forms of public mockery, although high status may make it easier for that group to absorb or deflect it. My point is not to compare public criticism of elites with verbal abuses directed at low-income groups and minorities, but to emphasize that such incivilities are in an important sense indiscriminate and that all Americans, rich or poor, must learn to deal with them.

Third, the informal social norms condemning such conduct are stronger than ever before. They are now reinforced by political and market mechanisms, not to mention legal ones, that punish apparent violators. Public and private critics of the Boy Scouts' antigay policy, for example, have moved swiftly against the organization. Business, political, religious, and civic leaders almost reflexively denounce and sanction antiminority slurs by celebrities, employees, and others. Much of this public pressure is desirable; some important social changes occur in just this way. Much of this pressure, however, is stultifying, if not unconstitutional—laws against hate speech, for example. By suppressing diversity, such pressure may inhibit socially valuable innovations and information.

Finally, all of the alternatives to developing thicker skins are unappealing, unconstitutional, or unworkable. Consider some examples. Employment discrimination law punishes speech and conduct by workers that may offend some coworkers' sensibilities but that do not otherwise harm them. This well-intentioned remedy, however, has introduced formality, legalisms, and incentives that stifle enjoyable and productive interactions, making matters worse for all but the most prickly employees.[64] Campus and other institutional speech codes supposedly adopted to respect diversity have regulated thought and conduct in ways likely to reduce viewpoint and behavioral diversity. Similar orthodoxies in the nation's newsrooms are, by some accounts, impeding the more diverse journalistic coverage that they were supposed to generate.[65] Political correctnesss—on- and off-campus, by left, right, and center—tends to suppress and flatten the eccentricity, heterodoxy, obliqueness, and complexity so essential to realizing the diversity ideal and to living in a dynamic, creative, and interesting society.[66]

This diversity ideal is still in its infancy, and all of us are responsible for guiding it to maturity and beyond. Like all abstract conceptions, the diversity ideal will be rudely buffeted by the brute experiences of actually living with it. Indeed, as I showed in Part II, particular versions of that ideal have already generated strong resistance that should chasten anyone who embraces these particular versions and should humble any others who want government to pursue different ones. Yet these failures have not much tarnished the lustre of the ideal itself; it retains a powerful, compelling allure.

Much in American culture demands and nourishes diversity, even as we grope to understand what it means, how much it costs, whether law can effectively manage it, and whether and when other social processes, if any, might do it better. We have only begun to ask these immensely difficult questions. I take some comfort from the conviction that no other society in history has been better equipped to answer them than twenty-first-century America.

Notes

1. FIRST THOUGHTS

1. K. Anthony Appiah argues that America's diversity is less a diversity of culture than of identity, which exploits a "politics of nostalgia" that "offers the promise of forms of recognition and of solidarity that could make up for the loss of the rich, old kitchen comforts of ethnicity." "The Multiculturalist Misunderstanding," *New York Review of Books*, 30, 32–33 (Oct. 9, 1997). For a contrarian view, see Edward L. Rubin, "Puppy Federalism and the Blessings of America," 574 *Annals of the American Association of Political and Social Science* 37, 45 (2001) (United States a "socially homogenized and politically decentralized nation").

2. See, e.g., Michael Pollak, "World's Dying Languages, Alive on the Web," *New York Times*, G13 (Oct. 19, 2000); Stephen Labaton, "F.C.C. Offers Low-Power FM Stations," *New York Times*, C1 (Jan. 29, 1999); "The Fashion for 'Tracking Stocks,'" *The Economist*, 68 (Aug. 5, 2000); Leslie Kaufman, "The Opposite of Amazon.com," *New York Times*, C1 (Sept. 22, 2000) (specialty book stores).

3. See Robert W. Fogel, *The Fourth Great Awakening and the Future of Egalitarianism*, 54 (2000). For example, "[b]etween 1810 and 1860, the time of the [transatlantic] journey was reduced by 75 percent (to about seven days), the average risk of death as a result of the journey was reduced by up to 90 percent, and passage charges were reduced by 90 percent."

4. Arthur M. Schlesinger, Jr., *The Disuniting of America: Reflections on a Multicultural Society* (1992).

5. John A. Hall and Charles Lindblom, *Is America Breaking Apart?*, 146–147 (1999).

6. See, e.g., Tamar Jacoby, "Adjust Your Sets," *The New Republic*, 21 (Jan. 24, 2000) (segregation of television markets).

7. Nathan Glazer, *We Are All Multiculturalists Now*, 99 (1997) (quoting Philip Gleason).

8. See, e.g., Tamar Lewin, "Women's Health Is No Longer a Man's World," *New York Times*, A1 (Feb. 7, 2001).

9. The classic statement of this view, of course, is Jane Jacobs, *The Death and Life of Great American Cities* (1961); see also Jacobs's more recent account, *Cities and the Wealth of Nations: Principles of Economic Life* (1984).

10. See, e.g., Iver Peterson, "Newest Immigrants Head Straight to New Jersey's Suburbs," *New York Times*, B1 (Mar. 10, 2001) (2000 census shows "diversification of the suburbs around the state"); Michael Pollan, "The Triumph of Burbopolis," *New York Times Magazine*, 51, 55 (Apr. 9, 2000) (diversity of Nassau County; "more people now live in suburban America than rural and urban America combined"); see generally Alan Wolfe, *One Nation, After All: What Middle-Class Americans Really Think about God, Country, Family, Racism, Welfare, Immigration, Homosexuality, Work, the Right, the Left, and Each Other* (1998) (describing American attitudes on a range of issues, including diversity).

11. This is detailed in Lauren B. Edelman, Sally Riggs Fuller, and Iona Mara-Drita, "Diversity Rhetoric and the Managerialization of Law," 106 *American Journal of Sociology* 1589 (2001).

12. Leon E. Wynter, *American Skin: Pop Culture, Big Business, and the End of White America* (2002).

13. Repression of gays may be taking a new form but this is surely an advance over earlier forms. See Kenji Yoshino, "Covering," 111 *Yale Law Journal* 769 (2002).

14. See, e.g., Suzanna Danuta Walters, *All the Rage: The Story of Gay Visibility in America* (2001).

15. In popular culture, see, e.g., television programs like *Ellen, Will and Grace, Dawson's Creek,* and the *Rosie O'Donnell Show,* movies like *My Best Friend's Wedding, Gods and Monsters,* and *The Birdcage,* and musicals such as *Rent.* In religious culture, see, e.g., "Presbyterian Assembly Favors Lifting Ban on Ordination of Gays," *New York Times*, A11 (June 16, 2001).

16. On social attitudes, see Wolfe, *One Nation, After All.* On government attitudes, see, e.g., Eric Schmitt, "U.S. Agency Plans to Hire a Specialist on Gay Issues," *New York Times*, A19 (June 20, 2001) (Department of Agriculture). On the military, see James Dao, "Antigay Behavior in Military Has Dipped a Bit, Report Says," *New York Times*, A22 (Mar. 15, 2001) (10% decline in reports of harassment). See also Andrew Sullivan, "They Also Served," *New York Times Magazine*, 13 (June 17, 2001) (more than doubling of discharge rate in six years may be due to straight soldiers seeking discharges for a status that is now less shameful).

17. See Stanley Rothman and Amy E. Black, "Media and Business Elites: Still in Conflict?" *The Public Interest*, 72, 83 (Spring 2001) (35% of business elites say homosexuality as acceptable a lifestyle as heterosexuality).

18. See, e.g., James B. Jacobs and Kimberly Potter, *Hate Crimes: Criminal Law and Identity Politics,* chap. 5 (1998).

19. See generally U.S. General Accounting Office, "Sexual-Orientation-Based Employment Discrimination: State and Federal Status," GA0-02-665R (Washington, D.C., 2002) (thirteen states bar discrimination for sexual orientation). An effort to repeal Miami's 1998 ordinance barring discrimination against gays is strongly opposed by all racial and ethnic groups. Dana Canedy, "Miami Sees Challenge on Gay Rights, Again," *New York Times*, A18 (Sept. 5, 2002). At least one court has extended civil rights protection to transsexuals. Maria New-

man, "New Jersey Appeals Court Bars Firing of Transsexual," *New York Times,* B5 (July 4, 2001).

20. Politicians have picked up on the widespread public opposition to the Boy Scouts' antigay policy; in June 2001, the Senate narrowly defeated an amendment that would have penalized school districts that barred the Boy Scouts from using their facilities. Edward Wyatt, "Education Bill May Omit Its Provision on Boy Scouts," *New York Times,* 22 (June 17, 2001); also, compare President Bush's courtship of the Log Cabin Republicans and Vice President Cheney's refusal to oppose same-sex unions to presidential candidate Bob Dole's dismissive return of the gay conservative group's donations. Ellen Gamerman, "President Reaches Gay Conservatives; Quiet Effort Has Them Hoping for Fuller Role," *Baltimore Sun,* 1A (Apr. 19, 2001).

21. Stuart Elliott, for example, notes that Absolut vodka and other products are increasingly doing so. Elliott, "Advertising," *New York Times,* D6 (Feb. 22, 2001).

22. See Andrew Sullivan, "Us and Them," *The New Republic,* 8 (Apr. 2, 2001) (comparing coverage of crimes committed by and against gays).

23. See, e.g., Maureen Dowd, "'Will & Will,' 24/7," *New York Times,* 17 (Jan. 13, 2002); Bill Carter, "MTV and Showtime Plan Cable Channel for Gay Viewers," *New York Times,* C1 (Jan. 10, 2002).

24. See, e.g., "Surprise Church Vote on Same-Sex Blessing," *New York Times,* A21 (Mar. 15, 2001) (most presbyteries allowing same-sex unions); H.B. 847, 2000 Gen. Assem. Reg. Sess. (Vt. 2000) (Vermont law allowing "civil unions" entitling gay couples to rights and benefits available under state law to heterosexual married couples); Baker v. Vermont, 744 A.2d 864 (Vt. 1999) (holding that under the state constitution, state must give gay couples access to material benefits similar to those provided to heterosexual couples); Robert Whereatt, "Senate OKs Bill Dealing with Labor Pacts," *Star Tribune,* 5B (Mar. 5, 2002) (reporting that Minnesota state senate authorized labor contracts that include insurance benefits for state employees' same-sex partners); David G. Savage, "U.S. Lays Out Aid for Kin of Terror Attack," *Los Angeles Times,* A1 (Dec. 21, 2001) (reporting that same-sex partners can receive compensation from various Sept. 11–related funds); Michael Cooper, "Cheney's Marriage Remarks Irk Conservatives," *New York Times,* A23 (Oct. 10, 2000) (discussing Cheney's support of some form of gay union and his willingness to stand firm despite opposition from Republican right). But see Pamela Ferdinand, "With Vermont in the Lead, Controversy Progresses; Battle over Same-Sex Unions Moves to Other States," *Washington Post,* A3 (Sept. 4, 2001) (describing heated political battles in many states).

25. See Gertrude Himmelfarb, "Religion in the 2000 Election," *The Public Interest,* 20, 25 (Spring 2001) (analyzing report by Ethics and Public Policy Center, Washington, D.C., 2001). A recent study finds a causal relation between gay population and high-tech prosperity. Richard Florida and Gary Gates, "Technology and Tolerance: Diversity and High-Tech Growth," 20 *Brookings Review* 32, 35–36 (2002).

26. For one solution to this nomenclature problem, see Orlando Patterson, *The Or-*

deal of Integration: Progress and Resentment in America's "Racial" Crisis, x–xi (1997). The term "black" is also objectionable; still, I prefer it to the term "African American," as I have explained in Peter H. Schuck, "Reflections on the Effects of Immigrants on African Americans—and Vice Versa," in Daniel S. Hamermesh and Frank D. Bean, eds., *Help or Hindrance? The Economic Implications of Immigration for African Americans,* 361–363 (1998). For a forceful statement of this position, see Albert Murray, *From the Briarpatch File: On Context, Procedure, and American Identity,* 191 (2001) ("I don't like being called 'black American' because it so often implies *less American.* And I absolutely despise being called 'African-American.' I am not an African. I am an American. And I still can't believe my ears when I hear educated people calling themselves a *minority*-something, by the way, which uneducated people never do") (emphasis in the original).

27. See the debate sparked by Robert Putnam, *Bowling Alone: The Collapse and Revival of American Community* (2000). For a recent review, see Book Note, 111 *Yale Law Journal* 1031 (2002).

28. To some intellectuals, however, tolerance is a discourse of repression and inequality "that carries repugnance at its heart." Wendy Brown, author's note introducing "The Governmentality of Contemporary Tolerance" (Feb. 14, 2002) (unpublished manuscript presented to Yale Legal Theory Workshop).

29. Orlando Patterson, *The Ordeal of Integration: Progress and Resentment in America's "Racial" Crisis,* 18–19 (1997). Patterson points to a cross-national survey in 1991 comparing attitudes of several nations' majority populations toward their main domestic minorities. He does not mention whether the survey included Canada and the Netherlands, two reputedly tolerant societies.

30. Jill Lepore, *A Is for American: Letters and Other Characters in the Newly United States,* 28 (2002) (emphasis in the original). On the remarkable diversity of colonial America, see Jon Butler, *Becoming America: The Revolution before 1776* (2000).

31. John Higham, *Strangers in the Land: Patterns of American Nativism* (2d ed. 1988).

32. Rogers M. Smith, *Civic Ideals: Conflicting Visions of Citizenship in U.S. History* (1997).

33. In more recent work, Philip A. Klinkner and Rogers M. Smith argue that diversity's recent gains are but fragile, tentative advances against a perpetual conservative campaign against inclusion. Klinkner and Smith, *The Unsteady March: The Rise and Decline of Racial Equality in America* (1999).

34. E. M. Forster, *Two Cheers for Democracy* (1951).

35. See, e.g., Seth Mydans, "Indonesia May Crumble without Falling Apart," *New York Times,* 1 (July 29, 2001) (independence movements temporarily stalled).

36. In Belgium, political devolution may have gone about as far as it can go without actual separation. "A Worrying European Paradox," *The Economist,* 47 (July 7, 2001). See generally Michael J. Kelly, "Political Downsizing: The Re-Emergence of Self-Determination, and the Movement toward Smaller, Ethnically Homogenous States," 47 *Drake Law Review* 209 (1999) (discussing Russia's

secessionist conflict with Chechnya, France's efforts to manage self-determination movements in Corsica and Brittany, the Basque independence movement in Spain, and the United Kingdom's devolution of power to Scotland, Northern Ireland, and Wales).

37. Jonathan Rauch, "Diversity in a New America: Charting the Changes," 20 *Brookings Review* 5 (2002).

38. See, e.g., Jerry Vincent Nix, "Assessing the Existence of Social Distance and Factors That Affect Its Magnitude at a Southern University," *http://www.sspp .net/archive/papers/1(1)nix.htm* (last visited Feb. 14, 2002) (reviewing earlier studies and making new findings).

39. Id.

40. For an exploration of the expressive uses of conduct and law, see, e.g., Richard H. McAdams, "An Attitudinal Theory of Expressive Law," 79 *Oregon Law Review* 339 (2000); Eric A. Posner, *Law and Social Norms* (2000).

41. Sanford Levinson, "Diversity," 2 *University of Pennsylvania Journal of Constitutional Law* 573, 582–584 and note 49 (2000).

42. David A. Hollinger, *Postethnic America: Beyond Multiculturalism,* chap. 2 (rev. ed. 2000).

43. See, e.g., Clara E. Rodriguez, *Changing Race: Latinos, the Census, and the History of Ethnicity in the United States* (2000).

44. See, e.g., Matthew Frye Jacobsen, *Whiteness of a Different Color: European Immigrants and the Alchemy of Race* (1998). For a devastating review of some of this "whiteness" scholarship, see Eric Arnesen, "A Paler Shade of White," *The New Republic,* 33 (June 24, 2002) (review of David R. Roediger, *Colored White: Transcending the Racial Past* (2002)).

45. See Willy Forbath, "When Jews, Italians, Greeks, and Slavs Belonged to Races Different from 'We, the People': Race, Class, and National Identity in Immigration Law and Policy, 1882–1924" (June 2002) (unpublished manuscript, University of Texas Law School).

46. See, e.g., Rodriguez, *Changing Race.*

47. The fourteen are geographic origin; migratory status; race; language or dialect; religion; ties that transcend kinship, neighborhood, and community; shared traditions, values, and symbols; literature, folklore, and music; food; settlement and employment patterns; special political interests either in the homeland or in the settlement home; group institutions; internal sense of distinctiveness; and external perception of distinctiveness. Stephan Thernstrom, ed., *Harvard Encyclopedia of American Ethnic Groups,* vi (1980). See also the entry for "Concepts of Ethnicity," id., 234–242.

48. Id., 234–235.

49. See generally, e.g., *Temporary Workers or Future Citizens: Japanese and U.S. Migration Policies* (M. Weiner and T. Hanami, eds., 1998).

50. See, e.g., Eric Schmitt, "New Census Shows Hispanics Are Even with Blacks in U.S.," *New York Times,* A1 (Mar. 8, 2001).

51. Seymour Martin Lipset and Gary Marks, *It Didn't Happen Here: Why Socialism Failed in the United States,* 267 (2000).

52. Although many have attributed this failure to the first-past-the-post rule, Lipset and Marks carefully consider and reject this explanation on historical and empirical grounds. Id., 44–48, 264–265.

53. Jim Chen, for example, instances an esthetic, or at least nonfunctional, kind of diversity ideal: "[E]ven if the Navajo tongue had provided no national service in the Pacific theater of World War II, the aboriginal languages of North America are worth preserving." Chen, "Is Affirmative Action Fair? Diversity in a Different Dimension: Evolutionary Theory and Affirmative Action's Destiny," 59 *Ohio State Law Journal* 811, 831 (1998).

54. After developing this distinction and well into my writing, I came upon Stanley Fish's "new distinction between multiculturalism as a philosophical problem and multiculturalism as a demographic fact." Stanley Fish, *The Trouble with Principle,* 63 (1999). There is considerable overlap between our two distinctions.

55. Diversity value should be distinguished from "value diversity," which is a domain of diversity—for example, a classroom in which students possess different values—that may best be thought of as cultural or ideological in nature.

56. Anthony T. Kronman, "The Democratic Soul," sec. IX, DeVane Lecture Series at Yale University (Jan. 9, 2001).

57. See Levinson, "Diversity," at 573, 578, 581.

58. President William J. Clinton, State of the Union Address, Jan. 27, 2000, available at *http://www.access.gpo.gov/congress/sou/sou00.html* (last visited Mar. 15, 2002) ("Within 10 years, there will be no majority race in our largest state of California. In a little more than 50 years, there will be no majority race in America. In a more interconnected world, this diversity can be our greatest strength. Just look around this chamber. We have members in this Congress from virtually every racial, ethnic, and religious background. And I think you would agree that America is stronger because of it").

59. Robin Toner, "A Closer Look at the Planks," *New York Times,* A24 (July 30, 2000).

60. Reprinted in the *New York Times,* 14–15 (Jan. 21, 2001).

61. President George W. Bush, Address to the Joint Session of Congress, Sept. 20, 2001, available at *http://www.whitehouse.gov/news/releases/2001/09/20010920–8.html* (last visited Mar. 15, 2002) ("I ask you to uphold the values of America, and remember why so many have come here. We are in a fight for our principles, and our first responsibility is to live by them. No one should be singled out for unfair treatment or unkind words because of their ethnic background or religious faith").

62. See, e.g., Donald Galloway, "The Dilemmas of Canadian Citizenship Law," in *From Migrants to Citizens: Membership in a Changing World,* chap. 3 (T. Alexander Aleinikoff and Douglas Klusmeyer, eds., 2000).

63. See K. Anthony Appiah, "The Multiculturalist Misunderstanding," at 32 ("To an outsider, few groups in the world looked as culturally homogeneous as the various peoples—Serb, Croat, Muslim—of Bosnia. (The resurgence of Islam in Bosnia is a result of the conflict, not a cause of it.) Hutus and Tutsis speak the same language, have long lived side by side, and (racial ideology notwithstand-

ing) it is often extremely hard, even for Hutus and Tutsis, to tell them apart. Different identities can appear to require at least as much toleration as different cultures").

64. See James D. Fearon and David D. Laitin, "Ethnicity, Insurgency, and Civil War" (Sept. 18, 2001) (unpublished manuscript, Political Science Department, Stanford University). Another cross-national study finds no trade-off between the greater ethnic and religious heterogeneity of larger polities and their scale economies. Alberto F. Alesina, Reza Baqir, and Caroline Minter Hoxby, *Political Jurisdictions in Heterogeneous Communities,* Harvard Institute of Economic Research Paper No. 1949 (Mar. 2002). A recent study of Indian cities finds that the existence of nongovernmental civic organizations is a major factor in preventing ethnic violence. Ashutosh Varshney, *Ethnic Conflict and Civic Life: Hindus and Muslims in India* (2002).

65. See, e.g., Donald L. Horowitz, *Ethnic Groups in Conflict* (1985); Amy L. Chua, "Markets, Democracy, and Ethnicity: Toward a New Paradigm for Law and Development," 108 *Yale Law Journal* 1 (1998).

66. See, e.g., Anthony DePalma, "Canada's Eskimos Get a Land of Their Own," *New York Times,* A3 (Apr. 2, 1999) (establishment of the new territory of Nunavut); Warren Hoge, "Inside the Arctic Circle, an Ancient People Emerge," *New York Times,* A3 (Mar. 18, 2001) (Sami legislature in Norway).

67. See, e.g., Alan Cowell, "After Black Teenager Is Slain, Norway Peers into a Mirror," *New York Times,* A1 (Jan. 3, 2002).

68. See, e.g., Will Kymlicka, *Multicultural Citizenship: A Liberal Theory of Minority Rights,* 23, 87–88 (1995).

69. See James Brooke, "Pokemon Wins a Battle but Not the Language War," *New York Times,* A4 (Mar. 15, 2000) (describing Quebec's language law, immigration policy, and 30% conversion rate each generation).

70. Donald G. McNeil, Jr., "French McDonald's Bombed; Breton Terrorists Suspected," *New York Times,* A8 (Apr. 20, 2000).

71. See, e.g., Yaakov Kop and Robert E. Litan, *Sticking Together: The Israeli Experiment in Pluralism* (2002).

72. See, e.g., Amnesty International, Annual Report 2000: Turkey, available at *http://www.web.amnesty.org/web/ar2000web.nsf/countries/* (last visited Mar. 18, 2002).

73. See, e.g., Open Society Institute, *Racism in Central and Eastern Europe and Beyond: Origins, Responses, Strategies,* Rapporteur's Notes (July 19, 2000); Human Rights Watch World Report 2001, available at *http://www.hrw.org/wr2k1/europe/index.html* (last visited Sept. 8, 2001). For a detailed account of the Roma's plight from the Holocaust through the 1990s, see Barry A. Fisher, "No Roads Lead to Roma: The Fate of the Romani People under the Nazis and in Post-War Restitution," 20 *Whittier Law Review* 513 (1999).

74. See Gianni Zappala and Stephen Castles, "Citizenship and Immigration in Australia," 13 *Georgetown Immigration Law Journal* 273 (1999); "Australia's Populist Bites Back," *The Economist,* 41 (Feb. 24, 2001) (resurgence of xenophobic One Nation party in run-up to 2001 elections).

75. Cited in James F. Hollifield, "The Politics of International Migration: How Can

We 'Bring the State Back In'?" in *Migration Theory: Talking across Disciplines,* 149 (James. F. Hollifield and Caroline B. Brettell, eds., 2000). Gerald Neuman traces the quote to Max Frisch, "Überfremdung I," in *Schweiz als Heimat?* 219 (1990). See also Philip Martin, "There Is Nothing More Permanent Than Temporary Foreign Workers" (Center for Immigration Studies, Washington, D.C., Apr. 2001) (U.S. and German experiences).

76. Victor Homola, "Germany: Rightists on Rise," *New York Times,* A9 (Feb. 8, 2001) (neo-Nazi and rightist crimes rose 40% in 2000); Roger Cohen, "Germany's Financial Heart Is Open but Wary," *New York Times,* A1 (Dec. 30, 2000); Roger Cohen, "German Faults 'Silence' about Attacks on Immigrants," *New York Times,* A9 (Aug. 1, 2000).

77. Roger Cohen, "Rightists to Join Austria's Cabinet," *New York Times,* A1 (Feb. 4, 2000); Donald G. McNeil, Jr., "Austria Politician Sometimes Down but Never Out," *New York Times,* A3 (July 23, 2000). See also Roger Cohen, "Austrian School Drama: Crucifix Meets Ramadan," *New York Times,* A3 (Mar. 20, 2001) (antiforeigner sentiment rising, especially outside Vienna).

78. Craig R. Whitney, "France Blasts European Parliament for Attacking Immigration Bill," *New York Times,* A4 (Feb. 27, 1997).

79. Emma Daly, "Brutal Death of Immigrant Shakes Faith of Spaniards," *New York Times,* A9 (Feb. 13, 2002); Suzanne Daley, "African Migrants Risk All on Passage to Spain," *New York Times,* A1 (July 10, 2001); "Unwelcome to Iberia," *The Economist,* 51 (Feb. 10, 2001); Marlise Simons, "Between Migrants and Spain: The Sea That Kills," *New York Times,* A3 (Mar. 30, 2000); George Stolz, "Europe's Back Doors," *Atlantic Monthly,* 26 (Jan. 2000).

80. See, e.g., Peter Finn, "A Turn from Tolerance," *Washington Post,* A1 (Mar. 29, 2002) (reviewing anti-immigrant party gains in Denmark, Netherlands, Germany, and other EU states).

81. Elizabeth Olson, "Swiss Voters Will Assess Immigrants, Stirring Alarm," *New York Times,* 15 (Mar. 12, 2000).

82. Elizabeth Olson, "Swiss Voters Reject Limit on Number of Foreigners," *New York Times,* A16 (Sept. 25, 2000).

83. James Brooke, "Canada Is Taking a Tougher Line with Illegal Chinese Migrants," *New York Times,* A14 (Sept. 30, 1999).

84. "Unwelcome to Iberia," *The Economist,* 51 (Feb. 10, 2001) (new restrictive law adopted in Spain; number of illegal migrants entering European Union doubled between 1996 and 1999, to 500,000).

85. Indeed, Germany has sharply limited the number of visas for ethnic Germans from eastern Europe. *Paths to Inclusion: The Integration of Migrants in the United States and Germany,* chap. 6 (Peter H. Schuck and Rainer Munz, eds., 1998).

86. Steven Komarow, "Germany Looks Outside to Fill High-Tech Jobs," *USA Today,* 24A (June 16, 2000); "Work in Germany? No Way, Say Indian IT Experts," *Straits Times,* 5 (May 24, 2000); Ralph Atkins and Carlos Grande, "Work Permit Plan Opens Up Global Jobs Market," *Financial Times,* 3 (Mar. 23, 2000).

87. See, e.g., Bagehot, "Speak No Evil," *The Economist,* 60 (Apr. 28, 2001) ("no senior Conservative dares these days to put immigration on the list of things that

endanger British identity"); Warren Hoge, "British City Defines Diversity and Tolerance," *New York Times*, A1 (Feb. 8, 2001). But see Sarah Lyall, "The Immigrant Journey Gets No Easier in Britain," *New York Times*, A3 (July 13, 2001) (race riots in cities despite integration programs).

88. In the United States this discursive tradition probably begins with Zechariah Chafee, *Freedom of Speech* (1920).

89. On speech codes, see Cass R. Sunstein, *Democracy and the Problem of Free Speech*, 180–208 (1993) (supporting codes in order to combat racism and sexism). But for two cases striking down campus speech codes, see UWM Post, Inc. v. Board of Regents, 774 F. Supp. 1163 (E.D. Wis. 1991) (invalidating system-wide university code as vague and overbroad), and Doe v. University of Michigan, 721 F. Supp. 852 (E.D. Mich. 1989) (voiding speech code as vague and overbroad, in violation of the First Amendment). On workplace speech, see Jeffrey Rosen, *The Unwanted Gaze: The Destruction of Privacy in America* (2000). On hate crimes, see James B. Jacobs and Kimberly Potter, *Hate Crimes: Criminal Law and Identity Politics* (1998). On journalism, see William McGowan, *Coloring the News: How Crusading for Diversity Has Corrupted American Journalism* (2001).

2. TAXONOMIES, SOURCES, AND LEGAL STRUCTURES

1. See generally Anthony W. Marx, *Making Race and Nation: A Comparison of South Africa, the United States, and Brazil* (1998) (comparing colonization, slavery, racial protests, and contemporary racism in the three countries); Charles V. Hamilton, ed., *Beyond Racism: Race and Inequality in Brazil, South Africa, and the United States* (2001) (covering similar material).

2. I say upper limit because the costs of group formation and maintenance prevent some groups from forming or surviving despite the existence of common attributes that would otherwise suffice. The classic account is Mancur Olson, *The Logic of Collective Action* (1971).

3. K. Anthony Appiah, "The Multiculturalist Misunderstanding," *New York Review of Books*, 30, 32–33 (Oct. 9, 1997).

4. Amartya Sen, "Other People," *The New Republic*, 23–30 (Dec. 18, 2000).

5. Jim Sleeper, "Yankee Doodle Dandy," *Los Angeles Times*, BR6 (July 2, 2000) (review of Norman Podhoretz, *My Love Affair with America* (2000)).

6. See Jim Chen, "Is Affirmative Action Fair? Diversity in a Different Dimension: Evolutionary Theory and Affirmative Action's Destiny," 59 *Ohio State Law Journal* 811, 825, 830 (1998).

7. Hunt v. Cromartie, 526 U.S. 541 (1999).

8. See, e.g., Clara E. Rodriguez, *Changing Race: Latinos, the Census, and the History of Ethnicity in the United States* (2000), esp. chaps. 7–8; Stephan Thernstrom, "American Ethnic Statistics," in *Immigrants in Two Democracies: French and American Experience* (Donald Horowitz and Gerard Noiriel, eds., 1992); Peter Skerry, *Counting on the Census?: Race, Group Identity, and the Evasion of Politics* (2000).

9. See Skerry, *Counting on the Census?*

10. See, e.g., Judith Resnik, "Dependent Sovereigns: Indian Tribes, States, and the Federal Courts," 56 *University of Chicago Law Review* 671, 712–727 (1989).

11. Skerry, *Counting on the Census?* 52, 149.

12. Resnik, "Dependent Sovereigns."

13. See Gregory Rodriguez, "The Race to End Race," *The Economist: The World in 2002,* 31 (2002).

14. Census enumerators often ascribed race on the basis of their observation, a neighbor's report, or the racial composition of the neighborhood in which the subject lived. Scott Malcolmson, *One Drop of Blood: The American Misadventure of Race,* 110 (2000). See also Lawrence Wright, "One Drop of Blood," *New Yorker,* 53 (July 25, 1994) (describing results from a National Center for Health Statistics (NCHS) study in which nearly one-third of those people who identified themselves as Asian were classified by observers as white or black). For some other complications, see also Eduardo Porter, "Even 126 Sizes Don't Fit All," *Wall Street Journal,* B1 (Mar. 2, 2001).

15. See, e.g., Malcomson, *One Drop of Blood;* Orlando Patterson, *The Ordeal of Integration: Progress and Resentment in America's "Racial" Crisis,* 68–72 (1997). As David Hollinger notes, the one-drop rule persists in the popular mind that thinks a white mother can give birth to a black child but not the reverse. David A. Hollinger, *Postethnic America: Beyond Multiculturalism,* 27 (rev. ed. 2000) (quoting Barbara Fields).

16. The literature is large. For a very recent example, see Paul Gilroy, *Against Race: Imagining Political Culture beyond the Color Line* (2000).

17. Natalie Angier, "Do Races Differ? Not Really, Genes Show," *New York Times,* F1 (Aug. 22, 2000) (analyzing debate). On the other hand, some genetically influenced disease patterns are peculiar to discrete ethno-racial groups, and awareness of these differences has clinical significance. See Nicholas Wade, "Race Is Seen as Real Guide to Track Roots of Disease," *New York Times,* F1 (July 30, 2002).

18. "Fewer and fewer Americans believe in the biological reality of races, but they are remarkably willing to live with an officially sanctioned system of demographic classification that replicates precisely the crude, colloquial categories, black, yellow, white, red, and brown. . . . [C]ategories deriving their integrity not from culture but from a history of political and economic victimization based on bad biology were frequently treated as cultures." Hollinger, *Postethnic America,* 8. Orlando Patterson, after attacking the notion of race, observes: "The paradox is that the two groups of Americans now most committed to its survival are 'white' supremacists and most Afro-American intellectual and political leaders!" *The Ordeal of Integration,* 69.

19. For elaboration of this idea in the context of earlier naturalization law's requirement of "whiteness," see Ian Haney Lopez, *White by Law: The Legal Construction of Race* (1996); John Tehranian, "Performing Whiteness: Naturalization Litigation and the Construction of Racial Identity in America," 109 *Yale Law Journal* 817 (2000).

20. See, e.g., Luigi Luc Cavalli-Sforza, *Genes, Peoples, and Languages,* 25–27 (2000)

(genetic variation between any racial groups ever identified far less than variation within any single population).

21. For an exploration of the daunting administrative issues, see Christopher A. Ford, "Administering Identity: The Determination of 'Race' in Race-Conscious Law," 82 *California Law Review* 1231 (1994).

22. Hollinger, *Postethnic America*, 39.

23. Ford, "Administering Identity," 1285. See also Ford, "Symposium on Affirmative Action: Challenges and Dilemmas of Racial and Ethnic Identity in American and Post-Apartheid South African Affirmative Action," 43 *UCLA Law Review* 1953 (1996).

24. Jon Butler, *Becoming America: The Revolution before 1776,* 22 (2000).

25. See Stanley Lieberson and Mary C. Waters, *From Many Strands: Ethnic and Racial Groups in Contemporary America* (1988); Justin Kaplan and Anne Bernays, *The Language of Names* (1997); see also "The Melting Pot Works Its Magic on Baby Names," *New York Times,* B1 (Jan. 12, 2001) (most popular baby names differ among ethnic groups in the United States, but immigrants do not prefer names familiar in their native countries).

26. A classic study is Mary C. Waters, *Ethnic Options: Choosing Identities in America* (1990).

27. Natalie Angier, "The Bush Years: Confessions of a Lonely Atheist," *New York Times Magazine,* 34 (Jan. 14, 2001).

28. For an interesting example, see Anatole Broyard, *Intoxicated by My Illness: And Other Writings on Life and Death* (Alexandra Broyard, ed., 1992). For a fictional example explored with great insight, see Philip Roth, *The Human Stain* (2000).

29. See, e.g., Marjorie Garber, *Vested Interests: Cross-Dressing and Cultural Anxiety* (1992).

30. See, e.g., Philip J. Hilts, "Is Nicotine Addictive? It Depends on Whose Criteria You Use," *New York Times,* C3 (Aug. 2, 1994).

31. See, e.g., Eric Posner, *Law and Social Norms* (2000).

32. See, e.g., Myron Magnet, *The Dream and the Nightmare: The Sixties' Legacy to the Underclass* (1993).

33. President Clinton used his last message to Congress for this purpose. Steven A. Holmes, "In His Last Week, Clinton Issues Proposals on Race," *New York Times,* A11 (Jan. 15, 2001).

34. The U.S. census adopted this coinage as recently as 1980, although it made earlier efforts to classify this remarkably heterogeneous population, which descends from some two dozen nations, may be of any race, and is sharply differentiated between the U.S.-born and the foreign-born.

35. James Sterngold, "Move to Secede Splits Latinos in the Valley," *New York Times,* A14 (June 10, 2002).

36. On the former Yugoslavia, see, e.g., Robert D. Kaplan, *Balkan Ghosts* (1993).

37. See, e.g., Peter H. Schuck, *Citizens, Strangers, and In-Betweens: Essays on Immigration and Citizenship,* chap. 12 (1998) (reviewing Thomas Sowell, *Migrations and Cultures: A World View* (1996)); Sanford Levinson, "Diversity," 2 *University of Pennsylvania Journal of Constitutional Law* 573, 586–587 (2000) (noting

that if differences in "tastes" among ethnic groups are as large as alleged, we could expect different propensities for various types of jobs and other experiences).

38. Few, however, would go as far as the philosopher Leibniz, who defined reality to include the diversity of all existent things—past, present, and future—and found this diversity, including evil, to constitute God's creation and thus the best of all possible worlds. See generally Benson Mates, *The Philosophy of Leibniz: Metaphysics and Language,* 69–73 (1986).

39. Michael Walzer, *Spheres of Justice: A Defense of Pluralism and Equality,* 38–39 (1983).

40. See, e.g., George J. Borjas, *Friends or Strangers: The Impact of Immigrants on the U.S. Economy,* 169–174 (1990).

41. Contrary to public legend, however, Eskimos do not use a large number of words to describe snow. Geoffrey K. Pullam, *The Great Eskimo Vocabulary Hoax* (1991).

42. See David Berreby, "How, but Not Why, the Brain Distinguishes Race," *New York Times,* F3 (Sept. 5, 2000) (discussing studies).

43. See Chapter 1, note 63.

44. E.g., Posner, *Law and Social Norms;* Richard H. McAdams, "Cooperation and Conflict: The Economics of Group Status Production and Race Discrimination," 108 *Harvard Law Review* 1003 (1995).

45. See, e.g., Daniel Kahneman and Amos Tversky, "Prospect Theory: An Analysis of Decision under Risk," 47 *Econometrica* 263 (1979); Christine Jolls, Cass R. Sunstein, and Richard Thaler, "A Behavioral Approach to Law and Economics," 50 *Stanford Law Review* 1471, 1478 (1998) ("[E]xpected utility theory is not a good description of actual decisionmaking"); Cass. R. Sunstein, "How Law Constructs Preferences," 86 *Georgetown Law Journal* 2637 (1998); Amos Tversky and Daniel Kahneman, "Rational Choice and the Framing of Decisions," 59 *Journal of Business* 251 (1986).

46. Aristotle, *The Politics* (Ernest Barker, ed., 1962).

47. See, e.g., Montesquieu, *The Spirit of the Laws* (Anne M. Cohler et al., trans. and eds., 1989); Thomas Jefferson, *Notes on the State of Virginia* (1788); for a classic *annaliste* historical account, see Fernand Braudel, *The Mediterranean and the Mediterranean World in the Age of Philip II* (1972); on environmental history, see, e.g., William Cronon, *Changes in the Land: Indians, Colonists, and the Ecology of New England* (1983); William Cronon, *Nature's Metropolis: Chicago and the Great West* (1991); Jared Diamond, *Guns, Germs, and Steel: The Fates of Human Societies* (1997).

48. See Alan Finder, "Upstate Prosecutors Often Turn to Death Penalty," *New York Times,* A1 (Jan. 21, 1999) (cultural differences help explain why upstate New York prosecutors seek death penalty far more often than New York City prosecutors); Benjamin Soskis, "Tale of Two Cities," *The New Republic,* 23 (Oct. 9, 2000) (differences between Philadelphia and Pittsburgh).

49. Bernard Bailyn, *The Peopling of British North America: An Introduction* (1986); David Hackett Fisher, *Albion's Seed: Four British Folkways in America* (1989).

50. See Peter J. Klenow and Mark Bils, "The Acceleration in Variety Growth," 91

American Economic Review 274 (2001) (shift from "static" to "dynamic" goods and services).

51. See, e.g., Thorstein Veblen, *The Theory of the Leisure Class* (1899); Vance Packard, *The Hidden Persuaders* (1957); John Kenneth Galbraith, *The Affluent Society* (1958).

52. See Sherwin Rosen, "Markets and Diversity," 92 *American Economic Review* 1 (2002) (explaining how market mechanisms accommodate diversity).

53. Benjamin M. Friedman, *The Moral Consequences of Economic Growth* (forthcoming). See also Robert W. Fogel, *The Fourth Great Awakening and the Future of Egalitarianism* (2000) (economic growth has increased spiritual cravings).

54. See generally Henry Hansmann, "The Role of the Non-Profit Enterprise," 89 *Yale Law Journal* 835 (1980) (array of economic roles nonprofits play in modern economy).

55. Bob Jones University v. United States, 461 U.S. 574, 609 (1983) (Powell, J., quoting Brennan, J., in Walz v. Tax Commission, 397 U.S. 664, 689 (1970) (concurring opinion)).

56. Butler, *Becoming America*.

57. See, e.g., Jack N. Rakove, *Original Meanings: Politics and Ideas in the Making of the Constitution* (1996).

58. See Akhil R. Amar, *The Bill of Rights: Creation and Reconstruction* (1998).

59. See Dickerson v. United States, 530 U.S. 428 (2000).

60. E.g., United States v. Morrison, 529 U.S. 598 (2000) (Commerce Clause); Medtronic, Inc. v. Lohr, 518 U.S. 470, 485 (1996) (Supremacy Clause). But see Geier v. American Honda Motor Co., Inc., 529 U.S. 861 (2000) (preempting state law airbag litigation).

61. For the view that the parties are not subconstitutional institutions but are constitutionally protected *qua* parties and not simply by virtue of individual rights of speech and association, see Larry D. Kramer, "Putting the Politics Back into the Political Safeguards of Federalism," 100 *Columbia Law Review* 215 (2000); Larry D. Kramer, "The Confidence of the People: Political Parties and the Constitution" (2002) (unpublished manuscript, New York University Law School).

62. See, e.g., the Federal Tort Claims Act, 28 U.S.C. §2674 (1994), and, to a lesser extent, 42 U.S.C. §1983 (1994). Under Erie R.R. Co. v. Tompkins, 304 U.S. 64 (1938), state procedural rules govern, and under Klaxon Co. v. Stentor Elec. Mfg. Co., 313 U.S. 487 (1941), state choice-of-law rules hold sway.

63. See, e.g., Peter H. Schuck, *The Limits of Law: Essays on Democratic Governance*, chap. 5 (2000).

64. See, e.g., Duncan Kennedy, "Form and Substance in Common Law Adjudication," 89 *Harvard Law Review* 1685 (1976).

65. Robert C. Post, "Democratic Constitutionalism and Cultural Heterogeneity," 20 *Australian Journal of Legal Philosophy* 65 (2000).

66. See generally Peter H. Schuck, *Suing Government: Citizen Remedies for Official Wrongs* (1983), esp. chaps. 1–2.

67. Post, "Democratic Constitutionalism and Cultural Heterogeneity," 72.

68. Boy Scouts of America v. Dale, 530 U.S. 640 (2000).

69. On the issue of whether, and in what sense, equal protection is a right of individ-

uals or groups, compare Owen M. Fiss, "Groups and the Equal Protection Clause," 5 *Philosophy and Public Affairs* 107 (1976), with Peter H. Schuck, "Groups in a Diverse, Dynamic, Competitive, and Liberal Society: A Comment on Owen Fiss," *http://demo2.bepress.com/fiss/articles.html*, and with other articles in the symposium posted there.

70. Peter H. Schuck, "Diversity Demands Exclusivity," *The American Lawyer*, 67–69 (Sept. 2000).
71. Post, "Democratic Constitutionalism and Cultural Heterogeneity," 75.
72. Id., 76.

3. A NEW IDEAL AND WHY IT MATTERS

1. See Amy L. Chua, "Markets, Democracy, and Ethnicity: Toward a New Paradigm for Law and Development," 108 *Yale Law Journal* 1 (1998). See also Donald L. Horowitz, *The Deadly Ethnic Riot* (2001).
2. This *"commerce doux"* tradition in political economy is reviewed in Albert O. Hirschmann, *The Passions and the Interests: Political Arguments for Capitalism before Its Triumph*, 55–66 (1977). See also Alan Macfarlane, *The Riddle of the Modern World: Of Liberty, Wealth, and Equality* (2000). On live-and-let-live tolerance, see Alan Wolfe, *One Nation, After All: What Middle-Class Americans Really Think about God, Country, Family, Racism, Welfare, Immigration, Homosexuality, Work, the Right, the Left, and Each Other* (1998).
3. James Romm, *Herodotus*, 100 (1998).
4. Peter H. Schuck, "The Perceived Values of Diversity, Then and Now," 22 *Cardozo Law Review* 1915 (2001).
5. See, e.g., Thomas J. Archdeacon, *Becoming American: An Ethnic History* (1983); John Higham, *Strangers in the Land: Patterns of American Nativism, 1860–1925* (1955); Winthrop D. Jordan, *White over Black: American Attitudes toward the Negro, 1550–1812* (1968); Rogers M. Smith, *Civic Ideals: Conflicting Visions of U.S. Citizenship* (1997).
6. Michael W. McConnell, "The Origins and Historical Understanding of Free Exercise of Religion," 103 *Harvard Law Review* 1409, 1449 (1990).
7. Jefferson even composed his own highly selective version of the Gospels that reflected his beliefs. See Thomas Jefferson, *The Life and Morals of Jesus of Nazareth* (1804). For Jefferson's heretical views on Christ and Scripture, see "Letter from Thomas Jefferson to Peter Carr (Aug. 10, 1787)," in *The Life and Selected Writings of Thomas Jefferson*, 429, 431–433 (Adrienne Koch and William Peden, eds., 1944).
8. McConnell, "Free Exercise of Religion," 1451.
9. Id.
10. Paul Finkelman, *Slavery and the Founders: Race and Liberty in the Age of Jefferson*, 106 (1996); David Brion Davis, *The Problem of Slavery in the Age of Revolution, 1770–1823*, at 178 (1975); Robert McColley, *Slavery and Jeffersonian Virginia*, 131 (2d ed. 1973). But see Thomas G. West, *Vindicating the Founders: Race, Sex, Class, and Justice in the Origins of America* (1997). A more guarded defense of Jefferson, which argues that Jefferson's racism was tempered by his

conviction that blacks and whites had equal moral sense, is Gary Wills, *Inventing America: Jefferson's Declaration of Independence* (1978).

11. See, e.g., Finkelman, id.; McColley, id.; Leonard W. Levy, *Jefferson and Civil Liberties: The Darker Side* (2d ed. 1989).

12. See Donald A. Grinde, Jr., "Thomas Jefferson's Dualistic Perceptions of Native Americans," in *Thomas Jefferson and the Education of a Citizen*, 193, 194–199 (James Gilreath, ed., 1999).

13. Thomas Paine, *The Rights of Man*, 268 (1791; Henry Collins, ed., 1984) ("All national institutions . . . [are] set up to terrify and enslave mankind"); see also Jack Fruchtmann, Jr., *Thomas Paine: Apostle of Freedom*, 152–153 (1994).

14. Patricia U. Bonomi, *Under the Cope of Heaven: Religion, Society, and Politics in Colonial America*, 101 (1986); Drew R. McCoy, *The Last of the Fathers: James Madison and the Republican Legacy*, 229 (1989).

15. Compare Finkelman, *Slavery and the Founders*, 52–53 (emphasizing Madison's support for the Northwest Ordinance, which did not bar slavery), with McCoy, *The Last of the Fathers*, 260.

16. See, e.g., Levy, *Jefferson and Civil Liberties*.

17. See Mary L. Dudziak, *Cold War Civil Rights: Race and the Image of American Democracy* (2000).

18. See, e.g., Patricia A. Cain, *Rainbow Rights: The Role of Lawyers and Courts in the Lesbian and Gay Civil Rights Movement* (2000). But see the discussion of changing attitudes toward homosexuality in Chapter 1, text accompanying notes 13–25.

19. See generally Werner Sollors, "Literature and Ethnicity," in *Harvard Encyclopedia of American Ethnic Groups*, 647–655 (Stephan Thernstrom, ed., 1980).

20. See David A. Hollinger, *Postethnic America: Beyond Multiculturalism*, 87–89 (rev. ed. 2000) (quoting Crèvecoeur, Emerson, and Melville); Ben J. Wattenberg, *The First Universal Nation: Leading Indicators and Ideas about the Surge of America in the 1990s* (1991).

21. Whitman glorified commonality in both of its senses: shared destiny and non-elitism. For a provocative discussion of Whitman's philosophical and poetic commitments to diversity, see Anthony T. Kronman, "Is Poetry Undemocratic?" 16 *Georgia State University Law Review* 311, 327–333 (1999).

22. For surveys of this history, see, e.g., Archdeacon, *Becoming American*; see also Smith, *Civic Ideals*.

23. Bonnie Honig, *Democracy and the Foreigner* (2001).

24. Nathan Glazer, *We Are All Multiculturalists Now* (1997).

25. See discussion in Michael Lind, *The Next American Nation: The New Nationalism and the Fourth American Revolution*, 73–74 (1996).

26. Hollinger, *Postethnic America*.

27. Cited in Nathan Glazer, *Ethnic Dilemmas, 1964–1982*, at 106 (1983).

28. Milton M. Gordon, *Assimilation in American Life: The Role of Race, Religion, and National Origins*, 88–114 (1964).

29. See John Miller, *The Unmaking of Americans: How Multiculturalism Has Undermined the Assimilation Ethic* (1998); see also Peter D. Salins, *Assimilation, American Style* (1997).

30. See James Crawford, ed., *Language Loyalties: A Sourcebook on the Official English Controversy* (1992).

31. Glazer, *We Are All Multiculturalists Now,* chap. 6.

32. Lind, *The Next American Nation,* 237.

33. Hollinger, *Postethnic America,* 93–95.

34. Id., 101–102.

35. See, e.g., Peter Brimelow, *Alien Nation: Common Sense about America's Immigration Disaster* (1995). Brimelow's book received very wide attention. For a critical review, see Peter H. Schuck, *Citizens, Strangers, and In-Betweens: Essays on Immigration and Citizenship,* chap. 14 (1998).

36. Joel S. Fetzer, *Public Attitudes toward Immigration in the United States, France, and Germany* (2000).

37. See Schuck, *Citizens, Strangers, and In-Betweens,* 4–11.

38. I am indebted to Robert Fischman for pointing out this feature of environmentalism in the United States. E-mail to author (Feb. 6, 2001).

39. George Santayana, "Reason in Common Sense," in *The Life of Reason,* 218 (2d ed. 1936).

40. The quotation is from Rita J. Simon, "Immigration and Public Opinion," paper presented before the National Legal Conference on Immigration and Refugee Policy (Washington, D.C., Mar. 30, 1995). See also Schuck, *Citizens, Strangers, and In-Betweens,* 9.

41. See generally Robert William Fogel, *The Fourth Great Awakening and the Future of Egalitarianism* (2000).

42. See, e.g., Schuck, *Citizens, Strangers, and In-Betweens,* chap. 4.

43. Id., 127.

44. Steven Greenhouse, "Immigrants Flock to Union Banner at a Forum," *New York Times,* 29 (Apr. 2, 2000).

45. The most authoritative recent study on this question is James P. Smith and Barry Edmonston, eds., *The New Americans: Economic, Demographic, and Fiscal Effects of Immigration* (1997). For a journalistic discussion of this point, see John Cassidy, "The Melting-Pot Myth," *The New Yorker,* 41–42 (July 14, 1997) ("These numbers suggest that the natives who benefit most from immigration are the ones who purchase the services of cooks, housekeepers, and gardeners on a regular basis, which is to say the rich"). A telling exception is the opposition by well-educated information technology workers to the steadily expanding H-1B program for highly skilled foreign workers.

46. See Salins, *Assimilation, American Style;* see also Miller, *The Unmaking of Americans.*

47. Schuck, *Citizens, Strangers, and In-Betweens,* chap. 14.

48. For some sobering realism about the good old days, see Nancy Foner, *From Ellis Island to JFK: New York's Two Great Waves of Immigration* (2000).

49. See Richard Brookhiser, *The Way of the WASP: How It Made America, and How It Can Save It, So to Speak* (1991).

50. Glazer, *We Are All Multiculturalists Now,* 101 (Higham's emphasis in the original).

51. See, e.g., Peter Skerry, "The Racialization of Immigration Policy," in *Taking*

Stock: American Government in the Twentieth Century (Morton Keller and R. Shep Melnick, eds., 1999).

52. Ironically, some of these criteria show that assimilating certain American values may not be such a good thing: illegitimacy and divorce rates, for example, tend to increase the longer immigrants live in the United States. See discussion in Schuck, *Citizens, Strangers, and In-Betweens,* 345.

53. I review the evidence at id., 343–344. See also Geoffrey Nunberg, "Lingo Jingo: English Only and the New Nativism," *The American Prospect,* 40–47 (July-Aug. 1997).

54. See generally Schuck, *Citizens, Strangers, and In-Betweens,* 341–353.

55. Archdeacon, *Becoming American.*

56. See Taylor Branch, *Parting the Waters: America in the King Years, 1954–63* (1989); E. Franklin Frazier, *The Negro in the United States* (1957); A. Leon Higginbotham, *Shades of Freedom: Racial Politics and Presumptions in the American Legal Process* (1996); Jordan, *White over Black.*

57. See, e.g., James Baldwin, *The Fire Next Time* (1963); Frederick Douglass, *A Narrative of the Life of Frederick Douglass* (1845); Malcolm X, *The Autobiography of Malcolm X* (1965). Note that popular culture (e.g., film, soul, rap music) exhibits similar conflicts and ambivalences.

58. The political dynamics of this change are well captured in James Q. Wilson, *Negro Politics: The Search for Leadership* (1960), where Wilson compares the political styles of William Dawson, a congressman allied with the Daley machine in Chicago, and Adam Clayton Powell, the flamboyant and rhetorically polarizing congressman from Harlem.

59. See Alan Wolfe, "Strangled by Roots," *The New Republic,* 30 (May 28, 2001) (review of Gary Gerstle, *American Crucible: Race and Nation in the Twentieth Century* (2001)).

60. See, e.g., Heather MacDonald, *The Burden of Bad Ideas: How Modern Intellectuals Misshape Our Society,* 13–16 (2000).

61. Glazer, *Ethnic Dilemmas,* 103–109.

62. Reynolds Farley, ed., *State of the Union: America in the 1990s* (1995).

63. See, e.g., Peter Skerry, *Mexican-Americans: The Ambivalent Minority* (1993).

64. Lau v. Nichols, 414 U.S. 563 (1974). See also Schuck, *Citizens, Strangers, and In-Betweens,* chap. 4.

65. Regents of University of California v. Bakke, 438 U.S. 265 (1978).

66. See, e.g., Michael Novak, *The Rise of the Unmeltable Ethnics: Politics and Culture in the Seventies* (1972).

67. Mary C. Waters, *Ethnic Options: Choosing Identities in America* (1990).

68. U.S. Census Bureau, *Statistical Abstract of the United States, 1999,* at 411, 459 (1999).

69. I discuss this development in Schuck, *Citizens, Strangers, and In-Betweens,* 337–341, 354–358.

70. See, e.g., Bruce J. Schulman, *The Seventies: The Great Shift in American Culture, Society, and Politics* (2001); David Frum, *How We Got Here: The 70s, the Decade That Brought You Modern Life, for Better or Worse* (2000); Wolfe, *One Nation, After All.*

71. Lauren B. Edelman, Sally Riggs Fuller, and Iona Mara-Drita, "Diversity Rhetoric and the Managerialization of Law," 106 *American Journal of Sociology* 1589, 1618–1619 (2001).

72. Id., 1626. This rhetoric is often used to compare the artificial, coercive character of civil rights law unfavorably with the natural, voluntary character of the diversity ideal. Id., 1620–1621.

73. I thank Alan Hyde for pointing out these increasingly common usages.

74. Schuck, *Citizens, Strangers, and In-Betweens*, 147.

75. Fogel, *The Fourth Great Awakening*, 36.

76. John D. Skrentny, "Republican Efforts to End Affirmative Action: Walking a Fine Line," in *Seeking the Center: Politics and Policymaking in the New Century*, 132–171 (Martin A. Levin, Marc Karnis Landy, and Martin M. Shapiro, eds., 2001).

77. David Hollinger's fine book, *Postethnic America*, comes closest to doing so, and I discuss it in Chapter 4. The paradigms he uses—multiculturalism, cosmopolitanism, pluralism, and universalism—enable him to contrast certain broad orientations toward diversity. My effort to canvass the array of values that diversity implicates requires a different analytical structure.

78. See generally Stephen Holmes, *Passions and Constraint: On the Theory of Liberal Democracy* (1995) (discussing self-interest's displacement of earlier ethos emphasizing glory and hierarchy).

79. But see William A. Galston, *Liberal Pluralism: The Implications of Value Pluralism for Political Theory and Practice* (2002) (diversity, not autonomy, is the central liberal value).

80. See, e.g., Jerry Z. Muller, *Adam Smith in His Time and Ours: Designing the Decent Society* (1995), esp. chap. 10.

81. Joseph A. Schumpeter, *Capitalism, Socialism, and Democracy* (1942).

82. Henry Hansmann, *The Ownership of Enterprise* (1996).

83. The two—groups and their members—are by no means the same. The classic account of the divide between organizational bureaucracies and their members is Robert Michels, *Political Parties: A Sociological Study of the Oligarchical Tendencies of Modern Democracy* (Eden and Cedar Paul, trans., 1999).

84. See Peter H. Schuck, *The Limits of Law: Essays on Democratic Governance*, chap. 7 (2000).

85. See, e.g., James M. Buchanan and Gordon Tullock, *The Calculus of Consent: Logical Foundations of Constitutional Democracy* (1962); Mancur Olson, *The Logic of Collective Action: Public Goods and the Theory of Groups* (1965); Thomas C. Schelling, "On the Ecology of Micromotives," *The Public Interest* (Fall 1971). For a discussion of the tension between a liberal property rights regime and collective environmental goals, see, e.g., Joseph Sax, "Property Rights and the Economy of Nature," 45 *Stanford Law Review* 1433 (1993).

86. See, e.g., Francis Fukayama, *Trust: The Social Virtues and the Creation of Prosperity* (1995); Robert D. Putnam, *Bowling Alone: The Collapse and Revival of American Community* (2000).

87. For a review of the literature, see Katherine Y. Williams and Charles A. O'Reilly

III, "Democracy and Diversity in Organizations: A Review of 40 Years of Research," 20 *Research in Organizational Behavior* 77 (1998).

88. I briefly discuss this issue in Chapter 7.

89. Boy Scouts of America v. Dale, 530 U.S. 640 (2000). For a very brief comment on this issue, see Peter H. Schuck, "Diversity Demands Exclusivity," *The American Lawyer*, 67–69 (Sept. 2000).

90. For a more extended discussion of this issue, see Peter H. Schuck, "Liberal Citizenship," in *Handbook of Citizenship Studies: Foundations, Approaches, Histories, Forms* (Engin F. Isin and Bryan S. Turner, eds., 2002). See generally Schuck, *Citizens, Strangers, and In-Betweens*, esp. part 4.

91. Michael J. Sandel, *Democracy's Discontent: America in Search of a Public Philosophy*, 278 (1996).

92. See, e.g., Linda S. Bosniak, "Exclusion and Membership: The Dual Identity of the Undocumented Worker under United States Law," 1988 *Wisconsin Law Review* 955 (1988).

93. For the ways in which Americans in the past succumbed to these feelings and the forms that this took, see Smith, *Civic Ideals*.

94. Several qualifications are in order. First, the ultimate interests may be those of third-party nonmembers. An army, for example, serves the interests of society's members, not individual soldiers. Second, a group seeking to reflect its members' interests must often use some method of interest aggregation (e.g., majority rule) that sacrifices the interests of some members in order to satisfy the interests of others. Even so, it is the members' interests that count, not some distinct collective interest. Third, none of this denies the fact that groups that in principle are member-oriented often become self-serving and even oligarchic in fact.

95. See, e.g., Will Kymlicka, *Multicultural Citizenship: A Liberal Theory of Minority Rights* (1995), esp. chap. 3; Kymlicka, *Politics in the Vernacular: Nationalism, Multiculturalism, and Citizenship* (2000).

96. For an overly strong form of this argument, not limited to the United States, see Brian M. Barry, *Culture and Equality: An Egalitarian Critique of Multiculturalism* (2001).

97. See, e.g., Andrew Sharp, "Are Group Rights Compatible with Liberal Democracy? The Case of the Maori in New Zealand" (Feb. 2001) (unpublished manuscript, Department of Political Studies, University of Auckland).

98. Robert E. Lane, "Putting People at the Centre of Things," in *Redefining Roles and Relationships*, 131–162 (Harry Bohan and Gerard Kennedy, eds., 2001).

99. So do at least some of its adherents. A prominent example is Amitai Etzioni, *The Spirit of Community: Rights, Responsibilities and the Communitarian Agenda* (1993).

100. See Frank K. Upham, *Law and Social Change in Postwar Japan*, 78–123 (1987) (discussing Burakumin and Ainu). Analysts like John Lie, *Multiethnic Japan* (2001), insist on Japan's diversity.

101. For one response to these fears, see Mario Vargas Llosa, "The Culture of Liberty," *Foreign Policy*, 66–71 (Jan.-Feb. 2001). For another, see Amartya Sen,

"Other People," *The New Republic*, 23 (Dec. 18, 2000) (wider contacts expand the reach of our sense of justice).

102. The fame of this particular offering may be relatively recent. Larry D. Kramer, "Madison's Audience," 112 *Harvard Law Review* 611 (1999).

103. Federalist No. 10.

104. See, e.g., the discussion in Cass Sunstein, "Beyond the Republican Revival," 97 *Yale Law Journal* 1539, 1558–1564 (1988).

105. See Nicholas D. Kristof, "Japan's Invisible Minority: Better Off Than in Past, but Still Outcasts," *New York Times*, A18 (Nov. 30, 1995).

106. See, e.g., Judith Resnik, "Dependent Sovereigns: Indian Tribes, States, and the Federal Courts," 56 *University of Chicago Law Review* 671 (1989) (membership rules favoring males).

107. A classic exploration of this impulse to retreat is Robert M. Cover, "Foreword: Nomos and Narrative," 97 *Harvard Law Review* 4 (1983).

108. See, e.g., Cover, id.

109. See, e.g., Roger Cohen, "Shifts in Europe Pose Prickly Challenge to U.S.," *New York Times*, 4 (Feb. 11, 2001).

110. See, e.g., Buchanan and Tullock, *The Calculus of Consent*.

111. See Stephen Jay Gould (with R. C. Lewontin), "The Spandrels of San Marco and the Panglossian Paradigm: A Critique of the Adaptationist Programme," *Proceedings of the Royal Society of London B 205*, at 581–598 (1979). See also, e.g., Talcott Parsons, *The Social System* (1951).

112. This was a central theme of Friedrich von Hayek's work. See Friedrich A. von Hayek, *The Constitution of Liberty* (1960). See also Muller, *Adam Smith in His Time and Ours*; Charles E. Lindblom, *Inquiry and Change: The Troubled Attempt to Understand and Shape Society* (1990).

113. E.g., Natalie Angier, "Confessions of a Lonely Atheist," *New York Times Magazine*, 34, 38 (Jan. 14, 2001).

114. See William K. Stevens, "Lost Rivets and Threads, and Ecosystems Pulled Apart," *New York Times*, F4 (July 4, 2000) (summarizing studies); Carol Kaesuk Yoon, "Study Jolts Views on Recovery from Extinctions," *New York Times*, A20 (Mar. 9, 2000) (summarizing study).

115. See Carol Kaesuk Yoon, "Simple Method Found to Increase Crop Yields Vastly," *New York Times*, F1 (Aug. 22, 2000) (summarizing study).

116. Fogel, *The Fourth Great Awakening*, 173. This reformism is by no means limited to evangelical groups; it was true of most Christian and Jewish congregations in nineteenth- and twentieth-century America. E-mail from Jon Butler, Yale University, to author (Aug. 24, 2002).

117. See, e.g., Milt Freudenheim, "States' Drug Subsidy Programs Have Troubles of Their Own," *New York Times*, A30 (Oct. 6, 2000) (state programs affecting debate in presidential campaign).

118. See Robin Toner, "Political Battle Lines Are Clearly Drawn in Fight over Medicare Drug Coverage," *New York Times*, A12 (July 24, 2000); Robin Toner, "The 2000 Campaign: The Ad Campaign; Battle on Prescription Drugs," *New York Times*, A24 (Sept. 21, 2000).

119. Robert Pear, "Senators Agree on Measure to Overhaul Voting System," *New York Times*, A12 (Mar. 23, 2002).

120. Sanford Levinson, "Diversity," 2 *University of Pennsylvania Journal of Constitutional Law* 573, 590–591 (2000).
121. The point discussed in this paragraph was suggested by my colleague Bill Eskridge.
122. Stanley Fish is perhaps the most playful and rigorous of these. See, e.g., *The Trouble with Principle* (1999).
123. Cover, "Nomos and Narrative."

4. IMMIGRATION

1. Janny Scott, "Foreign Born in U.S. at Record High," *New York Times*, A26 (Feb. 7, 2002).
2. Rogers M. Smith, *Civic Ideals: Conflicting Visions of Citizenship in U.S. History*, 15 (1997).
3. This section borrows very liberally from Thomas Archdeacon, *Becoming American: An Ethnic History* (1983); Roger Daniels, *Coming to America: A History of Immigration and Ethnicity in American Life* (1990); Thomas Aleinikoff, David Martin, and Hiroshi Motomura, *Immigration and Citizenship: Process and Policy*, 152–182 (4th ed. 1998); and Jon Butler, *Becoming America: The Revolution before 1776* (2000). Unless indicated, I do not cite a specific source or page to support a particular point.
4. Archdeacon, *Becoming American*, 19–20; Butler, *Becoming America*, 49.
5. This date is decades later than has generally been thought. See Roger Finke and Rodney Stark, *The Churching of America, 1776–1980*, at 110–115 (1992).
6. Gerald Neuman, "The Lost Century of Immigration Law (1776–1875)," 93 *Columbia Law Review* 1833 (1993).
7. See, e.g., Willy Forbath, "When Jews, Italians, Greeks, and Slavs Belonged to Races Different from 'We, the People': Race, Class, and National Identity in Immigration Law and Policy, 1882–1924" (June 2002) (unpublished manuscript, University of Texas Law School) (emphasizing concerns about dependency and servility of "unfree" contract laborers).
8. Kenneth Prewitt, "Demography, Diversity, and Democracy: The 2000 Census Story," 20 *Brookings Review* 6, 8 (2000).
9. See Stephen H. Legomsky, *Immigration and Refugee Law and Policy*, 399 (3d ed. 2001).
10. The development of racial and ethnic categories is itself an interesting tale combining bureaucratic imperatives, public attitudes, pseudo-scientific taxonomies, and group politics. See, e.g., Joel Perlmann, "Race or People: Federal Race Classifications for Europeans in America, 1898–1913," Jerome Levy Economics Institute Working Paper No. 320 (Jan. 2001).
11. Archdeacon, *Becoming American*, 142.
12. Id., 168.
13. Gordon A. Craig, "The X-Files," *New York Review of Books*, 57 (Apr. 12, 2001) (reviewing Joseph W. Bendersky, *The "Jewish Threat": Anti-Semitic Politics of the US Army* (2000)).
14. Immigration and Nationality Act Amendments of 1965, Pub. L. No. 89-236, 79 Stat. 911.

15. Refugee Act of 1980, Pub. L. No. 96-212, 94 Stat. 102.
16. The developments described in this paragraph are detailed in Peter H. Schuck, *Citizens, Strangers, and In-Betweens: Essays on Immigration and Citizenship,* chaps. 1, 4, and 5 (1998).
17. Immigration Reform and Control Act of 1986, Pub. L. No. 99-603, 100 Stat. 3360.
18. See, e.g., INS v. St. Cyr, 533 U.S. 289 (2001) (reducing retroactive effect of certain restrictions), and S. 955, the Immigrant Fairness Restoration Act, introduced in 2001.
19. Immigration Act of 1990, Pub. L. No. 101-649, 104 Stat. 4978.
20. Thomas J. Espenshade and Katherine Hempstead, "Contemporary American Attitudes toward U.S. Immigration," 30 *International Migration Review* 535 (1996). On public attitudes on immigration, see generally Schuck, *Citizens, Strangers, and In-Betweens,* 4–11.
21. Gallup press release (Sept. 22, 2000), at *http://www.gallup.com/poll/releases/pr000922.asp.//enottxt//.*
22. Leo R. Chavez, *Covering Immigration: Popular Images and the Politics of the Nation* (2001), esp. chap. 4 (study of seventy-six magazine covers between 1965 and 1999).
23. See generally Leah Haus, *Unions, Immigration, and Internationalization: New Challenges and Changing Conditions in the United States and France* (2002).
24. Pat Buchanan, *The Death of the West: How Dying Populations and Immigrant Invasions Imperil Our Country and Civilization* (2002). For the view that anti-immigrant sentiment is rife in the United States, see David M. Reimers, *Unwelcome Strangers: American Identity and the Turn against Immigration* (1998); Chavez, *Covering Immigration.*
25. See, e.g., Schuck, *Citizens, Strangers, and In-Betweens,* chap. 5.
26. See Eric Schmitt, "To Fill Gaps, Cities Seek Wave of Immigrants," *New York Times,* A1 (May 30, 2001).
27. Hugh Davis Graham, *Collision Course: The Strange Convergence of Affirmative Action and Immigration Policy in America,* 62 (2002).
28. Gabriel J. Chin, "The Civil Rights Revolution Comes to Immigration Law: A New Look at the Immigration and Nationality Act of 1965," 75 *North Carolina Law Review* 273, 276–277 (1996) (emphasis in the original).
29. Id., 305–306. Kennedy's prediction, Chin shows, related only to Asians already living in the Western Hemisphere who would migrate to the United States Id., 321–325.
30. See, e.g., Peggy Levitt, *The Transnational Villagers* (2001).
31. Eric Schmitt, "Census Data Show a Sharp Increase in Living Standards," *New York Times,* A1 (Aug. 6, 2001).
32. See Peter T. Kilborn and Lynette Clemetson, "Gains of 90's Did Not Lift All, Census Shows," *New York Times,* A1 (June 5, 2002); "Census Finds 'American' Identity Rising in U.S.," *New York Times,* 27 (June 9, 2002); *1998 Statistical Yearbook of the Immigration and Naturalization Service,* table 2 (2000).
33. *1999 Statistical Yearbook of the Immigration and Naturalization Service,* 120 (2002).

34. American Competitiveness in the Twenty-First Century Act of 2000, 106 Pub. L. No. 106-313, 114 Stat. 1251.

35. Talk about a new economy is not new. See Jeffrey Madrick, "Economic Scene," *New York Times,* C2 (May 10, 2001) (research on use of the term historically).

36. Because this slowdown continued in fiscal year 2002, only half as many H-1B visas were approved in that year. 79 *Interpreter Releases* 1239 (Aug. 19, 2002). But see Rick Green, "As the Tech Economy Goes, So Go Special Visas," *New York Times,* 4 (June 16, 2002) (slowdown caused decline in applications and approvals). Australia relies on foreign labor for a quarter of its workforce, Switzerland for nearly a fifth, and the United States for about a sixth. "Let the Huddled Masses In," *The Economist,* 15 (Mar. 31, 2001). Germany and other EU states with shrinking populations have not been nearly as successful as the United States in attracting skilled workers. See, e.g., "Bridging Europe's Skills Gap," *The Economist,* 55 (Mar. 31, 2001) (Germany created a special program for 30,000 computer scientists but fewer than 5,000 have come, mostly from eastern Europe, not from India as planned).

37. See generally Gabriel J. Chin, "Virtual Immigrants: The Evolution of the H-1B Program" (2001) (unpublished manuscript, University of Cincinnati Law School). See also Angelo A. Paprelli and Susan K. Wehrer, "Update on Mergers and Acquisitions: Congress Toys with the H-1B," 78 *Interpreter Releases* 1401 (Aug. 31, 2001).

38. Both estimates (totals and number of Mexicans) are well above earlier ones and exceed INS estimates by 1.5 million. Schmitt, "Census Data"; e-mail messages from Jeffrey Passel, a demographer at the Urban Institute, Washington, D.C., to author (Mar. 26, 2001).

39. See generally Legomsky, *Immigration and Refugee Law and Policy,* 607–611.

40. See Eric Schmitt, "U.S.-Mexico Talks Produce Agreement on Immigration Policy," *New York Times,* A1 (Aug. 10, 2001).

41. See *http://www.immigrationlinks.com/news/news576.htm* (INS report on the effects of earlier amnesties on illegal immigration).

42. Steven Greenhouse, "In U.S. Unions, Mexico Finds Unlikely Ally on Immigration," *New York Times,* A1 (July 19, 2001).

43. Legal Immigration Family Equity (LIFE) Act of 2000, Pub. L. No. 106-553, 114 Stat. 2762, 2762A-345.

44. See Section 245(i), Extension Act of 2001, Pub. L. No. 107-116, 115 Stat. 2220 (2001). As of October 2002, the deadline had not been further extended.

45. See Eric Schmitt, "Salvadorans Illegally in U.S. Are Given Protected Status," *New York Times,* A7 (Mar. 3, 2001).

46. See Schmitt, "U.S.-Mexico Talks Produce Agreement."

47. Eric Schmitt, "You Can Come In. You Stay Out," *New York Times,* Week in Review at 1 (July 29, 2001).

48. For INS figures, see Migration News, *http://migration.ucdavis.edu* (Aug. 2002).

49. See "Possession of Social Security Number Not Required for Driver's License, Texas AG Says," 78 *Interpreter Releases* 1501 (Sept. 24, 2001); David Firestone, "In U.S. Illegally, Immigrants Get License to Drive," *New York Times,* A1 (Aug.

4, 2001). The California legislature passed such a statute but Governor Gray Davis vetoed it. Nancy Vogel and Dan Morain, "No Licenses for Illegal Immigrants," *Los Angeles Times,* A1 (Oct. 1, 2002).

50. See Jennifer Steinhauer, "Rulings on Medicaid for Immigrants Step Up the Pressure on Albany," *New York Times,* B2 (June 9, 2001).

51. "Some Illegal Immigrants to Get a Tuition Break in California," *New York Times,* A18 (Jan. 18, 2002); "In-State Tuition for Immigrants," *New York Times,* B3 (Aug. 10, 2002).

52. David Barstow, "Final Rules for Federal Victims' Fund Increase Aid to Families of Sept. 11 Dead," *New York Times,* B4 (Mar. 8, 2002).

53. See discussion and sources in Schuck, *Citizens, Strangers, and In-Betweens,* 336.

54. Scott, "Foreign Born in U.S. at Record High."

55. Bruce Lambert, "40 Percent in New York Born Abroad," *New York Times,* B1 (July 24, 2001).

56. Jose Casanova and Aristide R. Zolberg, "Religion and Immigrant Incorporation in New York" (2001) (unpublished manuscript, New School University).

57. Thomas J. Espenshade, ed., *Keys to Successful Immigration: Implications of the New Jersey Experience,* 5, table 1.1.c (1997).

58. See, e.g., Susan Sachs, "A Hue, and a Cry, in the Heartland," *New York Times,* WK5 (Apr. 8, 2001) (mentioning West Virginia, Georgia, Iowa, and Nevada).

59. This paragraph closely follows Nancy Foner, *From Ellis Island to JFK: New York's Two Great Waves of Immigration,* chap. 1 (2000).

60. Jason Begay, "Native New Yorkers (the Original Kind)," *New York Times,* B1 (Aug. 29, 2002) (2000 census data).

61. Foner cites an INS estimate of about 425,000 illegal immigrants in New York City in 1996, the vast majority of them with expired visas. *From Ellis Island to JFK,* 17. This number is probably a conservative estimate of the current figure.

62. Nicholas Kulish, "U.S. Asian Population Grew and Diversified, Census Shows," *Wall Street Journal,* B4 (May 15, 2001).

63. Foner, *From Ellis Island to JFK,* 12, 15, 95.

64. Audrey Singer et al., "The World in a Zip Code: Greater Washington, D.C. as a New Region of Immigration" (Brookings Institution Survey Series, Apr. 2001).

65. Gregory Rodriguez, "Where the Minorities Rule," *New York Times,* WK6 (Feb. 10, 2002); Dana Canedy, "Florida Has More Hispanics Than Blacks, Census Shows," *New York Times,* A1 (Mar. 28, 2001).

66. Tamar Lewin, "Child Well-Being Improves, U.S. Says," *New York Times,* A14 (July 19, 2001).

67. Rodriguez, "Where the Minorities Rule"; Todd S. Purdum, "Non-Hispanic Whites a Minority, California Census Figures Show," *New York Times,* A1 (Mar. 30, 2001) (less than one-fifth of Hispanic growth due to new immigration; however, most of the Asian growth is due to this).

68. See, e.g., Peter Brimelow, *Alien Nation: Common Sense about America's Immigration Disaster* (1995).

69. See generally Schuck, *Citizens, Strangers, and In-Betweens.*

70. See Diana L. Eck, *A New Religious America: How a "Christian Country" Has Now Become the World's Most Religiously Diverse Nation* (2001).

71. Daniel Pipes and Khalid Durán, "Muslim Immigrants in the United States" (Center for Immigration Studies, Washington, D.C., Aug. 2002).
72. Gregory Rodriguez, "Forging a New Vision of America's Melting Pot," *New York Times*, WK1 (Feb. 11, 2001). The greater fluidity of Latino conceptions of race and ethnicity is analyzed in Clara E. Rodriguez, *Changing Race: Latinos, the Census, and the History of Ethnicity in the United States*, chap. 1 (2000).
73. Id. See discussion in Chapter 5 of mixed-race designations in the 2000 census.
74. For some reason, black-white intermarriage is more common in the United Kingdom. "Alone, Together," *The Economist*, 53 (July 14, 2001).
75. See Migration News, *http://migration.ucdavis.edu* (Sept. 2002).
76. David A. Hollinger, *Postethnic America: Beyond Multiculturalism*, 206–208 (rev. ed. 2000).
77. See Nathan Glazer, "American Diversity and the 2000 Census," *The Public Interest*, 3, 14–15 (Summer 2001). On whiteness studies, see Chapter 1, note 44.
78. See, e.g., Paula D. McClain and Joseph Stewart, Jr., *"Can We All Get Along?": Racial and Ethnic Minorities in American Politics* (2d ed. 1999).
79. See Peter H. Schuck, "Law and the Study of Migration," in Caroline B. Brettell and James F. Hollifield, *Migration Theory: Talking Across Disciplines*, 187, 197–200 (2000). I say "rough approximation" because some unknown portion of illegal immigration is not controllable as a practical matter.
80. See *www.ins.gov/graphics/aboutINS/statistics/IMM2001* (Oct. 2002).
81. Id.
82. See *1999 Statistical Yearbook*, 169–171.
83. See generally Peter H. Schuck and Rogers M. Smith, *Citizenship without Consent: Illegal Aliens in the American Polity* (1985).
84. See Nguyen v. INS, 533 U.S. 53 (2001).
85. See generally Patrick Weil, "Access to Citizenship: A Comparison of Twenty-five Nationality Laws," in *Citizenship Today: Global Perspectives and Practices*, chap. 1 (T. Alexander Aleinikoff and Douglas Klusmeyer, eds., 2001).
86. See generally Smith, *Civic Ideals*.
87. On naturalization of women, see Rogers M. Smith, "'One United People': Second-Class Female Citizenship and the American Quest for Community," 1 *Yale Journal of Law and the Humanities* 229 (1989).
88. 8 U.S.C. §1423.
89. See the Senior Citizenship Act, H.R. 964, 107th Cong. (2001).
90. *2000 Statistical Yearbook*, 202, table 46; e-mail from John Bjerke, chief, Demographic Statistics, Statistics Division, Office of Policy and Planning, INS, to author (July 10, 2002).
91. *2000 Statistical Yearbook*, 199–200.
92. 8 U.S.C. §1448(a).
93. Stanley Renshon, "Dual Citizenship and American National Identity" (Center for Immigration Studies, Washington, D.C., Dec. 2001).
94. Michael Jones-Correa, "Under Two Flags: Dual Nationality in Latin America and Its Consequences for Naturalization in the United States," 35 *International Migration Review* 997 (2001).
95. For analyses of dual citizenship, see, e.g., Schuck, *Citizens, Strangers, and In-*

Betweens, chap. 10; Peter J. Spiro, "Dual Nationality and the Meaning of Citizenship," 46 *Emory Law Journal* 1411 (1997).

96. Jim Chen, "Is Affirmative Action Fair? Diversity in a Different Dimension: Evolutionary Theory and Affirmative Action's Destiny," 59 *Ohio State Law Journal* 811, 830 (1998).

97. J. Hector St. John de Crèvecoeur, *Letters from an American Farmer,* 69–70 (1781; Penguin Books ed., 1963).

98. See, e.g., Lawrence Fuchs, *The American Kaleidoscope: Race, Ethnicity, and the Civic Culture* (1990).

99. Ben J. Wattenberg, *The First Universal Nation: Leading Indicators and Ideas about the Surge of America in the 1990s* (1991).

100. A recent book argues, wrongly, that the United States is more culturally homogeneous than ever, but maintains, correctly, that concerns about disunity are exaggerated. John A. Hall and Charles Lindblom, *Is America Falling Apart?* (1999).

101. See Alberto Alesina, Rafael Di Tella, and Robert MacCulloch, "Inequality and Happiness: Are Europeans and Americans Different?" (Feb. 2001) (unpublished manuscript, Department of Economics, Harvard University).

102. I have discussed at length the issues mentioned in this paragraph. See Schuck, *Citizens, Strangers, and In-Betweens,* esp. chaps. 8, 10, and 14.

103. Even America's standard of living, traditionally the most palpable symbol of its exceptionalism, is more easily taken for granted today after a decade of steady economic growth. Moreover, some other nations like Finland and Switzerland now equal or exceed the American standard.

104. Robert Frank, "Checks in the Mail," *Wall State Journal,* A1 (May 22, 2001).

105. See, e.g., Schuck, *Citizens, Strangers, and In-Betweens,* 180–181.

106. See, e.g., Stephen D. Krasner, *Sovereignty: Organized Hypocrisy* (1999).

107. Countries unaccustomed to immigrants but experiencing rapid demographic change face an even greater identity problem. See, e.g., Warren Hoge, "Britain's Nonwhites Feel Un-British, Report Says," *New York Times,* A13 (Apr. 4, 2002) (Britain's population now 7.1% nonwhite).

108. The U.S. Commission on Immigration Reform (known as the Jordan Commission, after its chair, Barbara Jordan) deliberated before deciding to use the term "Americanization" to describe its policy recommendations on how to help immigrants become full members of American society. See U.S. Commission on Immigration Reform, *Becoming an American: Immigration and Immigrant Policy,* 26–27 (1997).

109. Alan Wolfe, "Alien Nation," *The New Republic,* 30–31 (Mar. 26, 2001).

110. See generally Werner Sollors, "Literature and Ethnicity," in *Harvard Encyclopedia of American Ethnic Groups,* 647–655 (Stephan Thernstrom et al., eds., 1980).

111. Nathan Glazer, *We Are All Multiculturalists Now,* 96–97 (1997).

112. Stanley Lieberson, *A Matter of Taste: How Names, Fashions, and Culture Change* (2000).

113. Alejandro Portes and Ruben G. Rumbaut, *Legacies: The Story of the Immigrant Second Generation* (2001).

114. See Richard Rothstein, "Achievers and Delinquents via Melting Pot Recipe," *New York Times,* B9 (Apr. 24, 2002) (reviewing Zhou-Bankston study of Vietnamese children in New Orleans). Some groups are more successful at positive assimilation than others. See Alejandro Portes and Min Zhou, "The New Second Generation: Segmented Assimilation and Its Variants," 530 *Annals of the American Academy of Political and Social Science* 74 (1993) (comparing assimilation patterns among Cuban, Haitian, and Mexican immigrant enclaves in South Florida and California).

115. K. Anthony Appiah, "The Multiculturalist Misunderstanding," *New York Review of Books,* 30, 32 (Oct. 9, 1997). For another analysis of its contested meaning, see Will Kymlicka, *Politics in the Vernacular: Nationalism, Multiculturalism, and Citizenship,* esp. chaps. 1, 8 (2000).

116. See, e.g., "Pope Condemns Xenophobia in a Global Age," *New York Times,* A6 (Jan. 2, 2001).

117. See, e.g., Report of the Commission on the Future of Multi-ethnic Britain, discussed in Amartya Sen, "Other People," *The New Republic,* 23, 25–26 (Dec. 18, 2000).

118. See, e.g., Romesh Ratnesar, "London Diarist," *The New Republic,* 54 (Oct. 9, 2000) ("[m]ulticulturalism is practically a civic religion" in London).

119. Even here, one can question whether the demand for respect really concerns the culture or the individual. In Appiah's view, individuals in today's "edgy" climate often respond to perceived disrespect "in the name of all black people, all women, all gays, as the case may be, taking the high road of Kantian principle. But the truth is that what mostly irritates us in these moments is that we, as individuals, feel diminished. . . . Culture is not the problem, and it is not the solution." "The Multiculturalist Misunderstanding," 36.

120. On conservative multiculturalism, see Angela D. Dillard, *Guess Who's Coming to Dinner Now?: Multicultural Conservatism in America* (2000).

121. Will Kymlicka's illustrative list of multicultural policies includes affirmative action; reserved seats in public institutions; revised public school curricula; religious accommodation in secular settings; revised dress codes; programs to encourage toleration; antiharassment codes; diversity training for officials; efforts to reduce ethnic stereotyping; public funding of ethnic festivals and programs; multilingual social services; and bilingual education. *Politics in the Vernacular,* 163.

122. Nathan Glazer notes that "[a]lmost every book in the Harvard University libraries listed as containing the word 'multiculturalism' in its title in the 1970s and 1980s is Canadian or Australian." Glazer, *We Are All Multiculturalists Now,* 8.

123. Id.

124. Hollinger, *Postethnic America,* 209.

125. Id., 68 (italics original).

126. Will Kymlicka, *Multicultural Citizenship: A Liberal Theory of Minority Rights* (1995); Kymlicka, *Politics in the Vernacular.*

127. Hollinger might have added that Puerto Ricans already enjoy special economic and cultural rights and have recently rejected both statehood and independence, while Native Americans possess quasi-sovereignty—two facts that Kymlicka rec-

ognizes and applauds. Economic equality, as Kymlicka also recognizes, is a separate issue.

128. Kymlicka, *Politics in the Vernacular*, 24–27.

129. Hollinger, *Postethnic America*, 215–216.

130. Michael Lind, *The Next American Nation: The New Nationalism and the Fourth American Revolution* (1995). Oddly, given their similar views, Hollinger does not cite Lind in his revised edition published five years after Lind's book appeared.

131. Wolfe, "Strangled by Roots," *The New Republic*, 33 (May 28, 2001) (review of Gary Gerstle, *American Crucible: Race and Nation in the Twentieth Century* (2001)). On the multiplicity of ideas that pass as multiculturalism, see Glazer, *We Are All Multiculturalists Now*, chap. 1.

132. Amartya Sen provides an arresting example: "the so-called 'cultures' do not reflect anything like some monolithic and uniquely defined set of attitudes and beliefs. Indian traditions, for example, are often taken to be intimately associated with religion—and yet Sanskrit and Pali have a larger literature in defense of atheism and agnosticism than can be found in any other classical language." Sen, "Other People," 28.

133. See Schuck, *Citizens, Strangers, and In-Betweens*, chap. 14.

134. For descriptions of the Americanization movements in the early twentieth century, see John J. Miller, *The Unmaking of Americans: How Multiculturalism Has Undermined the Assimilation Ethic* (1998); Alejandro Portes and Ruben G. Rumbaut, *Immigrant America: A Portrait* (1996); Philip Gleason, "American Identity and Americanization," in *Harvard Encyclopedia of American Ethnic Groups*, 31, 39–41, 57–58; Milton M. Gordon, *Assimilation in American Life* (1964).

135. U.S. Commission on Immigration Reform, *Becoming an American*, 25–45.

136. Lind's much longer book also disappoints on many points—not least, the simplistic quality and strident tone of his political critique, some of his ill-considered, reflexively populist policy proposals (including zero net immigration), and his apocalyptic predictions of social catastrophe. Even his indictment of racial preferences, a position I share, is too tendentious, failing to acknowledge the nuances and merits of competing arguments. For all this, Lind's book remains impressive in its historical sweep, interesting details, and many astute judgments.

137. See Graham, *Collision Course*, 12, 129–130.

138. George J. Borjas, *Strangers and Friends*, 169–174 (1990).

139. Increases in linguistic diversity in Europe largely take the form of English acquisition, and the trends are striking: in 1999, 78% of the Dutch, 77% of Swedes, 41% of Germans, 30% of the French, and 28% of Italians claimed to speak English. See Alessandra Stanley, "English without Tears, Thanks to TV," *New York Times*, A4 (Sept. 14, 2000) (citing EU study). See also James Fallows, "He's Got Mail," *New York Review of Books*, 4 (Mar. 14, 2002) (English as universal lingua franca).

140. The next two paragraphs draw heavily on Aristide R. Zolberg, "Language Policy: Public Policy Perspectives," in *International Encyclopedia of the Social and*

Behavioral Sciences, vol. 12, pp. 8365–8373 (Neil J. Smelser and Paul B. Baltes, eds., 2001).

141. Id., 8365.
142. Nell Lake, "Language Wars," *Harvard Magazine,* 12 (Mar.-Apr. 2002).
143. Fallows, "He's Got Mail," 4–6 (but noting that proportion of English-language pages is falling).
144. Gregory Rodriguez, "The Overwhelming Allure of English," *New York Times,* WK3 (Apr. 7, 2002).
145. Lake, "Language Wars," 11.
146. Meyer v. Nebraska, 262 U.S. 390 (1923).
147. Zolberg, "Language Policy," 8368.
148. Rosalie Pedalino Porter, "The Case against Bilingual Education," *http:// www.ceousa.org.* According to another source, more than 140 languages are spoken in the United States. "Labels in English Pose Risks in a Multilingual Country," *New York Times,* 30 (May 20, 2001).
149. Bilingual Education Act of 1968, Pub. L. No. 90-247, 81 Stat. 816.
150. Voting Rights Act Amendments of 1975, Pub. L. No. 94-73, 89 Stat. 400.
151. For the background of these laws before 1980, see "Language: Issues and Legislation," in *Harvard Encyclopedia of American Ethnic Groups,* 619–629.
152. The primary issues have been the costs to local communities of preparing bilingual ballots, the resistance by those communities to Justice Department scrutiny of their electoral processes, and the number of groups that should be included as linguistically disadvantaged.
153. John David Skrentny, *The Minority Rights Revolution,* chap. 7 (2002).
154. Glazer, *We Are All Multiculturalists Now,* 89.
155. See Jorge Ruiz-de-Velasco and Michael Fix, *Overlooked and Underserved: Immigrant Students in U.S. Secondary Schools* (2000); Karen W. Arenson, "Scaling the Barriers of Literacy and Language," *New York Times,* 1 (Mar. 12, 2000).
156. See discussion and studies cited in Schuck, *Citizens, Strangers, and In-Betweens,* at 343–344. See also Rodriguez, "The Overwhelming Allure of English." Rodriguez also notes that Latinos increasingly prefer English-language television shows and films.
157. Ruiz-de-Velasco and Fix, *Overlooked and Underserved,* 2.
158. Ron Unz, "Bilingual Education Lives On," *New York Times,* A23 (Mar. 2, 2001). Some prefer the term "English language learner" (ELL), thinking it less pejorative. See Chancellor's Report on the Education of English Language Learners (New York City Board of Education, Dec. 19, 2000), i.
159. "Labels in English Pose Risks in a Multilingual Country," *New York Times,* 30 (May 20, 2001).
160. See note 139.
161. The historical account that follows draws on Skrentny, *Minority Rights Revolution,* and Linda Chavez, *Out of the Barrio: Toward a New Politics of Hispanic Assimilation* (1991), chap. 1. See also James Crawford, *Bilingual Education: History, Politics, Theory, and Practice* (1989).
162. According to Skrentny, historians are uncertain how similar to current bilingual

education these practices were, but they note that Germans, the major group seeking such education, did not really look to the public schools for cultural maintenance and that the programs were controversial. Id.

163. See Peter D. Salins, *Assimilation, American Style,* 38 (1997).

164. Chavez, *Out of the Barrio,* 11.

165. National Defense Education Act of 1958, Pub. L. No. 85-864, 72 Stat. 1580.

166. Elementary and Secondary Education Act of 1965, Pub. L. No. 89-10, 79 Stat. 27.

167. Civil Rights Act of 1964, Pub. L. No. 88-352, 78 Stat. 241.

168. See, e.g., United States v. State of Texas, 342 F. Supp. 24 (E.D. Tex. 1991).

169. 414 U.S. 563 (1974).

170. Equal Educational Opportunity Act of 1974, Pub. L. No. 93-380, 88 Stat. 514.

171. Skrentny, *Minority Rights Revolution,* chap. 7.

172. Aspira of New York, Inc. v. Board of Education of the City of New York, 72 Civ. 4002 (S.D.N.Y. Aug. 29, 1974) (unreported consent decree).

173. See, e.g., Frank J. Macchiarola, "The Courts in the Political Process: Judicial Activism or Timid Local Government?" 9 *St. John's Journal of Legal Commentary* 703, 715 (1994); Rachel F. Moran, "Bilingual Education, Immigration, and the Culture of Disinvestment," 2 *Journal of Gender, Race, and Justice* 163, 176–177 (1999).

174. Quoted in Chavez, *Out of the Barrio,* 13 (emphasis in the original).

175. The AIR survey and the reaction to it are discussed in John Rhee, "Theories of Citizenship and Their Role in the Bilingual Education Debate," 33 *Columbia Journal of Law and Social Problems* 33, 41–42 (1999).

176. An apparent exception is the Native American Languages Act of 1990, which seeks to preserve and enhance America's indigenous languages, although this statute may signify that Congress views Native Americans, unlike Hispanics, as so politically and culturally marginal that maintaining their cultures poses no threat to the dominant one. See Pub. L. No. 101-477, 104 Stat. 1152.

177. Bilingual Education Improvement Act of 1984, Pub. L. No. 98-511, 98 Stat. 2369.

178. See, e.g., Mark Colon, "Line Drawing, Code Switching, and Spanish as Second-Hand Smoke: English-Only Workplace Rules and Bilingual Employees," 20 *Yale Law and Policy Review* 227 (2002) (reviewing cases).

179. See Alexander v. Sandoval, 532 U.S. 275 (2001) (no private remedy under Title VI against state's policy on driver's examination); Yniguez v. Arizonans for Official English, 520 U.S. 43 (1997) (dismissing challenge as moot). See Laura A. Cordero, "Constitutional Limitations on Official English Declarations," 20 *New Mexico Law Review* 17 (1990).

180. Rodriguez, "The Overwhelming Allure of English."

181. See Jack Citrin, "Official English and the Symbolic Politics of Language in the United States," 43 *Western Political Quarterly* 535, 546 (1990).

182. Schmitt, "Census Data."

183. Ruiz-de-Velasco and Fix, *Overlooked and Underserved,* 18, figure 1.

184. Id. at 24, tables 8 and 26, figure 6.

185. See National Clearinghouse for Bilingual Education, *http://www.ncbe.gwu.edu/ncbepubs/reports/state-dta/us.htm*.
186. Rodriguez, "The Overwhelming Allure of English."
187. Id., 3. See also U.S. General Accounting Office, "Title I Services Provided to Students with Limited English Proficiency," GAO/HEHS-00-25 (Washington, D.C., 1999).
188. Ruiz-de-Velasco and Fix, *Overlooked and Underserved*, 2.
189. U.S. Department of Education appropriations figures.
190. Estimate based on $373 median per-student cost differential for bilingual instruction, times 4.1 million students ($1.5 billion), compared to a total of $446 million for combined bilingual and immigrant education. The state spending figures come from Paul J. Hopstock, Bonnie J. Bucaro, Howard L. Fleischman, Annette M. Zehler, and Hongsook Eu, "Descriptive Study of Services to Limited English Proficient Students, Volume II," report by Development Associates, Inc. to Office of the Undersecretary, U.S. Department of Education, at 96 (June 1993).
191. Id., 21.
192. E-mail from Michael Fix, principal research associate at the Urban Institute's Population Studies Center, Washington, D.C., to author (May 23, 2001) (hereafter Fix e-mail).
193. Hopstock et al., "Descriptive Study," 96.
194. See Michael Fix and Wendy Zimmerman, "The Integration of Immigrant Families in the United States," 51, table 4 (Urban Institute, Washington, D.C., Mar. 2001).
195. See testimony by Delia Pompa, director, Office of Bilingual Education and Minority Languages Affairs, U.S. Dept. of Education, hearing on appropriations for 2000 before House Appropriations Committee, Subcommittee on Departments of Labor, Health and Human Services, Education, and Related Agencies, 148, 160 (Mar. 9, 1999).
196. Ruiz-de-Velasco and Fix, *Overlooked and Underserved*, 28, table 13; Fix e-mail.
197. Zolberg, "Language Policy," 8370.
198. *Valeria G. v. Wilson*, 12 F. Supp. 2d 1007 (N.D. Cal. 1998).
199. Jennifer Medina, "Bilingual Education on Ballot in Two States," *New York Times*, A18 (Oct. 8, 2002).
200. See Jacques Steinberg, "Increase in Test Scores Counters Dire Forecasts for Bilingual Ban," *New York Times*, 1 (Aug. 20, 2000) (test scores for LEP students in first year under Proposition 227 increased for every grade except fourth-grade math).
201. See, e.g., Kevin Clark, "From Primary Language Instruction to English Immersion: How Five California Districts Made the Switch" (Institute for Research in English Acquisition and Development (READ), Washington, D.C., 1999); Keith Baker, "Structured English Immersion: Breakthrough in Teaching Limited-English-Proficient Students," 80 *Phi Delta Kappan* 199–204 (1998).
202. See, e.g., Jorge Amselle, ed., *The Failure of Bilingual Education* (1996).
203. A leading academic supporter of bilingual education is Stanford professor Kenji

Hakuta, who chaired a National Academy of Sciences study on the subject. See Hakuta, "The Education of Language Minority Students," testimony to U.S. Commission on Civil Rights (Apr. 13, 2001).

204. For example, a recent governmental report on the four federal bilingual programs found the evidence of effectiveness to be inconclusive. U.S. General Accounting Office, "Bilingual Education: Four Overlapping Programs Could Be Consolidated," GAO-01-657 (Washington, D.C., May 14, 2001).

205. The remainder of this paragraph draws on Frank Newport, Poll Release, "Americans Support Elimination of Bilingual Education," *Gallup News Service,* 1–2 (June 6, 1998); and Public Agenda, "A Lot to Be Thankful For: What Parents Want Children to Learn about America" (Sept. 1998), available at *http://www .publicagenda.org/specials/thankful/thankful.htm* (last accessed Oct. 22, 2001).

206. See, e.g., Mark Barabak, "Bilingual Education Gets Little Support," *Los Angeles Times,* 1 (Oct. 15, 1997); Ramon McLeod, "Prop. 227 Got Few Latino Votes," *San Francisco Chronicle,* A19 (June 5, 1998); Ron Unz, "California and the End of White America," *Commentary,* 17, 26 (Nov. 1999). Among Asian-Americans, 57% voted for Proposition 227. Barabak, id.

207. Amy Goldstein and Roberto Suro, "A Journey in Stages: Assimilation's Pull Is Still Strong, but Its Pace Varies," *Washington Post,* A1 (Jan. 16, 2000).

208. See, e.g., Roberto Suro, "Hispanic Views Defy Predictions," *Dallas Morning News,* 1A (Dec. 15, 1992) (Latino National Political Survey).

209. See Michael Barone, "Debating Bilingual Education," *U.S. News and World Report* (Feb. 8, 2002), available at *http://www.usnews.com/usnews/opinion/ baroneweb/mb_020208.htm.*

210. The description that follows draws on the Chancellor's Report on the Education of English Language Learners (New York City Board of Education, Dec. 19, 2000) (hereafter Chancellor's Report); Mireya Navarro, "For Parents, One Size Doesn't Fit All in Bilingual Education," *New York Times,* B1 (Feb. 24, 2001); and Jacques Steinberg, "City's Bilingual Education Debated at Spirited Hearing," *New York Times,* B4 (Oct. 18, 2000).

211. See Peter Duignan, *Bilingual Education: A Critique,* 9 (1998).

212. Nationally, more than 70% of LEP students speak Spanish at home. Porter, "The Case against Bilingual Education." About 74% of Latino students are *not* considered LEP and are not enrolled in such classes. Navarro, "For Parents, One Size Doesn't Fit All."

213. Chancellor's Report, 4.

214. See Moran, "Bilingual Education," 175–181.

215. Chancellor's Report, 7–8.

216. Salins, *Assimilation, American Style,* 75. The drop-out rate has increased sharply since the state adopted higher standards, leading some immigrant advocates to demand special Regents tests for LEP students. Jennifer Medina, "Critics Say Regents English Tests Push Immigrants to Drop Out," *New York Times,* A25 (natl. ed., June 23, 2002).

217. Chancellor's Report, 6–7.

218. In addition to his support for an amnesty for undocumented Mexicans and an

expanded guestworker program and other Latino-friendly actions described earlier, Bush has proposed restoring food stamp benefits to legal immigrants denied them by the 1996 welfare reform law. Robert Pear, "Bush Plan Seeks to Restore Food Stamps for Noncitizens," *New York Times*, A1 (Jan. 10, 2002).

219. "OMB Requests Information on Costs, Benefits of Services for Persons with Limited English Proficiency," 78 *Interpreter Releases* 1864 (Dec. 10, 2001). Further guidance was published at 67 Fed. Reg. 7692 (Feb. 20, 2002).

220. See "In Spanish, Bush Focuses on Working with Mexico," *New York Times*, 36 (May 6, 2001).

221. Jim Yardley, "One Texas Candidate Cools on a Debate in Spanish," *New York Times*, A14 (Mar. 1, 2002).

222. See, e.g., Chancellor's Report, at 5 (in light of globalization, urging that *all* students have multiple language skills). Pressures are growing for multilingual product warnings. See "Labels in English Pose Risks in a Multilingual Country," *New York Times*, 30 (May 20, 2001).

223. Yardley, "One Texas Candidate."

224. Citrin, "Official English."

225. See, e.g., Jim O'Grady, "A Shortage of Seats to Learn Miss Liberty's Tongue," *New York Times*, CY4 (May 6, 2001) (estimate of 50,000 English-language class slots for the million immigrants who need them).

226. Chancellor's Report, 14–16 and appendix D. The proposal's budgetary fate is still unclear. See Edward Wyatt, "Levy Warns Budget Cuts May Threaten Bilingual Plan," *New York Times*, B4 (July 18, 2001).

227. For a summary of the research on vouchers, see Jay P. Greene, "The Hidden Consensus for School Choice," in *Charters, Vouchers, and Public Education*, chap. 5 (Paul E. Peterson and David E. Campbell, eds., 2001). For a brief discussion of the arguments, see Peter H. Schuck, "The Classroom Clash," *The American Lawyer*, 63 (Feb. 2001).

228. A properly designed and scrupulously neutral program providing vouchers to parents rather than to institutions should satisfy constitutional standards. See Good News Club v. Milford Central School, 533 U.S. 98 (2001). See also Nicole Stelle Garnett and Richard W. Garnett, "School Choice, the First Amendment, and Social Justice," 4 *Texas Review of Law and Politics* 301 (2000).

229. See Walter P. Jacob, "Note: Diversity Visas: Muddled Thinking and Pork Barrel Politics," 6 *Georgetown Immigration Law Journal* 297, 298 (1992).

230. As this book was going to press, I read Anna O. Law, "The Diversity Visa Lottery—a Cycle of Unintended Consequences in United States Immigration Policy," 21 *Journal of American Ethnic History* 3, 11–14 (2002), which recounts these early proposals.

231. Id., 19–21.

232. The discussion of the legislative history and structure of the original diversity visas program draws on Aleinikoff et al., *Immigration and Citizenship*, 290–292; and Thomas Saenz, "The Development of 'Diversity' Immigration Laws" (May 28, 1991) (unpublished manuscript, Yale Law School).

233. For a biting critique of their argument, see Stephen H. Legomsky, "Immigration, Equality, and Diversity," 31 *Columbia Journal of Transnational Law* 319 (1993).

234. Codified at 8 U.S.C. §1151.

235. See Jan C. Ting, "Other Than a Chinaman: How U.S. Immigration Law Results from and Still Reflects a Policy of Excluding and Restricting Asian Immigration," 4 *Temple Political and Civil Rights Law Review* 301, 309 (1995).

236. For the details, see "State Department, INS Preparing for Diversity Immigrant Visa Program," 70 *Interpreter Releases* 1590 (Dec. 6, 1993).

237. The one recent bill introduced to eliminate the lottery quickly also sought to place a moratorium on all immigration until 2007 or later. That bill is currently languishing in committee. "A Bill to Effect a Moratorium on Immigration," H.R. 2712, 107th Cong. (2001). Rep. Thomas Tancredo (R-Colo.) introduced the bill in August 2001. Rep. Tancredo is chairman of the Congressional Immigration Reform Caucus, a group that has called for elimination of the diversity lottery but has not taken significant strides toward that result.

238. Commission on Immigration Reform, *U.S. Immigration Policy: Restoring Credibility* (1994).

239. Conversation with congressional aide (Feb. 28, 2002).

240. Conversation with congressional aide (Nov. 15, 2001).

241. Some congressional aides consider smaller changes to the lottery program possible. For example, one observed that certain countries will be excluded from the lottery based on their lack of cooperation with the United States in the war on terrorism. The lottery requirements might be changed to require spouses and children over 18 years old to have completed a high school education or possess a certain level of professional experience. Conversation with congressional aide (Feb. 28, 2002).

242. E.g., personal interviews with immigration lawyers Allan Kaye and Theodore Ruthizer (May 24, 2001) (hereafter Kaye and Ruthizer interviews); with Charles Oppenheim, U.S. State Department (May 25, 2001) (hereafter Oppenheim interview), and Mark Krikorian, Center for Immigration Studies (Mar. 25, 2001) (hereafter Krikorian interview).

243. See 68 *Interpreter Releases* 139 (Feb. 4, 1991).

244. Legomsky, *Immigration and Refugee Law and Policy,* 241 (emphases in the original).

245. Louis Anthes, "The Island of Duty: The Practice of Immigration Law on Ellis Island," 24 *New York University Review of Law and Social Change* 563, 572–573 (1998).

246. The government has not attempted to collect data or conduct research on the fate of diversity immigrants once they arrive. Oppenheim interview.

247. The following description is based on the Kaye, Ruthizer, Oppenheim, and Krikorian interviews.

248. For discussion of these systems, see, e.g., Demetrios Papademetriou and Stephen Yale-Loehr, *Balancing Interests: Rethinking U.S. Selection of Skilled Immigrants,* 124–139 (1996); Stephen Yale-Loehr and Christoph Hoashi-Erhardt, "A Comparative Look at Immigration and Human Capital Assessment," 16

Georgetown Immigration Law Journal 99 (2001) (describing failed efforts in the United States to adopt a point system). In March 2003, a revised, somewhat more demanding point system goes into effect in Canada.

249. See Papademetriou and Yale-Loehr, *Balancing Interests*. See also Lenni B. Benson, "Breaking Bureaucratic Borders: A Necessary Step toward Immigration Law Reform," 54 *Administrative Law Review* 197 (2002).

250. A number of analysts have proposed this approach in some form. See, e.g., Julian Simon, *The Economic Consequences of Immigration,* 329–335 (1990); Gary Becker, "An Open Door for Immigrants: The Auction," *Wall Street Journal,* A14 (Oct. 14, 1992); Alan O. Sykes, "The Welfare Economics of Immigration Law: A Theoretical Survey with an Analysis of U.S. Policy," in *Justice in Immigration,* 158, 181–183 (Warren F. Schwartz, ed., 1995); Howard F. Chang, "Liberalized Immigration as Free Trade: Economic Welfare and the Optimal Immigration Policy," 145 *University of Pennsylvania Law Review* 1147, 1221–1229 (1996). For other approaches, see Michael J. Trebilcock with Benjamin Alarie, "Why Aren't People More Like Commodities: The Case for a Liberalized Immigration Policy" (Jan. 16, 2002) (unpublished manuscript, University of Toronto Law School) (proposing to eliminate quotas but require immigrants to carry social program insurance). See also Committee on Economic Development, *Reforming Immigration: Helping Meet America's Need for a Skilled Workforce,* 35–36 (Washington, D.C., 2001) (proposing auction of some H-1B visas).

251. In 2000, Congress did take a small step in this direction when it imposed a $1,000 fee on employers who file an H-1B petition, and then earmarked much of the proceeds—$138 million by mid-2002—to train Americans in affected industries. The law also expedited temporary visas for certain high-skill workers in exchange for a special $1,000 "premium processing" fee, with many of the proceeds going to improve other immigration services. Eric Schmitt, "Immigration Agency Offers Expedited Visas for $1000," *New York Times,* A12 (June 1, 2001).

252. The government has subsidized some bidders in FCC spectrum auctions. See Chapter 5.

253. Diversity visas now enjoy a processing priority because of their one-year expiration period, but that priority, which delays the processing of other visas, need not apply if the auction winners are treated just like other visa petitioners, as they should be. Those who would have won the diversity visa lottery would be worse off, of course, but their chances are minuscule to begin with (55,000/ 13,000,000, or 0.42%).

254. See generally Peter H. Schuck, *The Limits of Law: Essays on Democratic Governance,* esp. chaps. 1 and 13 (2000).

5. AFFIRMATIVE ACTION

1. Legalized abortion under *Roe v. Wade* is a possible exception, but there are some important differences. *Roe*'s foundation is judicial, not political. *Roe,* decided in 1973, has not been in place quite as long as affirmative action. Public opinion

about abortion is not as sharply divided, though in both cases the precise division depends on the formulation and context of the questions. Finally, *Roe*'s legal status is reasonably secure for now. President Bush and his attorney general, John Ashcroft, have disclaimed any serious effort to reverse it. In contrast, affirmative action is beleaguered as never before both in politics, where several states have limited it, and in the courts, where it is under intense challenge.

2. My reasons for using the unsatisfactory term "blacks" rather than the even more unsatisfactory term "African-Americans" are discussed in Chapter 1, note 26.

3. The data are presented and analyzed at length in Orlando Patterson, *The Ordeal of Integration: Progress and Resentment in America's "Racial" Crisis,* 15–82 (1997). See text accompanying notes 271–278, 400–405 for further discussion.

4. See text accompanying notes 23–25 and notes 112–125.

5. Eric Schnapper, "Affirmative Action and the Legislative History of the Fourteenth Amendment," 71 *Virginia Law Review* 753 (1985). This claim is sharply disputed by Paul Moreno, "Racial Classifications and Reconstruction Legislation," 61 *Journal of Southern History* 271 (1995) (relying on legislative history and the administration of the preferential statute). Moreno's position is buttressed by evidence of Frederick Douglass's strong opposition to affirmative action during Reconstruction. Seymour Martin Lipset, "Two Americas, Two Value Systems: Blacks and Whites," 13 *Tocqueville Review* 137, 170 (1992).

6. I say "possible" because deciding whether such an exception is wise and just will depend on a number of considerations that will appear in my analysis.

7. E.g., City of Richmond v. J. A. Croson Co., 488 U.S. 469, 493–498 (1989) (discussing judicial requirements for remedially based preferences); United States v. Paradise, 480 U.S. 149 (1987) (same).

8. For a more extended description, see John David Skrentny, *The Ironies of Affirmative Action,* 6–8 (1996). For discussion of competing definitions, including Skrentny's, see Deborah C. Malamud, "Race, Culture, and the Law: Values, Symbols, and Facts in the Affirmative Action Debate," 95 *Michigan Law Review* 1668, 1691–1694 (1997).

9. This equivalence is endorsed by some affirmative action enthusiasts like Stephen Steinberg, not just by opponents. David A. Hollinger, "Group Preferences, Cultural Diversity, and Social Democracy: Notes toward a Theory of Affirmative Action," in *Race and Representation: Affirmative Action,* 97 (Robert Post and Michael Rogin, eds., 1998).

10. On its outcome-determinativeness, see, e.g., Samuel Issacharoff, "Can Affirmative Action Be Defended?" 59 *Ohio State Law Journal* 669, 671–672 (1998).

11. For my analysis of age discrimination, see Peter H. Schuck, "The Graying of Civil Rights Law: The Age Discrimination Act of 1975," 89 *Yale Law Journal* 27 (1979).

12. In the race context, this is sometimes called "color-blindness." Skrentny, *Ironies of Affirmative Action,* 7–8. See generally Andrew Kull, *The Color-Blind Constitution* (1992).

13. Its psychological contours are doubtless complex and opaque. See, e.g., Linda Hamilton Krieger, "Civil Rights Perestroika: Intergroup Relations after Affirma-

tive Action," 86 *California Law Review* 1251, 1329 (1998) ("When a person is color-blind, there is simply much he will not see").

14. Patterson, *The Ordeal of Integration,* 15–16 ("Viewed from the perspective of comparative history and sociology, it can be said, unconditionally, that the changes that have taken place in the United States over the last fifty years are unparalleled in the history of minority-majority relations").

15. Alan Wolfe, "Strangled by Roots," *New Republic,* 33 (May 28, 2001) (review of Gary Gerstle, *American Crucible: Race and Nation in the Twentieth Century* (2001)).

16. Malamud, "Race, Culture, and the Law," 1691; see also text accompanying notes 112–125.

17. See, e.g., Hollinger, "Group Preferences," 101.

18. Even a rule merely requiring regulated companies to report the number of minorities who apply and who are hired is not impact-neutral, as it makes it more likely that the agency will investigate and impose sanctions. See, e.g., Stephen Labaton, "Court Rules Agency Erred on Mandate for Minorities," *New York Times,* A16 (Jan. 17, 2001). By the same token, giving dyslexic test-takers advantages such as additional time and spell-check programs may do more than merely equalize opportunity. See, e.g., Daniel Golden, "Disabled Students Gain More Aid on Tests," *Wall Street Journal,* B2 (Feb. 1, 2001) (settlement of lawsuit demanding accommodation for special education students).

19. See, e.g., David Neumark and Wendy A. Stock, "The Effects of Race and Sex Discrimination Laws," National Bureau of Economic Research, Working Paper No. 8215, at 39 (Cambridge, Mass., Apr. 2001) (numerical guidelines now affect both Title VII and affirmative action program enforcement); Eric Schnapper, "The Varieties of Numerical Remedies," 39 *Stanford Law Review* 851 (1987).

20. Personal communication with Derek Bok, President Emeritus, Harvard University (Aug. 11, 2001).

21. E.g., Iris Marion Young, *Justice and the Politics of Difference,* 193–198 (1990).

22. See text accompanying notes 240–252.

23. It is also central to Americans' views of procedural fairness. See, e.g., E. Allen Lind and Tom R. Tyler, *The Social Psychology of Procedural Justice* (1988); John Thibaut and Laurens Walker, *Procedural Justice: A Psychological Analysis* (1975).

24. Krieger, "Civil Rights Perestroika," 1291–1302.

25. See, e.g., Jacques Steinberg, "Usefulness of SAT Test Is Debated in California," *New York Times,* A11 (Nov. 17, 2001) (some schools dropping main SAT requirement); Jodi Wilgoren, "Mount Holyoke Drops SAT Requirement," *New York Times,* A28 (June 7, 2000).

26. David A. Hollinger, *Postethnic America: Beyond Multiculturalism,* 8 (1995).

27. Eduardo Porter, "Even 126 Sizes Don't Fit All," *Wall Street Journal,* B1 (Mar. 2, 2001).

28. Romer v. Evans, 517 U.S. 620 (1996) (rejecting claim that Colorado's Amendment 2 merely barred "special rights" for homosexuals).

29. Even a law that prohibits most affirmative action may leave some limited space

for using it. But see Hi-Voltage Wire Works, Inc. v. City of San Jose, 24 Cal. 4th 537, 562–568 (2000) (Proposition 209 bars "targeted outreach").

30. The authoritative study is Charles Moskos and John Sibley Butler, *All That We Can Be: Black Leadership and Racial Integration the Army Way* (1996). See also David K. Shipler, *A Country of Strangers: Blacks and Whites in America*, 532–559 (1997).

31. See, e.g., Aileen Cho, "Uneasy Path for Diversity Effort in Building Industry," *New York Times*, B6 (Apr. 8, 2001). For a detailed account of how these programs actually operated in New York, Detroit, and Atlanta during the 1990s, see Tamar Jacoby, *Someone Else's House: America's Unfinished Struggle for Integration* (1998).

32. This enthusiasm, however, appears to conceal much faculty opposition. Stephen H. Balch, "What Professors Really Think of Preferences," *NAS Update* (Dec. 1996) (indicating widespread opposition); Carl Auerbach, "The Silent Opposition of Professors and Graduate Students to Preferential Affirmative Action Programs: 1969 and 1975," 72 *Minnesota Law Review* 1233 (1988). Auerbach notes that law professors were strongly opposed to potent affirmative action for minorities in 1969 and 1975 responses to a survey by the Carnegie Commission. Only 9% of them favored strict goals and timetables for admissions, and only 7% favored such a program for faculty hiring. Id. at 1237 and note 10. A further 30% favored a less restrictive program of preferences in admissions. Id. at 1238 and note 14.

33. See, e.g., Amy Dockser Marcus, "The New Battleground over Race and Schools: Younger Students," *Wall Street Journal*, B1 (Dec. 29, 1999); "Latin Lesson," *New Republic*, 7 (Dec. 14, 1998) (Boston Latin case).

34. Sally L. Satel, "Science by Quota," *New Republic*, 14 (Feb. 27, 1995). Satel cites an NIH estimate that the new law would necessitate multiplying the size of treatment studies by "a factor of 5 to 10 with a stultifying effect on budget . . . and, paradoxically, could hamper planned investigations of racial/ethnic differences." Id.

35. Community Reinvestment Act of 1977, Pub. L. No. 95-128, 91 Stat. 1147.

36. For an account of why affirmative action got off to a slow start in federal housing programs, see Chris Bonastia, "Why Did Affirmative Action in Housing Fail during the Nixon Era? Exploring the 'Institutional Homes' of Social Policies," 47 *Social Problems* 523 (2000) (detailing bureaucratic politics as impediment).

37. This is affirmative action, but with a difference. Here, unlike in most other affirmative action domains, there is no "natural" or normatively compelling standard like merit to which one can compare the preference. Line-drawers must use some more or less arbitrary criteria to do so; the question is how much weight they may (or must) give to race. See generally Richard H. Pildes, "Principled Limitations on Racial and Partisan Redistricting," 106 *Yale Law Journal* 2505 (1997).

38. See, e.g., Samuel Issacharoff, Pamela S. Karlan, and Richard H. Pildes, *The Law of Democracy: Legal Structure of the Political Process*, 582 (1998). See also Voting Rights Act Amendments of 1982, Pub. L. No. 97-205, 96 Stat. 131.

39. The Court's latest word on this subject is Hunt v. Cromartie, 532 U.S. 234

(2001) (upholding redistricting despite lower court finding that "race, not politics" determined boundaries).

40. Charles S. Bullock III and Richard E. Dunn, "The Demise of Racial Districting and the Future of Black Representation," 48 *Emory Law Journal* 1209 (1999).

41. See, e.g., Robert Hanley, "Judges Uphold New Districts in New Jersey," *New York Times,* B1 (May 3, 2001) (upholding dismantling of majority-minority districts); Robert Pear, "Race Takes Back Seat as States Prepare to Redistrict," *New York Times,* 17 (Feb. 4, 2001). Such racial gerrymandering of legislative districts in the name of affirmative action has led some states to do likewise for jury districts. Randall Kennedy, "The Racial Rigging of Juries," *American Experiment,* 1 (Fall 1994). But see United States v. Nelson, 277 F.3d 164 (2d Cir. 2002) (reversing trial court's effort to balance jury racially).

42. In contrast, the Supreme Court, applying less than strict scrutiny, upheld an FCC preference program authorized by statute. Metro Broadcasting, Inc. v. FCC, 497 U.S. 547 (1990), overruled by Adarand Constructors, Inc. v. Pena, 515 U.S. 200 (1995) (overruling the level-of-scrutiny point).

43. Stephen Labaton and Simon Romero, "A Flawed Wireless Auction," *New York Times,* A30 (Feb. 13, 2001) (reporting that despite bidding subsidies, auction failed to attract small firms).

44. MD/DC/DE Broadcasters Assn. v. FCC, 236 F.3d 13 (D.C. Cir. 2001).

45. Labaton, "Court Rules Agency Erred on Mandate for Minorities"; Stephen Labaton, "Deregulation Called Blow to Minorities," *New York Times,* C1 (Dec. 12, 2000) (summarizing studies).

46. Stephen Labaton, "Bush Appoints Powell's Son to Lead F.C.C.," *New York Times,* C1 (Jan. 23, 2001) (reporting that Michael Powell, chairman of the FCC and Colin Powell's son, is skeptical about a link between ownership diversity and programming diversity).

47. Ian Ayres, *Pervasive Prejudice? Unconventional Evidence of Race and Gender Discrimination,* 315–395 (2001). According to Ayres, the designated bidders in the set of auctions he studied (for regional narrowband licenses in 1994) agreed to pay the government, net of the bid subsidy, $151.9 million over time at submarket interest rates. The subsidy's value is probably $60–75 million. Ayres argues, interestingly and counterintuitively, that designated bidders actually increase government auction revenue by fostering bidding competition, and that the fiscal effects of bidding subsidies could be extended to government procurement. His overall efficiency analysis, however, seems too complicated, contextual, and ultimately indeterminate to support firm policy conclusions.

48. Jonathan Rauch, "Color TV," *New Republic,* 9–10 (Dec. 19, 1994).

49. Michael Kinsley, "The Spoils of Victimhood," *The New Yorker,* 62, 69 (Mar. 27, 1995).

50. Stephen Labaton and Simon Romero, "F.C.C. Auction Hit with Claim of Unfair Bids," *New York Times,* A1 (Feb. 12, 2001) (legal challenges to this practice). The FCC auctions have also encountered other problems. NextWave Personal Communications Inc. v. FCC, 254 F.3d 130 (D.C. Cir. 2001), cert. granted, FCC v. NextWave Personal Communications Inc., 122 S. Ct. 1202 (2002).

51. See, e.g., Local 28, Sheet Metal Workers' Intl. Assn. v. EEOC, 478 U.S. 421, 481–483 (1986); Pennsylvania v. Local 542, Intl. Union of Operating Eng'rs, 619 F. Supp. 1273, 1275 and note 4 (E.D. Pa.), aff'd, 770 F.2d 1068 (3d Cir. 1985).

52. James Podgers, "New Diversity Initiatives," *American Bar Association Journal*, 97 (April 2000).

53. Michael Walzer, *Spheres of Justice*, 3–33 (1983).

54. For an exploration of this point in the context of affirmative action in higher education, see Akhil R. Amar and Neal Katyal, "*Bakke*'s Fate," 43 *UCLA Law Review* 1745 (1996).

55. The U.S. Supreme Court rejected an equal protection challenge to this system. Personnel Administrator v. Feeney, 442 U.S. 256, 279 (1979) (upholding a Massachusetts law considering veterans for state civil service ahead of non-veterans because its purpose was not to exclude women). President Franklin Roosevelt apparently opposed the preference as well but could not defeat it politically. Skrentny, *Ironies of Affirmative Action*, 41–42.

56. See, e.g., James L. Shulman and William G. Bowen, *The Game of Life* (2001). The authors calculate that in 1999 at one school in their sample, legacies had even more of an advantage than "minorities" with the same SAT scores. Id., 40–41. This was not generally true in the years covered by the Bowen-Bok study discussed later in this chapter. See text accompanying notes 81–92.

57. Including capital costs, intercollegiate sport is seldom a moneymaker, and Shulman and Bowen find that large donors generally prefer to reduce emphasis on athletics. Andrew Hacker, "The Big College Try," *New York Review of Books*, 52 (Apr. 12, 2001) (citing sources, including Shulman and Bowen).

58. See also Jim Chen, "Is Affirmative Action Fair? Diversity in a Different Dimension: Evolutionary Theory and Affirmative Action's Destiny," 59 *Ohio State Law Journal* 811, 893–894 (1998).

59. Russell Thornton, "What the Census Doesn't Count," *New York Times*, A19 (Mar. 23, 2001) (Native Americans); Eric Schmitt, "Multiracial Identification Might Affect Programs," *New York Times*, A20 (Mar. 14, 2001); Eric Schmitt, "For 7 Million People in Census, One Race Category Isn't Enough," *New York Times*, A1 (Mar. 13, 2001).

60. Peter Skerry, *Counting on the Census?: Race, Group Identity, and the Evasion of Politics*, 51–54 (2000).

61. For a full explanation, see U.S. Census Bureau, *Census 2000 Brief: Overview of Race and Hispanic Origin* (2001).

62. Quoted in Amitai Etzioni, *The Monochrome Society*, 30 (2001).

63. The census has issued different allocation rules for purposes of legislative districting and other government decisions using such demographic categories. Nathaniel Persily, "Color by Numbers: Race, Redistricting, and the 2000 Census," 85 *Minnesota Law Review* 899, 932 note 127 (2001) (brief discussion).

64. Office of Management and Budget, *Bulletin No. 00-02*, rule 2 (Mar. 2000). It is not clear whether the Bush administration will retain these rules.

65. Eric Schmitt, "Census Data Show a Sharp Increase in Living Standard," *New York Times*, A1 (Aug. 6, 2001).

66. Steven A. Holmes, "The Confusion over Who We Are," *New York Times,* WK1 (June 3, 2001) (discussing National Health Interview Survey data).

67. Gallup poll (Sept. 1, 2000), available at *http://www.gallup.com/poll/fromtheed/ ed0009.asp.*

68. For an exploration of the implications of multiracialism, see Rachel F. Moran, *Interracial Intimacy: The Regulation of Race and Romance,* 154–178 (2001).

69. Kenneth Prewitt, "Demography, Diversity, and Democracy: The 2000 Census Story," *Brookings Review* 6, 9 (Winter 2002). The color-coding in Brazil, which is proposing to create racial quotas for universities, civil service jobs, and other areas, is likely to be far more complex and perhaps unworkable. Larry Rohter, "Multiracial Brazil Planning Quotas for Blacks," *New York Times,* A3 (Oct. 2, 2001) (over 300 terms for different skin colors and more elastic racial categories).

70. Etzioni, *The Monochrome Society,* 26–27.

71. See, e.g., Persily, "Color by Numbers." But see Joshua R. Goldstein and Ann J. Morning, "Back in the Box: The Dilemma of Using Multiple-Race Data for Single-Race Laws" (Mar. 9, 2001) (unpublished manuscript, Office of Population Research, Princeton University) (noting that allocation rule will disadvantage Asian-Americans and reassign many who traditionally self-identified as white).

72. On racial profiling, see Peter H. Schuck, "A Case for Profiling," *American Lawyer,* 59 (Jan. 2002); Samuel R. Gross and Debra Livingston, "Racial Profiling under Attack," 102 *Columbia Law Review* 1413 (2002).

73. Gregory Rodriguez, "When Perception Is Reality," *New York Times,* WK1 (June 3, 2001) (quoting Margo J. Schlanger).

74. Id.

75. The phrase was popularized by Justice Blackmun. Regents of University of California v. Bakke, 438 U.S. 265, 407 (1978) (Blackmun, J., concurring in judgment and dissenting in part).

76. See, e.g., Issacharoff, "Can Affirmative Action Be Defended?" 690.

77. See, e.g., Paul M. Sniderman and Edward G. Carmines, *Reaching beyond Race,* 23–27 (1997) (discussing "Two Meanings Experiment"). But see Martin Gilens, Paul M. Sniderman, and James H. Kuklinski, "Affirmative Action and the Politics of Realignment," 28 *British Journal of Political Science* 159, 167 (1998) (finding that over 37% oppose affirmative action even in its milder, extra outreach forms).

78. Issacharoff, "Can Affirmative Action Be Defended?" 675–676 (discussing effect on debate at University of Texas).

79. This point has been made by a number of commentators, including Malamud, "Race, Culture, and the Law."

80. See text accompanying notes 319–338 ("The Resegregation Nightmare").

81. William G. Bowen and Derek Bok, *The Shape of the River: Long-Term Consequences of Considering Race in College and University Admissions* (1998).

82. Id., 15; see also Thomas J. Kane, "Racial and Ethnic Preferences in College Admissions," in *The Black-White Test Score Gap,* 431, 436 (Christopher Jencks and Meredith Phillips, eds., 1998) (in a sample of 36,000 high school students from

1,000 high schools, over 90% who applied to colleges in the bottom three-fifths were admitted).

83. Robert Lerner and Althea K. Nagai, *Pervasive Preferences: Racial and Ethnic Discrimination in Undergraduate Admissions across the Nation* (Center for Equal Opportunity, 2001) (study of forty-seven public colleges and universities).

84. For one thing, we do not know the test scores of the white and Asian-American students in the Bowen-Bok sample who would have been admitted in place of the blacks who were admitted because of preferences. For another, Bowen and Bok only had adequate test-score data for five of the twenty-eight institutions, though they believe that these are roughly representative of the larger group.

85. Kane, "Racial and Ethnic Preferences," 431–432.

86. For discussion and citations, see Terrance Sandalow, "Minority Preferences Reconsidered," 97 *Michigan Law Review* 1874, 1877 and note 4 (1997). This fact is also acknowledged by Nathan Glazer, "The Case for Racial Preferences," *Public Interest*, 45, 57 (Spring 1999), who is a prominent advocate of affirmative action for blacks.

87. Sandalow, "Minority Preferences Reconsidered," 1880–1881 (citing to Bowen and Bok, *The Shape of the River*).

88. Bowen and Bok, *The Shape of the River*, 27.

89. Gratz v. Bollinger, 135 F. Supp. 2d 790 (E.D. Mich. 2001), cert. granted 123 S. Ct. 602 (2002).

90. Elizabeth S. Anderson, "From Normative to Empirical Sociology in the Affirmative Action Debate: Bowen and Bok's *The Shape of the River*," 50 *Journal of Legal Education* 284, 287 (2000).

91. Lerner and Nagai, *Pervasive Preferences*, figure 5.

92. For discussion of these issues, compare Richard O. Lempert et al., "Michigan's Minority Graduates in Practice: The River Runs through Law School," 25 *Law and Social Inquiry* 395 (2000), with Richard Sander, "The Tributaries to the River," 25 *Law and Social Inquiry* 557 (2000), and Richard O. Lempert et al., "Michigan's Minority Graduates in Practice: Answers to Methodological Queries," 25 *Law and Social Inquiry* 585 (2000).

93. Sandalow, "Minority Preferences Reconsidered," 1891–1894 (reviewing Linda F. Wightman, "The Threat to Diversity in Legal Education: An Empirical Analysis of the Consequences of Abandoning Race as a Factor in Law School Admissions Decisions," 72 *New York University Law Review* 1 (1997)).

94. Sandalow, "Minority Preferences Reconsidered," 1895–1896 (reviewing Linda F. Wightman, "LSAC National Longitudinal Bar Passage Study," *Law School Admission Council Research Report Series* (1998)). Some of this difference reflects greater persistence in whites taking the examination over and over.

95. See, e.g., Anderson, "From Normative to Empirical Sociology," 286–287; Lempert et al., "Methodological Queries," 586.

96. Bowen and Bok, *The Shape of the River*, 37 (citing Wightman study of law school admissions).

97. Lempert et al., "Law School," 401.

98. Sander, "The Tributaries to the River," 562; see also id. at 561.

99. See, e.g., Issacharoff, "Can Affirmative Action Be Defended?" 675–676.

100. See text accompanying notes 292–318 ("The Incidence and Distribution of Costs").

101. Stanley Fish, *The Trouble with Principle*, 32 (1999).

102. Patterson, *The Ordeal of Integration*, 147–169.

103. Nathan Glazer, "In Defense of Preference," *New Republic*, 18 (Apr. 6, 1998). See also text accompanying notes 104–106.

104. E.g., Boris I. Bittker, *The Case for Black Reparations* (1993).

105. For an exploration of the need principle, see Walzer, *Spheres of Justice*, 25–26.

106. In Gratz v. Bollinger, 135 F. Supp. 2d 790, 796–801 (E.D. Mich. 2001), for example, a white applicant who was rejected by the University of Michigan challenged its preferential admissions policy. Although the university seemed to concede that it has been "a passive participant" in past subordination, id. at 801, the court found no evidence of this. The Supreme Court is reviewing this decision.

107. See, e.g., Stephanie Wildman et al., *Privilege Revealed: How Invisible Preference Undermines America* (1996); Frances Lee Ansley, "Stirring the Ashes: Race, Class, and the Future of Civil Rights Scholarship," 74 *Cornell Law Review* 993, 1005–1023 (1989); compare Thomas Ross, "Innocence and Affirmative Action," 43 *Vanderbilt Law Review* 297 (1990) (describing "rhetoric of innocence" used by whites claiming to be victims of affirmative action).

108. To cite just one of many complications, evidence suggests that discrimination against a group, while damaging in the short run, often strengthens its economic and perhaps social positions in the long run. Peter H. Schuck, *Citizens, Strangers, and In-Betweens: Essays on Immigration and Citizenship*, 273–275 (1998) (reviewing evidence cited by Thomas Sowell).

109. Hugh Davis Graham, *Collision Course: The Strange Convergence of Affirmative Action and Immigration Policy in America*, 2 (2002) (drawing on James S. Robb, *Affirmative Action for Immigrants: The Entitlement Nobody Wanted* (1995)). Peter Schrag estimated that more than 75% of the post-1965 immigrants immediately qualified for affirmative action benefits. Schrag, "So You Want to Be Color-Blind: Alternative Principles for Affirmative Action," *American Prospect*, 41 (Summer 1995).

110. See, e.g., Fullilove v. Klutznick, 448 U.S. 448 (1980); Franks v. Bowman Transportation Co., 424 U.S. 747, 777 (1976) (when effectuating a properly tailored remedy to cure effects of prior discrimination, "a sharing of the burden" by innocent parties is permissible). For more recent decisions by the Court that strictly limit the scope and nature of the discrimination that affirmative action may remedy, see Adarand Constructors, Inc. v. Pena, 515 U.S. 200 (1995); City of Richmond v. J. A. Croson Co., 488 U.S. 469 (1989); United States v. Paradise, 480 U.S. 149 (1987).

111. See, e.g., Issacharoff, "Can Affirmative Action Be Defended?" 681–682.

112. See, e.g., Young, *Justice and the Politics of Difference*, esp. 192–225.

113. Nicholas Lemann, *The Big Test*, 345 (1999).

114. Fish, *The Trouble with Principle*, 30.

115. See, e.g., Patterson, *The Ordeal of Integration*, 155–165.

116. Sandalow, "Minority Preferences Reconsidered," 1914 (quoting Richard Delgado). Some critics of this radical challenge to the merit principle view it as

thinly veiled anti-Semitism. See, e.g., Daniel A. Farber and Suzanna Sherry, *Beyond All Reason: The Radical Assault on Truth in American Law*, 52–71 (1997). For a thoughtful review of this position, see Edward L. Rubin, "Jews, Truth, and Critical Race Theory," 93 *Northwestern University Law Review* 525 (1999).

117. Ronald Dworkin, *Sovereign Virtue: The Theory and Practice of Equality*, 327 (2000).

118. See, e.g., Glenn C. Loury, *One by One from the Inside Out: Essays and Reviews on Race and Responsibility in America* (1995); Shipler, *A Country of Strangers*, 506.

119. Kinsley, "The Spoils of Victimhood," 65 ("Republicans, who were slow to approach the C.B.E.O. [color-blind equal opportunity principle] in the 1960s, have often charged past it in the years since. If color blindness is a virtue, hypocrisy is in this case the tribute virtue pays to vice").

120. Jeffrey Rosen, "Without Merit," *New Republic*, 20 (May 14, 2001).

121. See, e.g., John Feinstein, *The Last Amateurs: Playing for Glory and Honor in Division I College Basketball* (2000) (neglect of academics in college basketball programs); Shulman and Bowen, *The Game of Life*; Robert Lipsyte, "Backtalk: The Devil and an Angel Envision a Revolution in College Sports," *New York Times*, 11 (Feb. 4, 2001) (effort of beleaguered female professor at University of Tennessee to curb academic abuses by scholar-athletes and athletic department).

122. See, e.g., John H. McWhorter, *Losing the Race: Self-Sabotage in Black America* (2000) (recounting personal experiences).

123. George A. Akerlof, "The Market for 'Lemons': Quality Uncertainty and the Market Mechanism," 84 *Quarterly Journal of Economics* 488 (1970).

124. See, e.g., Sander, "The Tributaries to the River," 561 (example of law graduates).

125. Fish, *The Trouble with Principle*, 32–33.

126. See, e.g., Philip A. Klinkner and Rogers M. Smith, *The Unsteady March: The Rise and Decline of Racial Equality in America* (1999); Cass R. Sunstein, *Designing Democracy*, 177–182 (2001); Bryan K. Fair, "Review Essay: America's Equality Promise—Where Do We Go from Here?," 19 *Journal of American Ethnic History* 94, 96 (2000); Owen M. Fiss, "Groups and the Equal Protection Clause," 5 *Philosophy and Public Affairs* 107 (1976); Jed Rubenfeld, "Affirmative Action," 107 *Yale Law Journal* 427, 456 (1997).

127. See, e.g., Elizabeth S. Anderson, "Integration, Affirmative Action, and Strict Scrutiny," 77 *New York University Law Review* 1195 (2002).

128. Chang-Lin Tien, "Diversity and Excellence in Higher Education," in *Debating Affirmative Action*, 237, 239 (Nicolaus Mills, ed., 1994).

129. Amar and Katyal, "*Bakke*'s Fate," 1779 (quoting Kenneth Karst).

130. Patterson, *The Ordeal of Integration*, 161–162.

131. Martin Duberman, "The 'New' (1997) Scholarship on Race Relations," in *Left Out: Politics of Exclusions—Essays/1964–1999*, at 369, 385 (1999).

132. Regents of University of California v. Bakke, 438 U.S. 265, 407 (1978) (Blackmun, J., concurring in judgment and dissenting in part).

133. See note 5.

134. Patterson, *The Ordeal of Integration*, 65–66.

135. Jack Citrin, "Affirmative Action in the People's Court," *Public Interest*, 39, 48 (Winter 1996).

136. Affirmative action's political origins are discussed in the text accompanying notes 235–239. For a much fuller account, see Skrentny, *Ironies of Affirmative Action*.

137. See, e.g., Deborah C. Malamud, "Affirmative Action, Diversity, and the Black Middle Class," 68 *University of Colorado Law Review* 939, 953 (1997).

138. Patterson details this progress, *The Ordeal of Integration*, 17–51, although he still favors continuing affirmative action for fifteen years, then to be transformed into class-based programs, id. at 147–169. I discuss this further in the text accompanying notes 361–364 ("Time Limits"). See also Stephan Thernstrom and Abigail Thernstrom, *America in Black and White: One Nation, Indivisible*, 183–202 (1997).

139. See, e.g., Thomas Sowell, *Migrations and Cultures: A World View* (1996). I have explored some of the complexities of this comparison. See Peter H. Schuck, "Reflections on the Effects of Immigrants on African Americans—and Vice Versa," in Daniel S. Hamermesh and Frank D. Bean, eds., *Help or Hindrance? The Economic Implications of Immigration for African Americans*, 361–363 (1998).

140. See, e.g., Patterson, *The Ordeal of Integration*, 147–203.

141. Robert William Fogel, *The Fourth Great Awakening and the Future of Egalitarianism* (2000).

142. Sunstein, *Designing Democracy*, 181.

143. For a recent review of these inequalities, see Angela Glover-Blackwell, Stewart Kwoh, and Manuel Pastor, *Searching for the Uncommon Ground: New Dimensions on Race in America* (2002).

144. See, e.g., text accompanying notes 103–106, 126–131.

145. Christopher Lasch, for example, opposes affirmative action because, among other reasons, it would strengthen the dominant position of the middle class, further estranging it from lower-income people. Christopher Lasch, *The Revolt of the Elites and the Betrayal of Democracy*, 79, 137 (1995).

146. Bowen and Bok, *The Shape of the River*, 116.

147. The Bowen-Bok data do reveal a substantial, persistent, and unexplained earnings gap between white and black male graduates of the sampled institutions, though not for females. See also Sandalow, "Minority Preferences Reconsidered," 1908–1910 (discussing possible explanations). And some studies do find performance differentials. See, e.g., John R. Lott, "Does a Helping Hand Put Others at Risk? Affirmative Action, Police Departments, and Crime," 38 *Economic Inquiry* 239 (2000). On the other hand, a study of Michigan Law School's white and minority graduates shows their earnings, arguably a proxy for performance, to be quite comparable. Lempert et al., "Law School," 447–453. But see Sander, "The Tributaries to the River" (discussing response rate, cohort, aggregation, and other methodological considerations).

148. Issacharoff, "Can Affirmative Action Be Defended?" 684–688.

149. As Sandalow puts it, "It is entirely predictable . . . that African-American students at those institutions will, in their later lives, be actively involved in civic or-

ganizations. The importance of attending a selective college lies elsewhere, not in leading students to engage in civic activities, but in enhancing the quality of their efforts." Sandalow, "Minority Preferences Reconsidered," 1909–1910.

150. Bowen and Bok, *The Shape of the River,* 48–49. Stephan and Abigail Thernstrom question the causal assumption of the leadership cadre rationale. Rather than these schools creating a black middle class, they say, the black middle class sends its children to these schools. Thernstrom and Thernstrom, *America in Black and White;* see also Stephan Thernstrom and Abigail Thernstrom, "Racial Preferences: What We Now Know," 107 *Commentary* 44, 44–50 (1999) (reviewing the Bowen-Bok study).

151. Lerner and Nagai, *Pervasive Preferences.* Some of these other institutions, it now appears, also use preferences. Id.

152. Thernstrom and Thernstrom, "Racial Preferences," 49. These colleges educate 15% of black college students and produce 30% of all black graduates. Darien A. McWhirter, *The End of Affirmative Action,* 150 (1996). For an argument that these institutions may now be unconstitutional, see Mark Strasser, "*Plessy, Brown* and HBCUs: On the Imposition of Stigma and the Court's Mechanical Equal Protection Jurisprudence," 40 *Washburn Law Journal* 48 (2000).

153. Diana Jean Schemo, "Black Colleges Lobby Hard to Lure the Best and Brightest," *New York Times,* A10 (Mar. 8, 2001).

154. See, e.g., Jack Citrin, "Scores Do Measure Talent, Berkeley Professor Insists," *San Jose Mercury News* (Mar. 4, 2001); see text accompanying note 332.

155. See, e.g., Stewart Schwab, "Is Statistical Discrimination Efficient?" 76 *American Economic Review* 228 (1986).

156. Issacharoff, "Can Affirmative Action Be Defended?" 682.

157. See text accompanying notes 365–389 ("Voluntary Programs").

158. Issacharoff, "Can Affirmative Action Be Defended?" 690–692.

159. See, e.g., Sanford Levinson, "Diversity," 2 *University of Pennsylvania Journal of Constitutional Law* 573, 577–578 (2000); Rubenfeld, "Affirmative Action," 471.

160. For this reason, some have seen the diversity rationale as a diversion from the anticaste project. See, e.g., Barbara Phillips Sullivan, "The Gift of *Hopwood:* Diversity and the Fife and Drum March Back to the Nineteenth Century," 34 *Georgia Law Review* 291, 298 (1999).

161. Samuel Issacharoff, "Law and Misdirection in the Debate over Affirmative Action," 2002 *University of Chicago Legal Forum* 11.

162. California's Proposition 209, passed in the November 1996 election, dismantled affirmative action in public education and public employment; Washington State's Proposition 200, passed in the November 1998 election, yielded a similar outcome.

163. Terrance Sandalow observes that "the importance of racial diversity in the educational process has become something of a mantra in higher education circles in the years since Justice Powell's pivotal opinion in *Bakke.*" Sandalow, "Minority Preferences Reconsidered," 1905. Sanford Levinson likens this to a game of "Simon Says" in which the Court tells the players that "Simon says, 'Start talking

about diversity—and downplay any talk about rectification of past social injustice.'" Levinson, "Diversity," 578.

164. Regents of University of California v. Bakke, 438 U.S. 265, 311–313 (1978) (Powell, J., concurring in result) (quoting Sweezy v. New Hampshire, 354 U.S. 234, 263 (1957)). As Issacharoff points out, Powell's discussion of diversity was abstract, as it was not an issue in *Bakke*. Issacharoff, "Can Affirmative Action Be Defended?" 677. The Supreme Court had alluded to the benefits of diversity in higher education long before *Bakke*, though not in so many words, not as a rationale for affirmative action, and only as to how blacks would benefit from being with whites, not the reverse. Sweatt v. Painter, 339 U.S. 629, 634 (1950); McLaurin v. Oklahoma State Regents, 339 U.S. 637, 641 (1950). For an argument that Powell's diversity rationale did not command majority support among the Justices, see Thomas E. Wood and Malcolm J. Sherman, "Race and Higher Education: Why Justice Powell's Diversity Rationale for Racial Preferences in Higher Education Must Be Rejected, Part I," *http://www.nas.org/rhe.pdf* (May 2001).

165. Michael Selmi, "The Facts of Affirmative Action," 85 *Virginia Law Review* 697, 729 (1999) (reviewing Bowen and Bok, *The Shape of the River*).

166. Id., 733; see also id. at 729 notes 152–153 (citing sources). As Michael S. Greve, an opponent of affirmative action, notes of the successful challenge to the University of Texas Law School's preferential admissions system, "if the Law School with its notorious past cannot rely on historical discrimination as a predicate for preferential admissions, then no institution of higher learning . . . can rely on a remedial rationale for affirmative action." Greve, "*Hopwood* and Its Consequences," 17 *Pace Law Review* 1, 6 (1996).

167. See, e.g., Sheila Foster, "Difference and Equality: A Critical Assessment of the Concept of 'Diversity,'" 1993 *Wisconsin Law Review* 105, 107; Ronald Dworkin, "Race and the Uses of Law," *New York Times*, A17 (Apr. 13, 2001).

168. Eugene Volokh, "Diversity, Race as Proxy, and Religion as Proxy," 43 *UCLA Law Review* 2059, 2060 (1996).

169. Quoted in Chen, "Is Affirmative Action Fair?" 815.

170. Malamud, "Affirmative Action, Diversity, and the Black Middle Class," 953 ("[The] diversity rationale makes it unnecessary to answer the hardest question about . . . affirmative action: the question of when it is time to stop").

171. Kenneth L. Karst, *Law's Promise, Law's Expression: Visions of Power in the Politics of Race, Gender, and Religion*, 105–107 (1993) (emphasizing "enacted narrative" of "doing things together over a period of time").

172. See, e.g., Karl Zinsmeister, "The Shame of America's One-Party Campuses," *The American Enterprise*, 18–25 (Sept. 2002). Based on a 1993–1994 survey of 710 law faculty at the top 100 law schools and the AALS data from 1996–1997, 80% of law faculty are Democratic or lean Democratic (compared with 46% of the working population). Although about 15% of full-time working women are Republicans, only 0.5% of women law professors are Republicans. James Lindgren, "Measuring Diversity," table 2 (January 1, 1999) (unpublished manuscript, Northwestern University Law School). See also Center for the Study of

Popular Culture, "Political Bias in America's Universities" (Los Angeles, n.d.) (reviewing surveys and other evidence, including commencement speakers).

173. Rachel F. Moran cites two recent surveys finding that "university faculty in general, and law faculty in particular, express high levels of support for diversity and affirmative action." "Symposium on Law in the Twentieth Century: Diversity and Its Discontents—the End of Affirmative Action at Boalt Hall," 88 *California Law Review* 2241, 2267 note 137 (2000). She cites American Council on Education and American Association of University Professors, *Does Diversity Make a Difference? Three Research Studies on Diversity in College Classrooms* (2000), and Richard A. White, "Preliminary Report: Law School Faculty Views on Diversity in the Classroom and the Law School Community" (May 2000). But see Balch, "What Professors Really Think of Preferences" (indicating opposition).

174. I say few of the costs, not none. Some of their students who receive preferences are less well prepared academically and thus harder to teach. Institutions may pressure faculty not to fail minority students. In addition, affirmative action in faculty hiring and promotion introduces more conflict and tension, acknowledged or not, into relations with colleagues and students. Sandalow, "Minority Preferences Reconsidered," 1902–1905. It also bears noting that a diversity rationale for admission preferences would not necessarily justify preferences for faculty hiring and promotion. Indeed, Derek Bok, a supporter of admission preferences, opposed them in hiring and tenure decisions while Harvard University's president and in his writing. Id.

175. "Diversity value" is the sum of any of the social values associated with diversity. Diversity value should be distinguished from "value diversity," which is a domain of diversity—for example, a classroom in which students possess different values—that may best be thought of as "cultural-ideological." These concepts and distinctions are developed in Chapter 2.

176. See Chapter 2 of this book; see also Martha Minow's discussion of the "dilemma of difference" in her "The Supreme Court, 1986 Term—Foreword: Justice Engendered," 101 *Harvard Law Review* 10, 12 (1987). On equality, see Peter Westen, "The Empty Idea of Equality," 95 *Harvard Law Review* 537 (1982).

177. Foster, "Difference and Equality," at 109. For an unusually thoughtful exception, see Guido Calabresi, "Diversity in Faculty Hiring" (July 31, 1990) (unpublished manuscript, Yale University Law School).

178. Including, but by no means limited to, these: race is a spurious category; miscegenation has occurred since colonial times and is common today, producing a very large number of mixed-race individuals; even recent immigrants are included in preference programs; Hispanics are a language group, not a racial one; and Asians are a composite of many ethnic, religious, linguistic, and national origin groups with little or nothing in common with one another, and indeed histories of deep conflict.

This last, however, is not the reason why pressures are growing to exclude Asians from diversity programs. The usual grounds for doing so are that Asians are already well represented on university campuses, their average family income is relatively high, they would qualify for admission on a race-neutral basis, and giving them preferences would leave few slots left for more deserving minorities, notably blacks. Not surprisingly, these grounds are disputed by Asian groups complaining that such "model minority" stereotypes overlook the many disadvantages these groups face. See, e.g., Chris Hedges, "Fighting a Happy Image of Self-Sufficiency," *New York Times*, B2 (Mar. 6, 2001) (Asian Americans for Equality group in New York City).

179. James Lindgren, "What Groups Think: Viewpoint Diversity among Demographic Groups" (Aug. 1, 2001) (unpublished manuscript, Northwestern University Law School).

180. Volokh argues that religious preferences under a diversity rationale would be unconstitutional for the same reason he thinks racial preferences are—though the lack of religious diversity at many schools is "at least as severe as the lack of racial diversity." Volokh, "Diversity, Race as Proxy, and Religion as Proxy," 2072.

181. Hollinger, *Postethnic America*, 120.

182. See Chapter 7 of this book.

183. Indeed, Volokh contends that affirmative action that covers race while not covering religion casts doubt on the integrity of this use of the diversity rationale and thus would also be unconstitutional. Noting this conflict between the core principles of antidiscrimination law and of affirmative action law, he asks the law, "How exactly does what you praise differ from what you damn?" Volokh, "Diversity, Race as Proxy, and Religion as Proxy," 2076.

184. James Lindgren's survey of law professors during the 1990s indicates that nearly 27% were Jewish, and another 26% professed no religion, compared with 2% and 8%, respectively, in the full-time working population. Protestants accounted for 32% and Catholics for 14%, compared with 60% and 26%, respectively, in the full-time working population. Lindgren, "Measuring Diversity."

185. Some argue that because test-score differences between religious groups are not as great as between racial ones, affirmative action for the former is unnecessary to assure diversity; it will take care of itself. E-mail from Nathan Glazer to author (Aug. 24, 2001). But even if this were true as to students, it cannot explain why university employment preferences, particularly in faculty hiring, show no interest in religious diversity.

186. Levinson, "Diversity," 603 note 120.

187. Hollinger, *Postethnic America*, 177–178.

188. Amar and Katyal see the need for a "critical mass." "*Bakke*'s Fate," 1777. See also Chen, "Is Affirmative Action Fair?" 883–884 (justification of "comfort level" for minority students "conflates diversity with the distinct and doctrinally unsound role model rationale").

189. See, e.g., Chen, "Is Affirmative Action Fair?" 825–826 (reviewing the case law).

190. See, e.g., Christopher A. Ford, "Administering Identity: The Determination of 'Race' in Race-Conscious Law," 82 *California Law Review* 1231 (1994); Levinson, "Diversity," 599–601.

191. Compare, e.g., the majority and dissenting opinions in Grutter v. Bollinger, 288 F.3d 732 (6th Cir. 2002). For my criticism of *Grutter*, now before the Supreme Court, see Peter H. Schuck, "Diversity Dodge," *The American Lawyer*, 75 (July 2002).

192. *Grutter,* 288 F.3d 732. This issue is also analyzed in Johnson v. Board of Regents of the University of Georgia, 263 F.3d 1234 (11th Cir. 2001).

193. Regents of University of California v. Bakke, 438 U.S. 265, 315–318 (1978). This emphasis on "the whole person," with race merely one consideration among many, is echoed by some commentators sympathetic to affirmative action. See, e.g., Amar and Katyal, "*Bakke*'s Fate," 1772–1773.

194. Some programs purport to do so. Tien, "Diversity and Excellence," 243–244 (stating that Berkeley's admissions policy "assures that our doors are open to low-income, older, immigrant, disabled, special talent," and geographically diverse students).

195. *Bakke,* 438 U.S. at 316–317, 322–323.

196. For a careful—but for the reasons presented here and others, unconvincing—argument that affirmative action in higher education meets the strict scrutiny test, see Goodwin Liu, "The Diversity Rationale as a Compelling Interest," 33 *Harvard Civil Rights-Civil Liberties Law Review* 381 (1998).

197. Adarand Constructors v. Pena, 515 U.S. 200 (1995) (overruling Metro Broadcasting, Inc. v. FCC, 497 U.S. 547 (1990), for failing to apply strict scrutiny). Some commentators doubt that this decision, which dealt with minority set-asides in government contracting, should apply to higher education. See, e.g., Amar and Katyal, "*Bakke*'s Fate," 1746–1749. The Court has been more deferential to preferences favoring Native Americans, viewing them not as racial but as political due to tribal sovereignty. Morton v. Mancari, 417 U.S. 535, 554 (1974). See also Ellen D. Katz, "Race and the Right to Vote after *Rice v. Cateyano,*" 99 *Michigan Law Review* 491 (2000).

198. Kirk Kennedy, "Race-Exclusive Scholarships: Constitutional Vel Non," 30 *Wake Forest Law Review* 759, 774 (1995); see also McWhirter, *The End of Affirmative Action,* 152.

199. See, e.g., Issacharoff, "Can Affirmative Action Be Defended?" 678–679 (describing the process at the University of Texas).

200. Not everywhere. According to Bowen and Bok, America's most selective institutions reject about 25% of black applicants with SAT scores between 1400 and 1500. Bowen and Bok, *The Shape of the River,* 27.

201. "All" may be too strong. If only a small percentage of a group's members lack the desired quality, it may still be worthwhile to confer the benefit on all members in order to avoid the administrative costs of identifying the few who lack it.

202. Volokh, "Diversity, Race as Proxy, and Religion as Proxy," 2062.

203. Hollinger, *Postethnic America,* 32. For a lively and passionate development of this idea, see Jim Sleeper, *Liberal Racism,* 1–21 (1997).

204. E. John Gregory, "Dunwoody Commentary: Diversity Is a Value in American Higher Education, but It Is Not a Legal Justification for Affirmative Action," 52 *Florida Law Review* 929, 950 (2000). For my views on profiling, see Peter H. Schuck, "A Case for Profiling," *American Lawyer,* 59 (Jan. 2002).

205. Anthony T. Kronman, "Is Diversity a Value in American Higher Education?" 52 *Florida Law Review* 861 (2000).

206. See, e.g., Amar and Katyal, "*Bakke*'s Fate," 1773–1776 (but insisting that pro-

grams meet certain other criteria); Paul Brest and Miranda Oshige, "Affirmative Action for Whom?" 47 *Stanford Law Review* 855, 862 (1995).

207. Levinson, "Diversity," 577.
208. Id., 592–608.
209. Selmi, "The Facts of Affirmative Action," 725.
210. The evidence is summarized in Selmi, id. at 724 note 141.
211. Bowen and Bok, *The Shape of the River,* 236; see also id. at 220–227, 231–240.
212. For a development of this argument with respect to workers, see Cynthia L. Estlund, "The Workplace in a Racially Diverse Society: Preliminary Thoughts on the Role of Labor and Employment Law," 1 *University of Pennsylvania Journal of Labor and Employment Law* 49 (1998).
213. Expert Report of Patricia Gurin, at *http://www.umich.edu/~urel/admissions/ legal/expert/gurintoc.html* (last updated Oct. 2001).
214. Wood and Sherman, "Race and Higher Education," part IV.
215. Thernstrom and Thernstrom, *America in Black and White,* 386–492.
216. Thernstrom and Thernstrom, "Racial Preferences," 47; see also Patterson, *The Ordeal of Integration,* 45 (57% of blacks claimed to have a good Euro-American friend "to whom they felt they could really say anything they thought"). Patterson emphasizes that workplace contacts matter more to friendships than neighborhood ones, noting a recent study in "hypersegregated Detroit" finding "a level of personal friendships with people from the other group that was wholly inconsistent with the dismal accounts of hypersegregation being reported by spatially oriented scholars." Id. at 44–46.
217. Thernstrom and Thernstrom, "Racial Preferences," 47.
218. See, e.g., D'Vera Cohn and Ellen Nakashima, "Crossing Racial Lines," *Washington Post,* A1 (Dec. 13, 1995) (newspaper poll indicating that more than three-quarters of Washington-area 12- to 17-year-olds say they have a close friend of another race); Corey Takahashi, "Selling to Gen Y: A Far Cry from Betty Crocker," *New York Times,* WK3 (Apr. 8, 2001) (in 1997, 57% of teens who dated said they had dated interracially and another 30% had no objection to doing so). But see Gary Orfield and Dean Whitla, "Diversity and Legal Education: Student Experiences in Leading Law Schools," *http://www.law.harvard .edu/groups/civilrights/publications/lawsurvey.html* (The Civil Rights Project, Harvard University, Aug. 1999) (blacks and Hispanics admitted to elite colleges had more interracial contacts in high school than whites did).
219. Here Sandalow cites to none other than Derek Bok, when president of Harvard University. Sandalow, "Minority Preferences Reconsidered," 1906 and note 78.
220. Id., 1906–1907. If I may indulge in a personal anecdote, I once stated in a seminar discussion of affirmative action that any experienced, conscientious teacher, regardless of race, could and would get on the table any of the arguments that ought to be there, including ideas normally associated with racism or other analogous experiences not personally experienced by the teacher. One of my best students responded, "Yes, but you wouldn't say it with the same conviction or affect as one who had experienced it personally." This is a point I had to concede, as Sandalow docs: "At times, the importance of what is said depends less

upon the idea expressed than upon the identity of the speaker and the manner of expression." Id., 1907; see also Levinson, "Diversity," 596–597 (race and ethnicity may be good proxies for probability of interest and knowledge about an issue).

221. Neil Gotanda, "A Critique of 'Our Constitution Is Color-Blind,'" 44 *Stanford Law Review* 1, 64–68 (1991).

222. Mary Ann Case, "Lessons for the Future of Affirmative Action from the Past of the Religion Clauses?" *2000 Supreme Court Review* 325, 337 note 48.

223. McWhirter, *The End of Affirmative Action*, 151.

224. Sandalow, "Minority Preferences Reconsidered," 1906–1907; see also Orfield and Whitla, "Diversity and Legal Education."

225. Issacharoff, "Law and Misdirection in the Debate over Affirmative Action" (citing studies of effects of workplace diversity).

226. See, e.g., Wygant v. Jackson Board of Education, 476 U.S. 267, 315–317 (1986) (Stevens, J., dissenting).

227. Moran, "Diversity and Its Discontents," 2331–2342 (large classes, focus on abstract concepts and universal principles, intense competition, and hierarchy prevent schools from capitalizing on diversity).

228. Malamud makes the point in the workplace context: "The diverse candidates must do their jobs, be role models, and teach the rest of the workforce how the world looks from their diverse perspectives. They can never be at peace in the same way as those whose right to be on the job is socially constructed as based on their pure individual merit." "Race, Culture, and the Law," 1709. But as Derek Bok points out, we don't worry about this as to musicians, students from rural areas, and other "diversity" admissions. Personal communication (Aug. 11, 2001).

229. Bowen and Bok, *The Shape of the River*, 193–198.

230. Patterson, *The Ordeal of Integration*, 157.

231. Citrin, "Scores Do Measure Talent." This emphasis on differences in academic preparation, program, and performance, however, neglects the psychological and other factors that surely contribute to this separation. Richard Lempert, a law and society scholar at the University of Michigan and a strong advocate for affirmative action, argues that the "academic caste system" mentioned by Citrin antedated affirmative action and was not worsened by it. Personal communication (June 16, 2002).

232. Anderson, "Integration, Affirmative Action, and Strict Scrutiny." Anderson imaginatively argues that diversity, so reconceived, can satisfy the Supreme Court's "compelling interest" and "narrowly tailored" tests for strict scrutiny, which she also reconceives.

233. Robert Post, "Introduction" to *Race and Representation: Affirmative Action*, 21–24 (Robert Post and Michael Rogin, eds., 1998).

234. In a notorious recent example, Clinton v. Jones, 520 U.S. 681 (1997), events proved that the majority had vastly underestimated the potential burden on the president of private litigation.

235. See, e.g., Lemann, *The Big Test*, 161–165, 200–211, 277–283; McWhirter, *The End of Affirmative Action*; Sunita Parikh, *The Politics of Preference: Democratic*

Institutions and Affirmative Action in the United States and India (1997); Jeremy Rabkin, *Judicial Compulsions: How Public Law Distorts Public Policy* (1989); John D. Skrentny, ed., *Color Lines: Affirmative Action, Immigration, and Civil Rights Options for America* (2001); Skrentny, *Ironies of Affirmative Action;* John D. Skrentny, *The Minority Rights Revolution* (2002); Bob Zelnick, *Backfire: A Reporter's Look at Affirmative Action* (1996).

236. Peter H. Schuck, "Affirmative Action: Past, Present, and Future," 20 *Yale Law and Policy Review* 1, 46–62 (2002).

237. Civil Rights Act of 1991, Pub. L. No. 102-166, 105 Stat. 1071.

238. City of Richmond v. J. A. Croson Co., 488 U.S. 469 (1989).

239. Adarand Constructors v. Pena, 515 U.S. 200 (1995).

240. Howard Schuman, Charlotte Steeh, Lawrence Bobo, and Maria Krysan, *Racial Attitudes in America: Trends and Interpretation,* 182 (rev. ed. 1998). These authors report that, depending on question phrasing, "support has ranged from at most a third of the white public down to just a few percentage points." See also Benjamin Page and Robert Y. Shapiro, *The Rational Public: Fifty Years of Trends in Americans' Policy Preferences,* 74 (1992) (public opinion stable over time).

241. Schuman et al., *Racial Attitudes in America,* 182; this is in accord with Charlotte Steeth and Maria Krysan, "Affirmative Action and the Public, 1970–1995," 60 *Public Opinion Quarterly* 128, 132 (1996) (decline in support during mid-1990s) ("Attitudes about affirmative action policies for which we have continuous data have not shifted dramatically for whites since 1965, and, even among African Americans, they remain constant for the most part").

242. Citrin, "Affirmative Action in the People's Court," 43–44 (reviewing American National Election Studies). Other surveys find much higher levels of opposition among blacks. Stuart Taylor, Jr., "Do African-Americans Really Want Racial Preferences?" *National Journal,* Dec. 20, 2002.

243. Sniderman and Carmines, *Reaching beyond Race,* 145.

244. Id. Not all researchers agree with this interpretation. See, e.g., David O. Sears, "Symbolic Racism," in *Eliminating Racism: Profiles in Controversy, Perspectives in Social Psychology* 53 (Phyllis A. Katz and Dalmas A. Taylor, eds., 1988) (emphasizing symbolic racism); Lawrence D. Bobo, "Race, Interests, and Beliefs about Affirmative Action: Unanswered Questions and New Directions," in *Color Lines,* 91 (emphasizing interest-group conflict).

245. For thorough reviews of the methodological issues, see Schuman et al., *Racial Attitudes in America,* 58–98, and Donald R. Kinder and Lynn M. Sanders, *Divided by Color: Racial Politics and Democratic Ideals,* 163–195 (1996).

246. Nor is the simple "angry white male" story a credible explanation for this opposition. See, e.g., Sniderman and Carmines, *Reaching beyond Race,* 144–145 ("[Y]ounger men are less, not more, likely than older men to oppose it, and women are overwhelmingly opposed to it as well. Opposition to affirmative action is one-sided, intense, and remarkably invariant over time"); Gilens et al., "Affirmative Action and the Politics of Realignment." Oddly, Orlando Patterson seems to endorse this hypothesis even while emphasizing, correctly, that only 7% of whites claim to have been personally injured in any way by affirmative action. *The Ordeal of Integration,* 64. Most uncharacteristically, Patterson here joins

other affirmative action proponents in retreating to reductionist explanations of complex phenomena.

247. Sniderman and Carmines, *Reaching beyond Race,* 40–45; Sam Howe Verhovek, "In Poll, Americans Reject Means but Not Ends of Racial Diversity," *New York Times,* A1 (Dec. 14, 1997). John D. Skrentny contends that repeal of affirmative action is an issue of low salience among whites. Skrentny, "Republican Efforts to End Affirmative Action: Walking a Fine Line," in *Seeking the Center: Politics and Policymaking at the New Century,* 141–142 (Marc Landy et al., eds., 2001).

248. Skrentny, id., 163; see also id. at 161.

249. Sniderman and Carmines, *Reaching beyond Race,* 17–18.

250. Id., 141–155.

251. Jacoby, *Someone Else's House,* 432–462 (expansion of Atlanta's set-asides before and after *Croson*).

252. Nathan Glazer, *Affirmative Discrimination* (1975).

253. Peter H. Schuck, *The Limits of Law: Essays on Democratic Governance,* 91–138 (2000) (reviewing *The Politics of Regulation* (James Q. Wilson, ed., 1980)); see also Citrin, "Affirmative Action in the People's Court," 48 ("In the American political system, policies that distribute important material and psychological benefits to intense, restricted constituencies can survive and flourish despite the opposition of a majority of voters. The story of affirmative action fits this pattern").

254. See the paragraph accompanying notes 298–300.

255. Lemann, *The Big Test,* 165.

256. Even the conservative George W. Bush administration is defending a federal affirmative action program that the Supreme Court invalidated earlier as unconstitutional. Brief of Respondents Norman Mineta, Secretary of Transportation, et al., Adarand Constructors, Inc. v. Mineta, 532 U.S. 941 (2001) (grant of certiorari), available at *http://supreme.lp.findlaw.com/supreme_court/briefs/00-730/2000-0730.mer.aa.pdf* (accessed Oct. 14, 2001). The Supreme Court subsequently dismissed the writ of certiorari as improvidently granted. 534 U.S. 103 (2001) (per curiam).

257. See, e.g., Jodi Wilgoren, "Michigan: Diversity Grant for University," *New York Times,* A12 (July 13, 2001) (Ford Foundation grants $600,000 to University of Michigan to finance research to support its defense of affirmative action in the courts).

258. There, the Republicans argue and litigate in favor of mandating majority-minority districts. See, e.g., Hanley, "Judges Uphold New Districts."

259. Skrentny, "Republican Efforts to End Affirmative Action," 132–171.

260. See, e.g., Susan Welch and John Gruhl, *Affirmative Action and Minority Enrollments in Medical and Law Schools,* 153 (1998). A number of Fortune 500 firms have filed amicus briefs defending the programs in the pending University of Michigan cases. Jim Sleeper notes that Boeing, Microsoft, and other corporate giants were the major defenders of preferences in Washington State's 1998 referendum, "a fact that made some on the left wonder whether the color-coding of American identity is really so 'progressive' after all, and some on the right to

wonder whether private-sector bureaucrats can be just as stultifying as public ones." Sleeper, "Yankee Doodle Dandy," *Los Angeles Times,* July 2, 2000 (reviewing Norman Podhoretz, *My Love Affair with America* (2000)).

261. See, e.g., Bowen and Bok, *The Shape of the River,* 11–13.

262. See, e.g., Nelson Lund, "Reforming Affirmative Action in Employment: How to Restore the Law of Equal Treatment," The Heritage Foundation Committee Brief No. 17, at 8 (1995).

263. Similar reasons may have motivated Philip Morris to advocate federal regulation of tobacco. Gordon Fairclough, "Philip Morris Pushes for FDA Tobacco Regulation," *Wall Street Journal,* A2 (Apr. 11, 2001). In addition, the settlement of state suits over tobacco has created significant barriers to new competition over both cheaper and safer cigarettes.

264. See, e.g., Frederick R. Lynch, *The Diversity Machine: The Drive to Change the "White Male Workplace"* (1997); compare this to David E. Bernstein, "Color Bind," *Reason,* 69 (May 1996).

265. McWhirter, *The End of Affirmative Action,* 14.

266. See, e.g., Skrentny, "Republican Efforts to End Affirmative Action"; see also Robert K. Detlefsen, *Civil Rights under Reagan,* 136–138 (1991); Lemann, *The Big Test,* 278–279; McWhirter, *The End of Affirmative Action,* 43–44.

267. Neal Devins, "Congressional Factfinding and the Scope of Judicial Review: A Preliminary Analysis," 50 *Duke Law Journal* 1169, 1203–1205 (2001); Skrentny, *Minority Rights Revolution.*

268. Jacoby, *Someone Else's House,* 541.

269. Charles Fried, "Uneasy Preferences: Affirmative Action, in Retrospect," *The American Prospect,* 55 (Sept.-Oct. 1998).

270. See discussion at text accompanying notes 81–98.

271. Patterson, *The Ordeal of Integration,* 15. The major exception is the rising illegitimate birth rate, especially to teenagers. Id., 35–38. However, the teenage birth rate has declined slightly in recent years. Id., 36.

272. John J. Donohue III and James Heckman, "Continuous versus Episodic Change: The Impact of Civil Rights Policy on the Economic Status of Blacks," 29 *Journal of Economic Literature* 1603 (1991).

273. Neumark and Stock, "The Effects of Race and Sex Discrimination Laws."

274. See, e.g., James P. Smith and Finis R. Welch, "Black Economic Progress after Myrdal," 27 *Journal of Economic Literature* 519 (1989) (black-white wage gap closed more rapidly before than after affirmative action); Thomas Sowell, *Civil Rights: Rhetoric or Reality?* (1984) (similar).

275. On the need to distinguish the contributions of nondiscrimination and affirmative action, see Richard A. Epstein, *Forbidden Grounds: The Case against Employment Discrimination Laws,* 245–262 (1992).

276. See, e.g., Schnapper, "The Varieties of Numerical Remedies" (classifying remedies cases).

277. Farrell Bloch, *Antidiscrimination Law and Minority Employment* (1994). Like Donohue and Heckman, "Continuous versus Episodic Change," Bloch emphasizes that because existing employees are much more likely to file civil rights

complaints than people applying for jobs in the first instance, employers have an incentive to avoid hiring potentially litigious minorities. Bloch, *Antidiscrimination Law,* 88–116.

278. Harry Holzer and David Neumark, "Assessing Affirmative Action," 38 *Journal of Economic Literature* 483, 558–559 (2000) (summarizing literature).

279. See discussion at text accompanying note 150.

280. See discussion at text accompanying note 94.

281. See, e.g., U.S. General Accounting Office, *Small Business Administration: 8(A) Is Vulnerable to Program and Contractor Abuse* (1995); Edmund L. Andrews and Geraldine Fabrikant, "The Black Entrepreneur at a Firestorm's Center," *New York Times,* D1 (Feb. 10, 1995) (tax benefits for sales of cable properties to minority-owned company received by a company with significant nonminority investment); Paul M. Barrett, "Foes of Affirmative Action Target SBA's 8(a) Program," *Wall Street Journal,* B2 (Mar. 18, 1996); see also Ian Ayres, "Symposium on Affirmative Action: Narrow Tailoring," 43 *UCLA Law Review* 1781, 1823 note 113 (1996) (minority-owned broadcasters hired higher proportions of minority workers than nonminority ones; however, Ayres found little information on this trend in other fields).

282. See, e.g., Cho, "Uneasy Path for Diversity Effort" (preferences for female-owned construction and engineering firms).

283. See, e.g., U.S. General Accounting Office, *Small Business Administration;* Barrett, "Foes of Affirmative Action"; Steven A. Holmes, "What Is a Minority-Owned Business?" *New York Times,* C4 (Oct. 12, 1999) (efforts to expand definition); Dirk Johnson, "Chicago Minority Program Aids Firm Run by White Men," *New York Times,* A15 (Jan. 4, 2000); Jane Larson, "Woes Plague Program for Minorities," *Arizona Republic,* D1 (July 20, 1997).

284. But see María E. Enchautegui et al., *Do Minority-Owned Businesses Get a Fair Share of Government Contracts?* (Urban Institute, Washington, D.C., Dec. 1997), available at *http://www.urban.org/civil/civil1.htm* (reviewing post-*Croson* "disparity studies" and finding large disparity, especially absent affirmative action programs, between share of minority-owned firms and share of contracts received—but not testing for discrimination).

285. See, e.g., Cho, "Uneasy Path for Diversity Effort" (contracts to female-headed firms send "alarm bells ringing in many minority business communities").

286. Mary Anne Case's contrived analogy of ethno-racial preferences to the free exercise of religion, noted earlier, also founders on her failure to recognize that the former are zero-sum and the latter is not. Case, "Lessons for the Future," 329.

287. See, e.g., Carol M. Swain, *Black Faces, Black Interests: The Representation of African-Americans in Congress* (1993); Charles Cameron et al., "Do Majority-Minority Districts Maximize Substantive Black Representation in Congress?" 90 *American Political Science Review* 794 (1996); Bernard Grofman et al., "Drawing Effective Minority Districts: A Conceptual Framework and Some Empirical Evidence," 79 *North Carolina Law Review* 1383 (2001). Indeed, as white voters increasingly support moderate black candidates, such candidates are also being elected from majority-white districts. See, e.g., David Grann, "Close Races," *New Republic,* 11 (Mar. 9, 1998); Robert Hanley, "Expert Backs New Districts

as Unbiased," *New York Times*, B5 (May 2, 2001) (giving examples); Fred Siegel, "Fair Philly," *New Republic*, 13 (Nov. 1, 1999). For a contrary view, see, e.g., Pamela S. Karlan, "Loss and Redemption: Voting Rights at the Turn of the Century," 50 *Vanderbilt Law Review* 291 (1997).

288. David Lublin, *The Paradox of Representation: Racial Gerrymandering and Minority Interests in Congress* (1997).

289. See Chapter 6.

290. See, e.g., Will Kymlicka, *Politics in the Vernacular: Nationalism, Multiculturalism, and Citizenship*, 198 (2000).

291. See, e.g., Marc Galanter, *Competing Equalities: Law and the Backward Classes in India* (1984); Thomas Sowell, *Preferential Policies: An International Perspective* (1990); Myron Weiner, *Sons of the Soil: Migration and Ethnic Conflict in India* (1978); Sunita Parikh, "Affirmative Action, Caste, and Party Politics in Contemporary India," in *Color Lines*, 297.

292. Patterson, *The Ordeal of Integration*, 148–149.

293. Kristin Bumiller, *The Civil Rights Society*, 99–100 (1988).

294. See, e.g., Frederick R. Lynch, *Invisible Victims: White Males and the Crisis of Affirmative Action*, 51–91 (1989).

295. Bowen and Bok, *The Shape of the River*, 36.

296. Id., 33–34 (without affirmative action, blacks' chance of admission would decline from 42% to 13%; their percentage of the student body would decline from 7.1% to 2.1%).

297. For an argument that Allan Bakke was in this position and thus had no standing, see Goodwin Liu, "The Causation Fallacy: *Bakke* and the Basic Arithmetic of Selective Admissions," 100 *Michigan Law Review* 302 (2002).

298. Extrapolating from Bowen and Bok's figures, almost 2,000 more white students in the 1976 cohort would have been admitted to the schools that were studied.

299. See, e.g., Bill Ong Hing, *Making and Remaking Asian America through Immigration Policy* (1993); Charles L. McClain, Jr., *In Search of Equality: The Chinese Struggle against Discrimination in Nineteenth-Century America*, 10–11 (1994); Lucy Salyer, *Law Harsh as Tigers: Chinese Immigrants and the Shaping of Modern Immigration Law* (1995); Ronald Takaki, *Strangers from a Different Shore: A History of Asian Americans*, 85 (1989); John Hayakawa Torok, "Reconstruction and Racial Nativism: Chinese Immigration and the Debates on the Thirteenth, Fourteenth, and Fifteenth Amendments and Civil Rights Laws," 3 *Asian Law Journal* 55 (1996).

300. Chinese Exclusion Case (Chae Chan Ping v. United States), 130 U.S. 581 (1889); Korematsu v. United States, 323 U.S. 214 (1944). Neither case has been overruled; both are occasionally cited by the Court. See, e.g., Zadvydas v. Davis, 533 U.S. 678, 695 (2001) (citing Chinese Exclusion Case); Missouri v. Jenkins, 515 U.S. 70, 121 (1995) (Thomas, J., concurring) (citing *Korematsu*).

301. For experimental evidence on these feelings, see, e.g., Frederick R. Lynch, "Casualties and More Casualties: Surviving Affirmative Action (More or Less)," in *Affirmative Action: Social Justice or Reverse Discrimination?*, 90 (Francis J. Beckwith and Todd E. Jones, eds., 1997).

302. Bowen and Bok found that graduates rejected by their first-choice schools were

as supportive of diversity efforts as those who were admitted. *The Shape of the River,* 251–252. On the other hand, almost all applicants to selective schools apply to a large number of them and presumably do not expect to get into their first choices (commonly called a "reach") anyway.

303. See generally Schuck, *The Limits of Law,* 419–479. Despite methodological and interpretive difficulties, some researchers have studied the effects, if any, of affirmative action on behaviors in "micro" policy contexts. Results are mixed. See, e.g., Brandice J. Canes and Harvey S. Rosen, "Following in Her Footsteps: Women's Choices of College Majors and Faculty Gender Composition," 48 *Industrial and Labor Relations Review* 486 (1995) (adding more female role models to three faculties had no effect on gender composition of undergraduate majors); Lott, "Does a Helping Hand Put Others at Risk?" (increasing black and minority police officers increased crime rates, especially in heavily black neighborhoods, by lower hiring standards for both minority and nonminority officers; no effect found with female recruits); C. J. Chivers, "From Court Order to Reality: A Diverse Boston Police Force," *New York Times,* A1 (Apr. 4, 2001) (positive effects on policing); Barbara Whitaker, "When California Lights Dim; Utilities' Turmoil Also Hits Program That Aids Concerns Owned by Women and Minorities," *New York Times,* C1 (Feb. 28, 2001) (describing "Women, Minority, and Disabled Veterans Business Enterprises Program for Public Utilities" as a "national model for minority contracting efforts" but also an example of the perils of dependence on particular revenue sources).

304. See generally Bowen and Bok, *The Shape of the River,* 258–259; Thernstrom and Thernstrom, *America in Black and White,* 405–412; Sandalow, "Minority Preferences Reconsidered," 1884–1891. Although the former chancellor of the University of California at Berkeley claims that it is a "myth" that students admitted under affirmative action do not succeed academically, his own figures from his own campus belie this claim: the five-year graduation rate for blacks was 46%, for Chicanos 56%, for Latinos 59%, for Filipinos 63%, for whites 76%, and for non-Filipino Asians 78%. Tien, "Diversity and Excellence," 245.

305. Shelby Steele, "Affirmative Action Must Go," *New York Times,* A19 (Mar. 1, 1995) (arguing that opponents of affirmative action can gain moral authority by criminalizing discrimination).

306. See, e.g., Shelby Steele, *The Content of Our Character* (1990); see also Missouri v. Jenkins, 515 U.S. 70, 122 (1995) (Thomas, J., concurring) ("'Racial isolation' itself is not a harm; only state-enforced segregation is. After all, if separation itself is a harm, and if integration therefore is the only way that blacks can receive a proper education, then there must be something inferior about blacks. Under this theory, segregation injures blacks because blacks, when left on their own, cannot achieve. To my way of thinking, that conclusion is the result of a jurisprudence based upon a theory of black inferiority"); Alex M. Johnson, "Bid Whist, Tonk, and *United States v. Fordice:* Why Integrationism Fails African-Americans Again," 81 *California Law Review* 1401 (1993). See text accompanying notes 122–125.

307. Even so, many of their frontline shock troops may be having second thoughts. One survey of professors suggests that they reject group preferences by over-

whelming margins. Balch, "What Professors Really Think of Preferences," 2. Competitive trends at the elite schools may also reduce the schools' enthusiasm for preferences. As one economist said in 1997, "if affirmative action raised hackles in the 1980's and 1990's, watch what happens when a third more students are competing for the same number of places in class." Peter Passell, "Economic Scene," *New York Times,* D2 (May 1, 1997).

308. On the importance of corporate support for affirmative action, see discussion at text accompanying notes 260–265. See also Judith H. Dobrzynski, "Some Action, Little Talk," *New York Times,* D1 (Apr. 20, 1995) (noting that executives prefer a low-key, behind-the-scenes approach).

309. Steinberg, "Usefulness of SAT Test."

310. Lexington, "Disabling the National Education Defence System," *The Economist,* 36 (Feb. 24, 2001).

311. The achievement tests, after all, were devised to enable colleges to compare applicants from high schools with extraordinarily diverse programs, standards, and student bodies. Under pressure by the many groups that hope for more minority admissions, the tests have often been revised in order to minimize their supposed cultural and other biases. See generally Lemann, *The Big Test.*

312. For examples, see Zelnick, *Backfire,* 107–118 (police and fire departments).

313. See, e.g., G. Kindrow, "The Candidate: Inside One Affirmative Action Search," in *Debating Affirmative Action,* 140; Lynch, *The Diversity Machine,* 51–82; Issacharoff, "Can Affirmative Action Be Defended?" 675 note 14 (attorney general of Texas falsely denied preferences' role even though law school had admitted it). See also Jacques Steinberg, "Using Synonyms for Race, College Strives for Diversity," *New York Times,* p. 1 (Dec. 8, 2002) (evasions by Rice University).

314. See text accompanying notes 321–322.

315. Glazer, "The Case for Racial Preferences," 59 (quoting Bowen and Bok's statement that stigmatization helps explain institutions' reluctance to discuss the degree of preference given black students).

316. For a careful review of the psychological evidence, see Krieger, "Civil Rights Perestroika." For more anecdotal evidence, see, e.g., Lynch, *The Diversity Machine* and *Invisible Victims.*

317. See text accompanying note 125.

318. Patterson, *The Ordeal of Integration,* 2–4.

319. Welch and Gruhl, *Affirmative Action and Minority Enrollments.*

320. Marta Tienda, "College Admission Policies and the Educational Pipeline: Implications for Medical and Health Professions," in *The Right Thing to Do, the Smart Thing to Do: Enhancing Diversity in Health Professions,* 117, 128–129 (Brian D. Smedley et al., eds., 2001). See also Jim Yardley, "The 10 Percent Solution," *New York Times Education Life,* 26 (Apr. 14, 2002) (more low-income students admitted; share of University of Texas, Austin, freshmen with SAT scores below 990 (school mean is 1202) has doubled; share of blacks has declined slightly).

321. James Traub, "The Class of Prop. 209," *New York Times Magazine,* 44, 78 (May 2, 1999). Some argue that this "top X% solution" may not simply increase minority admissions but, by altering parents' incentives, may also improve the

quality of the weaker high schools. David Orentlicher, "Affirmative Action and Texas' Ten Percent Solution: Improving Diversity and Quality," 74 *Notre Dame Law Review* 181 (1998).

322. University of California, "New California Freshman ADMITS," Fall 1997 through 2001, at *http://www.ucop.edu/news/factsheets/2001/ethnicity.pdf* (accessed June 26, 2001).

323. Barbara Whitaker, "Admission Up for Minorities in California," *New York Times,* 25 (Apr. 7, 2002).

324. Rick Bragg, "Minority Enrollment Rises in Florida College System," *New York Times,* A18 (Aug. 30, 2000).

325. Tienda, "College Admission Policies," 128.

326. Id., 139. See also Michelle Adams, "Isn't It Ironic? The Central Paradox at the Heart of 'Percentage Plans,'" 62 *Ohio State Law Journal* 1729 (2002).

327. Nate Tabak, "Acceptance Policies May See Major Changes," *Daily Californian,* 1 (July 3, 2001).

328. See, e.g., Daniel Golden, "College Entry in U.S. Inspires New Calculation," *Wall Street Journal* (European ed.), 34 (May 16, 2000) (describing schools' manipulations); see Issacharoff, "Can Affirmative Action Be Defended?" 687 (without affirmative action, public universities in Texas will lower standards "as far as necessary to avoid re-segregation").

329. Citrin, "Scores Do Measure Talent" (among students with same credentials and family income and background, black and Latino students are more likely to receive higher holistic ratings; faculty opponents of affirmative action excluded from admissions committees).

330. The rest of this paragraph is based on Daniel Golden, "Admission: Possible— Language Test Gives Hispanic Students a Leg Up in California," *Wall Street Journal,* A1 (June 26, 2001).

331. For the situation in 1997, the first post-affirmative action year there, see John E. Morris, "Boalt Hall's Affirmative Action Dilemma," *American Lawyer,* 73 (Nov. 1997). For the situation in 2000, see University of California at Berkeley School of Law (Boalt Hall), "2000 Annual Admissions Report." The entering class in 2000 contained only seven blacks (twenty-eight received offers) and ten Chicanos (thirty-two received offers), constituting 3% and 4% of the class, respectively. Id. at first page (unnumbered). The number of blacks who applied to Boalt declined almost 50% between 1996 and 2000; the Chicano application decline was about 30%. Id. at 5. The share of those who accepted Boalt's offer dropped only slightly for blacks (26% to 25%) but substantially for Chicanos (42% to 31%). Id. at 9. Those who declined the offer almost certainly went to comparable or higher ranked law schools. Morris, "Boalt Hall's Affirmative Action Dilemma" (eleven of the fifteen who received offers in 1997 went "to schools with more cachet than Boalt"). Boalt's problem was that the pool of blacks and Chicanos who met their minimum standards was exceedingly small to begin with—only sixteen blacks and forty-five Hispanics *nationwide* even came close to the median for whites entering Boalt (id. at 74)—and most of those in that pool chose to attend other schools.

332. University of California, "Distribution of New California Freshman Admit Offers," Fall 1997 through 2001, at *http://www.ucop.edu/news/factsheets/2001/campus.pdf* (accessed June 26, 2001).

333. The evidence on how attending institutions of varying selectivity affects future earnings is mixed and hard to interpret. Compare Bowen and Bok, *The Shape of the River*, 128 (without controlling for pre-college aptitude, finds wage premium for attending selective institution), with Stacy Berg Dale and Alan B. Krueger, "Estimating the Payoff to Attending a More Selective College: An Application of Selection on Observables and Unobservables," Working Paper #409, Industrial Relations Section, Princeton University (July 1999) (controlling for pre-college aptitude, finds no wage premium for attending selective institution for either whites or blacks, though sample of blacks was small). Recent studies indicate that the returns for additional years of schooling are now about equal for blacks and whites. Alan Krueger, Michael Boozer, and Shari Wolkon, "Race and School Quality since *Brown vs. Board of Education*," in *Brookings Papers on Economic Activity: Microeconomics*, 269–326 (Martin N. Baily and Clifford Winston, eds., 1992).

334. Stephan Thernstrom and Abigail Thernstrom, "Racial Preferences in Higher Education: An Assessment of the Evidence," in *One America? Political Leadership, National Identity, and the Dilemmas of Diversity*, 206–207 (Stanley A. Renshon, ed., 2001).

335. "U. of California Alters Admission Policy," *New York Times*, A12 (July 20, 2001) (starting in fall 2003, top 12.5% of high school class assured eventual place at a university campus; most of those between 4% and 12.5% must first complete two years at community college); Barbara Whitaker, "University of California Moves to Widen Admissions Criteria," *New York Times*, A26 (Nov. 15, 2001) (replacing two-tier system with "comprehensive review" system that considers applicant's success in overcoming disadvantages); Daniel Golden, "To Get into UCLA, It Helps to Face 'Life Challenges,'" *Wall Street Journal*, A1 (July 12, 2002) (examples of arbitrariness and manipulation of system).

336. For a decidedly less optimistic prediction based on cognitive psychology research, see Krieger, "Civil Rights Perestroika," which leads her to advocate continued affirmative action. Krieger shows that subtle cognitive biases make discrimination hard to detect and remedy, in part because of the salience and persistence of intergroup distinctions. The psychological literature she cites is complex; it indicates that racial preferences may magnify these distinctions in some ways while reducing them in others. Krieger believes that effective legal remedies can deal with such unconscious biases, but I am not fully persuaded. E-mail from Linda Hamilton Krieger, Professor of Law, University of California at Berkeley, School of Law (Boalt Hall), to author (Mar. 9, 2001).

337. See, e.g., Michael Fix and Margery Austin Turner, eds., *A National Report Card on Discrimination in America: The Role of Testing* (1998); Ayres, *Pervasive Prejudice?*, 396–427.

338. See, e.g., Linda Hamilton Krieger, "The Content of Our Categories: A Cognitive Bias Approach to Discrimination and Equal Employment Opportunity," 47

Stanford Law Review 1161 (1995) (favoring goals and timetables as well as preferences); Vicki Schultz, "Reconceptualizing Sexual Harassment," 107 *Yale Law Journal* 1683 (1998).

339. Nathan Glazer is most prominently associated with this position. Nathan Glazer, *We Are All Multiculturalists Now* (1997).

340. According to a leading expert on affirmative action, employment preferences do not make such a distinction. Hugh Davis Graham, "Affirmative Action for Immigrants," in *Color Lines,* 54 (noting that 19% of the black faculty recruited under the university's affirmative action program were foreign-born).

341. See, e.g., Kymlicka, *Politics in the Vernacular,* 197–198; Peter Skerry, *Mexican Americans: The Ambivalent Minority* (1995); see also Brest and Oshige, "Affirmative Action for Whom?" (distinguishing Latino claims from black claims).

342. Patterson, *The Ordeal of Integration,* 193.

343. Daria Roithmayr, "Direct Measures: An Alternative Form of Affirmative Action," 7 *Michigan Journal of Race and Law* 1 (2001).

344. See, e.g., Drew S. Days III, "Fullilove," 96 *Yale Law Journal* 453 (1987).

345. See, e.g., City of Richmond v. J. A. Croson Co., 488 U.S. 469, 493–494 (1989) (explaining "strict scrutiny" test).

346. Schuck, "Affirmative Action: Past, Present, and Future," 52–53.

347. See, e.g., Richard D. Kahlenberg, *The Remedy: Class, Race, and Affirmative Action* (1996); Patterson, *The Ordeal of Integration,* 193.

348. Carol M. Swain, Kyra R. Greene, and Christine Min Wotipka, "Understanding Racial Polarization on Affirmative Action: The View from Focus Groups," in *Color Lines,* 214.

349. Malamud, "Race, Culture, and the Law," 1707 (agreeing with others on this point).

350. See also Tanya K. Hernandez, "An Exploration of the Efficacy of Class-Based Approaches to Racial Justice: The Cuban Context," 33 *University of California at Davis Law Review* 1135 (2000) (arguing that Afro-Cuban disadvantage and subordination persist despite class-based redistribution in Cuba).

351. Sarah Kershaw, "California's Universities Confront New Diversity Rules," *New York Times,* A10 (Jan. 22, 1996) (up to half of applicants meeting minimum academic standards to be evaluated on basis of "special circumstances," including social disadvantage).

352. Jacques Steinberg, "University of Vermont Builds Pool of Recruits in the Bronx," *New York Times,* 1 (Dec. 26, 2001).

353. Some proponents apparently ignore this problem. Patterson, for example, would include those of "lower class background," without noting that the meanings of both "lower class" and "background" are highly debatable in this context. Patterson, *The Ordeal of Integration,* 193.

354. Richard D. Kahlenberg has responded to these and other criticisms, unpersuasively in my view. *The Remedy: Class, Race, and Affirmative Action* (1996).

355. Kinsley, "The Spoils of Victimhood," 66.

356. See, e.g., Paul M. Barrett and Michael K. Frisby, "'Place, Not Race' Could Be Next Catch Phrase in Government's Affirmative-Action Programs," *Wall Street Journal,* B16 (Oct. 19, 1995).

357. Lani Guinier, "Democracy's Conversation: Beyond Winner Take All," *Nation*, 88 (Jan. 23, 1995). For another lottery proposal, see Jack Citrin, "For True Diversity, Universities Should Consider a Lottery," *Sacramento Bee* (editorial, July 22, 2001).

358. See, e.g., Paul M. Barrett, "Birmingham's Plan to Help Black-Owned Firms May Be Alternative to Racial Set-Aside Programs," *Wall Street Journal*, A14 (Feb. 27, 1995); see also Lemann, *The Big Test*, 348–349 (favoring restraints on regulation of local schools); Rubenfeld, "Affirmative Action," 471 (favoring "a massive capital infusion into inner-city day care and educational facilities").

359. This problem is discussed in James Q. Wilson, *Thinking about Crime*, 51, 73 (1975).

360. States have substantially increased spending on public elementary and secondary education in recent years; their per-pupil expenditures increased almost 50% in constant dollars between 1980 and the late 1990s. U.S. Census Bureau, *Statistical Abstract of the United States: 2000*, at 164, table 262, available at *http://www.census.gov/statab/www/* (last accessed Dec. 3, 2001). Their general-fund spending in fiscal 2002 will increase 3.7% above 2001 levels. Jessica L. Sandham, "States Slowing Spending for Public Schools," *Education Week* (Sept. 5, 2001), available at *http://www.edweek.org/ew/newstory.cfm?slug=01downturn.h21* (last accessed Oct. 15, 2001). At the same time, federal elementary and secondary education spending will enjoy its largest rise ever, with a 20% increase in Title I spending, outstripping Bill Clinton's previous record increase of $3.6 billion for fiscal year 2001. The new legislation also increases teacher and school accountability. Adam Clymer, "Congress Reaches Compromise on Education Bill," *New York Times*, A1 (Dec. 12, 2001).

361. According to John Jeffries, Lewis Powell's biographer, Justice Stevens speculated during the Supreme Court's deliberations in *Bakke* that blacks might not need preferences much longer. Justice Marshall "broke in to say that it would be another hundred years." John C. Jeffries, Jr., *Justice Lewis F. Powell, Jr.*, 487 (2001).

362. The U.S. Supreme Court has confronted this question but only in the special context of the dismantling of previously segregated school systems that have been under court order. United States v. Fordice, 505 U.S. 717 (1992).

363. Patterson, *The Ordeal of Integration*, 192–193.

364. Sowell, *Preferential Policies;* Erik Bleich, "The French Model: Color-Blind Integration," in *Color Lines*, 270; Parikh, *The Politics of Preference;* Steven M. Teles, "Positive Action or Affirmative Action? The Persistence of Britain's Antidiscrimination Regime," in *Color Lines*, 241.

365. It seems unlikely, for example, that banks would voluntarily invest in distressed neighborhoods where it seems unprofitable, nor would many companies regulated by the FCC and other agencies co-venture with, or give stock to, members of favored groups if that did not help them to obtain government licenses.

366. Welch and Gruhl, *Affirmative Action and Minority Enrollments.*

367. On corporations, see, e.g., Thernstrom and Thernstrom, *America in Black and White*, 452–453; Lauren B. Edelman et al., "Diversity Rhetoric and the Managerialization of Law," 106 *American Journal of Sociology* 1589 (2001); Levin-

son, "Diversity," 585–589 (example of Coca-Cola); Dobrzynski, "Some Action, Little Talk"; Alan Wolfe, "Affirmative Action, Inc.," *The New Yorker,* 106, 107 (Nov. 25, 1996) ("[T]he support of business for affirmative action is one of the better-kept secrets of the debate").

368. Edelman et al., "Diversity Rhetoric," 1581 (managers and their consultants believe that "diversity is directly valuable to organizational efficiency and important in its own right rather than because it might promote legal ideals").

369. Elizabeth Lasch-Quinn, *Race Experts: How Racial Etiquette, Sensitivity Training, and New Age Therapy Hijacked the Civil Rights Revolution,* 163 (2001). Lasch-Quinn's assessment of these programs is very negative. Id. at chap. 8.

370. See, e.g., Christopher Edley, Jr., *Not All Black and White: Affirmative Action, Race, and American Values* (1996) (written as a defense of the Clinton administration's essentially standpat position on affirmative action).

371. Wolfe, "Affirmative Action, Inc.," 114–115.

372. See, e.g., Kinsley, "The Spoils of Victimhood," 67.

373. "Symposium on the Public/Private Distinction," 130 *University of Pennsylvania Law Review* 1289 (1982).

374. See, e.g., Brentwood Academy v. Tennessee Secondary School Athletic Assn., 531 U.S. 288, 295 (2001).

375. Schuck, *The Limits of Law,* 419–479.

376. The classic exploration of this distinction is Albert O. Hirschman, *Exit, Voice, and Loyalty: Responses to Declines in Firms, Organizations, and States* (1970).

377. See generally Schuck, *The Limits of Law,* 434–454.

378. See Gregory Rodriguez, "Where the Minorities Rule," *New York Times,* WK6 (Feb. 10, 2002). The demographic change caused the San Diego City Council to ban the word "minority" from official documents and discussions. Id.

379. See, e.g., Richard H. McAdams, "An Attitudinal Theory of Expressive Law," 79 *Oregon Law Review* 339 (2000).

380. For a discussion of what these values might be, see Levinson, "Diversity," at 592–608.

381. Jacoby, *Someone Else's House,* 541.

382. Id.

383. See, e.g., Kent Greenawalt, "Hands Off! Civil Court Involvement in Conflicts over Religious Property," 98 *Columbia Law Review* 1843, 1901 (1998) (rejecting extreme deference to church decisions).

384. Boy Scouts of America v. Dale, 530 U.S. 640 (2000). For my initial reaction to this decision, see Peter H. Schuck, "Diversity Demands Exclusivity," *American Lawyer,* 67 (Sept. 2000).

385. Compare David E. Bernstein, "The Right of Expressive Association and Private Universities' Racial Preferences and Speech Codes," 9 *William and Mary Bill of Rights Law Journal* 619 (2001), with Mark Tushnet, "The Redundant Free Exercise Clause?" 33 *Loyola University of Chicago Law Journal* 71 (2001) (noting possible limits on defense).

386. For an exploration of considerations sometimes favoring opacity, see Guido Calabresi and Philip Bobbitt, *Tragic Choices* (1978).

387. Rubenfeld, "Affirmative Action," 471.

388. Personal communication with Derek Bok (Aug. 11, 2001).

389. See text accompanying notes 8–25 ("Definitions").
390. See text accompanying notes 313–330.
391. See, e.g., McAdams, "An Attitudinal Theory."
392. For example, Edelman et al., "Diversity Rhetoric," explains how civil rights and affirmative action law have influenced diversity management in organizations, and vice versa.
393. Justice Blackmun's opinion in *Bakke* is an example. Post, "Introduction," 18 (Blackmun "fails to engage Powell's central point, which is that when it comes to state action the country's history has made race and ethnicity special and problematic categories").
394. Many leading scholars, however, take this view. See, e.g., Laurence H. Tribe et al., "Constitutional Scholars' Statement on Affirmative Action after *City of Richmond v. J. A. Croson Co.*," 98 *Yale Law Journal* 1711 (1989) (statement signed by thirty scholars).
395. See text accompanying note 132.
396. Lasch, *The Revolt of the Elites*, 17.
397. John Rawls, *A Theory of Justice* (1971).
398. Within the Rawlsian logic, of course, one could posit that the Framers knew additional things about the society's inequality that I believe to be true—for example, that the disadvantaged made enormous progress even before preferences were instituted; that the society firmly believed in the principles of individualism and merit; and so forth. This knowledge, I suggest, would make even more unlikely a behind-the-veil choice for racial preferences. On the other hand, if one posited that current inequalities were caused primarily by racism on the part of the society today (which I do not believe), the choice might be otherwise. But of course such a society would not propose preferences as an option in the first place.
399. My claim that a society behind the veil would not choose such a rule, while contestable, is not refuted by the observation that some societies, including the United States, have in fact done so. The whole point of the Rawlsian thought experiment, after all, is to test the justice of that choice.
400. The 2000 census reports a marked improvement in absolute levels of living standards among all groups. Schmitt, "Census Data Show a Sharp Increase in Living Standard."
401. See, e.g., Patterson, *The Ordeal of Integration*; Schuck, *Citizens, Strangers, and In-Betweens*, 441 note 17 (citing studies). To choose just one of many indicators of this change, 95% of Americans say that they would vote for a black nominated by their party, up from 38% in 1958 and 79% as recently as 1987. Glover-Blackwell et al., *Searching for the Uncommon Ground*, figures 2–3.
402. Yolanda Woodlee, "Top D.C. Aide Resigns over Racial Rumor," *Washington Post*, B1 (Jan. 27, 1999).
403. Patterson, *The Ordeal of Integration*, 17–27.
404. On the virtual equality of black women on many indicators, see, e.g., Orlando Patterson, *Rituals of Blood: Consequences of Slavery in Two American Centuries*, 3–168 (1998). Patterson emphasizes the reasons why it will be difficult to close the black male–black female and black male–white male gaps. Id.
405. Edward L. Glaeser and Jacob L. Vigdor, "Racial Segregation in the 2000 Cen-

sus: Promising News" (The Brookings Institution, Center on Urban and Metropolitan Policy, Survey Series, Apr. 2001). Overall migration patterns, however, have increased racial isolation in the public schools since the 1980s. Diana Jean Schemo, "U.S. Schools Turn More Segregated, a Study Finds," *New York Times,* A14 (July 20, 2001) (70% of black children attended predominantly minority schools in 1998–1999, up from 63% in 1980–1981).

406. See generally John E. Roemer, *Equality of Opportunity* (1998) (new methodology for measuring equality of opportunity and showing that remaining inequality is great). For one recent example, see Sheryl Gay Stolberg, "Race Gap Seen in Health Care of Equally Insured Patients," *New York Times,* A1 (Mar. 21, 2002).

407. For a contrary view, see Anderson, "Integration, Affirmative Action, and Strict Scrutiny" (positing that a well-designed program based on integration rationale could satisfy strict scrutiny).

408. See discussion at text accompanying notes 38–41.

409. For a longer version of Chapter 6, see Peter H. Schuck, "Judging Remedies: Judicial Approaches to Housing Segregation," 37 *Harvard Civil Rights-Civil Liberties Law Review* 289 (2002).

410. See, e.g., Michael Klausner, "Market Failure and Community Investment: A Market-Oriented Alternative to the Community Reinvestment Act," 143 *University of Pennsylvania Law Review* 1561 (1995).

411. I say "initial" because it is much harder to make the case that once minorities are hired or admitted through preferences, have an equal opportunity to perform, and are treated without discrimination, they should receive yet another preference in being considered for promotion or graduate school. This distinction should be especially important to those who favor affirmative action only as a temporary expedient.

412. See discussion at text accompanying notes 255–270.

413. Hollinger, *Postethnic America,* 187.

414. See, e.g., Seymour Martin Lipset and Gary Marks, *It Didn't Happen Here: Why Socialism Failed in the United States,* 282–283 (2000); Alberto Alesina, Rafael Di Tella, and Robert MacCulloch, "Inequality and Happiness: Are Europeans and Americans Different?" National Bureau of Economic Research, Working Paper No. W8198 (Cambridge, Mass., Apr. 2001) (finding a large negative effect of inequality on happiness measures in Europe but not in the United States).

415. Rogers M. Smith, *Civic Ideals: Conflicting Visions of Citizenship in the U.S.* (1997).

6. RESIDENTIAL NEIGHBORHOODS

1. The discussion of the *Mount Laurel* litigation draws primarily on two decisions, Southern Burlington County NAACP v. Mount Laurel Township, 336 A.2d 713 (N.J. 1975), appeal dismissed and cert. denied, Township of Mount Laurel v. Southern Burlington County NAACP, 423 U.S. 808 (1975); and Southern Burlington County NAACP v. Mount Laurel Township, 456 A.2d 390 (N.J. 1983).

2. Hills v. Gautreaux, 425 U.S. 284 (1976).

3. United States v. Yonkers Board of Education, 518 F. Supp. 191 (D.C.N.Y. 1981).

4. This section draws on Robert C. Ellickson and Vicki L. Been, *Land Use Controls: Cases and Materials,* 20 (2d ed. 2000). Ellickson and Been report that the nation's largest homebuilder in 1993, Centex Corporation, accounted for under 1% of the total national housing starts. Id. Concentration is usually greater in specific metropolitan areas; one study found that the combined market share of the four largest builders in several metropolitan areas was about 50%. Id.

5. U.S. Census Bureau, *Statistical Abstract of the United States: 2000,* at 713, table 1195; 716, tables 1201 and 1202; 718, table 1207 (2000). See also David Leonhardt, "More Falling Behind on Mortgage Payments," *New York Times,* A4 (June 12, 2001).

6. Edward L. Glaeser and Joseph E. Gyourko, *The Impact of Zoning on Housing Affordability,* Harvard Institute of Economic Research, Paper No. 1948 (Mar. 2002), available at *http://papers.nber.org/papers/w8835.pdf.*

7. See Vicki L. Been, "'Exit' as a Constraint on Land Use Exactions: Rethinking the Unconstitutional Conditions Doctrine," 91 *Columbia Law Review* 473 (1991) (describing market forces).

8. U.S. Census Bureau, *Statistical Abstract of the United States: 2000,* at 28, table 26 (16% of households move each year).

9. Davis-Bacon Act, 40 U.S.C. §§276a–276a-5 (2000) (establishing a high floor under wages of construction workers in federally subsidized projects).

10. Fair Housing Act §804, 42 U.S.C. §3604 (1994) (barring discrimination in the sale or rental of housing and other prohibited practices).

11. Anthony Downs, *A Re-evaluation of Residential Rent Controls,* 61–63 (1996). There are dignity-based arguments favoring rent controls—see, e.g., Margaret Jane Radin, "Market-Inalienability," 100 *Harvard Law Review* 1849 (1987)— though, in my view, the advantages claimed by such arguments are outweighed by their disadvantages.

12. See, e.g., Andrew Jacobs, "New Jersey's Housing Law Works Too Well, Some Say," *New York Times,* A1 (Mar. 3, 2001).

13. See Ingrid Gould Ellen, *Sharing America's Neighborhoods: The Prospects for Stable Racial Integration,* 176 (2000) (finding that homeowners are more resistant to residential community integration).

14. See Christopher Howard, *The Hidden Welfare State: Tax Expenditures and Social Policy in the United States* (1997).

15. See Joseph Gyourko and Todd Sinai, *The Spatial Distribution of Housing-Related Tax Benefits in the United States,* National Bureau of Economic Research, Working Paper No. 8165 (Cambridge, Mass., 2001), available at *http://papers.nber.org/papers/w8165.pdf.*

16. Fair Housing Act §804, 42 U.S.C. §3604 (1994).

17. See, e.g., Minn. Stat. §363.03 (2000).

18. See Robert C. Ellickson, "The Irony of Inclusionary Zoning," 54 *Southern California Law Review* 1167, 1202 (1981) (annual income, the measure used by inclusionary zoning programs, often unreliable indicator of class status).

19. See Witold Rybczynski, "City Lights," *New York Review of Books*, 68–69 (June 21, 2001) (reviewing Pietro S. Nivola, *Laws of the Landscape: How Policies Shape Cities in Europe and America* (1999)).

20. See, e.g., Howard Husock, "A Critique of Mixed Income Housing: The Problems with 'Gautreaux,'" 5 *Responsive Community* 34 (1995). For a discussion of black community classist resistance to public housing, see Bruce D. Haynes, *Red Lines, Black Spaces: The Politics of Race and Space in a Black Middle-Class Suburb*, 105–108 (2001).

21. Nathan Glazer, *We Are All Multiculturalists Now*, 146 (1997).

22. Douglas S. Massey and Nancy A. Denton, *American Apartheid: Segregation and the Making of the Underclass* (1993).

23. Id., 109–110.

24. Id., 221. Others find more, albeit still limited, integration. See, e.g., David M. Cutler, Edward L. Glaeser, and Jacob L. Vigdor, "The Rise and Decline of the American Ghetto," 107 *Journal of Political Economy* 455 (1999).

25. William H. Frey, *Melting Pot Suburbs: A Census 2000 Study of Suburban Diversity*, 1, 13 (The Brookings Institution, Center on Urban and Metropolitan Policy, Census 2000 Series, June 2001), available at *http://www.brook.edu/dybdocroot/es/urban/census/frey.pdf*.

26. Id., 1, 6.

27. Id., 1, 12.

28. Among the favorable reviews are Lawrence H. Fuchs, "Book Review," 99 *American Journal of Sociology* 1342 (1994); Roberta Johnson, "Book Review," 534 *Annals of the American Academy of Political and Social Science* 203 (1994); and Michael Schill, "Race, the Underclass, and Public Policy," 19 *Law and Social Inquiry* 433 (1994).

29. See, e.g., Reynolds Farley and William H. Frey, "Changes in the Segregation of Whites from Blacks during the 1980s: Small Steps toward a More Integrated Society," 59 *American Sociological Review* 23 (1994); Florence Wagman Roisman, "The Lessons of *American Apartheid:* The Necessity and Means of Promoting Residential Racial Integration," 81 *Iowa Law Review* 479 (1995); Wilbur Rich, "Book Review," 108 *Political Science Quarterly* 574 (1993); Nathan Glazer, "A Tale of Two Cities," *The New Republic*, 40 (Aug. 2, 1993) ("When it comes to causes, they present only prejudice"); Abraham Bell and Gideon Parchomovsky, "The Integration Game," 100 *Columbia Law Review* 1965, 1982–1985 (2000).

30. See generally Massey and Denton, *American Apartheid*.

31. Janny Scott, "Rethinking Segregation beyond Black and White," *New York Times*, §4, at 1 (July 29, 2001).

32. Pietro S. Nivola, *Laws of the Landscape: How Policies Shape Cities in Europe and America* (1999). See also Peter Grant, "Sprawl Thins Populations of Older Suburbs," *Wall Street Journal*, A2 (July 9, 2001) (densities decreasing in most suburbs, especially in Northeast and Midwest).

33. Rybczynski, "City Lights," 70 (quoting Nivola, *Laws of the Landscape*). See also Janny Scott, "Amid a Sea of Faces, Islands of Segregation," *New York Times*, A1 (June 18, 2001) (examining ethnic clustering in diverse communities).

34. See, e.g., Paul A. Jargowsky, "Take the Money and Run: Economic Segregation in U.S. Metropolitan Areas," 61 *American Sociological Review* 984 (1996).

35. See Thomas C. Schelling, "On the Ecology of Micromotives," *The Public Interest,* 59 (Fall 1971).

36. Id., 88. See generally Malcolm Gladwell, *The Tipping Point: How Little Things Can Make a Big Difference* (2000). But see Bell and Parchomovsky, "The Integration Game," 1988–1996 (criticizing Schelling's model).

37. "Tipping" refers to a disequilibrium dynamic in which whites would leave a neighborhood, project, or school, making it "blacker," thus encouraging more whites to leave, and so on until it might become entirely black.

38. Glazer, "A Tale of Two Cities," 40. But see Richard P. Taub, D. Garth Taylor, and Jan D. Dunham, *Paths of Neighborhood Change: Race and Crime in Urban America,* 150 (1984) (finding that the wording of survey questions affects the preferences expressed by blacks, that "[t]he percentage of blacks who are tolerant of all racial mixtures up to extreme minority or extreme majority status for themselves is quite high," and that this affects models predicting the dynamics of tipping).

39. United States v. Starrett City Associates, 840 F.2d 1096 (2d Cir. 1988).

40. Id. See also Davis v. New York City Housing Authority, 278 F.3d 64 (2d Cir. 2002). In an interesting variation on the quota theme, the Second Circuit recently invalidated a trial court's effort to racially configure a jury in a criminal case. United States v. Nelson, 277 F.3d 164 (2d Cir. 2002).

41. Ellen, *Sharing America's Neighborhoods,* 2–3.

42. I can think of only two ways to avoid such an absurd characterization. One would be to evaluate the preferred levels directly: a white person who preferred, say, fewer than 50% of her neighbors to be black would be considered, perhaps only presumptively, to be a racist. But any number (even an extremely low one) would be quite arbitrary, especially since we would be unable to determine the extent to which that number took into account the preferences of others and hence the risk of a perverse tipping. The second way would be to try to distinguish between good and bad motives for having such a preference. In the real world, however, it is difficult to imagine how one might go about doing this. Again, would selecting a preferred level by taking into account the tipping-relevant preferences of others be a good motive or a bad one?

43. Jonathan Rieder, *Canarsie: The Jews and Italians of Brooklyn against Liberalism* (1985).

44. Ellickson, "The Irony of Inclusionary Zoning," 1198–1202 (citing studies).

45. Taub et al., *Paths of Neighborhood Change,* 186–190 (1984).

46. Id., 186.

47. See id.

48. See Ellen, *Sharing American Neighborhoods,* 4–5.

49. See Taub et al., *Paths of Neighborhood Change,* 186–188.

50. Jayson Blair, "Failed Disney Vision: Integrated City," *New York Times,* A31 (Sept. 23, 2001).

51. See San Antonio Independent School District v. Rodriguez, 411 U.S. 1, 19 (1972) (noting that "under the Constitution, the class of disadvantaged poor cannot be identified or defined in customary equal protection terms").

52. Id.
53. See Ellickson, "The Irony of Inclusionary Zoning," 1198–1202 (reviewing empirical studies).
54. See Howard, *The Hidden Welfare State,* 27–28 ("Subsidies for home ownership comprise almost all housing tax expenditures, to the tune of $90 billion per year. Tax subsidies for rental housing and low-income housing come to a few billion dollars at most").
55. See generally David Rusk, *Cities without Suburbs* (1993) (arguing that, in many ways, the poverty problem is a race problem).
56. Hazelwood School District v. United States, 433 U.S. 299, 307–308 (1977) ("Where gross statistical disparities can be shown, they alone may in a proper case constitute . . . proof of a pattern or practice of [racial] discrimination"). The law sometimes tries to manage this indeterminacy by barring unbiased practices that nevertheless have a "disparate impact" on minorities. For example, the implementing regulations of Title VI of the Civil Rights Act of 1964 prohibit educational programs that receive federal assistance from acting in ways that "have the effect of defeating or substantially impairing accomplishment of the objectives of the program as respect individuals of a particular race, color, or national origin." 34 C.F.R. §100.3(b)(2) (1999).
57. See, e.g., James E. Ryan, "Schools, Race, and Money," 109 *Yale Law Journal* 249, 279 note 132 (1999) (discussing the residential isolation of blacks).
58. A similar asymmetry contributes to the stigma borne by blacks in selective schools that are suspected of using racial preferences. See generally George A. Akerlof, "The Market for Lemons: Quality Uncertainty and the Market Mechanism," 84 *Quarterly Journal of Economics* 488 (1970).
59. See Charles M. Tiebout, "A Pure Theory of Local Expenditures," 64 *Journal of Political Economy* 416 (1956). The following discussion of Tiebout draws as well from William A. Fischel, "Municipal Corporations, Homeowners, and the Benefit View of the Property Tax," in *Property Taxation and Local Public Finance,* 33, 33–68 (Wallace E. Oates, ed., 2001).
60. Fischel, "Municipal Corporations," 33–36.
61. Id., 35.
62. Id., 33–68.
63. Ellickson and Been, *Land Use Controls,* 922–923.
64. Id., 923.
65. Jane Jacobs, *The Death and Life of Great American Cities* (1961).
66. See generally id. at 143–240.
67. On the importance of the idea of nature in Jacobs's work, see generally Jane Jacobs, *The Nature of Economies* (2000).
68. Jacobs, *The Death and Life of Great American Cities,* 273.
69. James C. Scott, *Seeing Like a State: How Certain Schemes to Improve the Human Condition Have Failed,* 138 (1998).
70. Andres Duany, Elizabeth Plater-Zyberk, and Jeff Speck, *Suburban Nation: The Rise of Sprawl and the Decline of the American Dream* (2000).
71. Id., 43–55.
72. Anthony Downs, *Opening Up the Suburbs: An Urban Strategy for America* (1973).

73. Compare id. at 138–139 (discussing priority of economic over racial integration), with William Julius Wilson, *When Work Disappears: The World of the New Urban Poor* (1996); Gerald E. Frug, *City Making: Building Communities without Building Walls*, 143–164 (1999); Michael H. Schill, "Deconcentrating the Inner City Poor," 67 *Chicago-Kent Law Review* 795 (1991); and Richard Thompson Ford, "The Boundaries of Race: Political Geography in Legal Analysis," 107 *Harvard Law Review* 1843 (1994).

74. Southern Burlington County NAACP v. Mount Laurel Township, 336 A.2d 713 (N.J. 1975), appeal dismissed and cert. denied, 423 U.S. 808 (1975) (hereafter *Mount Laurel I*), and Southern Burlington City NAACP v. Mount Laurel Township, 456 A.2d 390 (N.J. 1983) (hereafter *Mount Laurel II*).

75. Hills v. Gautreaux, 425 U.S. 284 (1976).

76. In addition to the *Mount Laurel* opinions, this section refers to several secondary sources. These include J. Peter Byrne, "Are Suburbs Unconstitutional?" 85 *Georgetown Law Journal* 2265 (1997), which in turn reviews the two leading books on *Mount Laurel*, Charles M. Haar, *Suburbs under Siege: Race, Space, and Audacious Judges* (1996), and David L. Kirp, John P. Dwyer, and Larry A. Rosenthal, *Our Town: Race, Housing, and the Soul of Suburbia* (1995). Henry A. Span, "How the Courts Should Fight Exclusionary Zoning," 32 *Seton Hall Law Review* 1 (2001), is a recent analysis of the effects of *Mount Laurel* and of reform efforts in other states.

77. See text accompanying notes 18–21 and 51–58.

78. The mayor of Mount Laurel issued a statement to this effect in the speech that triggered the *Mount Laurel* litigation: "If you people can't afford to live in our town, then you just have to leave." See Kirp et al., *Our Town*, 2.

79. See *Mount Laurel I*, 336 A.2d at 713.

80. For a different view, see David L. Kirp, *Almost Home: America's Love-Hate Relationship with Community*, chap. 3 (2000).

81. The same court exhibited similar creativity a year later in Robinson v. Cahill, 360 A.2d 400 (N.J. 1976), which invoked the New Jersey constitution's "thorough and efficient [public education]" clause, rather than the equal protection clause, to invalidate the state's school finance system, unleashing a "three-decade saga." See Michael Heise, "Preliminary Thoughts on the Virtues of Passive Dialogue," 34 *Akron Law Review* 73, 99 (2000).

82. *Mount Laurel I*, 336 A.2d at 731–732.

83. Id. at 724.

84. *Mount Laurel II*, 456 A.2d 390.

85. Id. at 410.

86. Id.

87. Id.

88. Id.

89. E-mail from John M. Payne, Professor of Law, Rutgers School of Law, to author (Sept. 20, 2000) (hereafter Payne, Sept. 2000 e-mail).

90. *Mount Laurel II*, 456 A.2d at 419.

91. Id. at 442.

92. Id. at 443.

93. Id. at 452.

94. Id. at 420.
95. See Andrew Jacobs, "New Jersey's Housing Law" (developers are the main enforcers).
96. *Mount Laurel II,* 456 A.2d at 453.
97. Haar, *Suburbs under Siege,* 50.
98. See Alan Mallach, "The Tortured Reality of Suburban Exclusion: Zoning, Economics, and the Future of the Berenson Doctrine," 4 *Pace Environmental Law Review* 37, 119 (1986); Payne, Sept. 2000 e-mail. Payne recounted the summation of a much older case filed by the Urban League against Middlesex County towns and consolidated in *Mount Laurel II.* The judge sequestered almost two dozen planning experts in a conference room where they met in a nonjudicial forum without the participation of the attorneys representing the parties. The judge ordered them to work out the relevant formulas on regional needs, fair shares, growth areas, and so forth. After several months, the planners agreed on formulas that the judges then used throughout the state.
99. See Haar, *Suburbs under Siege,* 55–86; Kirp et al., *Our Town,* 83–111.
100. Haar, id.; Kirp et al., id.
101. See, e.g., Byrne, "Are Suburbs Unconstitutional?"; John M. Payne, "Lawyers, Judges, and the Public Interest," 96 *Michigan Law Review* 1685, 1705, 1712–1713 (1998) (book review); Ellickson and Been, *Land Use Controls,* 934 note 5 (citing other sources).
102. See Kirp et al., *Our Town,* 112–136.
103. Fair Housing Act, N.J. Stat. Ann. §§52:27D-301 to 52:27D-329 (West 2001).
104. N.J. Stat. Ann. §52:27D-305 (West 2001).
105. N.J. Stat. Ann. §52:27D-307 (West 2001).
106. I have proposed an analogous scheme for the allocation of refugee burden-sharing obligations. See Peter H. Schuck, *Citizens, Strangers, and In-Betweens: Essays on Immigration and Citizenship,* chap. 13 (1998).
107. See Edward A. Zelinsky, "Metropolitanism, Progressivism, and Race," 98 *Columbia Law Review* 665, 688 (1998) (reviewing Kirp et al., *Our Town*). For commentary on RCAs, see sources cited in Ellickson and Been, *Land Use Controls,* 938 note 5.
108. Hills Development Co. v. Bernards Township in Somerset County, 510 A.2d 621 (N.J. 1986) ("Mount Laurel III").
109. Payne, "Lawyers, Judges, and the Public Interest," 1698.
110. The summary that follows draws on Span, "How the Courts Should Fight Exclusionary Zoning," and a telephone interview with Sidna B. Mitchell, deputy director of the New Jersey Council on Affordable Housing (July 17, 2001). But see Robert W. Burchell, a housing policy analyst and *Mount Laurel* enthusiast, cited by Andrew Jacobs, "New Jersey's Housing Law."
111. For a discussion of the numbers problem, see Ellickson and Been, *Land Use Controls,* 937–938.
112. Id. In 1991 it was estimated that 675,000 households exceeded the 30%-of-income standard. Id. COAH defines need as the number of households living in decrepit units (which constantly decreases as substandard housing is retired) plus an estimate of needed new construction over a six-year period. Id.
113. Haar, *Suburbs under Siege,* 115.

114. Naomi Bailin Wish and Stephen Eisdorfer, "The Impact of *Mount Laurel* Initiatives: An Analysis of the Characteristics of Applicants and Occupants," 27 *Seton Hall Law Review* 1268 (1997).

115. Id., 1298–1299.

116. Id., 1295–1296.

117. Id., 1304.

118. E-mail from John M. Payne, Professor of Law, Rutgers School of Law, to author (May 29, 2001). While criticizing overreliance on inclusionary zoning, Payne believes that it can be a useful tool when, for example, localities approve large-tract, high-density developments. Id.

119. A leading developer's law firm, for example, maintains a website featuring a wallet filling up with dollars, a list of 196 towns that are fair game, and an exhortation that developers "contract for land in one of them, decide what you would like to build, and sue." See, e.g., Andrew Jacobs, "New Jersey's Housing Law," B5. Jacobs reports that forty-seven municipalities are now in *Mount Laurel* litigation, many of them rural or agricultural, and most will probably lose. Id.

120. Payne, "Lawyers, Judges, and the Public Interest," 1702.

121. Id., 1696.

122. Id., 1707.

123. Id., 1710.

124. Id., 1710–1711.

125. Id., 1713.

126. Id.

127. See, e.g., Thomas J. Espenshade, ed., *Keys to Successful Immigration: Implications of the New Jersey Experience* (1997).

128. See Peter H. Schuck, "Affirmative Action: Past, Present, and Future," 20 *Yale Law and Policy Review* 1, 14–16 (2002).

129. Village of Arlington Heights v. Metropolitan Housing Development Corp., 429 U.S. 252, 265 (1977) ("Arlington Heights I").

130. See, e.g., Metropolitan Housing Development Corp. v. Village of Arlington Heights, 558 F.2d 1283 (7th Cir. 1977) ("Arlington Heights II").

131. See Payne, "Lawyers, Judges, and the Public Interest," 1706–1707 (analyzing litigation strategy).

132. See, e.g., Downs, *Opening Up the Suburbs,* chap. 12.

133. See Span, "How the Courts Should Fight Exclusionary Zoning," 37–85 (discussing Pennsylvania, New York, New Hampshire, New Jersey, Oregon, and California).

134. Ellickson, "The Irony of Inclusionary Zoning," 1203.

135. Payne agrees with this assessment. See Payne, Sept. 2000 e-mail.

136. See Downs, *Opening Up the Suburbs.*

137. Toll Brothers, Inc. v. Township of West Windsor, 173 N.J. 502, 803 A.2d 53 (2002). This decision is destined to be known as "Mount Laurel IV."

138. See Hills v. Gautreaux, 425 U.S. 284 (1976).

139. The summary that follows draws heavily on Leonard S. Rubinowitz and James E. Rosenbaum, *Crossing the Class and Color Lines: From Public Housing to White Suburbia* (2000).

140. Id., 1.

141. Id., 1–2; Gautreaux v. Chicago Housing Authority, 304 F. Supp. 736 (N.D. Ill. 1969), enforcing Gautreaux v. Chicago Housing Authority, 296 F. Supp. 907 (N.D. Ill. 1969).

142. Rubinowitz and Rosenbaum, *Crossing the Class and Color Lines,* 27.

143. Id., 36; Gautreaux v. Romney, 448 F.2d 731 (7th Cir. 1971).

144. Gautreaux v. Romney, 448 F.2d 731.

145. Rubinowitz and Rosenbaum, *Crossing the Class and Color Lines,* 2; Hills v. Gautreaux, 425 U.S. 284 (1976).

146. Housing and Community Development Act of 1974, §201(a), 42 U.S.C. §1437d (Supp. IV 1998) (as amended).

147. William P. Wilen and Wendy L. Stasell, "*Gautreaux* and Chicago Public Housing Crisis: The Conflict between Achieving Integration and Providing Decent Housing for Very Low-Income African Americans," 34 *Clearinghouse Review* 117, 126 notes 79–82 (2000).

148. The research on which this paragraph draws is discussed in Rubinowitz and Rosenbaum, *Crossing the Class and Color Lines.*

149. Id.

150. U.S. General Accounting Office, "Costs and Characteristics of Federal Housing Assistance," GAO-01-901R, at 4, 47–52 (Washington, D.C., 2001), available at *http://www.gao.gov/new.items/d01901r.pdf.*

151. Id.

152. Dennis Hevesi, "Cracks in a Pillar of Affordable Housing," *New York Times,* §11, at 1 (Nov. 18, 2001).

153. Housing and Community Development Act of 1992, Pub. L. No. 102-550, §152, 106 Stat. 3672, 3716–3717 (1992).

154. U.S. Department of Housing and Urban Development, "Study on Section 8 Voucher Success Rates: Volume 1," at i–ii (Nov. 2001).

155. See Office of Policy Development and Research, U.S. Department of Housing and Urban Development, *Moving to Opportunity for Fair Housing Demonstration Program: Current Status and Initial Findings* (1999).

156. Margery Austin Turner, Susan Popkin, and Mary Cunningham, *Section 8 Mobility and Neighborhood Health: Emerging Issues and Policy Challenges* (2000), available at *http://www.urban.org/community/sec8_mobility.pdf.*

157. An even more detailed account of the Yonkers litigation appears in Peter H. Schuck, "Judging Remedies: Judicial Approaches to Housing Segregation," 37 *Harvard Civil Rights-Civil Liberties Law Review* 289, 324–364 (2002). For the events up to 1989, this section draws on my own extensive interviews and research on the *Yonkers* case, which are unpublished. For events after 1989, it draws on a variety of sources, including the following: Lisa Belkin, *Show Me a Hero: A Tale of Murder, Suicide, Race, and Redemption* (1999); telephone interview with Xavier de Souza Briggs, Assistant Professor of Public Policy, Kennedy School of Government, Harvard University (July 1, 2001); telephone interviews with Andrew Beveridge, Professor of Sociology, Queens College, and former president of Yonkers School Board (July 11 and 16, 2001), and e-mail from Andrew Beveridge (Sept. 11, 2001); e-mail from Diane Houk, Housing and Civil Enforcement Section, Civil Rights Division, U.S. Department of Justice (July

12, 2001); telephone interviews with Jerrold M. Levy, General Counsel of Enhanced Section 8 Outreach Program, Department of Housing and Urban Development (Oct. 12, 2001, and Oct. 3, 2002); telephone interview with Peter
Smith, executive director of the Yonkers Municipal Housing Authority (Oct. 19,
2001); e-mails from Ming-Yuen Meyer-Fong, Housing Section, Civil Rights Division, U.S. Department of Justice (Dec. 26, 2001, and Oct. 20, 2002); and
public documents.

158. See United States v. Yonkers Board of Education, 624 F. Supp. 1276 (S.D.N.Y.
1985). The length of the docket sheet alone, which simply lists the court filings
only to the middle of 1986 (that is, only through the liability phase in the district court and before the remedial phase really got under way), runs to forty-
three pages.

159. Lisa Foderaro, "Neighborhood Groups Wield Influential Role in Yonkers," *New
York Times*, §12 (Westchester Weekly), at 1 (Aug. 21, 1988). The account of
these groups that follows is taken directly from this article.

160. Village of Arlington Heights v. Metropolitan Housing Development Corp., 429
U.S. 252, 264–268 (1977). The *Arlington Heights* case simply applied to housing cases the principle announced a year earlier in Washington v. Davis, 426 U.S.
229 (1976). A decade before that, the same principle had been applied in another Fourteenth Amendment challenge to public housing siting policy. See
Gautreaux v. Chicago Housing Authority, 265 F. Supp. 582 (N.D. Ill. 1967).

161. Personal interview with Drew S. Days, III, Professor of Law, Yale Law School
(Sept. 26, 1988).

162. Id.

163. See United States v. Yonkers Board of Education, 624 F. Supp. at 1295 (Judge
Sand's discussion of the reasons for community opposition).

164. Id. at 1294–1363.

165. Interview with Angelo Martinelli, former mayor of Yonkers, conducted in Yonkers, New York (Feb. 8, 1989).

166. See United States v. Yonkers Board of Education, 624 F. Supp. at 1294–1363.
Here, as elsewhere, the parallels between the anxieties in Yonkers and those described by Jonathan Rieder in his study of Canarsie are interesting.

167. Id. at 1298–1300, 1304.

168. Id.

169. Id. at 1312.

170. Interview with Michael H. Sussman, counsel for NAACP, in Goshen, New York
(Aug. 21, 1988).

171. Housing and Community Development Act of 1974, Pub. L. No. 93-383, 88
Stat. 633 (codified as amended in various sections of Titles 12 and 42 of the
U.S. Code).

172. Interview with John Herold, Office of General Counsel, U.S. Department of
Housing and Urban Development, in Washington, D.C. (Mar. 9, 1989).

173. United States v. Yonkers Board of Education, 624 F. Supp. at 1347. Judge Sand
had made the same point in an earlier opinion. See United States v. Yonkers
Board of Education, 611 F. Supp. 730, 738 (S.D.N.Y. 1985).

174. United States v. Yonkers Board of Education, 624 F. Supp. at 1347.

175. Interview with Drew S. Days, III. HUD Secretary Moon Landrieu, the former mayor of New Orleans, later refused to allow HUD to join the suit as a plaintiff. Id.; interview with Michael H. Sussman.
176. Interview with John Herold.
177. Id.
178. United States v. Yonkers Board of Education, 624 F. Supp. at 1356.
179. United States v. Yonkers Board of Education, 518 F. Supp. 191 (S.D.N.Y. 1981).
180. In fact, the school case has been even more protracted; it was only settled in the spring of 2002.
181. Interview with Drew S. Days, III.
182. Interview with Michael H. Sussman.
183. Id.
184. United States v. Yonkers Board of Education, 624 F. Supp. at 1329.
185. Id.
186. The case law on the authority of trial courts to grant far-reaching structural relief was (and remains) uncertain. See Missouri v. Jenkins, 515 U.S. 70, 100 (1995).
187. United States v. Yonkers Board of Education, 611 F. Supp. at 742.
188. Id. at 743–744.
189. United States v. Yonkers Board of Education, 594 F. Supp. 466, 476 (S.D.N.Y. 1984).
190. United States v. Yonkers Board of Education, 611 F. Supp. at 737.
191. Id. In August 1985, the court denied HUD's subsequent motion to modify the order compelling HUD compliance.
192. Interview with Peter Smith, executive director of the Yonkers Municipal Housing Authority, in Yonkers, New York (Feb. 15, 1989).
193. Interview with Angelo Martinelli; interview with Henry Spallone, Vice Mayor of Yonkers and member of the Yonkers City Council, in Yonkers, New York (Mar. 9, 1989).
194. Interview with Victoria Holmes, United States Department of Housing and Urban Development, in Washington, D.C. (Mar. 9, 1989).
195. Interview with John Herold.
196. Id.
197. United States v. Yonkers Board of Education, 624 F. Supp. at 1376.
198. Id. at 1369.
199. See United States v. Yonkers Board of Education, 837 F.2d 1181 (2d Cir. 1987).
200. See Yonkers Board of Education v. United States, 486 U.S. 1055 (1988).
201. See, e.g., Lawrence D. Bobo and Michael P. Massagli, "Stereotyping and Urban Inequality," in *Urban Inequality: Evidence from Four Cities,* 89–163 (Alice O'Connor et al., eds., 2001) (analyzing racial and economic stereotypes).
202. Peter H. Schuck, *The Limits of Law: Essays in Democratic Governance,* 428 (2000).
203. Rieder, *Canarsie,* 216.
204. See Hills v. Gautreaux, 425 U.S. 284, 297–300 (1976). In so doing, the Court

distinguished its remedial plan from the interdistrict relief that it had rejected two years earlier in Milliken v. Bradley, 418 U.S. 717 (1974).

205. United States v. Yonkers Board of Education, 635 F. Supp. 1577 (S.D.N.Y. 1986).

206. United States v. Yonkers, No. 80 CIV 6761, 1986 WL 6159, at *1–*3 (S.D.N.Y. May 28, 1986).

207. See generally United States v. Yonkers Board of Education, 635 F. Supp. 1577.

208. Id.

209. Id.

210. Id. at 1581.

211. Id. at 1581–1582.

212. Id. at 1582. These might include write-downs of the price of city-owned land, subsidized development costs, infrastructure improvements, or interim construction loans; rental or mortgage subsidies to tenants or buyers; and rehabilitation funds to low- and moderate-income families. Id. The order included special allocation formulas to assure compliance with the CDBG rules. See id. at 1583.

213. Id. at 1582.

214. The decision joins the ranks of the district court decision in Missouri v. Jenkins, 1991 WL 538841 (W.D. Mo. 1991), which imposed a broad tax as part of the remedy for a desegregation challenge in Kansas City. The Supreme Court later rejected the district court's sweeping decision in Missouri v. Jenkins, 515 U.S. 70 (1995).

215. See discussion in Alexander Polikoff, "*Gautreaux* and Institutional Litigation," 64 *Chicago-Kent Law Review* 451, 461 (1988).

216. "High Court Blocks Stay for Yonkers," *New York Times,* B4 (Aug. 21, 1986).

217. James Feron, "Contempt Ruling Urged over Yonkers Housing," *New York Times,* 30 (Dec. 6, 1986).

218. James Feron, "Housing Design Argued in Yonkers Bias Case," *New York Times,* §22 (Westchester Weekly), at 1 (May 3, 1987).

219. Id.

220. James Feron, "Judge Warns Yonkers of Big Fines If Housing Integration Is Delayed," *New York Times,* A1 (July 2, 1987).

221. James Feron, "Site Questions Could Upset Housing Plan in Yonkers," *New York Times,* §22 (Westchester Weekly), at 1 (July 19, 1987).

222. James Feron, "Citing Bias Order, U.S. Curbs Yonkers on Aid to Builders," *New York Times,* A1 (Nov. 20, 1987).

223. "When a City Defies a Judge," *New York Times,* A26 (Nov. 25, 1987) (editorial).

224. United States v. Yonkers Board of Education, 837 F.2d at 1186.

225. James Feron, "Yonkers Said to Propose an Accord on Bias Suit," *New York Times,* B1 (Jan. 9, 1988).

226. Sara Rimer, "Yonkers, Ending 2-Year Battle, Agrees to Low-Income Housing," *New York Times,* B1 (Jan. 26, 1988).

227. Id.

228. Sara Rimer, "Council Backs Housing Order in Yonkers," *New York Times,* B1 (Jan. 29, 1988).

229. James Feron, "Yonkers Racial Suit Settled in Court, Not in Community," *New York Times,* §4, at 6 (Mar. 27, 1988).

230. United States v. City of Yonkers, 856 F.2d 444 (2d Cir. 1988), rev'd, Spallone v. United States, 493 U.S. 265 (1990).

231. Two months later, he also won a legal victory when the Supreme Court ruled, over four Justices' impassioned dissent, that Judge Sand had abused his discretion by sanctioning the two councillors without waiting to see whether they would comply with the new ordinance. See Spallone v. United States, 493 U.S. 265.

232. Xavier de Souza Briggs (with Joe T. Darden and Angela Aidala), "In the Wake of Desegregation: Early Impacts of Scattered-Site Public Housing on Neighborhoods in Yonkers, New York," 65 *Journal of the American Planning Association* 27, 43 (1999). The study acknowledges that its analysis is subject to methodological difficulties and the property value effects are uncertain.

233. E-mail from Andrew Beveridge, Professor of Sociology, Queens College, and former president of Yonkers School Board, to author (July 17, 2001); e-mail from David Sheingold, former reporter for the *Herald Statesman* in Yonkers, to author (Jan. 14, 2002); telephone interview with David Sheingold (Jan. 14, 2002).

234. Xavier de Sousa Briggs, "Social Capital and the Cities: Advice to Change Agents," 86 *National Civic Review* 111, 116 (1997).

235. Belkin, *Show Me a Hero,* 321.

236. Giddins v. Secretary of Housing and Urban Development, 91 Civ. 7181 (S.D.N.Y., Nov. 10, 1993) (entry of consent decree).

237. Telephone interview with Jerrold M. Levy (Oct. 3, 2002).

238. E-mail from Ming-Yuen Meyer-Fong (Oct. 20, 2002).

239. Belkin, *Show Me a Hero,* 322–324.

240. At the same time, Judge Sand terminated Oscar Newman, his longtime special master for the housing remedy, because his high fees, inability to secure the affordable housing, and political tin ear made him a growing liability. He replaced Newman with a business executive from Washington who had experience with development of low-income housing.

241. United States v. Secretary of Housing and Urban Development, 239 F.3d 211 (2d Cir. 2001).

242. Id. at 219–220.

243. City of Yonkers v. United States, 122 S. Ct. 643 (2001).

244. E-mail from Ming-Yuen Meyer-Fong (Oct. 20, 2002).

245. Jennifer Hochschild and Michael N. Danielson, "Analyzing the Demise of a Dinosaur: School and Housing Desegregation in Yonkers," in *Race, Urban Poverty, and Domestic Policy* (Michael Henry, ed., forthcoming).

246. See generally Peter H. Schuck, "Benched," *The Washington Monthly,* 35 (Dec. 2000).

247. Zelinsky, "Metropolitanism," 691.

248. David W. Chen, "Yonkers Desegregation Plan Clears Hurdle in High Court:

Justices Let Stand a Ruling against the City," *New York Times*, D5 (Dec. 4, 2001).

249. Winnie Hu, "No More Raging at a Yellow Bus," *New York Times*, §1, at 29 (Jan. 13, 2002). Immigration can account for only a small part of this decline. The school side of the case was settled in late March 2002. Winnie Hu, "Judge Approves Settlement in Yonkers Desegregation Suit," *New York Times*, B8 (Mar. 27, 2002).

250. A possible contender is school finance litigation. See Heise, "Preliminary Thoughts," 99–101.

251. Federal law permits states and localities to bar landlords from discriminating against voucher-holders as such. 24 C.F.R. §982.52 (1995).

252. See generally Schuck, *The Limits of Law*, chap. 13.

253. See generally David M. Halbfinger, "Yes, in Our Backyard: Accepting a Shelter Can Be a Lucrative Deal," *New York Times*, §1, at 29 (Feb. 24, 2002).

7. RELIGION

1. Ted G. Jelen, *To Serve God and Mammon: Church-State Relations in American Politics*, 7, table 1.1 (2000).

2. Diana L. Eck, *A New Religious America: How a "Christian Country" Has Now Become the World's Most Religiously Diverse Nation* (2001). Eck is an expert on religious diversity in India, which is the only serious competitor for this distinction.

3. Peter L. Berger, "Foreword," in Charles L. Glenn, *The Ambiguous Embrace: Government and Faith-Based Schools and Social Agencies*, xi (2000).

4. See, e.g., Jon Butler, *Awash in a Sea of Faith: Christianizing the American People* (1990).

5. Quoted in Barbara Goldsmith, *Other Powers: The Age of Suffrage, Spiritualism, and the Scandalous Victoria Woodhull*, 85 (1998).

6. See generally John T. Noonan, Jr., *The Lustre of Our Country: The American Experience of Religious Freedom*, chap. 2 (1998).

7. Eck, *A New Religious America*, 36–40.

8. Even today, atheists and agnostics feel beleaguered by intolerance. See, e.g., Natalie Angier, "Confessions of a Lonely Atheist," *New York Times Magazine*, 34 (Jan. 14, 2001).

9. Alan Wolfe, *One Nation, After All: What Middle-Class Americans Really Think about God, Country, Family, Racism, Welfare, Immigration, Homosexuality, Work, the Right, the Left, and Each Other* (1998).

10. For a summary of this episode in American legal and religious history, see John T. Noonan, Jr., and Edward M. Gaffney, Jr., *Religious Freedom: History, Cases, and Other Materials on the Interaction of Religion and Government*, chap. 9 (2001).

11. See John T. Noonan, Jr., "Religious Liberty at the Stake," 84 *Virginia Law Review* 459, 466 (1998).

12. For an account of this document and its evolution, see Noonan, *The Lustre of Our Country*, 348–353.

13. Steven D. Smith, *Getting over Equality: A Critical Diagnosis of Religious Freedom in America,* 21 (2001).

14. Some commentators argue that there really is but one religion clause and that this affects its interpretation. See, e.g., Akhil Reed Amar, "The Supreme Court, 1999 Term: Foreword—the Document and the Doctrine," 114 *Harvard Law Review* 26, 120 (2000); Stephen L. Carter, "Religious Freedom As If Religion Matters: A Tribute to Justice Brennan," 87 *California Law Review* 1059, 1061 (1999); Richard. J. Neuhaus, "A New Order of Religious Freedom," 60 *George Washington Law Review* 620, 626–627 (1992) (stating that there is only one religion clause and as a result there is no need to balance between free exercise and establishment). Others argue that the Free Exercise Clause is essentially redundant because of the large zone of protection afforded to religious exercise by other constitutional provisions, especially the Fourteenth Amendment. See Mark Tushnet, "The Redundant Free Exercise Clause?" 33 *Loyola University of Chicago Law Review* 71 (2001); Kenji Yoshino, "Covering," 111 *Yale Law Journal* 769, 927–930 (2002).

15. Stanley Fish, *The Trouble with Principle,* chap. 9 (1999).

16. Daryl J. Levinson, "Framing Transactions in Constitutional Law," 11 *Yale Law Journal* 1311 (2002).

17. Employment Division, Department of Human Resources of Oregon v. Smith, 494 U.S. 872 (1990). For an extended argument applauding *Smith* on philosophical grounds, see Brian Barry, *Culture and Equality* (2001).

18. See James E. Ryan, "*Smith* and the Religious Freedom Restoration Act: An Iconoclastic Assessment," 78 *Virginia Law Review* 1407 (1992) (reviewing cases).

19. For a nonexhaustive list of them, see Noonan, *The Lustre of Our Country,* 236–237.

20. See, e.g., Brown v. Gilmore, 258 F.3d 265 (4th Cir.), cert. denied, 122 S. Ct. 465 (2001) (upholding Virginia's "minute of silence" law).

21. See Gregg Easterbrook, "Religion in America," *Brookings Review,* 45, 48 (Winter 2002) (vast majority of Americans view atheists much less favorably than religionists of any denomination).

22. Eck, *A New Religious America,* 3.

23. Id., 5.

24. See generally H. Richard Niebuhr, *The Social Sources of Denominationalism* (1929).

25. Jon Butler, *Becoming America: The Revolution before 1776* (2000).

26. Robert W. Fogel, *The Fourth Great Awakening and the Future of Egalitarianism,* 123 (2000).

27. See, e.g., Gustav Niebuhr, "With Texas Group's Proposal, Struggle among Baptists Enters a New Phase," *New York Times,* A8 (Oct. 28, 2000) (conflict between national and Texas Baptist conventions); Gustav Niebuhr, "Carter Seeking Alliance of Moderate Baptists," *New York Times,* A26 (June 30, 2001; Peter Steinfels, "Beliefs," *New York Times,* B8 (Oct. 7, 2000) (Vatican's issuance of "Dominus Iesus" challenging some ecumenism); Barbara Carton, "Protestants

Look to Their Roots," *Wall Street Journal,* B1 (Oct. 19, 2000) (quest for sectarian identities).

28. Peter Berger, *The Sacred Canopy: Elements of a Sociological Theory of Religion,* 137, 141, 145 (1967).

29. Wade Clark Roof, *Spiritual Marketplace: Baby Boomers and the Remaking of American Religion* (1999). See also Richard Cimino and Don Lattin, *Shopping for Faith: American Religion in the New Millennium* (1998).

30. On the tension between competition, "ecumenicity," and "cartelization" among religions, see Berger, *The Sacred Canopy,* 140–144. The recent agreement between the Evangelical Lutheran Church in America and the Episcopal Church to share clergy, facilities, and missionary work, a move apparently prompted as much by changing demographics and economic factors as by theology, probably does not presage any genuine interdenominational merger. Laurie Goodstein, "Episcopalians Inaugurate Alliance with Lutherans," *New York Times,* 12 (Jan. 7, 2001). In contrast to formal mergers, informal collaborations have been common in American Protestantism. E-mail from Mark Silk, director of the Leonard E. Greenberg Center for the Study of Religion in Public Life and Adjunct Associate Professor of Religion, Trinity College, to author (Oct. 26, 2001).

31. See Gustav Niebuhr, "Humanist Jewish Group Reaches New Milestone," *New York Times,* A10 (Oct. 20, 2001) (growing number of ordinations).

32. See Norimitsu Onishi, "Africans Fill Churches That Celebrate Wealth," *New York Times,* A1 (Mar. 13, 2002) (U.S. Pentecostal groups leading boom in Africa).

33. Glenn, *The Ambiguous Embrace,* 20–21.

34. Andrew Kohut, John C. Green, Scott Keeter, and Robert C. Toth, *The Diminishing Divide: Religion's Changing Role in American Politics,* 18–19 (2000).

35. Richard N. Ostling, "America's Ever-Changing Religious Landscape," in *What's God Got to Do with the American Experiment?,* 21–22 (E. J. Dionne, Jr., and John J. DiIulio, Jr., eds., 2000). See also Gustav Niebuhr, "Catholic Bishops Elect First Black President," *New York Times,* A14 (Nov. 14, 2001) (thirteen black bishops in U.S. Catholic Church).

36. Kohut et al., *The Diminishing Divide,* 63–64.

37. Ostling, "America's Ever-Changing Religious Landscape," 19.

38. Russell Shorto, "Belief by the Numbers," *New York Times Magazine,* 60 (Dec. 7, 1997).

39. Ostling, "America's Ever-Changing Religious Landscape," 18.

40. Id.

41. See "Largest Denominational Families in U.S., 2001," *www.adherents.com/rel_USA.html* (last visited Dec. 20, 2001).

42. Russell Shorto, *Gospel Truth: The New Image of Jesus Emerging from Science and History, and Why It Matters,* 234 (1997). In England, the Anglican Church has lost 10% of its rolls in five years. Id. See also Laurie Goodstein, "Conservative Churches Grew Fastest in 1990s, Report Says," *New York Times,* A22 (Sept. 18, 2002).

43. Goodstein, id.; Gustav Niebuhr, "Vietnamese Immigrants Swell Catholic Clergy," *New York Times,* A11 (Apr. 24, 2000).

44. Stability in the overall Baptist share masks a decline outside the Southern Baptist Convention. Goodstein, "Conservative Churches Grew Fastest in 1990s." Judaism's share, when including those unaffiliated with synagogues, increased 2.7%, to 6.1 million, but the share of those affiliated declined. See Goodstein, id.; *www.adherents.com/rel_USA.html* (last visited Dec. 20, 2001).

45. See *www.adherents.com/rel_USA.html;* Goodstein, id. At the same time, the evangelical movement has entered the intellectual mainstream. See Alan Wolfe, "The Opening of the Evangelical Mind," *Atlantic Monthly,* 55 (Oct. 2000).

46. Easterbrook, "Religion in America," 46.

47. Even so, mainstream and especially evangelical Christian groups are expanding rapidly in South America, Asia, and Africa. Gustav Niebuhr, "At Conference, Billy Graham's Torch Moves South," *New York Times,* 6 (July 30, 2000).

48. Stephen Prothero, "Church Spires and Minarets," *Wall Street Journal,* A16 (June 20, 2001).

49. See Gustav Niebuhr, "Studies Suggest Lower Count for Number of U.S. Muslims," *New York Times,* A16 (Oct. 25, 2001); Gustav Niebuhr, "Study Finds Number of Mosques Up 25% in 6 Years," *New York Times,* A12 (Apr. 27, 2001). Earlier statements that Muslims in the United States exceed either Presbyterians or Episcopalians, e.g., Eck, *A New Religious America,* 3, were probably based on erroneous estimates.

50. Ostling, "America's Ever-Changing Religious Landscape," 23; Blaine Harden, "Saudis Seek to Add U.S. Muslims to Their Sect," *New York Times,* A1 (Oct. 20, 2001); Michelle Cottle, "Native Speakers," *The New Republic,* 16 (Nov. 19, 2001) (tensions between black and Arab-origin Muslims).

51. See generally Yvonne Yazbeck Haddad and John L. Esposito, eds., *Muslims on the Americanization Path?* (2000). The number of mosques increased by 25% between 1994 and 2000. Gustav Niebuhr, "Study Finds Number of Mosques Up 25% in 6 Years." As "archetypal swing voters" in politically important states, Muslims' influence is growing. Lexington, "The Birth of an Arab-American Lobby," *The Economist,* 41 (Oct. 14, 2000).

52. Eck, *A New Religious America,* chap. 4, traces the various Buddhist traditions in the United States.

53. Id., 3. On the stupa, see Gustav Niebuhr, "Towering Buddhist Shrine Is Consecrated in Rockies," *New York Times,* A12 (Aug. 20, 2001). See also Gustav Niebuhr, "A Monk in Exile Dreams of Return to Vietnam," *New York Times,* A8 (Oct. 16, 1999) (citing report by Don Morreale, *The Complete Guide to Buddhist America* (1998)); Gustav Niebuhr, "Zen on the Prison Grapevine," *New York Times,* B1 (May 30, 2001).

54. Eck, *A New Religious America,* 336.

55. David B. Barrett, *World Christian Encyclopedia* (2001); *1996 Britannica Book of the Year,* Table: Non-Christian Religious Adherents in the United States. Estimates, however, vary considerably.

56. Gustav Niebuhr, "Pagans' Spiritual Umbrella Opens Wide," *New York Times,*

A12 (Sept. 19, 2000). See also Eck, *A New Religious America* (describing Wiccan groups).

57. Gustav Niebuhr, "Makeup of American Religion Is Looking More Like Mosaic, Data Say," *New York Times,* 14 (Apr. 12, 1998).

58. See generally Peter H. Schuck, *The Limits of Law: Essays on Democratic Governance,* chap. 3 (2000).

59. Garry Wills, "Jesuits in Disarray," *New York Review of Books,* 12 (Mar. 28, 2002) (reviewing Peter McDonough and Eugene C. Bianchi, *Passionate Uncertainty: Inside the American Jesuits* (2002)).

60. Gustav Niebuhr, "Across America, Immigration Is Changing the Face of Religion," *New York Times,* A18 (Sept. 23, 1999).

61. For a reprise of this great work, see Charles Taylor, *Varieties of Religion Today: William James Revisited* (2002).

62. See James R. Lewis, *The Encyclopedia of Cults, Sects, and New Religions* (1998).

63. Alan Wolfe, *One Nation, After All,* 83.

64. See, e.g., R. Stephen Warner, "The Congregation in American Society," in *American Congregations,* vol. 2 (James Wind and James Lewis, eds., 1994).

65. See Frank Bruni, "Sins of the Church," *New York Times,* A1 (Apr. 8, 2002).

66. See Robert Wuthnow, *Restructuring American Religion: Society and Faith since World War II,* chap. 6, esp. 130–131 (1988).

67. Laurie Goodstein, "Search for the Right Church Ends at Home," *New York Times,* 1 (Apr. 29, 2001) (number of home churches apparently growing).

68. The statistics are taken from Jelen, *To Serve God and Mammon,* 7, table 1.1; Shorto, "Belief by the Numbers"; and Natalie Angier, "Confessions of a Lonely Atheist."

69. Susan Stellin, "Many Are Using Internet to Seek Spiritual Aid," *New York Times,* C3 (Dec. 24, 2001) (Pew survey).

70. Many of the countries with lower church attendance, moreover, have state or state-favored religions. See Christopher Shea, "Too Few in the Pew?" *Lingua Franca,* 10 (March 2001). Blacks appear to be the most devout group in the United States.

71. See Robert Wuthnow, *The Struggle for America's Soul: Evangelicals, Liberals, and Secularism,* 50 (1989) (comparing number of Bibles purchased and churches and clergy per capita in Europe).

72. Jose Casanova, *Public Religions in the Modern World,* 135 (1994).

73. Bill Broadway, "Are the Faithful Misinformed? Americans Hold 'Errant' Theological Positions, Survey Finds," *Washington Post,* B9 (Aug. 5, 2000) (40% believe that the Holy Spirit and Satan do not exist, and more than 20% deny Jesus' physical resurrection and say Jesus the man was a sinner).

74. See, e.g., Fogel, *The Fourth Great Awakening* (describing the present period as "the Fourth Great Awakening").

75. See Richard Parker, "Progressive Politics and Visions and, Uh, Well . . . God," in *What's God Got to Do with the American Experiment?,* 63 (citing study that 86% of Washington press corps seldom or never attend religious services).

76. Kohut et al., *The Diminishing Divide,* 19–20; Ostling, "America's Ever-Changing Religious Landscape," 23.

77. Shorto, *Gospel Truth,* 234.
78. Id., 25–28, 31–32.
79. See, e.g., Easterbrook, "Religion in America," 48.
80. Id. (discussing Pew survey).
81. Wolfe, *One Nation, After All,* 71–72.
82. The research and debate are summarized in Christopher Shea, "Supply and Demand among the Faithful," *New York Times,* B9 (Mar. 24, 2001).
83. See Carton, "Protestants Look to Their Roots."
84. See, e.g., Freeman J. Dyson, "Science and Religion: No Ends in Sight," *New York Review of Books,* 4 (Mar. 28, 2002).
85. Eck, *A New Religious America,* 22–25, 69–77.
86. Kenneth L. Karst, *Law's Promise, Law's Expression: Visions of Power in the Politics of Race, Gender, and Religion,* 150 (1993).
87. Mother Katherine Drexel, renowned for celebrating diversity for this reason, is being canonized by the Catholic Church even though it holds that nonbelievers are in fundamental error. Diana Jean Schemo, "Pope Announces Sainthood for Champion of Minorities," *New York Times,* A9 (Mar. 11, 2000).
88. The Federalist, No. 10.
89. See Gustav Niebuhr, "Keeping Friends and the Faith," *New York Times,* Week in Review at 6 (Sept. 17, 2000); Peter Steinfels, "Beliefs"; Laurie Goodstein, "A.C.L.U. Sues a School District for Closing on the Jewish High Holy Days," *New York Times,* A2 (Sept. 9, 1999).
90. E-mail from Nicole Stelle Garnett, Assistant Professor of Law, University of Notre Dame Law School, to author (Nov. 12, 2000).
91. The Federalist, No. 51.
92. The Federalist, No. 10.
93. Gordon S. Wood, "Give Me Diversity or Give Me Death," *The New Republic,* 34, 38 (June 12, 2000) (review of Jon Butler, *Becoming America: The Revolution before 1776* (2000)).
94. See Philip Gleason, *Keeping the Faith: American Catholicism Past and Present* (1987); Jonathan M. Butler, *Softly and Tenderly Jesus Is Calling: Heaven and Hell in American Revivalism, 1870–1920* (1991); Oscar Handlin, *The Uprooted: The Epic Story of the Great Migrations That Made the American People* (1951); Howard M. Sachar, *A History of the Jews in America* (1992).
95. See, e.g., Noonan, *The Lustre of Our Country,* chap. 13; Stephen Macedo, *Diversity and Distrust: Civic Education in a Multicultural Democracy,* 7, 131–138 (2000).
96. Jose Casanova and Aristide R. Zolberg, "Religion and Immigrant Incorporation in New York" (2001) (unpublished manuscript, New School University). For some other specific examples, see Gustav Niebuhr, "Across America, Immigration Is Changing the Face of Religion"; David Gonzalez, "Leaders of 11 Orthodox Churches in America Plan Unity Move," *New York Times,* A22 (Dec. 9, 1994) (unification reflects Americanization of their immigrant members).
97. See discussion in Robert C. Ellickson, "Property in Land," 102 *Yale Law Journal* 1315, 1357–1362 (1993).
98. This paragraph and the next draw on Noonan and Gaffney, *Religious Freedom,*

391–417, and Kent Greenawalt, "All or Nothing at All: The Defeat of Selective Conscientious Objection," 1971 *Supreme Court Review* 31, 35–47.

99. United States v. Seeger, 380 U.S. 163 (1965).

100. Welsh v. United States, 398 U.S. 333 (1970). In 1971, however, it denied relief to a selective conscientious objector who opposed only the Vietnam War. United States v. Gillette, 401 U.S. 437 (1971).

101. Noonan and Gaffney, *Religious Freedom,* 408. See generally Kent Greenawalt, "Religion as a Concept in Constitutional Law," 72 *California Law Review* 753 (1984). On Scientology, see Paul Horwitz, "Scientology in Court: A Comparative Analysis and Some Thoughts on Selected Issues in Law and Religion," 47 *DePaul Law Review* 85 (1997). On the Unification Church, see Anne Berrill Carroll, "Religion, Politics, and the IRS: Defining the Limits of Tax Law Controls on Political Expression by Churches," 76 *Marquette Law Review* 217 (1992).

102. Alan Wolfe, "Judging the President," in *What's God Got to Do with the American Experiment?,* 90.

103. This discussion draws on Jelen, *To Serve God and Mammon,* chap. 1. Stephen Carter asserts that all theories of church-state relations are about "either neutrality or accommodationism." Stephen L. Carter, *God's Name in Vain: The Rights and Wrongs of Religion in Politics,* 159 (2000).

104. For example, Brennan wrote the majority opinion in Sherbert v. Verner, 374 U.S. 398 (1963), while dissenting in Lyng v. Northwest Indian Cemetery Protective Assn., 485 U.S. 439 (1988), noted later. I thank Kent Greenawalt for this point. Telephone conversation (Dec. 14, 2001).

105. Employment Division, Department of Human Resources of Oregon v. Smith, 494 U.S. 872 (1990). On this point, see Michael W. McConnell, "The Origins and Historical Understanding of Free Exercise of Religion," 103 *Harvard Law Review* 1409, 1451 (1990). The Court's free speech doctrines may render this distinction redundant. See Tushnet, "The Redundant Free Exercise Clause?"

106. Philip Hamburger, *Separation of Church and State* (2002). Stephen Carter traces the source of the wall metaphor to a theological distinction developed by Roger Williams, the seventeenth-century religious dissenter, between two divinely ordained realms—the wilderness (secular) and the garden (spiritual). The wall, Carter holds, protects the garden from the wilderness, not the reverse. Carter, *God's Name in Vain,* 74–81. Everson v. Board of Education, 330 U.S. 1 (1947), the first Supreme Court decision invalidating a law on Establishment Clause grounds, is often criticized for misreading and misusing the metaphor.

107. See also, e.g., Michael W. McConnell, "Accommodation of Religion: An Update and a Response to the Critics," 60 *George Washington Law Review* 685 (1992).

108. 2002 WL 1370796. For my brief analysis of this decision, see Peter H. Schuck, "The Pledge on the Edge," *The American Lawyer,* 65 (Sept. 2002).

109. See, e.g., Macedo, *Diversity and Distrust,* 220–226 (describing Carter's "illiberal" tendencies and asserting that "Carter's political sectarian cannot be a good citizen" in the liberal sense).

110. I could have chosen other disputants. Compare, e.g., separatist Brian Barry in

Culture and Equality (2001) with accommodationist William A. Galston in "Who's a Liberal?" *The Public Interest,* 100 (Summer 2001) (reviewing Barry).

111. Carter, *God's Name in Vain,* 72–74, 159–162.

112. Macedo, *Diversity and Distrust,* chap. 6.

113. For a recent statement of this verity, see William P. Marshall, "The Culture of Belief and the Politics of Religion," 63 *Law and Contemporary Problems* 453 (2000).

114. Goldman v. Weinberger, 475 U.S. 503 (1986).

115. Macedo, *Diversity and Distrust,* 8–12. Other neutrality skeptics include Jelen, *To Serve God and Mammon,* 123.

116. See, e.g., Ira C. Lupu, "The Trouble with Accommodation," 60 *George Washington Law Review* 743 (1992).

117. For book-length studies of this important case, see Garrett Epps, *To an Unknown God: Religious Freedom on Trial* (2001); Carolyn N. Long, *Religious Freedom and Indian Rights: The Case of Oregon v. Smith* (2000).

118. I am hardly the first to point this out. See, e.g., Marshall, "The Culture of Belief and the Politics of Religion," 464–465; Ira C. Lupu, "Threading between the Religion Clauses," 63 *Law and Contemporary Problems* 439, 451 (2000).

119. Ryan, "*Smith* and the Religious Freedom Restoration Act," 1445–1451 (reviewing statutes).

120. Pub. L. No. 103-141, 107 Stat. 1488 (1993). For a brief account of the politics that preceded the RFRA, see Epps, *To an Unknown God,* 227–234.

121. See Ryan, "*Smith* and the Religious Freedom Restoration Act." Government agencies at all levels, however, did seek to de-fang the RFRA. See Lupu, "Threading between the Religion Clauses," 443.

122. Church of Lukumi Babalu Aye, Inc. v. City of Hialeah, 508 U.S. 520 (1993).

123. City of Boerne v. Flores, 521 U.S. 507 (1997).

124. Macedo, *Diversity and Distrust,* 38.

125. Id., 38–39, 138.

126. Political support for the two positions within Protestantism has shifted dramatically since the 1960s. For a fascinating account, see John C. Jeffries, Jr., and James E. Ryan, "A Political History of the Establishment Clause," 100 *Michigan Law Review* 279, 338–365 (2001).

127. Carter, *God's Name in Vain,* chap. 11.

128. Macedo, *Diversity and Distrust.*

129. See Rosemary C. Salamone, *Visions of Schooling: Conscience, Community, and Common Education,* 233–240 (2000) (defining national civic values).

130. Carter, *God's Name in Vain,* 167.

131. 494 U.S. 872 (1990).

132. This test was elaborated and applied in Sherbert v. Verner, 374 U.S. 398 (1963), and reaffirmed in Wisconsin v. Yoder, 406 U.S. 205 (1972).

133. For example, the Court has allowed government actions that could "devastate" religious practices. Lyng v. Northwest Indian Cemetery Protective Assn., 485 U.S. 439 (1988).

134. Macedo, *Diversity and Distrust,* 200–201.

135. Mozert v. Hawkins County Public Schools, 827 F.2d 1058 (6th Cir. 1987), cert. denied, 484 U.S. 1066 (1988).
136. Macedo, *Diversity and Distrust*, 160.
137. Id., 202.
138. Carter, *God's Name in Vain*, 182–183.
139. Noonan and Gaffney, *Religious Freedom*, 546.
140. This problem is discussed in Macedo, *Diversity and Distrust*, 198–200; Salamone, *Visions of Schooling*, 216–223. See generally Peter H. Schuck, "When the Exception Becomes the Rule: Regulatory Equity and the Formulation of Energy Policy through an Exceptions Process," 1984 *Duke Law Journal* 165.
141. Pub. L. No. 106-274, 114 Stat. 803 (2000).
142. A recent review of post-*Smith* decisions indicates that the lower courts are interpreting it narrowly and accommodating many exceptions. Carol M. Kaplan, "The Devil Is in the Details: Neutral, Generally Applicable Laws and Exceptions from *Smith*," 75 *New York University Law Review* 1045 (2000).
143. "Thus far, dissenting secular beliefs, no matter how sincerely held or central to a group's identity, have not moved either the courts or the educational bureaucrats." Stephen Arons, *Compelling Belief: The Culture of American Schooling*, 181 (1983).
144. Goldman v. Weinberger, 475 U.S. 503 (1986).
145. Indeed, Congress later did so. See Noonan and Gaffney, *Religious Freedom*, 462.
146. See, e.g., Ali v. Alamo Rent-A-Car, Inc., 246 F.3d 662 (4th Cir.), cert. denied, 122 S. Ct. 323 (2001) (no adverse employment action).
147. For an argument that balancing is not what courts really do in these cases, see Smith, *Getting over Equality*, 92–96.
148. See Lupu, "Threading between the Religion Clauses," 445–446.
149. Compare, e.g., Leonard W. Levy, *The Establishment Clause: Religion and the First Amendment* (1994); William L. Miller, *The First Liberty: Religion and the American Republic* (1986); and Douglas Laycock, "'Nonpreferential Aid to Religion: A False Claim about Original Intent," 27 *William and Mary Law Review* 875 (1986), with McConnell, "The Origins and Historical Understanding of Free Exercise of Religion."
150. Jeffries and Ryan, "A Political History of the Establishment Clause."
151. Lemon v. Kurtzman, 403 U.S. 602 (1971).
152. See, e.g., Noonan and Gaffney, *Religious Freedom*, 740–742, and the Court's decision in Mitchell v. Helms, 530 U.S. 793 (2000) (upholding state distribution of educational materials and equipment to all public and private schools on an enrollment basis, but dividing sharply on the appropriate test).
153. This might be accomplished under "federal RFRA," assuming it survives *City of Boerne*. See Gregory P. Magarian, "How to Apply the Religious Freedom Restoration Act to Federal Law without Violating the Constitution," 99 *Michigan Law Review* 1903 (2001).
154. Civil Rights Act of 1964, 42 U.S.C. §2000e(j).
155. See, e.g., Wisconsin v. Yoder, 406 U.S. 205 (1972). This is so even though the

government is intentionally advancing religion. See Edwards v. Aguillard, 482 U.S. 578, 610 (1987) (Scalia, J., dissenting). The fact that some states or localities have accommodated a minority practice strongly suggests that other jurisdictions lack a compelling interest in refusing to do so. See, e.g., Francis X. Clines, "Traffic Ticket Spurs Fight on Religion," *New York Times,* A18 (June 6, 2002) (law requiring bright reflector triangle on vehicle burdens Amish who oppose secular symbols on buggies and prefer gray tape, which some other states accept); Dana Canedy, "Lifting Veil for Photo ID Goes Too Far, Driver Says," *New York Times,* A16 (June 27, 2002) (Muslim cannot lift her veil as law requires; many states waive requirement for religious reasons).

156. Good News Club v. Milford Central School, 533 U.S. 98 (2001) (school cannot exclude religious club from using facilities after hours); Rosenberger v. Rector and Visitors of University of Virginia, 515 U.S. 819 (1995) (university cannot exclude from funding student publication addressing issues from religious perspective); and Lamb's Chapel v. Center Moriches Union Free School District, 508 U.S. 384 (1993) (school cannot exclude group presenting films although it discusses them from religious perspective). See also Gentala v. Tucker, 122 S. Ct. 340 (2001) (in light of *Good News Club,* Court vacated lower court decision allowing city to waive its park-use fees for all groups but religious ones).

157. Kiryas Joel Village School District v. Grumet, 512 U.S. 687 (1994).

158. The precedent was Aguilar v. Fenton, 473 U.S. 402 (1985) (invalidating use of Title I funds to send public school teachers to teach on parochial school premises). It was overruled in Agostino v. Felton, 521 U.S. 203 (1997) (upholding same).

159. After three new laws to establish the special district without running afoul of the Court's ruling were struck down by state and federal courts, a fourth law has been upheld by a state trial court. Abby Goodnough, "Ruling Favors Public School in Hasidic Village," *New York Times,* B3 (Feb. 20, 2001).

160. Lee v. Weisman, 505 U.S. 577 (1992).

161. Santa Fe Independent School District v. Doe, 530 U.S. 290 (2000). See also Doe v. School Board of Ouachita Parish, 274 F.3d 289 (5th Cir. 2001) (invalidating state law allowing vocal classroom prayer). But see Diana Jean Schemo, "After a Surge, Limits Return to School Prayer," *New York Times,* A16 (Oct. 23, 2001) (widespread defiance of decision in wake of Sept. 11 attack).

162. On this point, see the powerful dissenting opinion of Justice Scalia in *Lee,* 505 U.S. at 631.

163. See Michael Janofsky, "Colorado Children's Deaths Rekindle Debate on Religion," *New York Times,* A10 (Feb. 21, 2001) (state considering law to eliminate defense to prosecution, created by 46 states, for parents withholding medical treatment from children for religious reasons; study found 172 cases of children dying this way between 1975 and 1995, more than 30 in Colorado).

164. See, e.g., Prince v. Massachusetts, 321 U.S. 158 (1944); Application of President and Directors of Georgetown College, 331 F.2d 1000 (D.C. Cir.), cert. denied, 377 U.S. 978 (1964).

165. Perhaps the hardest cases involve parental withholding of medical treatment. See Richard W. Garnett, "Taking *Pierce* Seriously: The Family, Religious Education,

and Harm to Children," 76 *Notre Dame Law Review* 109, 116–117 (2000) (expressing doubt about how to "strike the balance").

166. See Marshall, "The Culture of Belief and the Politics of Religion," 457–458 (62% of Americans in 1993 believed religion is losing its social influence, up from 14% in 1957, but explaining volatility in such views).

167. Pub. L. No. 105-292, 112 Stat. 2787 (1998).

168. 42 U.S.C. §1996a (1994). This statute would not protect one of the *Smith* plaintiffs who was not an Indian. E-mail from Garrett Epps, Associate Professor of Law, University of Oregon, to author (Oct. 28, 1991).

169. Pub. L. No. 104-155, 110 Stat. 392 (1996).

170. See, e.g., Pam Belluck, "Many States Ceding Regulations to Church Groups," *New York Times*, A1 (July 27, 2001) (states passing and considering RFRA-type laws and state supreme courts are doing so by interpretation); Noonan and Gaffney, *Religious Freedom*, 535–536 (state statutory and constitutional protections).

171. For an exhaustive list, see Marci A. Hamilton, "Religion and the Law in the Clinton Era: An Anti-Madisonian Legacy," 63 *Law and Contemporary Problems* 360 (Winter-Spring 2000). See also Marshall, "The Culture of Belief and the Politics of Religion," 453–454 (listing others and noting that House majority approved a school prayer amendment for the first time in almost thirty years).

172. Carter, *God's Name in Vain*, 7.

173. See, e.g., Lyng v. Northwest Indian Cemetery Protective Assn., 485 U.S. 439 (1988) (allowing government to build road through national forest traditionally used by Indian tribes).

174. See Blaine Harden, "Religious and Public Stations Battle for Share of Radio Dial," *New York Times*, 1 (Sept. 15, 2002) (religious stations dominating many public stations in ratings and in power of radio signal).

175. See Wolfe, "The Opening of the Evangelical Mind"; David D. Kirkpatrick, "Evangelical Sales Are Converting Publishers," *New York Times*, B9 (June 8, 2002).

176. Personal communication with Wade Clark Roof, chair, Department of Religious Studies, University of California at Santa Barbara, and Jackson W. Carroll, director of Ormond Center, Divinity School, Duke University (Aug. 15, 2001).

177. Church of Lukumi Babalu Aye, Inc. v. City of Hialeah, 508 U.S. 520 (1993). For a critical view of the reasoning, not the result, in this case, see Smith, *Getting over Equality*, 122–139.

178. See Marci Hamilton, "Free? Exercise," 42 *William and Mary Law Review* 823 (2001) (cataloging them).

179. Review of Carter's book, *The New Republic*, 4 (Sept. 13, 1993).

180. To an extent, I have done so elsewhere. See, e.g., Schuck, *The Limits of Law*, chap. 7; Schuck, *Citizens, Strangers, and In-Betweens: Essays on Immigration and Citizenship*, chap. 14, esp. 355–358 (1998).

181. The social science and religious literature on this is enormous. On the social science side, see, e.g., James Q. Wilson, *The Moral Sense* (1993); Robert N. Bellah et al., *Habits of the Heart: Individualism and Commitment in American Life* (1996); Fogel, *The Fourth Great Awakening*. On the religion side, see, e.g., Max

L. Stackhouse, *Covenant and Commitments: Faith, Family, and Economic Life* (1997).

182. See, e.g., Wuthnow, *The Struggle for America's Soul;* Martin Marty, *Modern American Religion* (1986); Marty, *The Public Church: Mainline-Evangelical-Catholic* (1981).

183. See generally, Fogel, *The Fourth Great Awakening,* chap. 3.

184. Some claim that recent presidents, especially Clinton, have whitewashed this danger. See, e.g., Hamilton, "Religion and the Law in the Clinton Era," 361–363, 389; Levy, *The Establishment Clause.*

185. Kansas, which decided in 1999 to remove evolution as the sole explanation of man's origins, reinstated it in 2001. John W. Fountain, "Kansas Puts Evolution Back into Public Schools," *New York Times,* A18 (Feb. 15, 2001).

186. Macedo, *Diversity and Distrust,* chaps. 2, 6.

187. Carter, *God's Name in Vain,* 5–6.

188. The study is summarized in Ram Cnaan and Gaynor I. Yancey, "Our Hidden Safety Net," in *What's God Got to Do with the American Experiment?,* 153.

189. Mark Chaves, "Religious Congregations and Welfare Reform: Who Will Take Advantage of Charitable Choice?" 64 *American Sociological Review* 836 (1999).

190. "Compassionate Conservatism Takes a Bow," *The Economist,* 29 (Feb. 3, 2001).

191. See *Finding Common Ground: 29 Recommendations of the Working Group on Human Needs and Faith-Based and Community Initiatives,* table 1 (Jan. 2002) available at *www.working-group.org* (typology ranging from "faith-saturated" to "secular").

192. Stephen V. Monsma, *When Sacred and Secular Mix: Religious Nonprofit Organizations and Public Money,* xi (1996). By way of comparison, the Canadian government has supported FBOs for almost a century. See Anthony DePalma, "Canada Cuts Back Funds for Faith-Based Charities," *New York Times,* A3 (July 24, 2001).

193. Letter from Judge John T. Noonan to author (Nov. 13, 2001) ("[T]he Supreme Court did not even blink, as *Worcester v. Georgia* shows").

194. See Macedo, *Diversity and Distrust,* 41–147 and sources there cited.

195. Monsma, *When Sacred and Secular Mix,* 4–10 (using extensive survey of nonprofit organizations).

196. Id., 68.

197. See Hamilton, "Religion and the Law in the Clinton Era."

198. Chaves, "Religious Congregations and Welfare Reform."

199. Laurie Goodstein, "Many Churches Slow to Accept Government Money to Help the Poor," *New York Times,* A1 (Oct. 17, 2000) (slow, lukewarm response to 1996 law by states and churches); Marc Lacy and Laurie Goodstein, "Bush Fleshes Out Details of Proposal to Expand Aid to Religious Organizations," *New York Times,* A15 (Jan. 31, 2001) (participants mostly black urban churches).

200. White House, "Unlevel Playing Field: Barriers to Participation by Faith-Based and Community Organizations in Federal Social Service Programs" (Aug. 2001), available at *http://purl.access.gpo.gov/gpo/lps16590.*

201. See Elizabeth Becker, "House Backs Aid for Charities Operated by Religious Groups," *New York Times,* A1 (July 20, 2001); Democrats were split on the bill.

Elizabeth Becker, "Democrats Stand on Both Sides of Faith Bill," *New York Times*, A16 (July 18, 2001).

202. Corporation of Presiding Bishop v. Amos, 483 U.S. 327 (1987).

203. This concern is widely shared, even among supporters of the legislation. See Laurie Goodstein, "Support for Religion-Based Plan Is Hedged," *New York Times*, A14 (Apr. 11, 2001) (survey shows widespread opposition to funding such churches; blacks, Hispanics, and younger people more favorable to legislation in general).

204. See Laurie Goodstein, "Bush Aide Tells of Plan to Aid Work by Churches," *New York Times*, A10 (Mar. 8, 2001); Laurie Goodstein, "Bush's Charity Plan Is Raising Concerns for Religious Right," *New York Times*, A1 (Mar. 3, 2001); John Gibeaut, "'Welcome to Hell,'" *American Bar Association Journal*, 44 (Aug. 2001) (reviewing FBO abuse scandal in Texas). The Methodist leadership and Catholic bishops, however, voted to support the proposal. E-mail from Mark Silk, director of the Leonard E. Greenberg Center for the Study of Religion in Public Life and Adjunct Associate Professor of Religion, Trinity College, to author (Oct. 26, 2001).

205. Elizabeth Becker, "Head of Religion-Based Initiative Resigns," *New York Times*, A11 (Aug. 18, 2001); Elisabeth Bumiller, "New Leader Picked for Religion-Based Initiative," *New York Times*, A14 (Feb. 2, 2002).

206. See Easterbrook, "Religion in America," 47 (discussing Pew survey).

207. See, e.g., Amy Sherman, "Should We Put Faith in Charitable Choice?" 10 *The Responsive Community* 22 (2000), and comments by others, id. at 31–39.

208. See Laurie Goodstein, "Church-Based Projects Lack Data on Results," *New York Times*, A12 (Apr. 24, 2001) (experts, including University of Pennsylvania colleague of DiIulio, discuss studies).

209. For a pending conflict, see Freedom from Religion Foundation, Inc. v. McCallum, 2002 WL 24246 (W.D. Wis. 2002) (challenging faith-based substance-abuse program).

210. See, e.g., Jane Fritsch, "Chief Judge Calls for Measures to Thwart Guardianship Abuses," *New York Times*, D7 (Dec. 6, 2001).

211. See, e.g., Nina Bernstein, *The Lost Children of Wilder: The Epic Struggle to Change Foster Care* (2001).

212. A diverse, blue-ribbon group studying FBOs has endorsed this principle, albeit with some misgivings. *Finding Common Ground*, 24. But see Laura B. Mutterperl, "Employment at (God's) Will: The Constitutionality of Antidiscrimination Exemptions in Charitable Choice Legislation," 37 *Harvard Civil Rights-Civil Liberties Law Review* 389 (2002) (arguing, unpersuasively in my view, that such exemptions are unconstitutional). The legality of coreligionist discrimination by FBOs that receive federal funds is being litigated. See Adam Liptak, "A Right to Bias Is Put to the Test," *New York Times*, A30 (Oct. 11, 2002).

213. Elisabeth Bumiller, "Accord Reached on Charity Aid Bill after Bush Gives In on Hiring," *New York Times*, A19 (Feb. 8, 2002).

214. For a forceful development of this point, see Arons, *Compelling Belief*.

215. Elementary and Secondary Education Act of 1965, Pub. L. No. 89-10, 79 Stat. 27.

216. Expenditures since 1965 under Title I alone amount to nearly $130 billion, ac-

cording to the House Committee on Education and the Workforce. See Press Release, "'No Child Left Behind' Education Bill Introduced as H.R. 1," Committee on Education and the Workforce (Mar. 22, 2001), available at *http:// edworkforce.house.gov/press/press107/nclbintro32201.htm*. State and local program expenditures are much greater.

217. Quoted in Michael Heise, "Choosing Equal Educational Opportunity: School Reform, Law, and Public Policy," 68 *University of Chicago Law Review* 1113, 1136 (2001).

218. James S. Coleman, Thomas Hoffer, and Sally Kilgore, *High School Achievement: Public, Catholic, and Private Schools Compared* (1982).

219. Id., 200–213.

220. Id., 31–38, 74–79, 99–113, 122–146; James S. Coleman and Thomas Hoffer, *Public and Private High Schools: The Impact of Communities* (1987); James S. Coleman, "Changes in the Family and Implications for the Common School," 1991 *University of Chicago Legal Forum* 153, 161–167 (1991).

221. See Joseph G. Altonji, Todd E. Elder, and Christopher R. Taber, "Selection on Observed and Unobserved Variables: Assessing the Effectiveness of Catholic Schools" (Apr. 30, 2001) (unpublished manuscript, Department of Economics, Yale University) (finding large effects on probability of graduation and college attendance, but not test scores).

222. See, e.g., James E. Ryan and Michael Heise, "The Political Economy of School Choice," 111 *Yale Law Journal* 2043, 2063–2085 (2002) (reviewing public school and private school choice programs).

223. See Milton Friedman, *Capitalism and Freedom,* chap. 6 (1962); John E. Coons and Stephen D. Sugarman, *Education by Choice: The Case for Family Control* (1978).

224. The public favors the religious school option. More surprising, so do most voucher opponents! Diane Ravitch, "The Right Thing," *The New Republic,* 34 (Oct. 8, 2001) (review of Terry M. Moe, *Schools, Vouchers, and the American Public* (2001)).

225. Jeffries and Ryan, "A Political History of the Establishment Clause," 338.

226. Zelman v. Simmons-Harris, 122 S. Ct. 2460 (2002).

227. Jacques Steinberg, "Cleveland Case Poses New Test for Vouchers," *New York Times,* A1 (Feb. 8, 2002) (view of analyst for National Conference of State Legislatures).

228. See, e.g., Hamburger, *Separation of Church and State,* chap. 8.

229. Lloyd Jorgenson, *The State and the Non-Public School, 1825–1925,* at 69 (1987). For a more benign view of this disinheritance, see Macedo, *Diversity and Distrust,* chap. 2.

230. Jeffries and Ryan, "A Political History of the Establishment Clause," 283, 349. The authors note that the political future of school prayer and other practices raising Establishment Clause issues is different. Id., 367–368.

231. Id., 351.

232. Abby Goodnough, "Teachers at Catholic Schools Strike over Pay and Pensions," *New York Times,* A1 (Nov. 30, 2001) (budget deficit has already forced school closures in diocese).

233. Ravitch, "The Right Thing," 37 (quoting Greeley).

234. Id., 35. On international comparisons, see also sources cited in Joseph P. Viteritti, "A Truly Living Constitution: Why Educational Opportunity Trumps Strict Separation on the Voucher Question," 57 *New York University Annual Survey of American Law* 89, 112 note 127 (2000).

235. Ravitch, "The Right Thing," 31.

236. See, e.g., Paul E. Peterson and David E. Campbell, eds., *Charters, Vouchers, and Public Education* (2001).

237. Jay P. Greene, "The Hidden Research Consensus for School Choice," in *Charters, Vouchers, and Public Education,* chap. 5.

238. See Brian Gill et al., "Rhetoric versus Reality: What We Know and What We Need to Know about Vouchers and Charter Schools" (2001), available at *http://www.rand.org/publications/MR/MR1118;* Indiana Center for Evaluation, "Evaluation of the Cleveland Scholarship Program, 1998–2000," Summary Report (Sept. 2001).

239. See *http://www.jointcenter.org/databank/NOP/NOP_98/Education/VOUCHERS.htm* (last visited Feb. 5, 2002).

240. Greene, "The Hidden Research Consensus for School Choice," 90.

241. Zelman v. Simmons-Harris, 122 S. Ct. at 2464.

242. The new law merely allows children in failing schools to transfer to other in-district public or charter schools or receive additional services. Adam Clymer, "Congress Reaches Compromise on Education Bill," *New York Times,* A1 (Dec. 12, 2001). Since few seats are available in the better public schools, however, transfer is not a meaningful choice. Diana Jean Schemo, "Officials Say School Choice Often Just Isn't an Option," *New York Times,* A13 (Dec. 22, 2001).

243. Greene, "The Hidden Research Consensus for School Choice," 90 (citing U.S. Department of Education estimate); Ryan and Heise, "The Political Economy of School Choice," 2064 (citing Jeffrey R. Henig and Stephen D. Sugarman estimate).

244. See, e.g., Indiana Center for Evaluation, "Evaluation of the Cleveland Scholarship Program," 6–8.

245. Greene, "The Hidden Research Consensus for School Choice," 91.

246. Caroline M. Hoxby, "Analyzing School Choice Reforms That Use America's Traditional Forms of Parental Choice," in Paul E. Peterson and Bran C. Hassel, eds., *Learning from School Choice,* 148 (1998) (emphasis in the original). Greene reached similar results. "The Hidden Research Consensus for School Choice," 92 (study of Florida schools).

247. See Peterson and Campbell, *Charters, Vouchers, and Public Education,* chaps. 9–11. A negative factor for the community, according to one analysis, is that by dispersing students geographically, vouchers reduce adults' "community-specific capital." William A. Fischel, "An Economic Case against Vouchers: Why Local Public Schools Are a Local Public Good" (Feb. 2002) (unpublished manuscript, Department of Economics, Dartmouth College).

248. For a thumbnail summary of this history, see Ravitch, "The Right Thing," 36.

249. For a detailed discussion of housing subsidies, see Chapter 6 of this book.

250. Ravitch, "The Right Thing," 34.

251. This discussion draws on Macedo, *Diversity and Distrust,* 232–240.

252. Id., 244.

253. Salamone, *Visions of Schooling,* 6.

254. Ravitch, "The Right Thing," 34; Michael Leo Owens, "Why Blacks Support Vouchers," *New York Times,* A25 (Feb. 26, 2002) (surveys show strong support especially among young adults, but opposition by black officials). Many evidently favor other structural changes as well. See "City to Vote on Secession from Los Angeles School District," *New York Times,* A14 (Nov. 2, 2001) (revolt against "disturbingly dysfunctional" schools in working-class, racially mixed city).

255. Macedo, *Diversity and Distrust,* 252.

256. See generally Albert O. Hirschman, *Exit, Voice, and Loyalty: Responses to Decline in Firms, Organizations, and States* (1970).

257. Ravitch, "The Right Thing," 35.

258. Macedo, *Diversity and Distrust,* 324 note 28 (calling the earlier evidence to this effect "scanty and rather soft").

259. The studies are summarized in Greene, "The Hidden Research Consensus for School Choice," 93–97, and in Peterson and Campbell, *Charters, Vouchers, and Public Education,* chaps. 12, 13. See also Salamone, *Visions of Schooling,* 253–255.

260. Compare Diana Jean Schemo, "Study Finds Church Schools Racially Segregated," *New York Times,* A18 (June 27, 2002) (Harvard Civil Rights Project finding more segregation in private schools), with Jay P. Greene, "Choosing Integration," *Wall Street Journal,* A22 (July 8, 2002) (Harvard data show more integration in private schools at classroom, lunchroom, and high school levels).

261. See Edward A. Zelinsky, "Metropolitanism, Professionalism, and Race," 98 *Columbia Law Review* 665, 692 (1998) ("The community unwilling to zone for low-income housing might take a more favorable view of low-income students who bring dollars with them and who go home after the school day").

262. Steinberg, "Cleveland Case Poses New Test for Vouchers."

263. Ryan and Heise, "The Political Economy of School Choice," 2081–2082.

264. The nation's 2,400 charter schools, for example, account for barely 1% of the 48 million children in public schools. Timothy Egan, "Failures Raise Questions for Charter Schools," *New York Times,* A15 (Apr. 5, 2002). Under 1% of all public school students go to schools outside their districts. Ryan and Heise, "The Political Economy of School Choice," 2066.

265. On the politics of school vouchers, see Jeffries and Ryan, "A Political History of the Establishment Clause," 358–365. For an example, see Michael Winerip, "In Suburbia, Suicide by Vouchers," *New York Times,* D1 (Nov. 7, 2001) (suburban opposition to voucher proposal by New Jersey gubernatorial candidate).

266. Denis P. Doyle, "Where Connoisseurs Send Their Children to School," in *A Choice for Our Children: Curing the Crisis in America's Schools,* 40–41 (Alan Bonsteel and Carlos A. Bonilla, eds., 1997) (noting that 40% of the children of Cleveland public school teachers go to private schools, compared with 25% of all children; in Milwaukee, the percentages are 33 versus 23, and in Boston 45 versus 29). See also Jennifer Garrett, "Another Look at How Members of Congress

Exercise School Choice," *www.heritage.org/library/backgrounder/bg1553.html* (May 22, 2002) (over 40% of members of Congress send at least one child to private school compared with 10% of general population).

267. Ryan and Heise, "The Political Economy of School Choice," 2079–2083.

268. See, e.g., Lizette Alvarez, "House Democrats Block Voucher Provision," *New York Times,* A18 (May 3, 2001). Many Republicans joined the opposition to Bush's proposal.

269. See Richard Rothstein, "A Third Way on Schools, Mixing Public and Private," *New York Times,* B9 (Mar. 20, 2002) (citing examples of mixed systems).

270. Salamone, *Visions of Schooling,* 257–262, discusses these and other regulatory issues.

271. New Zealand's market-based school reforms, which encourage competition but do not include vouchers, have had mixed results. See Edward D. Fiske and Helen F. Ladd, "Lessons from New Zealand," in *Charters, Vouchers, and Public Education,* chap. 4. For reviews of the Fiske and Ladd study, see, e.g., Bill J. Johnston and Kaye Pepper, "Book Review," 30 *Journal of Law and Education* 379 (2001) (mixed results); John Jewett, "Left Back," 103 *Policy Review* 67 (2000) (emphasizing optimistic findings); Dorothy Shipps, "Book Review," 103 *Teachers College Record* 77 (2001) (similar); Howard Gardner, "Paroxysms of Choice," *New York Review of Books,* 44 (Oct. 19, 2000) (emphasizing class-based differentials).

272. Egan, "Failures Raise Questions for Charter Schools" (nationwide, 4.5% of charter schools have closed or had their charters revoked; failure rate in Arizona is nearly 10%).

273. See, e.g., Ira C. Lupu and Robert Tuttle, "Sites of Redemption: A Wide-Angle Look at Government Vouchers and Sectarian Service Providers," 18 *Journal of Law and Politics* (Summer-Fall 2002).

274. Some recent evidence suggests that student performance improves more in states that permit wider school choice. Jay P. Greene, "School Choice = Higher Test Scores," *Wall Street Journal,* A22 (Jan. 23, 2002) (using Manhattan Institute's "Education Freedom Index").

8. CONCLUDING THOUGHTS

1. I do not include the ethnic preferences that India and some other multiethnic states adopted after independence because these preferences were generally solidaristic gestures supporting nation-building projects, not expressions of the kind of diversity ideal that has recently emerged in the United States.

2. See generally Samuel Issacharoff, Pamela S. Karlan, and Richard H. Pildes, *The Law of Democracy: Legal Structure of the Political Process,* 417–448 (2d ed. 2001).

3. See, e.g., International Ladies' Garment Workers' Union v. NLRB, 366 U.S. 731 (1961).

4. See, e.g., Norfolk Southern Railroad Co. v. Shanklin, 529 U.S. 344 (2000). See also, e.g., Unum Life Insurance Co. of America v. Ward, 526 U.S. 358 (1999) (holding that Employee Retirement Income Security Act preempted a Califor-

nia rule allowing policyholder-employer to be deemed agent of insurer in administering group insurance policies).

5. Remarks at symposium on affirmative action, Whitney Humanities Center, Yale University (Oct. 17, 1996).

6. See, e.g., "A Symposium on Finding a Path to Gender Equality: Legal and Policy Issues Raised by All-Female Public Education," 14 *New York Law School Journal of Human Rights* 1 (1997).

7. United States v. Starrett City Associates, 840 F.2d 1096 (2d Cir.), cert. denied, 488 U.S. 946 (1988).

8. See, e.g., Amy Dockser Marcus, "The New Battleground over Race and Schools: Younger Students," *Wall Street Journal*, B1 (Dec. 29, 1999); "Latin Lesson," *The New Republic*, 7–8 (Dec. 14, 1998).

9. James Lindgren, "Measuring Diversity" (Jan. 1, 1999) (unpublished manuscript, Northwestern University School of Law).

10. See Robert M. Cover, "Foreword: Nomos and Narrative," 97 *Harvard Law Review* 4 (1983).

11. Rogers Smith, *Civic Ideals: Conflicting Visions of Citizenship in U.S. History* (1997).

12. Id., 15 (footnote omitted).

13. Peter H. Schuck, *Citizens, Strangers, and In-Betweens: Essays on Immigration and Citizenship,* chap. 2 (1998).

14. James Lindgren found that Jewish professors and those with no religion were overrepresented on the top 100 law faculties. The most underrepresented gender was female, the most underrepresented minority was Hispanic, the most underrepresented large U.S. religious affiliation was Christian, and the most underrepresented political group was Republican, particularly Republican women, who were almost absent from law teaching. Lindgren, "Measuring Diversity."

15. Yochai Benkler, "Siren Songs and Amish Children: Autonomy, Information, and Law," 76 *New York University Law Review* 23, 107–112 (2001) (favoring "distributed" information environment).

16. See, e.g., Robert V. Avery et al., "Credit Scoring: Statistical Issues and Evidence from Credit-Bureau Files," 28 *Real Estate Economics* 523 (2000).

17. This episode is detailed in James Fallows, "He's Got Mail," *New York Review of Books,* 4 (Mar. 14, 2002) (reviewing Cass Sunstein, *republic.com* (2001)).

18. See, e.g., Frederick R. Lynch, *The Diversity Machine: The Drive to Change the "White Male Workplace"* (2000).

19. See, e.g., Yaakov Kop and Robert E. Litan, *Sticking Together: The Israeli Experiment in Pluralism* (2002).

20. See, e.g., Peter Schuck and Rainer Munz, eds., *Paths to Inclusion: The Integration of Migrants in the United States and Germany* (1998).

21. United States v. Mercedes, 2002 WL 537032 (2d Cir. 2002).

22. United States v. Starrett City Associates, 840 F.2d 1096 (2d Cir.), cert. denied, 488 U.S. 946 (1988).

23. See, e.g., United States v. Eichman, 496 U.S. 310 (1990) (flag burning); R.A.V. v. City of St. Paul, 505 U.S. 377 (1992) (hate speech); Brandenburg v. Ohio,

395 U.S. 444 (1969) (incendiary speech). Hate-crime laws, however, are permitted to regulate hate speech when coupled with criminal behavior. See generally James B. Jacobs and Kimberly Potter, *Hate Crimes: Criminal Law and Identity Politics* (1998); Frederick M. Lawrence, *Punishing Hate: Bias Crimes under American Law* (1999). The political pressure to expand the scope of hate-crime laws continues. See Christopher Marquis, "Man Is Charged in Two Killings That U.S. Calls Hate Crime," *New York Times*, A27 (Apr. 11, 2002) (Senator Kennedy pressing administration to support bill covering sex, sexual orientation, and disability).

24. See, e.g., Ashcroft v. Free Speech Coalition, 122 S. Ct. 1389 (2002) (striking down federal statute restricting child pornography on the Internet).

25. See, e.g., David M. Herszenhorn, "Two Feuding Indian Tribes Are Recognized, but as One," *New York Times*, B5 (June 25, 2002); Timothy Egan, "Lawsuit in California Asks, Whose Tribe Is It, Anyway?" *New York Times*, A24 (Apr. 10, 2002) (woman and her two children claim to be tribe); Brent Staples, "The Seminole Tribe, Running from History," *New York Times*, WK12 (Apr. 21, 2002) (dispute over quantity of "Seminole blood"). See generally Jeff Benedict, *Without Reservation: The Making of America's Most Powerful Indian Tribe and Foxwoods, the World's Largest Casino* (2000).

26. See generally Peter Skerry, *Counting on the Census?: Race, Group Identity, and the Evasion of Politics* (2000).

27. See generally Cover, "Nomos and Narrative."

28. Robert W. Fogel, *The Fourth Great Awakening and the Future of Egalitarianism*, 214 (2000).

29. The rest of this paragraph draws on Peter H. Schuck, *The Limits of Law: Essays on Democratic Governance*, chap. 13, esp. 427–432 (2000).

30. The analogy here is to John Hart Ely, *Democracy and Distrust: A Theory of Judicial Review* (1980), which justifies the use of judicial power to open the channels of political change.

31. The dominant group in one community may be a minority elsewhere—the Mormons in Utah, for example. For international examples, see Amy L. Chua, "Markets, Democracy, and Ethnicity: Toward a New Paradigm for Law and Development," 108 *Yale Law Journal* 1 (1998).

32. Civil Rights Act of 1964, Pub. L. No. 88-352, 78 Stat. 241; Americans with Disabilities Act of 1990, Pub. L. No. 101-336, 104 Stat. 327.

33. For examples, see David E. Bernstein, "Antidiscrimination Laws and the First Amendment," 66 *Montana Law Review* 83, 106–107 (2001).

34. Id. at 102 (discussing religious and small firm exemptions, balancing factors, and other limitations). For a discussion of the tension between the two jurisprudences of equal protection and religious protection, see Kenji Yoshino, "Covering," 111 *Yale Law Journal* 769, 927–930 (2002).

35. The seminal cases are Hurley v. Irish-American Gay, Lesbian and Bisexual Group of Boston, 515 U.S. 557 (1995), and Boy Scouts of America v. Dale, 530 U.S. 640 (2000).

36. See Diana Jean Schemo, "White House Proposes New View of Education Law to Encourage Single-Sex Schools," *New York Times*, A26 (May 9, 2002).

37. For a very brief discussion of this case and this issue, see Peter H. Schuck, "Diversity Demands Exclusivity," *The American Lawyer*, 67 (Sept. 2000).

38. See Bruce A. Ackerman and Ian Ayres, *Voting with Dollars: A New Paradigm for Campaign Finance*, 12–24 (2002). The campaign reform law enacted in March 2002 will do none of this.

39. See, e.g., Mark G. Yudof, *When Government Speaks: Politics, Law, and Government Expression in America* (1983).

40. See, e.g., Legal Services Corp. v. Velazquez, 531 U.S. 533 (2001) (federally funded lawyers represent their clients' interests, not the government's).

41. The struggle over multiracial options in the 2000 census described in Chapter 5 suggests just how difficult it will be politically to move in this direction.

42. The variable scope of political conflict is the theme of E. E. Schattschneider, *The Semi-Sovereign People: A Realist's View of Democracy in America* (1975).

43. The rest of this paragraph draws on Schuck, *The Limits of Law*, chap. 3.

44. See generally Guido Calabresi and Philip Bobbitt, *Tragic Choices* (1978).

45. See, e.g., Francis X. Clines, "Ohio Board Hears Debate on an Alternative to Darwinism," *New York Times*, A16 (Mar. 12, 2002).

46. See generally Peter H. Schuck, "When the Exception Becomes the Rule: Regulatory Equity and the Formulation of Energy Policy through an Exceptions Process," 1984 *Duke Law Journal* 165 (1984).

47. See, e.g., Stephen G. Breyer, *The Vicious Circle: Toward Effective Risk Regulation* (1993).

48. See, e.g., Hal R. Varian, "Economic Scene," *New York Times*, C1 (Feb. 14, 2002) (analyzing investor choices among 401(k) plans).

49. Alan Wolfe, *One Nation, After All: What Middle-Class Americans Really Think about God, Country, Family, Racism, Welfare, Immigration, Homosexuality, Work, the Right, the Left, and Each Other*, chap. 7 (1998).

50. See Peter H. Schuck, "A Case for Profiling," *American Lawyer*, 59 (Jan. 2002).

51. For some recent empirical work bearing, at least indirectly, on the nature and magnitude of this trade-off, see, e.g., Alberto Alesina and Eliana La Ferrara, *The Determinants of Trust*, National Bureau of Economic Research, Working Paper No. 7621 (Cambridge, Mass., Mar. 2000) (finding that minorities trust other people less and that racially diverse communities display less trust).

52. Elisabeth Lasch-Quinn, *Race Experts: How Racial Etiquette, Sensitivity Training, and New Age Therapy Hijacked the Civil Rights Revolution*, chap. 6 (2001).

53. Barbara Stewart, "Museum May Rethink 3 Works in Holocaust Show," *New York Times*, B3 (Feb. 28, 2002).

54. Michelle Rosenthal, "Yale Employee's Racial Remark Elicits Hardened Response," *Yale Daily News*, 3 (Feb. 6, 2002). A subsequent "letter to the editor" by an American instructor of English in Korea, after noting that dogs and kimchi are in fact normal ingredients of both traditional and modern Korean cuisine, wonders whether the worker's joke reflected cultural ignorance or cultural awareness. Letter from David Woods, *Yale Daily News*, 2 (Feb. 11, 2002).

55. Winnie Hu, "Road Sign Urging Tolerance Manages to Turn Many Off," *New York Times*, B1 (Feb. 9, 2002).

56. Letters to the Editor, *The American Lawyer*, 12 (Mar. 2001).

57. Yolanda Woodlee, "Top D.C. Aide Resigns over Racial Rumor," *Washington Post*, B1 (Jan. 27, 1999).

58. Kate Zernike, "Free-Speech Ruling Voids School District's Harassment Policy," *New York Times*, A10 (Feb. 16, 2001) (policy invalidated by federal appeals court). Several states have passed laws against "bullying," and others are considering them. See Lucio Guerrero, "Bullying No Longer Seen as a Rite of Passage," *Chicago Sun-Times*, A12 (May 6, 2001). For a recent proposal to make hate speech more actionable in tort law, see Victor C. Romero, "Restricting Hate Speech against 'Private Figures': Lessons in Power-Based Censorship from Defamation Law," 33 *Columbia Human Rights Law Review* 1 (2001).

59. Aisha D. Gayle, "Whiplash: Race Still Matters at Yale," *Yale Daily News* (Oct. 10, 2000).

60. "University of Virginia Law Professor Sued over Lesson on Assault," *Associated Press* (Mar. 25, 2002).

61. N. R. Kleinfeld, "The Elderly Man and the Sea? Test Sanitizes Literary Texts," *New York Times*, 1 (June 2, 2002).

62. For similar views, see Jonathan Rauch, "Offices and Gentlemen," *The New Republic*, 22 (June 23, 1997), and Randall Kennedy, *Nigger: The Strange Career of a Troublesome Word*, chap. 3 (2002).

63. The tort of intentional infliction of emotional distress through extreme and outrageous behavior is an example. See, e.g., Daniel J. Givelber, "The Right to Minimum Social Decency and the Limits of Evenhandedness: Intentional Infliction of Emotional Distress by Outrageous Conduct," 82 *Columbia Law Review* 42 (1982). The torts of defamation, where one's reputation is unfairly injured, and invasions of privacy involve different kinds of offenses than those under discussion here.

64. See, e.g., Jeffrey Rosen, *The Unwanted Gaze: The Destruction of Privacy in America* (2000); Walter Olson, *The Excuse Factory: What Happened When America Unleashed the Lawsuit* (1997).

65. See, e.g., William McGowan, *Coloring the News: How Crusading for Diversity Has Corrupted American Journalism* (2001).

66. See, e.g., John Leo, *Incorrect Thoughts: Notes on Our Wayward Culture* (2001).

INDEX